SACRED WATERS

Describing sacred waters and their associated traditions in over thirty countries and across multiple time periods, this book identifies patterns in panhuman hydrolatry. Supplying life's most basic daily need, freshwater sources were likely the earliest sacred sites, and the first protected and contested resource. Guarded by taboos, rites and supermundane forces, freshwater sources have also been considered thresholds to otherworlds. Often associated also with venerated stones, trees and healing flora, sacred water sources are sites of biocultural diversity. Addressing themes that will shape future water research, this volume examines cultural perceptions of water's sacrality that can be employed to foster resilient human–environmental relationships in the growing water crises of the twenty-first century. The work combines perspectives from anthropology, archaeology, classics, folklore, geography, geology, history, literature and religious studies.

Celeste Ray is Professor of Environmental Arts and Humanities at the University of the South, USA. She is the author of *The Origins of Ireland's Holy Wells* and *Highland Heritage: Scottish Americans in the American South*, and the editor of volumes considering ethnicity and historical ecology.

SACRED WATERS

A Cross-Cultural Compendium of Hallowed Springs and Holy Wells

Edited by Celeste Ray

Routledge
Taylor & Francis Group

LONDON AND NEW YORK

First published 2020
by Routledge
2 Park Square, Milton Park, Abingdon, Oxon OX14 4RN

and by Routledge
52 Vanderbilt Avenue, New York, NY 10017

Routledge is an imprint of the Taylor & Francis Group, an informa business

British Library Cataloguing-in-Publication Data
A catalogue record for this book is available from the British Library

Library of Congress Cataloging-in-Publication Data
Names: Ray, R. Celeste, editor.
Title: Sacred waters: a cross-cultural compendium of hallowed springs and holy wells / edited by Celeste Ray.
Description: Abingdon, Oxon; New York, NY: Routledge, 2020. | Includes bibliographical references and index.
Identifiers: LCCN 2019044846 (print) | LCCN 2019044847 (ebook) | ISBN 9780367445126 (hardback) | ISBN 9780367445133 (paperback) | ISBN 9781003010142 (ebook)
Subjects: LCSH: Holy wells. | Springs—Religious aspects. | Springs—Folklore.
Classification: LCC GR690 .S23 2020 (print) | LCC GR690 (ebook) | DDC 398.26—dc23
LC record available at https://lccn.loc.gov/2019044846
LC ebook record available at https://lccn.loc.gov/2019044847

ISBN: 978-0-367-44512-6 (hbk)
ISBN: 978-0-367-44513-3 (pbk)
ISBN: 978-1-003-01014-2 (ebk)

Typeset in Bembo
by codeMantra

CONTENTS

FIGURES

TABLES

CONTRIBUTORS

Michael Agnew is a Postdoctoral Research Fellow at the MacPherson Institute for Leadership, Innovation and Excellence in Teaching at McMaster University in Hamilton, Canada. He received his Ph.D. in Religious Studies from McMaster University. His doctoral research included extensive ethnographic fieldwork at the Catholic shrine of Lourdes in southwestern France. His research interests include caregiving, material religion, ritual healing, and religion and film.

Victor Ajisola Omojeje holds B.A Ed., M. Phil and Ph.D. degrees in History from the Obafemi Awolowo University, Ile-Ife and the University of Ibadan, Ibadan, Nigeria. He is a Senior Lecturer in the Department of History, Adeyemi College of Education in Ondo, Nigeria. His most recent publication appeared in *Yoruba Studies Review*.

Wojciech Bedyński completed his Ph.D. at the Institute of Ethnology and Cultural Anthropology at the University of Warsaw and Université Paris-IV (Sorbonne). He is a cultural historian and ethnologist at the Centre for Migration Research at the University of Warsaw, Poland. He is the co-author of *The Tree, the Well and the Stone: Sacred Places in the Cultural Space of Central-Eastern Europe* (2011) and co-editor of *Landscape as a Factor in Creating Identity* (2014).

John Björkman, M.A., is a doctoral student in Nordic folklore at the Åbo Akademi University in Turku, Finland. His research focuses on different types of historic vernacular sacred sites in Southwest Finland as part of the cultural and social landscape. Björkman is a regional researcher in the Museum Centre of Turku.

Liam M. Brady is Associate Professor and Australian Research Council Future Fellow at Flinders University. For the last 15 years, he has been working in partnership with Indigenous communities in northern Australia, Canada and the United States exploring the cultural and relational contexts of cultural heritage sites. He is the recipient of postdoctoral fellowships from the Australian Research Council and the University of Western Australia, and co-editor of *Relating to Rock Art in the Contemporary World*.

Margaret Jean Cormack is Professor Emeritus of Religious Studies at the College of Charleston, South Carolina and Affiliate Professor in the Faculty of Theology and Religious Studies at the University of Iceland. She has published *The Saints in Iceland: Their Veneration from the Conversion to 1400* and edited *Sacrificing the Self: Perspectives on Martyrdom and Religion; Saints and Their Cults in the Atlantic World*, and *Muslims and Others in Sacred Space*.

Jane Costlow is the Clark A. Griffith Professor of Environmental Studies at Bates College, Maine, where she teaches courses in Environmental Humanities and Russian literature. Her book *Heart-Pine Russia: Walking and Writing the Nineteenth Century Forest* (2013) won the USC Prize for Best Book in Literary and Cultural Studies. Her other works include co-edited volumes on water in Russian culture and animals in Russian history; essays on film, classic Russian fiction and Russian women writers; and translations of literary prose.

Kate M. Craig is an Assistant Professor of History at Auburn University and a former Fulbright scholar. She received her B.S. in Applied Physics and History from the California Institute of Technology and her Ph.D. in History from UCLA. Her research focuses on central medieval religious history, and her current project examines relic journeys in northern France and Flanders.

Marco Curatola Petrocchi is Professor of History, Department of Humanities, and directs the Andean Studies Program in the Graduate School of the Pontificia Universidad Católica del Perú. He is Director of the Andean Studies Series of the PUCP Press. He received his Ph.D. in Archaeology and Ancient Art History from the University of Genoa. He has been a visiting professor at the University of Chicago (2014) and the École des Hautes Études, Paris (2018). Specializing in the history of Andean culture, he has focused his research on native religion in pre-Columbian and Colonial times.

Jean DeBernardi is Professor and Acting Chair of Anthropology at the University of Alberta. She is the author of two books with Stanford University Press considering the Chinese in Malaysia: *Rites of Belonging: Memory, Modernity and Identity in a Malaysian Chinese Community* (2004) and *The Way that Lives in the Heart: Chinese Popular Religion and Spirit Mediums in Penang, Malaysia* (2006). Her current interests include religious and cultural pilgrimage to the Daoist temple complex at Wudang Mountain in South-Central China and contemporary Chinese tea culture.

Nicholas P. Dunning is a geoarchaeologist, paleoecologist and archaeologist currently teaching in the Department of Geography and GIS at the University of Cincinnati. He has worked in the Maya Lowlands since he was a college student in the late 1970s. Along the way, he has published several books and some 150 journal articles and book chapters. In his spare time, he is an organic gardener.

Snežana Filipova is a faculty member in the Department of Art History and Archaeology at Saints Cyril and Methodius University in Skopje, Macedonia (UKIM). She received her doctorate in Art History at the University of Belgrade. She has written television programs on Macedonian heraldry, has authored over 50 scholarly articles, and is author or co-author of four books considering heraldry, Macedonian sculpture, monumentality in Skopje, and social memory and memorial mythologies. She teaches medieval art history, methodologies of art history and heraldry.

Gedef Abawa Firew is an Assistant Professor at Barhir Dar University, Ethiopia. He holds an M.Phil. and Ph.D. in Archaeology (University of Bergen, Norway) and a bachelor's degree in History. His main research areas are agricultural history and transitions, environment and human adaptation, sociocultural aspects of local food, and culture and development in Ethiopia. He is involved in the Amhara History Research Project.

Ronan Foley is a Senior Lecturer at the Department of Geography at Maynooth University, Ireland. He has written on the broad area of therapeutic landscapes, including the 2010 monograph, *Healing Waters: Therapeutic Landscapes in Historic and Contemporary Ireland*, as well as papers on holy wells in *Social Science & Medicine, Culture & Religion* and the *Journal of Medical Humanities*. He is currently Principal Investigator on an Irish Environmental Protection Agency project on Green/Blue Spaces and Health and an advisory partner on a University of Exeter project on Sensing Nature.

Richard I. Ford retired as Professor of Anthropology and Botany from the University of Michigan. Research took him to Poland, Tunisia, Kenya, Mexico, Canada, the Bahamas, China and the Western U.S. Publishing 135 essays and nine research monographs, he received numerous awards including India's Amal Amique Award, "Distinguished Ethnobiologist" from the North American Society of Ethnobiology, the Society of American Archaeology's Fryxell Award, the Franz Boas Award from the American Anthropological Association and election to the American Academy of Arts and Sciences. He now serves as a legal expert witness for several Pueblos in their land and water cases.

Ahmad Ghabin is a lecturer in Islamic Studies at Al-Qasemi Academic College of Education in Haifa, Israel. He has written extensively about Arts and Crafts in observance of Islamic principles (Hisba), architecture and building according to the Quran, and also about the Zamzam well.

Laurence Gill is a Professor in Environmental Engineering in the School of Engineering, Trinity College Dublin. His research interests involve studying the fate and transport of both air and water-borne pollutants in the natural and built environment, the development of passive treatment processes, the ecohydrology of wetlands and the characterisation of karst hydrological catchments. Much of the work involves extensive field studies which are then used to develop mathematical models to gain further insight into the processes.

Ramiro Alfonso Gómez Arzapalo Dorantes is Director of the Master's Program in Philosophy and Culture Critique at Intercontinental University in Mexico City. He also teaches at the Catholic University *Lumen Gentium* and is a member of the National

Council of Science and Technology (*Consejo Nacional de Ciencia y Tecnología*), the Philosophical Mexican Association, the Mexican Academy for Dialogue on Science and Faith, and the Interdisciplinary Group for Studies of Popular Religion. Arzapalo also serves as Academic Director of the journal *Intersticios* and is President of the Intercontinental Observatory on Popular Religiousness.

Evy Johanne Håland is a Lifetime Government scholar in Norway. Linking ancient sources with fieldwork on religious festivals and life-cycle rituals, her publications include *Greek Festivals, Modern and Ancient: A Comparison of Female and Male Values*; *Rituals of Death and Dying in Modern and Ancient Greece: Writing History from a Female Perspective*; and the edited *Women, Pain and Death: Rituals and Everyday-Life on the Margins of Europe and Beyond*. She was formerly a lecturer/research fellow with the University of Bergen, Norway and a Marie Curie Fellow at the National and Kapodistrian University of Athens, Greece.

Martin Haigh is Emeritus Professor of Geography at Oxford Brookes University, Oxford, England. He is a National Teaching Fellow and a Senior Fellow of the U.K.'s Higher Education Academy. He also taught at the Universities of Chicago and Oklahoma, Jawaharlal Nehru University, Keele University, and most recently, at Nagaland University. Co-Founder of the International Association for Headwater Control and former Vice-President of the World Association for Soil and Water Conservation, his recent research considers "connective practices" that foster global citizenship, sustainability and landscape conservation.

Yan Jie is a Ph.D. candidate in Anthropology at the University of Alberta. Her B.A. is in Chinese Literature and her M.A. is in Folklore (Peking University). Her research focuses on the revival of Buddhist temples in Hangzhou, Zhejiang province, and the cultural practices of the Jingshan temple, including Chan tea culture. She also investigates the relationship of religious places and urban space, and the niche construction of folk traditions in processes of Chinese modernization.

Ma Junhong is a Ph.D. candidate in Anthropology at the University of Alberta. She received a B.Econ. in the Department of Finance at Fudan University, where she also completed an M.A. degree in Chinese Classical Literature. Her doctoral thesis focuses on gongfu tea practice as a new lifestyle mode for a cosmopolitan middle class in the context of a post-socialist China.

Jens Kreinath is Associate Professor of Socio-Cultural Anthropology at Wichita State University, U.S.A. He conducted ethnographic and historical research on shared pilgrimage sites and Christian-Muslim relations in Hatay, Turkey. His fields of interest include concept formation in the study of ritual and the aesthetics of religion with a focus on visual culture and historical discourse analysis. Kreinath co-edited *Dynamics of Changing Rituals* (2004) and *Theorizing Rituals* (2006–2007), and edited *The Anthropology of Islam Reader* (2012).

Vera Lazzaretti is a Post-Doctoral Fellow at the Department of Culture Studies and Oriental Languages at the University of Oslo. Her research deals with everyday negotiations of religious heritage and the politics of the past in urban contexts of

Northern India. She also worked on patterns in the sanctification of space in Hinduism as part of her doctoral and post-doctoral research at the Universities of Turin, Milan and Heidelberg.

Elizabeth McAlister is a Professor of Religion at Wesleyan University in Connecticut. She is author of *Rara! Vodou, Power and Performance in Haiti and its Diaspora* (University of California Press, 2002), and *Race, Nation, and Religion in the Americas* (Oxford University Press, 2004), and the albums *Rhythms of Rapture: Sacred Musics of Haitian Vodou* (Smithsonian/Folkways, 1995) and *Angels in the Mirror: Vodou Music of Haiti* (Ellipsis Arts 1997).

Christopher M. McDonough holds the Alderson-Tillinghast Chair of Humanities at the University of the South in Sewanee, Tennessee, having previously taught at Boston College and Princeton. He has published widely on ancient religion—notably on Ovid's *Fasti*—as well as on classical reception and film. His co-authored translation *Servius' Commentary on* Aeneid *Book Four* (Bolchazy-Carducci) was published in 2004. His forthcoming monograph is *Pontius Pilate on Screen: Sinner, Soldier, Superstar* (Edinburgh University Press).

Cora McKenna is Technical Officer in Geology at Trinity College Dublin. Her research specializes in bulk and in-situ trace element geochemistry.

Bruce Misstear is an Associate Professor and Fellow of Trinity College Dublin, and a specialist in groundwater resources development. Prior to joining Trinity College, he worked as a consultant hydrogeologist and became Director of Water Resources Division for the Global Engineering Firm Mott MacDonald. During this period, he undertook groundwater resources projects in the U.K., Nigeria, Sudan, Oman, Myanmar, Pakistan and Saudi Arabia. Both a Chartered Geologist and Chartered Engineer, he is Secretary General of the International Association of Hydrogeologists.

Cailín E. Murray is Associate Professor of Anthropology and Director of Native American Studies at Ball State University in Indiana. She is co-editor of *Explorations in Cultural Anthropology* (2011) and of *Phantom Past, Indigenous Presence: Native Ghosts in North American Culture and History* (2011). Her research interests also include river restoration and tribal sovereignty along North America's Northwest Coast, and NAGPRA (Native Americans Grave Protection and Repatriation).

Terje Oestigaard is Senior Researcher with the Department of Archaeology and Ancient History at Uppsala University and the Nordic Africa Institute in Uppsala, Sweden. In the Nile Basin, he has mainly worked in Egypt, Ethiopia, Tanzania and Uganda. His main field of interest is water studies with the aim of understanding the role of water in history, society and civilization with a particular emphasis on culture and comparative religion in changing environments.

Raheem Oluwafunminiyi recently rounded off a Research Fellowship in the 5-Year (2012–2017) European Research Council *Knowing Each Other* project on "Everyday Religious Encounter in Southwest Nigeria." His research interests cover areas such as Yoruba Islam and Yoruba Cultural History and have been published in the *Yoruba Studies Review*. Raheem is currently a Junior Research Fellow at the Centre for Black Culture and International Understanding, Abere, Osun State, Nigeria.

Robert Phillips is an Assistant Professor of Anthropology at Ball State. He lectures on ethnographic methods and the anthropology of technology and religion. His early fieldwork was in south India, but most of his empirical research was conducted in Singapore, focusing on how interactions on the Internet affect national and sexual subjectivity. More recently, Phillips has been conducting research in Brooklyn, NY and Jerusalem, Israel, focusing on religious subjectivity among Orthodox Jewish men.

Celeste Ray is Professor of Environmental Arts and Humanities and Anthropology at the University of the South in Sewanee, Tennessee. She is author of *The Origins of Ireland's Holy Wells* and *Highland Heritage: Scottish Americans and the American South*, and editor of five other volumes considering ethnicity and Historical Ecology. She has pursued fieldwork on sacred springs and holy wells in Appalachia, Austria, Cornwall, England, Iceland, Ireland, Northern Italy, Norway and Scotland.

Jeanmarie Rouhier-Willoughby is Professor of Russian and Folklore at the University of Kentucky and Department Chair, Modern and Classical Languages, Literatures and Cultures. Her Ph.D. is in Slavic Languages and Literatures from the University of Virginia. Her first book, *Village Values: Negotiating Identity, Gender and Resistance in Urban Russian Life-Cycle Rituals*, considered ten years of fieldwork on birth, wedding and funeral customs in Russian cities across the country. Her current research focuses on the religious revival in post-socialist Russia.

Ellen Schattschneider is an Associate Professor of Anthropology at Brandeis University, specializing in psychoanalytic, phenomenological and practice approaches to culture with ethnographic interests in East Asia, especially Japan. Her book, *Immortal Wishes: Labor and Transcendence on a Japanese Sacred Mountain* (Duke University Press, 2003) explores healing, self-fashioning and embodied psychodynamic processes on a sacred landscape associated with a Shinto shrine founded by a rural Japanese woman in the 1920s.

Rachelle M. Scott is an Associate Professor of Religious Studies at the University of Tennessee—Knoxville. Scott is the author of *Nirvana for Sale?: Buddhism, Wealth, and the Dhammakāya Temple in Contemporary Thailand*, and is currently working on a book project entitled, *Gifts of Beauty and Blessings of Wealth: The New Prosperity Goddesses of Thailand*. She is a co-editor of the journal, *Fieldwork in Religion*.

Andy Seaman is an Archaeologist and Senior Lecturer at Canterbury Christ Church University who specialises in early medieval Wales and Western Britain. His research interests focus on Christianity and the early Church, settlement and landscape, and patterns of power. He is currently leading a number of research projects in these areas, including a programme of excavation focused on the "lost" church of SS. Julius and Aaron near Caerleon.

Rana P.B. Singh was Professor of Cultural Landscapes and Heritage Studies at Banaras Hindu University, India, and is the founding Vice President of Asian Cultural Landscape Association (SNU Seoul, Korea), and Big History Association of India. In the last four decades, he has studied, lectured about and promoted cultural and sacred landscapes in India, and also conducted field studies in Japan, Italy, Korea and Sweden. His publications include 40 books and anthologies and over 290 research papers.

Astrid B. Stensrud is Associate Professor in Development Studies at the University of Agder. She holds a Ph.D. in Social Anthropology from the University of Oslo, and was a postdoctoral fellow at the Department of Social Anthropology, University of Oslo until 2018. She has published various articles and book chapters on water, climate change and world-making practices in the Peruvian Andes.

Vykintas Vaitkevičius is Senior Researcher at the Institute of Baltic Region History and Archaeology, Klaipėda University, Lithuania. Since 1992, his research has considered sacred sites, burials and other religious phenomena through the lenses of Archaeology, History, Linguistics and Cultural Anthropology. He is author or co-author of 14 monographs and more than 100 articles in peer-reviewed journals. He was awarded the "Dr. J. Basanavičius Prize" for his research by the Government of the Republic of Lithuania in 2011.

Heiki Valk is Senior Research Fellow and Head of Centre for Archaeological Research at the Institute of History and Archaeology, University of Tartu (Estonia). An essential aspect of his studies concerns Medieval and Post-medieval Archaeology, including connections between the archaeological record, folkloric data and ethnographic tradition. The topic of his Ph.D. thesis (1999) was *Rural Cemeteries of Southern Estonia 1225–1800 AD*. He researches sacred natural sites which were in use in Estonia until the twentieth century.

Hong-key Yoon is a Cultural Geographer and Associate Professor in the School of the Environment, University of Auckland. From a small South Korean village, with a Ph.D. from University of California, Berkeley, his books include *Maori Mind, Maori Land* (1986), *Relationships Between Culture and Nature in Korea* (1976) and *The Culture of Fengshui in Korea* (2006). Most recently, he edited *P'ungsu: A Study of Geomancy in Korea* (2017). His research considers Indigenous "folk" geographies in East Asia and Maori cultural geography in New Zealand.

Terese Zachrisson obtained her Ph.D. in History in 2017. Her research interests include the cult of saints, sacred space and materiality in pre-modern Europe. She is currently a researcher at the University of Gothenburg, as part of the project "Mapping Lived Religion." This five-year project, funded by the Swedish Research Council, is to map, catalogue, digitalise and analyse sources on the medieval cult of saints in Sweden and Finland.

HOLY WELLS AND SACRED SPRINGS

Celeste Ray

Nullus enim fons non sacer.
There is no spring which is not sacred.
Marius Servius Honoratus *ad Aen.* VII, 84

Water existed before any form of life as we know it. The earth's most abundant molecule is Dihydrogen Oxide or H_2O. A simple covalent bonding of two hydrogen atoms with one oxygen atom, water is *the* solvent mediating all molecular processes of life, and its movement as liquid and ice has also shaped earth's topography (Ball, 2001; Solomon, 2010:9). An adult human body consists of at least 60% water, the same water that has given form to other living bodies over and over again through the eons. Fresh water is continuously recycled as sea water evaporates and condenses into clouds which carry rain and snow over the land. Our blue planet is a watery world; yet, only 2.5% of the earth's water is fresh and almost 70% of that is locked in glaciers and ice caps—figures that stay relatively constant over time.[1] In societies where reliance on indoor plumbing is now multiple generations deep, water's actual scarcity makes little impression, but reverence for fresh water is likely as old as humanity. The spread of *Homo sapiens* around the globe was arguably driven by the search for fresh water springs (Finlayson, 2014; Cuthbert et al., 2017). Water sources were likely the earliest sacred sites—the first places at which people sought access to the supernatural (before they did so at other topographic features considered holy around the globe such as mountains, trees, rocks and caves). Water's obvious necessity meant that it was not only venerated, but protected, and access to it was no doubt contested between groups as it is today. People experienced, and then feared, the loss of their most precious resource. Guarded by taboos, rites and supermundane forces, some fresh water sources are considered thresholds to otherworlds. Taking a variety of physical forms around the world, such water sources are regularly called sacred springs or holy wells.[2]

Springs are, of course, places where groundwater issues at the earth's surface.[3] A holy well is most commonly a sacred spring, but can be any natural source of fresh water that is a focus for ritual practice and engagement with the supernatural. Containing the majority of the earth's liquid surface fresh water, lakes are sometimes called "holy wells," especially when spring-fed. Ponds, seepage pools and even natural rock crevices or cavities in trees left by broken branches, where dew and rain collect, can be holy wells and recipients of votives. Sometimes adorned with superstructures, or deepened and enhanced with stone impoundments and steps to aid water retention and access, these sacred "wells" remain distinct from human-excavated holes or shafts dug purposely for the collection of water for non-ritual use. Often perceived as curative, holy wells and sacred springs may be dedicated to deities or saints, or be considered the abodes of ancestors and marvelous genii loci. Most languages encode the sacrality and healing potential of fresh water springs: for example, *Heiliger Brunnen/Heilige Quelle* (German), *puit sacré/source sacrée* (French), *kisima kitakatifu* (Swahili), *pozo santo* (Spanish), *ayazmalar* (Turkish) or *yaksutŏ* in Korean. India has its hallowed pools (*kundas*) and *tirthas* (sacred places along rivers); Vārāṇasī alone has 60 sacred ponds and 31 sacred wells or *kūps*.[4] Mexico has its holy water *aguajes* and Mayan *cenotes* (which gave access to Mayan deities and the underworld). In a tribute to *Fontus* (a god of wells and springs), Roman wells and fountains were decorated with garlands every October 13th for Fontinalia.

Sacred springs and wells of some form have been venerated through time around the globe perhaps simply because, as the Greek philosopher Thales of Miletus noted in the sixth century BC, water is the originating principle of all things. The Romanian historian of religion Mircea Eliade expressed this as "water symbolises the whole of potentiality; it is *fons et origo*, the source of all possible existence" (1958:188). Water is not merely sacred where it is limited (the desertified Middle East or parts of Australia or Mongolia) or where it is bountiful (Ireland, Fiji or Bangladesh), but it is particularly sacred everywhere. No structuralist or Jungian formula is required to explain this cross-cultural commonality; global hydrolatry derives from the most basic material similarities of life. Servius' appealing aphorism that all springs are sacred still resonates around the world, but there are, of course, springs and other water sources that are considered cursed, or that have neither retained nor acquired sacrality; even many healing water sources are not considered holy. Those identified as places of hierophanies (manifestations of the sacred) are often in unusual landscape contexts or sometimes waters with distinctive mineral content—sites attractive to people of different times and ideologies.[5]

Veneration of the same spring site in different eras could be sponsored by quite distinct cosmologies and rituals, but around the globe and transtemporally, patterns emerge at sacred spring sites. Whether venerated by members of a state-level society or a hunting and gathering band, sacred water sources often have associations with other landscape features, and folk liturgies that relate to their unique topographic setting; these natural sites of sacrality are also linked to ancestors worldwide and to similar categories of genii loci. Understanding their veneration and stewardship is especially significant now that our ever-renewing amount of fresh water, which has supported all life on earth since "the beginning," is becoming inadequate for the new consumption levels demanded by a burgeoning human population.

Creation and renewal

Water is indicative of life's inception (a woman's "water breaks" before she gives birth); not surprisingly, water figures prominently in stories describing creation and demiurges cross-culturally. Just as Carl Linnaeus modeled his scientific classification of all living things on Swedish folk taxonomies, people around the world have long understood water's formative role in making life possible and encoded ethnoscientific understandings of its significance in religion long before the succinct epiphany of Thales of Miletus. Explaining creation, the second verse of Genesis describes an earth without form: "darkness was upon the face of the deep. And the Spirit of God moved upon the face of the waters" (KJV, 1:2). In the Babylonian creation epic (*Enuma Elish*), all life begins with a mingling of the salt waters of the mother-goddess Tiamat and the fresh waters of Apsu (a deep abyss). According to the Hindu Rig Veda, "in the beginning, all was water, and there was darkness which engulfed it" (Dwivedi, 1997). The Koran places God's throne upon the waters from which all living creatures emerge (de Châtel, 2007:25). Common to the folklore of Native Americans, the Siberian Chukchi, the Finno-Ugric-speaking peoples (Estonians, Finns and Hungarians) and the Turkic-speaking Tatars of Russia, "earth-diver" myths describe various animals selected by a creator being to gather mud or grains of sand from the depths of the primal waters and construct land.[6] Of the Greek Titans (the children of heaven and earth), Tethys was the source of all rivers and fresh water, and Rhea, whose name means "to flow, run, stream or gush," was the mother of all the Olympian gods (Håland, 2009:137).

Fresh waters are not only sites of creation, but are prototypical symbols of renewal during life. Called "the universal solvent" because water dissolves myriad substances visibly, it also washes away sin in many traditions. Varied forms of baptisms in multiple faiths represent a cleansing of vice and symbolic rebirth. Favored for such rituals, the ever-flowing waters of rivers were eponymous for deities around the world. In India, the ancient Sarasvati is an embodiment of the enlightenment-granting Rig Veda goddess, bathing in Yamuna's waters enables an easy death, and immersing oneself in the ever-renewing Ganga offers remission of sin.[7] Water from such sacred sources is carried around the world for rites of passage, as water from the River Jordan where Jesus was baptized is sometimes brought for christenings and Christian baptisms across the globe. Taoist pilgrims to China's Mount Lao drink from springs enclosed within temples of "great" and "supreme" purity that give imbibers a thousand lives (which is considered desirable rather than punishment). Ever-elusive on the ground, those springs that restore youth appear so frequently in global folklore as to merit their own genre. The Romances of Alexander the Great mention three magical fountains including one in the liminal "lands of the blessed" where the sun does not shine, but the spring's water does, and also flashes like lightning. A dried fish set in the spring revives, and those who drink the water, including Alexander's daughter Kalé, become immortal (Cook, 2009:113–117).[8] The tale is thought to have inspired one of the fourteenth-century well stories in *The Travels of Sir John Mandeville*. This fictional "travel memoir" places the well at the foot of a mountain in an ancient port city in contemporary India's southwestern state of Kerala. Describing a well that changes scent and taste with each hour, the fantasy traveler notes: "Some call it the Fountain of Youth, because whoever drinks often from it seems to be always young and lively without any illness, and they say that this spring comes from Paradise and that is why it is so powerful" (Higgins, 2011:106). The motif of youth-giving springs has continued to resonate through the ages. Ponce de León's fabled search for a Fountain of Youth left later generations claiming candidates among sacred fountains from Florida to Bimini, and Honduras to Jamaica.

FIGURE 0.1 St. Winifred's holy well, North Wales. A curative spring burst from the earth where the seventh-century Winifred was beheaded by a rejected suitor. Her uncle, St. Bueno, miraculously reattached her head and, bearing a small scar as testament to her martyrdom, Winifred became a nun as she had wished. Her cult spread to England by the twelfth century and her curative well became a site of international pilgrimage. Unusual compared with modifications of other holy well sites, the Perpendicular Gothic structure dates to the fifteenth century. An arcaded well chamber encloses the source beneath a second-story chapel. Bathing rites are still available daily in the outer pool. Photograph by author.

Around the world, water sources are celebrated as life-giving and even floods could bring bounty and renewal. The Nile's annual flood is still celebrated in mid-August. Before 1960s damming, the inundation deposited rich sediment that replenished agricultural fields in a desert environment and was anciently deemed a gift of the god Osiris—a personification of the river.[9] Yet, floods are also universally considered a particularly painful form of divine punishment (Dundes, 1988; Oestigaard, 2006; Doniger, 2010; Tvedt, 2016:68). Describing the otherwise inexplicable reversal of life-supporting water bringing death, flood myths are perhaps embellishments of folk memories of a widespread and recurring phenomenon, and commonly attribute disaster to supernatural displeasure. In the indigenous tradition of the hunter-gatherer

Andaman Islanders, the creator god Puluga sent a flood when his commands were ignored. In Yoruba legends of West Africa, the goddess of the oceans inundated the first dry land as her permission was not obtained for its creation. After wiping out the unruly products of his first attempt with a great flood, the creator deity Viracocha re-established humanity on islands of the vast Lake Titicaca—the sacred center of the Andes. Genesis, the Sumerian Epic of Gilgamesh and the Mayan *Popol Vuh* (the creation narrative of the K'iche') likewise describe world-ending floods and a cultural hero who restarts humanity and redirects its path. The Noah of the Hindu Puranas is Manu (humanity's progenitor) who builds a boat in preparation for the flood, and in Hawaiian mythology, Nu'u is the ark maker. In China, a legendary Great Flood lasting two generations plagued the third millennium BC reign of Emperor Yao. Stealing expanding soil from the supreme deity, the hero "Gun" fails to control the flood and turns into a dragon, but his virtuous son Yu succeeds and founds the possibly-mythical first dynasty. The banks of the Huang He (the Yellow River) were the favored abode of the pre-Taoist creator deity Hebo who blessed farmers' fields with floodwater silt, but vented his displeasure with disastrous inundations and required regular appeasement with sacrificial offerings.

Veneration and votive deposition

Spirits of springs and water holes have also required gifts to keep their blessings flowing. Veneration of water bodies in the past is evidenced archaeologically through the deposition of votives (objects left by petitioners to emphasize the sincerity of a request or in thanksgiving for a desired outcome). Due to the use and reuse of water sources and the decay process of varied types of votives (metal as opposed to organic gifts of wood, bread or cake, for example), the surviving record is partial (Ray, 2014, 2019). Detectable remains of offerings in watery places can reveal period-specific veneration, but also veneration of a site in different eras or even across the periods by which we divide "the past." To point out that many sites have been reused in different eras does not imply continuity of use or continuity of meaning. Reuse of sites for seemingly ritual purposes (the deposition of votives) can occur after long time gaps and presumed breaks in cultural knowledge about a site (Ray, 2014). As the sacrality of springs can endure through changing populations, elites, technologies and religions, their biographies can encapsulate local and regional societal trends across the *longue durée* (Ray, 2019). Research on springs in France, Hungary and England that were assumed to have first been venerated by Romans, for example, reveals that sacred places deemed significant enough to remake as part of Roman conquest, of course, yield evidence of previous Iron Age and earlier devotions (Andrews, 2007; Jerem, 2007; Roymans, 2009).[10]

Watery site propitiation could be long lived: one of the largest Iron Age artifact deposits in the Baltic region was found in an Estonian spring-fed site where deposition continued for close to a millennium (Oras et al., 2018). Ritual landscapes could also expand around and far from an original source of sacrality—a spring. The 2,000 acre palimpsest of over 400 Neolithic earthen and stone monuments now featuring Stonehenge may have Mesolithic origins at the sacred spring Blick Mead which received thousands of pristine stone tools as votives (Jacques et al., 2018; see also Lewis et al.,

2019). Among the Neolithic standing stone rows at Carnac is the healing well now belonging to St. Cornély, Brittany's patron of cattle. Not only offering votives, the Nuragic people of Bronze Age Sardinia embellished holy wells in their own characteristic style with a hypogeal chamber for water access and stone block, tholos-like superstructures with benches on their outer walls (Lilliu, 2006). In addition to being sites of votive deposition, sacred water sources have been monumentalized around the world. Ancient Egypt's Karnak, still the largest religious complex in the world, was built beside a spring-fed sacred lake representing the primordial site of creation. The spring sources of the Tigris River in Upper Mesopotamia were where Assyrian kings communed with the ancestors, accepted the submission of local kings, gave offerings to the gods and had reliefs carved on nearby rocks to illustrate their acts and divine connections (Harmanşah, 2014:150–154).[11] Similarly, springs and water-filled sinkholes received sacrifices as passages to the Mayan underworld and the world of ancestors, and were the landscape features to which monumental structures were often aligned (Brady and Ashmore, 1999:129; Scarborough, 2003). Susan Evans and Deborah Nichols have argued that the largest monuments in the western hemisphere, the pyramids of Teotihuacan, were built by water worshippers in conjunction with an elaborate hydrological grid system that harnessed the flow of the area's nearly 80 springs (a special place in a dry valley) and canalized a river to visually reference the Feathered Serpent cult (associated with rain and flowing water) and the power of the ruling elite.[12] Perhaps representing a watery underworld, the Ciudadela, an immense sunken square at the center of Teotihuacan, had at its core a well/pit that received diverted water and was a focus for rituals (2015:25–34).

Folk liturgies and the body politic

In many places and eras, state- and chiefdom-level authorities have sanctioned and perpetuated sacred water rituals when these bolstered public reception and legitimized power, but they have also contested rituals and beliefs associated with this most basic resource when folk devotions could be perceived as a source of popular resistance. At locally-sacred springs, contemporary rituals are more often folk liturgies. In contrast to liturgy (the officially prescribed form of public religious worship), folk liturgical practices are those accepted as efficacious through generations of repetition rather than through sanction from religious authorities. Heterodox and regularly renegotiated, folk liturgies may be challenged, qualified or supplemented by professional religious practitioners, but their ownership remains with the populace. Especially at natural sacred sites, place-based rituals literally arise organically and similarly respond to changes in their setting over time. Just as hydronyms are the oldest-lived placenames (because of water's centrality to life, they are more likely to persist through changes of powers, populations and languages), types of popular devotions associated with sacred waters, such as votive offerings, can be some of the most perdurable through changes in faiths. Even though beliefs and intentions may transition or be replaced, ritual visitation of a spring can continue.

In the year 452, the Second Council of Arles prohibited the "pagan" veneration of springs, trees and stones for Christians; yet in the sixth century, the Gallo-Roman Bishop Gregory of Tours complained that "rustics" offered bread, cheese, beeswax and clothing to lakes and St. Martin of Braga sermonized against ongoing Galician devotion to rivers and springs (Alcock, 1966; Richert, 2005:6). In the same century, the British Gildas likewise assessed popular attributions of supernatural presence to mountains and water sources, but a holy well is nonetheless dedicated to him at Saint-Gildas-de-Rhuys. Originally advocating destruction of native pagan shrines, Pope Gregory the Great (540–604) decided that their reuse for Christian worship would speed conversion and suggested that foodstuffs generally left at such sites should instead be eaten there to enhance "good fellowship" among believers (Demacopoulos, 2008:353). While sixth-century religious officials were clearly worried about water veneration, the fact that bans continued across Europe for over a millennium—into the twelfth century in England and after the Reformation into the seventeenth century in Sweden, for example, means that syncretic folk pieties endured (Stjernquist, 1997:84; Oestigaard, 2011:46). Sacred springs that already attracted devotion and provided ready baptismal water were some of the first locations of Christian churches, small and large. England's cathedrals at St. Alban's, Wells, Winchester and York, Scotland's St. Mungo's Cathedral in Glasgow, Germany's Regensburg Cathedral and St. Kunibert's Church in Cologne, Norway's Nidaros Cathedral in Trondheim, and the Cathedral of the Virgin at Gelati, Georgia (to mention only a few) were all built over or immediately adjacent to sacred springs.

Concerns over folk rituals waxed and waned with the power of religious authorities (and with the varieties of festive behaviors supplemental to gatherings at sacred watery places). Even nineteenth-century holy well practices were still discouraged in many countries such as Ireland where a recently emancipated Church sought to regain control over holy well devotions (converting local folk liturgies to prayers at the Stations of the Cross, for example) and to stamp out wellside "patterns" (gatherings on the patron saint's feast day) that could feature distinctly unrelated activities such as drinking and fights between factions of the assembled (Ray, 2015). Just a few decades after the height of ritual conversions and pattern day suppression, holy wells emerge in antiquarian journals and newspaper editorials as endangered symbols of national identity and by 1934, as the Irish Free State was still straining towards complete independence from the British Commonwealth and fashioning an Irish-focused school curriculum, holy wells were selected as the subject for Ireland's first national folklore survey. Similarly, some forms of Buddhism view the use of holy water as Brahmanic (Hindu) or indigenous and therefore un-Buddhist; yet, one of the most common practices in Thai and other East Asian forms of Buddhism is the pouring of "lustral" holy or mantra water (*nam mon*) (Olson, 1991:75). Sometimes antithetical to a faith, water devotions can endure within new belief systems and water sources can be persistently sacred places.

Some sacred springs are global pilgrimage centers such as at Tirta Empul in Bali, Lourdes in France or Zamzam in Mecca, Saudi Arabia. Lesser-known sources also attract international pilgrims who return home with bottles of restorative water from sites such as Miracle Spring in the tiny town of Natadradave, in eastern Fiji's Tailevu district. Since a local discovered its ameliorative properties in 2016, thousands of hopeful visitors can visit in a day. Holy wells associated with Marian apparitions in Poland attract visitors from across Europe and the Polish Diaspora. The international Greek Diaspora likewise visits the most important pilgrimage site in Greek Orthodoxy, the

Aegean Island of Tinos, where Mary is venerated as *Panagia* (the Life-giving Spring) and the nineteenth-century Church of the Annunciation was built over the ruins of a Byzantine church and a holy well. The world's largest pilgrimage gathering is also the largest sacred water festival. In a struggle over a bowl (*kumbh*) of sacred nectar (*amrita*), gods and demons spilled a drop at each of four river locations which host the Kumbha Mela in rotation. In 2019, the Mela drew 105 million people to Prayagraj (Allahabad) at the confluence of three rivers: the Ganga, Yamuna and the mythical Sarasvati.

Yet, sacred water pilgrimage is more often quite localized. Cross-culturally, water sources are perceived as liminal places (thresholds between the natural and supernatural) and visiting even a local sacred water hole requires an inward journey of reverent thought manifested through appropriate behaviors that pauses ordinary time.[13] Pilgrimage to engage with natural sacred sites, rather than to enter temples or view relics, usually entails localized or regionalized folk liturgies, but can also be similar around the world. Walking ceremonial circuits in the direction of the sun is the most predominant pattern in the human veneration of topographical features. Excepting China and Tibet, Yi Fu Tuan has noted the almost universal perspective of the left side as profane and the right and front as sacred (2005 [1977]:35, 42). Moving from east to west, "sunwise" or clockwise, is fortuitous; counterclockwise ritual can be dangerous or curse-invoking. Marshall Sahlins wrote that the Hawaiian "splashing water" ceremony in sacred chiefs' initiations occurred sunwise and sovereignty was annually renewed by carrying an image of the fertility god Lono on circumnavigations of each island in a "right circuit" that kept the land always on the right hand (Sahlins, 1987:118). Lisa Lucero, Jean Larmon and Aimée Carbaugh have noted that the Maya traditionally walk ceremonial circuits which mirrored the path of the sun to reaffirm their relationship with sacred places; their own study focuses on a ceremonial circuit between 25 pools that were underworld portals and pilgrimage destinations at Cara Blanca, Belize (2017:249; see also Lucero, 2018). Wherever they are found, such circuits incorporate ritual at accessory landscape features.

Thaumaturgy-supporting natural features in sacred well landscapes

Folk liturgies and traditions about sacred watery sites often subsume other topographical features such as trees, stones, caves and heights. Water has its own materiality, but these graspable, textured repositories for prayer offer a different sensory connection to belief. Perhaps also considered thaumaturgical (miracle-producing), these have at some point come within the orbit of the spring or well where ultimate power resides. Anthropology provides several interlinked concepts that undergird our understandings of folk liturgies at sacred water sites and their associated natural features around the globe. From the Latin *anima* for soul, animism is common to humanity and is the belief that aspects of the material world can possess a soul or supernatural force. While devotees often commune with a larger sacred power willing to manifest in natural features for veneration and supplication, trees and stones can also be perceived as sentient members of a spiritual community in which animals and humans are also a part. Many historically documented hunting and gathering societies and tribes view trees and stones as "elders" that require the respect given to ancestors or older relatives. Across the continents, traditions hold that sacred water sources, trees and stones can "move" (leave their sacred precincts) if offended. The commonality of such perceptions around the globe led Sir Edward Tylor (a formative thinker in socio-cultural anthropology) to argue that animism was everywhere the first form of religion (1871). In fact, some have argued that explaining perceptions of animated nature gave rise to the discipline of anthropology itself and that animism was perhaps its first concept (Bird-David, 1999:67). Seeing ourselves as *apart* from nature, rather than *a part* of it, is a product of agricultural subsistence strategies and the emergence of state-level societies (with a "state-state of mind") (Scott, 1999). Animism may still pervade folk traditions in states however, and sit alongside adherence to the world's major faiths in localized popular belief. Certain species of plants or trees, or particular rocks and stones in which the supernatural abides can become totems (spiritual symbols). Trees and stones have been totemic from prehistory, serving as emblems for clans, lineages and tribes. Totems are a reminder of a group's identity and beliefs, of mythic origins, and of ancestors and tutelary deities. Anthropologists borrowed the concept of "mana" from Austronesian languages to describe the power which animists believe some stones and trees contain. Mana is an impersonal force that can inhabit some objects, places, plants and people, but not others (for example, mana can reside in members of chiefly dynasties, but not other social classes; four-leaf clovers, but not those with three leaves; a horse shoe mounted above a door with heels up rather than heels down). Mana-possessing sacred trees and stones, particularly those perceived as totems, are loaded with taboos (prohibitions against actions/behaviors). Taboos prevent offense to the mana-possessor; transgressions bring supernatural punishment. Sacred trees and stones associated with holy wells are totemic and usually swathed in ritual taboos meant to protect and direct their mana towards thaumaturgy (miracle production/cures) and good fortune.

Trees

Venerable trees have been symbolic places of assembly, covenant and prophecy where vows taken were considered sacred and binding. With roots reaching underground and branches stretching towards the sky, trees are *axes mundi* par excellence.[14] As agriculture's Middle Eastern invention was accompanied by deforestation for crop production, early animist farmers reserved groves as the dwelling places of otherwise dispossessed spirits. Agriculture enabled a human population boom and these sacred groves could be whittled away to single sacred trees as farmlands, dwellings and livestock pastures gradually encroached on even tabooed sacred precincts. Today, a few individual sacred trees are world renowned such as Indra's paradisiacal and wish-granting Kalpavriksha which emerged from earth's primal waters, or Gautama Buddha's Enlightenment-inspiring Bodhi. The ash that links and shelters all worlds and planes of existence in Norse mythology, Yggdrasil, has three roots drawing from three wells: one to the wisdom-giving well of Mimir, another to the spring Hvergelmir and a third extending to Urd's well where the gods gather and from which the Norns (the Norse Fates) water Yggdrasil itself. The pairing or proximity of a life-giving tree and water source is ubiquitous around the globe. This coupling is not only practical (sacred trees survive longer with a constant water source), but mana and symbolism are intensified when they co-occur. Both trees (as *axes mundi*) and wells (as entrances to the otherworld) are boundaries between the supernatural plane and our own. As liminal landscape features, they are both places of dread and blessing. Recipients of votive offerings or rags (which symbolize an affliction), the venerated trees in healing springs' sacred landscapes are the points where illness or worry is symbolically left when seeking grace from the waters.[15]

Stones

In some places, natural landscape features where prayers are said or rituals are performed as constituent parts of a larger pilgrimage are called "stations." Stone stations offer a comforting materiality to faith, remind devotees of transgenerational ritual practice and may perform a crucial role in traditional healing rituals. When natural springside rocks and boulders are recipients of votive offerings, these are often foodstuffs, alcohol or oil. Not always amenable to official, orthodox visions of international faiths, particular stones are made holy worldwide by their shape or by indentions perceived to be imprints made by the foot, hand, fingers, elbow, back, head and even the tears or face of a saint, deity, hero or ancestor (see Bord, 2004). Aligning one's relevant body part in the stone's depressions can be part of their ritual visitation. Imprint stones can even be contested between folk interpretations, for example, at the summit of Sri Lanka's 2,243-meter high mountain called Adam's Peak; a sacred footprint is claimed to be that of Shiva by Hindus, the Lord Buddha by Buddhists, the apostle Thomas by some Christians and, for Muslims, it is the imprint left by Adam when exiled from paradise (Aksland, 2001:16). Other stones might be referenced as the "chairs," "beds" or "boats" of cultural heroes and supernatural figures. After symbolic purification by drinking or anointing themselves with sacred water, petitioners may anticipate the arrival of a curative moment while sitting or lying on these thaumaturgical stones.[16]

Like trees, stones have provided a focus for veneration, ritual, revelations and inaugurations cross-temporally and cross-culturally. Stone cairns in memory of the dead and of heroic deeds may be found worldwide. Repeatedly erecting stone pillars, the Biblical Jacob arose after his famous dream about a ladder to heaven and "took the stone that he had put for his pillow, and set it up for a pillar, and poured oil on the top of it" (Genesis 28:18 KJV) and "vowed a vow" (28:20). Jacob and Laban commemorated a covenant by building a cairn and offering a sacrifice on it (Genesis 31:45–47). The Phoenicians are thought to have worshipped at stones considered to be houses of God (baetyls) which were likely meteorites. The most venerated meteorite on earth would be that embedded in the Ka'ba at Mecca.[17] The much-debated Germanic "Irminsuls" (interpreted as universal pillars) seem to have been tree trunks re-erected in a space selected for ritual focus and sometimes replaced with stone pillars; Charlemagne notably ordered their destruction during his eighth-century wars with the Saxons (Dowden, 2002:118–119). Hinduism and some types of Buddhism have the lingam (a cosmic pillar without beginning or end). A complement to the female yoni, the lingam is associated with fertility and power, most commonly represented in stone (in both private shrines and temples), and offered flowers, milk, oil, fruit and rice. From New Guinea to India to Morocco, megaliths are often associated with power structures and memorializing the dead, but have also been associated with fertility into the twentieth century even at sites such as Men-an-Tol in Cornwall. When beside sacred water sources, natural or human-modified, mana-possessing stones can play supportive roles in water veneration.

Caves

Springs emanating from caves are special wherever they occur, their waters are considered the most miraculous and ritually pure from Greece to Mexico, and some have evidence of prehistoric veneration.[18] Bronze Age cults engaged the underground pool within the cave at Psychro on the edge of the Lasithi Plateau on the island of Crete (Rutkowski and Nowicki, 1996:18). Visited by Greeks in antiquity to cure leprosy, the two thermal springs of Kaiafas flow from within a cave at the foot of Mount Lapithas and the resulting pool is still frequented by contemporary spa-goers.

In the first officially Christian nation, Armenia, the missionizing saint who converted the populace in 301, "Gregory the Illuminator" founded a church at the site of a sacred spring within a cave at Geghard (the later medieval monastic complex is now a UNESCO World Heritage Site). Mexico's second most significant Roman Catholic pilgrimage site after the Basilica of Our Lady of Guadalupe is the spring, cave and tree complex at Chalma. Pilgrims immerse or splash themselves with sacred water from a spring-fed pool sheltered by an ancient Montezuma cypress tree near a cave that was dedicated in pre-Aztec times to Oztotéotl (the god of darkness and night). Surrounded by mountains, Chalma was an abode of Tláloc (the celestial waters) who was the god of water, rain and lightning, and Chalchiuhtlicue (the earthly waters) who was the goddess of running water (de Orellana, 1972:71; Claassen, 2011).

The oldest place of Christian pilgrimage in Norway is a cave/spring complex dedicated to a legendary Irish martyr who was Norway's first saint. Fleeing a marriage to an invader Viking chieftain, St. Sunniva was said to be an Irish queen who put to sea with her followers and landed on the island of Selja on Norway's western coast. Hiding in a cave there from a local Viking menace and praying for aid, their deliverance came in a quick demise when the cave collapsed (Mikaelsson, 2005:107). Sunniva was known from Finland to Germany and even in the Faeroe Islands; her sacred spring was a significant place of pilgrimage before the Reformation, and Lutherans continue to use Sunniva as feminine given name (ibid:104; Hommedal, 2018).

Built in veneration of a spring emerging from a cave, one of Bali's most famous water temples is Tirta Empul (meaning Holy Spring). Rather than a sacred place along a river, the Hindu concept of *tirtha* came to refer to holy springs on Bali, and from at least the ninth century, Balinese temples were located beside springs for the creation of sacred bathing pools (Lansing, 2006:51). A temple has existed at Tirta Empul, the spring source of the Pakerisan River, from the tenth century and the site now draws thousands of international pilgrims, new yoga enthusiasts and spiritual tourists who move between two pools of spring water to dip their heads under a row of waterspouts in each. Expanding accommodation for visitors has led to garbage and sewage pollution directly entering the water (causing boil notices most recently in 2017); *E. coli* contamination has now compromised the holy waters where pilgrims have sought ritual purification for over a thousand years (see Warren, 2002).

Archaeologists James Brady and Wendy Ashmore note that in karstic landscapes, caves are geological conduits for the movement of groundwater. In the cosmology of the Mayan Lowlands where they research, water surfaces were viewed like mirrors and were an aid to scrying (foretelling the future). Cenotes (sink holes) there are known for their sacrificial depositions and their attractive colors where surface bedrock has collapsed to reveal the water table (1999:137). At Dos Pilas, Guatemala, Mayan kings positioned public architectural complexes beside caves with springs—the largest is today called El Duende, but was in ancient times known as K'inalha' for the springs to which it orients (ibid:128–129; see also Brady, 2010). The rush of water within the caves would have been an aural manifestation of the sacred. The Inca regularly enabled auditory hierophany through their placements of Andean shrines beside flowing water (Curatola Petrocchi, 2016). Recent archaeological research on the ritual use of caves has focused on their multisensory perception (how ancients experienced them and not just viewed them) and has particularly considered the links between sound and manifestations of the divine. Caves with springs were sacred soundscapes where particular areas could offer optimum acoustics for ritual or listening for a divine presence (Yioutsos, 2019).

Genii loci

Springs and riverbanks around the world are favored venues for receiving ritual purification, blessing and wisdom and serve as boundary markers between territories, villages or towns, and also between this world and supermundane domains. Liminal places cross-culturally, sacred springs and holy wells also have a numinous quality—many were perhaps selected as special because their physical distinctiveness suggested a supernatural character or presence. Supernatural guardians monitor these watery portals between realms and assist petitioners in accessing grace and thaumaturgical power across perceived divides between the natural and the supernatural. The protective spirit of a place, the genius loci may be imagined as a tutelary deity, a variety of supernatural beings, a muse or a totemic animal. While a genius loci can also simply be the characteristic atmosphere of a place, similar forms of genii aquae appear worldwide and their form shapes expectations of place-appropriate behaviors.

Dug by the hooves of the divine, winged stallion Pegasus, the famous Hippocrene spring on Mt. Helicon was the haunt of the Muses and imbibers of its waters received poetic inspiration.[19] The Greeks associated so many supernatural beings with fresh water sources that they classified these Naiades by abode and power: the Crinaiae occupied wells and fountains, the Limnades lived in lakes and the trickster Eleionomae dwelled in marshes and wetlands. While these could manifest as youthful beauties, more common genii are fish, eels and dragons. Across many faiths, fish and eels residing in sacred waters are considered embodiments of the genius loci. Just seeing them is thought to indicate the success of a petition, and their movements are considered prophetic (foretelling a return of health or impending death). From Scotland to South Africa, a change in the color of special water sources is also thought to be oracular and to either indicate the mood of ancestral spirits or the answers to questions posed to an aid-giving genius loci. Regular cast members in Han Chinese water myths, dragons reside in spring-fed pools where important events transpire. Again, perhaps because waters have to break before a birth—explanatory tales of babies emerging from water sources are found in many parts of the world and the Pumi (an official minority in China's Yunnan Province) visit "dragon pools" on the first day of the lunar calendar to request babies from water-dragon deities (Yun, 2010:419). In Japan, the Shinto *kami* (spirits) are associated with springs and waterfalls and can appear as dragons in devotees' dreams (Schattschneider, 2003). Dragon deities are also honored at Korean sacred springs in a blend of indigenous shamanism and Buddhism.

Snakes are ubiquitous supernatural protectors and residents of sacred waters. Except in a few cases of obvious diffusion, water-dwelling serpentine beasts appear so regularly in tales around the world because of the centrality of water in mythic cosmologies and an almost panhuman fascination with the silently undulating and sidewinding snake. Routinely molting their skin (ecdysis), they seem to regenerate themselves and appear more vibrant after sloughing a layer. As sacred water sources also have renewing powers, and as many snakes prefer watery habitats, their conflation in legend is unsurprising—varieties of actual "water snakes" affirm the association on six continents. On the southern slope of Mt. Parnassos is the celebrated Castalian Spring where those seeking the oracle at Delphi stopped to purify themselves; Apollo famously killed the resident serpent (Juuti et al., 2015:2327). In the cosmology of the Tewa in New Mexico, all rivers, arroyos, springs and lakes are linked underground and are traveled by prayer-carrying sacred water serpents (Awenyus) which deliver requests to the relevant water spirits (Ford and Shapiro, 2017). In northern Swaziland, a seven-headed snake lives in the sacred Mantjolo pool and grants poolside requests for rain from the site's Mnisi clan stewards (van Vuuren et al., 2007:18). While ancestral snakes live in the bottom of Australian waterholes created in the Dreamtime, for the Mae Enga of New Guinea, ancestors coalesce into huge, invisible pythons that dwell in forest pools where they receive pig organs and fat and around which men position images of both ghosts and living clan members (Meggitt, 1965:118).

Historical and ethnographic accounts demonstrate that from Peru to Indonesia and Siberia, water sources are common venues for engaging the ancestors in a variety of forms.[20] In Madagascar, springs (and stones) are associated with the more-feared-than-venerated *vazimba* (the earth's first inhabitants) who require offerings and can cause illness and calamity if displeased or enable haleness and fertility if placated. Malagasy springs could be called into being wherever sacred ancestors were invoked (Radimilahy, 1994:83–86). Stephanie Bunn has described how Kyrgyzstan's sacred Lake Issyk-kul is protected by the Mistress of Water *Bugu enye* who is considered the ancestor spirit of local people. There and at sacred springs, waterfalls and pools associated with ancestors or Sufi Muslim saints, the Kyrgyz may wash their faces, collect restorative and fertility-inducing waters to carry home, and tie rags on nearby bushes and trees. In another example of how sacred water beliefs and folk liturgies can deviate from a majority faith, they may also roll around on the ground beside the source and sacrifice sheep to the resident *e'e*—the powers or masters of the water (Bunn, 2013:131–132).[21] Similarly, linked notions of ancestry and treating water sources respectfully are also found in the Limpopo Province of South Africa (Ratiba, 2013). The health-giving Lake Fundudzi (the only natural inland lake in Southern Africa) is the abode of the ancestral spirits of the Vhatavhatsindi (people of the pool) and of a python fertility god. The lake is considered "a sacred burial site in which their ancestors continue to live" so that irreverent swimmers may be dragged under the water by displeased spirits (Van der Waal, 1997; Van Vuuren et al., 2007; Sharfman, 2017:106). On the Southeast-Asian island of Timor, each descent group stewards a particular spring where the ancestors were traditionally addressed in water-drawing rituals that reaffirm consanguineal kinship at "the door" to their ancestors' world ("the threshold of the spring") (Traube, 1986:188–191; Jennaway, 2008:24). Protected also by sacred eels, crocodiles and pythons, health and fertility-granting springs there generally have an associated stone where offerings of live animals are made (Kehi and Palmer, 2012:460–464). In Hindu and Buddhist mythologies, a naga (nagini in female form) is one of an array of snakey-water deities that can adopt human form and protect springs, wells and rivers (though they can also cause these to flood).[22] With some parallels to European Melusina legends (in which fish-tailed supernatural women beget noble lines), serpent-tailed nagini are considered ancestors in parts of South Asia. One naga king, Mucilanda, sheltered the Buddha from rain and storms while he obtained Enlightenment, and now appears in Buddhist art and state ritual in Thailand. As in many places, sovereignty is still associated with holy water in Thailand and in 2019, sacred waters were collected from each of the 76 provinces across the country for a traditional purification shower in the new king's coronation ceremonies.

While not regularly ancestral themselves, varied forms of African mermaids may guard sacred watery thresholds to the realms of the ancients or the recently departed. Zulu speakers in South Africa consult the mermaid deity of healing and fertility, Inkosazana, at the edges of pools that she inhabits and through which she may drag the petitioner to an underwater land of ancestors (Bernard, 2008). In South Africa's Ukhahlamba Mountains, a series of waterfalls flow into Gxubuse Pool which is dangerous to visit without an invitation through a dream, or for rainmaking or therapeutic purposes. Mermaids (*abantu bomlambo*) dwell there with a giant mystical snake (Bernard, 2013:145–146). Mami Wata (derived from Pidgin English for "water as mother") has become the generalized name for healing spirits who inhabit a variety of water bodies in Cameroon, Ghana, Niger and Nigeria and now have a homogenized representation as mirror-using mermaids (Drewal, 2012). In Benin, favor-granting spirits dwell in sacred pools called *Íbú ódó* at numerous points along the Ouèmé and Okpara Rivers and receive cheese gifts or annual goat sacrifices (Ceperley, 2012:399–401). Notions of female water supernaturals moved abroad with the African Diaspora and Bettina Schmidt notes ongoing creolization in Brazilian Candomblé of water goddesses from the West African pantheon. The mother of living waters, Iemanjá, is also sometimes regarded as the mother of all Candomblé *orixás* (deities and spirits) and Oxum (a fresh water goddess of rivers, lakes, springs and waterfalls) is represented like Mami Wata as a mermaid with a mirror (2017). Many of these numens can drag unattended children into their realms; the "Water Woman" version of Inkosazana, who occupies a pool beneath a waterfall at the South African mountain gorge of Meiringspoort, can grab them from any nearby water hole (van Vuuren et al., 2007). Her stories echo those of *La Llorona* in Mexican myth who wails for her lost children near water, the serpent- or fish-tailed Greek Lamia who grieves for her lost children yet devours those of others, and the Catalonian *donas d'aigua* who snags children venturing too close to one of her wells with a hook and keeps them. Combing her hair by water like a mermaid, an Estonian water spirit also acts like a banshee in lamenting the impending deaths of locals though it is sometimes she who drowns them (Västrik, 1999:28, 33). The third-century Christian theologian Tertullian even commented about "those wells called 'snatching wells,' where malignant spirits violently snatch people" (Jensen, 1993:40). Transcultural characters like these all speak to a panhuman fear of child-loss and specifically to the dangers of water sources for the young.

At wells sacred in the Judeo-Christian and Muslim traditions, genii loci more regularly take the form of a monotheistically agreeable zaddik, saint or wali. Jerusalem had the healing Pool of Siloam and the Pool of Bethesda where angelic visits activated the waters' curative abilities. Divinely provided for Hagar who stewarded it, Mecca's Zamzam spring is thought to cure illness and hunger (now a part of the *hajj*, the well preceded Abraham's legendary construction of the Ka'ba which makes Mecca holy).[23] In Morocco at the ruins of Shalla in Rabat, a shaded spring beside a wali's tomb is inhabited by eels which children feed; the eels are understood to be the embodiments of jinns that have become servants of the wali or Muslim saint.[24] Arising in Christianity as early as the third century, "saint cults" may be briefly defined as systems of beliefs and rituals associated with a holy person's relics or frequented places that induce a saint's intercession with the divine on behalf of the devotee, and foster friendship and communion between patron and individual (Brown, 2014). At Lourdes, apparitions of the Blessed Virgin Mary instructed the nineteenth-century French teenager, Bernadette Soubirous, to dig the earth with her hands in a cave to reveal a healing spring that now yields up to 40 liters of pure water per minute.

Connectivities

Today, sacred wells, trees, stones and caves can be considered isolated oddities in many parts of the world because of the radical editing of the landscapes in which they happen to survive. More likely, they were part of an interconnected sacred topography which is now largely inaccessible to us. What we think of as numinous nodes on an otherwise disenchanted map may have once derived meaning by their connection to multiple seemingly discrete sites and landscapes. It is now popular to speculate about articulated placelore of sacred topographies—to consider "Dreamtimes" beyond Australia (Mallory, 2016). The "Dreaming" is an unending beginning or temporal continuum in which heroic Ancestral Beings created the land, its resources and lore about the same in a still-ongoing process. Songs about the Dreaming (Songlines), which describe the paths traveled by revered Creator Beings, not only encoded knowledge about seasonal changes in flora and fauna, but also provided nomadic hunters and gatherers with cognitive maps of water holes, rock shelters and landmarks to navigate in their own travels. The interconnectivity of landscapes is, of course, always punctuated with water sources—as such generationally layered Indigenous Knowledge is elsewhere.

While people everywhere might consider "their" well or spring as the most pure, the most powerful and the most ancient, adherents to international faiths might acknowledge a distant source as the ultimate sacred water and if fortunate enough to visit as a pilgrim, bring that water home to increase the mana of their local fountainhead. Almost literally iconic themselves, the blue and white bottles shaped like a statue of the Virgin Mary in which pilgrims carry away water from the Lourdes spring are regularly left at holy wells in Ireland and can also appear at those in Italy and Austria. The full bottle is placed somewhere near the access point to the well, bolstering the capabilities of the home site, perpetuating the intention of the distant pilgrimage, and also linking the numinosity perceived at Lourdes to the experience of one's local shrine. In an age of inexpensive airline travel, such long-distance links can replace older pilgrimage circuits. Linked sacred topographies are also still evident in saint cults elsewhere. Chalma water is poured on or placed beside shrines elsewhere in Mexico. This is particularly so in the towns of the region where different communities engage in an elaborately choreographed schedule of Lenten pilgrimages based on a hierarchy of local patron saints whose statues are brought to "visit" the Christ of Chalma in a set order (though on a slightly different calendar than the official Church reckonings of Lent) (Gómez Arzápalo, 2009). In Ireland, holy wells dedicated to saints remembered as siblings were often visited in conjunction, or the site of one was ritually acknowledged as a distant station while offering devotions at the other. Devotees performing ritual circuits at St. Elva's well at Derrysallagh, County Sligo used to bow toward the well of her sister, St. Lassair, in Kilronan, Co. Roscommon. The Shinto spirits/saints known as *kami* merged into Japanese Buddhism and, both the good and the bad, dwell at water sources, caves, stones and trees, particularly those on sacred mountains. Worshippers undertake vision-granting austerities at the shrines of various *kami* and Buddhist deities that reside at different locations and elevations of a sacred mountain, and through their asceticism, ritualists ascend a spiritual hierarchy embedded in a mountain's topography (Schattschneider, 2003).[25]

It also happens that devotees may acknowledge some transcendent sources as the ultimate origin of their local site, or as in some way linked to their sacred waters which makes them holier and more phenomenal. In various parts of the globe, sacred fresh waters are deemed extraordinary through perceived connections with saltwater seas. Springs of East Timor are thought to recede with the ocean's low tide and to fill at high tide (Kehi and Palmer, 2012:456). Likewise, the Tullaghan well in County Sligo (made famous by Yeats as "the Hawk's Well") is thought to be the holy well Gerald of Wales reckoned as one of Ireland's twelfth-century wonders because, despite its inland, hilltop location, it ebbed with the tides of the sea (which local residents still claim in the twenty-first century) (Wright, 1863:65). In eastern China's tea-growing area of Longjing (a placename meaning Dragon Well), waters of the eponymous well were believed to be connected with those of the Eastern Sea where dragons lived and from which rain could be requested.[26]

Waters deemed unusually powerful are thought to have paradisiacal origins. Gish Abay, or the source of the Blue Nile, in Ethiopia is thought to be "Gihon," one of the four rivers that flowed out of the Garden of Eden (the others being the Hiddekel or Tigris, the Euphrates and the Pishon). Genesis 2:13 describes Gihon as encircling the land of Cush which is identified elsewhere in the Bible with Ethiopia. Unlike the other rivers diverging across Mesopotamia from the primal Edenic source, Gish Abay emerges after a journey under the Red Sea. While Gish Abay is a center of pilgrimage, devotees do not have direct access to the ultra-holy water to avoid its defilement (attendants approved by the Ethiopian Orthodox Church provide water in bottles and cans) (Oestigaard and Gedef, 2011). The source of the White Nile in Uganda, by contrast, is more mundane, and while healing, it is not thought holy (Oestigaard, 2018). The most sacred waters for Muslims, those of Zamzam, are thought to mingle with those of every other spring in Islamic countries one night a year and refresh their mana; a pilgrim losing his drinking cup when reaching for Zamzam water claimed to have retrieved it from a well at a Cairo mosque (Canaan, 1927:65).[27] In what Rana Singh has called "*Gangaization,*" the Ganga is perceived as the ultimate source of all Hindu sacred waters. Other sacred rivers, all sacred *tirthas, kundas* (pools) and *kūps* (wells), are thought to ultimately derive from the Ganga which also sacralizes all that is between them (1987:316–317). This perspective traveled with nineteenth-century immigrants to the island of Mauritius off the southeast coast of Africa where in the 1890s, a local priest dreamed a crater lake called Talao in the island's mountainous center was linked to the Ganga. The idea gave comfort to indentured workers who had moved there, and temples now line the water's edge where fruit and incense offerings are made and devotees perform ritual purifications. In 1972, Ganga water was brought to pour into the sacred lake which was renamed Ganga Talao and now pilgrims walk barefoot to the lake during Shivaratri (the annual festival honoring Shiva). Whether Dreamtime-like interconnections or newly imagined links to the greatest sources of mana, cosmovisions of sacred water highlight the natural fact that, while ever renewing, fresh water is a limited and precious resource.

Sacred waters as a subject and their relevance for socioecological resilience

Until the arrival of plumbing, knowledge of water sources and their associated qualities was part of the most basic education for living and was acquired through oral traditions. The earliest "science" of life was encoded in religious creation stories and the earliest scholars whose works are known to us considered the meanings of water. James Smith's examination of the classical authorities on legends or locations of springs included Aeschylus, Apollodorus, Xenophon, Thucydides, Herodotus and Euripides, and many poets who also described their physical appearance and traditions (1922). Smith noted that Hesiod, Homer and Ovid wrote about magical transformations in the waters of springs (which count as the first landscape features in Ovid's description of creation). The second-century cultural geographer and travel writer Pausanias recorded traditions of ancient Greece as they edged from folk memory under Roman domination. Across his ten volumes, the names of springs that he documented still indicate the route of his travels (ibid:viii; see Elsner, 1992). While the secular Chinese scholar Wang Chong was accurately describing the hydrological cycle in the first century, the era of the Han Dynasty was also the period during which a growing body of topographical lore, the mythical geography of China known as *The Classic of Mountains and Seas*, was evolving into its set form in which spring and river waters are described as divine and immortal (see Birrell, 1999).

For the naturalist Pliny the Elder, sacred waters were interesting for their curative potential and he classified springs according to their remedies for eyes, ears, head, bones, stomach, infertility and miscarriage, gout and insanity. This focus also characterized Renaissance and post-Reformation studies of springs in Europe and impacted views of holy water in places to which European cultures were exported. Sixteenth-century Italians were intrigued with balneology (from the Latin for bath, *balneum*) or the study of bathing (particularly therapeutic), and revived interest in the theories of Galen (the second-century Greek physician) about bathing in natural spring waters. The English physician and Reformer chaplain William Turner began publishing on the virtues of the waters at Bath in the 1550s, crediting their health-giving power to brimstone.[28] Turner's publications ushered in an insular enthusiasm for analyzing mineral waters that, in turn, fostered "taking the waters" (both drinking and bathing) for health benefits and for socializing as a form of proto-vacation. During "the season," those with the leisure time and funds mixed with invalids at Tunbridge Wells, Bath and Malvern (where the source of medicinal water was a holy well known for cures in medieval times), or they traveled abroad (with the excuse of a spa visit for health).[29] The rationalism of Enlightenment thinkers had largely finished off vestiges of animism and reduced once numinous waters to resources valued for their mineral content and recreational potential. By the mid-nineteenth century, medicinal water spas numbered close to 250 in England and in the thousands across Europe and North America (Mather, 2013; Robins and Smedley, 2013). Likewise, in volcanically-active Japan, the *onsen* (a hot spring with bathing facilities and nearby inns) may have replaced much earlier Shinto conceptions of genii loci at thousands of springs. From Japan to Bulgaria to Argentina, multiple international associations now pursue balneology both in academic terms as Medical Hydrology, and to promote spa tourism.

A century ago, sacred wells were a scholarly interest. In 1918, Rustom Pestonji Masani published *Folklore of Wells: Being a Study of Water-Worship in East and West* and four years later, James Reuel Smith published a 722-page book on the legendary springs and wells in Greece, Asia Minor and Italy (mentioned earlier). Through the nineteenth and twentieth centuries, holy wells and sacred springs were regularly featured in folklore studies and in local history journals—so many that Arthur Gribben published a 114-page bibliography of works mentioning or dedicated to holy wells and sacred water sources just in Britain and Ireland (1992:31–150). Recently, it is sacred rivers that have attracted scholarly attention. Considering the paradox of India's rivers' enduring sacrality and their pollution, David Haberman focused on the Yamuna (2006). Peter Ackroyd examined the Thames from its prehistoric sacrality to the present (2008). Considering the Hudson, the Volga, the Seine, the Thames and the Shannon, Tricia Cusack (2010) has explored the significance of ancient river mythologies and painted riverscapes in shaping national identities in nineteenth- and early twentieth-century Europe and America. Rachel Havrelock (2011) considered the political and symbolic borders of the Jordan—one of the holiest rivers (from which, as mentioned, water is flown around the world for christenings and baptisms). Catherine Knight has offered an environmental history of New Zealand's rivers, some of which the Maori consider ancestral (2016). Terje Oestigaard's 2018 volume, *The Religious Nile*, considers how ancient and contemporary religious perspectives of the river have shaped the societies along its course.

While not focused on the sacrality of water, the subfield of wet site and wetland archaeology has grown particularly since the 1980s (Menotti and O'Sullivan, 2013).[30] Neither water bodies nor land, liminal wetlands have received both votive deposition and burials around the globe. Northern European bogs are famous for their Iron Age "bog bodies"—perhaps victims of sacrifice or executed criminals (Aldhouse-Green, 2015). Underwater burials in peat at Florida's much older, Archaic-period sites (such as Windover, Bay West, Little Salt Springs and Republic Grove) occurred over a millennium (see Purdy, 2017 [1991]). In both locations, bodies could be staked into the peat to prevent their re-emergence so that wetlands do attract some similar forms of ritual activity. The cross-cultural sacrality of marshes, fens, bogs and other wetlands deserves further attention. While interpreted and venerated differently than sacred water sources, such depositional locations are sacred waterscapes.

Employed since the mid-nineteenth century, "waterscape" is analogous to landscape and, as defined by Ben Orlove and Steven Caton, refers to "the culturally meaningful, sensorially active places in which humans interact with water and with each other" (2010:408). Whether we describe them as therapeutic, "ordinary," sacred or spiritually neutral, we can now speak of waterscapes, riverscapes, seascapes, lakescapes, blue spaces and waterworlds. Kirsten Hastrup's concept of waterworlds references the ways water connects all of life's different domains (2009; Orlove and Caton, 2010). In current and anticipated water crises, more aquacentric language can only be an aid to better stewardship. Beliefs, knowledge and traditions (Intangible Cultural Heritage) about sacred waters have fostered biocultural diversity around the globe. Cross-cultural similarities in visions and treatments of sacred waters, particularly those forms that can have either highly localized or international appeal (hallowed springs, holy wells, pools and water holes) can inspire adoptable paradigms for responsible water cultures.

Current academic, media and popular obsession with "difference" is hardly productive for a world population in excess of 7.7 billion which increasingly embraces lifestyles that overconsume and pollute basic resources. Understanding the myriad ramifications of culturally constructed categories of difference is essential for social and environmental justice, but so too is an appreciation of what we share in common. Anthropologist Peter Van der Veer has in fact specifically called for a revitalization of the comparative approach (2016).[31] Better understandings of shared values and of similarities between worldviews enable us not only to learn from each other more effectively across difference, but to collaboratively shape answers to environmental issues that impact us all. Sacred water sites and their traditions have many striking similarities around the world, and are also humanity's shared biocultural heritage. Their stewardship (only recently failed in many places) models routes to reconnecting communities to better treatment of water generally. Designating four main types of sacred places as World Heritage Sites (mountains, landscapes, forests and waters), UNESCO (the United Nations Educational, Scientific and Cultural Organization) deems the conservation of both their cultural and biological diversity to be significant for humanity (Dudley et al., 2009; Robson and Berkes, 2010:199). Sites of biocultural diversity are those where cultural beliefs and practices help protect and maintain habitats, ecosystems and stocks of particular flora and fauna (because these are perceived as curative, numinous, or as totems, metaphorical kin or valued resources). Likewise, those flora and fauna influence cultural traditions and identities, along with languages that encode local ecological knowledge and cultural worldviews about how to relate to landscape features, resources and biota (see Maffi, 2001). With the loss of animism and disenchantment of the natural world has come its anthropocentric abuse. Water sources were likely the first sites humans venerated and those that cross-culturally and cross-temporally have remained the most common category of sacred natural sites worldwide. Religious beliefs that perpetuate biodiversity conservation deserve our attention (Frascaroli, 2013; Lazzerini and Bonotto, 2014).

While we have the same amount of fresh water on earth as did all previous generations, we now overexploit our most important resource (70% of all drawn water is expended on agriculture and 20% on industry) so that what was an ample and self-renewing vital resource for smaller human populations is for much of ours, a limited or scarce one. The intensification of agriculture to meet increased food demands has caused significant depletion of aquifers and their pollution from the application of fertilizers and pesticides. The lowering of water tables through current consumption levels means that formerly reliable springs are running dry around the world. In 2010, the United Nations General Assembly recognized access to water as a human right and, in 2015, acknowledged the separate but equal right to water sanitation. Yet, close to two-sevenths of the world's population lacks access to safely managed drinking water (Klaver, 2012). This lack, combined with lack of education, cultural hygiene practices and changing weather patterns that result in changing water supplies, leads to millions of deaths each year from consumption of unsafe water (Grojec, 2017). Never reaching one billion until the first decade of the 1800s, the human population has exploded in 200 years by more than 700%. Neo-Malthusian worries are about water as much as food. The cultural devaluation and disempowerment of women that creates unsupportable overpopulation, coupled with human choices about settlement locations, urban expansion and consumption levels have created water crises that are now exacerbated by the shifting rainfall patterns accompanying environmental change. Megacities such as Cape Town, Sao Paulo, Beijing, Istanbul and Mexico City are all experiencing water stress and scarcity. In some cases, unmaintained infrastructure causes significant loss of water, in Bangalore rapid expansion and pollution are to blame, and in Jakarta aquifers have been drained by illegal well digging. No longer treated as something considered sacred, water is in short supply.

The United Nations Conference on Environment and Development first recommended an international observance "for" water in 1992. Anthropologists such as Veronica Strang (2009; 2015), John Richard Wagner (2013), and Kirsten Hastrup and Frida Hastrup (2015) have addressed the inequity issues prompting "World Water Day" and importantly considered watery environments in relation to settlement, ownership and subsistence. What is also needed is a greater understanding of the religious significance of water and what motivates people to steward water sources in ways that enable socioecological resilience. As protection of water sources came early in humanity's colonization of the globe, water sources are perhaps the oldest conservation areas.

Transdisciplinary efforts now link traditional ecological knowledge about sites of natural sacrality with solutions for water crises (Groenfeldt, 2013; Willems and van Schaik, 2015; Bryan, 2017; Jackson, 2018). How people view their world directly shapes how they act in it (Sharfman, 2017) and knowing how people value and use water can enable better stewardship, but we need to first understand water cultures. Sometimes, perceptions of Mother Nature or "God's Providence" can foster both veneration *and* a lack of responsibility. In March 2017, New Zealand granted the legal rights of a living entity to the 90-mile-long Whanganui River which is considered ancestral to the Maori people and will now be represented by two guardians in future legal matters. Inspired by this, and a few days later, the High Court in India's Uttarakhand State granted the Ganga and Yamuna Rivers (and the Gangotri and Yamunotri glaciers that feed them) the same legal rights as a person to protect them from pollution. Because the rivers extend beyond Uttarakhand, and because identifying and punishing polluters in the same ways as offenders committing assault or murder was deemed to be legally unsustainable, the Supreme Court quickly overturned the ruling in July (see O'Donnell and Talbot-Jones, 2018). Even though Hindu scriptures encourage environmental stewardship (Dwivdei, 1997), because the Ganga and Yamuna are both perceived as living goddesses, they are expected to receive not only the ashes from regular cremations along their banks (permitted in scripture), but human corpses (Sharma, 2004; see Haberman, 2006). They also receive trash, sewage and industrial waste. Yet perceiving them as self-renewing and inviolable, devotees still immerse themselves in their waters (see Colopy, 2012). As is known too well, sometimes religion backfires. When people believe in a "giving environment," as the very name "Ganga Mata"/Mother Ganga implies, the suggestion that they can protect or conserve what they view as the source of all life can seem inconceivable (Milton, 1996:118–120).

On the other hand, religious worldviews often explicitly require stewardship and conservation practices that ostensibly honor and please the supernatural, but also have practical benefits. Anthropologist Stephen Lansing has studied how the traditional Balinese production of rice in flooded fields depends on a precise control of water enabled by religious tradition (1987, 2012). Irrigation is regulated through a hierarchical network of water temples and festival calendars so that fields are irrigated during the temple visits of particular deities. A typical village can have between 10 and 50 temples that receive holy water from central Balinese lake temples for purifying irrigation water. Water rituals at each temple relate to nine stages of planting and harvesting rice. As the growing period of native Balinese rice is 105 days, major temple festivals occur at intervals of 105, 210 and 420 days—a cycle that allows enough algae growth for fertilization, yet not enough to attract unmanageable numbers of pests in the form of fish, insects and rodents. When the "Green Revolution" arrived in Bali in the 1970s to push new technologies for higher yields, Balinese famers were instructed to put away their incense and ignore the gods' temple visits around which irrigation was scheduled. Along with bacterial and viral diseases, rat and insect populations surged. The pesticidal remedies for these then killed fish and eels and some farmers (Lansing, 1987:339). "Celebrated" as they are, science and contemporary technology disregard religion and the biocultural heritage religion protects. Folk technologies are honed across centuries for fit with local environments. Bali's rice cultivation had been based on generationally layered ecological knowledge and farmers had enshrined best practice within religion so that it would not be forgotten. Dismissing religious tradition can eradicate a wealth of practical wisdom.

In the twentieth century, close to 800,000 dams were built worldwide and they now yield close to 20% of the world's electricity, but divert, or otherwise fragment, 60% of the world's largest rivers (Wu et al., 2004; Johnston, 2012; Hammersley et al., 2018).[32] Nehru identified dams with progress and famously called them the "temples of modern India"; yet with damming, river sediment is deposited in reservoirs rather than nourishing the floodplains. These reservoirs are breeding grounds for snails that harbor disease-causing parasites and mosquitoes that carry the viruses for the Yellow, West Nile, and Dengue fevers, Malaria and Zitka (Bartram, 2015). Dams are often damnation for traditional beliefs about water sources. Terje Oestigaard has described the hydropower project in the Bujagali Falls area of Uganda which encompasses multiple sites sacred to the Busoga including waterfalls, groves and rocks (2015). Years of opposition to damming the falls for hydroelectric power focused on the multiple resident waters spirits, but especially the waterfall-dwelling healer Budhagaali who had to be ceremonially relocated before the nearly one-billion-dollar dam project could be inaugurated. In Uttarakhand, India, a local version of the goddess Kali, Dhārī Devī, is venerated along the River Alaknanda with a temple and statue. Both were to be inundated by a hydropower project at Srinagar. Frances Niebuhr noted that the local resistance which emerged due to cultural epistemologies about water demonstrates the need for "water-based environmental dialogue" (2017:246, 257; see also Drew, 2017).

Brokering solutions or pre-emptions to the predicted water wars of climate change requires reasserting commonalities in human valuations of water. Our two most immediate needs are for air and water and while outdoor air quality is mostly beyond individuals' control, water must be gathered and can be owned and privatized by cities, states or corporations. John Wagner has suggested that "'imagining' water as a commons can help us build the types of institutional networks we need to manage water wisely, equitably, and sustainably" (2012:627). To do so, we need to identify and emphasize what is common in our evaluations and uses of water; panhuman perceptions of water's sacrality seem a good way to start. Understanding water cultures and how humans everywhere protect and manage sacred waters is constructive in promoting behaviors and policies that enhance socioecological resiliency—what religious practices at watery sites evolved to foster in the first place.

Notes

1 See Shiklomanov (1993) and Ball (2001).Thanks to Bruce Misstear for comments on a draft of this essay and his prompt to also note that, additionally, 97% of the world's unfrozen fresh water occurs beneath the land surface as groundwater while only 3% exists in lakes, rivers and the atmosphere.

2 Across two decades of researching holy wells in Ireland and Scotland (with field work in Wales, Cornwall, the South Tyrol, Norway and Austria), this book was a pause

from a longer project on Irish holy wells begun in the year 2000. As I read about comparative sites elsewhere to make sense of the Irish cases, I found colleagues from New Zealand to Iceland, and from China to Peru who were also fascinated with watery sites of natural sacrality. I contacted many to pose comparative queries and from those exchanges, this book emerged. Along the way, I organized a two-day workshop on sacred springs and holy wells with medievalist Shane Lordan in Waterford, Ireland which was generously hosted by Eamonn McEneaney of the Waterford Council and the Waterford Museum of Treasures. Eight of the presentations from that gathering were revised for inclusion in this volume. Many thanks are owed to Cari Shepherd Reynolds for global sourcing of interlibrary-loans and to David Syler for editing images across the volume. Thanks also to Hannah Marie Garcia and Kennedy Jones for reading drafts.

3   Springs are further classified by flow rate, mineral content and formation, for example, via a fissure in the earth's surface, as a seepage spring (where water has slowly filtered through permeable ground), within a cave ("tubular springs"), or through pressure in a confined aquifer creating artesian springs.

4   See Diana Eck's essay on *tirthas* (1981).

5   What Jacques et al. (2018): call "persistent places." For a discussion of natural sacred site selection, see Bradley (2000).

6   For the obvious reasons of their work ethic and building skills, ants are a kind of earth diver in many parts of the world. In Lithuania, they bring soil out of water and even in the Homer's *Illiad*, Achilles' Myrmidons created his island from the sea and were known as "ant people." (Their ancestress Eurymedousa was oddly seduced by Zeus in the appearance of an ant, and/or Zeus gave them ant-like immunity to the plagues Hera sent in punishment of her husband's lover.)

7   Yamuna's twin sister Yama is the deity of death.

8   Thanks to Christopher McDonough for this reference.

9   The Aswan High Dam has blocked the flow of sediment since the 1960s.

10 The hot springs at Bath are perhaps the most famous Iron Age water shrine because of their Roman reuse. Roman engineering eradicated native treatments of the site, excepting a possible pre-Roman gravel causeway to the spring. Pairing or equating native deities with their own as part of imposing *Romanitas*, Romans likened the indigenous genius loci Sulis with Minerva. Sulis is cognate with the Irish súil (meaning eye, but also hope/expectation and sometimes gap). Rather than a proper name for a singular divinity, the name may reference perceptions of the sacred spring; the water, like an eye, reflected an image and was an orifice to the otherworld (Ray, 2014:41–42). Viewing the surface of sacred waters as reflecting special visions is common elsewhere and the Mayan perception is noted in this chapter.

11 "Sources" of rivers refer not only to an originating spring, but feeder springs along the course of a river.

12 The largest, the Pyramid of the Sun as known by a later Aztec name, was built over an artificial cave and what was thought to have been a former spring.

13 Most works on pilgrimage have focused on journeys to distant sites (Turner and Turner, 1978; Eade and Sallnow, 1991; Morinis, 1992; Badone and Roseman, 2004; Di Giovine and Picard, 2015). Pilgrimage to local sites of natural sacrality is in many ways distinct. Even when a site is overlain with an international faith, the biocultural setting shapes devotions and belief.

14 Water sources are often considered in similar ways as axes mundi, but their fluid materiality means that they have not been generally referenced as such.

15 For a wonderful comparative essay about tying rags on trees, see Dafni (2002).

16 Folk liturgies can, of course, vary; such engagements can precede physical contact with sacred spring water.

17 Debate continues as to whether the Ka'ba's "Black Stone" is a meteorite or pseudometeorite (a terrestrial rock attributed with meteoritic origins) or possibly basalt lava or pumice.

18 Writing about pilgrimage in Western Europe, the Nolans argued that if a shrine has three such topographic features (for example, a mountain cave with a curative spring or a sacred tree and stone beside a holy well), then chances are "twelve to one that additional evidence proves or strongly suggests that the place was holy before the advent of Christianity in the region" (1989:303).

19 Pegasus was the creator of many such springs (Smith, 1922). Another is the famous "wellspring of Western Civilization," the Peirene Fountain in Classical Corinth (Robinson, 2011).

20 On Siberia, see Breyfogle (2017).

21 While the *hajj* to Mecca is a pillar of the faith, voluntary pilgrimages such as these are "ziarat" which Bhardwaj might call "parallel Islam" (1998). On the Indonesian island of Lomboka, both Hindu and Muslim pilgrims undertake a *tirtha yatra* (a sacred water journey) to the home of a Hindu-Balinese goddess Dewi Anjani, a crater lake on a volcanic mountain that is considered the center of the world. Along their route, they pray, ritually purify themselves in hot springs and gather water at local springs, waterfalls and the lake to bring home. This sacred site-sharing is tense, but combines localizations of both Hinduism and Islam (Gottowik, 2016).

22 Before Spanish colonization, Philippine nagini were snakey mermaids and in Cambodia and Laos, they were water serpents.

23 The Saudi Arabian government prohibited Zamzam water's commercial export, but bottles (often fakes) are sold globally. Testing purported Zamzam water sold in London, Britain's environmental agency found high arsenic levels (de Châtel, 2007:27).

24 Thanks to anthropologist Emilio Spadola for this account.

25 Links between sacred places are more readily researched in documented religions where gods traveled between them (and humans imitated their circuits). Kaljürgen Feuerherm has described the "daisy chain" of divine travels of Ancient Mesopotamian deities who frequented the stones and trees and water sources people should venerate; their "descents to the lake" were marked with festivals (2011).

26 Thanks to Jean deBernardi for this reference.

27 Thanks to Ahmad Ghabin for this reference.

28 As noted by B.W. Richardson in an article "The Medical History of England" for *The Medical Times and Gazette*, March 18, 1865 (p. 292).

29 The Latin phrase *sanitas per aquas* is sometimes referenced as the origin of the concept, as is Belgium's fourteenth-century discovery of a curative thermal spring in the town of Spa.

30 Barbara Purdy organized an International Conference on Wet Site Archaeology in 1986 at the University of Florida that she and, my then graduate student idol, Lee Newsom kindly allowed me to attend as an undergraduate. Hearing Byrony Coles and John Coles, Sander E. van der Leeuw, Tom Dillehay and William Watts there fanned an early interest in watery sites that became instead a fixation on sacred water. The Coles went on to found the Wetland Archaeology Research Project (an international network of researchers in wetland archaeology).

31 The comparative approach, for some, remains tied to Lewis Henry Morgan's thoughts on unilineal social evolution, Van der Veer instead calls for post-Durkheimian, post-Weberian endeavors with historical grounding.

32 NASA even estimated that the weight of the water and trapped sediment behind the thirty-billion-dollar Three Gorges Dam in China could slow the earth's rotation and lengthen each day by 0.06 microseconds. https://www.jpl.nasa.gov/news/news.php?feature=716.

References

Ackroyd, Peter. 2008. *Thames: Sacred River*. London: Vintage.

Alcock, Joan. 1966. Celtic Water Cults in Roman Britain. *Archaeological Journal* 122:1–12.

Aldhouse-Green, Miranda. 2015. *Bog Bodies Uncovered: Solving Europe's Ancient Mystery*. London: Thames and Hudson.

Aksland, Markus. 2001. *The Sacred Footprint: A Cultural History of Adam's Peak*. Bangkok: Orchid Press.

Andrews, Phil. 2007. Springhead: Late Iron Age Ceremonial Landscape to Roman Healing Centre? In *Continuity and Innovation in Religion in the Roman West (Vol. 1)*, edited by Ralph Haeussler and Anthony King, 31–36. Portsmouth, RI: Journal of Roman Archaeology Supplementary Series No. 67.

Badone, Ellen and Sharon Roseman. 2004. *Intersecting Journeys: The Anthropology of Pilgrimage and Tourism*. Urbana: University of Illinois Press.

Ball, Philip. 2001. *Life's Matrix: A Biography of Water*. Berkeley: University of California Press.

Bartram, Jamie, ed. 2015. *Routledge Handbook of Water and Health*. London: Routledge.

Bernard, Penny. 2008. "The fertility goddess of the Zulu: reflections on a calling to Inkosazana's pool." In *Deep Blue: Critical Reflections on Nature, Religion and Water*, edited by Sylvie Shaw and Andrew Francis, 49–65. London: Equinox.

Bernard, Penelope S. 2013. "Living Water" in Nguni Healing Traditions, South Africa. *Worldviews* 17(2):138–149.

Bhardwaj, Surinder M. 1998. Non-Hajj Pilgrimage in Islam: A Neglected Dimension of Religious Circulation. *Journal of Cultural Geography* 17(2):69–87.

Bird-David, Nurit. 1999. 'Animism' Revisited: Personhood, Environment, and Relational Epistemology. Special issue, Culture: A Second Chance? *Current Anthropology* 40(suppl.1):67–91.

Birrell, Anne, trans. 1999. *The Classic of Mountains and Seas*. London: Penguin.

Bord, Janet. 2004. *Footprints in Stone*. Loughborough: Heart of Albion.

Bradley, Richard. 2000. *An Archaeology of Natural Places*. London: Routledge.

Brady, James E. 2010. Offerings to the Rain Gods: The Archaeology of Maya Caves. In *Fiery Pool: The Maya and the Mythic Sea*, edited by Daniel Finamore and Steven D. Houston, 218–222. New Haven, CT: Yale University Press.

Brady, James E. and Wendy Ashmore. 1999. Mountain, Caves, Water: Ideational Landscapes of the Ancient Maya. In *Archaeologies of Landscape: Contemporary Perspectives*, edited by Wendy Ashmore and A. Bernard Knapp, 124–148. Oxford: Blackwell.

Breyfogle, Nicholas. 2017. Sacred Waters: The Spiritual World of Lake Baikal. In *Meanings and Values of Water in Russian Culture*, edited by Jane Costlow and Arja Rosenholm, 32–50. New York: Routledge.

Brown, Peter. 2014. *The Cult of the Saints: Its Rise and Function in Latin Christianity*. Chicago, IL: University of Chicago Press.

Bryan, Michelle. 2017. Valuing Sacred Tribal Waters within Prior Appropriation. *Natural Resources Journal* 57(1):139–181.

Bunn, Stephanie. 2013. Water as a Vital Substance in Post-Socialist Kyrgyzstan. *Worldviews* 17(2):125–137.

Canaan, Taufik. 1927. *Muhammadan Saints and Sanctuaries in Palestine*. London: Luzac and Co.

Ceperley, Natalie. 2012. The Role of Íbú ódó Sacred Pools in Preserving Riparian Forest Structure and Diversity along the Ouèmé and Okpaa Rivers of Central Benin. In *Sacred Species and Sites: Advances in Biocultural Conservation*, edited by Gloria Pungetti, Gonzalo Oviedo and Della Hooke, 399–402. Cambridge: Cambridge University Press.

Claassen, Cheryl. 2011. Waning Pilgrimage Paths and Modern Roadscapes: Moving through Landscape in Northern Guerrero, Mexico. *World Archaeology* 43(3):493–504.

Colopy, Cheryl. 2012. *Dirty, Sacred Rivers: Confronting South Asia's Water Crisis.* Oxford: Oxford University Press.

Cook, Brad L. 2009. A Watery Folktale in the Alexander Romance: Alexander's Byzantine NERAÏDA. *Syllecta Classica* 20:105–134.

Curatola Petrocchi, Marco. 2016. La voz de la huaca. Acerca de la naturaleza oracular y el transfondo aural de la religión andina antigua. In *El Inca y la huaca. La religion del poder y el poder de la religión en el mundo andino antiguo,* edited by Marco Curatola Petrocchi and Jan Szemiñski, 259–316. Lima: Fondo Editorial de la Pontificia Universidad Católica del Perú and The Hebrew University of Jerusalem.

Cusack, Tricia. 2010. *Riverscapes and National Identities.* Syracuse, NY: Syracuse University Press.

Cuthbert, Mark O., Tom Gleeson, Sally C. Reynolds, Matthew R. Bennett, Adrian C. Newton, Cormac J. McCormack and Gail M. Ashley. 2017. Modelling the Role of Groundwater Hydro-refugia in East African Hominin Evolution and Dispersal. *Nature Communications* 8:15696.

Dafni, Amots. 2002. Why Are Rags Tied to the Sacred Trees of the Holy Land? *Economic Botany* 56(4):315–327.

de Châtel, Francesca. 2007. *Water Sheiks and Dam Builders: Stories of People and Water in the Middle East.* New Brunswick, NJ: Transaction Publishers.

de Orellana, Margarita. 1972. The Worship of Water Gods in Mesoamerica. *Arqueologia Subacuatica*: 152:70–74.

Demacopoulos, George. 2008. Gregory the Great and the Pagan Shrines of Kent. *Journal of Late Antiquity* 1(2):353–369.

Di Giovine, Michael and David Picard, eds. 2015. *The Seductions of Pilgrimage: Sacred Journeys Afar and Astray in the Western Religious Tradition.* London: Ashgate.

Doniger, Wendy. 2010. Flood Myths. In *A History of Water, Vol. I,* edited by Terje Tvedt and Terje Oestigaard, 424–439. London: I.B. Tauris.

Dowden, Ken. 2002. *European Paganism: The Realities of Cult from Antiquity to the Middle Ages.* London: Routledge.

Drew, Georgina. 2017. *River Dialogues: Hindu Faith and the Political Ecology of Dams on the Sacred Ganga.* Tucson: University of Arizona Press.

Drewal, Henry John. 2012. Beauteous Beast: The Water Deity Mami Wata in Africa. In *The Ashgate Research Companion to Monsters and the Monstrous,* edited by Asa Simon Mittman and Peter Dendle, 77–102. Surrey: Ashgate.

Dudley, Nigel, Liza Higgins-Zogib and Stephanie Mansourian. 2009. The Links between Protected Areas, Faiths, and Sacred Natural Sites. *Conservation Biology* 23(3):568–577.

Dundes, Alan, ed. 1988. *The Flood Myth.* Berkeley: University of California Press.

Dwivedi, Onkar Prasad. 1997. Vedic Heritage for Environmental Stewardship. *Worldviews: Global Religions, Culture, and Ecology* 1(1):25–36.

Eade, John and Michael J. Sallnow, eds. 1991. *Contesting the Sacred: The Anthropology of Christian Pilgrimage.* New York: Routledge.

Eck, Diana L. 1981. India's "Tirthas": "Crossings" in Sacred Geography. *History of Religions* 20(4):323–344.

Eliade, Mircea. 1958. (Translated by Rosemary Sheed). *Patterns in Comparative Religion.* London: Sheed and Ward.

Elsner, John. 1992. Pausanias: A Greek Pilgrim in the Roman World. *Past and Present* 135:3–29.

Evans, Susan and Deborah Nichols. 2015. Water Temples and Civil Engineering at Teotihuacan, Mexico. In *Human Adaptation in Ancient Mesoamerica,* edited by Nancy Gonlin and Kirk D. French, 25–51. Boulder: University Press of Colorado.

Feuerherm, Kaljürgen. 2011. Have Horn, Will Travel: The Journeys of Mesopotamian Deities. In *Travel and Religion in Antiquity*, edited by Philip A. Harland, 83–97. Waterloo, ON: Wilfrid Laurier University Press.

Finlayson, Clive. 2014. *The Improbably Primate: How Water Shaped Human Evolution*. Oxford: Oxford University Press.

Ford, Richard I. and Jason Shapiro. 2017. The Sacred Environment of Arroyo Hondo. In *The Arroyo Hondo Project, A Comprehensive Review and Evaluation*, edited by Douglas W. Schwartz. Sante Fe, New Mexico: School for Advanced Research (eBook: *arroyohondo.org*).

Frascaroli, Fabrizio. 2013. Catholicism and Conservation: The Potential of Sacred Natural Sites for Biodiversity Management in Central Italy. *Human Ecology* 41:587–601.

Frérot, Antoine. 2011. *Water: Towards a Culture of Responsibility*. Durham: University of New Hampshire Press.

Gómez Arzapalo, Dorantes and Ramiro Alfonso. 2009. *Los santos, mudos predicadores de otra historia: la religiosidad popular en los pueblos de la región de Chalma*. No. Sirsi) i9786077527084. Xalapa, Veracruz, México: Editora de Gobierno del Estado de Veracruz.

Gottowik, Volker. 2016. In Search of Holy Water: Hindu Pilgrimage to Gunung Rinjani on Lombok, Indonesia, as a Multi-religious Site. In *Religion, Place and Modernity: Spatial Articulations in Southeast Asia and East Asia*, edited by Michael Dickhardt and Andrea Lauser, 205–243. Leiden: Brill.

Gribben, Arthur. 1992. *Holy Wells and Sacred Water Sources in Britain and Ireland: An Annotated Bibliography*. London: Garland Publishing.

Groenfeldt, David. 2013. *Water Ethics: A Values Approach to Solving the Water Crisis*. London: Routledge.

Grojec, Anna. 2017. *Progress on Drinking Water, Sanitation and Hygiene*. Geneva: World Health Organization.

Haberman, David L. 2006. *River of Love in an Age of Pollution: The Yamuna River of Northern India*. Berkeley: University of California Press.

Håland, Evy Johanne. 2009. 'Take, Skamandros, My Virginity': Ideas of Water in Connection with Rites of Passage in Greece, Modern and Ancient. In *The Nature and Function of Water, Baths, Bathing, and Hygiene from Antiquity through the Renaissance*, edited by Kosso, Cynthia and Anne Scott, 109–148. Leiden: Brill.

Hammersley, Mia, Christopher Scott and Randy Gimblett. 2018. Evolving Conceptions of the Role of Large Dams in Social-ecological Resilience. *Ecology and Society* 23(1):40.

Harmanşah, Ömür. 2014. Event, Place, Performance: Rock Reliefs and Spring Monuments in Anatolia. In *Of Rocks and Water: Towards and Archaeology of Place*, edited by Ömür Harmanşah, 140–168. Oxford: Oxbow.

Hastrup, Kirsten. 2009. Waterwords: Framing the Question of Social Resilience. In *The Question of Resilience: Social Responses to Climate Change*, edited by Kirsten Hastrup, 11–30 Copenhagen, Denmark: Royal Danish Academy of Sciences and Letters.

Hastrup, Kirsten and Frida Hastrup, eds. 2015. *Waterworlds: Anthropology in Fluid Environments*. New York: Berghahn.

Havrelock, Rachel. 2011. *River Jordan: The Mythology of a Dividing Line*. Chicago, IL: University of Chicago Press.

Higgins, Iain Macleod, ed. 2011. *The Book of John Mandeville with Related Texts*. Indianapolis, IN: Hackett Publishing Company.

Hommedal, Alf Tore. 2018. A Holy Cave and Womb: The Sanctuary on the Island of Selja and the Birth of the First Norwegian Saints. In *Caves and Ritual in Medieval Europe, AD 500–1500*, edited by Knut Andreas Bergsvik and Marion Dowd, 63–84. Oxford: Oxbow.

Jackson, Sue. 2018. Indigenous Peoples and Water Justice in a Globalizing World. In *The Oxford Handbook of Water Politics and Policy*, edited by Ken Conca and Erika Weinthal, 120–141. Oxford: Oxford University Press.

Jacques, David, Tom Phillips, and Tom Lyons. 2018. *Blick Mead: Explaining the 'first place' in the Stonehenge Landscape.* Oxford: Peter Lang.

Jennaway, Megan. 2008. Aquatic Identities, Fluid Economies: Water Affinities and Authenticating Narratives of Belonging in East Timorese Myth and Ritual. *Oceania* 78(1):17–29.

Jensen, Robin. 1993. What Are Pagan River Gods doing in Scenes of Jesus' Baptism? *Bible Review* 9(1):35–41; 54–55.

Jerem, Elizabeth. 2007. Applying Interdisciplinarity in Research on Celtic Religion: The Case of the Eravisci. In *Continuity and Innovation in Religion in the Roman West (Vol. 1)*, edited by Ralph Haeussler and Anthony King, 128–134. Portsmouth, RI: Journal of Roman Archaeology Supplementary Series No. 67.

Johnston, Barbara Rose, ed. 2012. *Water, Cultural Diversity, and Global Environmental Change.* New York: Springer.

Juuti, Petri S., Georgios P. Antoniou, Walter Dragoni, Fatma El-Gohary, Giovanni De Feo, Tapio S. Katko, Riikka P. Rajala, Xiao Yun Zheng, Renato Drusiani and Andreas N. Angelakis. 2015. Short Global History of Fountains. *Water* 7(5):2314–2348. doi:10.3390/w7052314

Kehi, Balthasar and Lisa Palmer. 2012. Hamatak Halirin: The Cosmological and Socio-Ecological Roles of Water in Koba Lima, Timor. *Journal of the Humanities and Social Sciences of Southeast Asia* 168(4):445–471.

Klaver, Irene J. 2012. Placing Water and Culture. In *Water, Cultural Diversity, and Global Environmental Change*, edited by Barbara Rose Johnston, 9–29. New York: Springer.

Knight, Catherine. 2016. *New Zealand's Rivers: An Environmental History.* Christchurch, New Zealand: Canterbury University Press.

Lansing, J. Stephen. 1987. Balinese "Water Temples" and the Management of Irrigation. *American Anthropologist* 89:326–341.

———. 2006. *Perfect Order: Recognizing Complexity in Bali.* Princeton, NJ: Princeton University Press.

Lazzerini, Fáabio Tadeu and Daniel Marcos Bonotto. 2014. Brazilian "holy" Spring Waters. *Ciência e natura, suppl. Edição Especial 35 anos Vol. II*, 36:559–572.

Lewis, Jodie, Caroline Rosen, Rona Booth, Paul Davies, Martyn Allen and Matt Law. 2019. Making a Significant Place: Excavations at the Late Mesolithic Site of Langley's Lane, Midsomer Norton, Bath and North-East Somerset. *Archaeological Journal* 176(1):1–50.

Lilliu, Giovanni. 2006. *Sardegna Nuragica.* Nuoro, Sardinia: Il Maestrale.

Lucero, Lisa J. 2018. A Cosmology of Conservation in the Ancient Maya World. *Journal of Anthropological Research* 74(3):327–359.

Lucero, Lisa, Jean T. Larmon and Aimée E. Carbaugh. 2017. The Ancient Maya Ceremonial Circuit of Cara Blanca, Belize. *Research Reports in Belizean Archaeology* 14:249–259.

Maffi, Luisa, ed. 2001. *On Biocultural Diversity: Linking Language, Knowledge, and the Environment.* Washington, DC: Smithsonian Institution Press.

Mallory, James Patrick. 2016. *In Search of the Irish Dreamtime: Archaeology and Early Irish Literature.* London: Thames and Hudson.

Masani, Rustom Pestonji. 1918. *Folklore of Wells: Being a Study of Water-Worship in East and West.* Bombay: D. B. Taraporevala Sons and Co.

Mather, John D. 2013. Britain's Spa Heritage: A Hydrogeological Appraisal. *Geological Society, London, Special Publications* 375:243–260.

Meggitt, Mervyn J. 1965. The Mae Enga of the Western Highlands. In *Gods, Ghosts and Men in Melanesia*, edited by P. Lawrence and M.J. Meggitt, 105–131. Melbourne: Oxford University Press.

Menotti, Francesco and Aidan O'Sullivan. 2013. *Oxford Handbook of Wetland Archaeology*, edited by Francesco Menotti and Aidan O'Sullivan, 811–826. Oxford: Oxford University Press.

Milton, Kay. 1996. *Environmentalism and Cultural Theory: Exploring the Role of Anthropology in Environmental Discourse*. London: Routledge.

Mikaelsson, Lisbeth. 2005. Locality and Myth: The Resacralization of Selja and the Cult of St. Sunniva. *Numen* 52(2):191–225.

Morinis, Alan, ed. 1992. *Sacred Journeys: The Anthropology of Pilgrimage*. Westport, CT: Greenwood Press.

Niebuhr, Frances A. 2017. Resettling a River Goddess. In *Water, Knowledge and the Environment in Asia: Epistemologies, Practices and Locales*, edited by Ravi Baghel, Lea Stepan and Joseph K. W. Hill, 246–260. London: Routledge.

Nolan, Mary Lee and Sidney Nolan. 1989. *Christian Pilgrimage in Modern Western Europe*. Chapel Hill: University of North Carolina Press.

O'Donnell, Erin L. and Julia Talbot-Jones. 2018. Creating Legal Rights for Rivers: Lessons from Australia, New Zealand, and India. *Ecology and Society* 23(1):7.

Oestigaard, Terje. 2006. Heavens, Havens, and Hells of Water: Life and Death in Society and Religion. In *Water: Histories, Cultures, Ecologies*, edited by Marnie Leybourne and Andrea Gaynor, 94–105. Crawley, Western Australia: University of Western Australia.

———. 2011. Water. In *The Oxford Handbook of the Archaeology of Ritual and Religion*, edited by Tim Insoll, 38–50. Oxford: Oxford University Press.

———. 2015. *Dammed Divinities: The Water Powers at Bujagali Falls, Uganda*. Uppsala: The Nordic Africa Institute.

———. 2018. *The Religious Nile: Water, Ritual and Society since Ancient Egypt* London: I.B. Tauris.

Oestigaard, Terje and Gedef Abawa Firew. 2011. Gish Abay: The Source of the Blue Nile. *Water and Society* 153:27–38.

Olson, Grant A. 1991. Cries over Spilled Holy Water: "Complex" Response to a Traditional Thai Religious Practice. *Journal of Southeast Asian Studies* 22(1):75–85.

Oras, Ester, Aivar Kriiska, Andres Kimber, Kristiina Paavel and Taisi Juus. 2018. Kohtla-Vanaküla Weapons and Tools Deposit: An Iron Age Sacrificial Site in North-East Estonia. *Estonian Journal of Archaeology* 22(1):5–31.

Orlove, Ben and Steven C. Caton. 2010. Water Sustainability: Anthropological Approaches and Prospects. *Annual Review of Anthropology* 39:401–415.

Purdy, Barbara A. 2017 [1991]. *The Art and Archaeology of Florida's Wetlands*. [ebook] New York: Routledge.

Radimilahy, Chantal. 1994. Sacred Sites in Madagascar. In *Sacred Sites, Sacred Places*, edited by David Carmichael, Jane Hubert, Brian Reeves and Audhild Schanche, 82–88. London: Routledge.

Ratiba, Matome M. 2013.The Gods will Get You – A Plea, Exploration and Assessment of Possibilities for the Rescuing of Phiphidi Waterfalls and Other Sacred Cultural Sites. *Indilinga African Journal of Indigenous Knowledge Systems* 12(1): 142–159.

Ray, Celeste. 2014. *The Origins of Ireland's Holy Wells*. Oxford: Archaeopress/Oxbow.

———. 2015. Paying the Rounds at Ireland's Holy Wells. *Anthropos* 110:415–432.

———. 2019. Sacred Wells across the *Longue Durée*". In *Historical Ecologies, Heterarchies and Transtemporal Landscapes*, edited by Celeste Ray and Manuel Fernández-Götz, 265–286. London: Routledge.

Richert, Elizabeth A. 2005. *Native Religion under Roman Domination: Deities, Springs and Mountains in the North-West of the Iberian Peninsula*. BAR International Series 1382. Oxford: Archaeopress.

Robins, Nicholas S. and Pauline L Smedley. 2013. Groundwater—Medicine by the Glassful? *Geological Society, London, Special Publications* 375:261–267.

Robinson, Betsey. 2011. *Histories of Peirene: A Corinthian Fountain in Three Millennia*. Princeton, N.J.: The American School of Classical Studies at Athens.

Robson, James P. and Fikret Berkes. 2010. Sacred Nature and Community Conserved Areas. In *Nature and Culture: Rebuilding Lost Connections*, edited by Sarah Pilgrim and Jules Pretty, 197–216. London: Earthscan.

Roymans, Nico. 2009. Hercules and the Construction of a Batavian Identity in the Context of the Roman Empire. In *Ethnic Constructs in Antiquity: The Role of Power and Tradition*, edited by Ton Derks and Nico Roymans, 219–238. Amsterdam: Amsterdam University Press.

Rutkowski, Bogdan and Krzysztof Nowicki. 1996. *The Psychro Cave and Other Sacred Grottoes in Crete*. Warsaw: Art and Archaeology.

Sahlins, Marshall. 1987. *Islands of History*. Chicago, IL: University of Chicago Press.

Scarborough, Vernon L. 2003. *The Flow of Power: Ancient Water Systems and Landscapes*. Sante Fe, NM: School for Advanced Research Press.

Schattschneider, Ellen. 2003. *Immortal Wishes: Labor and Transcendence on a Japanese Sacred Mountain*. Durham, NC: Duke University Press.

Schmidt, Bettina. 2017. Mermaids in Brazil: The (ongoing) Creolization of the Water Goddesses *Oxum* and *Iemanjá*. In *Anthropology and Cryptozoology: Exploring Encounters with Mysterious Creatures*, edited by Samantha Hurn. London: Routledge.

Scott, James C. 1999. *Seeing Like a State: How Certain Schemes to Improve the Human Condition Have Failed*. New Haven, CT: Yale University Press.

Sharfman, Jonathan. 2017. *Troubled Waters: Developing a New Approach to Maritime and Underwater Cultural Heritage in Sub-Saharan Africa*. Leiden: Leiden University Press.

Sharma, Dinesh. 2004. Human Corpses Pollute India's Holy Rivers. *Frontiers in Ecology and the Environment* 2(5):229.

Shiklomanov, Igor. 1993. World fresh water resources. In *Water in Crisis*, edited by Peter Gleick, 13–24. Oxford: Oxford University Press.

Singh, Rana P.B. 1987. Towards Myth, Cosmos, Space and Mandala in India. *National Geographical Journal of India* 33(3):305–326.

Smith, James Reuel. 1922. *Springs and Wells in Greek and Roman Literature: Their Legends and Locations*. New York: G.P. Putnam's Sons.

Solomon, Steven. 2010. *Water: The Epic Struggle for Wealth, Power, and Civilization*. New York: HarperCollins.

Stjernquist, Berta. 1997. *The Röekillorna Spring: Spring-cults in Scandinavian Prehistory*. Stockholm: Almquist and Wiksell.

Strang, Victoria. 2015. *Water: Nature and Culture*. London: Reaktion Books.

———. 2009. *Gardening the World: Agency, Identity and the Ownership of Water*. New York: Berghahn.

Traube, Elizabeth G. 1986. *Cosmology and Social Life: Ritual Exchange among the Mambai of East Timor*. Chicago, IL: University of Chicago Press.

Tuan, Yi Fu. 2005 [1977]. *Space and Place: The Perspective of Experience*. Minneapolis: University of Minnesota Press.

Turner, Victor and Edith Turner. 1978. Image and Pilgrimage in Christian Culture. New York: Columbia University Press.

Tvedt, Terje. 2016. *Water and Society: Changing Perceptions of Societal and Historical Development*. London: I.B. Tauris.

Tylor, Edward Burnett. 1871. *Primitive Culture: Researches into the Development of Mythology, Philosophy, Religion, Art, and Custom*. London: J. Murray.

Van der Veer, Peter. 2016. *The Value of Comparison*. Durham, NC: Duke University Press.

Van der Waal, B. C. W. 1997. Fundudzi, a Unique, Sacred and Unknown South African Lake. *Southern African Journal of Aquatic Sciences* 23(1):42–55.

Van Vuuren, Lani, Marlese Net, Sibonfile van Damme and Eberhard Braune. 2007. *Our Water Our Culture: A Glimpse into the Water History of the South African People*. Gezina, South Africa: Water Research Commission of South Africa.

Västrik, Ergo-Hart. 1999. The Waters and Water Spirits in Votian Folk Belief. *Folklore (Tartu)* 12:16–37.

Wagner, John Richard, ed. 2012. Water and the Commons Imaginary. *Current Anthropology* 53(5):617–641.

———. 2013. *The Social Life of Water*. New York: Berghahn Books.

Warren, Carol. 2002. Tanah Lot: The Cultural and Environmental Politics of Resort Development in Bali. In *The politics of environment in Southeast Asia*, edited by Philip Hirsch and Carol Warren, 243–275. London: Routledge.

Willems, Willem J. H. and Henk P. J. van Schaik, eds. 2015. *Water and Heritage. Material, Conceptual and Spiritual Connections*. Leiden: Sidestone Press.

Wright, Thomas, ed. 1863. *The Historical Works of Giraldus Cambrensis*. London: H.G. Bohn.

Wu, Jianguo, Jianhui Huang, Xingguo Han, Xianming Gao, Fangliang He, MingxiJiang, Zhigang Jiang, Richard B. Primack and Zehao Shen. 2004. The Three Gorges Dam: An Ecological Perspective. *Frontiers in Ecology and Environment* 2(5):241–248.

Yioutsos, Nektarios-Petros. 2019. Pan Rituals of Ancient Greece Revisited. In *Between Worlds: Understanding Ritual Cave Use in Later Prehistory*, edited by Lindsey Büster, Eugène Warmenbol and Dimitrij Mlekuž, 113–136. Cham, Switzerland: Springer.

Yun, Zheng Xiao. 2010. Shaping Beliefs, Identities and Institutions: The Role of Water Myths among Ethnic Groups in Yunnan, China. In *A History of Water, Vol.I: Ideas of Water from Ancient Societies to the Modern World*, edited by Terje Tvedt and Terje Oestigaard, 405–423. London: I.B. Tauris.

PART I

Ancient influences

Individually, and as the sources of civilization-shaping rivers, numinous springs were ubiquitous in the cosmologies of ancient states around the world. The Sumerians, Akkadians and Babylonians all venerated Enki/Ea (the god of water and wisdom and the lord of springs) whose temples across ancient Mesopotamia were often beside pools. Ancient Greeks could seek the mysteries of the universe from the Muses' famously inspirational Hippocrene spring on Mount Helicon. Christopher McDonough opens the volume by examining the significance of water in general and springs in particular for classical Greek and Roman imaginations. McDonough considers the gendered and sometimes violent spring creation legends in classical antiquity that appealed across social classes, and their likewise bloody oblations. Focusing on springs within caves, Evy Håland next examines links between pre-Christian spring sites and contemporary Greek water rituals. She especially discusses those with persistent sacrality which are now dedicated to *Panagia* (the Virgin Mary in her identity as *Zōodochos Pēgē*, or the Life-giving Spring). Similarly, Nicholas Dunning examines the sacred waters of deep caves and cenotes that figure in the Mayan cosmologies of the Yucatan Peninsula. Portals to the watery underworld and the deities, these ritual sites were formative of place identity and also served as sacred omphaloi for the orientation of sacred architecture.

1

FONS ET ORIGO

Observations on sacred springs in classical antiquity and tradition

Christopher M. McDonough

In 476 BC, the Greek lyric poet Pindar famously intoned Ἄριστον μὲν ὕδωρ, or "the best of things is water" (*Olympians* 1.1; see Glover and Castle, 1945:1). It is hardly possible to overstate the significance of water in general and springs in particular to the classical imagination. From symbolic images for inspiration and mythological stories featuring deities and their exploits to the various official ceremonies performed for their maintenance and the less formal worship activities conducted on their locations, springs occupied a significant place in the religious mentality of the Greeks and Romans and have remained an important point of contact with classical tradition and its religious sentiment ever since.

The story of the origin of the cosmos and the gods told by one of the earliest European epics, Hesiod's *Theogony* (ca. 700 BC), opens with an appeal to the Muses, whom the poet imagines dancing and bathing on Mount Helicon around the spring called the Hippocrene. Since its evocation by Hesiod, this particular spring has been alluded to ever after in Western literature as a token of inspiration, as, for instance, by John Keats (*Ode to a Nightingale*, 15–18, composed in 1819 AD):

> O for a beaker full of the warm South
> Full of the true, the blushful *Hippocrene*,
> With beaded bubbles winking at the brim,
> And purple-stained mouth.

Less overt than Keats in its allusiveness, though firmly rooted in this Hesiodic tradition, is "The Pasture," the poem with which the American poet Robert Frost begins his first collection of poems, *North of Boston* (1915):

> I'm going out to clean the pasture spring;
> I'll only stop to rake the leaves away
> (And wait to watch the water clear, I may):
> I sha'n't be gone long.—You come too.

In the otherwise harsh and rocky terrain of the Boeotian mountains (or in Northern London, or North of Boston), the Hippocrene comes as a surprise in the landscape, offering an ever-flowing source of refreshment whose ultimate origin is hidden in wonder and mystery. That such an image should suggest itself to ancient and later poets as a metaphor for poetic creativity seems especially apt.

Beyond its afterlife in the poetic tradition, the creation of the Hippocrene is of particular importance as well (see McDonough, 2002 for a discussion of classical sources). According to Pausanias, a geographer of the second century AD, "They say that the earth sent up the water there when the horse Pegasus struck the ground with his hoof" (*Description of Greece*, 9.31.3 and 2.31.9). The story of a spring breaking forth where the ground has been hit was widespread in classical antiquity: the worshippers of Bacchus beat the earth to cause not just water, but even wine, milk and honey to issue forth. But more often, it is a powerful male figure who performs the task, as, for instance, Poseidon bringing forth a salt spring on the Athenian Acropolis with the stroke of his trident, a scene famously depicted on the West Pediment of the Parthenon. In like fashion, the springs of Thermopylae—the so-called "Hot Gates" where Leonidas and the Spartans made their famous stand against Xerxes' Immortals—were created when Heracles struck the mountain-top with his club. The topos is not limited to the Greeks and Romans, of course. One thinks of Moses hitting the rock of Horeb with his staff in order to create a spring in the desert (Exodus 17.6 and Numbers 20.1–13), and similar miracles recorded in Ireland, China and France according to Stith Thompson's 1955 *Motif-Index of Folk- Literature* (A941.3 & D1567.6). The association of violence with the creation of springs is not entirely surprising. As one can readily infer for antiquity from the etymology of the English word "rival"—derived from the Latin *rivalis*, "one who shares a common riverbank"—the control of water sources has been and is one of the persistent causes of conflict.

The violence prevalent in the depiction of springs—which are without fail figured as females called nymphs or naiads—gives rise to some troubling myths of domination and rape. In his *Metamorphoses* (5.552–641), the poet Ovid recounts the story of the virgin nymph Arethusa who one day took a bath in a clear stream in Arcadia, not realizing that it was in fact the river-god Alpheus. Startled by the god's sudden appearance, she flees and he chases after her intending to rape her. Although she is hidden in a cloud from her pursuer by the goddess Diana, the nymph's nervous sweating causes her to be transformed into a pool. Alpheus, seeing this, himself transforms back into a river to mingle with her waters, but Diana then opens the ground to give her a means of escape; she eventually re-emerges on the island of Ortygia, in the heart of the city of Syracuse in Sicily (where a fountain of fresh water by the harbor has been called Fonte Aretusa since antiquity). Ovid tells another story of abduction and escape in his poem of the Roman calendar, the *Fasti* (2.583–616)—in which Jupiter has conceived a desire for the Roman spring-goddess Juturna, but is stymied by her sister, Lara, who reveals his plan to Juno. The god rips out Lara's tongue and consigns her to the Underworld, although her sister indeed escapes.

Juturna herself, better known from her vivid depiction in battle in Book 12 of Virgil's *Aeneid*, was a quintessential Italian goddess of springs and as such was ritually celebrated every January 11th by "those whose work involves water," *qui artificium aqua exercent* (Scullard, 1981:64). Among the most important of Roman springs was that which fed the Lacus Juturnae, the Pool of Juturna, in the Roman Forum. Water from this pool was used for all official sacrifices of the Roman state religion. After military victories in 496 and 168 BC, the gods Castor and Pollux had been seen watering their horses at the Lacus Juturnae, an event commemorated on coins from the late Republic. The city of Rome itself is plentifully supplied by water, the sources of which were subjects of particular worship. "Esteem for springs still continues, and is observed with veneration. They are believed to bring healing to the sick," writes the first-century author Frontinus, whose work, *On Aqueducts*, is a rich storehouse of information on this topic (1.4; Bennett, 1925:339). On the Ides of October, all of the city's springs were honored in the festival of the Fontinalia during which "garlands were thrown into the springs and wells crowned with them," an especially fitting tribute for the water by which flowers are nourished (Scullard, 1981:192). A gate in the Servian Wall that surrounded the city was called the Porta Fontinalis, the Gate of Springs, after the Tullianum spring that was located alongside it by the northwest corner of the Capitoline Hill. This spring is still visible today, in the lowest level of the church of S. Pietro in Carcere situated above it. The cistern constructed in the seventh century BC for gathering water from this particular spring was later repurposed as the Mamertine, Rome's most notorious dungeon: foreign captives such as Vercingetorix and Jugurtha were incarcerated here before their executions, as was Saint Peter who used the spring-water of the Tullianum to baptize his jailers, according to the Passion of Saints Processus and Martinianus (Lapidge, 2017:385).

Located near the Porta Fontinalis, it has been posited, was a shrine to the spring-god, Fons, reckoned the son of Juturna by some authorities. While its site is ultimately unknown, the story behind this shrine's dedication is related by a historian of the Byzantine era who indicates that it was built by the general C. Papririus Maso in 231 BC from the spoils of the Roman victory in Corsica in commemoration of the fortunate discovery of a water source. A similar story is told about the discovery of the Aqua Virgo, so called "because a young girl pointed out certain springs to some soldiers hunting for water, and when they followed these up and dug, they found a copious supply. A small temple, situated near the spring, contains a painting which illustrates this origin of the aqueduct" (Frontinus, *On Aqueducts,* 1.10; Bennett, 1925:351).

The Aqua Virgo is even today the most beloved of all Roman water sources and its termination in the city is celebrated by Niccolo Salvi's famous Trevi Fountain (1744). Behind the Baroque statuary of Oceanus, Tritons, and hippocamps (around and over which the waters from the aqueduct joyously burst forth) can be seen a bas relief depiction of the maiden showing the soldiers the spring's point of origin. No tourist leaves Rome without tossing a coin or two into the Trevi, in imitation of ancient practice. The 1954 film, *Three Coins in a Fountain,* and its Oscar-winning theme song, sung by Frank Sinatra, made much of the tradition and assured its continuation in the post-war period. The Trevi Fountain remembers the good luck of the soldiers in its sculptural program, and in its ritual practice promises good luck for lovers.

The fact that springs dispense not just good water but also good fortune is a commonplace in classical thinking. The fact that the dispensation of these benefits is not free of charge, however, but rather dependent upon a regular cycle of ritual maintenance is the subject of a justly famous ode by Horace, a great poet of the Augustan era, which is worth looking at in its original Latin. As the poet writes (*Odes* 3.13; translation mine),

O fons Bandusiae, splendidior vitro,	O Spring of Bandusia, clearer than glass,
dulci digne mero non sine floribus,	worthy of sweet wine not without flowers,
cras donaberis haedo,	Tomorrow you will be presented a kid
cui frons turgida cornibus	whose forehead swells with its first horns
primis et venerem et proelia destinat.	promising Love and Battle
Frustra: nam gelidos inficiet tibi	in vain. For tomorrow the offspring
rubro sanguine rivos	of the wanton flock will stain
lascivi suboles gregis.	your cold waters with red blood.
Te flagrantis atrox hora Caniculae	The season of the blazing Dog Star
nescit tangere, tu frigus amabile	cannot touch you. You provide
fessis vomere tauris	cold relief to the bulls, weary
praebes et pecori vago.	from the plough, and [to] the
	wandering herd.
Fies nobilium tu quoque fontium,	You will become a famous spring,
me dicente cavis impositam ilicem	when I tell of the holm-oak which
saxis, unde loquaces	overhangs the hollow rocks
lymphae desiliunt tuae.	where your babbling waters leap down.

The critical axis upon which Horace's odes turns is found in the paired verbs *donaberis* (you will be presented) and *praebes* (you provide). Ancient religion operates on the principle of reciprocity between the human and divine realms, summed up in the phrase *do ut des* (I give so that you give). Horace's spring offers respite to his exhausted bulls and wandering cattle but must itself receive payment if it is to continue offering its services. At the heart of the poem is Horace's emphasis on the spectacular moment of bloodshed, *nam gelidos inficiet tibi/rubro sanguine rivos* (foreshadowed by the *dulci mero*, sweet wine with which the ode begins): this sudden red stain in the crystal clear water is intended to jolt us out of complacency in the presence of even so small a deity as that of this minor spring. We do well to recall Walter Burkert's remark that in sacrifice, there is a "shock caused by the sight of flowing blood"—an astonishment which heightens and solemnizes the ritual act (1983:21). In this context, it is worth pointing out how often the appearance of blood at a river, lake or spring was taken for a prodigy (an omen demanding action) according to numerous historical accounts (see especially the historian Livy, *From the Founding of the City*, 22.1.10, 24.10.7, 27.11.3, etc.). Sources of water as well as wonder, springs evidently served as conduits of communication between gods and humans.

The bloody spring, whether deemed as an offering or an omen, might perhaps point back to an implicit idea of the violence of the spring's inception, and yet we should not forget the deep appeal a spring in its rustic setting might convey. There is a charming description found in a letter by the early second-century AD author, Pliny the Younger, which tells us much about the way ancient people experienced the natural and cultic setting of a spring in rural Umbria. "Have you ever seen the spring at Clitumnus? If no, and I think you have not, or else you would have told me about it," Pliny writes to his friend, Romanus (*Epistles* 8.8; translation modified from that of Firth 1900: 121–123). "I only regret that I did not visit it before." He goes on to describe the spring's hillside location, the cypress trees growing up around it and the various streams emanating from it in "a broad sheet of pure and crystal water, so clear that you can count the small coins and pebbles that have been thrown into it." He then turns to the "built environment" of religious edifices surrounding the spring:

> Hard by is an ancient and sacred temple, where stands Jupiter Clitumnus himself clad and adorned with a toga and the oracular responses delivered there prove that the deity dwells within and foretells the future. Round about are sprinkled a number of little chapels, each containing the statue of a god. There is a special cult for each and a particular name, and some of them have springs dedicated to them, for in addition to the one I have described, which may be called the parent spring, there are lesser ones separated from the chief one.

What he describes is a complex of temples, large and small, that mimics the hydrological landscape with its parent and children springs. "Upon every column and every wall," Pliny continues, are found numerous inscriptions to the various divinities of the place. "Most of them you will commend, but a few will make you laugh. But, wait, I am forgetting that you are so kind-hearted that you will laugh at none," he concludes, with a kind compliment to his friend after a less-than-kind assessment of the homeliness of some of the epigraphic evidence.

People from every walk of life visited springs in antiquity, and they did so for a variety of reasons, from the simple physical needs of quenching their thirsts or soaking away their illnesses to the more spiritual demands of inspiration, prophecy and communication with the divine. While the evidence of poetry and literary epistles necessarily reflects the tastes and interests of the elite, inscriptions such as those Pliny references (mentioned earlier) reveal the wider scope of religious activity to be found at springs. One of the most famous sites in the Roman world was the hot springs of Aquae Sulis, the modern city of Bath in Somerset, England. From the bubbling brook of sulfurous water at its center arose one of the great beauty-spots of England, the site not just of Iron Age and Roman settlements but also of royal medieval and elegant Georgian-era towns. Here, we find not only funerary monuments of rich and poor Romans alike but also numerous offerings to the patron goddess of the spring, Minerva Sulis (as the Romans called her). As at ancient Clitumnus and the modern Trevi Fountain, coins are among the most common votives, but in addition an enormous number of leaden *defixiones*, "curse tablets," have been recovered. One of these, written in rough style with the words reversed, reads as follows ("RIB 154. Curse." 2014): May he who carried off Vilbia from me become as liquid as water.

(May) she who obscenely devoured her (become) dumb, whether Velvinna, Exsupereus, Verianus, Severinus, A(u)gustalis, Comitianus, Catus, Minianus, Germanilla (or) Jovina.

Well might we imagine Pliny and his friend quietly chuckling to themselves over this no doubt heartfelt, but decidedly vulgar appeal to the goddess of the spring for help with a difficult predicament. What exactly is being sought is unclear—is Vilbia a woman, an article of clothing or something else? Scholars are uncertain—and the long list of possible suspects reveals a cagey and even suspicious frame of mind. Yet, we should consider that for many of the non-elite, to whom regular avenues of justice were cut off by expense, appeal to the divine might be the only recourse, and springs—with their hidden sources deep in the earth—were among the most popular places to entrust these direct addresses to the gods, untold thousands of which have been found in springs all over the classical world. As the epigraphic record indicates, members of every class went to springs, and not very far from where this *defixio* was found, in the Roman reservoir below the King's Spring, we are also able to read an inscription in the Neo-Classical pediment over the Royal Pump Room: written in large bronze letters at the entrance, the phrase from Pindar with which we began can be seen: Ἄριστον μὲν ὕδωρ, "the best of things is water."

References

Bennett, Charles E., trans. 1925. *Frontinus: The Stratagems, and the Aqueducts of Rome*. Loeb Classical Library. New York: William Heinemann-G.P. Putnam's Sons.

Burkert, Walter. 1983. *Homo Necans: The Anthropology of Ancient Greek Sacrificial Ritual and Myth*. Trans. Peter Bing. Berkeley: University of California Press.

Firth, John B., trans. 1900. *The Letters of the Younger Pliny*. Vol. 2. Newcastle-upon-Tyne: Walter Scott Publishing Co., Ltd.

Glover, Terret Reaveley and Sydney Castle. 1945. *The Springs of Hellas, and Other Essays*. Cambridge: Cambridge University Press.

Lapidge, Michael. 2017. *The Roman Martyrs: Introduction, Translations, and Commentary*. Oxford: Oxford University Press.

McDonough, Christopher M. 2002. Hercle and the Ciminian Lake Legend: Source Study for an Etruscan Mirror. *Classical Journal* 98(1): 9–19.

"RIB 154. Curse." 2014. *Roman Inscriptions of Britain*. Administrators of the Haverfield Bequest, University of Oxford. https://romaninscriptionsofbritain.org/inscriptions/154

Scullard, Howard Hayes. 1981. *Festivals and Ceremonies of the Roman Republic*. Ithaca, NY: Cornell University Press.

Thompson, Stith. 1955. *Motif-index of Folk-literature: A Classification of Narrative Elements in Folktales, Ballad, Myths, Fables, Medieval Romances, Exempla, Fablaux, Jest-books and Local Legends-Volume 1: D-E*. Bloomington: Indiana University Press.

2

WATER SOURCES AND THE SACRED IN MODERN AND ANCIENT GREECE

Evy Johanne Håland

Springs in caves have shaped and featured prominently in Greek religious beliefs and practices. In ancient times, springs represented water nymphs. Today, springs are dedicated to the *Panagia*, that is, the Virgin Mary, under her attribute of *Zōodochos Pēgē* (the Life-giving Spring). Baptisms today also significantly employ water from one of the many sacred springs which are dedicated to the *Panagia*. These personified healing springs were and are considered most efficacious during the festivals dedicated to their supernatural patrons. This is reflected today in the modern festival dedicated to the Life-giving Spring, which is celebrated on the first Friday after Easter Sunday. During this festival, Athenians come to the *Panagia*'s chapel inside a circular spring house hewn in the rock on the southern slope of the Akropolis to fetch "life-giving water." The sacred spring is situated inside a cave over which a church is constructed. Throughout antiquity, this cave and its spring were dedicated to different deities, until it became part of a Byzantine Church-complex. This essay will compare particular cave spring sites in contemporary ritual and ancient cults.

There are two cave-churches on the southern slope of the Akropolis, and the first of these is called *Zōodochos Pēgē* (the Life-giving Spring). "Saint" in Greek is *Agios* (m.) or *Agia* (f.) and *Agioi* (pl.), and this spring is dedicated to *Agioi Anargyroi*, the patron saints of healing (Loukatos, 1982:153; cf. Håland, 2005, 2009a, 2009b, 2017). When pilgrims reach the cave, everyone washes in the spring and drinks the miracle-working water. Of the many icons in the cave, the most holy represents the *Panagia* and is situated next to the spring itself. Visitors arrange flowers and light candles and olive-oil lamps in front of this icon and one that depicts the *Panagia* and Child. While the cave is dedicated to *Agioi Anargyroi*, in reality, the *Panagia* is the one who gets the gifts. *Tamata* (metal plaques depicting a vow or request) are mainly placed near the icons of the *Panagia*, even though the icon of *Agioi Anargyroi* is still in the cave. The most common votive offering is a silver- or gold-plated ex-voto representing a person or body part for which a cure has been sought. In recent times, people claim to be cured of allergies, eczema and arthritis, illnesses that doctors could not diagnose, eye ailments, nervous problems and also credit pregnancies to the spring water. Taught by their mothers since early childhood to revere and collect the holy water, devotees believe that this site is the oldest church in Greece and that St. Paul preached there.

The second of the two caves, situated higher on the Akropolis rock, is dedicated to the *Panagia Chrysospēliōtissa* and is known as the Chapel of Our Lady of the Golden Cavern. Today, a lamp is lit there every evening. The cave was also important for the ancients. On the walls of the cave-church are faded Byzantine paintings. A local legend unfolds the origins of the cult as follows. *Agios* Luke (the Evangelist) was to have painted a miraculous icon of Mary during her lifetime and it came to be left in the cave. In the fourth century, Roxane, the daughter of a pagan medical doctor, had three dreams in which the *Panagia* asked to be freed from her imprisonment. The dream was the voice of the *Panagia* residing in the buried icon. With other Christians, Roxane dug in the cave until the icon was found. Then, the *Panagia* appeared to her in a vision and promised to liberate Athens. When the Visigothic leader Alaric invaded in 395 CE and planned to destroy the city, he saw a light and the *Panagia* on the city wall and departed instead (cf. Hdt. 8.65, 8.84; Xen. *Hell.* 2.4,14 f.; Diod. 14.32,2 f. and Clem. Al. *Strom.* 1.24,163,1–3 for other pre-Christian parallels). As the invasion was routed in August, this local miracle has become an added layer to the August 15th celebration of the Dormition of the *Panagia* (*Ē Koimēsis tēs Theotokou*, that is, the "Falling Asleep" of the Mother of God). Formerly, the festival of the Life-giving Spring engaged both cave-churches on the slope of the Akropolis. Devotees began their rituals at the Life-giving Spring, and sometimes continued the celebration in the *Chrysospēliōtissa* (where mothers came particularly to pray for ill children). While a very close relationship exists between the official Orthodox religion and the popular religion, some priests will not officiate at such popular observances. This conflict between official religion and folk liturgies (very strong in the 1990s) is now changing, which may be due to the fact that the priests are more educated and tolerant today (cf. Håland, 2014, 2019).

"New" Friday in the "White Week": the celebration of the Life-giving Spring

Easter celebrations in Greece last throughout the week that follows Easter Sunday. This week is known as the "White Week" or the "Bright Week." On "New" Friday in the "White Week," the Greeks celebrate the *Theotokos* (Mother of God) under her attribute of *Zōodochos Pēgē*, the Life-giving Spring. She acquired this epithet in a ninth-century hymn.[1] In several places, on this day there are special services and processions, followed by folk dances (see also Tsotakou-Karbelē, 1991:98–99; Megas, 1992:184–187). On the island of Karpathos in southern Greece, the festival actually begins Thursday evening in Diaphanē (a small port town) and in the island's main village *Pēgadia* (from *pēgadi* or "spring"). In Olympos (served by Diaphanē's port), the icon of the *Panagia* is immersed in the water during a procession on "White" Tuesday (cf. Håland, 2005).

At the Life-giving Spring in the Akropolis cave, a two-hour celebration includes choir singing and the Divine Liturgy with Communion (especially for the ill). This service attracts people of all ages who collect the holy water. Outside the entrance of the cave-church, several tables are set up. They are laid with a variety of special breads[2] brought by the participants who make offerings of a round holy bread, called *prosphoro*. In addition, sweet breads and cakes sprinkled with icing sugar also appear and are typical at annual festivals dedicated to saints. Inside the church, the air over the spring is fragranced by a suspended censer. The priest officiates at the altar in front of the spring which is visible to participants. The Divine Liturgy ends with the priest blessing the bread offerings and distributing them to participants. The popular liturgy then begins as people anoint themselves at the spring and drink the water. A person sits by the spring and continually fills bottles brought to him by attendees who queue for this service. Other people sprinkle their heads, or fill small bottles they have brought for just this purpose by putting the bottles directly into the spring. These may be taken home to keep in case of illness or taken to the sick who cannot attend the service.

The cults in the Akropolis caves at Athens: continuity and change

In ancient Greece, water in grottos/caverns was thought to be the manifestation of a divinity. Later, most water-retaining caves were transformed into churches, as in Athens. At the church dedicated to the Life-giving Spring, the *Panagia* has taken over the healing power of ancient water nymphs. Ancient votive reliefs and votive offerings (*anathēmata*) were dedicated to these nymphs, while in parallel at the same site today, visitors attach ex-votos to Christian icons or to the embroidered cloths placed under the icons. The holy spring is behind a low wall in the cavern church. Thus, the Athenian chapel dedicated to the *Panagia* under her attribute of the Life-giving Spring is situated on a site sacred to water-divinities in antiquity. The original round spring house enclosing the site dates to the late sixth century BCE. Pan was also worshipped there from the fifth century BCE onwards (Hdt. 6.105, cf. Håland, 2009a). Furthermore, a large altar or altar-table of Hymettian marble with an inscription datable to the first century BCE bears the names of other gods who were jointly worshipped there along with the former: Pan, Hermes, Aphrodite and the Egyptian goddess Isis (*IG* II^2 4994) in addition to the nymphs. Sometime before the middle of the first century, a modest shrine for Isis was also established on a slope just south of the Archaic spring house, beside an even smaller temple of the Titan goddess Themis who was associated with natural law. The original cult of the spring was therefore followed by the construction of the Archaic spring house which was itself later situated within the Asklepieion (the sanctuary of Asklepios) dedicated in 419/418 BCE by Telemakhos of Acharnai, a devout private donor (Travlos, 1971:127). Artemis was especially connected with springs (Håland, 2009b) and was worshipped in the upper Akropolis cave with her brother Apollo. The sacred territory of the spring was only officially delimited in the fifth century BCE, the era of Telemakhos' beneficence, with the erection of a marble boundary stone inscribed with the words *horos krenes* (boundary of the spring) (see Figure 2.1).

Asklepios was the god of medicine and healing and one of his daughters was known simply as Hygieia (Health). Asklepios' original cult centre at Epidauros drew hordes of visitors seeking miracle cures and gave rise to a regular health business (cf. Paus. 2.26,8). The cult of Asklepios arrived in Athens at the time of the "great plague" of 429 BCE. A "cure" was ritually obtained. Patients washed in the sacred

FIGURE 2.1 (L): Within the archaeological quarter of the Sanctuary of Asklepios (the ancient healer), the entrance to the Sacred spring of the Akropolis cave at Athens is today barred and generally locked. (R): *Horos krenes* (boundary of the spring) the Akropolis area. Photographs by author.

spring, presented offerings at an altar and then retired to the *stoa*, a porch or portico not attached to a larger building, where the mysterious process of "incubation" (*egkoimēsis*) was assisted by incense from the altars (cf. Paus. 2.27,1–2). Those seeking healing washed in the spring and slept in the sanctuary hoping that Asklepios would visit them in their dreams to effect his cure. Ex-voto tablets to Asklepios and Hygieia have been recovered from the site that represent the portion of the anatomy treated. The second-century traveller and writer Pausanias describes votive offerings he saw when he was visiting the Akropolis cave (Paus. 1.21,4–7).

In the fifth century or in the beginning of the sixth century CE, all previous structures were demolished and Athenians built a large three-aisled Christian basilica on their foundations. The church was dedicated to *Agioi Anargyroi* who are the doctor saints or the patron saints of healing (Travlos, 1939/41:35–68, cf. 1971:128). The remains of the Asklepieion, the sanctuary dedicated to the ancient god of healing, transformed into a Byzantine Church. Under the patronage of *Agios* Kosmas and *Agios* Damianos, the process of incubation assisted by incense and the miracle-working nature of the sacred spring continued under the Christian aegis. When the area around the Asklepieion was excavated in 1876, the cave with holy water was dedicated to the *Panagia* as well (Travlos, 1939/41:68). Therefore, the cult in the cave around a curative spring and dedicated to a female supernatural (or holy person) is not so much exemplifying "continuity" but perhaps rather "revival" of cult. According to the Greek scholar, Dēmētrios Loukatos, who examines the cult-continuity from Asklepios to

Agioi Anargyroi, the cave is still dedicated to the doctor saints (1982:153). But, even though the icon of *Agioi Anargyroi* is still in the cave, the *tamata* (ex-votos) are mainly dedicated to the *Panagia* today.

Contemporary rituals are documented from the eighteenth century. The English architects James Stuart and Nicholas Revett visited Athens from 1751 to 1753 and later published a five-volume survey of classical architecture. They provide a drawing of the site that represents people sitting on a rock wall at the cave awaiting the arrival of a priest, attended by a boy who carries a wax candle, followed by a man and a woman leading a child (Revett and Stuart, 1762–1816:33 and plate 1; Travlos, 1971:565, Fig. 707). The scene is very similar to the modern cult. Cult activity at the site thus has pre-Christian documentation, a related fourth-century Christian legend, and an early modern account provided by Revett and Stuart. In antiquity, the two Akropolis caves were dedicated to the water nymphs and Artemis, respectively, and later they became the *Panagia's* churches. In the two caves, there have been cults dedicated to female fertility-bestowing and healing divinities in ancient and modern times, even if the names of the divinities and the religions have changed. Male elements in the Classical era and the Byzantine period were intermezzos (even Asklepios was together with Hygieia). Even with the ideological transition from paganism to Christianity, exemplified by Christian saints taking over the fields of responsibilities of the ancient goddesses and gods, the spring's associations endure or re-emerge and their waters are still ritually approached and collected.

Tinos, the *Panagia* as the Life-giving Spring, and the *Agiasma* in Greece

The ritual patterns encountered at the Akropolis cave of the Life-giving Spring are like those found in all Greek holy springs, but the story behind the cult in the upper cave is reminiscent of the one found on the Aegean island of Tinos, the greatest shrine of Greek Orthodoxy. Similar to the account of the buried icon of the *Panagia Chrysospēliōtissa*, here a miraculous icon of the Annunciation of the *Panagia* was buried. According to the tradition, a nun (later sanctified as *Agia* Pelagia) experienced repeated visions of the *Panagia*, who ordered her to find her icon, and to build her church on the site. The icon was unearthed in a field in 1823, two years after the great Greek War of Liberation broke out.

The sanctuary on Tinos has a chapel dedicated to the *Panagia* as the Life-giving Spring and rituals connected with water are important as in all Greek churches. The first excavations on Tinos revealed the foundation ruins of a Byzantine Church and, most importantly, a deep but dry well. Some months later, in 1823, the cornerstone of the church of the Life-giving Spring was laid. Later, the icon was found approximately 2 m from the well. After the icon's rediscovery, it was decided to build a larger church above that dedicated to the Life-giving Spring. The chapel or church dedicated to the Life-giving Spring, which is formed as a cave, is now situated below the Church of the Annunciation (Håland, 2009b, 2012, 2017). On the day the cornerstone of the church was laid, the formerly dry well became filled to the brim with water. The source is seen as a miracle, and according to the tradition, it is one of the most important miracles of the *Panagia* of Tinos. Pilgrims from around the world take home bottles of this precious water and they keep it as a talisman.

Upon entering the Church of the Annunciation, pilgrims first perform their *proskynēma*, that is, the required set of devotions, the most important being to kiss the miraculous icon itself. Then, they seek out the chapel of holy water below the church. Here, they queue to obtain holy well water in small bottles or drink directly from the tap. Baptisms are not performed in the church itself but in the baptistry, which is located off the Chapel of the Life-giving Spring. Particularly during the Dormition of the *Panagia*, on 15th August, many children are baptised in the chapel, in holy water, from the Life-giving Spring (Håland, 2009b).

Holy water, *agiasma*, is found in most modern Greek sanctuaries, but some sanctuaries offer particularly miracle-working water with its own attached legend, and several caves with springs dedicated to ancient goddesses and gods, particularly water nymphs, are now transformed to chapels dedicated to the *Panagia*. One may argue

FIGURE 2.2 The Chapel of the Life-giving Spring on Tinos has an adjacent baptistery. Baptisms there employ water from the holy well beneath the main church. Photograph by author.

for a continuous association of water sources with the sacred in the area. Rituals connected with water are very important, both in modern and ancient Greece, as exemplified by the festival dedicated to the *Panagia*, under her attribute of the Life-giving Spring. Recalling the Konstantinople origins of the *Panagias'* epithet, the festival was established by the Orthodox Patriarch in 1833 (Loukatos, 1985:165).

The Greek ritual carried out on "New" Friday is a part of the spring festivals, and may also be regarded as a purification ritual before the new season, which starts with Christ's Resurrection. Water has fertility-enhancing, healing, purifying and protecting powers; in the form of holy water, it is central to many rituals designed to ward off evil and to ensure blessings. It is also used in conjunction with different magical remedies. In an account from modern Greece, it is said that the spring at the Church of Christ at Spata lends power to stones gathered there. When added to holy water and passion flowers, these stones make a charm which protects a house from illness (Blum and Blum, 1970). A spring may also be a place to which one is directed by a dream for a cure (see Hp. *Insomn.* 90, see also *Aër.* 7–10; Blum/Blum, 1970:137; Håland, 2009b).

Through the important blessing of the *agiasma*, we meet holy water or a very old purification symbol, which, on one level, was "reinvented" in the service of the national ideology in 1833, during the same year that the Greek struggle for independence came to a successful conclusion and the Kingdom was established. This may be regarded as an example of ideological reuse of old popular symbols in the service of the Greek nation state. At intervals, this has occurred throughout Greek history (cf. the aforementioned resistance to Alaric's invasion in 395 CE). Simultaneously, people have carried out their own rituals in connection with the life-cycle passages of death, birth, baptism and weddings, as well as other rituals in connection with the cycle of nature.[3] We have seen how the same spring with holy water has been dedicated to ancient water nymphs and the Christian *Panagia* in the same Akropolis cave across religious and political changes. People have always fetched miracle-working water and have probably not been very affected by what has been introduced from "above" by official authorities. One may suggest that even if the official Orthodox Church or the nation state, two institutions with a very close connection in Greece,[4] sometimes try to dictate to the people, the populace carries out its own rituals as it has always done, despite changes within the "Great History." Particular forms of Greek water veneration surely illustrate the Braudelian *longue durée* (cf. Håland, 2005). Hence, the two sometimes contradictory views, the official and the popular, are both complementary and interdependent.

Notes

1 Kontogiannēs/Bolakēs/Chintziou-Kontogiannē (2005:218). The legend behind the first church dedicated to the *Zōodochos Pēgē* is due to the supernatural revelation of the location (called *Pēgē*) of a sacred spring to a solider named Leo Marcellus in Valoukli, Konstantinople. The solider later became the Byzantine Emperor Leo I (457–474) and built the Church of the *Zōodochos Pēgē* over the site. An alternative story relates that the Emperor Justinian had a vision at the spring while hunting and later built a monastery at the site; see Migne, Vol. 147:72–77.

2 In Greek, the word *psōmi* refers to everyday bread, and *artos*, pl. *artoi* indicates special ritual breads.

3 For the similarities between life-cycle passages and the rituals performed in connection with important passages during the cycle of nature, see Håland (2006, 2017), esp. Chapter 6.
4 That is, in a patriotic sense, and this is probably also why the official and popular religions have a close relationship, despite some problematical incidents, cf. above.

References

Blum, Eva and Richard Blum. 1970. *The Dangerous Hour. The Lore of Crisis and Mystery in Rural Greece.* London: Chatto and Windus.
Clem. Al. *Strom*=Clément d'Alexandrie, *Les Stromates, Vol. I*, trans. Marcel Gaster and Claude Mondésert 1951. Sources Chrétiennes. Paris: Les Éditions du Cerf.
Diod.=Diodorus of Sicily, *Vol. VI*, trans. Oldfather Charles H. 1954. The Loeb Classical Library. London: Heinemann.
Hdt.=Herodotus, *Vols. III–IV*, trans. Godley A. D. (1946, 1950 [1922, 1925]). The Loeb Classical Library. Cambridge, MA: Harvard University Press.
Hp.=Hippocrates, *Vol. I: Aër.=Airs, Waters, Places, Vol. IV: Insomn.=Dreams*, trans. Jones, William Henry Samuel. 1948, 1953 [1923, 1931]). London: Heinemann.
Håland, Evy J. 2005. Rituals of Magical Rain-Making in Modern and Ancient Greece: A Comparative Approach. *Cosmos: The Journal of the Traditional Cosmology Society* 17(2):197–251.
———. 2006. The Ritual Year as a Woman's Life: The Festivals of the Agricultural Cycle, Life-cycle Passages of Mother Goddesses and Fertility-Cult. In *Proceedings from the First International Conference of the SIEF working group on The Ritual Year, in association with the Department of Maltese University of Malta, Junior College, Msida, Malta*, edited by Mifsud-Chircop, George, 303–326. Malta: PEG Ltd.
———. 2009a. Water Sources and the Sacred in Modern and Ancient Greece and Beyond. *Water History* 1(2):83–108.
———. 2009b. Take Skamandros, My Virginity: Ideas of Water in Connection with Rites of Passage in Greece, Modern and Ancient. In *The Nature and Function of Water, Baths, Bathing, and Hygiene from Antiquity through the Renaissance. Technology and Change in History 11*, edited by Kosso, Cynthia and Anne Scott, 109–148. Leiden: Brill.
———. 2012. The Dormition of the Virgin Mary, on the Island of Tinos: A Performance of Gendered Values in Greece. *The Journal of Religious History* 36(1):89–117.
———. 2014. *Rituals of Death and Dying in Modern and Ancient Greece: Writing History from a Female Perspective.* Newcastle upon Tyne: Cambridge Scholars Publishing.
———. 2017. *Greek Festivals, Modern and Ancient: A Comparison of Female and Male Values*, 2 vols. Newcastle upon Tyne: Cambridge Scholars Publishing.
———. 2019. *Competing Ideologies in Greek Culture, Ancient and Modern.* Newcastle upon Tyne: Cambridge Scholars Publishing.
IG=Inscriptiones Graecae. 1927–1977. Consilio et auctoritate. Academiae litterarum Borussicae editae. Inscriptiones Atticae Euclidis anno posteriores. Berolini: Walteri de Gruyter et Soc.
Kontogiannēs, Giōrgos N., Bolakēs, Panagiōtēs and Sophia Chintziou-Kontogiannē. 2005. *Ellēnismos kai Orthodoxia.* Athens: Ekdoseis Politeia.
Loukatos, Dēmētrios S. 1982. *Ta Phthinopōrina.* Laographia-Paradosē 4. Athens: Ekdoseis Philippotē.
———. 1985. *Symplērōmatika tou Cheimōna kai tēs Anoixēs.* Laographia-Paradosē 5. Athens: Ekdoseis Philippotē.
Megas, Geōrgios A. 1992 [1956/1957]. *Ellēnikes Giortes kai Ethima tēs Laïkēs Latreias.* Athens: Odysseas. (English edition: *Greek Calendar Customs.* Athens 1982).

Migne, Jacques-Paul. 1857–1866. *Patrologiae Graecae Cursus Completus. Series Græca*, Vol. 147. Paris: Imprimerie Catholique.

Paus.=Pausanias, *Description of Greece. Vol. I*, trans. Jones, William Henry Samuel (1954 [1918]). *Description of Greece. Vol. I.* London: Heinemann.

Revett, Nicholas and James Stuart. 1762–1816. On the Choragic Monument of Thrasyllus. In *The Antiquities of Athens, Measured and delineated*, edited by J. Stuart and Revett, N. Vol. 2, 29–36. London: Johan Haberkorn, London.

Travlos, John. 1939/41. *Ē palaiochristianikē basilikē tou Asklēpieiou tōn Athēnōn.* Athens: *Archaiologikē Ephēmeris.*

———. 1971. *Pictorial Dictionary of Ancient Athens.* London: Thames and Hudson.

Tsotakou-Karbelē, Aikaterinē. 1991 [1985]. *Laographiko Ēmerologio: Oi dōdeka mēnes kai ta ethima tous.* Athens: Patakē.

Xen. *Hell.*=Xenophon, *Hellenica, Vol. I*, trans. Brownson, Carleton Lewis. 1947 [1918]. *Vol. I.* The Loeb Classical Library. Cambridge, MA: Harvard University Press.

3

LIFE AND DEATH FROM THE WATERY UNDERWORLD

Ancient Maya interaction with caves and cenotes

Nicholas P. Dunning

In the pre-dawn hours, shaman Faustino Xiu and two apprentices labor in hypoxic darkness near the subterranean pool at the heart of Actun Xoch, a labyrinthine cave underlying the monumental core of an ancient Maya city in the Puuc Hills of Yucatan, Mexico. The year is 1835 CE. Severe drought has continued into a second year (Mendoza et al., 2007), jeopardizing the all-important germination and survival of maize recently planted in fields surrounding Xcoch, part of the lands of the nearby town of Santa Elena Nohcacab.[1] These lands include some of the richest soils in the Yucatan, but lie barren without sufficient rainfall in this karst region with no rivers or lakes.

Faustino has followed a path worn into the cave floor by his predecessors for 2,500 years. The descent begins in a yawning sinkhole where the sheer wall above the cave entrance leers like the open-mouthed face of the *Witz*, or Earth Monster, of Maya cosmology—the perceived entrance to the underworld (see Figure 3.1). The mouth draws its breath daily, sucking in air overnight, and then expelling it in a fierce wind as the following day progresses. The monster has a long throat, necessitating a crawl on hands and knees before giving access to the first of a series of open chambers littered with thousands of wooden torch fragments and areas replete with the decaying remains of ritual offerings.

Faustino and his companions lower a ceramic water jar into a small pool of water lying within the lowest chamber at the base of the cave system, securing a vital substance, *zuhuy ha* or virgin water, for the day's forthcoming ceremony. Faustino will lead the community in the day-long *Ch'a-Cháak*, a rain-summoning ritual that has been practiced by the Maya for millennia (see Figure 3.2). If this fails to bring rain, the crops will be lost and disaster will ensue. Although Faustino's efforts on behalf of his community are relatively humble, they hearken back to times when Xcoch was a ritual center of immense importance (Dunning et al., 2014; Smyth et al., 2017). On the lip of the sinkhole, above the mouth of the cave, is a complex of altars linked by a causeway to Aguada La Gondola, the principal reservoir of ancient Xcoch. It is easy to imagine generations of shamans laboriously ascending

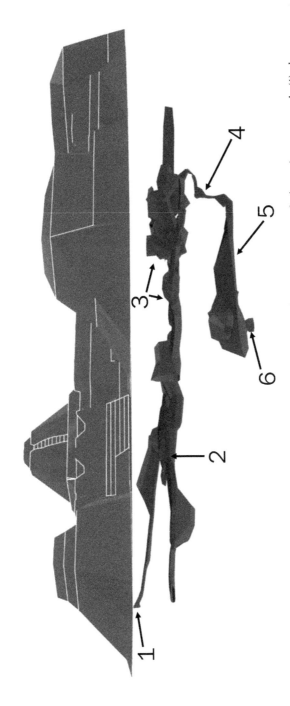

FIGURE 3.1 Schematic view of part of the Xcoch acropolis and the labyrinthine cave system below. Arrows mark (1) the cave entrance at left—a pit in bottom of sinkhole leading into a long crawlway, (2) the intersection of two passageways marked by an inverted conical stone altar, (3) a warren of passages and chambers, (4) a series of vertical shafts, (5) the penultimate chamber with altar complex and deep deposit of ritually killed ceramic vessels, and (6) the water pool in the lowest chamber. Courtesy of Eric Weaver.

FIGURE 3.2 A Maya shaman engaged in a *Ch'a Cháak*, or rain-summoning ceremony in Santa Elena, Yucatan. The ritual offerings tethered to the four-
quartered altar include *zuhuy ha* obtained from the deep pool in Xcoch
Cave. Photograph by author.

from the depths of the cave and carrying their precious liquid offering to the end
of the reservoir and casting it in, an act of imitative magic to symbolically initiate
the beginning of the rainy season.

Geography played a critical role in the development of Maya beliefs about water.
The Maya world was essentially bounded on four sides by water between the Gulf of
Mexico, Caribbean Sea and Pacific Ocean. The Yucatan Peninsula formed the heartland of Ancient Lowland Maya Civilization, its karst nature limiting the availability
of surface water—a situation made critical by the highly seasonal nature of regional
rainfall, including a five-month-long dry season. As noted by Finamore and Houston:

> Surrounded by the sea in all directions, the ancient Maya people of Central
> America viewed their world as one bounded by and integrally tied to water.
> To the Maya, oceans, rivers, springs, clouds and rain were a unity, enveloping
> and infusing the terrestrial world with its influence. Water was more than the
> essential compound that sustained people and the food they ate. It was the
> fundamental and vital medium from which the earthly world emerged, gods
> arose and returned to at death, and where ancestors resided.
>
> *(2010:15)*

Among the Yukatek Maya, there is a belief that subterranean water is akin to the
blood of the Earth, and that there is a current of underground water (*sayab'*) flowing

like an artery under the peninsula from east to west—from the eastern sea, that is the source of all water including clouds, wind and rain (Taube, 2010).

Maya beliefs about water are remarkably akin to the modern concept of the hydrologic cycle (Dunning, 2003). In the humid tropics, the forest steams in the morning sun; evapotranspiration is clearly visible; clouds are born, rising above the eastern sea and above the forest, then moving westward across the sky and delivering rain—often in the form of thunderstorms, the perceived voice of rain gods. Fallen rain, in turn, reenters the earth, and in doing so ensures life. So too, key Maya deities, such as the Sun and Venus gods, make a similar journey, rising in the east and reentering the watery realm of death in the west—only to repeat the cycle again reemerging, resurrected in the east. In Classic Maya script, the expression *och-ha* ("enter the water") is used for death (Taube, 2010). People too, especially royal people, could make the journey of the Sun and Venus, passing through the watery underworld, and eventually rising to be seated as deified ancestors in the sky.

The word *ha'* (or *ja'*) and its cognates designate "water" across the Mayan language family and also appear in Maya glyphic script of the Classic period (Kettunen and Helmke, 2013). In Classic period texts, *ha'al* refers specifically to rainfall, and *nahb* references bodies of water, most commonly "pools" of water (*aguadas*/reservoirs). Water and water bodies, including those in caves, form fundamental components of Maya cosmology, reflective of the tropical karst environment of the Maya Lowlands (Dunning, 2003). Across the lower-lying coastal plains of the Yucatan Peninsula, the dissolution of limestone has created many openings that penetrate to the permanent water table lying variously two to twenty meters below the surface. Many of these openings are sheer-sided sinkholes (*dzono't* in Yukatek Mayan, or, more commonly *cenote*, a Hispanicized form). Many are more cave-like, typically sloping downward such that little or no sunlight reaches the water. In the Elevated Interior Region (EIR) of the peninsula, the depth to groundwater ranges from thirty to two hundred or more meters and very few caves, like Xcoch, penetrate to these depths.

Water-related landscape features became closely associated with the sacred places of origin (*ch'en*). At its most mundane, *ch'en* ("well") simply refers to any water-bearing cenote or cave. But its meaning can be much more profound, referencing the symbolic birthplaces of Maya lineages and dynasties as documented in Classic period inscriptions (Tokovinine, 2013), or the sanctified territory controlled by a divine king (Bíró, 2011). This fundamental link between Maya culture, society, place-based identity and water reflects the critical nature and seasonal scarcity of this resource across much of the Maya Lowlands. Almost all ancient Maya agriculture was rainfall dependent and in many areas water for consumption and other needs had to be "harvested" and stored in the rainy season and meted out through the dry. This relationship was most pronounced in the EIR where Maya water collection and storage technology evolved over many centuries. Unlike the northern karst plain of Yucatan where cenotes (sinkholes with perennial water) and caves offered easy access to groundwater, or the southern parts of the Maya Lowlands where non-karst rivers provided perennial water, the EIR posed greater water management challenges for its ancient inhabitants (Dunning, Beach and Luzzadder-Beach, 2012).

In Maya cosmology, water functions as a transformative boundary, simultaneously separating and connecting cosmic planes. In particular, the boundary of the underworld is manifest as a watery surface, reflective of events past, present and future (Scarborough, 1998). Where natural water sources were not present, the ancient Maya created them as focal points in their communities, typically as central reservoirs within urban areas (Dunning, 2019). The creation, or enhancement of such surfaces within an ancient Maya community undoubtedly had tremendous symbolic power replicating cosmic structure at the hands of the Maya rulers (Dunning et al., 1999). At Xcoch, the east–west celestial journey was recreated via a cave-mouth altar complex, elevated causeway and enormous reservoir mimicking the western sea. Notably, in Maya cosmology, such causeways (or *sakbe'ob*) were conceptually linked to the idea of celestial umbilical ropes connecting significant cosmic points (Dunning and Weaver, 2015). Central reservoirs, of course, also had a great pragmatic role as well, helping urban populations to survive the annual dry season.

Water indeed played a central role in both Maya cosmological and pragmatic understanding of the world; thus, perceived divine and elite political control of this substance became intertwined as Maya Civilization evolved (Scarborough, 1998; Dunning, 2003; Lucero, 2006; Houston, 2010). This complex relationship is evident in the incorporation of water collection and storage features in the elite-sponsored monumental architecture within site cores from the Middle Preclassic (c. 800 BCE) onward, for example, the shedding of water from the Brisa Group, an early ritual and elite residential complex, into the Brisa reservoir at Yaxnohcah (Dunning, 2019). While the precise meaning and function of many Maya pyramid temples remain unclear, at least some of these buildings were apparently manifestations of the pan-Mesoamerican concept of a "water mountain" (Lucero, 2006). Conceptually tied to mountain caves and springs, the architectural creation of such symbolically potent places was another symbol of the cosmologically endowed authority of rulers. The symbolic recreation of water mountains as plastered pyramids and associated plazas and structures allowed these features to literally produce water as rain was shed, which could, in turn, be collected in reservoirs (Scarborough, 1998).

In Maya cosmology, water-bearing caves are believed to be the home of the rain deity, Chaak (Brady, 2010). Caves that penetrate to the permanent groundwater table are extremely rare in the EIR, including the Puuc Hills, at the heart of the Yucatan Peninsula. One such cave is located at Xcoch, where a tortuous series of narrow passageways drops, and wider chambers eventually reach a small pool of water. Archaeological evidence indicates that this pool was a focus of rain-related rituals from at least as early as 800 BCE—and continuing into the modern era (Stephens, 1841; Smyth and Ortegón Zapata, 2008; Dunning et al., 2014; Weaver, Dunning and Smyth, 2015; Smyth et al., 2017). Above the cave, the Great Pyramid of Xcoch and an associated acropolis and plaza complex grew incrementally over many centuries beginning in the Middle Preclassic (c. 800 BCE). Numerous rebuilding episodes reinvigorated this sacred site and literally created a "water mountain," that shed rain which was captured in plazas below, essentially harvesting water from the sky. Over time, a city grew around and over the cave, which remained at its ceremonial heart and the geomantic centering point for the community, its public architecture, its water management infrastructure and its identity creation. Plastered channels funneled rain water collected in several plazas into the city's largest reservoir, Aguada La Gondola. A causeway (*sakbe*) was constructed connecting an altar complex at the cave entrance to a temple group on the eastern lip of the reservoir. Rare polychrome water jars are found only deep within the cave and on the successive buried floors of the reservoir. These specialized jars were likely used to bring *zuhuy ha* to the reservoir to symbolically initiate the refilling of the reservoir by the perceived combined actions of a shaman/ruler and the rain gods being called forth from the cave and sky.

The repetition of the urban pattern of pyramid, plazas and reservoirs in the core areas of Maya cities and towns in the EIR is indicative of the pervasiveness of a belief system that included the close relationship between rulers and rain deities that persisted from the Middle Preclassic through Terminal Classic periods. Many of these water catchment systems continued to evolve as central architectural complexes grew (e.g. a system documented at Nakum: Kozskul and Žralka, 2013). Whether natural or created, water sources at the heart of Maya communities were intrinsically tied to place identity and the authority of dynastic rulership (Dunning et al., 1999; Tokovinine, 2013; Dunning and Weaver, 2015).

While the individual elements that combine to make Xcoch a sacred place are unique in detail, these elements all reflect broader Maya and Mesoamerican patterns and traditions and share some common ground with traditional conceptions of space and place in many other parts of the world. Paul Wheatly used René Berthelot's term "astro-biological" to describe this type of world model and its characteristics: Terrestrial space was initially generated by, and subsequently structured about, an existentially centered point of ontological transition between cosmic planes…the orientation of the sacred enclave surrounding the *axis mundi* should be achieved in relation to the cardinal directions. From that *enceiente*, enclosing the holy of holies, the four horizons were projected outwards…thus assimilating the group's territory to the cosmic order and constructing a sanctified space (Wheatley, 1977:53).

The Maya *ch'en* represents just such a concept, a simple word for cave or well, but that was also conceptualized variously as an opening in the sky and earth, a place of dynastic origin, a home of gods and deified ancestors, and as the sanctified territory of a ruler or dynasty symbolically tethered to this centering point (Bíró, 2011). Sanctified, politically reified space was projected outward from this point of origin and set in order according to cosmic principles, beginning with the careful arrangement of public architecture, in an attempt to recreate the perceived order of the cosmos within the landscape and, in doing so, helping to ensure the proper working of the universe and the prosperity of humans (Dunning and Weaver, 2015).

A great deal of Maya ritual activity, both ancient and contemporary, involves the maintenance of perceived cosmic order. For many Maya peoples today, the natural environment is alive with vital forces, in ways consistent with what appears in Classic-period iconography and texts (Dunning and Houston, 2011). The Maya do not believe themselves to be passive participants in the behavior of these forces, but critical agents of maintenance, as well as, when necessary, of change.

In the present day, the principal forces that are addressed in caves and cenotes, identified by Maya peoples as "the first temples of the world" (Brady, 2010), are rain, wind and even hurricanes, with many beliefs apparently carrying over from ancient Maya times (Dunning and Houston, 2011). The essence of contemporary Yukatek Maya rituals tied to the agricultural cycle is to maintain the proper order of things in time and space (Hanks, 1990:361–391; Gubler, 2012). This order includes the bringing of rain at beneficial times and in appropriate quantities. Proper order also ordains that the great wind beneath the sea should stay in its place and push the subterranean currents that filter sweet water into the cenotes. Such order even dictates that venomous serpents should stay out of the gardens and paths of humans. However, sometimes chaos prevails: snakes are in the paths, winds are dislodged from their proper places and rage above ground as hurricanes and tornados—indeed, "snakes" then swirl in the air. Similar beliefs are found among contemporary Ch'orti' Maya, including that rain and wind are controlled by the Noh Chih Chan, a great cosmic serpent residing in the subterranean waters of a spring or well that is the navel or heart of the world (Girard, 1995:115–116). This snake and its subsidiary kin have the power to release or withhold rain and wind. Ch'orti' shamans attempt to control winds and rain by bringing stones from water sources located at the four world directions, forming the stones and a central canoe filled with water into a quincunx, then using this altar to call forth and "arrange" benevolent winds and rains to the benefit of humanity. Evil winds are also called to the altar, captured and stored in jugs—though these sometimes escape.

The aforementioned *Ch'a Cháak* ceremony is another example of ritual intervention, essentially seeking to keep the universe on track by bringing rain when it is needed and expected. These ceremonies are held all across rural Yucatan today, though with place-to-place variation in their particulars and frequency (Love, 2012). In some communities, the ceremony has become essentially an annual event, held to keep the celestial rhythms in proper sync, whereas some communities hold it only during drought years—in an attempt to get those rhythms back on track.

The cave at Xcoch is far from being the only sacred well in the Maya Lowlands (Brady, 2010). In ancient times, the landscape was replete with them, including the famous Cenote of Sacrifice (or Sacred Cenote) at Chichen Itza, a place famous for sacrificial offering in the Maya Terminal Classic and Postclassic periods (Coggins, 1984). The importance of these places has waxed and waned over time, partly in keeping with the fortunes of the communities that grew, flourished and declined there. Xcoch was a place of paramount ritual importance between about 800 BCE and 850 CE during which time a large community grew around it. However, like many Maya cities in the EIR of the peninsula, Xcoch was abandoned in the Terminal Classic period—at least in part because of severe and extended droughts (Smyth et al., 2017). Nevertheless, the cave and its regionally unique source of virgin water remained important in the minds of surrounding communities, diminished though they might be. The deep pool continued to be tapped through the Postclassic and Colonial eras, and is still used today. The impressive architectural infrastructure from the city's heyday has crumbled, and even the wooden ladders used to assist access within the cave that were noted in the mid-nineteenth century (Stephens, 1843) have fallen apart. Today, nylon ropes and flashlights are used to navigate the labyrinthine cave and descend to its lowest chambers. Even without the smoke of the torches used by past visitors, the lower chambers are hypoxic and one is left gasping for breath. In shimmering light, the heaps of ritually smashed ceramics and other offerings emerge from the darkness, and reflected beams dance off the surface of the sacred pool. Even for those non-Maya visitors not attuned to the deep cultural meaning of this place, its special nature is apparent. Yes, this was, and is, a place to converse with the gods.

Note

1 The vignette encompassing the first three paragraphs in this chapter is historical fiction, based on a known acute drought, a known Maya ritual response to such droughts and the known use of the deep cave at Xcoch as a source of sacred water used in such rituals. The name of the shaman is fictional.

References

Bíró, Péter. 2011. Politics in the Western Maya Region. *Ajawil/Ajawel* and *Ch'e'n*. *Estudios de Cultura Maya* 38: 43–73.

Brady, James. 2010. Offerings to the Rain Gods: The Archaeology of Maya Caves. In *Fiery Pool: The Maya and the Mythic Sea*, edited by Daniel Finamore and Steven D. Houston, 218–222. New Haven, CT: Yale University Press.

Coggins, Clemency C. 1984. *Cenote of Sacrifice: Maya Treasures from the Sacred Well at Chichen Itza*. Austin: University of Texas Press.

Dunning, Nicholas P. 2003. Birth and Death of Waters: Environmental Change, Adaptation, and Symbolism in the Southern Maya Lowlands. In *Espacios Mayas: Representaciones, Usos, Creencias*, edited by Alain Breton, Aurore Monod-Becquelin and Mario Humberto Ruz, 49–76. Mexico City: Universidad Autonoma de México.

———. 2020. Water Harvesting and Urbanization in the Maya Heartland. In *La Gestión y Manejo del Agua en las Tierras Mayas*, edited by Josep Ligorred, Berlin: Springer.

Dunning, Nicholas P. and Stephen D. Houston. 2011. Hurricanes as a Disruptive Force in the Maya Lowlands. In *Ecology, Power, and Religion in Maya Landscapes*, edited by Christian Isendahl and Bodine L. Persson, 49–59. Möckmühl, Germany: Verlag Anton Sauerwein.

Dunning, Nicholas P. and Eric Weaver. 2015. Final Thoughts: Space, Place, Ritual, and Identity in Ancient Mesoamerica. In *Memory Traces: Sacred Space at Five Mesoamerican Sites*, edited by Laura Amrhein and Cynthia Kristen-Graham, 203–218. Boulder: University of Colorado Press.

Dunning, Nicholas P., Timothy Beach and Sheyrl Luzzadder-Beach. 2012. *Kax* and *Kol*: Collapse and Resilience in Lowland Maya Civilization. *Proceedings of the National Academy of Sciences* (USA) 109: 3652–3657.

Dunning, Nicholas P., Vernon Scarborough, Fred Valdez, Sheryl Luzzadder-Beach, Timothy Beach and John G. Jones. 1999. Temple Mountains, Sacred Lakes, and Fertile Fields: Ancient Maya Landscapes in Northwestern Belize. *Antiquity* 73: 650–660.

Dunning, Nicholas P., Eric Weaver, Michael P, Smyth and David Ortegón Zapata. 2014. Xcoch: Home of Ancient Maya Rain Gods and Water Managers. In *The Archaeology of Yucatan: New Directions and Data*, edited by Travis Stanton, 65–80. Oxford: BAR International Series.

Girard, Raphael. 1995. *People of the Chan*. Trans. by Bennett Preble. Chino Valley, AZ: Continuum Foundation.

Gubler, Ruth. 2012. Yucatec Maya Agricultural Ritual Survivals. In *Fanning the Sacred Flame: Mesoamerican Studies in Honor of H. B. Nicholson*, edited by Matthew A. Boxt and Brian D. Dillon, 489–518. Boulder: University Press of Colorado.

Hanks, William F. 1990. *Referential Practice: Language and Lived Space among the Maya*. Chicago, IL: University of Chicago Press.

Houston, Stephen D. 2010. Living Waters and Wondrous Beasts. In *Fiery Pool: The Maya and the Mythic Sea*, edited by Danial Finamore and Steven D. Houston, 66–79. New Haven, CT: Yale University Press.

Kettunen, Harri and Christophe Helmke. 2013. Water in Maya Imagery and Writing. *Contributions to New World Archaeology* 5:17–38.

Kozskul, Wieslaw and Jaroslaw Žralka. 2013. El manejo ritual y práctico del agua: el caso del Edificio 14 de Nakum, Guatemala. *Contributions to New World Archaeology* 5: 101–124.

Love, Bruce. 2012. *Maya Shamanism Today: Connecting with the Cosmos in Rural Yucatan*. San Francisco, CA: Mesoweb Press.

Lucero, Lisa J. 2006. *Water and Ritual: The Rise and Fall of Classic Maya Rulers*. Austin: University of Texas Press.

Mendoza, Blanca, Virginia García-Acosta, Victor Velasco, Ernesto Jáuregui and Rosa Díaz-Sandoval. 2007. Frequency and Duration of Historical Droughts from the 16th to the 19th Centuries in the Mexican Maya Lands, Yucatan Peninsula. *Climatic Change* 83: 151–168.

Scarborough, Vernon L. 1998. Ecology and Ritual: Water Management and the Maya. *Latin American Antiquity* 9: 135–159.

Smyth, Michael P. and David Ortegón Zapata. 2008. A Preclassic Center in the Puuc Region: A Report on Xcoch, Yucatan, Mexico. *Mexicon* 30: 63–68.

Smyth, Michael P., Nicholas P. Dunning, Eric Weaver, Philip van Beynen and David Ortegón Zapata. 2017. The Perfect Storm: Climate Change and Ancient Maya Response in the Puuc Hills Region, Yucatan, Mexico. *Antiquity* 91: 490–509.

Stephens, John Lloyd. 1841. *Incidents of Travel in Yucatan*. Vol. 1. New York: Harper and Rowe.

Taube, Karl A. 2010. Where the Earth and Sky Meet: The Sea in Ancient and Contemporary Maya Cosmology. In *Fiery Pool: The Maya and the Mythic Sea*, edited by Danial Finamore and Steven D. Houston, 202–222. New Haven, CT: Yale University Press.

Tokovinine, Alexandre. 2013. *Place and Identity in Classic Maya Narratives: Studies in Pre-Columbian Art and Archaeology 37*. Washington, DC: Dumbarton Oaks.

Weaver, Eric, Nicholas P. Dunning and Michael P. Smyth. 2015. Investigation of a Ritual Cave Site in the Puuc Region of Yucatan, Mexico: Actun Xcoch. *Journal of Cave and Karst Studies* 77:120–128.

Wheatley, Paul. 1977. The Suspended Pelt: Reflections on a Discarded Model of Spatial Structure. In *Geographic Humanism, Analysis, and Social Action*, edited by Dennis R. Deskins, 47–108. Ann Arbor: University of Michigan Geographical Publications 17.

PART II

Stewarding curative waters and caring for pilgrims

In many parts of the world, sacred springs and holy wells have local individuals or families who serve as their stewards. In some cases, they might require a token fee for admission or for the service of water-drawing for devotees. This fee can remind visitors of the site's special qualities or serve in place of a votive offering, and finance the upkeep of a site shrine. Other locals may begrudge, but tolerate, such payments when they form the stewards' main source of income. Stewarding sacred watery sites that draw international pilgrims requires an elaborate infrastructure which can even be governmentally supported. Michael Agnew offers an overview of the nineteenth-century Marian apparitions that brought forth the miraculous waters of Lourdes and created one of Roman Catholicism's most prominent pilgrimage shrines. Exploring the shrine's rituals and pilgrims' engagement with the waters, Agnew discusses the "infrastructure of care" provided to pilgrims traveling to Lourdes. Likewise, the supernatural provision of the Zamzam spring for Hagar led to the settlement and eventual sacrality of Mecca and the *hajj* required of Muslims at least once in a lifetime. Ahmad Ghabin examines access to the well and "Watering the Pilgrims"—a stewardship role Hagar performed, that was sanctioned in the Koran, and is perpetuated today by state authorities which make Zamzam water available to mosques in both Mecca and Medina. The largest gathering of humanity anywhere in the world is a water pilgrimage: the Kumbha Mela. This gathering draws pilgrims in larger figures than the populations of either São Paulo or Mexico City (two of the world's largest megacities). Rana Singh notes the infrastructural organization required to host the mass gathering within a chapter that examines Hindu valuations of different water forms as sacred, and the mythology and rituals associated with waterfront sacred places along the Ganga. As even the Ganga has been recklessly polluted, he emphasizes the role that reawakened sacred water beliefs can play in environmental stewardship more generally.

4

"GO DRINK FROM THE SPRING AND WASH THERE"

The healing waters of Lourdes

Michael Agnew

In 1858 on the edge of the small town of Lourdes, situated in the foothills of the Pyrénées in southwestern France, a 14-year-old girl named Bernadette Soubirous reported a series of 18 visions of a figure who was quickly understood by several townspeople to be the Virgin Mary. Bernadette's visions began on February 11 when she joined her sister and a friend to collect wood along the riverbank of the Gave de Pau, at a site where there was a small cave or grotto called Massabielle by locals. While Bernadette removed her stockings in order to cross the river, she heard a sudden gust of wind. As she later wrote: "I went on taking off my stockings. I heard the same sound again. As I raised my head to look at the grotto, I saw a Lady dressed in white, wearing a white dress, a blue girdle and a yellow rose on each foot, the same color as the chain of her rosary; the beads of the rosary were white" (McEachern, 2005:20). No words were exchanged and the lady, who Bernadette initially referred to as *aquerò*, a term in the local dialect meaning "that one" or "that thing," soon disappeared.

Over the following days, Bernadette and a growing number of friends and townspeople returned to the grotto of Massabielle, but only Bernadette was able to witness the "thing" in the rock niche. It was not until the third apparition on February 18 that the lady first spoke to Bernadette. The lady asked Bernadette if she would do her the favor of going to the grotto each day for a fortnight, and told Bernadette that she did not promise to make her happy in this world, but in the next. For her next trek to the grotto the following day, Bernadette brought a lighted candle, which became the precedent for the tradition of lighting candles at the grotto and holding them during the Marian torchlight procession which continues at the shrine today.

During what is often called the "fortnight of the apparitions," the visions on February 25 and March 2 were particularly crucial in bringing Lourdes to national and later global prominence as a healing shrine with a miraculous spring at its center. When Bernadette arrived at the grotto on February 25, joined by over three hundred witnesses, she was instructed by the lady to "Go drink from the spring and wash there." Seeing no spring at the grotto, Bernadette began to move toward the river when the lady interrupted, telling her that the spring was not there, and pointing instead to the base of the rock wall at the back of the grotto. Bernadette crawled on her hands and knees into the grotto and found a small patch of mud, and began scraping at the earth with her hands. The water she was first able to extract was too dirty and she threw it away, but by her fourth attempt, the water was still muddy but clear enough that she could drink some of it and smear it on her face. Bernadette was also directed to eat some of the plants growing near the grotto, and did so, without knowing why. She was ridiculed by many in the crowd who were shocked and repulsed by her actions and disheveled appearance. Some onlookers now believed the series of apparitions to be a childish fabrication. Yet, the muddy patch at the base of the grotto soon developed into a clear, flowing spring, and several began to bottle the water from the spring to take home with them, as contemporary pilgrims still do at the shrine. On March 1, the first recognized miracle cure at Lourdes occurred, when Catherine Latapie, a woman from the neighboring village of Loubajac who was nine months pregnant, walked the 9-km trail to Lourdes to dip her paralyzed arm in the spring. Healed immediately, she returned home to give birth to a son. Her cure was recognized four years later in 1862 as the first of 70 miracles occurring at Lourdes officially approved by the Catholic Church. The most recent *miraculée* (those persons declared officially cured by the Church) was a French nun who was inexplicably cured of severe complications of acute sciatic nerve pain a few days after returning from a pilgrimage to Lourdes. The cure was recognized by the church on the feast day of Our Lady of Lourdes, February 11, 2018 (Paone, 2018).

On March 25, Bernadette once again experienced an apparition of the lady. Determined to learn the identity of the vision, Bernadette asked the lady thrice for a name, and thrice the only response she received was a smile. Finally, on the fourth attempt, her persistence was rewarded. As Bernadette wrote: "She stopped smiling. With her arms down, she raised her eyes to heaven and then, folding her hands over her breast she said, 'I am the Immaculate Conception'" (McEachern, 2005:25). Many believed that this statement confirmed that the figure Bernadette communed with in the grotto was indeed the Virgin Mary. Her identification as the Immaculate Conception (*Que soy era Immaculada Concepciou* in the local dialect) was later celebrated by Church officials as validation of the dogma of the Immaculate Conception of Mary which had become official doctrine only four years previously.[1] While the identity-revealing episode served as the dramatic climax of the apparition cycle, Bernadette would see the Lady twice more, on April 7 and on July 16. Her final vision was from across the river as town officials had barricaded access to the grotto by that time.

This greatly condensed account provides the general sequence of reported apparitions of the Virgin Mary to Bernadette that would together form the Lourdes story and inspire the sick and disabled, the faithful, the skeptical and the curious to travel to the grotto at Lourdes and "drink from the spring and wash there." The general details of the story of Bernadette Soubirous and the 18 visions of the Virgin Mary she is believed to have witnessed, as well as the early development of the shrine have been chronicled by several popular writers and academics. Bernadette's visions serve as the natural starting point for an incredible range of devotional,

FIGURE 4.1 Pilgrims move in-line through the Grotto of Massabielle at Lourdes, where Bernadette reported receiving her visions of the Virgin Mary. Photograph by author.

apologetic and historical treatments of Lourdes.[2] The overview provided here, however, lends context to the factors that motivate pilgrims who travel to Lourdes and their engagement with the sacred geography of the shrine.[3]

The sacred geography of Lourdes

The Sanctuary of Our Lady of Lourdes, referred to as the *Domaine*, that gradually developed around the Grotto of Massabielle in the latter decades of the nineteenth century continues to attract millions of pilgrims each year. The large diocesan "pilgrimages" (referencing groups of pilgrims), and those organized by various Catholic charitable organizations, travel to Lourdes primarily during the height of the pilgrimage season from April through October. However, significant numbers of pilgrims go to the shrine outside of this period for the Feast of the Immaculate Conception on December 8 and to mark the anniversary of the first apparition to Bernadette on February 11. The most recent estimates place the total number of shrine visitors at nearly 6.3 million per year, with pilgrims predominantly traveling from western Europe, but also from as far away as China and Argentina.

The sacred geography of Lourdes which these pilgrims encounter is indeed vast and consists of grand basilicas, intimate chapels, Stations of the Cross, walking paths that run along the river bank, accommodations for the sick and disabled, first aid posts, administrative offices, an information center and a bookshop. Any description of the Lourdes *Domaine* would be incomplete, however, without mention of its physical and spiritual heart, the Grotto of Massabielle, where Bernadette's dramatic visionary episodes occurred and from where the spring she unearthed began to flow. Although the several gates ringing the Sanctuary are locked at midnight and do not reopen until 5:00 AM, one small gate is left open throughout the year, granting access to what pilgrims call the "zig-zag path" which leads down the hill directly to the grotto. This is important for many pilgrims, who report that their favorite time to visit the grotto was around 2 or 3 in the morning, when activity around the sacred area was relatively still and quiet. The grotto then seems to take on an especially numinous aura with the glistening rock walls illuminated by the glow of a large, continuously lit candelabra. Except when pilgrimages are holding their masses at its stone altar, access to the shallow cave is also provided at various times of the day when long lines of eager pilgrims quickly form. Pilgrims occupying wheelchairs do not wait in line, but are granted special admission by a shrine volunteer acting as a gatekeeper.

As pilgrims file through the grotto, most will touch, kiss and run their hands along the stone surface, now worn smooth by the millions of pilgrims who have come before and physically engaged with the grotto. Some will enter the grotto with rosaries, religious medals and prayer cards in hand, pressing them to the rock wall and blessing them through contact with this most auspicious site in Lourdes. Pilgrims may leave written prayer petitions as they enter the grotto and then view (through a glass portal) the original source of the miraculous spring revealed by Bernadette scraping the earth with her hands. The portal is often surrounded by flowers and notes left in thanksgiving for a favor received by means of the spring water. As pilgrims begin to exit the grotto, they will often turn around and gaze up toward the statue of Our Lady of Lourdes in the rock niche above, where Bernadette claimed the Virgin appeared, and cross themselves, genuflect, or say a quick prayer before they are moved along by the line of pilgrims following them through the grotto. Often, there are light trickles of water flowing from the crevices of the rock just below the statue, and pilgrims scoop some small amounts into their hands with which they quickly wash their face, or might press their lips to the wet rock. There are rows of metal benches in front of the grotto where some choose to stay and continue their prayers and watch the seemingly endless flow of pilgrims move through the shallow cave.

Alternatively, they may proceed down toward the row of taps recently positioned to the right of the grotto. Lining up and waiting for their turn, pilgrims fill whatever bottles they have with water drawn from the spring uncovered by Bernadette, which is believed by pilgrims to have the potential to effect miraculous cures of illnesses ranging from tuberculosis, and cancer, to rheumatism and paralysis. Receptacles include small bottles in the shape of Our Lady of Lourdes with her crown as the twist cap, more conventional water bottles and flasks, large soda bottles and even gasoline cans are filled with the miraculous spring water. Pilgrims often take

FIGURE 4.2 Pilgrims from the United Kingdom carry a statue of the Virgin Mary toward the main basilica of Lourdes during the Marian torchlight procession. Photo by author.

the water back home with them and drink it or use it as a sort of topical medicine, and some also use it to bless their homes. Lourdes water, it could be said, is a translocative symbol (Tweed, 1997), that can be easily transported from Lourdes and possessed within the home, and with which one can physically engage and directly apply to the body. Long after their visit to Lourdes, pilgrims can still experience an especially potent element of the shrine, the water from the spring and the miraculous potential it holds.

In addition to the grotto, pilgrims cite the *piscines* or baths as central to the Lourdes experience and as the most spiritually meaningful place at the shrine for them. The baths open each day from 9:00 AM to 11:00 AM and again from 2:00 PM to 4:00 PM, and are located in a rather inconspicuous gray stone building further down the river past the grotto and taps. There are 17 separate baths: 11 for women (of which one is reserved for children) and six for men. The lack of gender parity relates simply to the fact that more women than men go to Lourdes on pilgrimage, and far more women than men use the baths, at a ratio of 289,600 women to 130,200 men during the course of the pilgrimage season. Like the taps, the baths are fed by the miraculous spring and allow pilgrims to honor the Virgin's request in the apparitions to not only drink the water issuing from the spring but also to wash there. The water is continually topped-up, circulated by a pump and irradiated for hygiene. When it is their turn to enter the baths, pilgrims are directed to a small cubicle to undress and are covered with a cloth or robe. They are then ushered to a shallow rectangular pool of water, where they are assisted by lay volunteers who ask if they would like to present their prayer petitions to Our Lady. Pilgrims are then slowly immersed into the water up to the neck, and asked by the volunteers whether they would like to make the sign of the cross and recall their baptism. They are then invited to kiss a statue of Our Lady of Lourdes, and together recite the invocation: "Our Lady of Lourdes, pray for us. St. Bernadette, pray for us. O Mary, conceived without sin, pray for us who have recourse to you." The pilgrim is then assisted out of the bath and returned to the cubicle to dress (without drying themselves) and they exit the bathing facility, often smiling widely or with tears in their eyes, overwhelmed by what is for many pilgrims an emotional and sometimes transformational experience.

The liturgical calendar of Lourdes

Key rituals and services punctuating the liturgical calendar at Lourdes include the International Mass, the Blessed Sacrament Procession and the Marian Torchlight procession. The International Mass is held each Sunday and Wednesday at 9:30 AM during the pilgrimage season (April through October), at the Underground Basilica of St. Pius X which is a massive church seating over 25,000 pilgrims and consecrated by Cardinal Angelo Roncalli in March 1958, seven months before he would be elected as the recently canonized Pope John XXIII. The service brings together all of the pilgrimage groups in Lourdes at one time to celebrate mass together, with readings and prayers in several languages.

The Blessed Sacrament Procession occurs each day at 5:00 PM, as pilgrims march from the square in front of the Rosary Basilica, along the esplanade, and into the Underground Basilica with the "host" (the bread or wafer believed by Catholics to transform into the literal body of Jesus). During Gospel readings and hymn-singing in the incense-scented church, pilgrims venerate the Eucharistic wafer displayed on the altar in a monstrance (an elaborate gold and jeweled vessel with a clear window through which the host can be seen). The service concludes with a Benediction or blessing of the pilgrims with the Eucharist, as priests slowly make their way around the basilica giving special attention to the ill and holding the monstrance aloft as pilgrims bow toward it and make the sign of the cross. Several of the miraculous cures at Lourdes recognized by the Church, and many more that have not received official sanction, have been reported as occurring at this point when sick pilgrims were blessed with the Eucharist.

The principal procession for which Lourdes is renowned, however, is the Marian Torchlight Procession, which begins at 9:00 PM each night. Soon after dinner in their hotels, pilgrims begin making their way back to the shrine, purchasing candles for the procession at shops along the way. The candles are sheathed by a white and blue paper cone-shaped lantern to shelter the flame. Images of the Virgin Mary appearing to Bernadette are printed on the paper lantern, along with the lyrics to Ave Maria, which is sung during the procession. As the sunlight fades, the glow of thousands of individual candles brightens while the line of pilgrims weaves its way from the grotto down the main esplanade of the *Domaine* and back as hymns are sung and decades of the rosary are recited. Many pilgrims choose not to participate in this ritual and instead angle for prime vantage points for viewing the procession along the massive archways and rooftop of the Rosary Basilica. The candlelight procession presents an impressive spectacle. As it slowly makes its way toward its destination point at the front steps of the Rosary Basilica, the pilgrims are directed to march in a zig-zag pattern toward the front. This pattern creates a stunning, almost serpentine, effect when viewed from above. Once all pilgrims have come to a stop, with sick and disabled pilgrims at the front as they always are for processions and services, the Salve Regina hymn is sung and a final blessing is given. Pilgrims then slowly begin splintering off from the square, some to the grotto, some to walk alone or in small groups along the river, and others back into the town to unwind in the many cafés situated around the shrine.

"Let me be as Christ to you": Lourdes and an infrastructure of care

From the earliest claims of dramatic, miraculous cures by the first pilgrims who traveled to Lourdes, who visited the makeshift shrine and drank and washed in the water flowing from the spring uncovered by Bernadette, Lourdes has become renowned as a sacred place of potential healing, drawing millions of sick and disabled pilgrims each year. Even for the casual day-tripper quickly passing through Lourdes as part of a larger itinerary, it becomes readily apparent that care and concern for the sick is *the* central animating ethos sustaining the activity of the shrine. This has been the case from the very outset, as shrine officials and pilgrimage organizers have tried to facilitate travel, accommodations and medical care for sick pilgrims for their journeys to Lourdes and for their stay. As Ruth Harris explains, the first serious contingent of around 50 *malades* (the historical term used to refer to sick pilgrims at Lourdes) joined the French national pilgrimage in 1875. Two years later, the ratio had reached 366 *malades* out of a total of 1,200 pilgrims, the numbers of both *malades* and total pilgrims rapidly increasing in subsequent years (1999:258).

An extensive spiritual and medical infrastructure is now in place at the shrine to support these pilgrims during their stay in town. Professional medical staff are joined by hundreds of volunteer caregivers or "helpers," tasked with pushing wheelchairs, assisting with bathing and dressing, and simply providing companionship (Agnew, 2015). *Malades*, now sometimes referred to by English-speaking pilgrimages as "assisted pilgrims" who require help, will often stay in one of two large facilities provided by the shrine: the Accueil Marie Saint-Frai and the Accueil Notre-Dame. The Accueil St. Frai was the first hospital facility for sick pilgrims in Lourdes, established in 1874 by Marie Saint-Frai and Fr. Dominique Ribes, who also founded the Order of the Daughters of Our Lady of Sorrows that is still charged with operating the Accueil. Situated outside the shrine domain in the town of Lourdes, just up the street from one of the principal entrances into the Sanctuary, it can accommodate up to 414 sick and disabled pilgrims and was significantly remodeled in 1998. It is not quite a hospital nor is it a hotel, but rather has been designed as accommodation with the sick, disabled and elderly in mind. The design of each floor is akin to a hospital ward however, with rooms of six beds each and a nurses' station lining the halls, which open up onto a six-story atrium where sunshine streams through the skylight above. The Accueil St. Frai also includes a chapel, meeting rooms and a terrace which allows for impressive views of the Château Fort de Lourdes (an eleventh-century castle).

Similarly, the Accueil Notre-Dame is a massive state-of-the-art facility, built in 1997 along the riverbank of the Gave de Pau, opposite the grotto. Containing 904 beds in rooms that can accommodate one to six pilgrims, it replaced the outdated building it once occupied, now renamed the Accueil Jean-Paul II which includes a first aid post, the Lourdes Medical Bureau, meeting rooms and chapels, and the headquarters of the Hospitalité Notre-Dame de Lourdes. Rooms in the Accueil Notre-Dame are fitted with accessible toilets and showers, are connected to an oxygen supply system and have alarms at each bed for assistance during the night. Like the St. Frai, it has dining rooms and nurses' stations, as well as storage areas for wheelchairs and other equipment. Pope John Paul II stayed in the Accueil Notre-Dame during his visit to Lourdes in August 2004, to mark the 150th anniversary of the promulgation of the Roman Catholic dogma of the Immaculate Conception of Mary. This, his final visit to Lourdes, was less than a year before his death, at a time when he was quite ill himself.

For many volunteer caregivers, and also for many assisted pilgrims, what is critical to their experience at Lourdes and what often inspires return visits to the shrine is not necessarily the story of the apparitions to Bernadette, or the reports of miraculous cures stemming from the water flowing at the base of the grotto. Rather, it is the connections formed between caregivers and Assisted Pilgrims at the Accueil St-Frai and the Accueil Notre-Dame and the ways these relationships reflect the core of their faith.[4] Indeed, Lourdes has been described as having at its heart an "economy of caring exchange" (Goldingay et al., 2014:316). This is the ideal frame within which caregivers and assisted pilgrims operate. The act of caregiving can be a deeply moving moral act, but can also be incredibly challenging. The invitation extended at Lourdes in the words of a Christian hymn are "let me be as Christ to you." Love and service of one's neighbor can be awkward, messy and complex. Yet for many volunteer caregivers, the potential for an experience of what they understand to be the "Christian love command" draws them to Lourdes and informs their practice.

Notes

1 The dogma of the Immaculate Conception was defined in an Apostolic Constitution of Pope Pius IX, *Ineffabilis Deus*, on December 8, 1854. For further context on the importance of Lourdes for the Church in confirming the Pope's proclamation of the doctrine, see Thomas A. Kselman, *Miracles and Prophecies in Nineteenth-Century France* (New Brunswick, NJ: Rutgers University Press, 1983), 92–93.

2 For a representative sample of early apologetic and devotional accounts of the Lourdes story, see Henri Lasserre, *Notre-Dame de Lourdes* (Paris: Victor Palmé, 1870); Léonard Cros, *Histoire de Notre-Dame de Lourdes* (Paris: Beauchesne, 1925), and J. K. Huysmans, *Les Foules de Lourdes* (Paris: Tresse and Stock, 1907). For English renderings see Robert Hugh Benson, *Lourdes* (London: Manresa Press, 1914) and Ruth Cranston, *The Miracle of Lourdes* (New York: McGraw-Hill, 1955).

3 This brief overview of the apparitions draws from more recent historical accounts, namely the excellent work of Ruth Harris in her definitive text on the early development of the Lourdes shrine, *Lourdes: Body and Spirit in the Secular Age* (New York: Viking, 1999), that of Sandra Zimdars-Swartz, *Encountering Mary: Visions of Mary from La Salette to Medjugorje* (Princeton, NJ: Princeton University Press, 1991), and Therese Taylor's *Bernadette of Lourdes: Her Life, Death and Visions* (London: Continuum, 2008).

4 See also John Eade, "Order and Power at Lourdes: Lay Helpers and the Organization of a Pilgrimage Shrine," in *Contesting the Sacred: The Anthropology of Christian Pilgrimage*, ed. John Eade and Michael J. Sallnow (London: Routledge, 1991), Alana Harris, "'A Place to Grow Spiritually and Socially': The Experiences of Young Pilgrims to Lourdes," in *Religion and Youth*, ed. Sylvia Collins-Mayo and Ben Pink Dandelion (Aldershot: Ashgate, 2010), Catrien Notermans, "Loss and Healing: A Marian Pilgrimage in Secular Dutch Society," *Ethnology* 46 (2007), Catrien Notermans, Maya Turolla and Willy Jansen, "Caring and Connecting: Reworking Religion, Gender and Families in Post-Migration Life," in *Contemporary Encounters in Gender and Religion*, ed. Lena Gemzoe, Marja-Liisa Keinänen and Avril Madrell (Palgrave Macmillan, 2016), and Michael Agnew, "'Spiritually, I'm Always in Lourdes:' Perceptions of Home and Away among Serial Pilgrims," *Studies in Religion* 44:4 (2015).

References

Agnew, Michael. 2015a. 'Let Me Be as Christ to You:' Pilgrimage and Volunteer Caregiving at Lourdes. In *Religious Diversity Today: Experiencing Religion in the Contemporary World* (Vol. 2), edited by Jean-Guy Goulet, 65–88. Santa Barbara, CA: Praeger.

Agnew, Michael. 2015b. 'Spiritually, I'm Always in Lourdes:' Perceptions of Home and Away among Serial Pilgrims. *Studies in Religion* 44: 516–535.

Benson, Robert Hugh. 1914. *Lourdes*. London: Manresa Press.

Cranston, Ruth. 1955. *The Miracle of Lourdes*. New York: McGraw-Hill.

Cros, Léonard. 1925. *Histoire de Notre-Dame de Lourdes*. Paris: Beauchesne.

Eade, John. 1991. Order and Power at Lourdes: Lay Helpers and the Organization of a Pilgrimage Shrine. In *Contesting the Sacred: The Anthropology of Christian Pilgrimage*, edited by John Eade and Michael J. Sallnow, 51–76. London: Routledge.

Goldingay, Sarah, Paul Dieppe and Miguel Farias. 2014. 'And the Pain Just Disappeared into Insignificance:' The Healing Response in Lourdes Performance, Psychology, and Caring. *International Review of Psychiatry* 26: 315–323.

Harris, Alana. 2010. 'A Place to Grow Spiritually and Socially': The Experiences of Young Pilgrims to Lourdes. In *Religion and Youth*, edited by Sylvia Collins-Mayo and Ben Pink Dandelion, 149–158. Aldershot: Ashgate.

Harris, Ruth. 1999. *Lourdes: Body and Spirit in the Secular Age*. New York: Viking.

Huysmans, J. K. 1907. *Les Foules de Lourdes*. Paris: Tresse and Stock.

Kselman, Thomas A. 1983. *Miracles and Prophecies in Nineteenth-Century France*. New Brunswick, NJ: Rutgers University Press.

Lasserre, Henri. 1870. *Notre-Dame de Lourdes*. Paris: Victor Palmé.

McEachern, Patricia. 2005. *A Holy Life: The Writings of Saint Bernadette of Lourdes*. San Francisco, CA: Ignatius Press.

Notermans, Catrien. 2007. Loss and Healing: A Marian Pilgrimage in Secular Dutch Society. *Ethnology* 46:217–233.

Notermans, Catrien, Maya Turolla and Willy Jansen. 2016. Caring and Connecting: Reworking Religion, Gender and Families in Post-migration Life. In *Contemporary Encounters in Gender and Religion*, edited by Lena Gemzoe, Marja-Liisa Keinänen and Avril Maddrell, 241–258. London: Palgrave Macmillan.

Paone, Anthony. 2018. French Nun Speaks of Lourdes 'miracle' that Ended Crippling Disability. *Reuters*, February 13.

Taylor, Therese. 2008. *Bernadette of Lourdes: Her Life, Death and Visions*. London: Continuum.

Tweed, Thomas. 1997. *Our Lady of the Exile: Diasporic Religion at a Cuban Catholic Shrine in Miami*. New York: Oxford University Press.

Zimdars-Swartz, Sandra. 1991. *Encountering Mary: Visions of Mary from La Salette to Medjugorje*. Princeton, NJ: Princeton University Press.

5

THE WELL OF ZAMZAM

A pilgrimage site and curative water in Islam

Ahmad Ghabin

Zamzam is the name of a much-venerated well, situated 20 m to the east of the Ka'ba. The focus of the *hajj*, the Ka'ba, is Islam's most sacred structure (said to have been built by Abraham and Ishmael and around which the Great Mosque of Mecca was constructed). The now subterranean Zamzam is within the area pilgrims circumambulate around the Ka'ba. The well was a part of pilgrimage practices of pre-Muslim Arabs and continues to be venerated by Muslim pilgrims year-round, but particularly in the annual *hajj* (the main pilgrimage has set dates each year) and the *'umra* (the "lesser" pilgrimage which may be undertaken at any time). Stories about the Zamzam prior to the advent of Islam all come from Islamic sources and may be divided into two periods. Accounts relating to the first of these periods tell about the water's initial eruption, for the benefit of Hagar and her infant son Ishmael. The second period is concerned with the well's rediscovery by the grandfather of the Prophet Muhammad, Abd al-Muttalib (480–578). The well stories from both periods explain Islamic pilgrimage practices and connect Islam with Abraham, whom Muslims regard as the founder of monotheism on the Arabian Peninsula.

Origins

Obeying God's instruction, Abraham, his wife Hagar and their infant son Ishmael wandered to the barren valley of Mecca. Seeking water for her son, Hagar jogged seven times between two hills, the Safa and the Marwa (located 400 m from each other), and heard a voice (that of Archangel Gabriel) instructing her to return to her son and find water that would erupt from the ground near him.[1] The same story, with varying details, is related in Genesis 21:17–19. On seeing the water, Hagar collects it in an earthen pool and the water accordingly remains there in the form of a well. Without Hagar's structure, the Zamzam would have turned into a spring whose waters flowed on to no useful purpose. According to one tradition, the angel announced that the water of the Zamzam would suffice for the area's inhabitants

FIGURE 5.1 The well of Zamzam, now within a museum setting and inaccessible to pilgrims. (Source: Flickr, Creative Commons Attribution-Share Alike 2.0 Generic license).

as well as for future guests of God (pilgrims).[2] This foundation story explains how Mecca became a center of pilgrimage and its great sanctity in Islam.

The *siqaya* (the giving of drink to pilgrims) was first Hagar's purview. The well attracted the south Yemenite tribe of Jurhum, and Hagar negotiated their settlement in Mecca on the condition that Ishmael and his progeny were guaranteed ownership of the well. As time went by, Ishmael married a Jurhum woman and thus his descendants were "Arabized." Ishmael's descendants continued the *siqaya* including one named Hashim (464–497) (from whom the Prophet Muhammad descended). When the people of Jurhum began to neglect the Ka'ba and its sanctity (stealing gifts offered there among other sins), the well dried up, disappeared and remained forgotten until the time of the grandfather of Prophet Muhammad Abd al-Muttalib (d. 578) who rediscovered it through "Divine guidance" (al-Azraqi, 1858:46; Ibn Hisham, 1999, 1:82; al-Tabari, 1:523; Gaudefoy-Demombynes, 1923:72).

The sanctity of the waters of Zamzam links beliefs about water with histories related to the well. Firstly, the Quran indicates that water is the source of every living thing (Q21:30) and that it is the best and only means by which people purify themselves before prayers. Zamzam supplies the "water of life" and also provides the context for important events in the establishment of Islam. Secondly, since Zamzam's waters saved the life of Hagar and her son Ishmael, the waters spared the life of the great progenitor of Muhammad and his tribe. Thirdly, Zamzam's appearance alongside the building of the Ka'ba spurred the foundation of the city of

Mecca and both pre-Islamic and Islamic pilgrimages there. The main rite that commemorates the appearance of the well is that of *sa'i*. Immediately after finishing the *tawaf* (circuiting the Ka'ba), every pilgrim "jogs" seven times between the two hills of al-Safa and al-Marwa just as Hagar did (Porter and Saif, 2013:3). During or after that, every pilgrim should consume a large draught of Zamzam water.

The well's significance for Islam also relates to the site's rediscovery by Muhammad's grandfather Abd al-Muttalib just prior to the advent of Islam. Abd al-Muttalib was commanded, via a series of four dreams, to arise and dig the Zamzam. His dreams contained a riddle that pointed him to the well's location (it had vanished during the time of the Jurhum).[3] The dream-induced rediscovery becomes a means of connecting the Prophet to Abraham. With the aid of his son and "Divine intervention," Abd al-Muttalib excavated the well and was recognized in the office of *siqaya* as a descendant of Hashim (Ibn Hisham, 1999:143–145). He rejected a claim to a share in the well by the people of Quraish and then proceeded to build an impoundment to hold the water in a pool so that it could be given to the pilgrims. In this way, the custom of *siqaya* for pilgrims to Mecca was renewed (al-Azraqi, 1858:281–287).

Notwithstanding the substantial legendary/mythological dimension of the pre-Islamic Zamzam stories, the well itself did indeed exist and enjoyed a certain degree of sanctity and veneration (Muir, 1912: xcix–cv; Burton, 1926, 2:162; *EI*[2]). In the traditions are the religious-"historical" roots of the Islamic Zamzam and *hajj* rituals: the Zamzam's connection to Abraham and his family, a total obscuring of any pagan influences, the water's appearance, the well's disappearance and rediscovery—all in accordance with the Divine will. The story merges seamlessly into Islamic monotheistic thought and is an important link between Islam and Abraham/Ishmael. The well has subsequently attracted additional legends. One is the belief that the waters of the Zamzam overflow copiously in the night of the middle of the Islamic month of Sha'ban. On pilgrimage to Mecca in 1183, the geographer and traveler Ibn Jubayr (1145–1217) and his companions investigated this claim by climbing down into the well on that night and discovered that the water level had lowered, because of a then-popular practice of people spraying water excitedly on each other in honor of the supposed mid-month outflow (Ibn Jubayr, 1984:118–119). With no footing in Islam, such a practice disappeared totally. However, Zamzam has remained an inseparable part of daily religious practice in the area of the Ka'ba and a feature of both the *hajj* and the *umra*.

The special qualities of the Zamzam waters

Qualities ascribed to the Zamzam and its water are mentioned in prophetic sayings (*hadith*) or have been circulated in popular traditions. The Qur'an does not mention the Zamzam explicitly, but verses like Q14:37, in which Abraham asked God to secure his family and their place (Mecca) and to provide them with livelihood, indirectly relate to the well's story. In contrast, the *hadith* literature is replete with references to the qualities of the Zamzam, some of which were known to Arabs prior to Islam. Pre-Islamic Meccans customarily gathered around the Zamzam with their children during the morning hours and drunk its water for breakfast; for this reason, they called it *al-Shabba'ah* (Azraqi, 1858:291). A well-known tradition ascribed to the Prophet also says that the waters of Zamzam are blessed and drinking them is a substitute for food (Bakdash, 2001:103–104).

The water of Zamzam has two main powers: it has curative properties for those seeking physical healing and exerts religious influence on all believers and pilgrims who drink it. The blessed waters give nourishment and health and are cooling for those with fever (Ibn Maja, 2:1017; Daraqutni, 2004, 2:288, al-Buhkari, n.d., 1/2:219). Drinking Zamzam water is said to distinguish believers from hypocrites. Drinking copiously from the Zamzam purifies the body and the soul. The main *hadith* ascribed to the Prophet says, "The waters of the Zamzam are good for any purpose for which they are drunk" (Ibn Maja, n.d., 1018). Meaning, if you drink its water to be healed, God will heal you, and if you drink it to obtain forgiveness for transgressions, God will forgive you (al-Azraqi, 1858:290; al-Fakihi, 1858:27). The qualities that Zamzam waters will hold for an individual (and their efficacy) relate to one's *al-niyya* (intention) and this should be carefully considered before drinking. Clerics and pilgrims would customarily ask for beneficial knowledge, financial prosperity or good health (Ibn Zahira, 1921:275). People believe strongly in the healing properties of the water and pilgrims do their best to get Zamzam water directly from the well in Mecca and to bring it home as gifts. Family members expect pilgrims to bring back containers of Zamzam water to drink for blessings and cures, or to sprinkle on their shrouds and into their grave when they die (Siraj and Tayab, 2017:26). Some bring enough home to allocate to sick people in their community as a form of charity.

A significant number of works of *hadith* devote entire chapters to the qualities and the powers of the waters of the Zamzam (al-Azraqi, 1858:289; Ibn Hisham, 1999:150; Ibn Maja n.d., 2:1017). One *hadith* offers a story from the Prophet about the well:

> When I was in Mecca the ceiling of my house opened up and the angel Gabriel (peace be unto him) descended and he opened up my chest and bathed it with Zamzam water; afterward he came with a golden tray laden with wisdom and emptied it into me.
>
> *(Bukhari, n.d., 1/1:283; Muslim, 1994:488–492)*

This kind of *hadith* undoubtedly played an important role in elevating the Zamzam in terms of its sacred status and in terms of the special properties associated with it. The *hadith* describes the Prophet's tasting of the Zamzam water as part of the preparation for his great mission, and for his journey to Jerusalem and ascension to heaven (*al-Isra' wal-mi'raj*). The Zamzam waters bestowed physical and spiritual purity on the Prophet, thereby encouraging his believers to behave in a similar manner. The *hadith* was an important tool in the hands of those who believed in the supernatural powers of the Zamzam water. It increased the sanctity of the Zamzam and made it the only well that Muslims should venerate, taste and interact with as the Prophet did.

The way in which the Prophet and his companions used the waters of Zamzam became in time a kind of ritual that people called *Sunnah*. This ritual interaction with well water found its way into the ceremonies of the *hajj* and reached the status equal to that of obligatory rites like circling the Ka'ba. For instance, it is believed that just looking into the Zamzam brings forgiveness and removes sins (Ibn Zahira, 1921:255–259; al-Fakihi, 2:41). As the Prophet sipped the water of Zamzam from a standing position, pilgrims are also expected to do so. Some claimed that the Prophet's manner of drinking from the well provides instruction on how to eat and drink in general (Ibn Maja, n.d., 2:1017; Ibn Hanbal, 1950, 3:252, 276). Another tradition provides step-by-step guidance to those drinking from the Zamzam: "When drinking from the Zamzam turn toward the Ka'ba, pronounce the name of God, take three breaths, and drink your fill, ending with thanks to God" (Ibn Maja, n.d., 2:1017; Ibn Zahira, 1921:275).

The *Siqaya*, watering the pilgrims

In Islam, only the waters of Zamzam are sanctified – in contrast to other cultures which accord sacred status to water sources of many different kinds. "The best well for people is the Zamzam" (al-Azraqi, 1858:292; Abu al-Baqa' n.d.:145); "the best water on earth is the water of Zamzam" (al-Mundhiri, 1994, 1:132–133). From a Muslim point of view, the Zamzam-based *siqaya* had its origins with Hagar and Ishmael inasmuch as the water's revelation was meant to save Ishmael and to revivify an arid place in anticipation of the arrival of settlers and pilgrims. Originally, Ishmael was to have conducted the pilgrimage to the Ka'ba and been responsible for providing water to pilgrims, a role that Hagar had performed when she permitted the Jurham tribe to settle in Mecca.

FIGURE 5.2 Containers of Zamzam water in Al-Masjid an-Nabawi or the Prophet's Mosque in Medinah. Face intentionally blurred to protect identity. ID 34077529 © Ahmad Faizal Yahya/Dreamstime.com.

During the period of the Zamzam's disappearance, knowledge of the *siqaya* continued to circulate, referring to the task of providing water to those visiting the Ka'ba, but its link with the Zamzam took place in the time of Abd al-Muttalib. He bore responsibility for the office and when he discovered the Zamzam, he centered *siqaya* around it (citing Divine command) (Ibn Sa'd, 1970, 1:83). Later, the Prophet sanctioned the office (Ibn Hisham, 1999:187–189). The *siqaya* of pilgrims, not necessarily from the Zamzam, is mentioned in Quran 9:19, where the zeal for watering the pilgrims is dampened and its importance for the Arabs is questioned. By contrast, the *hadith* of the Prophet attaches great religious and political importance to the function of *siqaya*. In one tradition, the Prophet proceeded during the *hajj* journey to the Zamzam; there, he encouraged the sons of Abbas family in watering the pilgrims and he assured them that their work was sacred and should continue (Muslim 1994, 4:429–433; al-Bukhari n.d., 1/1:283). Later, the Abbasids took political advantage of their role using it as religious support for their claim to be the rightful heirs of Muhammad, and to the caliphate that they won 132/750 (al-Tabari, 1991, 4:433).

The function of *siqaya* continues to exist in Mecca and in Medina. In both cities, it is well-managed by the authorities. In Mecca, Zamzam water is pumped directly from the well to taps around the Great Mosque. Tankers carry Zamzam water from Mecca to Medina where the water is distributed in thousands of jugs in and around the Nebawi Mosque (the Mosque of the Prophet). Saudi authorities established a special factory to produce Zamzam water containers which are distributed equally and freely to all pilgrims. An indirect extension of the *siqaya* in Islam is the *sabil* system, water devices built mostly by benefactors on public roads and sometimes attached to shrines in order to serve every thirsty passerby (but this water has no special sanctity). *Siqaya* is still practiced in recently constructed mosques where modern devices (water fountains, taps and bottles) for drinking water are installed by authorities or by benefactors as charity.

Zamzam and perceptions of watercourses in the Islamic world

While the well of Zamzam is the only source of water with "built-in sanctity" for the rites of the *hajj*, popular legends and superstitions have developed over time around the Zamzam and other water sources in different places. The rites around the well in Mecca came to remind the believers of the miraculous gushing of water for the sake of Hagar and her son and also to bring life into the barren place of Mecca in response to Abraham's invocation to God (Q:14). Aside from drinking, other ritual uses of Zamzam water outside of Mecca derive from legends and popular beliefs that are unrelated to those sanctioned at the well. Some traditions in the *hadith* codices refer to the Nile and Euphrates Rivers as originating from Paradise (Muslim, 2005:1302–1303; al-Bukhari, 2002:1856). Yet, this gave no special sanctity to their waters and resulted in no special rites around them.

The case is different in the Shi'a/Shi'a sect of Islam, in which Muhammad's legal successor is considered to have been Imam 'Ali. In their codices, one finds numerous traditions, mostly ascribed to 'Ali and his descendants, considering the water of the Euphrates River as holy and attributing different qualities to it. The Arabic name of the Euphrates, *furat*, means the most fresh water and was referenced in the Q23:50 by the word *ma'in* (spring of flowing water). Several qualities are attributed to the Euphrates: it is one of the rivers of Paradise, drinking from it means that one supports the 'Alid family, its waters are the best in this world and in the next world, and that it receives an angelic delivery of seven drops of water from Paradise each night (al-Majlisi, 1430, 22:66–69; al-Kullayni, 1928: 6:388–389; al-Qummi, 1996:106–112). In order to benefit from these qualities, a real Shi'i should drink, wash and rinse the mouth with the water of the Euphrates. Rinsing the mouths of young boys especially, using the water of Euphrates, is a kind of rite of passage by which they enter the Shi'a community (al-Kullayni, 1928, 6:389). The great sanctity attributed to Euphrates water stemmed from its association with historical events of the 'Alid family: the killing of the caliph 'Ali in the Muslim year 40 (661) in Najaf, the tragic killing of his son al-Husayn in Karbala' in the year 61 (680) and other events that took place in the neighborhood of the Iraqi Euphrates.

Springs and wells in Palestine have also developed popular legends. First, in Jerusalem, there is 'Ayn al-Silwan (the Pool of Siloam). According to a tradition from the fundamentalist theologian Ahmad b. Hanbal (780–855), any pilgrim who visits Jerusalem should swim in it since it is one of the springs of the Garden of Eden. In the time of Bani Israil (the sons of Israel), women accused of adultery were forced to drink from the spring of al-Silwan; if they felt sick, they were guilty (Ibn al-Jawzi, 1980:97–98). A legend says that its waters visit the waters of Zamzam in the night of the halting at Mount 'Arafa (Mount Arafat) (Yaqut n.d., 4:178). Locals therefore bathed with its waters on Fridays and poured it over the ill seven times to banish a fever (Canaan, 1927:110–112). In 'Akka (the Acre of Palestine), there is a spring visited by Muslims, Jews and Christians called 'Ayn al-Baqar from which a bovine first emerged, and Adam domesticated it for tilling the land (Yaqut, 4:176; al-Harawi, 2002:30). Around this well, there is a lengthy tradition transmitted by 'Aisha, the wife of the Prophet. She noted that camphor from Paradise was sprinkled in the well of 'Ayn al-Baqar and that the Prophet had said washing and drinking from that well and from the well of Silwan or from the Zamzam will keep one's body from the fires of Hell (Kister, 1996:74-48).[4] Special springs or wells are often in the vicinity of the shrines of *walis* (Muslim saints) in Palestine. The waters take their sanctity and supernatural powers from the remains of the *walis*. Watercourses in Palestine were also widely believed to be inhabited by demons. Researching the so-called "Palestinian demonology" in 1921, Taufik Canaan examined about 180 wells and springs and noted the good and bad demons and spirits inhabiting them. Two of them, Hammam 'Ashura/al-Shifa' (curing bath) and the spring of Silwan, are distinctive because of the beliefs that they mixed with the waters of Zamzam. (The former was thought to be the water that cured the Prophet Job of his skin disease.)

Legends of the mixing of local water sources with the waters of Zamzam impute greater sanctity to nearby pools and springs. A generalized story suggests that the water of Zamzam mixes with those of every spring in the Islamic world during the night of 'Ashura', the tenth of the month Muharram and thus supernatural powers are bestowed to their waters (Canaan, 1927:65). In nineteenth-century Egypt, for example, some clerics at the Hanafi mosque in Cairo publicized such legends, saying that the water of Zamzam flowed together with those of their mosque. Accordingly, one Egyptian pilgrim, who lost his drinking cup in the well of Zamzam, claimed that when he returned to Cairo, he found it in the well of that mosque! (al-Batanuni, 1990:181–182).

While water sources have become venerated due to local and historical conditions, or the burial nearby of a saint, their supernatural qualities have not always been remembered. Of those mentioned earlier, the only spring that still attracts Islamic veneration is that of Silwan in Jerusalem, most likely because of its location within the holy city for Jews and Muslims (Ghabin, 2012:116–135). The Zamzam is the only source of water that all Muslims, Sunna and Shi'a, agree must have a formal place in the rites of the *hajj* and *umra*. Further, its religious-historical and geographical connection with the Ka'ba made it particular and resistant to imitation elsewhere.

Notes

1 See: al-Azraqi (1858, 1:279–283); al-Nahrawali (1858, 3:33); al-Tabari (1991, 1:152–155); al-Ya'qubi (1970, 1:255).
2 See: al-Tha'labi n.d., 72; Ibn Kathir n.d., 144–145; al-Nahrawali, 1858:33–34; al-Tabari, 1:154.
3 See: Ibn Hisham (1999, 1:142–141); Ibn Sa'd (1970, 1:83); Fakihi (1998:12).
4 Another Prophetic utterance on 'Akka tells that God will fill with light the abdomen of one who drinks from the well of 'Ayn al-Baqar and those pouring its water on themselves will remain pure until the Day of Resurrection (al-al-'Asqalani 2001:64). In 'Asqalani, there is the well which Abraham dug with his hands and in Tabariyya (Tiberias), there is a well in which 'Isa b. Maryam (Jesus) made his first miracle.

References

Abu al-Baqa', Muhammad Baha' al-Din. (n.d.). *Tarikh Makka al-Musharrafa wal-Masjid al-Haram wal-Madina al-Sharifa wal-Qabr al-Sharif.* Beirut: Dar al-Kutub al-'Ilmiyya.

al-'Asqalani, Ibn Hajar. 2001. *al-Khisal al-mukaffira lil-dhunub,* edited by 'Amru 'Abd al-Mun'im Salim. Jidda: Dar Majid 'Asiri al-Azraqi, Muḥammad B. Abdallah. 1858. *Akhbar Makka,* in *Die Chroniken der Stadt Mekka,* edited by Ferdinand Wüstenfeld. Leipzig: F. A. Brockhaus.

Bakdash, Said. 2000. *Fadl ma' Zamzam.* Beirut: Dar al-Basha'ir al-Islamiyya.

al-Bukhari, Muhammad B. Isma'il. a) n.d. *al-Sahih.* Cairo: Dar Ihya' al-Kutub al-'Arabiyya. b) Damascus: Dar Ibn Kathir 1423/2002.

Burton, Richard Francis. 1924–1926. *Personal Narrative of a Pilgrimage to al-Madinah and Meccah.* Memorial Edition, London: G. Bill and Sons.

Canaan, Taufik. 1920–1921. Haunted Springs and Water Demons in Palestine. *Journal of the Palestine Oriental Society* 1:153–170.

Canaan, Taufik. 1927. *Muhammadan Saints and Sanctuaries in Palestine.* London: Luzac and Co.

Chabbi, Jacqueline. 2002. Zamzam. *EI²: The Encyclopedia of Islam* 2:440–442. Leiden: Brill.

al-Daraqutni, Ali bin 'Umar. 2004. *al-Sunan,* edited by Shu'ayb al-Arna'ut. Arna'ut. Beirut: Mu'ssasat al-Risala.

Ghabin, Ahmad. 2012. The Zamzam Well Ritual in Islam and its Jerusalem Connection. In *Sacred in Israel and Palestine,* edited by Marshal J. Berger, Yitzhak Reiter and Leonard Hammer, 116–135. London: Routledge.

Gaudefoy-Demombynes, Maurice. 1923. *Le Pèlerinage à la Mekke, Étude d'hitoire religieuse*. Paris: Geuthner.

al-Fakihi, Muhammad B. Ishaq. 1998. *Akhbar Makka*, edited by 'Abd al-Malik Dhaysh. Beirut: Dar Khadr.

al-Harawi, Abu al-Hasan. 2002. *al-Ishara ila ma'rifat al-ziyara*, edited by 'Ali 'Umar. Cairo: Maktabat al-Thaqafa al-Diniyya.

IbnHanbal, Ahmad. 1950. *Musnad*. Cairo: Dar al-Ma'arif.

Ibn Hisham, 'Abd al-Malik. 1999. *al-Sirah al-nabawiyyah*, edited by Mustafa al-Saqqa. Damascus: Dar Ibn Kathir.

Ibn al-Jawzi, 'Abd al-Rahman. 1980. *Fada'il al-Quds*, edited by Jibra'il Jabbur. Beirut: Dar al-Afaq al-Jadida.

Ibn Jubayr, Muhammad. 1984. *al-Rihla*. Beirut: Dar Sadir.

Ibn Kathir, Abu al-Fida Isma'ill. n.d. *Qiṣaṣ al-anbiya'* edited by Muhammad A. 'Abd al-'Aziz. Cairo: Dar al-Hadith.

Kister, Meir Jacob. 1990. Sanctity Joint and Divided: On Holy Places in the Islamic Tradition. In *Jerusalem Studies in Arabic and Islam* 20:18–65.

al-Kullayni al-Razi. 1928. *Kitab al-Kafi*, edited by 'Ali Akbar al-Ghafari. Tehran: Dar al-Kutub al-Islamiyya.

Ibn Maja, Abu 'Abdallah Muhammad. n.d. *al-Sunan*. Cairo: Dar Ihya' al-Kutub al-'Arabiyya.

Ibn Sa'd, Muhammad. 1970. *al-Tabaqat al-kubra*. Beirut: Dar Sadir.

Ibn Zahira, al-Qurashi. 1921. *al-Jami' al-latif fi fadl Makka wa-ahlaha wa-bina'al bayt al-sharif*. Cairo: Dar Ihya' al-Kutub al-'Arabiyya.

al-Majlisi, Muhammad Baqir. 2008. *Bihar al-Anwar*. Iran: Mu'assasat Ihya' al-Kutub al Islamiyya.

Al-Mas'ūdi, Abual-Hasan 'Ali. 1982. *Muruj al-dhahab wa-ma'adin al-jawhar*. Beirut: Dar al-Kitab al-Lubnani.

Muir, William. 1912. *The Life of Muhammad from Original History*. Edinburgh: John Grant.

al-Mundhiri, al-Hafiz. 1994. *al-Targhib wal-Tarhib*. Cairo: Dar al-Hadith.

Muslim b. al-Hajjaj. 2005. *Sahih* edited by Muhammad al-Farabi. Riyadh: Dar Tiba.

Muslim b. al-Hajjaj. 1994. *Sahih Muslim bi-Sharh al-Nawawi*. Cairo: Dar al-Hadith.

al-Nahrawali, Qutub al-Din. 1858. *al-I'lam bi-a'lam bayt Allah al-haram*, edited by Ferdinand Wüstenfeld, *Die Chroniken der Stadt Mekka*. Leipzig.

Omghar, Samir Ayat. n.d. *al-Ma'budat al-Ma'iyya fi al-Maghrib*. Rabat: Mominoun without Borders.

Porter, Venetia and Saif Liana. eds. 2013. *The Hajj: Collected Essays*. London: The British Museum Press.

al-Qummi, Abu al-Qasim b. Qulawayh. 1996. *Kamil al-Ziyaratt*, edited by Jawad al QayumÐ. Qum: Nashr al-Faqaha.

Siraj, M. A. and Tayab, M. A. K. 2017. Water in Islam. In *Water and Scriptures*, edited by Konduru Raju and Manasi Subramaniam, 15–58. New York: Springer International Publishing AG.

al-Tabari, Muhammad bin Jarir. 1991. *Tarikh al-umam wal-muluk*. Beirut: Dar al-Kutub al-'Ilmiyya.

al-Tha'labi, Ahmad b. Ibrahim al-Naysaburi. n.d. *Qisas al-anbiya'*. Beirut: al-Maktaba al-Thaqafiyya.

Ya'qubi, Ahmad bin Ja'far. 1970. *Tarikh* Beirut: Dar Sadir.

Yaqut al-Hamawi. n.d. *Mu'jam al-Buldan*. Beirut: Dar Sadir.

6

SACRALITY AND WATERFRONT SACRED PLACES IN INDIA

Myths and the making of place

Rana P.B. Singh

The ancient Indian (Hindu) mythologies refer to water as the container of life, strength and eternity, but most commonly it is perceived as the purifier and water sites are sacred places. The three most common factors enhancing the popularity of sacred places along rivers *(tirthas)* and water pools *(kundas)* are: their unique natural landscape and beauty, the unusual physical features of the body of water and the watery place's association with some great sage or site-based mythology. The psychic attachment to a place and the maintenance of its associated cultural traditions and water-related rituals reflect the belief in divine manifestations there and the site's intrinsic values; this is maintained by a huge mass of festivities and rituals even today. The Ganga (the Ganges River) is the sacred fluid, an essential element for all the Hindu rites and rituals. The Ganga is known as "the mother who bestows prosperity *(sukh-da)*, and secures salvation *(moksha-da)*"; she represents joy in this life and hope for the life to come (Zimmer, 1991:110). This essay describes the Ganga, the river's waterfront sacred places and related sacred waters.

Sacrality and water: metaphysical context

The *Puranas* are a genre of ancient literature (in Sanskrit) considering myths, legends and lore. The creation theory of Puranic mythology conveys the spirit of sustainability in Hinduism. Among the five fundamental organic elements of Nature *(mahabhutas)*, water is given primal importance. According to the *Bhagavata Purana* (1.3.2–5), an eighth-century text, Primordial Man was lying down in the water of the universe. The *Mahabharata* (12.182.14–19), a circa-fourteenth-century BCE text, states that the Supreme God created Primordial Man who first made sky; from sky, water was then made; and the seed of water, together with fire and air, made the earth; hence in a metaphysical sense, these elements are not separated from each other (Singh, 1992:142). Not only are these elements related to one another by their intrinsic nature, but they foster bonds among creatures. In fact, "water plays a cardinal role in most creation myths, frequently associated with the female element, in reciprocal relationship with the male elements of sky and earth" (Buttimer, 1989:265). The *Rig Veda* (10.90. 11–14), a circa-fifteenth-century BCE text, describes water as a unifying fluid between sky/heaven and earth (Singh, 1996:87). In a part of the *Rig Veda*, the *Shatapatha Brahmana* (1.8.1.1–6), the protector of the Hindu Trinity, Vishnu, has a fish incarnation that symbolizes the origin of life in water. In a fish form, he saved organic life-seeds from the great cosmic flood (Singh, 1992:77). The water is regarded as the primary materialization of Vishnu's *maya* (energy) and is therefore a visible manifestation of the divine essence (Zimmer, 1991:34).

The first reference of cosmic evolution is given in the *Purushasukta* of the *Rig Veda* (10.129), and is considered to be the earliest description of the mystery of the cosmos (Singh, 1993:114). In ancient Hindu mythology (circa 800 BCE), water is described as the foundation of the whole world, the essence of plant life and the elixir of immortality (cf. *Shatapatha Brahmana* 6.8 2.2; 3.6.1.7). The *Atharva Veda* (2.3.6), a circa-tenth-century BCE text, prays, "May the water bring us well-being!" There are many such descriptions about the quality, use, sanctity and symbolism of water (Eliade, 1958:188). In a later period of Hindu mythology, water becomes a symbol for life, and a liquid spirit of sustainability. Water is said to be a healer (*Atharva Veda* 6.91.3). Metaphorically and metaphysically, the ancient mythologies refer to water as the container of life, strength and eternity, but most commonly it is perceived as the purifier. However, to reach the source and receive the merit of "living water" involves a series of consecrations, rituals and religious activities such as pilgrimages and sacred baths. The cult of living water is described in the Vedic literature and is continued vividly in the Puranic literature. The *Rig Veda,* in its famous "River Hymn" (10. 75.5–6), mentions the divine power of the Ganga. The text also eulogizes the Ganga as Gangeya, which means the "giver of all sorts of prosperity and peace"—the liquid spirit of sustainability (*Rig Veda* 6.45.3 1). Similar sentiments are echoed in the *Padma Purana* (Shristi 60.64–65), a circa-ninth-century CE text: "We pray to you O! the Liquid-energy of the Ganga–the universal form of supreme Lord Vishnu."

In Hindu mythology, water is considered as the first sacred fluid for purification ritual. The *Yajur Veda* (2.1) states: "Human offerings in *yajnas* (sacrifices) purify the water sucked by the sun in clouds with the air. Then that water rains and makes the medicines on earth sound." In the *Chandyogya Upanishadaa* (7.10.1), water is described as an attribute linking subtler fire and grosser earth in different forms: "This earth, the air, the heavens, the mountains, gods and men, domestic animals and birds, vegetables and trees, wild creatures down to worms, flies and ants, are nothing but this water under solid conditions."

Environmental ethics and concern about water pollution were present in Hindu thoughts of the ancient period. One of the hymns of the *Rig Veda* (7.9) states: "The water in the sky, the waters of rivers, and the waters in wells whose source is ocean, may all these sacred waters protect me." The *Manu Smriti* (4.6) clearly states that to maintain the sacred power of water, one should not cause urine, stool or even coughs to enter the water: "anything which is mixed with these impious objects; blood and poison should not be thrown into water." The importance of water is fully elaborated in the *Mahabharata* (12.83–84): "The creator first produced water for the maintenance of life among human beings. The water enriches life and its absence destroys all creatures and plant-life."

Sacred waters vis-à-vis holy places

The "wash away sins" quality of water has many cosmological connotations in various mythologies. Says Eliade (1958:131), "Everything that is *form* manifests itself above the waters, by detaching itself from the waters." Running water in general and the waters of the Ganga in particular are described as bestowing sanctity and miracles. From mythology to tradition, a common chain of interrelationships between the river and human society is maintained by a wide variety of performances and rituals. The psychic attachment to a place and the maintenance of cultural traditions reflect the appreciation for the divine manifestation at the place and the intrinsic value of sustainability. The intensity and level of this sacrosanct power is greater in certain places. Such specific places are known as *tirthas* (holy sites or sacred places). The unique natural landscape and appearance of a site, together with the topographical context of the water source and its association with a famous sage all enhance the appeal of a sacred watery place. Hinduism records a strong and ancient tradition of pilgrimage, called *tirtha yatra* (meaning "tour to the sacred fords") that denoted pilgrimage to take a holy dip in water bodies at special places as a purification rite.

The Vedic literature (ca. 2000–500 BCE) does not refer directly to pilgrimages, but traveling was considered an essential part of rite fulfillment (e.g. *Aitareya Brāhmana*, 7.15). In Vedic literature, the Sanskrit word *yātrā* referred to "travel" rather than "pilgrimage," but the Puranic literature (ca. 500 BCE–CE 900) did accept *yātrā* as meaning "pilgrimage" and provides detailed information about sacred sites and pilgrimages. The *Mahabharata* (ca. 300 BCE) may be considered the first Hindu book providing glorious descriptions of sacred places. It clearly indicates that going on pilgrimages (*tirtha yatras*) is superior to sacrifice (Bhardwaj, 1973:29). The *Matsya Purana* (ca. CE 400) enumerates a large number of sacred places with descriptions of associated schedules, gestures, dreams and auspicious signs and symbols. Similarly, other *Puranas* describe sacred places and pilgrimages.

Motives for pilgrimages, as stipulated in the *Puranas*, may be categorized into four broad groupings: *putreshanā* (desire for a son), *vitteshanā* (desire for wealth), *mukteshanā* (desire for liberation or atonement from sin) and *lokeshanā* (desire for worldly gain). But all centers of pilgrimage have the merits of general purification and bliss. In most cases, the act of pilgrimage is performed as an expression of devotion to a deity and ultimately to gain blissful satisfaction through the fulfillment of a particular desire (Singh, 1997:192).

It is a common tradition in Hinduism to endow more sacredness to some places than to others, even though no single system defines which place is the most sacred for all times, for all sects and for all regions. In general, sacred waters have been the most attractive holy sites. Today, the most popular pan-Hindu pilgrimage destinations are Kashi (Varanasi/ Banaras, along the Ganga River), Prayagraj (Allahabad, at the confluence of the Ganga and Yamuna Rivers) and Gaya (along the Phalgu River), which together are eulogized as the three ladders to the heaven. The "Braj Mandala," an area around the temple towns of Mathura and Vrindavan (in Uttar Pradesh, along the Yamuna River), is also important. Among pan-Indian pilgrimage places, there are seven sacred cities, all attached to waterfront sites, including Mathura, Dvarka, Ayodhya, Haridvar, Varanasi, Ujjain and Kanchipuram and, similarly, scattered across India are 12 important Jyotir Linga *tirthas* of Lord Shiva, four abodes of Lord Vishnu (the Preserver God), one major temple devoted to Lord Brahma (The Creator God) at Pushkar and 51 special sites sacred to the Goddess (Motivation and Power) (see Figure 6.1). According to the *Kalyana Tirthank* (1957), out of 1,820 Hindu holy places, 35% are associated with the Lord Shiva, followed by Lord Vishnu (16%) and the Goddess (12%). In addition, there are layers upon layers of more local and regional shrines; most of them are attached to water bodies at different scales.

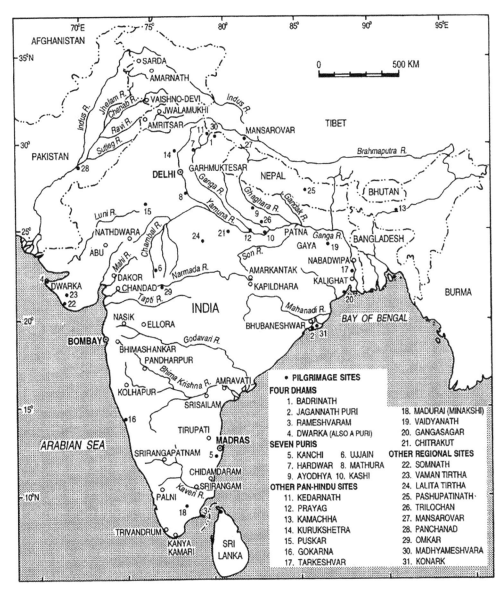

FIGURE 6.1 India: important pilgrimage sites (after Singh, 2013:59; reprinted with permission).

The Ganga River: mythology and intrinsic value

In Hindu mythology, all the rivers are revered as removers of pollution, but the Ganga is the most prominent purifying liquid power. The Ganga is the greatest example of perceiving divine-energy *(shakti)* in nature: through our experience of *shakti*, she stretches out our spirit-consciousness. That is why the Ganga is called *Adi-shakti*, the "Primordial Divine-Energy." The Ganga is the river of the water of life, immortality and healing derived from the very presence of God (Singh, 1996:88).

No river in the world's history has achieved the same fame of the sacred river Ganga. In fact, the Ganga River "is the archetype of sacred waters and participates in that spatial transposition that is so typical of Hindu sacred topography, pervading the sacred waters of all of India's great rivers" (Eck, 2012:159). This is especially true since the third century CE, when the Ganga began to play a vital role in Hindu ceremonies and worship—in rituals of birth and initiation, of purification and religious merit, of marriage and death. The Ganga is known as Mother Ganga *(Ganga Mai)*, bringing life in the form of sacred water (Darian, 1978:31). The Ganga's sacred fluid is an essential element for all the Hindu rites and rituals. Personifying and directing the terrestrial water, the goddess Ganga River preserves the seed of the world. The *Mahabharata* (3.85.88–97) describes the Ganga as the savior of life.

As the savior of life and the divine-energy interlinking the three realms, the Ganga manifests the spirit of sustainability. Its spatial form is manifested in five territories lying in different parts of India where regional sacred rivers are known as the Ganga of that direction, i.e. the Mandakini (the Ganga of the North), the Mahanadi (the East), Kaveri (the South), the Narmada (the West) and the Godavari (the center). According to another classification, the seven streams symbolizing the Ganga include Bhagirathi, Vriddha Ganga, Kalindi, Sarasvati, Kaveri, Narmada and the Veni. Another grouping of rivers considered merit-givers and equal to the Ganga include the Yamuna, Godavari, Sarasvati, Kaveri, Narmada and the Sindhu (Indus). Since the Ganga received special importance in the religious ethos as "purifier" (Singh, 2013:167), this tradition of perceiving the other regional rivers as symbols of the Ganga may be called "*Gangaization*" (Singh, 1987:316–317, see Figure 6.2). This makes the whole of India intensely sacralized, and is an example of spatial transposition. The Ganga is considered "a prototype of all the rivers of India; and her magic power of salvation is shared—only to a lesser degree—by all the bodies of water in the land" (Zimmer, 1991:111). A circa-ninth-century text, the *Matsya Purana* (102), says that "without purificatory rite by the holy water, the mind cannot be purified, therefore a sacred bath is the first necessity before any religious act." As the Ganga is not everywhere, Hindus believe that if a person remembers the Ganga with faith and reverence, any body of water can provide the sacrosanct divine-energy that the Ganga transmits. The real Ganga lies out there in the hearts and minds of many Hindus who have the faith to cherish any other river as the manifestation of the Ganga whenever they take their holy dip.

The Ganga is a "liquid *axis mundi*, a pathway connecting all spheres of reality, a presence at which or in which one may cross over to another sphere of the cosmos, ascend to heavenly worlds, or transcend human limitations" (Kinsley, 1987:193).

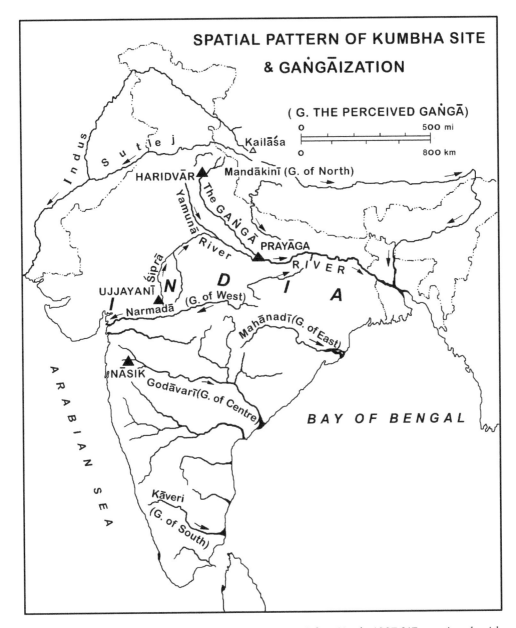

FIGURE 6.2 India: Kumbha sites and Gangaization (after Singh 1987:317; reprinted with permission).

The Ganga is the power center of liquid energy where one can realize the true spiritual source of power. This essentially means that the natural place has physical, mental, emotional and spiritual power (energy) beyond an economic value. That is how the Ganga is vital to the life force of earth. Pilgrimage to, and religious activities along, the Ganga provide a positive and natural return of power and energy, by recharging and recycling energy back to its original source. These activities serve as a means to help keep creation alive. The Ganga River should not be seen as an ordinary water stream; it is to be seen with the eyes of faith. A Hindu has binary vision: recognizing the ordinary as extraordinary and the extraordinary as ordinary. Hindus see the Ganga with a hermeneutical lens, which allows a correspondence to the alternative world of sacrality and power.

Only after walking along the Ganga's bank does one realize that the great-great-grandparents of today's Hindus once walked that very bank and had certain experiences, manifestations and revelations. Revealing the Ganga as a living organism requires specific forms of communication, interaction, environmental sensitivity and transpersonal ecological feelings. That is how the Ganga is known as the mother and soul of India. The Ganga possesses a unique history and mythology, a deep faith and divine landscape, and its own individuality together with multiplicity.

The stories of the Ganga may change, but the motherly river lives on. The story of the Ganga is the story of Indian people catching up to the older social ideals and values of the more devout Hindu world. She is a cultural symbol where every visitor has experiences and feels their harmonic relationship with nature. The story of the Ganga tells us everything about Hindu society, history, culture and religion—their possibilities and their future. However, a living mythology is not enough; real understanding and preservation are the call of the time.

There are many sacred sites and centers of pilgrimage along the Ganga River from the source to the mouth. These include Gomukha, Gangotri, Devaprayaga, Rishikesh, Haridvara, Kankhala, Soron, Bithura, Prayagraj/Allahabad, Vindhyachal, Chunar, Varanasi, Patna, Sultanganj and Gangasagara (see Figure 6.3). Ritualistic pilgrimage to the historic and sacred sites along the Ganga is a spiritual form of recharging and recycling energy back to its original source.

Given the current threat of urbanization and population pressures in the Ganga basin (where more than 600 million people, or 45% of the country's population resides), achieving a clean-flowing Ganga and regenerating the riverine ecosystem is bound to be a gargantuan task; nevertheless by public participation and mass awakening, this could be achieved (Das and Tamminga, 2012:1664). To paraphrase Carl Jung: "The people of India will never find true peace until they can come into a harmonious relationship with and cultivate deeper feelings of reverence for the Ganga River, which is the cradle and identity of India's culture and civilization since time immemorial" (Swan, 1991:304).

The waterfront holy cities

Holy sites possess some peculiarity together with sacral spirit and a power of place that qualify them as salvific points where human beings can seek contact with the divine (see Jacobsen, 2013). In India, the most significant sacred places did not become such because of the presence of a particular temple (alone), but rather because the geography of such holy places was significant (and, of course, most are associated with rivers or other water bodies) (see Figure 6.1). At the pan-Indian level, there are 1,820 main sacred sites associated with Hindu

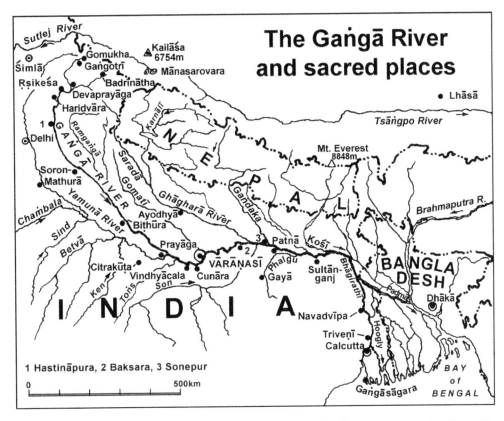

FIGURE 6.3 The Ganga River basin and location of holy places (after Singh, 1994:211; reprinted with permission).

gods, of which 1,362 (74.8%) are associated with water attributes (i.e. rivers, river banks, river's confluences, sources of rivers, lakes and pools/tanks) (based on *Kalyana-Tirthanka*, 1957).

The idea of sacrosanct energy at the junction of the two heavenly powers is preserved in the tradition of the special sacred bath. On the special, astrologically auspicious occasion of Kumbha, when Jupiter enters into Aries or Taurus, and the Sun/Moon into Capricorn, India's greatest fair is held at Prayagraj (Allahabad), at the confluence of the Ganga and Yamuna. This takes place about every 12 years. Among all the sacredscapes and holy centers, Prayagraj (Allahabad) is eulogized as "the king of holy centres" (*tirtharaja*), and is famous for the greatest sacred bath festival that takes place at the meeting point of the Ganga and Yamuna Rivers every 11 years (Dubey, 2001). A Canadian visitor, who has grasped the meanings and feelings evolved there, of course at a certain level and in his own way, expresses his views based on his experiences: "It went on as it has for centuries, I found myself wondering if I was watching an eternal drama, one that would continue as long as humanity remains aware of its need for renewal, for purification, for the revival of the spirit. I wondered as I watched again as the streaming water of the Ganga met the streaming masses of humanity in the wonderful dance where outer meets inner and becomes a living symbol of something more" (Bryant, 1994:39).

The Kumbha Mela, the world's largest pilgrimage gathering, owes its origin/ location and timing to two traditions. The first establishes its timeframe through astrological calculations, while the second emerges from the *Puranas*. The Puranic account tells of a battle between gods and demons during which four drops of sacred nectar (*amrita*) fell at each of the *mela* sites. The Kumbha Mela is held four times every 12 years and its location rotates between Prayagraj (Allahabad) at the confluence of the Rivers Ganga, Yamuna and mythical Sarasvati, Nasik on the Godavari River, Ujjain on the Shipra River and Haridvar on the Ganga River (Singh, 1987:316–318; cf. Figure 6.2). Taking a holy dip in these rivers at the Kumbha Mela is considered to bring great merit and to cleanse both body and spirit (see Eck, 2012:155). At these sites, purification by bathing reaches the highest level of auspiciousness when re-actualization of life-giving cosmic events occurs. The Ganga in its perceived spatial form represents "the whole" (either in India or as a river of the three realms), and as mother goddess, she blesses those who take part in the baths (Singh, 1996:89).

The Kumbha Mela has great antiquity, the Chinese Buddhist pilgrim, Xuanzang (Hiuen Tsiang), described a Magha Mela at Prayagraj (Allahabad) in 643 CE, but the modern festival was shaped by the ninth-century philosopher Shankaracharya (Dubey, 2001). Shankaracharya, leader of the non-dualist Advaitist School of Vedanta, called Hindu ascetics, monks and sages to meet at these places to exchange philosophical views and build mutual understanding, while the laity followed, in increasing numbers, to benefit from association with these assembled sages (Singh and Haigh, 2015:792). In 2017, Kumbha Mela was inscribed by UNESCO in its Representative List of the Intangible Cultural Heritage of Humanity. The last Kumbha Mela festival held in 2013 brought around 75 million visitors to Prayagraj (Allahabad). The most recent Mela was held between 15 January and 4 March 2019, under the direct patronage of the state government, and recorded around 105 million visitors. It is the greatest sacred water festival through which the Hindu philosophy of life is propagated. The Mela ground spread over an area of 45 sq km and an 8-km length of bathing ghats. Twenty-two million people resided in a temporary tent city divided into 22 sectors. To support this mass gathering, the infrastructural facilities included 122,500 toilets, 20,000 sanitation workers, 20,000 dustbins, 90 parking lots for 500,000 vehicles, 22 pontoon bridges on the two rivers (Ganga and Yamuna), 250 km of roads, 500 shuttle buses, 5,000 e-rikshas (three-wheelers) for travel within the Mela grounds, 22 hospitals (450 beds each), 40,700 LED lights, and ferry and boating services.

Varanasi

Varanasi (Banaras/Kashi) is known as the holiest place and the cultural capital of India. There, the Ganga flows past the splendor and beauty of 84 ghats (water-steps) and over 3,300 Hindu shrines, and also several Buddhist, Jain and Sikh shrines.

People from all parts of India came and settled along the river resulting in a complex web of social space. Rich persons, lords and kings from all parts of the country came and erected palatial buildings to serve as their resorts for performing rituals on special occasions. Thus, lofty and beautiful architecture developed along the Ganga ghats. In archetypal connotation, each ghat represents one *lākh* (100,000) of the organic species described in Hindu mythology; that is how in total all the 8.4 million species are symbolized along the 84 ganga ghats in Varanasi. Further, 12 zodiacs × 7 layers of atmosphere comes to 84; thus, the annual cycle of the cosmic journey is completed by taking sacred baths at the 84 ghats. At these sacred sites, there exist 96 waterfront sacred spots. The number 96 indicates the cosmic frame linking 12 zodiacs/months and 8 directions of space; thus, the product, 12 × 8, comes to 96. Among the 84 ghats, five are considered as more auspicious; from South to North, they are: Asi, Dashasvamedha, Manikarnika, Panchaganga and Adi Keshava (cf. Figure 6.4). These five ghats symbolize the microcosmic body of Vishnu, respectively, as his head, chest, navel, thighs and feet. This reminds us that Vishnu first placed his holy feet in Varanasi; this is why the area along the Ganga River is Vishnu's body. These five ghats, called the *Panchatirthis* (the five most sacred water spots), are eulogized in the Puranic mythologies, and serve as the nexus for most of the purification rituals.

Gaya is eulogized as the most sacred place for ancestral rituals. These aim to help ancestral spirits (who, through *karma* or premature death, are trapped in limbo) become free and reach the realm of the ancestor spirits. This site, which attracts over a million pilgrims each year, is mentioned in the ancient *Rig Veda* (1.22.17), while the rites in the Vishnupad Temple are described in texts dating from the fifth century CE and claim continuity of tradition since the eighth century CE. Presently, 84 of the original 324 sites, related to ancestral rites, are identifiable in nine sacred clusters, but modern pilgrims rarely visit more than 45. More than three-fourths of pilgrims perform their ancestral rites at the Phalgu River, the Vishnupad Temple and its associated sacred centers (Vidyarthi, 1978). The cosmogony of Gaya's faithscape contains three territorial layers: Gaya *Mandala*, Gaya *Kshetra* (literally "field") and Gaya *Puri* (township), through which shrines and rituals chart a complex of interweaving themes concerning birth, fertility, life and death (Singh, 2009). Lord Vishnu's footprints, enshrined in the Vishnupad Temple, serve as the *axis mundi* for the Gaya *mandala* whose cardinal and solstitial points are marked by hills, including Pretashila (the hill of the ghosts).

Ayodhya

The ancient city of Ayodhya lies at the bank of Sarayu (Ghaghara), a major tributary of Ganga River that manifests the evolutionary story of this waterfront sacred city (Kumar and Singh, 2013). The city possesses 1,161 Hindu temples and shrines, five Jain temples, two Buddhist shrines, seven Sikh gurudvaras, two churches and 186 Muslim shrines. The Sarayu River is also perceived as a goddess like many other great rivers of India. Every *ghat* (stairway)

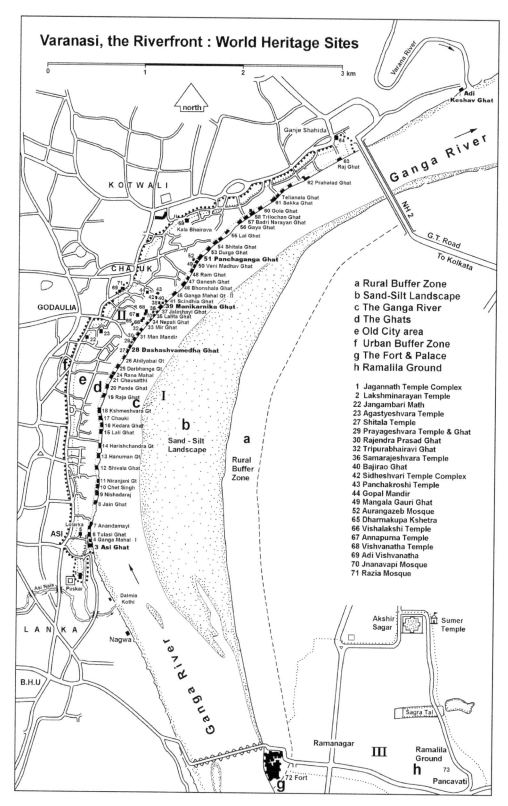

FIGURE 6.4 Varansi's ghats (after Singh, 2013:177; with permission).

possesses individual historical, mythological, religious folk tales and spiritual importance. The riverfront also consists of sacred places like monastic temples, *ashrams* and *chhavanis* (encampments of monks). Every year on the special occasion of pilgrimages, devotees perform the first ritual (bathing) before completing pilgrimage journeys. The waterfront landscape of Ayodhya represents the historical, mythological, architectural, cultural, religious and heritage values of the ancient city (see Figure 6.5). These manifested forms consist of four kinds of "*scapes*": first, the Sacredscape that contains the various sacred places, temples, *chhavanis* and *ashrams*; second, the Ritualscape containing the variety of rituals performed by the pilgrims (e.g. bathing, offering, cremation, etc.); third, the Riverfrontscape consisting of the 27 *ghats*, steps; and fourth the Holy Tankscapes/Kundscapes (pools) that number 64. These waterfront sites are associated with various forms of divinities and eulogized in ancient mythologies and folklore.

Sustainability vs. sacred water

The river symbolizes fertility by its liquidity ("living water") in which life, strength and eternity are contained; that is how all the sacred waters inherently possess the power of progeny and spiritual energy. A touching question that was asked by a journalist is an issue of serious concern: "How can Indians pollute Ganga yet at the same time worship her as a goddess? How can so many millions take a 'holy dip' every morning to wash away their sins in a river that is polluted by so much waste, both human and industrial? How does one explain this paradox?" (Hollick, 2007:1).

Let us change our attitude and orientation to search for ethical answers and awaken our "Self-realization" for deeper understanding and re-establishment of the "sacred power" of the water bodies! Political action alone would not work to revive this spirit without mass consciousness and active participation. Religion (*dharma*) plays a vital role in the Hindu quest for understanding and practicing harmony between nature and humanity to achieve a cosmological awakening. In eco-spirituality, sacred waters play a vital role. As such, pilgrimage of the ancient Hindu tradition—marches from realization towards revelation (Singh and Rana, 2016:79).

In closing, let me cite an ancient sage:

> May the waters from the snowy mountains bring health and peace to all people. May the spring waters bring calmness to you; may the swift currents be pleasing to you; and may the rains be a source of tranquillity to all. May the waters of Oasis in the desert be sweet to you; and so be the waters of ponds and lakes. May the waters from the wells dug by humans be good to them, and may the healing powers of water be available to all human beings.
> *(see Atharva Veda, Prithvi Sukta 12.11–12)*

After all, let us think *cosmically*, see *globally*, but act *locally* and *insightfully*. This is an appeal for cosmic vision, global humanism and Self-realization (Singh, 2017:223).

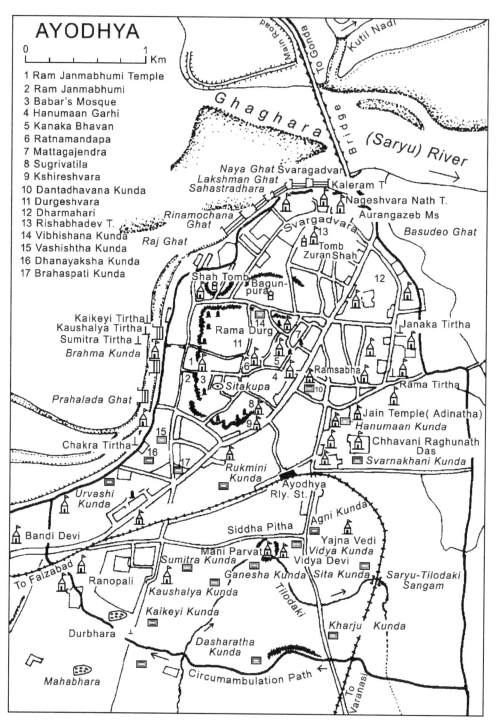

FIGURE 6.5 Ayodhya: sacred spots along the Sarayu's bank and the Holy Tank (Kunda) (after Kumar and Singh, 2013:13; reprinted with permission).

References

AV, *Atharva Veda*, 1895. Bombay: Venkateshvara Press.

Bryant, M. Darrol. 1994. River of Grace: The Kumbha Mela as Sacred Place. *Environments* 22(2):35–40.

Buttimer, Anne. 1989. Nature, Water Symbols and the Human Quest for Wholeness. In *Dwelling, Place and Environment*, edited by David Seamon and Robert Mugerauer, 257–280. New York: Columbia University Press.

Darian, Steven G. 1978. *The Ganges in Myth and History*. Honolulu: University of Hawaii Press.

Das, Priyam and Tamminga Kenneth R. 2012. The Ganges and the GAP: An Assessment of Efforts to Clean a Sacred River. *Sustainability* 4:1647–1668. doi:10.3390/su4081647.

Dubey, Devi Prasad. 2001. *Prayaga: The Site of the Kumbha Mela*. New Delhi: Aryan International.

Eck, Diana L. 2012. *India: A Sacred Geography*. New York: Harmony Book.

Eliade, Mircea. 1958. *Patterns in Comparative Religion*. Princeton, NJ: Princeton University Press.

Hollick, Julian C. 2007. *Ganga, A Journey Down the Ganges River*. New Delhi: Random House India.

Jacobsen, Knut A. 2013. *Pilgrimage in the Hindu Tradition*. London & New York: Routledge.

Kalyana-Tirthanka. 1957. Annual no. 31. Gorakhpur: Gita Press. [in Hindi].

Kinsley, David. 1987. *Hindu Goddesses*. Delhi: Motilal Banarasidass.

Kumar, Sarvesh and Singh Rana P. B. 2013. Waterfront Cultural Landscape of Ayodhya (India), an Ancient Sacred Abode of Gods. *South Asian Affairs* 9:6–17.

SBr, *Satapatha Brahmana*.1882. Trans. J. Eggeling. Sacred Books of the East, vols. 12, 26, 41, 43, 44. Oxford: The Claredon Press, reprinted. Delhi: Motilal Banaridass, 1989.

Singh, Rana P. B. 1987. Towards Myth, Cosmos, Space and Mandala in India. *National Geographical Journal of India* 33(3):305–326.

———. 1992. Nature and Cosmic Integrity: A Search in Hindu Geographic Thought. *GeoJournal* 26(2):139–147.

———. 1993. Cosmos, Theos, Anthropos: An Inner Vision of Sacred Ecology in Hinduism. *National Geographical Journal India* 39:113–130.

———. 1994. Water Symbolism and Sacred Landscape in Hinduism: A Study of Benares (Varanasi). *Erdkunde* (Bonn, Germany), Bd. 48(3):210–227.

———. 1996. The Ganga River and the Spirit of Sustainability in Hinduism. In *Dialogues with the Living Earth. New Ideas from Spirit of Place from Designers, Architects and Innovators*, edited by James Swan and Roberta Swan, 86–107. Wheaton, IL: Quest Books.

———. 1997. Sacred space and Pilgrimage in Hindu society: The Case of Varanasi. In *Sacred Places, Sacred Spaces: The Geography of Pilgrimages*. [*Geoscience & Man*, vol. 34], edited by Robert H. Stoddard and Alan Morinis, 191–207. Baton Rouge: Louisiana State University Press.

———. 2009. *Cosmic Order and Cultural Astronomy. Sacred Cities of India*. Newcastle upon Tyne: Cambridge Scholars Publishing.

———. 2013. *Hindu Tradition of Pilgrimage: Sacred Space and System*, 159–194. New Delhi: Dev Publishers.

———. 2017. Sacred Ecology and Transformative Consciousness in Hinduism. *IJTC, International Journal for the Transformation of Consciousness* (GIT, Chethimattom, Pala, Kerala) 3(1): 209–233.

Singh, Rana P. B. and Haigh Martin J. 2015. Hindu Pilgrimages: The Contemporary Scene. In *The Changing World Religion Map, CWRM: Sacred Places, Identities, Practices and Politics*, edited by Stanley D. Brunn, 783–801. Dordrecht and New York: Springer Science and Business Media B.V.

Singh, Rana P. B. and Rana Pravin S. 2016. Indian Sacred Natural Sites: Ancient Traditions of Reverence and Conservation explained from a Hindu Perspective. In *Asian Sacred Natural Sites: Ancient Philosophy and Practice in Conservation and Protected Areas*, edited by Bas Verschuuren and Naoya Furuta, 69–80. London and New York: Routledge.

Swan, James A., ed. 1991. *The Power of Place*. Wheaton, IL: Quest Books.

Vidyarthi, Lalita P. 1978. *The Sacred Complex in Hindu Gaya* (2nd Ed). New Delhi: Concept Publishing.

Zimmer, Heinrich. 1991. *Myths and Symbols in Indian Art and Civilization*. Princeton, NJ: Princeton University Press.

PART III

Genii loci and ancestors

Sacred waters around the globe have spiritual guardians as well as human stewards. As noted in the introduction, supernatural protectors of liminal watery places can take a variety of forms and are often considered ancestors. Describing the powerful symbolism of freshwater sources for Indigenous Australians, Liam Brady opens this section with an examination of the deep-time contexts through which people engage sacred waters and recall the songs of their creation by Ancestral Beings. These interconnected environmental features link kinship through space and time so that totemic wells associated with clans and spirit beings give order to sentient, Indigenous landscapes. Offering a compelling explanation of Incan sanctuaries and living landscapes, Marco Curatola Petrocchi employs early Spanish chronicles to explain the ubiquitous association of stone and water as an inseparable and animistic duo. Running water was perceived as the voice of the supernatural presence in stone. Oracular shrines for speaking springs had similar features and were linked through pilgrimage routes across the empire. Many of China's sacred springs and wells traditionally had dragon protectors who provided health, rain and babies. Jean DeBernardi, Yan Jie and Ma Junhong consider the sacred wells still commonly found in Daoist and Buddhist temples and monasteries which have spiritual efficacy and curative powers. While the Communist Party discourages the so-called feudal superstitions, the government has developed some sites as tourist destinations. As dragons were consulted for rain in China, so too are ancestors in other parts of the world. Richard Ford writes about the ritual work of Women's Societies among the Tewa of New Mexico. In their origin story, the Tewa were created under a spring (*Sipofene*). All bodies of water (springs, rivers and arroyos) are connected to that watery creation site, to each other and also to the ancestors. Women's sodalities stewarded the sacred springs where they requested rain from ancestors and primordial spirits.

7

FRESHWATER SOURCES AND THEIR RELATIONAL CONTEXTS IN INDIGENOUS AUSTRALIA

Views from the past and present

Liam M. Brady

Much like elsewhere around the world, freshwater sources in Australia are referred to using a range of terms including waterholes, soaks, rockholes, wells, springs, lakes, billabongs (ponds where creeks or rivers formerly flowed), claypans (water found in shallow clay depressions) and gnammas (water found in hollows in granite domes, often protected with a rock slab covering) (see Tindale, 1974; Bayly, 1999). Indigenous engagement with freshwater resources occurs in a range of contexts such as: subsistence pursuits; religious and kin-based relationships; mobility; trade and exchange; patterns of occupation; aesthetic qualities; recreation; artistic and literary inspiration; and varying forms of contact with Europeans including frontier violence and enslavement of Aboriginal people by explorers to help search for freshwater.[1] A brief consideration of previous studies of Australian freshwater sources and their deep-time use (the longevity of their human occupation) will preface a description of their sacrality and their significance in Indigenous worldviews, and relational networks.

At present, no figures are available for the number of freshwater sources across the continent; however, a recent mapping project in Martu Country in the Western Desert (part of the *Martu Living Deserts Project*) has identified 1,118 waterholes through site visits and helicopter surveys (Jupp et al., 2015:579). Likewise, in central Australia, June Ross and Leo Abbott (2004) have collected quantitative data about the geology and reliability of freshwater sources in the MacDonnell Ranges as a means to explore the contexts of rock art production, while in the Central Desert, Donald Thomson (1962:274) noted how Pintupi men recited the names of over 50 waterholes (wells, rockholes and claypans) in their country. This data suggests not only a high-quantity of freshwater sources in arid landscapes, but also the extensive knowledge about them held by Aboriginal men and women.

A focus of previous study is the well-known and highly significant Ooldea Soak—a permanent water source surrounded by steep red sand dunes—at the southern edge of the Great Victoria Desert in South Australia. Much like other freshwater sources around the country, the Soak was said by Aboriginal people to be created

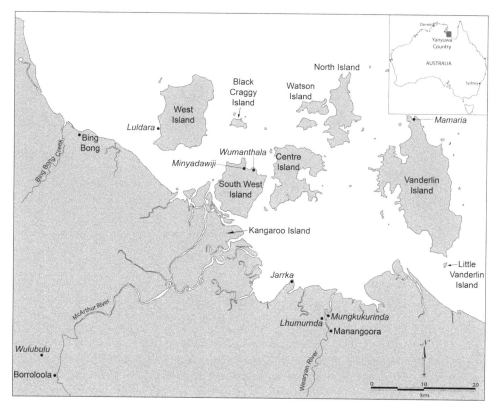

FIGURE 7.1 Map of the Sir Edward Pellew Islands showing places mentioned in Yanyuwa Country.

by travelling Ancestral Beings also known as Dreamings (which take many forms including animals, plants and natural phenomena and the term also encompasses a body of moral and social laws for people to live by) (Bates, 1920, 1938). Aboriginal people would gather at the Soak and similar sites when other semi-permanent water sources from desert regions ran dry or during periods of drought. As a large and reliable water source, the Soak became a key meeting place that was used for trade, exchange and other social and cultural activities (see Brockwell et al., 1989). Given the size, location and cultural significance of the Soak, it has also been the focus of historical, ethnographic and archaeological observations and research for well over a century.[2] Ronald and Catherine Berndt (pioneering Australian anthropologists who produced some of the most detailed, localised ethnographic studies of Aboriginal people across many parts of the continent) offered useful quantitative data about Aboriginal interaction with the Soak including the seasonal variability in the number of people encamped in its vicinity and the location and structuring principles of Aboriginal campsites in the area.[3] Archaeological studies of artefacts (e.g. stone tools, animal bone, European objects) at the Soak also reveal a wide range of cultural activities occurring here. Raw materials used in stone artefact manufacture found at the Soak clearly reflect interaction with others given the lack of local stone sources, while the appearance of flaked stone artefacts from the "Australian Small Tool Tradition" suggests that encampments at the site extend back at least "6000–7000 years"[4] (Brockwell et al., 1989:73).

Freshwater sources and deep-time contexts

Permanent and reliable freshwater resources have played a critical role for archaeological models of human colonisation, especially in terms of mobility and settlement behaviour (Veth, 1989, 2005).[5] When Aboriginal people arrived in Australia around 65,000 years ago, the climate was relatively favourable, cool and humid, with freshwater resources found in large lakes (e.g. Lake Gregory, Lake Eyre) across much of the continent and would likely have allowed for broadscale exploration (Hiscock and Wallis, 2005:41). However, beginning around 30,000 BP, the climate became increasingly arid with poorer rainfall, being driest during the Last Glacial Maximum (23,000–17,000 BP). These changes meant a dramatic reduction in freshwater sources leading Aboriginal people to aggregate at the remaining reliable well-watered locales, termed refugia, in inland ranges of the Pilbara, Kimberley and central Australia regions (Veth, 1989:84). People's movements during this harsh climatic period would have been "tethered to a series of restricted localities where water was available year round" and with fewer visits to "outlying sites...as [people's] foraging contracts" (Smith, 2013:123). However, the role of resource-rich aggregation sites with access to permanent freshwater in deep-time contexts was not simply about survival—they also had an important social function in helping to facilitate various cultural activities including ritual, exchange of goods and language diffusion (Veth, 2006). As the climate began to warm from the early Holocene (10,000 BP), freshwater sources began to increase and, no longer constrained to their refugia, Aboriginal people began to disperse throughout the continent. Excavations at freshwater sites around the country also reveal aspects of their significance. For example, Blackfellow's Waterhole in Wotjobaluk Country in southwestern Victoria is a deep, semi-permanent waterhole on a flood plain in a semi-arid environment. Research here has documented a 9,000-year record of occupation that continues into post-European contact times. This evidence suggests that this freshwater source remained an important feature in the cultural landscape of the Wotjobaluk (Richards, 2013:35; see also Porter, 2004).[6]

Ancestral Beings and the ancestral past

Freshwater sources are socially and culturally complex places. They mediate relationships with Ancestral Beings and engagements between and within Indigenous communities. In the Ancestral Past before humans existed—the "Dreaming"—Ancestral Beings created, shaped and named the land and sea, and left parts of their bodies and knowledge in geographical features. Indigenous narratives and songs relate the travels of Ancestral Beings and their creative activities:

> *"Every water got a song"*
> *(Joe Brown, Aboriginal contributor to the Canning Stock Route Project,*
> *quoted in LaFontaine and Buttler, 2008:15)*

In Aboriginal Australia, narratives and songs carry the stories of Ancestral Beings and their journeys and creative acts across land- and seascapes. For example, the epic journey of the Seven Sisters Ancestral Beings across the Central and Western Deserts contains many references to their visits to, and activities at, waterholes across the landscape (see Neale, 2017). For over 40 years in northern Australia's Gulf of Carpentaria region, anthropologist John Bradley and the Yanyuwa (an island- and coastal-based Aboriginal community from the Sir Edward Pellew Islands) have been documenting the travels and activities of Ancestral Beings in this area with freshwater springs and wells (*wayuru*) featuring prominently in their recorded material. For example, at Karruwa (Little Vanderlin Island), the Spirit People and Sea Turtle Ancestral Beings travelled over the island leaving a freshwater well. At Vanderlin Island, the Dugong Hunter Ancestral Beings rested at Mamarla and "created a freshwater well and stream" (Yanyuwa Families et al., 2003:65), while at North Island they left another freshwater well before continuing on their journey.

In other instances, narratives and songs provide specific details of the features used by Ancestral Beings to create freshwater sources (e.g. eyes). For example, the groper (spelled grouper outside Australia; *Promicorps lanceolatus*) is a large bony fish usually found in coral reefs and is one of the major Ancestral Beings for the Yanyuwa. The Songline (*kujika*) belonging to the Groper Ancestral Being describes her creation of a waterhole as she travels across South West Island:

> Here I am at my country, I am naming it Wumanthala.
> It is my country and I am placing water reed corms here…
> They are my eyes.
> I am placing my eyes again and water will flow…
> It is a fresh water well.[7]

Other examples include the Tiger Shark making a well using his eye and calling it Dungkurrumaji (Yanyuwa Families et al., 2003:182; see also Yanyuwa People and Bradley, 1988:12), while at West Island, after being chased by the Osprey Ancestral Being, the Sea Turtle Ancestral Beings "moved slowly and sang slowly and came to Luldarra where they left their eyes and made a fresh water well" (Yanyuwa Families et al., 2003:113).

Agency and Ancestral Beings

Ancestral Beings can also exert agency in relation to freshwater sources they created such as at Minyadawiji on South West Island where the Jabiru Ancestral Being created a freshwater well. Yanyuwa men and women note that at "high tide it is not possible to get fresh water only salt water, but when it is low tide the fresh water comes up and it is very good. It is because of the Dreaming that this happens, at low tide we can obtain water but not at high tide" (Yanyuwa People and Bradley, 1988:58).

On the coastal mainland at Jarrka, the Olive Python and Rock Cod Ancestral Beings "came up out of the ground and created a well"; the well represents the mouth of the Rock Cod, while the Olive Python is coiled inside the well (Yanyuwa People and Bradley, 1988:41, 2003:214, 2016:452–453, 2017:504). While the well is the result of a creative act, the role of the Olive Python is essential to understanding further relational contexts. Across Yanyuwa Country, freshwater wells tend to have real Olive Pythons living at or near them, and Yanyuwa say that they "maintain the water level in the well. If people kill the python or it is burnt in a bushfire the well waters may dry up" (ibid, 2003:214). The contemporary, visible presence of Olive Pythons at freshwater wells reinforces ideas of relational dependency, the relationship between an Ancestral Being and a freshwater source, and their role in matters concerning the well's health and maintenance. A similar example of the agency of Ancestral Beings involves the Tiger Shark's activities at Mungkukurinda lagoon where he "placed a small bundle of untreated cycad food" near the water's edge. Cycad palm fruit is an important food source for Yanyuwa, but if not processed properly, it can be poisonous. Yanyuwa state that this untreated bundle of cycad fruit is the reason why "the water of this lagoon is always cloudy and not that good to drink" (ibid:182).

The Jarrka well is also related to the health and wellbeing of Yanyuwa families. The well is associated with one of four Yanyuwa clans, the Mambaliya-Wawukarriya, and clan members have a responsibility to care for this country and all that it contains including the well. However, by 1982, all Mambaliya-Wawukarriya clan members responsible for Jarrka had moved to the central township of Borroloola. While some

FIGURE 7.2 Mambaliya-Wawukarriya clan member Johnson Babarramila Timothy sitting at the Jarrka well and surrounded by a shell midden, 1985. Photograph by John Bradley and reproduced with permission.

Mambaliya-Wawukarriya clan members occasionally visited Jarrka (including one attempt at setting up an outstation here), the well's health began to suffer with increasing salt content. Eventually, the well went dry and "people believe that this is because too many of the senior men and women associated with this place have died and the country is sad, it is crying for them" (Yanyuwa Families et al., 2003:216). Mambaliya-Wawukarriya clan members' interpretation of the absence of freshwater is built around kinship and relational understandings. When people are away from their country for long periods of time, spirits become sad and take things away, in this instance freshwater, but they are also known to take away other features in the landscape including rock paintings in similar circumstances (Brady et al., 2016).

Other freshwater sources in Yanyuwa Country are related to "increase rituals" (designed to enhance the population of a particular species). On the coastal mainland at Lhumurnda is a freshwater well created by the Yam Ancestral Being. Here, the *jungkayi* ("guardians" or "bosses" of specific tracts of country) would "clean out the well and call out the names of country where they wanted the yam to grow" (Yanyuwa Families et al., 2003:184). As a result, this site forms part of a complex web of relationships involving the state of the freshwater well, kinship obligations and a ritual associated with the potency of the Yam Ancestral Being.

Interacting with freshwater sources

Interaction with freshwater sources can take many forms such as visitation, drinking or bathing, and carrying out specific obligations, as well as showing feelings and emotions such as fear, worry and joy. Each form of interaction plays a role in referencing the nature of relationships people have and hold with their freshwater resources. People's interaction with freshwater sources may be examined through the lens of fear and distress, and performance and reciprocity.

Sandy Toussaint et al. recently noted that "[a] particular etiquette is required when 'looking after' or approaching a water source, either to assist with its renewal or to introduce a new person to the site" (2005:67; see Jarrka example provided earlier). They use the example of the composite Ancestral Beings *kalpurtu* (both man and snake) from the southwest Kimberley region who inhabit permanent waterholes to highlight what structures and shapes people's engagement with the freshwater sources. They note that the *kalpurtu* are "dangerous to approach" and if disturbed, they "can bring misfortune or death" (Sullivan et al., 2012:48–49). To appease the *kalpurtu* and make them "happy," the Wajamari Traditional Owners (those individuals with the correct kinship relationship to the Ancestral Being in question) must approach by singing the songs handed down to them by Ancestral Beings. In doing so, the *kalpurtu* know that they remain in the memory of Wajamari (ibid).

A second example is from the flat desert landscape of central Australia where the highly distinctive monolith known as Uluru (Ayers Rock) is found. The site is home to numerous waterholes that are laden with meaning and symbolism, and act to structure people's engagement and interaction with them. A particular waterhole, itself known as Uluru, is one of the most culturally significant sites here and is home to the powerful and greatly feared serpent, Wanambi. During a visit to the waterhole in 1961, anthropologist Charles Pearcy Mountford recorded the reaction of one of the Traditional Owners with whom he visited the site:

> If an Aboriginal drinks at Uluru rockhole, or lights a fire near by he will so offend the wanambi that it will rise in the air in the form of a rainbow, and kill the offender by biting his kuran (spirit) with its long teeth. As a still further punishment, the wanambi will take the water, not only from the Uluru rockhole, but from all the other springs and waterholes around the base of Ayers Rock … [t]he Ayers Rock wanambi is so greatly feared that old Balinga would not let me go near the Uluru rockhole…Balinga was sure that, had I disobeyed him, the wanambi would have transformed himself into a rainbow, and killed us both.
>
> *(Mountford, 1965:154)*

Balinga's fear and apprehension concerning Wanambi's potential reaction to their visit signal an affective response firmly anchored in Aboriginal ontology and epistemology. To anger Wanambi could have potentially dangerous consequences that threaten people's lives.

William E. Harney, a ranger at Uluru in the late 1950s, also recorded stories and events concerning Wanambi. His records reveal other dimensions of people's engagement with Wanambi as well as interpretations by Traditional Owners of specific events. Harney describes how a group of hunters arrived at Uluru in the dry season expecting it to be empty but instead found it full (1960:75). Their interpretation of this occurrence was shaped by a recent event whereby a senior man was killed by the Native Police. While Wanambi was capable of taking life, he could also cry and grieve for people, it was his tears for that man that filled the rockhole.

A second form of interaction with the Uluru waterhole concerns performance. Harney recorded how, when the rockhole was dry and people were thirsty, they would call out Wanambi: "Kuka…Kuka…Kuka (meat…meat…meat)" (1968:11). Upon hearing this chant, Wanambi would move and disgorge "water from within it, which flows down to the thirsty people" (ibid). Thus, an important bond can be seen to exist between people, the Uluru rockhole and an Ancestral Being with the power to control the environment. This bond not only reinforces the complex web of relationships the rockhole creates, but also the idea of relational dependency occurring here through performance.[8]

A final example concerns a freshwater spring at Wulubulu (formerly Binbingka Country, now cared for by Yanyuwa) just outside the township of Borroloola. This waterhole is intimately related to the Hill Kangaroo Ancestral Beings; on their creative journey, they stopped here and dug the freshwater spring which is also home to the *ardirri* (spirit child) of the Hill Kangaroos (Yanyuwa Families and Bradley, 2016:443–444; see also 79–80). With the *ardirri* of the Hill Kangaroos, Wulubulu becomes a potent place, one with the capacity to increase the quantity of hill kangaroos for hunting through specific rituals. Kearney et al. (2019) provide details of a conversation with senior Yanyuwa woman Violet Hammer in 2013 where she describes how her husband would not go hunting until he visited the spring and performed a small ritual in which he smeared his sweat on a little stone and threw it into the water calling out for kangaroos to make themselves visible to hunt. However, this type of engagement with Wulubulu and its potency for hunting has changed over time. With people becoming increasingly sedentary, they did not rely on hunting as much as in the past. Instead, Wulubulu is now visited by younger generations of Yanyuwa who venture here to swim in the wet season, thus adding another layer of significance to this place and, in doing so, creating new relational contexts.

Kinship, totemic wells and the cultural landscape

In the ethnographic examples presented earlier, kin-based relationships with freshwater sources are a common feature. For example, each of the Yanyuwa *kujika* and geographic location of freshwater sources discussed earlier belong to one of four clans: Wuyaliya, Wurdaliya, Rrumburriya and Mambaliya-Wawukarriya. As clan members, they have a kin-based obligation to look after these sites and their associated knowledge, and to pass on this knowledge to younger generations.[9]

In other areas of Australia, freshwater sources in the form of "totemic" or clan wells are used to describe and order the landscape. Rhys Jones' 1985 work in Gidjingali Country (northern Arnhem Land) draws attention to the complex relational sphere in which freshwater wells are enmeshed in terms of kinship, landscape, graphic designs and reproduction. Jones notes that the Gidjingali use wells rather than ecological units (e.g. desert, coast) as a framing device to describe their country; each well is owned by a specific patrilineal clan and given a name in accordance with its associated spirit being. The distribution of wells throughout the landscape reflects their ecological importance; that is, in arid and desert-like areas with few people, there are only a few named wells, while in rich coastal areas where there are larger populations and a need to "delineate and define social space more finely," totemic wells appear much more frequently (1985:202). Gidjingali's personal relationships with wells can be seen in several ways: (1) Gidjingali women believe that they fall pregnant by a spirit child, or "essence of the land entering their bodies from a totemic well or waterhole as they were near it"; (2) the individual then belongs to the set of totemic well(s) associated with that spirit child; (3) at different points in life (e.g. initiation, burial), the individual's relationship with their totemic well (Jones 1985: 1999) is reinforced through the use of specific clan-well designs painted on their bodies and hollow-log coffins; and (4) upon death, their hollow-log coffin is placed in close association with their totemic well (Rhys, 1985:199). Yanyuwa Families and Bradley (2017:504) also describe how individuals with an *ardirri* (spirit child) derived from the same freshwater source are close kin; for example, individuals with an *ardirri* from the Wurrumburramba well would say "*Nyangathi-wayurungu kumbu-ngka ngathangka Wurrumburramba.* = He is my kinsman, we share one water, he originated like me at Wurrumburramba." Thus, freshwater wells are intimately related to the human life cycle and represent critical features of the cultural construction of landscapes. The relational importance of a totemic well can be viewed through the lens of agency as it is by the agency of spiritual beings who guide and shape the web of relationships effecting each individual.

Communicating and memorialising freshwater sources

Aboriginal people also frequently included waterholes as part of their visual arts. While the designs and symbols used and communicated in various mediums (sand drawings, crayon drawings, rock art, canvas, sculpture and acrylic art) can be multi-referential, they are also embedded in a range of relational contexts including the activities of Ancestral Beings and knowledge of the cultural landscape.

One of the most recognisable symbols denoting freshwater sources are circle and concentric circle motifs. Nancy Munn's work into the Central Desert Warlpiri visual art system revealed that while circle motifs are multi-referential, they are oftentimes used to depict waterholes that feature in the activities and travels of Ancestral Beings or in narratives involving daily activities such as sitting around waterholes (Munn, 1962, 1973). Similarly, many crayon drawings made by Yolngu men at Yirrkala (northeast Arnhem Land) and collected by Ronald and Catherine Berndt also feature multi-referential circles oftentimes representing freshwater sources created by Ancestral Beings such as the powerful Djang'kawu sisters who are responsible for giving birth to Yolngu people (Morphy, 2013:29).

In 1957, anthropologist Donald Thomson collected carved spearthrowers from Pintupi men in the central Australian desert that featured carved geometric designs in the shape of circles and lines. Upon receiving the objects, he noted how one Pintupi man, Tjappanongo, pointed to and named each circle as a freshwater well or rock-hole. This event led Thomson to comment that what the Pintupi men showed him was "really a map, highly conventionalized, like the marks on a 'message' or 'letter' stick of the Aborigines, of the waters of the vast terrain over which the Bindibu [Pintupi] hunted" (1962:274; see also Tindale, 1974). What is significant here is the intimate knowledge Pintupi men held of their country, and waterholes specifically, and mechanisms to communicate this information via visual mapping practice.

Another example of an artwork reflecting a relationship with a freshwater source involves the Yawkyawk female spirit beings among the Kuninjku in western Arnhem Land. Yawkyawk spirits inhabit waterholes and freshwater streams, and people can "occasionally see their shadows as they flee the smell of humans who approach the water. They are imagined to have been girls who transformed into mermaid type figures with fishtails" (Taylor, 2005:190). Anthropologist Luke Taylor notes how many Kuninjku artists such as Owen Yalandja now depict the Yawkyawk as part of a sculptural wood carving tradition where long, sinuous bodies with "fishy" tails are used to represent the spirit beings travelling through the water (ibid).

Conclusion

The examples discussed here reveal freshwater sources to be complex entities but more importantly they epitomise an interconnected and relational world where people, environmental features, kinship and Ancestral Beings remain linked across space and through time. At a time when many of these sacred watery places are facing deterioration or are under threat from development, their cultural significance cannot be reduced to simple interpretations, but rather needs to be understood through their correct relational spheres. Perhaps most important in the consideration of freshwater resources is the role of Indigenous ontology and epistemology—as framing devices anchoring and orienting the observer among the complex relationships that these places command. In doing so, freshwater resources cannot be regarded as separate entities in the environment, but instead form part of a sentient cultural landscape, one that is embedded in complex notions of agency, symbolism and relational dependence.

Acknowledgements

This research has been supported by the Australian Research Council (DP170101083, FT180100038), the Wenner-Gren Foundation and the Australian Institute for Aboriginal and Torres Strait Islander Studies. Special thanks to John Bradley for sharing his knowledge about Yanyuwa waterholes and permission to reproduce Figure 7.2.

Notes

1 See, e.g., Barber and Jackson (2011); Bayly (1999:17); Buchler and Maddock (1978); Cane (1987); Caruana (2011); Elkin (1930); McConnel (1930); Langton (2006); Morton et al. (2013).
2 For example, see Bates (1920, 1921, 1923, 1938); Bolam (1923); Berndt and Berndt (1942); Brady (1999); Brockwell et al. (1989).
3 They noted considerable variability in the numbers of people at the site: after the wet season, the population decreased to around 80 people, but during ceremonial times and at times of drought, the population could swell to around 400. They also described the distances from the water source at which people would encamp or construct camps: "an average of three-quarters of a mile to one and a half miles distant." They described people moving their camps around the Soak regularly (noting 13 moves over six months) for various reasons including lack of firewood, sanitation, death and reduced vegetation through trampling, etc. (1942:310). The Soak also had spatial and socially driven structuring properties for Aboriginal visitors: people arriving from the south of the Soak would camp on its southern flank, while those arriving from the north would camp on the northern flank (Bates, 1921, 1938; Berndt, 1942).
4 The Australian Small Tool Tradition is now considered to date around 4500 BP (Hiscock and Attenbrow 1998).
5 See also Veth et al. (2014); Bird et al. (2016); Smith (2013).
6 Other freshwater sources feature much shorter periods of occupation. The Glen Thirsty rain-fed well in central Australia shows evidence of intense occupation beginning only around 1500 BP. Archaeological interpretations identify Glen Thirsty as a seasonal occupation site when people began travelling here regularly after wet season rains refilled the well (Smith and Ross, 2008).
7 Text from http://artsonline.monash.edu.au/countrylines-archive/the-groper-a-kuridi/; see also Yanyuwa Families et al. (2003:126).
8 See also, e.g., Gould (1969:126–127); Kearney et al. (2019).
9 See Bradley 1997 for details on Yanyuwa kinship.

References

Barber, Marcus and Sue Jackson. 2011. Aboriginal Water Values and Resource Development Pressures in the Pilbara Region of North-West Australia. *Australian Aboriginal Studies* 2:32–49.
Bates, Daisy M. 1920. Karrbiji Gabbi of Ooldilinga (The Legend of Ooldea Water). *Australasian* 25 April 1920:837–838, 1 May 1920:885–886.

Bates, Daisy M. 1921. Ooldea Water. *Proceedings of the Royal Geographical Society of Australasia, South Australian Branch* 21:73–78.

Bates, Daisy M. 1923. Central Australia: Underground Waters. *Australasian* 28 July 1923.

Bates, Daisy M. 1938. *The Passing of the Aborigines*. London: John Murray.

Bayly, Ian A.E. 1999. Review of How Indigenous People Managed for Water in Desert Regions of Australia. *Journal of the Royal Society of Western Australia* 82:17–25.

Berndt, Ronald and Catherine Berndt. 1942. A Preliminary Report of Field Work in the Ooldea Region, Western South Australia. *Oceania* 12(4):305–330.

Bird, Michael I., O'Grady Damien and Sean Ulm. 2016. Humans, Water, and the Colonization of Australia. *Proceedings of the National Academy of Sciences* 113(41):11477–11482.

Bolam, Anthony G. 1923. *The Trans-Australian Wonderland*. Melbourne: Modern Printing.

Bradley, John J. 1997. Li-Anthawirrayarra, People of the Sea: Yanyuwa Relations with their Maritime Environment. Unpublished PhD dissertation, Northern Territory University.

Brady, Liam M., Bradley John J and Amanda J. Kearney. 2016. Negotiating Yanyuwa Rock Art: Relational and Affectual Experiences in the Southwest Gulf of Carpentaria, Northern Australia. *Current Anthropology* 57(1):28–52.

Brady, Maggie. 1999. The Politics of Space and Mobility: Controlling the Ooldea/Yalata Aborigines, 1952–1982. *Aboriginal History* 23:1–14.

Brockwell, Sally, Gara Tom, Colley Sarah and Scott Cane. 1989. The History and Archaeology of Ooldea Soak and Mission. *Australian Archaeology* 28:55–78.

Buchler, Ira R. and Kenneth Maddock. eds. 1978. *The Rainbow Serpent: A Chromatic Piece*. The Hague: Mouton Publishers.

Cane, Scott. 1987. Australian Aboriginal Subsistence in the Western Desert. *Human Ecology* 15(4):391–434.

Caruana, Wally. 2011. History of the Canning Stock Route. In *Ngurra Kuju Walyja, One Country, One People: The Canning Stock Route Project 2006–2011*, edited by Monique LaFontaine and Elisha Buttler, 16–21. Perth: Form Publishing.

Elkin, A. Peter. 1930. The Rainbow-Serpent Myth in North-west Australia. *Oceania* 1(3):349–352.

Gould, Richard A. 1969. *Yiwara: Foragers of the Australian Desert*. London: Collins.

Harney, William E. 1960. Ritual Behaviour at Ayers Rock. *Oceania* 31(1):63–76.

Harney, William E. 1968. *The Significance of Ayers Rock for Aborigines*. Darwin: Northern Territory Reserves Board.

Hiscock, Peter and Val Attenbrow. 1998. Early Holocene Backed Artefacts from Australia. *Archaeology in Oceania* 33:49–62.

Hiscock, Peter and Lynley Wallis. 2005. Pleistocene Settlement of Deserts from an Australian Perspective. In *Desert Peoples: Archaeological Perspectives*, edited by Peter Veth, Mike A. Smith and Peter Hiscock, 34–57. Malden, MA: Blackwell Publishing.

Jones, Rhys. 1985. Ordering the Landscape. In *Seeing the First Australians*, edited by Ian Donaldson and Tamsin Donaldson, 181–209. Sydney: Allen and Unwin.

Jupp, Tony, Fitzsimons James, Carr Ben and Peter See. 2015. New Partnerships for Managing Large Desert Landscapes: Experiences from the *Martu Living Deserts Project*. *The Rangeland Journal* 37:571–582.

Kearney, Amanda, Bradley John and Liam M. Brady. 2019. Kincentric Ecology, Species Maintenance and the Relational Power of Place in Northern Australia. *Oceania* 89(3):316–335.

LaFontaine, Monique and Elisha Buttler. eds. 2008. *Ngurra Kuju Walyja, One Country, One People: The Canning Stock Route Project 2006–2011*. Perth: Form Publishing.

Langton, Marcia. 2006. Earth, Wind, Fire, Water: The Social and Spiritual Construction of Water in Aboriginal Societies. In *The Social Archaeology of Australian Indigenous Societies*, edited by Bruno David, Bryce Barker and Ian J. McNiven, 139–160. Canberra: Aboriginal Studies Press.

McConnel, Ursula. 1930. The Rainbow Serpent in North Queensland. *Oceania* 1(3):347–349.

Morphy, Howard. 2013. The art of the Yirrkala Crayon Drawings: Innovation, Creativity and Tradition. In *Yirrkala Drawings*, edited by Cara Pinchbeck, 27–33. Sydney: Art Gallery of New South Wales.

Morton, Steve, Martin Mandy, Mahood Kim and Jon Carty. 2013. *Desert Lake: Art, Science and Stories from Paruku*. Collingwood: CSIRO Publishing.

Mountford, Charles Pearcy. 1965. *Ayers Rock: Its People, their Beliefs and their Art*. Sydney: Angus and Robertson.

Munn, Nancy D. 1962. Walbiri Graphic Signs: An Analysis. *American Anthropologist* 64(5):972–984.

Munn, Nancy D. 1973. *Walbiri Iconography: Graphic Representation and Cultural Symbolism in a Central Australian Society*. Ithaca, NY: Cornell University Press.

Neale, Margo. ed. 2017 *Songlines: Tracking the Seven Sisters*. Canberra: National Museum of Australia Press.

Porter, Jenny. 2004. Blackfellow's Waterhole: A Study of Culture Contact. *The Artefact* 27:77–90.

Richards, Thomas. 2013. Early Holocene Aboriginal Occupation at Blackfellows Waterhole, Barrabool Flora and Fauna Reserve, South-West Victoria. *The Artefact* 36:32–38.

Ross, June and Leo Abbott. 2004 'These things take time': Central Australian Rock-art in Context. *Australian Aboriginal Studies* 2004(1):69–78.

Smith, Mike. 2013 *The Archaeology of Australia's Deserts*. Cambridge: Cambridge University Press.

Smith, Mike A. and June Ross. 2008. Glen Thirsty: The History and Archaeology of a Desert Well. *Australian Archaeology* 66:45–59.

Sullivan, Patrick, Boxer Hanson, Bujiman Warford and Doug Moor. 2012. The Kalpurtu Water Cycle: Bringing Life to the Desert of the South West Kimberley. In *Culture, Native Title and Ecology*, edited by Jessica Weir, 47–57. Canberra: ANU E-Press.

Taylor, Luke. 2005. Manifestations of the Mimih. In *The Power of Knowledge, the Resonance of Tradition*, edited by Luke Taylor, Graeme K. Ward, Graham Henderson, Richard Davis and Lynley Wallis, 182–198. Canberra: Aboriginal Studies Press.

Thomson, Donald F. 1962. The Bindibu Expedition: Exploration among the Desert Aborigines of Western Australia. *The Geographical Journal* 128(3):262–278.

Tindale, Norman. 1974. *Aboriginal Tribes of Australia*. Berkeley: University of California Press.

Toussaint, Sandy, Sullivan Patrick and Sarah Yu. 2005. Water Ways in Aboriginal Australia: An Interconnected Analysis. *Anthropological Forum* 15(1):61–74.

Veth, Peter. 1989. Islands in the Interior: A Model for the Colonisation of Australia's Arid Zone. *Archaeology in Oceania* 24:81–92.

Veth, Peter. 2005. Cycles of Aridity and Human Mobility: Risk Minimisation among Late Pleistocene Foragers of the Western Desert, Australia. In *Desert Peoples: Archaeological Perspectives*, edited by Peter Veth, Mike A. Smith and Peter Hiscock, 100–115. Malden, MA: Blackwell Publishing.

Veth, Peter. 2006. Social Dynamism in the Archaeology of the Western Desert. In *The Social Archaeology of Australian Indigenous Societies*, edited by Bruno David, Bryce Barker and Ian J. McNiven, 242–253. Canberra: Aboriginal Studies Press.

Veth, Peter, Williams Alan N. and Alistair Paterson. 2014. Australian Deserts: Extreme Environments in Archaeology. In *Encyclopedia of Global Archaeology*, edited by Claire Smith, 654–665. New York: Springer.

Yanyuwa people and John Bradley. 1988. *Yanyuwa Country: The Yanyuwa People of Borroloola Tell the History of their Land*. Richmond, VA: Greenhouse Publications Pty Ltd.

Yanyuwa Families and Bradley John J. 2016. *Wuka nya-nganunga li-Yanyuwa li-Anthawirrayarra: language for us, the Yanyuwa saltwater people (Vol. 1)*. Melbourne: Australian Scholarly Publishing.

Yanyuwa Families and Bradley John J. 2017. *Wuka nya-nganunga li-Yanyuwa li-Anthawirrayarra: language for us, the Yanyuwa saltwater people (Vol. 2)*. Melbourne: Australian Scholarly Publishing.

Yanyuwa Families, Bradley John J. and Nona Cameron. 2003. *Forget about Flinders: A Yanyuwa Atlas of the South West Gulf of Carpentaria*. Brisbane: J.M. McGregor Ltd.

8

INCA SHRINES

Deities in stone and water

Marco Curatola Petrocchi

Inca shrines of the fifteenth- through early sixteenth-centuries were sites where sacred beings dwelled, who communicated with people through an extra-human language. This "tongue" could only be understood by the priests in charge of their cults. Stone and water, the inseparable and animistic duo patterning every sanctuary, almost invariably were the essential and tangible elements of these sacred entities generically known as *huacas*. Each *huaca* featured a rock, a boulder or a crag (often with characteristically carved geometric motifs) and was associated with a spring, a fountain, a waterfall or a watercourse, which often was part of a sophisticated hydraulic system. Running water and its sound, which was believed to be the *huaca*'s "voice," was the perceived manifestation of stone's vitality and its sacred nature. The Incas were true masters in crafting stonework and managing water, and they built oracular shrines that had similar characteristics in many places of the heartland of their empire; this essay focuses on the shrines at Chuquipalta and Chuspiyoq.

The last Inca oracle: a huge white rock on top of a holy spring

Extending between the Urubamba and Apurímac Rivers to the northwest of Cuzco is the vast mountainous tropical forest region known as Vilcabamba. It was here that the last Inca kings and their retinues sought refuge after 1537, when the Spaniards secured their hold over the ancient imperial capital city. Manco Inca, the ruler who initially rose to power with the Spaniards' support, finally retreated in that year to the citadel of Vitcos. At more than 3,000 m above sea level, Vitcos was on a mountain spur that dominated the Vilcabamba River Valley. Manco Inca took with him there the relics and sacred items that the Incas most esteemed. These included the mummies of the Inca emperors Pachacuti, Tupa Yupanqui and Huayna Capac—his great-grandfather, his grandfather and his father (Titu Cusi Yupanqui, 2006 [1570]:122). He also brought the "Punchau," an anthropomorphic statuette depicting the young Sun god who was the supreme deity of the Inca Empire. The figure was originally kept in Cuzco's magnificent Temple of the Sun—the Coricancha. The hollowed core of the Punchau held a paste made out of gold dust and the ashes of hearts of deceased Inca kings (Julien, 2002). Associated with this remote shelter of Inca lords is Chuquipalta (or Chuquipalpa),[1] the last major Inca shrine.

The ruins of the sanctuary of Chuquipalta are linked to the Vitcos citadel by a path. The approximately 20-minute walk leads along a monumental complex of agricultural terraces that rise alongside a noisy and fast-flowing tributary stream of the Vilcabamba River known as Ñusta Hisp'ana (the Place where the Inca Princess pees). The exquisite architectural design of the terraces, which also include an elaborate hydraulic system with stone ducts and canals that are suggestive of waterfalls, shows that its execution was carefully planned. A big boulder stands out in the midst of the terrace complex. It boasts features characteristic of other sacred boulders: a finely carved wide bench and a small two-step stairway, that follows a pattern analogous to that found on other sacred stones like the "boulder shrine" at Chachabamba (Fejos, 1944:367, plate 35), the "carved stone with steps" at Saywite (Dean, 2010: plate 6) and the "ceremonial stone" in front of the so-called Watchman's Hut at Machu Picchu (Curatola Petrocchi, 2020, Figure 9.5). The sacred and ceremonial nature of the large rock in the Ñusta Hisp'ana terraces is also evinced by the remains of a niched wall that joins at one of its ends with a concavity in the boulder's base. There is another niche at the bottom of the cave that is associated with a spring and a small water canal. Hiram Bingham, the first researcher to locate and document the site, recorded local informants' reports that there was a spring close to the boulder (1912:84).

FIGURE 8.1   The sanctuary at Chuquipalta: the sacred rock called Yurac Rumi (at the back) and the fountain with double stream (forefront). Photograph by author.

FIGURE 8.2 The sacred rock at Chuspiyoq and the fountain and pond. Photograph by author.

It seems that the boulder conceptually replicates—albeit on a smaller scale and in a much simplified way—a much grander rock shrine some hundreds of meters up-hill, at a nook of the ravine. The giant white granite sculpted rock known as Yurac Rumi (White Rock), with dimensions of almost 21 m by 10 m and 8 m in height, lies at the center of the temple complex of Chuquipalta. The rock's main side, facing east, has a five-step stair motif carved in relief and a series of square protuberances, and the profile of its upper half looks like the shape of a hill. The White Rock's other sides and its upper section also have many perfectly carved seats, benches and shelves of different sizes and layouts.[2] At the southern side of the boulder's base, there is a natural concavity from which wells a spring. Another similarity between both sacred stones is that during the rainy season, a pool forms at their bases and in the contiguous areas. Yurac Rumi was surrounded by two sets of buildings that delimit two patios and by a plaza characterized by four small sculpted rocks. The ceremonial complex also comprises a canal that feeds an elegant, carefully carved stone fountain with a double spout (Bauer, Fonseca and Aráoz, 2015:44–58).

The Spanish chroniclers who mention the Chuquipalta sanctuary report that it was a Temple of the Sun (Murúa, 1987 [1590]:270)[3] and was attended by *acllas* (chosen ones) and *mamaconas* (mothers, older and higher-ranking *acllas*) (Ocampo, 2013 [1611]:31). They emphasize that it was oracular. The shrine was set on fire in 1570 by Augustinian missionaries Marcos García and Diego Ortiz (the latter was eventually killed by the Incas) (Bauer, 2012). Writing a history of the Augustinians in Peru and accessing testimonies his religious order had collected in 1595 to request the beatification of Ortiz, friar Antonio de la Calancha noted that "at Chuquipalpa place, close to Vitcos," there was a "house of the Sun" with a white rock above a spring of water worshipped "as a holy thing." He further recorded that a demon, who lived there, "gave answers and many times became visible" (Calancha, 1974–1982 [1638], V:1800 and 1827).[4] Summarizing Calancha's chronicle, another Augustinian friar, Bernardo de Torres, noted that this demon, "who answered the Indians at a white rock from which flowed a spring, near to the town of Vircos [Vitcos]," was called Paranti, i.e. "He-Who-Comes-with-Rain" (Calancha and Torres, 1972 [1653]:72).[5] Listing the major *huacas* (deities) worshipped by the Incas, the idolatry inspector Cristóbal de Albornoz states that on a mountain called "Uitcos [Vitcos] there was a sacred rock called 'Uiticos Guanacauri'" (Albornoz, 1984 [ca. 1585]:206). This is fully consistent with the testimony given by Titu Cusi Yupanqui, the son of Manco Inca and the third ruler of the Neo-Inca State of Vilcabamba. In his 1570 account, Tito Cusi listed Huanacauri as one of the images his ancestors kept at Vitcos (Titu Cusi Yupanqui, 2006 [1570]:122).[6] Huanacauri was identified with the homonymous high mountain near Cuzco. According to Inca narratives, standing at its summit after a long pilgrimage, Manco Capac, the mythical founder of the Inca dynasty, first saw the fertile valley where he would settle and found the city of Cuzco. This was the same spot where one of his brothers turned to stone and became the powerful oracle of Huanacauri. The latter was in fact the most important deity the Incas had prior to the rise of their empire, and it would later remain the specific tutelary deity of the Inca ethnic group (Szemiński, 1991). The young Inca nobles would go on pilgrimage to its shrine as part of the *huarachicuy*, the major initiation ritual that marked the passage to adulthood (Molina, 2008 [ca. 1576]:85–89).

To sum up, historical sources tell that the shrine of Chuquipalta was a Temple of the Sun, the main imperial god, whose "children" the Inca believed they were, and that Yurac Rumi, the huge sacred rock that distinguished the site and was its very center, was most likely identified with Huanacauri, the ancient tutelary deity of the lords of Cuzco. The shrine must have also housed the statuette of Punchau, the sacred figurine of the young Sun, which contained the remains of Inca rulers' hearts. From the final words of Tupa Amaru—the last Inca of Vilcabamba who was beheaded in Cuzco's main square in 1572—it can be inferred that this statue "spoke," and that Inca Titu Cusi Yupanqui frequently conferred with it (Salazar, 1867 [1596]:279).[7] The images of the past Inca kings must likewise have had a major role in the most solemn rituals performed at Chuquipalta, and were most likely placed on the granite bench right beside the Yurac Rumi. Everything seems to indicate that the Chuquipalta shrine was a true compendium of the religious cosmos of the last Incas, who tried to preserve and replicate in it the main elements of their system of beliefs, collective representations and ritual practices.

But why did the Inca choose precisely this site and what were the main, essential characteristics of the Chuquipalta shrine? The site appealed because of the rock—the Yurac Rumi—from whose base a well springs. The same elements are replicated in smaller dimensions at the boulder and water source on the lower terraces leading to the shrine. It can be inferred by analogy with the spatial organization and the functioning of other major Inca oracles (like those of Pachacamac, on the Peruvian coast, and Titicaca, on an island on the lake with the same name) that the rock with a bench and a small two-step stairway on the terraces was an "outer" representation/manifestation of the Yurac Rumi's god. This deity's alter-ego rock was visible from afar, and marked the point up to which faithful commoners and pilgrims could approach and the place where large numbers of Indians congregated during the state's major Sun festivals. Access to the shrine's oracular *sancta sanctorum*, i.e. to the Yurac Rumi, must have been limited to the Inca lords, priests and the *acllas* serving the temple.

The Cuzco *huacas*, deities in stone and water

For the Incas, much like for Andean peoples in general, the mineral world was not necessarily inanimate. Many outcrops, boulders and mountain peaks were believed to be powerful, extrahuman beings generically named *huacas*, who were able to communicate with human beings and exert a decisive influence over their life. These rocks usually had some striking features, because of their size, shape, landscape context or peculiar location. Their sacredness and significance were frequently emphasized with carefully carved and polished shelves, seats, benches, steps and other geometric motifs typical of, and symbolically relevant in, Inca art. These rocks were also almost invariably associated with a spring, a waterfall, a fountain or any other kind of streams of water, that were not accessory elements but instead absolutely essential in order to establish whether the rock was endowed with life, i.e. whether it had *camac* (the animating force) (Taylor, 2000:5) and was therefore a *huaca*. For the Inca in fact, a *huaca* was recognizable essentially in terms of its ability to "speak," so much so that if it became "mute," it had lost its power and its cult was abandoned (Castro and Ortega Morejón, 1974 [1558]:103); Álvarez, 1998 [1588]:74).[8] The *huaca*'s "speech" was a non-human language that consisted of sounds all could hear, but which only a few initiates—the deity's priests—could understand and thus translate into words for the faithful (Curatola Petrocchi, 2016). In this way, *huacas* were fully oracular deities, but were only deities (extrahuman entities endowed with life and power) insofar as they were able to speak. In general terms, in the Andean world, "sound" was—and still is among the most traditional communities—an expression of life itself. For instance, the herders of Macha in the Bolivian Plateau use the term *animu*—which apparently means the same as the ancient term *camac*—to indicate "the animating quality or essence of living things." For them, this applies not only to the animal kingdom, but also to natural phenomena like mountains and certain rocks, and as a generic term for all forms of sound (Stobart, 2007). For their part, the peasants of Huarochirí, in Peru's Central Highlands, describe the essence of their major traditional deity, Pariacaca—a high snow-capped mountain that sixteenth- and seventeenth-century sources claim was a powerful oracle in Inca times—as "a sound." "Pariacaca—they say—is the sound the water makes in the stream in winter. By listening to it, you can tell whether it will be a good year for crops" (Salomon and Niño-Murcia, 2011:232). The god of the high mountain manifests itself (and exists) in and through the sound of water that gushes forth and runs down the mountain.

In the valley of Cuzco, the imperial capital city and the sacred center of the world, there were hundreds of *huaca*-shrines that were believed to be arranged alongside 41 ideal lines (*ceques*) that spread outward radially from the Temple of the Sun. The *ceque* system, and the *huacas* laid out on it operated as a sophisticated ordering matrix by which the Incas regulated and matched the different planes of their political, economic, territorial and religious organizations; their geographical and astronomical knowledge; and their historical and cultural memories, in a grandiose operation of rationalizing and systematizing the social universe and its natural environment—probably without parallel in any other ancient civilization in history (Zuidema, 1995; Bauer, 1998). Employing a lost manuscript on the *ceque* system that was written about 1550 by Polo Ondegardo (a colonial official and expert in Indian affairs), the Jesuit Bernabé Cobo included a list of 328 *huacas* in his monumental *Historia del Nuevo Mundo* (1653).[9] The vast majority of the *huacas* are described in fairly general terms as rocks, mountains, springs and water sources, whilst the rest are sacred sites directly associated with the divine Inca kings and the mytho-historical events of their lives. Among the most important *huacas* of the Ondegardo-Cobo list are Huanacauri and the Coricancha itself (Bauer, 1998:23–24), which was the quintessential oracle of the Inca kings (Curatola Petrocchi, 2015:206–207). In the latter temple, there was a stone called Sabaraura (perhaps Sahuaraura), which was believed to be a metamorphosis of the chief of the *pururaucas*. The last ones were legendary warriors that the Sun god sent to Inca Pachacuti as help during his epic battle against the Chancas, which, according to Inca historical narratives, marked the beginning of Inca expansionism and of the formation of Tahuantinsuyu (the Inca empire) (Cobo, 1964 [1653], II:183[10]; MacCormack, 1991:288–289). This stone was the first *huaca* in the first *ceque* in the Cuntisuyu, one of the four sectors in which Cuzco and the entire empire were divided. From Cobo's concise description, it can be inferred that this sacred stone was located in the space delimited by the monumental curved wall that is still visible today on the outer side of the apse of the church of Santo Domingo (Gasparini and Margolies, 1977:240). The Sabaraura *huaca* was probably much like the rocky outcrops enclosed by the semi-circular walls of the Temple of the Sun (the Torreón) at Machu Picchu, and of the so-called Intihuatana at Pisac, in the sector bearing the same name. The chronicler Inca Garcilaso de la Vega (1991 [1609]:196, bk. III, chap. XXIII)[11] also states that there were five water fountains in the Coricancha. The only one that is preserved and still functional (thanks to a canal bearing water beneath the Temple) is in the terraces immediately below this curved wall (Hyslop, 1990:133, fig. 5.2). This is a fountain made out of finely carved and polished stones with a double stream, quite similar to that at Chuquipalta. Coricancha lies close to the confluence of the Huatanay and Tullumayo Rivers, and the temple as a whole seems to have had a sophisticated hydraulic system. The first to meticulously describe and record the remains of Coricancha in *Peru: Incidents of Travel and Exploration in the Land of the Incas* (1877) was the American archaeologist Ephraim George Squier who was well-versed in engineering (Barnhart, 2005:13–14). He noted that the temple's waterworks demonstrated the builders' very specific knowledge of fluid dynamics and communicating vessels (Squier 1877:442). Hence, the Coricancha had structures capable of giving out that gurgling noise or sound that was *the* quintessential and inherent attribute of Inca deities, and one of the basic elements of oracular rituals.

Some major sanctuaries in the Inca heartland: sacred outcrops and waterfalls

Of the various Inca monumental shrines where large sacred rocks are associated with water fountains, canals and cascades in the Cuzco region, the one in the sacred Intihuatana sector of Pisac is worth highlighting. The vast Inca archaeological site of Pisac is in the Vilcanota Valley, some 30 km to the northeast of the city of Cuzco. Its Intihuatana sector is characterized by the exquisite stonework of the structures, comparable to that of Coricancha, and the spectacular landscape that surrounds it. Near the aforementioned carved outcrop within a semi-circular wall (the site's *sancta sanctorum* and its *huaca*), there is an impressive stone fountain with two basins that are a few meters distant from each other and connected by a channel built with carefully hewn stones. This fountain, as well as other smaller ones lower down are fed by two water channels that meet at the entrance of the Intihuatana sector, that also includes a set of elegant terraces lying immediately below the sacred outcrop (Kaulicke et al., 2003:40, 45; Bray, 2013:172–174). Analogously, the main structures at the sacred core of the sanctuary of Tipón (more than 3500 m above sea level, in the Huatanay Valley, some 27 km to the southeast of Cuzco) were: (1) a jagged boulder atop a rocky spur that is fully stepped on all four sides, as if it was a small pyramid, and from whence the splendid terrace complex of the site is clearly visible and (2) a magnificent water fountain, which is located inside a restricted-access enclosure with niched walls, and fed by a water channel that goes over a long aqueduct (Wright, 2006:76). The same elements are present at the Quillarumiyoq shrine in the plain of Anta, some 50 km from Cuzco and at an altitude of over 3600 m. Here there is a spectacular fountain-waterfall at the foot of a gigantic rock, whose profile resembles that of a mountain. The waterfall was created between natural rocks, in front of which there is a ceremonial area delimited by niched walls of large stone blocks that have been particularly well crafted. A sacred place with analogous characteristics is found at the ancient Inca estate of Chinchero 30 km northwest of Cuzco. The site's most hidden sector is known as Chincana. The shrine there is dominated by a large rock with a sculpted staircase and shelves, and rectangular concavities and geometric carvings on the vertical sides. A waterfall on one side and a channel along the base of the rock produce engaging acoustic effects (Nair, 2015:48–54).

At the origins of the Inca empire: a speaking spring

Stone and water are also essential elements in an extraordinary *huaca* that lies at almost 3,700 m above sea level in the Chuspiyoq ravine, less than 3 km to the northeast of Coricancha. This *huaca* does not appear in the Cobo-Ondegardo list, but its location and shape suggest that in Inca sacred geography, it may have been the fountain of Susurpuquio. The foundation myths of Tahuantinsuyu tell that here the Sun god appeared before Inca Pachacuti and spoke to him through the water "from within the spring" to announce the future power and glory that awaited him and his people, and to request that they henceforth acknowledge and worship him as their main god (Molina, 2011 [ca. 1575]:17). The Chuspiyoq *huaca* is a huge rock with a large protuberance on its front-upper portion that faces southward, and an exquisite rectangular concavity on its frontal-lower part that evokes the shelter of Titicala, the sacred rock in the sanctuary of the island of Titicaca, or of the Sun, where, according to Inca mythology, the Sun first rose *in illo tempore* (Ramos Gavilán, 1988 [1621]:116 and 124).[12] The rock at Chuspiyoq is part of a sophisticated hydraulic system comprising water channels, a big fountain and other smaller ones, and an artificial pond formed with a stone dam some 210 m down the ravine. The sacred rock lies at the northernmost end of this former pond. If the site actually had a symbolic or formal correspondence with the Titicaca oracle, the pool may have been conceived as an equivalent of Lake Titicaca itself. In any case, it must have been envisaged as formed by water sprouting from the rock. The pond, in fact, lies at the *tinkuy* (meeting) of two stone channels. One of them runs in an east–southeast direction and passes along the rectangular concavity. The other sluice, whose water flow seems to have been controlled by some sort of fountain-gate, ran over the upper part of the rock to the west of a large ceremonial platform, and came down along its west–southwest side; its course is fully stepped and is flanked by a stairway also made completely of stone. The sluice comes to an end at a fountain that empties its waters in the pond close to the southernmost end of the rock, just at the same point where the other channel also discharges. It is possible that having the two channels run alongside the two sides of the rock, with their waters jointly discharging into the pond immediately in front of it, may have been to create the visual and symbolic image of water gushing forth from the base of the rock itself, much like the spring below the Yurac Rumi at Chuquipalta.

As at Chuquipalta and Coricancha, here also is a monumental fountain at the center of the pond's northernmost end and just a few meters away from Chuspiyoq's large rock. It was built with a huge white slab and finely worked stone blocks, and comprises an unusually large basin that empties directly into the pond. Immediately behind, to the north of the fountain and in front of a rectangular concavity in the Chuspiyoq rock is a courtyard with a large, also-rectangular, prismatic altar-like stone. The patio is bounded to the east and north by niched walls like those at other major Inca Sun cult sanctuaries. Behind the west, niched wall runs another water channel that likewise empties into the pond precisely in front of the discharge point of the two channels alongside the sacred rock. The latter has a long, deep and narrow fracture that partially separates it from an adjoining hill. The crevice is so narrow that only one person at a time can pass through. It is in fact practically invisible unless walking by its entrance. Its opening by the upper end of the stone staircase which flanks the channel on the west of the big rock does not seem to have been by chance. Rather, the stairway seems to have been built to accommodate someone who exited the crevice toward the pond, someone who had to appear as if out of nowhere in a perhaps dramatic ritual performance.

When viewed from the altar, what might otherwise appear to be just an odd, natural formation or erosion of the sacred rock at Chuspiyoq, looks like the upper part of an impressive human head in profile that points northward and is looking upward. The figure closely resembles some of the *huacas* with anthropomorphic heads drawn by the Indian chronicler Felipe Guaman Poma de Ayala (1980 [1615], I:235); Murúa, 2004 [1590]:96v.).[13] According to ancient and widespread Andean belief, particular rocks can be a metamorphic state of humans, and especially ancestors, whose traits can be observed in the stone by the attentive (Duviols, 1978; Dean, 2015:224). As Lisa Trever points out, in the Andes "seeing figures in stone *huacas* was, and remains, part of a process of visual imagination and active engagement between object and viewer" (2011:42). The site at Chuspiyoq where water "gushed" from the rock and formed an artificial pond, perhaps representing Lake Titicaca itself, may well have been the famed fountain of Susurpuquio. If that was the case, the Incas would have congregated there to evoke and relive that extraordinary founding moment in their history as chosen people, when the Sun god manifested himself to the Inca Pachacuti by speaking to him through a spring. If not, it was still an important *huaca* that they approached in order to listen to, and even meet, some stone being whose energy and powers could be perceived through the flow and sound of the water.

Notes

1 Chuquipalta perhaps means "overloaded with gold," or more likely "[stone] flattened with gold" (from *choqe*, gold, and *palta*, overload, or *p'alta*, "flat thing"). Chuquipalpa perhaps means "golden child" (from *choqe*, gold, and *phallpa*, "small boy").
2 The bench has a row of nine exquisitely carved cubic blocks, and the spaces between them form eight niches. They are aligned with the eastern side of the rock and oriented toward the rising sun. One end of the bench is 'inserted' inside the cavity at the base of the rock, much like the niched wall of the boulder on the terraces.
3 Murúa (1590, chap. LXXV).
4 Calancha (1638, bk. IV, chap. II, and bk. IV, chap. IV).
5 Calancha and Torres (1653, bk. V, chap. V).
6 This was written with the assistance of the aforementioned Marcos García and the mestizo scribe Martín Pando.
7 According to the 1596 account of Antonio Bautista de Salazar, the secretary of Viceroy Francisco de Toledo.
8 Álvarez (1588, chap. 133).
9 Cobo (1653, bk. XIII, chaps. XIII–XVI).
10 Cobo (1653, bk. XIII, chap. XVI).
11 Garcilaso de la Vega (1609, bk. III, chap. XXIII).
12 Ramos Gavilán (1621, chaps. XVII and XIX).
13 Guaman Poma (1615, I:262 [f. 264]; Murúa, 1590, n. 96v. [f. 90v]).

References

Albornoz, Cristóbal de. 1984 [ca. 1585]. Instrucción para descubrir todas las guacas del Pirú y sus camayos y haziendas, edited by Pierre Duviols. *Revista Andina* 3:194–222.
Álvarez, Bartolomé. 1998 [1588]. *De las costumbres y conversión de los Indios del Perú: Memorial a Felipe II*, edited by María del Carmen Martín Rubio, Juan J. R. Villarías Robles y Fermín del Pino Díaz. Madrid: Ediciones Polifemo.
Barnhart, Terry A. 2005. *Ephraim George Squier and the Development of American Anthropology.* Lincoln: University of Nebraska Press.
Bauer, Brian S. 1998. *The Sacred Landscape of the Inca. The Cusco Ceque System.* Austin: University of Texas Press.
Bauer, Brian S., Miriam Dayde Aráoz Silva and George S. Burr. 2012. The Destruction of the Yurac Rumi Shrine (Vilcabamba, Cusco Department). *Andean Past* 10:195–211.
Bauer, Brian S., Javier Fonseca Santa Cruz and Miriam Aráoz Silva. 2015. *Vilcabamba and the Archaeology of Inca Resistance.* Los Angeles: The Cotsen Institute of Archaeology at UCLA.

Bingham, Hiram. 1912. Vitcos, the Last Inca Capital. *Proceedings of the American Antiquarian Society* 22:135–196.

Bray, Tamara L. 2013. Water, Ritual, and Power in the Inca Empire. *Latin American Antiquity* 24(2):164–190.

Calancha, Antonio de la. 1974–1982 [1638]. *Corónica moralizada del orden de San Agustín en el Perú, con sucesos egemplares en esta monarquía*, edited by Ignacio Prado Pastor, 6 vols. Lima.

Calancha, Antonio de la and Bernardo de Torres. 1972 [1653]. Epitóme del Tomo I del P. Antonio de la Calancha (1639), reducido a compendio por el P. Bernardo de Torres (1653). In *Crónicas agustinianas del Perú*, 2 vols., edited by Manuel Merino, vol. I, 1–103. Madrid: Consejo Superior de Investigaciones Científicas.

Castro, Cristóbal de, y Diego de Ortega Morejón 1974 [1558]. La Relación de Chincha (1558), edited by Juan Carlos Crespo. *Historia y Cultura* (Lima) 8:91–104.

Cobo, Bernabé. 1964 [1653]. *Historia del Nuevo Mundo*. In *Obras del P. Bernabé Cobo*, vols. 1–2, edited by Francisco Mateos. Biblioteca de Autores Españoles, nos. 91–92. Madrid: Editorial Atlas.

Curatola Petrocchi, Marco. 2015. Oracles. In *Encyclopedia of the Incas*, edited by Gary Urton and Adriana von Hagen, 206–211. Lanham, MD: Rowman and Littlefield.

Curatola Petrocchi, Marco. 2016. La voz de la huaca. Acerca de la naturaleza oracular y el transfondo aural de la religión andina antigua. In *El Inca y la huaca. La religion del poder y el poder de la religión en el mundo andino antiguo*, edited by Marco Curatola Petrocchi and Jan Szemiński, 259–316. Lima: Fondo Editorial de la Pontificia Universidad Católica del Perú and The Hebrew University of Jerusalem.

Curatola Petrocchi, Marco. 2020. On the Threshold of the Huaca: Sanctuaries of Sound in the Ancient Andean World. In *Sacred Matter: Animacy and Authority in the Americas*, edited by Thomas B.F. Cummins, John W. Janusek and Steven Kosiba, 267–298. Washington, DC: Dumbartons Oaks.

Dean, Carolyn. 2010. *A Culture of Stone. Inka Perspectives on Rock*. Durham, NC: Duke University Press.

Dean, Carolyn. 2015. Men Who Would be Rocks. The Inka *Wank'a*. In *The Archaeology of Wak'as. Explorations of the Sacred in the Pre-Columbian Andes*, edited by Tamara L. Bray, 213–238. Boulder, CO: University Press of Colorado.

Duviols, Pierre. 1978. Un symbolisme andin du double: la lithomorphose de l'ancêtre. In *Actes du XVIIe Congres International des Américanistes. Congrés du Centenaire. París, 2–9 Septembre 1976*, vol. IV, 359–364. Paris: Société des Américanistes.

Fejos, Paul. 1944. *Archaeological Explorations in the Cordillera Vilcabamba, Southeastern Peru*. New York: Viking Fund Publications in Anthropology 3.

Garcilaso de la Vega, Inca. 1991 [1609]. *Comentarios reales de los Incas*, edited by Carlos Araníbar, 2 vols. Lima: Fondo de Cultura Económica.

Gasparini, Graziano and Luise Margolies. 1977. *Arquitectura inka*. Caracas: Centro de Investigaciones Históricas y Estéticas, Facultad de Arquitectura y Urbanismo, Universidad Central de Venezuela.

Guaman Poma de Ayala, Felipe. 1980 [1615]. *El primer nueva corónica y buen gobierno*, edited by John V. Murra and Rolena Adorno, 3 vols. Mexico City: Siglo Veintiuno.

Hyslop, John. 1990. *Inka Settlement Planning*. Austin: University of Texas Press.

Julien, Catherine. 2002. Punchao en España. In *El hombre y los Andes. Homenaje a Franklin Pease G.Y.*, edited by Javier Flores Espinoza and Rafael Varón Gabai, 709–715. Lima: Institut Francais d' Études Andines and Pontificia Universidad Católica del Perú.

Kaulicke, Peter, Ryujiro Kondo, Tetsuya Kusuda and Juliño Zapata. 2003. Agua, ancestros y arqueología del paisaje. *Boletín de Arqueología PUCP* 7:27–56.

MacCormack, Sabine. 1991. *Religion in the Andes. Vision and Imagination in Early Colonial Peru*. Princeton, NJ: Princeton University Press.

Molina, Cristóbal de. 2011 [ca. 1575]. *Account of the Fables and Rites of the Incas*, edited by Brian S. Bauer, Vania Smith-Oka and Gabriel E. Cantarutti. Austin: University of Texas Press.

Murúa, Martín de. 1987 [1590]. *Historia general del Perú*, edited by Manuel Ballesteros. Madrid: Historia 16.

Murúa, Martín de. 2004 [1590]. *Historia y genealogía real de los reyes ingas del Piru*. Madrid: Testimonio.

Nair, Stella. 2015. *At Home with the Sapa Inca. Architecture, Space, and Legacy at Chinchero*. Austin: University of Texas Press.

Ocampo Conejeros, Baltasar de. 2013 [1611]. Descripción de la Provincia de San Francisco de la Victoria de Vilcabamba. In *Baltasar de Ocampo Conejeros y la Provincia de Vilcabamba*, edited by Brian S. Bauer and Madeleine Halac-Higashimori, 19–56. Cusco: Ceques Editores.

Ramos Gavilán, Alonso. 1988 [1621]. *Historia del Santuario de Nuestra Señora de Copacabana*, edited by Ignacio Prado Pastor. Lima: Ignacio Prado.

Salazar, Antonio Bautista de. 1867 [1596]. Relación sobre el periodo de gobierno de los Virreyes Don Francisco de Toledo y Don García Hurtado de Mendoza. In *Colección de documentos inéditos relativos al descubrimiento, conquista y organización de las antiguas posesiones españolas de América y Oceania sacados de los archivos del Reino, y muy especialmente del de Indias*, edited by Luis Torres de Mendoza, 212–293. Madrid: Imprenta de Frías y Compañía.

Salomon, Frank and Mercedes Niño-Murcia. 2011. *The Lettered Mountain. A Peruvian Village's Way with Writing*. Durham, NC and London: Duke University Press.

Squier, E. George. 1877. *Peru: Incidents of Travel and Exploration in the Land of the Incas*. New York: Harper and Brothers.

Stobart, Henry. 2007. Ringing Rocks and Roosters. Communicating with the Landscape in the Bolivian Andes. *Proceedings of the Conference "Sound and Anthropology: Body, Environment and Human Sound Making,"* University of St. Andrews. www.st-andrews.ac.uk/soundanth/work/stobart/

Szemiński, Jan. 1991. Wana Kawri waka. In *El culto estatal del Imperio Inca*, edited by Mariusz S. Ziólkowski, 35–53. Varsovia: Centro de Estudios Latinoamericanos, Universidad de Varsovia.

Taylor, Gerald. 2000. *Camac, camay y camasca y otros ensayos sobre Huarochirí y Yauyos*. Lima: Institut Francais d'Études Andines.

Titu Cusi Yupanqui, Diego de Castro. 2006 [1570]. *History of How the Spaniards Arrived in Peru*, edited by Catherine Julien. Indianapolis/Cambridge, MA: Hackett Publishing Company, Inc.

Trever, Lisa. 2011. Idols, Mountains, and Metaphysics in Guaman Poma's Pictures of Huacas. *RES: Anthropology and Aesthetics* 59/60 (spring/autumn):39–59.

Wright, Kenneth R., with Gordon McEwan and Ruth M. Wright. 2006. *Tipon: Water Engineering Masterpiece of the Inca Empire*. Reston, VA: American Society of Civil Engineers.

Zuidema, R. Tom. 1995. *El sistema de ceques del Cuzco. La organización social de la capital de los Incas*. Lima: Fondo Editorial de la Pontificia Universidad Católica del Perú.

9

DRAGON WELLS AND SACRED SPRINGS IN CHINA

Jean DeBernardi, Yan Jie and Ma Junhong

In China, local historians have long described spring waters as divine or immortal waters (*shenshui* or *xianshui*, 神水or 仙水). Daoists used them to concoct elixirs of immortality, and Buddhists venerated the Dragon King of sacred wells and springs in their temples. In both cities and villages, people surrounded sacred pools and wells with gardens, pavilions and temples. After the Communist Party came to power in 1949, local officials discouraged the collection of sacred spring waters as "feudal superstitious activity" (Smith, 2006:1000). Today, however, spring-fed wells are found in restored temples and monasteries, and at tourist sites like Hangzhou's Running Tiger Spring and Dragon Well Village. At these sites, museum displays and open air signboards report folktales and local beliefs about the spiritual efficacy of spring water. Museum curators pair these narratives with displays explaining the special qualities of the water in light of geology and the water's chemical composition. This essay investigates the history, modern restoration, and use of some of China's many sacred springs and wells.[1]

Venerating the Dragon King

As early as three to five thousand years ago, the Chinese widely used wells to capture groundwater, allowing them to move away from riversides and settle anywhere that they could find a dependable water supply. When they moved to a new location, they built wells before anything else. Villagers used well water both for daily life and for irrigation, but the well was also a holy place where residents venerated the God of Water, typically represented as a dragon. People built decorated architectural structures above and around wells, which became village centers (Voudouris et al., 2018:10–12).

In a scholarly study of "famous springs and famous water," Zhan Luojiu provides details on 763 famous springs throughout China. The book's 44-page list of springs reveals that many names include terms that indicate their sacred powers (Zhan, 2003:139–183). Spring names include terms meaning spiritually efficacious (*ling*, 靈), immortal *(xian*, 仙), god *(shen*, 神), saint (*sheng* 聖 or *shengren* 聖人) and heaven (*tian*, 天).

Some are named for deities, including the God of Thunder (*Leigong*, 雷公) and the Goddess of Mercy (*Guanyin*, 觀音), who is often represented in paintings and porcelain statues holding a vase from which heavenly dew flows. Many names identify the springs with dragons, including a Dragon King Spring, and springs named for white, yellow, red, black or jade dragons (*long*, 龍). Some springs are given names that suggest the aesthetic qualities of the water, including gold, jade, incense, liquor and sweetness. One spring is identified as the "Serve the Nation Spiritually Efficacious Spring" (*Baoguo Lingquan*, 保國 靈泉) which suggests an attempt to accommodate and blend modern socialist and traditional values.

Practitioners of Chinese popular religion classify the cosmos into three realms: Heaven, Earth and Water. Water's rulers are dragons, imagined as living in the sea, rivers, lakes, springs and wells. The Chinese associated a water deity with the dragon by at least the Tang Dynasty (619–907), and Dragon Gods have been widely enshrined in village temples and Buddhist or Daoist monasteries since the Ming Dynasty (1368–1644) (Zhang, 2012). People prayed to the Dragon Kings of the four seas for rain, but the Dragon Kings also serve as territorial protectors, similar to the local deities known as Earth Gods (*Tudigong*, 土地公).[2]

Communities often built temples to the Dragon King near wells and spring-fed pools, and anthropologist Adam Chau provides us with a case study of the sixteenth-century construction and twentieth-century restoration of one such temple. When Shaanxi villagers rebuilt the Black Dragon King (*Heilong Dawang*, 黑龍大王) Temple in 1982, a local cultural worker composed a history that was engraved on a stone stele and installed on the new temple's wall. According to this text, the original temple had been built in the Ming Dynasty during the reign of the Zhengde Emperor (1505–1521) in Dragon King Valley, a secluded valley that the Dragon God had chosen for his dwelling place. The valley had nine pools, and "springs that flow and jump." To the northeast of this valley was a spring mouth called the Sea's Eye (*Haiyan*, 海眼) from which an inexhaustible thread of spring water dripped year round, resembling "a dragon spitting out a string of pearls" (Chau, 2006:93). The villagers built a temple dedicated to the Black Dragon King in the hills above the nine spring-fed pools. Over the years, the Dragon God proved his spiritual powers, providing timely rain for crops and for healing. The stele recorded that after the "violent calamity" of the temple's destruction in 1966 during the Cultural Revolution, "the god left and the water dried up" (ibid:94).

Sacred springs and wells: Daoism

Today, sacred wells are commonly found in Buddhist and Daoist temples and monasteries. Among the most impressive are wells in the courtyards of ancient temples and palaces at the Daoist temple complex at Wudang Mountain in Hubei Province. In 1994, UNESCO inscribed Wudang's temples in the list of World Heritage—temples built in valleys, on mountain peaks and slopes and on cliff edges. At one of the main temples, the Zixiao Palace (*Zixiaogong*, 紫霄宮), the ritual to invite the gods to descend to the altar begins by inviting the Dragon God Grandfather to provide blessed water (*fushui*, 福水). Although the ritual practitioners draw water from the temple's well, they imagine it as "sweet dew" falling from heaven.

FIGURE 9.1 (L): The Well of Sweet Dew, at the South Cliff Temple, Wudang Mountain, Hubei Province. Photograph by Jean De-Bernardi; (C): Dragon Spring Well, Jingshan Temple, Zhejiang Province. Photograph by Lyu Weigang with permission; (R) Dragon Well, Hangzhou, Zhejiang Province. Photograph by Jean DeBernardi.

At the Mysterious Emperor Palace (*Xuandi Dian*, 玄帝殿) at the Southern Cliff Temple, a large well identified as the Well of Sweet Dew (*Ganlu Jing*, 甘露井) stands in the front courtyard (Figure 9.1 [L]). Wudang Mountain is a UNESCO World Heritage Site, and a bilingual display in Chinese and English explains the ancient meaning of "sweet dew":

> The water in the well is so sweet that in antiquity it was named the Well of Sweet Dew. Chinese believed that dew, falling from the sky, was sweeter than water. The *Shanhaijing* (*The Book of Mountains and Seas*) recorded that the sweet dew, coming from Heaven above, had the spiritual efficacy (*lingqi*) of heaven and earth, and the essence (*jinghua*) of the sun and the moon, and that the person who drank it would have a long life or even become an immortal. It is said that this is the very water that Zhenwu [the Perfected Warrior, Wudang Mountain's patron deity] drank when he practiced fasting in his religious meditation. Since then the water in this well has been regarded as nectar and holy water. Daoism believers often draw water from the well and bring it to their family members and friends in hope that it will manifest spiritual efficacy (*lingyan*) and good luck (*jixiang*).

The author of this display describes the water as having *lingqi* (靈氣) and being *lingyan* (靈驗). *Ling* means both divine and efficacious, and *qi* means energy, referring to the water's exceptional cosmic properties. *Yan* means fulfill; thus, *lingyan* may be translated as spiritually efficacious.

This modern explication of "sweet dew" cites *The Classic of Mountains and Seas*, a mythical geography of China that reached its present form in the early Han Dynasty (c. 206 BCE). According to this classic text, the Divine Wind sent down sweet dew to the people, and on drinking it, all their wishes came true (Birrell, 1999:116). This mythical geography also reported that in the Country of Watering, people ate the eggs of a divine bird and drank sweet dew, and that each had whatever flavor they wished it to have (ibid:174).

Daoist adepts made use of spring water in their spiritual quests. According to a Ming Dynasty book compiled in 1554 by Tian Yiheng (a resident of Hangzhou), Daoists who sought the secret of eternal life favored rare springs, believing that drinking their waters could promote health and prolong life. The spring waters tasted sweet, and the author described different springs as having unique scents and flavors that he compared to jade, stone stalactites, cinnabar and mica (Zheng and Zhu, 2007:199). Daoist adepts drank spring water in their quest for longevity and immortality; today, devotees still prize water from Wudang Mountain's Well of Sweet Dew for its curative properties.

Sacred springs and wells: Buddhism

The Dragon God (or Dragon King) is not an orthodox Buddhist deity, but Chinese Buddhists regarded this deity as a Buddhist protector and believed him to control rain and water in their region. Buddhists incorporated sacred springs and wells into their monasteries and temples, and built shrines for dragon spirits.

Foundation accounts of famous Buddhist temples often begin with a virtuous monk miraculously producing a spring or rain, sometimes by influencing a dragon spirit to help him. For example, *The Biographies of Eminent Monks* (*Gaoseng Zhuan*) recorded that Master Huiyuan (334–416), the founder of Pure Land Buddhism, settled in Lushan in what is now northern Jiangxi Province. Lushan lacked water, but after he tapped the earth with his Buddhist walking stick, a spring gushed out and became a stream. The biography also reported that during a drought, Huiyuan recited *The Sutra of the Sea-Dragon King* by a pond. A giant snake emerged from the pond and flew to the sky, and a downpour soon followed. After this miracle, Master Huiyuan named his temple the Dragon Spring Temple.[3] Another biographical account reported that during the Qi Dynasty (479–502), Master Tanchao preached in a Buddhist temple in Hangzhou, and the Dragon God attended the sermon. As soon as the Dragon God clapped his hands, a spring came out. The temple was renamed the Jade Spring temple, and the spring was called Clapping Hands Spring (*Fuzhang Quan*).[4]

Today, the monks at the Buddhist Jingshan Temple in Hangzhou, Zhejiang Province, believe that the Dragon King donated his territory to the temple's founder during the Tang Dynasty (618–907). According to the collected historical records of Jingshan Temple, in 754, Master Faqin went to Jingshan, which is the northeastern peak of Tianmu Mountain. When he first arrived, he found that animals and birds of prey did not come near, and that the villagers had stopped fishing and hunting on Jingshan. A hunter tried to persuade the master to leave, explaining that a dragon lived on the mountain, but the master was not worried. One day, the dragon, who lived in a big pond, transformed into an old man to speak with the master. He told him: "I will give you this place as the Heavenly Eye Mountain (*Tianmu Shan*, 天目山)." After a stormy night, the dragon's pond became land, but a dragon well remained that still exists today (*Jingshanzhi* 2011:66, 690, 717, 1004). Both this story and that of Clapping Hands Spring suggest that the eminent masters' power and their good moral qualities deeply impressed the Dragon King, who was willing to serve the Buddhists.

Historically, the water from the Jingshan Dragon Well was believed to have miraculous healing properties. When a friend sent Su Shi (Su Dongpo, 1037–1101), a famous poet and scholar in the Northern Song Dynasty (960–1127), a bottle of Jingshan Dragon Well spring water as a gift, Su Shi replied with a poem, reporting that after he washed his eyes with this water, they were healed (Song, 2011:891). Some people still believe that water from sacred springs and ponds can cure eye ailments.

Today, the Jingshan Temple complex includes a shrine to the Dragon King and a Dragon Spring (*long quan*, 龍泉). According to local people, the spring that feeds the Jingshan Temple's Dragon Spring Well has never ceased flowing. Today, it is the primary source of the monks' potable water and they use it for making tea, even though it would be easier to use tap water. A locked gate protects the well, but its water is pumped into a courtyard for collection. Lay Buddhists and some tourists come to the well to get water to take home not only because of its good taste, but also because of its reputation for promoting health. Visitors who drive a long distance to fetch the water home share the same confidence in the Dragon King and the spring water's healing powers as Su Shi and his friend had almost a thousand years ago (Figure 9.1 [C]).

The Dragon King also controls the rain, and for that reason, the current abbot always opens outdoor events by thanking this deity. In a 2016 speech, he explained: "There are two efficacious Bodhisattvas in the Jingshan Temple. One is Wei Tuo Bodhisattva, who has been protecting Buddhism and Jingshan for thousands of years. The other is the Dragon King." The weather on top of the mountain changes quickly, but the abbot and monks are confident that the Dragon King will always provide clear skies for their outdoor gatherings.

Hangzhou: Running Tiger Spring and Dragon Well Village

Jingshan Temple is not far from the city of Hangzhou, which is the capital of Zhejiang Province. Hangzhou is the site of many famous wells and springs and also a famed tea-growing area. Hangzhou is a popular destination for domestic and international tourists, and in 2011, the West Lake Cultural Landscape of Hangzhou was inscribed in the UNESCO World Heritage List (Barmé, 2011).

During the Qing Dynasty (1644–1912), the Kangxi Emperor (who reigned from 1661 to 1722) visited Hangzhou five times, and named "Ten Scenic Spots of West Lake." His calligraphy was inscribed onto stelae at these locations, and elegant pavilions were built on the sites. His grandson, the Qianlong Emperor (who ruled from 1735 to 1796), also visited Hangzhou and erected stelae to celebrate "Scenic Spots of Dragon Well." The city government revived the practice of identifying scenic spots and adding architectural structures in 1985–1986 when they developed Ten New Scenes of West Lake (Barmé, 2011). Among these is the Hupao Spring, which became the focal feature of a park.[5]

The Running Tiger Spring (*Hupao Quan*, 虎跑泉) was once attached to a Buddhist temple complex, and the park still includes shrines to Jigong and Guanyin. According to Buddhist sources, tigers revealed the spring to a Buddhist monk (see Qian, 1990:3695). As visitor displays explain:

> A beautiful legend is related to the origin of Hupao Spring. In 819 (the 14th year of Yuanhe in the Tang Dynasty), a famous monk named Huanzhong (also named as Xingkong) came here and admired the wonderful landscape, but he was troubled by the lack of a water source nearby. Planning to set off, he was told by an immortal in a dream that two tigers would be dispatched to relocate Tongzi Spring of Nanyue Mountain to this spot. The next day he really saw two tigers digging the ground into a pit, where crystal clear spring water gushed out. The spring was thus named as Hupao Spring.

A modern sculpture of a tiger is associated with the original Hupao Spring, and another pool of water is the setting for a stone sculpture of the dreaming monk and the two tigers (Figure 9.2 [L]). At the same time, government-sponsored displays at springs formerly regarded as sacred note that these waters often have a special chemical composition, including high levels of minerals and radium as the consequence of seeping through rocks.

FIGURE 9.2 (L): Rock carving of the dreaming monk and the tigers by a pond at Hupao Springs, Hangzhou, Zhejiang Province. Photograph by Jean DeBernardi; (R) Eternal Life Spring, roadside collection site, Wuyi Mountain, Fujian Province. Photograph by Jean DeBernardi.

Only a few kilometers away from Hupao Springs is Longjing Village (Dragon Well Village) in a famed tea-growing area on the west side of Hangzhou's West Lake. Longjing tea is often referenced by the literal translation "Dragon Well tea." A variety of pan-roasted green tea, Longjing tea was given as a form of tribute to the Emperor during the Qing Dynasty, and is today one of China's premium teas. The tea and the village that produces it both take their name from a local Dragon Well. When the Hangzhou government added six additional scenic areas in 2005, they developed the Dragon Well tea-growing area into a park called "Enjoying Tea at Dragon Well" (龍井文茶, *Longjing Wen Cha*). The planners sought to "restore the old as the old," demolishing unapproved buildings and renovating building facades in the new scenic area.[6]

The park features a Dragon Well as a scenic destination (Figure 9.1 [R]). Site interpretation explains that in ancient times, people visited the well to pray for rain, believing that its waters were connected with those of the Eastern Sea where dragons lived. A Buddhist temple was built near an old well and, in 1438, relocated near the current Dragon Well. In the eighteenth century, the Emperor Qianlong visited the temple on multiple occasions to enjoy the scenery and the local tea. A postcard of the Dragon Well from the 1930s shows a simple structure and roof protecting the well, which is situated in an open grassy field. The site's redevelopment employed traditional open-sided wooden pavilions with tiled roofs in a garden setting. A stone gate identifies the entrance to the scenic area, and paths lead the visitor to the Dragon Well and Shenyun (Spiritual Harmony) Rock where historically villagers struck a sacred stone as a prayer to the Dragon God for rain. As with Running Tiger Spring, the spring water has multiple outlets including ponds, a well and a small square pool of water.

Sacred springs and wells: water connoisseurs

Buddhist monks established their monasteries in locations where spring water was found, and prayed to the Dragon King for protection. They also cultivated tea at their mountain monasteries and used it to stay alert while meditating, but also as a medicine or tonic (Benn, 2015:66–67). Just as the monks and abbots at the Jingshan Temple do today, they brewed tea with water drawn from sacred springs and dragon wells. Modern tea experts and practitioners of tea arts trace the history of Chinese tea culture to the so-called tea sage, Lu Yu (733–804), author of the *Classic of Tea* (written c. 760 CE). Lu Yu was an orphan raised in a Buddhist temple where he learned tea-drinking practices from the monk who had adopted him. Lu Yu left the temple and was patronized by a Confucian scholar, learning to read and write elegant prose. Through publication of *The Classic of Tea*, he introduced Buddhist tea-drinking practices to the wider society. Water was an important focus for the book, and he advised his readers that the best water for tea-brewing came from slow-flowing mountain springs and stone-lined pools (Lu, 1974:105). During the Ming Dynasty (1368–1644), authors continued to rank waters, including water drawn from sacred springs (Benn, 2015:184–197).

For centuries, the Imperial Court both received fine teas as "tribute tea" (貢茶, *gongcha)* and celebrated the famous spring waters used to brew them. Much as he did when he named scenic spots in Hangzhou, the Qianlong emperor visited China's famous springs and gave them honorary titles. These rankings have persisted. He declared the Baotu Spring in Jinan, Shandong province to be the Number One Spring under Heaven, and Jinan continues to be both a tourist destination and a major source of artesian spring water. Wuxi's "Second Best Spring in the World" (*Tianxia Dierquan*) is also a tourist site, but modern connoisseurs no longer rate its water as highly as the Qianlong Emperor did (Wang, 2015:41–42). Contemporary connoisseurs know the *Classic of Tea* and, like Lu Yu, prize spring water for brewing though they may not regard it as sacred. Some take tea leaves and elegant tea ware to the mountains in search of free-flowing spring water with which to brew tea. Modern tourist sites and Buddhist temples also offer visitors the opportunity to experience the pairing of fine tea and what tea experts describe as vital "living water" (*huo shui*, 活水) (Wang, 2015:41).

Conclusion

The Communist Party still discourages the so-called feudal superstitions, but since the end of the Cultural Revolution, spring water has been proven by science to have demonstrable health benefits. Even when tap water is available, many Chinese prefer to use well or spring water for drinking and cooking hoping to enhance their health and longevity. China has many famous springs that have long been recognized for their pure, inexhaustible waters, some of which have been developed as tourist destinations. But today, China's leaders also support the development of sites where people can collect spring waters for their personal use. Near Wuyi Star Village in north Fujian, for example, a local politician created a small well to collect spring water, directing it into a roadside pipe to make collection easy. A stone stele announced that this site was the "Eternal Life Spring" (永生泉, *Yong Sheng Quan*).[7] (Fig. 9.2 [R])

In 2016, the Hangzhou government opened a site at the Running Tiger Spring where the local people may now draw water. The site displays a life-sized bronze statue of a horse-drawn water cart. People wait beside this statue, for as long as an hour or two, to take their turn to fill plastic jugs with spring water for home use.

Because many are concerned about water safety, China is now the world's largest market for bottled water. But water falling from heaven and emerging from the earth can still be captured for free. Those who doubt its sacredness still value well and spring water for its purity and flavor, and drink it seeking to enhance their health and longevity. Meanwhile, despite secularization and the transformation of sacred sites to tourist destinations, Daoists still pray with water drawn from sacred wells, and Buddhists venerate the Dragon King in their temples.

Notes

1 We conducted ethnographic research in Zhejiang and Fujian Provinces with support from the Social Science and Humanities Research Council of Canada. Thanks are due to Yuhang local historian Mr. Lyu Weigang (吕偉剛) for help with illustrations of the Jingshan Temple's Dragon Spring and Hangzhou's Dragon Well, and Mr. Yu Jian'an (俞建安), the Director of the UNESCO World Cultural Heritage Inspection Center for his help at Wuyishan.
2 The Dragon King, who is sometimes known as Guangze, was also venerated as an earth god (Nikaido, 2015:55).

3 CBETA 2018, T50, no. 2059, 358a:21–28.
4 CBETA, B29, no. 161, 573a:6–8.
5 The Running Tiger Spring area has multiple springs, the largest being Hupao, Erfen and Zhenzhu (Pearl).
6 The government funded infrastructure development, while the villagers were responsible for the renovation of their own residences.
7 Mr. Yu explained that the auspicious name was based on the name of the village leader who developed the spring water collection site.

References

Barmé, Geremie R. 2011. A Chronology of West Lake and Hangzhou. *China Heritage Quarterly* 28:1–9.

Benn, James. 2015. *Tea in China: A Religious and Cultural History.* Honolulu: University of Hawai'i Press.

Birrell, Anne. 1999. *The Classic of Mountains and Seas (Shanhai Jing).* London: Penguin Books. CBETA [Chinese Electronic Tripitaka Collection]. (Version 2018).

Chau, Adam Yuet. 2006. *Miraculous Response: Doing Popular Religion in Contemporary China.* Stanford, CA: Stanford University Press.

Lu Yü [Lu Yu]. 1974. *The Classic of Tea.* Translated by Francis Ross Carpenter. Boston, MA and Toronto: Little Brown and Co.

Nikaido, Yoshihiro. 2015. *Asian Folk Religion and Cultural Interaction.* Taipei: National Taiwan University Press.

Qian, Shuoyou. 1990. *Xianchun Linan Zhi. (Historical Annals of Xianchun and Lin'an)* Beijing: Zhonghua Book Company.

Smith, Steve A. 2006. Local Cadres Confront the Supernatural: The Politics of Holy Water (*Shenshui*) in the PRC, 1949–1966. *The China Quarterly* 188:999–1022.

Song, Kuiguang, ed. 2011. *Jingshan zhi (The History of Jingshan).* Hangzhou: Zhejiang Ancient Books Publishing House.

Voudouris, Konstantinos, Mohammad Valipour, Asimina Kaiafa, Xiao Yu Zheng, Rohitashw Kumar, Katharina Zanier, Elpida Kolokytha and Andreas Angelakis. 2018. Evolution of Water Wells Focusing on Balkan and Asian Civilizations. *Water Science and Technology* 20 June 2018. doi:10.2166/ws.2018.114. Consulted 16 November 2018.

Wang, Kai. 2015. *Yuantou Huoshui: Haoshui yu Haochade Peihe* (The Source of Living Water: The Pairing of Good Water and Good Tea). *Shenghuo (Life)* No. 835:40–47.

Zhan, Luojiu. 2003. *Mingquan Mingshui Pao Haocha (Famous Springs and Famous Water make Good Tea).* Beijing: Zhongguo Nongye Chupanshe.

Zhang, Peifeng. 2012. Zhongguo Longwang Xinyang Yu Fojiao Guanxi Yanjiu (The Study of the Relationship between Dragon King Belief in China and Buddhism). *Literature and Culture Studies* 3:4–11.

Zheng, Peikai and Zizhen Zhu. 2007. *Zhongguo Lidai Chashu Huibian Jiaozhuben (The Annotated Collection of China's Historical Tea Books).* Hongkong: The Commercial Press.

10

SACRED SPRINGS OF THE TEWA PUEBLOS, NEW MEXICO

Richard I. Ford

The Pueblo Indian villages at Hopi, Arizona and Zuni, New Mexico are noted for their sacred springs where divinities reside, and many religious ceremonies are conducted (Hough, 1909; Wittfogel and Goldfrank, 1943). The ritual importance of these and other springs in their homeland is acknowledged by the care given to walls that keep them from being desecrated with windblown sand and trash, and the ceremonial offerings of small vases, prayer sticks, and stone and shell beads made to the deities of the water (Hough, 1909:169). Elsewhere, the six extant Tewa Pueblos of northern New Mexico are not known for their springs, but the ones they have are important to define their sacred landscapes. All their springs are interconnected by flowing water and allow messenger beings, e.g. Awenyu (horned serpents), other weather controlling spirits, and especially the deceased village ceremonial leaders, to accept the living peoples' offerings and prayers to benefit their agriculture, reproduction and general well-being. This essay will explain the significance of these sacred springs and their relationship to the social and religious organization of the Tewa people.

The Tewa speak six mutually intelligible languages of the Tanoan family. Today's Rio Grande Tewa share a common origin in southern Colorado. The currently occupied pueblos in the upper Rio Grande basin are Ohkay Owingeh, Santa Clara, San Ildefonso, Nambe, Pojoaque and Tesuque. They are all recognized as the Northern Tewa. However, until the Pueblo Revolt in 1680, there was a southern division in the Galisteo Basin south of Santa Fe. Some of those people were invited to migrate to First Mesa at Hopi as guardians against Ute and Navajo enemies on the Hopi's eastern front where their descendants reside today. Several other Tewa villages disappeared following the Revolt and their members joined other Tewa villages, other tribes, or never returned. Tewa archaeological sites are especially noted for their construction close to springs. For example, one of the most-studied archaeological sites in the American Southwest is Arroyo Hondo where the antiquity of the preeminent spring's veneration is indicated by the presence of broken pottery sherds (Ford and Shapiro, 2017). Among the Eastern Tewa, pueblos were situated by a stream that originated on a sacred mountain and was therefore perceived as bringing blessings to the village.

Origins

According to the Tewa Origin Legend, the world has three levels. The uppermost level contains the vital forces that control weather phenomena: thunder, lightning, rainbows, forms of precipitation and clouds. It is the abode of the Sun, Moon, Stars and other celestial beings. The second level is the surface of the earth. Here reside the animals, plants, people, helpful spirits and nefarious beings who also rose from the underworld at the time of Tewa emergence. Here also are the four sacred mountains and four associated lakes, caves considered sacred portals, hills which can be deified, and landscape beings. This second level, of course, also hosts the human-built environment ranging from villages, kivas (subterranean rooms for ritual and political gatherings) and shrines, to fields and agricultural features.

The lowest level is the dark underworld. The Tewa resided here under water with wild animals and their two Corn Mothers, White Corn Maiden (associated with winter) and Blue Corn Maiden (associated with summer). The Tewa were living in a place called *Sipofene* (the spring of tribal origin). When the world became welcoming, the Corn Mothers sent the Tewa up a ladder into the world, but it still was not ready for permanent residence. The surface was soft and would not support the migrants as they exited the watery underworld through a trapdoor entrance into the spring named Sandy Place Lake. The exact location of this spring is not known today, but its black waters are in a marshy area near Great Sand Dunes National Park in the southeast end of the San Luis Valley, Colorado.

Several times, the Tewa returned to the Corn Mothers to report the problems they encountered in their attempted migration and each time the Mothers resolved these by creating new societal leaders or culture heroes. In real time, these societal leaders are called *Paa Towa* which can be translated both as Made People and Fish People (in the metaphorical Tewa language, *Paa* can mean made or fish) (see Ortman, 2012:203–241). Like the world's three layers in cosmology, Tewa society also has three levels (Eggan, 1950). While the *Paa Towa* constitute the uppermost level, the lowest consists of the common Tewa who are called Dry Food People or *Fenyave Towa* (Weed People). They participate in dances and ceremonies and follow Tewa beliefs, but are not initiated into societies and do not become ritual leaders. At death, their souls go to shrines in their Tewa Pueblo and it is there where relatives can feed them with cornmeal and prayers and request favors from them. While they begin in the metaphorical spring of emergence, only a few who have undergone a ceremonial initiation would return there at death.

The second social level is the *Towa'e*. They represent the four pairs of ritual guardians who were sent by the Corn Mothers at the time of emergence to occupy the mountain tops and hills to guard the emerging ancestral people. They also protect and assure the purity of ritual activities. Through their life work, ritual participation and because of their accumulated ritual knowledge, they return to *Sipofene* at death (Ortiz, 1969). The third societal level, the *Paa Towa*, includes the initiated ritualists.

In life, they served and benefited the well-being of the people and it is expected that they will do so in death as well. At death, they enter the water ways and swim back to *Sipofene* ("like a fish" as their title affirms). Their souls remain in the lake where they are fed with cornmeal by living relatives, they are thanked with prayer sticks and feathers and, in return, they bring to the living the blessings of rain and precipitation, children, good health and well-being. Water is the basis of life and the deceased Made People assure its continuous availability for all the people.

Tewa sacred springs

Most Tewa Pueblos, archaeological and historic, are constructed near a sacred spring. As anthropologist Elsie Clews Parsons noted, "Around springs much ritual centers—prayer-sticks or prayer feathers are offered in or near them, and water is fetched from them to be used in altar ritual or to be poured out, as possessing peculiar virtue, upon the field" (1939:481–482). Sacred springs are religious shrines. Other shrines can be made in sacred locations by the ceremonial leaders or *Paa Towa*. These consist of ceramic bowls (*p'oekwin*) sometimes painted with water symbols, including dragonflies and Awenyu (horned serpent) messengers to the ancestral spirits (Martinez, 1982:38). A bowl of water on the altar represents a sacred spring (Parsons, 1939:213).

Village springs are under the ceremonial control of a Woman's Society (sodality) which also tends to their maintenance. Today, Ohkay Owingeh, San Ildefonso, Pojoaque and Nambe have major springs in their villages. Tesuque has numerous sacred springs venerated along the banks of the Rio Tesuque (see Hodges, 1938 for a description). Santa Clara has six flowing springs along the Rio Santa Clara and the Rio Grande (Hill, 1982:40–41). An ancient spring and a human-built reservoir at Santa Clara were also treated like sacred lakes at the ancestral site of Puje (Bandelier, 1882).

The Tewa words for spring and lake are the same. Each sacred lake is associated with the four sacred mountains recognized by each Tewa Pueblo. Two of the mountains are acknowledged as sacred mountains by all Eastern Tewa Pueblos— Sandia above Albuquerque and marking the South, and Tsekumo marking the West. However, the mountains of the North and East are different for each Tewa Pueblo. The male *Paa Towa* in each pueblo visit their sacred mountain and associated lake when they make July pilgrimages to bring rain. Only for San Ildefonso is a pattern of four sacred springs duplicated with lakes/springs in each cardinal direction around the pueblo (Harrington, 1916:44–45). These are *Busogepokwi* in the North, *Potsansennaepokwi* in the West, *Potsina'ege* in the South and *Potsiu'u* in the East. *Wopo* or medicine water was obtained from each for ceremonies or mixed in medicine water bowls called *woposa'i* (Harrington, 1916:44–45). Harrington's maps of San Ildefonso Pueblo indicate that these springs were not identical in size and this seems to be the only Tewa Pueblo built between nearby sacred springs in each cardinal direction. All are connected to the Spring of Emergence and are part of ceremonial cycle prayers by the male Made People. San Ildefonso has numerous other springs in its homeland, but we know little about them beyond their use to water livestock and to irrigate crops.

The Tewa Basin of northern New Mexico is considered a well-watered area. All the pueblos have access to numerous springs and rivers that rarely go dry, even if the surface is depleted. Each Tewa Pueblo has many springs in its homeland that are regarded as sacred. Their water is important for ceremonies and curing. The water is obtained in three ways: by collecting rainwater received in response to prayers to the *oxua* (cloud beings); dipping water directly from the pure spring and digging into the bottom of the spring to get artesian water from beneath. All sacred springs are connected to the spring of tribal origin—*Sipofene*. These flow from the lakes atop the sacred four mountains to the rivers closest to each pueblo and artesian water flowing beneath the rivers. Awenyus (sacred water serpents) can swim between all rivers, arroyos, lakes and springs. In the same way, ancestral spirits can swim throughout the aquatic network, receive the food and gifts from the living, and deliver their requested blessings. Each interlocking spring also shares a major spirit, "Blue Water Old Man," who offers life-sustaining benefits (Parsons, 1939:173). It is each pueblo's relation to this spiritual figure that leads to clean springs and pure water that can be used for ceremonies, agriculture and domestic purposes.

Woman's societies, warfare and springs

Each Tewa Pueblo had a Woman's Society that was within the *Paa Towa*. They are extinct now in all the pueblos, but in the past, they had important ceremonial functions. Primarily, they ground the corn for the two caciques, Summer and Winter, to use in the ceremonies they conducted. In Ohkay Owingeh, the last members of the society were organized by moiety with many ritual functions. One was to represent their moiety (villages were bifurcated on a social and ritual basis) as the *kiwi yo* (wise, respected old women) in the "Raingod ceremony" (Laski, 1959:15). Another was to assist in the initiation of the scalp society members, *tse'oke* (those who took scalps). They helped to care for the scalps the warriors returned to the pueblo. They fed them cornmeal, kept them clean and dry, and attended to their special needs. The Tewa believed that the scalps (*p'oesay*; translateable to "mist") would cry and help to bring rain to pueblo fields with their tears. After a return from war, the Woman's Society and the male Scalp Society members would dance in a circle together in the plaza around a pole suspending the new scalps often taken from Navaho, Utes or Apache who were the traditional enemies of Okay Owingeh (Parsons, 1929:138). The Scalp Dance (*pok'owa share*) celebrated the success of the warriors and the rain that the scalps would help to bring to the pueblo. The scalps were kept by the *tse'oke sendo* (the male head of the Scalp Society) in jars in his house or on his roof.

As far as is known, most pueblo springs were under the care of the village's Woman's Society. Just as the irrigation canals were cleaned by the men annually and ceremonially opened for water and closed by the caciques; so too, the springs were cleaned under the direction of the female society leader called the *Apienu*. Other offices were held by the "Blue Corn Girls" (Ortiz, 1969:89–90), but all society members assisted, as did non-member women volunteers from the pueblo. The trash they removed was carried to the nearest midden by male assistants. Once the spring was prepared after the Spring equinox, the officials of the Women's Society made prayer sticks and deposited them at the springs as a gift and a request to the spirits in the spring. Only after the opening ceremonies concluded could all the women and girls go to the spring to get water for domestic uses and did the ritual male leaders go to retrieve water for their ceremonies. They obtained the water in gourd vessels and brought it to the kiva where it was transferred to special pottery jars (which, again, were shrines themselves). All avoided polluting the spring. If the women wanted to wash wheat or clothes, they carried water with the help of their children from the spring to their workplace. Similarly, if they needed water for their kitchen gardens, the same work team carried water to irrigate the individual plants. In historic times, the women tended these gardens which included Spanish-introduced edible plants, including onions, garlic, lettuce, coriander, beets and tomatoes. In pre-Hispanic times, women may have similarly cared for wild vegetables and medicinal plants they wanted to have convenient to their homes. Simultaneously, there were other springs within walking distance of the pueblo. These were alternative sources of domestic water and perhaps ceremonial water if the major spring got too low. These springs were also accorded sacred respect because of their interconnectivity.

During monthly rituals, while the male *Paa Towa* retreated together in the kiva, the Women's Society members sat around their shrine to pray for the same benefits that the men requested for the pueblo. They employed portable shrines called *p'oekwin* that could be set up in any sacred location and which men still use today (Ford and Shapiro, 2017). When the men left the village to go to sacred mountains on "rain retreats," the Woman's Society traveled part of the way with them, stopping to pray along the trail under the watchful eyes of their *Towa'e* guardians. They never climbed the mountains or visited distant shrines. The women's spring had an outflow that resulted in the water connecting to the irrigation ditch, often to the *acequia madre*, which flowed near the spring. In this way, the sacred spring connected to the spring of emergence as did the other springs, local streams, arroyos and rivers, and made the spirits accessible for prayer requests, gifts of thanksgiving and ceremonial feeding.

In the late nineteenth century, all the New Mexico Tewa Pueblos had Women's Societies, but we know little about them since they were never studied by ethnologists. The three we know something about are Ohkay Owingeh (described earlier), and those of Santa Clara and San Ildefonso. At Santa Clara, the Women's Society was called the Women's Scalp Society and oversaw a dance called the *Punuha*. However, it had many elements of the Women's Society at Ohkay Owingeh and, as expected, was associated with the War Society. Membership was through family dedication of an infant at birth or could also be acquired in adulthood after being cured of an illness. Scalps had curative power and contact with a scalp could lead to wellness (Hill, 1982:347). In addition to grinding corn for the caciques, the other responsibilities of the society were to feed the scalps cornmeal, sing to them and to give them prayer plumes (feathers attached to prayer sticks) (Hill, 1982:348), and also to perform the *Punuha* initiation dance. The Women's Scalp Society assisted with the initiation of new Hunt Society members, new Scalp Society members, and assisted the Summer Moiety with the "water pouring" initiation. The climax of these initiation rites was the November performance of the *Pu'were* War Dance (a complex cycle that required four days to complete). It was directed by the *tse'oke kwiyo* (the war society old woman). This ceremony was a burlesque with men dressing as women, behaving as women and doing women's labor, while women imitated men. The ritual concluded with a community "giveaway" when the families of the new Scalp Society initiates baked bread for other residents (to acknowledge the power the scalps brought to the pueblo) and other gifts were dispersed around the village (Hill, 1982:347–351). The War Dance furthered community fertility; the scalps would help to produce abundant crops, many children, and horses and cattle (Parsons, 1939:681).[1]

Conclusion

Tewa springs and lakes were important portals to the underworld where the spirits of the Made People resided after death and where other supernatural beings dwelled. The Spring of Emergence was a supernatural portal and paradigm known by general location, not as a visitable place. However, religious pilgrimage did engage springs closer to Ohkay Owingeh that served in place of *Sipofene*. Until the 1920s, religious pilgrimages were still made to Ohkay Owingeh's main spring, and to Pagosa Springs in Colorado in the town of that name, and also to the spring at Ojo Caliente Pueblo in New Mexico. At these sites, pilgrims retrieved curative and ceremonial water, mud for ritual decoration and specially-regarded reeds. All flowing water sources were perceived as connected and were regularly navigated by the swimming *Paa Towa* spirits and Awenyus. Humans emerged on earth from springs and continued to engage the supernatural through their waters.

Note

1 San Ildefonso had *tseoke* and a 12-night scalp dance ceremonial. They also had a Blue Corn Woman ceremonial leader (Parsons, 1929:138). Although conceptually similar, Nambe and Tesuque had a Woman's Society chief called *naiw'akwiyo* (Sandstorm Wall Woman) and her assistants were the *kotsaianyo* (Blue Corn Girls). All three Tewa pueblos performed the burlesque *Puwaere dance* after the corn harvest. Despite the differences in specifics, all the Tewa pueblos had a connection of warfare, scalps and precipitation to benefit the growth of maize.

References

Bandelier, Adolph F. 1892. Final Report of Investigations among the Indians of the Southwestern United States Carried on Mainly in the Years from 1880 to 1885. 2 vols. Cambridge, MA: Archaeological Institute of America.

Eggan, Fred. 1950. *Social Organization of the Western Pueblos*. Chicago, IL: University of Chicago Press.

Ford, Richard I. and Jason Shapiro. 2017. The Sacred Environment of Arroyo Hondo. In *The Arroyo Hondo Project, A Comprehensive Review and Evaluation*, edited by Douglas W. Schwartz. Sante Fe, New Mexico: School for Advanced Research (eBook: *arroyo-hondo.org*).

Harrington, John Peabody. 1916. *The Ethnogeography of the Tewa Indians*. Twenty-ninth Annual Report of the Bureau of American Ethnology to the Secretary of the Smithsonian Institution, 1907–1908. Washington, DC: Government Printing Office.

Hill, Williard Williams. (Edited and Annotated by Charles H. Lange). 1982. *An Ethnography of Santa Clara Pueblo, New Mexico*. Albuquerque: University of New Mexico Press.

Hodges, Paul V. 1938. *Report on Irrigation and Water Supply of the Pueblos of New Mexico in the Rio Grande Basin*. Presented to the Bureau of Indian Affairs, Albuquerque.

Hough, Walter. 1909. Sacred Springs of the Southwest. *Records of the Past* 5(6):163–169.

Laski, Vera. 1959. Seeking Life. *Memoirs of the American Folklore Society* 50. Philadelphia, PA: American Folklore Society.

Martinez, Esther. 1982. *San Juan Tewa Dictionary*. San Juan Pueblo: San Juan Bilingual Program.

Ortiz, Alfonso. 1969. *The Tewa World: Space, Time, Being, and Becoming in a Pueblo Society*. Chicago, IL: University of Chicago Press.

Ortman, Scott. 2012. *Winds from the North*. Salt Lake City: University of Utah Press.

Parsons, Elsie Clews. 1929. Social Organization of the Tewa Indians of New Mexico. Volume 36 of American Anthropological Association: Memoirs.

———. 1939. *Pueblo Indian Religion*. 2 vol. Chicago, IL: University of Chicago press.

Wittfogel, Karl A. and Esther S. Goldfrank. 1943. Some Aspects of Pueblo Mythology and Society. *Journal of American Folklore* 56(219):17–30.

PART IV

Temporal powers, social identity and sacred geography

While water may productively be perceived as a commons for stewardship, its management often relates to social organization and both overtly hierarchical and heterarchical power flows. Opening this set of essays, Terje Oestigaard and Gedef Firew review the central role that Ethiopia's divine waters have played in the country's history and in the shaping of communities of varied faiths. They particularly examine myths and ritual practices associated with the source of the Blue Nile (Gish Abay) which, in cosmological geography, originates in the paradisiacal waters of Eden. In Yorubaland, Nigeria, the town of Ondo is home to a prophetic and weather-changing holy well called *Ori Aiye* (the peak or center of the earth) whose veneration transcends the Ondo Kingdom's religious divisions. Examining ritual observances, offerings and multiple festivals focused on the well, Raheem Oluwafunminiyi and Ajisola Omojeje detail how engagement with the well is always in line with Ondo's traditional civic power structures. Interactions, petitions and gifts must be mediated through a male hierarchy including the wells' gate-keepers, the head of warrior groups, the king's aides, the king's council and the king, who ultimately sanctions ritual performances that have limited viewers, but public significance. Next, Vera Lazzaretti considers well features in the sacred waterscape of Banaras, India. Her focus is the long-lived genre of literature called "glorifications" which provides a glimpse at the alternating promotion, neglect and assimilation of the city's sacred sites with changing preferences for particular deities and with Muslim Mughal rule. Security forces now monitor the area between the famed *Jnanavapi* (the Well of Knowledge) and the city's largest Islamic mosque nearby. Considering sacred mineral springs in South Korea (yaksutŏ), Hong-key Yoon discusses their cures, associated rituals and their guardian deities (the Mountain Spirit and the Dragon King) that illustrate how Korean Buddhism syncretized many aspects of Indigenous shamanism. Local women organize annual ceremonies for the deities of rural yaksutŏ, but rituals at sites on the margins of cities are often civic-oriented public displays. Ramiro Dorantes considers how the political, social, economic and religious lives of towns are connected through elaborately scheduled visits to Mexico's sacred spring/cave/tree complex at Chalma, which was venerated in pre-Aztec times and was Christianized in the sixteenth century. The spring waters are now part of a ritual complex that forms the heart of regional folk-liturgical practices. Diverse communities across the Mexican states of Morelos, México, Hidalgo and Guerrero are linked by a complex network of interrelations based on the patronage of saints and the hierarchical relationships of these saints with each other.

11

DIVINE WATERS IN ETHIOPIA

The source from Heaven and Indigenous water-worlds in the Lake Tana region

Terje Oestigaard and Gedef Abawa Firew

The source of the Blue Nile—Gish Abay—is the divine source from which the waters of Paradise flow—thus linking heaven and earth. In particular, this source has a special role in Christian mythology and cosmology, but Lake Tana has also been ascribed with wider religious significance. The source of the Blue Nile was also a stronghold for the traditional religion which involved lavish ox sacrifices. Nowadays, animal sacrifices to the river still take place, but they are a disappearing tradition. For the Indigenous group, the Negede-woyto, water is everything and their cosmological beliefs are structured around their river and lake lives. Their main and benevolent spirit, Abinas, lives in the water, and provides everything for his devotees and in the recent past, an omnipresent hippo-cult was part of Abinas' realm. This chapter will discuss different religious traditions and practices and the ways various divine waters are conceptualized and used in rituals. Through empirical case studies, it will also be argued that the omnipotence and omnipresence of water may have stronger cosmological roles when it is not holy, precisely because holiness implies restrictions, prohibitions and exclusiveness. Thus, the chapter will (1) discuss different types of divine waters, (2) describe Christian conceptions of Gish Abay as coming from Paradise and (3) give a short introduction to the rich Indigenous water cosmology among the Negede-woyto living around Lake Tana.

Holy and divine waters

Divine waters may have a number of different functions and inherent qualities and properties. Waters originating in divine spheres can be holy, sacred, neutral and even evil. Understanding the various processes at work may enable one to grasp the different significances water has in rituals and religions (Oestigaard, 2010, 2017, 2018; Tvedt and Oestigaard, 2010; Tvedt, 2016).

Holy water is the most common type of divine water associated with religion, but it is also to a large extent restricted to world religions, and it is, by definition, quite uncommon because it is exclusive and hence protected from defilement.

Theoretically, "holiness" refers to the divinity and what is derived from the divinity as attributes, whereas "sacredness" points to consecrated items, "respected or venerated objects but not the divine itself and not to persons as individuals" (Oxtoby, 1987:434). Thus, holiness implies a divine revelation or embodiment whereby godly powers are embedded in the water, which can be used for different benevolent practices by believers. It is an active divine medium in an otherworldly, dangerous and polluted world with malevolent forces. Sacred waters may also originate in divine spheres (like the earth and the life-giving waters being created by God, following the scriptures) and venerated because of being part of the divine creation, but it has no other inherent qualities which devotees can use for other religious practices. Neutral waters may also come in various forms, and the most common is rain. Although many cosmologies hold that rain is controlled by, or is the gift of divinities, and rain is often presented as the positive outcome of rituals, rain itself is not holy water, as such would imply that all things touched by rain become sanctified. Finally, there are also evil or malevolent waters, like the torturing waters in Hell, but also more ambiguous divine waters like the boiling hot waters of the Deluge.

In short, divine waters may take numerous forms and embody a wide range of godly or spiritual powers. Moreover, religious water at a certain spot having specific qualities may also change in form and substance as the water flows. Also, holiness implies restrictions and protection, because everything cannot be equally holy—not only would the holy lose its function as a divine medium here and

FIGURE 11.1 Gish Abay or the Source of the Nile: Photograph by Terje Oestigaard.

now, but an otherworldly substance embodying divine powers cannot be present everywhere for everybody at all times. If holiness was omnipresent in this daily world, the mundane world (which is sinful in a religious perspective) would literally be soaked in holiness if, for instance, rain was holy water. Particularly in monotheistic religions, the world is corrupted and sinful and hence holy water plays a fundamental role in belief.

The role of religious or divine waters in Indigenous cosmologies is often quite different. Most often, the various types of religious water are not holy, in the sense that the water itself is not embodying aspects or powers of divinities as such. However, precisely because the waters are not holy, their role in religion and cosmology can be more encompassing, omnipotent and omnipresent. The life-giving qualities are the essence of the divine powers in this world for humans, and hence the role of water in society and religion can encompass all spheres of life and well-being. The differences between cosmologies with holy water and omnipresent divine waters can be exemplified with Christianity and the Indigenous Negede-woyto religion.

Gish Abay—the source from Paradise

The Gish Abay spring in the Lake Tana region in Ethiopia is believed to be the source of the Blue Nile coming from Paradise. Since time immemorial, legends have been told about this holy place of utmost cosmological importance (Beke, 1844; Beckingham and Huntingford, 1954; Cheesman, 1968). For Christianity, the holiness of Gish Abay has its origin in both Old and New Testament contexts. In Genesis, it is written:

> A river watering the garden flowed from Eden; from there it was separated into four headwaters. The name of the first is the Pishon; it winds through the entire land of Havilah, where there is gold. The name of the second river is the Gihon; it winds through the entire land of Cush. The name of the third river is the Tigris; it runs along the east side of Asshur. And the fourth river is the Euphrates.
>
> *(Genesis 2:11–14)*

There is also a local myth giving Gish Abay its name; the story is about the introduction of Christianity to this area (Oestigaard and Gedef, 2011, 2013). Allegedly born at the end of the eighth century, Abune Zerabruk is known for performing miracles with the holy water at Gish Abay as a Christian practice, but Christianity is more generally thought to have come later to the Lake Tana region in the twelfth century. As the water comes from the Garden of Eden, and no place on earth is holier than Paradise itself, the powers of the water are immense and not of this world. It is believed that God bestows His mercy on descendants of devotees who make the pilgrimage to the source, pray, and use the water in rituals; this blessing may last for up to 70 generations. It is also thought that those being sprinkled with water from the Gihon River are cured of sins, sicknesses and misfortunes. Moreover, exorcisms often take place, and the holy water chases away the inner devils that possess and molest patients making them ill. Bottles of this water are also collected and carried for long distances and used later for other types of malignancies. Given that the water is of utmost holiness, its protection is imperative. Devotees belonging to Ethiopian Orthodox Church may even see other Christian denominations as impure and polluting to the source. Muslims, who also believe that the source derives from Eden's divine river Gihon, are prohibited from approaching the inner sanctuary where the source is located.

Beliefs about purity protection have co-existed with Christianity in the area. When Major Robert Ernest Cheesman (an English explorer and ornithologist) visited the source in the late 1920s and early 1930s, he received holy water from a priest. However, when the priest realized that Cheesman already had eaten that day, he insisted that he had to wait until the next day and drink the water before breakfast: devotees have to be fasting before approaching the source. If the water is consumed after having taken food, it can be deadly. According to stories, several people who had ignored this warning, and drank the holy water after a meal, died. In the same vein, when Cheesman's wife touched the water of the source with the end of her stick, the surrounding pilgrims shouted "Don't let her touch it, she is a woman." She asked the priest what would happen if she bathed in the spring, and the priest replied "You would die" (Cheesman, 1968:73). Polluting the most holy water at the pilgrimage site is a heinous sin. Today, Ethiopian women use the holy water from the source if they belong to the Ethiopian Orthodox Church, but restrictions mainly apply to foreigners or people of different faiths.

However, the Christian associations with Heaven are thought to be a late historic development, and prior to the eighteenth and nineteenth centuries, the water was a focus for pre-Christian practices. The first European to visit and document the source of the Blue Nile was the Portuguese Jesuit priest Pedro Paez (Lobo, 1789). The date of his visit is variously given as April 21, 1613 or 1615 or 1618 (Johnston, 1903:51). When James Bruce came to the source in November 1770, he referred in particular to the cult of sacrificing oxen:

> The Agows of Damot pay divine honour to the Nile; they worship the river, and thousands of cattle have been offered, and still are offered, to the spirit supposed to reside at its source … all the tribes … meet annually at the source of the river, to which they sacrifice, calling it by the name of the *God of Peace.*
>
> *(Bruce, 1790, Vol. 3:633)*

While this Indigenous tradition has disappeared a long time ago, the Negede-woyto cosmology still perpetuates both sacrifices to the Nile and ancient traditions of the former hippo-cult.

The Negede-woyto, Abinas and the hippo-cult

Throughout their written history, the Negede-woyto have occupied areas surrounding the shores and waters of Lake Tana and the Blue Nile near the outlet of the lake. Elders of the community unanimously state that wherever there is *Bahir* (literarily meaning Sea), there are the Negede-woyto. For the Negede-woyto,

Lake Tana in general and Abay in particular are their life, society and religion. According to their oral history, even the origin of the name Woyto is strongly associated with water. When the king of the Negede-woyto was defeated and chased by Egyptian Pharaohs, he sank into the water of the lake to hide himself. Hence, according to the Negede-woyto elders, the name Negede-woyto is literally similar to the Amharic word *watow*, meaning swallowed by the water. The Negede-woyto then settled around the water of Lake Tana from which they derive their livelihood by hunting and fishing (Oestigaard and Gedef, 2011, 2013; Gedef, 2014).

The Negede-woyto confidently state that since their life, birth and growth are made possible by Lake Tana and the River Abay—the Blue Nile—they cannot be consumed or endangered by them, even when they swim or navigate their papyrus boats into the deep waters of either. The Negede-woyto of Lake Tana, whose traditions and ways of life depend entirely on water, have different values and belief systems associated with fauna in the lake and Abay, such as the hippo and different types of fishes.

The hippo-cult and the water-traditions in general are widely recognized as parts of their living heritage, but this tradition is slowly disappearing. According to the Negede-woyto elders, the hippo is seen as a sacred animal, which has spiritual power that structures the social, cultural and economic lives of the Negede-woyto society. In particular, the hippo teeth, meat, hide and waste have in different ways great spiritual value and ritual importance for the Negede-woyto of Lake Tana. Hippo teeth protect people from attacks by bad and malignant spirits. They are also regarded as having the power to protect the good spirit (*Kole*). A hippo tooth or part of it is thus kept in the households for protection against malevolent spirits and to elicit the benevolence of the good spirit. Hippo meat is used as medicine in a number of ways for different treatments. Fat from the hippo may be smeared on the body for curative purposes. It is believed that hippo meat cures malaria and sufferers are therefore advised to eat raw hippo meat. Consumption of raw meat is also thought to help women conceive in the case of a couple's infertility.

Similarly, the hippo hide is assumed to increase the fertility and well-being of animals and to create wealth and prosperity for people and society. The Negede-woyto encouraged their cattle to taste or eat the hippo hide by spraying salt on the inside or on the fleshy sides of the hide, but these are practices that have disappeared. It was not only the flesh of the hippo which could bring prosperity and well-being. When the hippo is heard crying or making loud sounds early in the morning, it is considered as a sign of good fate or fortune. A successful hippo-hunt was also an essential part of marriage celebrations in the past (Gedef, 2014; Oestigaard, 2018).

The hippo is also seen as a sacred animal protecting their main god—Abinas, since they both live in the water and the animal is huge and strong. Abinas is the god of the Blue Nile or the spirit of the Abay, and he is a male spirit. He is the source of everything: it is from him that the Negede-woyto receive wealth, health, prosperity, natural resources and all that they need for living a good life. In return, they make sacrifices to Abinas, noting "unless you give it something, [the god] cannot give you anything" (Gedef, 2014:235, 245).

The main Negede-woyto sacrifice takes place before Lent starts, and sacrifices are conducted on both the Saturday and Sunday prior to the Christian fasting

FIGURE 11.2 Sacrifice of a calf to the Nile. Photograph by Gedef Abawa Firew.

period. This is the last day Christians eat meat before the fast begins. Since the Negede-woytos were once Christians, and also in respect for Christian neighbors, they conduct their main sacrifice before the Lenten fast starts. The festival is simply called the "Great" and involves sacrifices made by both family and community. Although the main sacrifice of a calf is for the well-being of the whole community, women are prohibited from participating. The calf must be without physical blemishes on its body or horns, and may be white or red, but never black. The sacrifice is conducted at the source of the river at the very outlet of the Nile at Lake Tana in Bahir Dar. While Abinas as a god can be anywhere, this is the place he prefers, and it is also where one of the biggest hippo colonies is located.

Conclusion

The divine waters in Ethiopia have a central role not only in the country's history and constitution of its societies, but in the myriad myths and ritual practices that have also been central to religious developments for centuries and perhaps even millennia. The source of the Blue Nile has a very special role in this history. For countless generations, it has fascinated scholars and believers, been a pilgrimage place for innumerable devotees and was in pre-Christian times a cult-place for lavish sacrifices. The water coming from Paradise is among the holiest waters on earth from a Christian perspective, but holiness usually implies exclusiveness, restrictions and utmost protection of its purity. Thus, concepts of holy water in theory and practice shape rituals and traditions in certain directions, whereas a water cosmology in an Indigenous tradition like the Negede-woyto may enable different roles of water in society and religion precisely because the water is not holy. While the holy and heavenly water at Gish Abay may be more efficient and stronger as a divine medium for specific purposes, in indigenous perspectives, the same water shapes all aspects of life. The Great Sacrifice and the hippo-cult give testimonies of a total water cosmology, which has been part of the legacy and heritage of water in Ethiopia since time immemorial.

References

Beckingham, Charles Fraser and George Wynn Brereton Huntingford. 1954. *Some Records of Ethiopia 1593–1646. Being Extracts from the History of High Ethiopia or Abassia by Manoel De Almeida. Together with Bahrey's History of the Galla.* London: The Hakluyt Society.

Beke, Charles Tilstone. 1844. Abyssinia: Being a Continuation of Routes in That Country. *Journal of the Royal Geographical Society of London* 14:1–76.

Bruce, James. 1790. *Travels to Discover the Source of the Nile, in the Years 1768, 1769, 1770, 1771, 1772, and 1773 in Five Volumes.* London: J. Ruthven.

Cheesman, Robert Ernest. 1968 [1936]. *Lake Tana and the Blue Nile. An Abyssinian Quest.* London: Frank Cass.

Gedef, Abawa Firew. 2014. *Archaeological Fieldwork around Lake Tana Area of Northwest Ethiopia and the Implication for an Understanding of Aquatic Adaptation.* Ph.D. Dissertation, University of Bergen.

Johnston, Harry. 1903. *The Nile Quest.* London: Lawrence and Bullen.

Lobo, Jerónimo. 1789. *A Voyage to Abyssinia, by Father Jerome Lobo, a Portuguese Missionary. Containing the History, Natural, Civil, and Ecclesiastical, of That Remote and Unfrequented Country, Continued Down to the Beginning of the Eighteenth Century: With Fifteen Dissertations… Relating to the Antiquities, Government, Religion, Manners, and Natural History, of Abyssina.* By M. Le Grand, translated from the French by Samuel Johnson, LL.D. To which are added, various other tracts by the same author, not published by Sir John Hawkins or Mr. Stockdale. London: Elliot and Kay, and Edinburgh: C. Elliot.

Oestigaard, Terje. 2010. Purification, Purgation and Penalty: Christian Concepts of Water and Fire in Heaven and Hell. In *A History of Water. Series 2, Vol. 1. The Ideas of Water. From Ancient Societies to the Modern World,* edited by Tvedt Terje and Oestigaard Terje, 298–322. London: I.B. Tauris.

Oestigaard, Terje. 2017. Holy Water: The Works of Water in Defining and Understanding Holiness. *WIREs Water* 2017. doi:10.1002/wat2.1205

Oestigaard, Terje. 2018. *The Religious Nile. Water, Ritual and Society since Ancient Egypt.* London: I.B. Tauris.

Oestigaard, Terje and Gedef Abawa Firew. 2011. Gish Abay– The Source of the Blue Nile. In *Water and Society,* edited by Pepper Darrell W. and Brebbia Carlos A., 27–38. Boston, MA: WIT Press.

Oestigaard, Terje and Gedef Abawa Firew. 2013. *The Source of the Blue Nile–Water Rituals and Traditions in the Lake Tana Region.* Newcastle: Cambridge Scholars Press.

Oxtoby, Willard G. 1987. Holy, Idea of the. In *The Encyclopaedia of Religion.* Vol. 6, edited by Mircea. Eliade, 431–438. New York: Macmillan.

Tvedt, Terje. 2016. *Water and Society–Changing Perceptions of Societal and Historical Development.* London: I.B. Tauris.

Tvedt, Terje and Terje Oestigaard. 2010. A History of the Ideas of Water: Deconstructing Nature and Constructing Society. In *A History of Water. Series 2, Vol. 1. The Ideas of Water. From Ancient Societies to the Modern World,* edited by Terje Tvedt and Terje Oestigaard, 1–36. London: I.B. Tauris.

12

ORI AIYE

A holy well among the Ondo of Southeastern Yorubaland, Nigeria

Raheem Oluwafunminiyi and Victor Ajisola Omojeje

The large concentration of holy well literature by Western scholars, particularly the focus on Britain and Ireland, relates to the available trove of textual materials and archaeological remains which have proved vital in reconstructing the antiquity of numerous wells and their roles or use both in pre-Christian and Christian periods (Logan, 1980; Meller, 2010; Ray, 2014; Atherton, 2016). This varies from parts of Africa where these wells, though extant, are generally memorialized through oral traditions (waiting to be unearthed), with virtually no documentation of their historicity. Additionally, local interest in holy wells is eroded by the penetrating influence of Islam and Christianity which continue to shift adherents' attention away from traditional devotion to them. Notwithstanding, this chapter adds to the growing discourse on holy well scholarship with voices from an African context.[1]

This essay examines a historically important holy well among the Ondo of Southeastern Yorubaland in Nigeria that is still venerated as *Ori Aiye* (peak of the earth). Across the Yoruba country (Akintoye, 2010),[2] there exist a handful of these wells, each with its enduring history, alluring powers, myths and roles.[3] Not only are these sites of daily, weekly or annual ritual devotions, but they remain places for votive offerings. While it is difficult to date their existence, they are mainly believed to be of great antiquity. In actual fact, according to Chief Julius Adepetu,[4] some Yoruba traditions hold that holy wells were molded during the creation of the earth by the Supreme Being, *Olodumare*, *Ori Aiye* being no exception. It is generally regarded as the peak of the earth because, according to tradition, it is located at the center of the earth. As Brenneman and Brenneman suggest, holy wells "take on the role of a centre," and often "radiate power to the surrounding area" (1995:793). Although *Ori Aiye* is not found on high ground as the meaning (peak of the earth) implies, and does not appear to be located in the middle of Ondo town, neither is the town itself in the heartland of Yorubaland, it is possible that its "radiating" power may have contributed to the well's attraction among locals who came from near and far. The appellation appears somewhat conjectural. Given the specific role played by the well, the Yoruba expression, *o ri abala'ye re* (one who sees his/her future) is the most likely etymology of the name *Ori Aiye*. These divergent meanings aside, the well is believed to forecast the future.

Ori Aiye is linked historically to the Ondo Kingdom or town founded in the six-teenth century in southeastern Yorubaland (Ajayi, 2014). The well is located along the popular Igele Maroko Street in Ondo town, and lies between the palaces of the Ondo king and the *Olobun* (Ondo female king). The well is protected by a strong square-shaped block wrapped on one side with an iron bar to ward off intruders. Two corrugated tin sheets are also placed under the iron bar to prevent meddling with the sacred well. A small opening is made on the side of the well which is spe-cifically reserved for votive offerings.

Based on its power to foretell the future, the well was often consulted while at the same time elevated as a revered space and deified through diverse forms of rit-ual practices and observances by specific traditional agencies in the town. While a visitor celebrated his luck in the event of an encouraging prediction, an inauspicious one often proved fatal. An agreement was therefore reached by its gatekeepers to shut the well indefinitely.[5] Nevertheless, *Ori Aiye*'s power is still reinforced at spe-cific times of the year through traditional festivals and sacrificial practices, among other rituals.

The Ondo: a brief historical background

Ondo town lies in the tropical rainforest belt of Nigeria (a town is an administrative division akin to a county elsewhere). It is bounded in the north by Akure, the state capital and Obokun Local Government Area (LGA) in Osun State; in the south by Ilaje/Eseodo LGAs; in the east by Owena River and in the west by the Ooni River. Mostly urban, Ondo is composed of a homogenous population of almost 300,000. Some villages and "towns within the town" include *Bolorunduro, Bagbe, Igbado, Losare, Oloruntedo* and *Oke Alafia*. Inhabitants of each of these towns speak the same language and also possess similar culture and traditions. The Ondo are not ethnically different from other sub-Yoruba groups in southwest Nigeria, but as in many Yoruba towns, have variations in language.

Ondo kingdom was founded by Pupupu, a princess of Ile-Ife origin. Her mother was forced to flee with her to the region since Pupupu was one of a set of twins and a rule then stipulated the instant death of such a child. Her wan-derings took her to several places until she finally settled at the location Ondo. She is popularly believed to have reigned between the year 1510 and 1530 and later "substituted" by *Airo* (1530–1561), one of her sons (Kolawole, 1997:57–58). Although Pupupu remains the first and only female king of the town (a separate, compensatory role some would argue), the equally powerful position or title referred to as *Olobun*[6] was conferred on all her female descendants (Iluyemi, 2014:50–54). Today, Ondo remains one of the very few Yoruba towns where both a male and female king, and palace chiefs rule simultaneously, each with multifarious functions or roles.

Well customs and religious rites

In past times, a visitor to *Ori Aiye* reached out to the *Odogun*[7] (gatekeeper) who, in turn, seeks the *Osemawe's*[8] (the paramount king's) consent after which an agreed date is chosen and then communicated to the visitor. The first process entails a visit to a small square-shaped roofless mud-house known as *Eminale* or *Esi*, located inside a fairly large compound close to *Ori Aiye*. In pre-colonial times, this enclave was hidden from public view. Inside the *Eminale*, the visitor is required to go through some ritual procedures. For instance, the visitor is handed a powdery material or, in other cases, a little amount of water (likely laced with charms), with which to wipe the face. It is also probable that the eyes of the visitor are beguiled by application of a local eye cosmetic (tiro) with varying medicinal and cultural purposes.[9] Though the *Odogun* interviewed was silent on this, this particular procedure may be carried out to enable the visitor to see through the well what an "ordinary" eye could not. Given that holy wells exist out of the ordinary and their water is powerful enough to perform feats not visible to the ordinary eye, the use of these materials perhaps becomes a necessary prerequisite. Other rituals are similarly observed after which the visitor is finally led by the *Odogun* to the well.

To identify a positive forecast, the visitor is said to see himself or herself in a colorful and very expensive piece of locally woven fabric (*Alarii* or *Aso Oke*). One who appears in ragged clothing, however, indicates a contrary forecast. It is pertinent to note here that *Ori Aiye's* forecast is not specific to wealth or lack of it alone, but could also reveal the mundane (bareness, sickness, a great harvest, an abundance of children, house flooding, disease, etc.). In actual fact, a traditional priest, Otunba Gbemisola Johnson, noted that *Ori Aiye* was finally closed to unaccompanied visitors after a maiden saw a forecast indicating she would be barren. Following a positive forecast, the visitor meets with waiting sympathizers to break the news after which merry-making ensues. This, however, is not the case for a negative forecast. Traditions hold that many of those who received adverse forecasts instantly plunged into the well. Although most respondents could not provide an exact death figure, Adesina Mary, a trader, claimed that tradition credited 7,000 deaths to the well. The validity, or otherwise, of these claims could not be independently verified since various and often conflicting figures ranging between 650, 800 and 2,000 were cited in interviews. Nevertheless, such large numbers underscore narratives that *Ori Aiye* has drawn various classes of peoples to their death from the nearby proximity and from distant parts of the town. Contrary to claims that holy wells were in the past visited by "the poorest members" within a locality (Jordan, 2000), in *Ori Aiye's* case, evidence showed that all classes of people were attracted to the well.[10]

Out of concern for the number of suicides, the *Osemawe* in concert with the *Odogun*, palace chiefs and other key traditional agencies in the town, agreed to seal off the well indefinitely.[11] For an important well as this, a full closure meant a disconnection or detachment from the history of the town. This was also certain to have grave implications for the town. Since *Ori Aiye* retained a degree of spirituality and was imbued with overwhelming powers, it required some befitting ritual attention so that, while no longer regularly accessible, the well would not be lost from popular memory. Agreements were reached by all traditional agencies in the town to dedicate, in effect, a special day and specific periods within the year to celebrate the well through votive offerings among other ritual observances. One of them is illustrated on the day after the popular *Odun Moko* festival (Akinkuolie, 2015),[12] where the *Olobun* with all her chiefs move in a procession from her palace to *Ori Aiye* to offer sacrifices and prayers.

Interestingly, in spite of the number of deaths linked to the well, accounts do not demonstrate whether individuals, even particularly well-known visitors to the well, are remembered through participation at *Ori Aiye* or at any ritual performance over it. A significant portion of the ritual performance at the well, including prayers, could be carried out to appease the dead and to avoid adverse consequences often linked with such fatalities in Yorubaland where suicide is forbidden (Awolalu, 1979:152–156).[13]

Taboos, myths and votive offerings

As sites of popular religious practices, holy wells are replete with myths and taboos. Taboos continually reinforce the covenant made with a sacred place or deity and sanctions and demands come with such a covenant (Awolalu and Dopamu, 1979:212). In the case of *Ori Aiye*, any form of bodily contact is considered a grave taboo, and even those oblivious to this injunction are not spared the repercussions until propitiation is adequately performed. The typical ritual or propitiation performed to counteract taboo violation is only known to *Ori Aiye*'s gatekeepers. Interestingly, the ritual items provided in the celebration of the well are also the same items required to carry out the propitiation. Even the *Odogun*[14] is required to adhere to some taboos. For instance, he is prohibited, according to Mulikat Babalola, from consuming yam each time a communal occasion or peculiar need demands him to enter the *Eminale*. A respondent who lives close to the well area, Ogunsola Akinkuowo, informed the authors that it was also forbidden to dig a well or build a latrine around the area.

FIGURE 12.1   (L) *Ori Aiye* prepared for propitiation. (R) A well gatekeeper (faces blurred for privacy). Photographs by author.

One of the mythical associations of *Ori Aiye* is its connection with the weather and other natural phenomena. For instance, Chief Olafemiwa Oluwasegun Michael observed that in the process of opening the well, the sky or clouds simultaneously darken or display a sudden flash of lightning. Another perspective links the well with the sea, although a few respondents disagreed, arguing that *Ori Aiye* was independent of any known sea goddesses or deities. Indeed, some holy wells are thought, as in Europe, to be portals to the "Other World" (Barrett, 2016). By this, we mean the most sacred of places which served as "both the land of the dead and the land of eternal youth" where the invited receive "constant renewal of youthful life" (Brenneman and Brenneman, 1995:797). The *Other World* is reputed for its power and wisdom and thought to be located in diverse, remote or hidden corners of the world. In relation to *Ori Aiye*, it is located beneath the earth. Incidentally, propitiations, votive offerings or ritual observances are rarely exerted over holy wells *per se*, but to an esoteric power believed to dwell around or inside it. A holy well is, therefore, connected—and within the context of how the *Other World* is locally conceived—to one deity or the other, particularly as they appear to embody the spiritual origin of the Earth (Molyneaux, 1995) and, at the same time, stand as the abode of the deity itself (Baker, 1985).

Remarkably, one of the well's gatekeepers, Lawrence Adeduro, claims that *Ori Aiye's* depth is boundless. Although the *Odogun* and the *Oshodi* (the Ondo king's aide) have unrestricted access to the well, both are limited by the boundaries set against even traditional insiders by *Ori Aiye* itself. Tradition suggests that the well's water is not only crystal clear but has never dried up. This is unusual, considering that many human-excavated wells across the country soon dry up during the harmattan season (a weather phenomenon in West Africa between late November and mid-March which is characterized by hot, dry and dusty north-easterly wind). *Ori Aiye's* continuous flow characterizes it as a holy well with the capacity of perpetual water flow through even the driest weather (Bord and Colin, 1994).

Votive offerings made at *Ori Aiye* can be classed into three: those offered by the *Odogun* and *Osemawe* through the *Oshodi* on an annual festival; those offered when observing the well's taboos and finally those on specific festival periods. However, at the annual festival honoring the well (see below), for instance, ewes are provided as votive offerings as are lesser materials such as kola nuts. Though a blessed bush—*Eminale* in this case—is closely associated with *Ori Aiye*, rag offerings do not form part of the well's votive materials, as is common elsewhere in the world. Offerings such as pebbles, pins, nails, buttons, necklaces, bottles and pottery found around or close to many renowned wells in Ireland, Britain and elsewhere, are also not found at *Ori Aiye*. An explanation for this is that votive offerings made at holy wells vary within the context of the sort of environment they are located and/or powers with which they are imbued. *Ori Aiye* is not a healing well, and so these types of small objects are not likely to suffice as offerings. Significantly, sacred places or springs in most Yoruba towns are propitiated with either consumable or non-consumable items such as corn pap, egg, palm oil, kola nut or gin.

Ori Aiye festival: kingship rites, ritual practices and observances

Historic monuments in Ondo and, most importantly, religious rituals are linked in various ways to the *Osemawe* (again, the paramount king). As Olupona noted, all festivals and rituals popular in many Ondo ritual songs are accomplished for, and in support of, the *Osemawe* (1992:13). *Ori Aiye* is no exception as the well's importance and religious symbolism are indicated in the annual *Ori Aiye* festival which is the very first festival held in the Ondo calendar in January and, as such, should attract the whole community. Indeed, as Alessandro Falassi observes, a festival is a social occasion celebrated periodically by all members within a particular community united not only by a common language, ethnicity, religion and history, but a similar worldview (1987). True as this may appear, festivals are arguably distinguished by "power, class structure and social roles," which, in some cases, are limited strictly to specific traditional agencies within a community (Falassi, 1987:3). For instance, while some Yoruba festivals are likely to draw vivacious public participation, a good number of the observances or religious rituals are held in private (Laitin, 1986:35). A closer look at the popular *Oro* festival among the Yoruba (a festival celebrating a community's departed spirit) actually excludes women and is usually celebrated late at night to limit broad participation. The *Ori Aiye* festival follows a similar path, with participation restricted to the *Osemawe* (the Ondo king), *Odogun* (*Ori Aiye* gatekeeper), *Oshodi* (the king's aide), *Eghae* (the king's council) and a tiny fraction of palace officials such as the royal flutist. Why this is so is unclear; yet, a festival such as this illustrates the boundaries between ritual performances and practices, part of which is strictly reserved for select groups, and indeed, for others which usually assume public meaning.

In addition to the ritual agencies listed earlier is the *Ayadi* who is the head of the 15 warrior groups (*Elegbe*) of the Ondo that play a significant role in the festival. The *Ayadi*'s role is to sound a note of warning expressed in the form of a threat of instant death to an "uninvited" or "unwanted" guest or resident at the festival.

> *Ogbeku o!*
> *Onile, alejo, a paramo o*
> *Eni wo, o ku boro, a ku fere*
> *Gbogbo obinrin, gbogbo okunrin*
> *Gbogbo okunrin, gbogbo obinrin*
> *Aiwo, eni wo boro a ku boro*

> Listen attentively!
> All residents and visitors should stay indoors
> A surreptitious glance invites instant death
> All women and men
> All men and women
>   Whoever attempts a glance faces instant death[15]

He returns to his seat, facing the king in obeisance to observe a short prayer of peace and tranquility. Interestingly, all surrounding areas are closed in deference to the *Ayadi*'s warning to actually enable what Cudny calls "separateness of the experiences" (2016:2). What this suggests is that all Ondo people, neighboring communities and anyone at all, are required to "isolate" themselves from the ritual and non-ritual experience of the festival. Similarly, women are not allowed to participate or attempt to come close to the ritual. This, nonetheless, was not the case in the closing stages of the festival where the researchers noticed the appearance of three elderly women who came out to give remnants of the bagged salt earlier used for rituals and who received cash gifts in return. The salt bags were arranged on a circular aluminum tray and taken to participants of their choice as a take-home gift. Rather than ritual in intent, this was likely done to avoid waste. Despite the exclusion of women in the *Ori Aiye* festival, the researchers observed that a female sheep (ewe) formed an important part of the ritual items or materials sacrificed before the well. Although the well's gatekeepers only explained the sacrifice as a custom dating back in time, it is possible that ewes were more suited culturally based on their ability to weaken menacing powers which manifest around sacred spaces when deities are invoked (Awolalu, 1973:91).

The *Odogun* kick-starts the next stage of the festival. Like the *Ayadi*, he pays obeisance to the king, performs a short prayer in concert with the *Oshodi*, using the required ritual materials, all of which, as tradition demands, the *Osemawe* must provide to the *Odogun* to propitiate the well. These materials include one matured live ewe, several pieces of kola nut, one keg of palm oil, one African land snail, one bag of salt, one keg of palm wine, three packs of Seaman's Schnapps, one matured live cock, one monkey arm (dried), one marine catfish (dried), one small pot and calabash, a few palm tree leaves and water drawn from a borehole. Significantly, all the consumable ritual items (except the ewe) are mixed and set for use at a later stage of the festival.

Once other rituals are completed, the well is ready to be opened. The *Oshodi* suggests that as soon as the well is thrown open, natural or atmospheric phenomena soon occur.[16] Virtually, all participants, except the *Odogun* and *Oshodi* who stand away from the well, turn their faces away at this instant. While this may possibly be a formal part of the ritual practice, the researchers, however, argue that this was most likely linked with health concerns. Since *Ori Aiye* is locked away throughout the year, the possibility that it may contain and as well emit toxic gases once exposed is high.

Votive offerings are one of the key aspects of the festival. Each of the ritual materials mentioned earlier is poured around the well and on the street in a similar fashion, following a cross-like form. The sheep then is placed on the well's slab and slaughtered, while its blood is allowed to flow freely inside the well after which the sheep's head is completely cut off and subsequently handed to the *Osemawe* for prayers. Other rituals are performed, but, significantly, each ritual practice centers on prayers. The prayers at such festivals stimulate an "endless celebration" and also invoke opportunities for newness and renewal (Makinde, 2012). Interestingly, unlike many festivals where traditional dances, songs or even incantations are performed, the *Ori Aiye* festival is linked to the pursuit of "newness" and "renewal" by specific traditional agencies in Ondo town. No traditional agency is likely to expressly assert itself without the invocation of these prayers. The Yoruba often express this sentiment at the end of a festival thus: *A seyi sa modun*, meaning "As we have celebrated this festival, so shall we celebrate another year" (Walsh, 1948:233).

As an important ritual material, each kola nut is broken into lobes by the *Odogun* and thrown at intervals into the well and across the street. Inscribed on each lobe are prayers for the king,[17] his immediate family, the palace chiefs, the Ondo people and the town—in that order. The last performance paves the way for the final closure of the well. At this juncture, an earlier prepared *Ero* (a material that protects against danger or evil) is sprinkled on the feet and hands of the king and each participant and also immediately along the street. This perhaps suppresses harm in the aftermath of opening the well. The practice is also believed to protect all participants and the Ondo people generally from any omen or danger surrounding the town. The king is, thereafter, summoned before the well to cap all ritual performances with royal blessings and prayers of peace and prosperity for the people and town. The festival comes to an end with drinking among the chiefs and other participants. Importantly, the festival has no specific starting or concluding period. From our observation, the festival closed some few hours after mid-day.

FIGURE 12.2 Priests stand just behind the well before the festival ritual to sort the kola nut (*obi abata*). The kola nut bag (with the chief priest in white attire) contains one white kola nut and several red ones. The white kola nut is primarily reserved to offer prayers at the well for the king (faces are intentionally blurred for privacy). Photograph by author.

Additionally, the January festival is the first and one of many times in the year that *Ori Aiye* is propitiated. Most festivals in the town usually begin with participants first visiting the well to give modest offerings and, second, to offer prayers. The centrality of these ritual observances to Ondo life underscores the life-giving powers of the well which these forms of ritual observances seek to maintain. Since the *Osemawe* in many ways profits from *Ori Aiye*'s sacrality, he must necessarily perform the kingship rituals and observances annually to benefit perpetually from the well's powers.

Conclusion

Ori Aiye's festival is celebrated in January each year on dates determined by traditional agencies in the town; the festival's endurance relates to the annual blessing of the local power structure. As mentioned earlier, each ritual item has individualistic powers that reinforce each prayer offered by participating traditional agencies at the festival. Ondo's traditional agencies and the king are also imbued with their own powers. Since the well is historically linked to the town, the traditional agencies must offer their powers in concert with the king to propitiate the well with offerings and thereby protect the town's people from real or perceived dangers. The well's attribution of protective powers could possibly explain why *Ori Aiye* is propitiated during all other annual town festivals, for example, the *Odun Obitun* or "new woman" festival, the *Odun Aje* or festival of the goddess of fertility and wealth, the *Odun Oba* or the king's festival and the *Odun Ogun* or the Ogun's festival.

Unlike some holy wells in Europe, for instance, where Christianity and saint patrons may have overtaken the previous pagan roles of sacred places, *Ori Aiye* maintains its traditional status despite Ondo's late-nineteenth-century religious conversion experience and its reputation as a town with a large Christian population today. Concord exists between tradition and modern religion in the town. Since kings in Yorubaland are favorably "at home" with all faiths, festival rites such as those for the well serve as a potent integrating factor that transcends the Ondo Kingdom's religious divisions (Olupona, 1992:21). Hence, while some Yoruba towns have now lost their traditional festivals with the passage of time, Ondo retains about 40 traditional festivals celebrated with pomp throughout the year.[18] *Ori Aiye* is venerated in line with Ondo's traditional power structures and by virtue of its historic attachment to the town. Having perhaps lost some of its previous observances with its closure for reasons highlighted earlier, the well's sacrality is still reinforced. It is hoped that this study might encourage further holy well discourse in Africa and among the Yoruba.

Notes

1 This essay is based on fieldwork conducted in Ondo Town between mid-2016 and early 2017.
2 The Yoruba, one of the largest ethnic groups in Africa, occupy southwestern and parts of north central Nigeria.
3 These holy wells include *Yeyemolu* Barrett and *Olokun* wells in Ile Ife, Ife Central LGA, Osun State, southwest Nigeria.

4 The term, chief (*Oloye* in Yoruba), is simply a traditional title bestowed (for positive contributions to a community) by a king on village heads, heads of lineages, a leader of a cult group or a worthy individual. It could be an inherited or honorary title within a particular community. The term to a larger degree retains its cultural meaning in spite of the changes emanating from the effect of Islam, Christianity and colonialism. Account of *Ori Aiye* in personal communication, January 22, 2017.

5 The period when this indefinite closure of *Ori Aiye* occurred is not known from tradition but it is probable that this happened before the mid-nineteenth century.

6 The *Olobun* (market head or female king) is a very powerful position or title. It applies to Pupupu, Ondo's first and only female "king," and all her female descendants. Like the *Osemawe*, the *Olobun* too has a palace and female chiefs under her.

7 *Odogun* is the title of *Ori Aiye*'s gatekeeper. This position in Ondo history is unclear. One story notes that the *Odogun* was one of the "slaves" who accompanied Pupupu from Ile-Ife to their present site. How he transitioned to a gatekeeper of *Ori Aiye* remains unknown.

8 *Osemawe* is the title of the paramount Yoruba king of Ondo kingdom instituted in 1510. Since the inception of the stool, 44 *Osemawe* have ruled the town. The current occupant, Oba Adesimbo Victor Kiladejo, became 44th in 2006.

9 *Tiro* is a fine black powder popular among the Yoruba and other ethnic groups in Nigeria. It is applied on the dermal surfaces of the eyelid to enhance beauty and for warding off "the evil eye" among other uses.

10 Europeans too, sources say, jumped into the well like their local counterparts. No evidence, however, exists to support this claim. The "European" theory is possibly an embellishment rather than an actual historical occurrence perhaps, made up to nourish a narrative of the well's power and potency.

11 Accounts elsewhere claimed the *Olobun* ordered the well's indefinite closure, having conferred with the *Osemawe, Odogun* and other chiefs.

12 *Odun Moko* lasts for a week and is the last of many festivals celebrated in the early part of November in Ondo town.

13 While suicide is prohibited among the Yoruba, an unpopular king or failed military leader might commit suicide rather than face ignominy at home. This was taking the path of honor for which such a figure was respected and sometimes deified.

14 There are three traditional houses in Ondo Kingdom dedicated to the service (gatekeepers) of the well. A house is expected to internally select the next *Odogun* once the position becomes vacant. Selection rotates through the three houses.

15 This warning is similar to those at other Yoruba festivals such as the *Agemo* festival among the Ijebu, in Ijebu-Ode LGA, Ogun State, southwest Nigeria.

16 The authors did not observe anything unusual at the ritual in 2017.

17 The white kola nut is used specifically to offer prayers for the king.

18 A number of these festivals are celebrated by the Ondo Diaspora who return home to join friends, families and neighbors.

References

Ajayi, Ibidayo, ed. 2014. *The Evolution of Ondo Kingdom over 500 Years (1510-2010+).* Ibadan: Spectrum Books Limited.

Akinkuolie, Victor. 2015. Ondo Women Barred from Public Glare over Moko Festival. *The Hope Newspaper,* November. Accessed December 21, 2016. www.thehopenewspapers.com/2015/11/ondo-women-barred-from-public-glare-over-moko-festival/

Akintoye, Stephen Adebanji. 2010. *A History of the Yoruba People.* Dakar: Amalion Publishing.

Atherton, Alex. 2016. *Walking between Worlds: A Secret Little Book of Devon's Ancient and Holy Wells.* United Kingdom: Meldon Art Studio.

Awolalu, J. Omosade. 1973. Yoruba Sacrificial Practice. *Journal of Religion in Africa* 5(2):91.

Awolalu, J. Omosade. 1979. *Yoruba Beliefs and Sacrificial Rites*. Essex: Longman, 152–156.

Awolalu, J. Omosade and Dopamu P. Ade. 1979. *West African Traditional Religion*. Ibadan: Onibonoje Press and Book Industries, 212.

Baker, G. M. Rowland. 1985. Holy Wells and Magical Waters of Surrey. *Source* 1.

Barrett, Suzanne. The Holy Wells of Ireland, Ireland for Visitors. Accessed November 10, 2016. www.irelandforvisitors.com/articles/holy_wells.htm.

Bord, Janet and Bord Colin. 1994. Living with a Holy Well. *Source* 1.

Brenneman, L. Walter and Mary G. Brenneman. 1995. The Circle and the Cross: Reflections on the Holy Wells of Ireland. *Natural Resources Journal* 45:793.

Cudny, Waldemar. 2016. *Festivalisation of Urban Spaces: Factors, Processes and Effects*. Switzerland: Springer International Publishing, 2.

Falassi, Alessandro. 1987. Festival: Definition and Morphology. In *Time Out of Time: Essays on the Festival*, edited by Falassi, Alessandro, 2. Albuquerque: University of New Mexico Press.

Iluyemi, Olufunke. 2014. Ondo Tradition and Culture: The Female Angle. In *The Evolution of Ondo Kingdom over 500 Years (1510 – 2010+)*, edited by Ibidayo Ajayi, 50–54. Ibadan: Spectrum Books Limited.

Jordan, Katty. 2000. Wiltshire Healing Wells and the Strange Case of Purton Spa. *Living Spring Journal*, (1).

Kolawole, Mary E. Modupe. 1997. *Womanism and African Consciousness*. Trenton, NJ: Africa World Press, 57–58.

Laitin, D. David. 1986. *Hegemony and Culture: Politics and Change among the Yoruba*. Chicago, IL: University of Chicago Press, 35.

Logan, Patrick. 1980. *The Holy Wells of Ireland*. Gerrards Cross: Colin Smythe.

Makinde, D. Olajide. 2012. Potentialities of the Egungun Festival as a Tool for Tourism Development in Ogbomoso, Nigeria. In *Management of Natural Resources, Sustainable Development and Ecological Hazards III*, edited by Carlos A. Brebbia and S.S. Zubir, 587. Issue 3. Southampton: WIT Press.

Meller, Walter. 2010. *Holy Wells*. Whitefish, MT: Kessinger Publishing.

Molyneaux, L. Brian. 1995. *The Sacred Earth*. Boston, MA: Little, Brown.

Olupona, K. Jacob. 1992. *Kingship, Religion and Rituals in a Nigerian Community: A Phenomenological Study of Ondo Yoruba Festivals*. Ibadan: Layday Limited, 13.

Ray, Celeste. 2014. *The Origins of Ireland's Holy Wells*. Oxford: Oxbow/Archaeopress.

Walsh, J. Michael. 1948. The Êdi Festival at Ile Ife. *African Affairs* 47(189):233.

13

SACRED WELLS OF BANARAS

Glorifications, ritual practices and healing

Vera Lazzaretti

As at many pilgrimage centers of the Indian subcontinent, water is foundational for Banaras (Varanasi), a notable Hindu pilgrimage destination in northern India. The city's waterscape includes the imposing Ganga River with its renowned *ghāṭs*—the flights of steps leading to the river waters (Singh, 1994; Jalais, 2014)—and its tributaries Varuna and Assi; however, it is also composed of a variety of minor water bodies entangled in the inner geography of the city, which are the focus of this chapter. It is this waterscape that fostered and sustained Banaras as a most renowned sacred center (*tīrtha*). One can describe Banaras as a *tīrtha* (literally a "ford" or "crossing place") *because* it is permeated with water: the term *tīrtha*, indeed, foregrounds the idea of sacredness as a quality linked to, and stemming from, water itself.

In Vedic literature, *tīrtha* was used to indicate places in which the magnificent rivers of South Asia could be crossed, as well as riverside localities in which bathing took place. Being perpetually mobile, Vedic gods originally had no connection with specific places (Angot, 2009). Over time, however, Brahmanical tradition assimilated a sense of divine presence at certain locations often associated with water—an idea that had originated in popular cults of deities associated with natural elements (Eck, 1981). The term *tīrtha*, then, came to identify "sacred centres," namely places in which a more metaphorical crossing is possible from the human shore to the divine. Lists of *tīrtha*s and descriptions of their qualities abound in various textual traditions; however, they are mostly developed in the Puranas, the "ancient recitations" of the Brahmans (Jacobsen, 2013:12–15). The term *tīrtha* continued to refer to water places themselves and is still in use today. Canonical texts on architecture prescribe that the location of a new shrine must be in the vicinity of a water place, because gods are said to be present where water flows (Jain-Neubauer, 1981:5).

Offering an account of Banaras' inner waterscape including sacred wells and stepwells, this chapter outlines the history and roles of minor water places as independent and autonomous sacred locations. It concludes by detailing the mythology, history and role of Jnanavapi (the Well of Knowledge) which is arguably the main sacred well of Banaras.

Inner waterscape and smaller water bodies: a short history

The dimensions and structures of Banaras' water places are the result of continuous interventions and changes to the urban fabric over time. These transitions impacted the highly changeable terminology through which authors of Sanskrit glorifications, historical accounts and modern pilgrims' guidebooks, as well as contemporary inhabitants, refer to smaller water places. Ponds, tanks and step-wells are variously called *kuṇḍ*s, *pokharā*s and *tālāb*s in Banaras. Although some have acquired superstructures and impoundments, these generally originated in natural features where rainwater was collected and then flowed into the Ganga (Singh, 1955). In many parts of India, ponds and step-wells are sites where the boundary between profane and sacred collapses, and where practical functions, leisure activities and irrigation practices meet with ritual and devotional uses of water (Jain–Neubauer, 1981; Dehejia, 2009). Many of these water bodies of Banaras are also known as *tīrtha*s and their waters grant specific boons to devotees.

Wells, which are usually somewhat smaller, are called *kūp*s, *kuāṃ*s or *vāpī*s. The last term may previously have referred to more elaborate structures than a simple well (Jain–Neubauer, 1981), but the term is in use synonymously with the others. Some of these wells are civic constructions from the Mughal and British periods (Rötzer, 1989). Others are of presumed antiquity and are the remnants of larger sacred water bodies that were reduced in size as part of British-era urban reshaping (Lazzaretti, 2017).

A history of Banaras' minor water places, such as wells, is difficult to trace. The first and very few sacred places of the city mentioned in the *Mahābhārata* were connected to water bodies, whose existence most likely predated that of actual shrines (Lazzaretti, 2017). In the progressive development of Sanskrit glorifications focused on Banaras, however, a growing number of sacred water places were incorporated into the lists of deities and places attached to the urban landscape that various anonymous scholars collected. "Glorification" refers to the genre of *māhātmya*s or *sthalapurāṇa*s which are sections of the Puranas that often circulate independently. They are centered on specific sacred objects, such as pilgrimage centers, shrines, water places or other holy areas.[1] Local glorifications culminated in the naming of dozens of sacred wells and ponds in the most extensive glorification of the city— the thirteenth-to-fourteenth-century *Kāśīkhaṇḍa* (henceforth KKh) (Bakker, 1996; Bakker and Isaacson, 2004; Smith, 2007).

Between the seventeenth and nineteenth centuries, regional sovereigns such as Marathas and Bengalis patronized the construction of riverfront palaces, *ghāṭ*s, temples and rest houses for pilgrims, to revitalize the city's sacred geography and ancient traditions (Couté and Léger, 1989; Freitag, 1989). During what Desai (2007) calls an architectural "resurrection" of the city, some of the pre-existing water places were equipped with more solid and sometimes monumental structures, or reshaped according to new directions and uses of the city's space (Singh, 1955). Major changes occurred again during colonial times, particularly in the first half of the nineteenth century, when indigenous epistemologies of water were challenged by, and at times attuned with, the projects of sanitation and development promoted by the British administration (Lazzaretti, 2017; Cf. Mosse, 2003).

Several current toponyms of urban areas come from water bodies which exist only in a reduced form or were drained during this time in the process of urban development.

Sacred wells and step-wells: types, locations and uses

In contemporary Banaras, most water places lie in a state of disrepair, with the exception of a few that have undergone sporadic "beautification" by governments or local associations. Whether mentioned in textual traditions or not, however, wells and their significance are known to elder inhabitants of the city, who still recall the diverse properties of their waters. The city's entire waterscape has been seen in fact as a framework through which inhabitants construct their own categories and understandings of time and space (Derné, 1998). Varied typologies, terminologies and practices associated with such water places have been documented by local scholars in their extensive cataloguing works about the city's sacred geography. Compilers of twentieth-century Hindī glorifications and guides to the city's various *tīrthas* (as they refer to water places) have registered a large number of names and locations of sacred watery sites, many of which are already said to be *lupta* (disappeared) (Vyas, 2011 [1987]:218–231; Cf. Sukul, 1977). These works have also acted as pilgrims' guides to the rituals and qualities of specific water places and have noted the auspicious moments of the calendar at which to bathe (*snān karnā*) and drink at these sites.

Sacred wells are today most often found inside temples or in temple compounds. Their waters are sprinkled over the divine icons of the deity who dwells there. An example of this kind of well is Kal *kūp*. This is located inside the Kaldand temple, which is dedicated to a form of Dandapani (one of the guardians of the city). The opening of the small square well is almost at ground level and Vyas describes it as a place whose waters can be used for ritual ablution and whose power is to remove the fear of time—in this context, a synonym for death (2011 [1987]:218). Other sometimes slightly bigger structures can be found in temple compounds. For example, Kalodak *kūp* (Figure 13.1) is a wide well located in the courtyard of what is today a unified temple compound that includes as major deities Mahamritunjaya, Mahakal and Vriddakal—three forms of the god Shiva associated with the defeat of death and time. Now usually visited as part of the compound, the well must have had in the past, and perhaps still has today, an independent nature. While the KKh describes it as a place whose waters dispel old age and sickness and grant liberation (24.74; 33.150), the well seems to have acquired more detailed qualities in the course of the centuries. For the last century at least, its waters have been employed against leprosy, psoriasis, colic, diabetes, dysentery, indigestion, urine infections, apparitions of ghostly creatures and for the eradication of various other diseases (Vyas, 2011 [1987]:218).

Apart from visiting various shrines of its deities and taking ablutions at notable bathing places along the river, Hindu pilgrims also come to Banaras to perform a series of rituals for the dead (*śraddhā*). Several larger tanks and step-wells retain a more visible status as autonomous destinations for specific rituals of this kind, especially the preparation of food offerings for the departed souls (*piṇḍa dān*). This ritual is performed annually after a death and at auspicious times of the Hindu calendar and it usually takes place at the river bank or at the side of water bodies, such as

FIGURE 13.1 Kalodak *kūp* and man receiving water at the *kūp*. Photograph by author.

*kuṇḍ*s. Under the guidance of a ritual specialist, the closest relative of the departed prepares the *piṇḍa*s (rice balls) that will then be placed in the water to nourish the departed, thus enabling their transition to the world of ancestors (Parry, 1994). Singh reports that there are three notable locations used for this purpose in Banaras: the Pishachmochana, Kapildhara and Chakrapushkarini *kuṇḍ*s (1994:223). Each specializes in pacifying particular types of deceased persons with offerings. Pishachmochana, for instance, is the right place to perform offerings for those who have turned into erratic goblins and haunting spirits (*bhūt, pret, piśac*) as a result of death due to illness or violent accidents. Offerings are performed here in order to set the deceased free from their ghostly form and enable them to access the realm of ancestors (*pitṛ*) (KKh 54.73–87). Kapildhara is recommended for the pacification of those who died in fires accidentally and those who were denied proper cremation because of a lack of male heirs (KKh 62.72–75), as well as those who had an unnatural death, drowned in water or committed suicide (KKh 62.75–76). The third watery location, Chakrapushkarini, is the cremation ground at Manikarnika *ghāṭ* which is noted by the KKh as originating at the time of creation (26.35–65). The KKh, however, mentions other wells as suitable for food offerings for the departed souls and some have other unique qualities. For example, Dharma *kūp* (see Figure 13.2) is praised extensively as a dispeller of sins and as a place where even glancing at one own's reflection in its water grants the results that would be obtained through performing a complete *śraddhā* ritual (KKh 81.21–36).

FIGURE 13.2 Dharma *kūp*. Photograph by author.

A well at the center of the pilgrimage city: Jnanavapi, the Well of Knowledge

The KKh mentions many water places of the city in passing even though they are said to be powerful locations. An important exception is Jnanavapi, the Well of Knowledge, to which the text dedicates two entire chapters (KKh 33 and 34). The well is today under a nineteenth-century arcaded pavilion, located in a wide *maidān* (open area) that separates the main temple of the city (dedicated to Shiva as Vishvanath or Vishveshvar, the Lord of the Universe) and the Gyan Vapi mosque (the central Islamic shrine of the city). Because of the mosque's controversial location on the site of what is considered to be a previous Vishvanath temple, the area is now managed by security forces.

The fact that the well is treated as a major destination by the KKh and is explicitly linked to the deity Vishvanath, fits well the project of the KKh compilers. This text has been seen as an attempt to re-write the city's myths and re-conceive its sacred geography as connected to the emerging deity, Vishvanath (Smith, 2007). While unknown to previous sources, during the twelfth century, Vishvanath most likely replaced and assimilated the city's first known major divine form, Avimukta (Bakker and Isaacson, 2004). This transition is clearly sanctioned by the KKh, in which Vishvanath is promoted as the new center of worship, drawing its power from connections with previously recognized powerful deities, such as Avimukta. Jnanavapi might well have been employed in the KKh to promote recognition of the newly established deity. The Well of Knowledge, in fact, has been identified as an important water place in existence well before the emergence of Vishvanath. As pointed out by Bakker and Isaacson (2004), the twelfth-century *Tirthavivechanakanda* (TVK), compiled by Lakshmidhara, locates the *vāpī* to the south of Avimukta (TVK:109–110). Both Avimukta and the *vāpī* have been tentatively located by Bakker (1996) in the area where the mosque and the *maidān* with the Well of Knowledge dwell today.

It is thus conceivable that the *vāpī* even predated Avimukta and, considering the principles highlighted earlier for the construction of shrines next to water, and the foundational role of water for sacredness, its presence there may even have been the reason for the establishment of an Avimukta shrine. The KKh, however, narrates a different story, in which an attempt to assimilate this water place into the tradition of Vishvanath is visible. The myth of the origins of the well tells that Ishana, the guardian of the north-east direction, and also identified as a terrifying form of Shiva, arrived at the great cremation ground that is the city of Kashi (a textual name of Banaras, still in use today) and saw the *liṅga* Vishveshvar (Vishvanath). This *liṅga*—an emblem of Shiva—was said to have previously erupted there to demonstrate the god's superiority and put an end to the rivalry between the fractious gods Brahma and Vishnu.[2] On seeing the *liṅga*, Ishana decided to bathe it with cool water and dug in the earth at a spot *to the south* of Vishveshvar, where water gushed forth allowing him to do so (KKh 33.16–18).

The qualities of these waters are then described in several verses (20–25) and the whole area around the well, called Jnanoda or Jnana *tīrtha,* is praised by Vishveshvar himself. The water of the well is seen as the liquid form of knowledge; it has the power of cleaning all sins and even dispenses *mokṣa* (liberation from rebirth)

(KKh 33.32–33; 45–46). The site is also identified as adequate for the performance of *śraddhā* rituals, which, at certain auspicious times, is equivalent to their performance in Gaya—a most renowned destination for such rituals (KKh 33.35–39). As is commonly found in the genre, the glorification continues narrating the greatness of Jnanavapi by reporting how one of the well's great devotees was even taken to the abode of Shiva (KKh 34).

The connection of Jnanavapi with the deity Vishvanath has been re-asserted over time since the KKh was composed. Vishvanath progressively gained popularity and a grand Vishvanath temple was later constructed during the reign of Mughal emperor Akbar next to the Well of Knowledge (Desai, 2017). In the seventeenth century, however, this temple was dismantled by order of the Mughal emperor Aurangzeb (Asher, 1992:254). Subsequent legends note that the deity fled the destruction by taking refuge in the well (Sherring, 1868:53–54; Prinsep, 2009 [1833]:71). Being perceived as the substitute location for the threatened divine image, and by hosting the *liṅga* in its water, Jnanavapi came to be seen as the new central divine abode. Even after the eighteenth-century installation of the *liṅga* in a new Vishvanath temple in a different location close to the well, the association of Jnanavapi with the "original" Vishveshvar continued to be acknowledged. Oral accounts collected in recent years testify that this association is still strong.

Research conducted at Jnanavapi and with the ritual specialists (the Vyas family) in charge of the well and the surrounding *maidān*, however, highlights how the area has also long been a ritual arena independent of Vishvanath, and one crucial to the performance of local urban pilgrimage (Gutschow, 2006; Gengnagel, 2011; Lazzaretti, 2015, 2017). Until recently, pilgrimage associations active in the promotion of these circuits would direct pilgrims to the Jnanavapi pavilion, where they would make a commencement vow (*saṅkalp lenā*). At the end of the pilgrimage, they would return here to mark the accomplishment of their vow and conclude the ritual performance (*saṅkalp choḍnā*). Members of the Vyas family used to perform these rituals for pilgrims.

The role of the well's pavilion, its waters and the ritual specialists connected to it has progressively become more peripheral due to security procedures and the management of the contested area in the last 30 years (Lazzaretti, 2015). The *maidān* first became just a space to be crossed, but today it and the Jnanavapi are completely obstructed by a controversial development plan for the expansion of the Vishvanath temple and its surroundings.

Conclusion

As seen from this brief exploration of the inner waterscape of Banaras, sacred water places exist in this pilgrimage city in a variety of forms and structures with their own rich terminology. The current locations of wells attached to temples has facilitated the use of their waters for *dharmik kām*—an expression that refers to religious purposes and devotional activities—and thus for the worship of nearby deities. The myth of Jnanavapi as recounted in the KKh also promotes the idea that the well was created to bathe and worship the *liṅga* Vishveshvar. However, we have also seen that the reputations of several water places have been enriched over time and that they have been and are still known as independent destinations sought for healing, and for the performance of specific rituals, such as *piṇḍa dān*.

As suggested by the history of the urban territory and by early glorifications focused on the city, water places are part of the first urban strata and their presence might well have stimulated the construction of major shrines. The case of Jnanavapi, in particular, speaks of a major well that has quite possibly been foundational for the promotion of both Avimukta and Vishveshvar, the two major deities in ancient and modern Banaras. Because of the constantly renovated "symbolic capital" of water (Fontein, 2008), the well has been continuously subject to attempts to assimilate it into the tradition of the nearby Vishvanath.

This account of wells and step-wells demonstrates that even apparently minor water bodies constitute important features of both historical and contemporary Hinduism. Water places were foundational for the development of notions of *tīrtha* and sacredness; despite now being found mostly in temple compounds, apparently in a peripheral role, they still represent autonomous sacred locations, whose distinctiveness is described by layered textual traditions and popular accounts.

Notes

1 See Bakker and Isaacson (2004) for an analysis of the layered glorification literature dedicated to Banaras.
2 The text locates the pan-Indian mythological episode of the eruption of Shiva as *jyotirliṅga* (*liṅga* of light) in Kashi (Banaras) and identifies the supreme light column of the *jyotirliṅga* with Vishveshvar/Vishvanath (KKh 33. 10–11).

References

Angot, Michel. 2009. Land and Location: Errant Gods, Erring Asuras and the Land of Men. Place and Space in Vedic Literature. In *Terra, territorio e società nel mondo indiano*, edited by Daniela Berti and Gilles Tarabout, *Etnosistemi* 10:10–27.

Asher, Catherine B. 1992. *Architecture of Mughal India*. Cambridge: Cambridge University Press.

Bakker, Hans T. 1996. Construction and Reconstruction of Sacred Space in Varanasi. *Numen* XLIII(1):32–55.

Bakker, Hans T. and Harunaga Isaacson. 2004. A Sketch of the Religious History of Vārāṇasī up to the Islamic Conquest and the New Beginning. In *The Skandapurāṇa*, vol. IIA (Adhyāyas 26-31.14), *The Varanasi Cycle*, edited by Hans T. Bakker and Harunaga Isaacson, 19–82. Gröningen: Egbert Forsten.

Couté, Pier Daniel and Jean-Michel Léger. 1989. *Bénarès. Un voyage d'architecture*. Paris: Editions Créaphis.

Derné, Steve. 1998. Feeling Water: Notes on the Sensory Construction of Time and Space in Banaras. *Man in India* 78(1 and 2):1–7.

Dehejia, Vidya. 2009. *The Body Adorned. Dissolving Boundaries between Sacred and Profane in India's Art*. New York: Columbia University Press.

Desai, Madhuri. 2007. *Resurrecting Banaras: Urban Spaces, Architecture and Religious Boundaries*. PhD thesis, University of California, Berkeley.

Desai, Madhuri. 2017. *Banaras Reconstructed. Architecture and Sacred Space in a Hindu Holy City*. Seattle: University of Washington Press.

Eck, Diana L. 1981. India's Tīrthas: "Crossings" in Sacred Geography. *History of Religions* 20(4):323–344.

Fontein, Joost. 2008. The Power of Water: Landscape, Water and the State in Southern and Eastern Africa: An Introduction. *Journal of South African Studies* 34(4):737–775.

Freitag, Sandra B. 1989. *Culture and Power in Banaras. Community, Performance and Environment, 1800–1980.* Berkeley: University of California Press.

Gengnagel, Jörg. 2011. *Visualized Texts. Sacred Spaces, Spatial Texts and the Religious Cartography of Banaras.* Wiesbaden: Harrassowitz Verlag.

Gutschow, Niels. 2006. *Benares. The Sacred Landscape of Vārānasī.* Stuttgart/London: Edition Axel Menges.

Jacobsen, Knut. 2013. *Pilgrimage in the Hindu Tradition. Salvific Space.* London: Routledge.

Jain-Neubauer, Jutta. 1981. *The Stepwells of Gujarat: In Art Historical Perspective.* New Delhi: Abhinav Publications.

Jalais, Savitri. 2014. Walking the Ghāṭs: A Measured Approach to the Banāras Riverfront. In *Banāras Revisited. Scholarly Pilgrimages to the City of Light,* edited by István Keul, 133–150. Wiesbaden: Harrassowitz Verlag.

Kāśīkhaṇḍa (Skanda Purāṇa), ed. 1991. *Karunapati Tripathi.* Varanasi: Sampurnanand Sanskrit University.

Kāśīkhaṇḍa (Skanda Purāṇa), ed. By G.V. Tagare, Motilal Banarsidass, Delhi, 1996.

Lazzaretti, Vera. 2015. Tradition versus Urban Public Bureaucracy? Reshaping Pilgrimage Routes and Religious Heritage around Contested Places. In *Religion and Urbanism: Reconceptualizing 'Sustainable Cities' for South Asia,* edited by Yamini Narayanan, 80–96. London: Routledge.

Lazzaretti, Vera. 2017. Waterscapes in Transition: Past and Present Reshaping of Sacred Water Places in Banaras. In *Water, Knowledge and the Environment in Asia: Epistemologies, Practices and Locales,* edited by Ravi Gabhel, Jospeh K.W. Hill and Lea Stepan, 230–245. London: Routledge.

Mosse, David. 2003. *The Rule of Water: Statecraft, Ecology and Collective Action in South India.* New Delhi: Oxford University Press.

Prinsep, James. 2009 [1833]. *Benares Illustrated in a Series of Drawings.* Varanasi: Pilgrims Publishing.

Rötzer, Klaus. 1989. Wells, Pokhara, Ghāṭ and Hammam. In *Bénarès, Un voyage d'architecture,* edited by Pier Daniel Couté and Jean-Michel Léger, 89–97. Paris: Editions Créaphis.

Sherring, Mathew A. 1868. *The Sacred City of the Hindoos: An Account of Benares in Ancient and Modern Times.* London: Trübner & Co.

Singh, Reginald Lal. 1955. *Banaras: A Study in Urban Geography.* Banaras: Nand Kishore and Bro.

Singh, Rana P. B. 1994. Water Symbolism and Sacred Landscape in Hindūism. A study of Benares (Varanasi). *Erdkuṇde* 48(3):210–227.

Smith, Travis L. 2007. Re-newing the Ancient: The Kāśīkhaṇḍa and Śaiva Vārāṇasī. *Acta Orientalia Vilnensia* 8(1):83–108.

Sukul, Kubernath. 1977. *Vārāṇasī Vaibhava.* Patna: Bihar Rashtrabhasha Parishad. *Tīrthavivecanakāṇḍa,* edited by K. V. Rangaswami Aiyangar. 1942. Gaekwad's Oriental Series 98, Baroda.

Vyas, Kedarnath. 2011 [1987]. *Pañcakrośātmaka jyotirliṅga kāśīmāhātmya evaṃ kāśī kā prācīna itihāsa.* Varanasi: Khandelavala Press.

14

YAKSUTŎ

Korean sacred mineral spring water

Hong-key Yoon

According to a survey carried out in 1995 by the South Korean Ministry of Environment, there are 1,460 yaksutŏ or "sacred mineral springs" scattered in different parts of South Korea.[1] As the context of a sentence indicates whether a subject is singular or plural in Korean, yaksutŏ does not have a pluralized form. Yaksutŏ means literally "the place of medicinal water" where yaksu means "medicinal mineral water" and tŏ means "the place of." Yaksu is supposed to contain minerals that enhance human health and which are not available in ordinary water. Yaksutŏ are usually considered sacred and are mostly located on wooded mountain slopes or in the foothills. Their waters often spring from the cracks of a rock and trickle down to a small pool [see Figure 14.1].

Although a sacred yaksutŏ is supposed to have mysteriously effective medicinal powers to heal certain illnesses, some of them are also known as good places for petitioning local deities. Mountain spirits and dragon kings are believed to abide there and control the waters. Koreans who pray to such deities believe that they can grant them blessings like a long healthy life, successful marriage arrangements or the birth of a son. Yaksutŏ can treat particular sicknesses such as indigestion, or can grant particular types of wishes such as successful university entrance. These specialist yaksutŏ remain famous for curing certain diseases or wish-granting today. Varying degrees of sacredness are assigned to different yaksutŏ depending on their efficacy.

Legends associated with the locations of yaksutŏ

Many Korean yaksutŏ have associated folklore affirming a spring's effective powers and how to employ the waters. Even more legends exist about the medicinal water's mysterious origins or discovery. Well-known yaksutŏ in the mountainous province of Kangwon-do, such as Osaek yaksu, are famed for treating stomach disorders, skin diseases and rheumatism, and are said to have been discovered by a sixteenth-century Buddhist monk who happened to drink the water that sprang from a crack

FIGURE 14.1 (L) Yŏngsiam Temple yaksutŏ. Water springs out of rock and trickles down to a small basin at Sŏraksan Mountain in Kangwŏn Province. At the top of a pagoda-styled rock cairn appears the dictum "Wash your mind [洗心.]" Photo by Professor In-choul Zho, used with permission. (R) A now-dried yaksutŏ partly hidden under a pile of tree leaves on a mountain slope behind Tŏksŏni village in Kosŏng County, South Kyŏngsang Province. The site is still visited when water re-emerges. Photograph by Professor Dowon Lee, used with permission.

in a boulder (Yi Kwang-yul, 2014:1). Another site in the same province, Sambong yaksu, is deemed effective for similar health complaints and depression. Its discovery came when Confucian scholar-teacher, Kwon Chŏn, noticed a wild crane fixing a damaged wing by soaking it in the stream's water; he went to the stream and also found the characteristic yaksutŏ source, a spring emerging from a crack in a boulder (Yi Kwang-yul, 2014:2).

Many yaksutŏ legends can draw on historical facts and these folk narratives are now utilized by the locals in promoting and marketing mineral springs to those with health issues and to tourists. For instance, the black-pepper-tasting Ch'ojŏngyaksu mineral water in Ch'ŏngwon County (North Ch'ungch'ŏng Province) is famous in Korea for its effectiveness in treating eye-related illnesses and skin diseases. The local people claim that the waters there are one of the three most effective mineral waters in the world. Two kings of the Chosŏn dynasty (King Sejong and King Sejo) cured their skin problems and poor health by bathing in the cold waters at Ch'ojŏngyaksu (No Sasin et al., 1969). As a part of their effort to promote the mineral water site and to attract more tourists, the locals organized an annual festival called "The Great King Sejong and Chojŏng mineral water festival" and set up restaurants and bath-houses using the mineral water (Yi Hakju et al., 2014:240).

The mysterious power of a yaksutŏ at the Koransa Buddhist Temple of Puyŏ County in South Ch'ungch'ŏng Province is related in the following legend:

> Once upon a time an old couple who lived in a village of Soburi (the ancient Capital District of the Paekche Kingdom) had no children of their own and the wife wished to conceive. One day a Buddhist monk from Ilsan (日山Sun Mountain) advised her that the mineral water in the Koransa Temple had revitalizing effects, because it sprang from a boulder surrounded by a special dew-collecting plant called, Korancho. On the next day at dawn, the wife sent her husband to the yaksutŏ for him to drink the mineral water. However, he did not return home. Early the next morning, the wife went to the yaksutŏ to find there a new born baby boy in her husband's old clothes. At that moment she realized that she had not told her husband what the Buddhist monk advised: "drinking a cup of the water will make him three years younger." Her husband had drunk so much water that he became a baby boy. She brought the baby home and raised him well. He grew to be a famous man and became a high ranking government officer of the Paekche Kingdom.[2]

The story explicitly presents Koransa Temple water as a youth-restoring tonic. Both funny and somewhat intimidating, the tale warns that the water's medicinal power is so effective that one should not consume too much.

Many traditional yaksutŏ are said to have been found by a worthy person, always after dreaming of an old man (a sage or a supernatural person) who instructs the dreamer about the medicinal spring site (Kim, 1995:351–355). For instance, the site of Ch'ugok yaksu at Ch'unch'ŏn owes its discovery to a traveler named "Mr. Kim" who happened to fall asleep in exhaustion at the place where he found the yaksutŏ. He dreamed of a mountain spirit scolding him: "why can't you recognize the medicinal water right here…why do you keep sleeping?" As he wakes, he finds a mineral water spring underneath a pile of tree leaves (Yi Hakju et al., 2014:330–301; Yi Hakju, 2014:245). Another well-known legend is associated with a famous Buddhist monk, Grand Master Wonhyo. The monk prayed hard to Buddha for good wells and in his dream an old man with gray hair (a mountain spirit? a sage?) appeared to tell him that his prayers were heard and instructed him about the location of the auspicious well sites at Yŏnghyŏlsa Temple and at Hongrŏn'am beside the Naksansa Temple (Kim Ŭisuk, 1995:353). Some yaksutŏ are associated with witnessing mysterious natural phenomena—such as the wild crane mending its wing that was mentioned earlier. Of the many legends associated with yaksutŏ, those retold today attract both supplicants in search of a cure and tourists curious about local folklore and popular religion.

Healing effects of the sacred medicinal spring water

Korean folklorist Kim Ŭisuk has noted 17 yaksutŏ with curative reputations in Kangwondo, a mountainous province of South Korea (1995:344). She notes that they have been credited with healing stomach disorders, cancer and skin diseases. These "medicinal effects" are listed in note form without further comments as what she learned from the locals during her field research on folk custom of the province. In the list of unproven folk-medicinal comments, 13 out of 17 yaksutŏ claim to be effective in treating stomach disorders as one of the principal medicinal benefits. Only four yaksutŏ were noted for primarily curing other concerns: cancer treatment, diabetes, skin diseases, pungbyong-paralysis or nerve system disorders, or for offering longevity and a life without sickness (1995:344).

A more elaborate and much older list of traditional yaksutŏ is found in Paek Namsin's encyclopedic *Sŏul Taekwan (A Grand Survey of Seoul)* (1955). The book is probably the first comprehensive description of Seoul and details the city's 24 yaksutŏ with their various health-improving effects (Paek Namsin, 1955:342–346). For example, the first two listings of the yaksutŏ and their brief description are as follows:

1. Changch'ungdan Yaksu (it is also known as Pŏtŏ Yaksu): located in the deep valley on the way to Hannamdong from Changch'ungdan. It produces plenty of water and many people come to this place to drink the water as well as to shower with the water. The water is the best in treating stomach problems such as indigestion.
2. Namsan Yaksu (it is also known as Pŏngbawi Yaksu): it springs out of a boulder on the middle slope of Namsan (the South mountain of Seoul), and it is generally called "Pŏngbawi Yaksutŏ" and is especially effective in curing stomach disorder (indigestion problems).

All of Seoul's 24 yaksutŏ are located in suburban areas and sprang from the usual crack in a boulder. None of them are in the city center, but they were reachable from the city via wooded footpaths. In most cases, people go to yaksutŏ to drink mineral water at the site and to carry it home in small bottles. At some exceptional yaksutŏ such as Changch'ungdan Yaksu (no. 1 above), the water flows at a higher volume and from a height so that visitors may also stand beneath the outflow to be showered in medicinal water. The most common cure sought at Seoul's 24 yaksutŏ is the treatment of stomach disorders including indigestion problems (the primary cure at 17 sites). Twelve of those 17 were deemed to exclusively specialize in treating ailments of the stomach, while six cured related conditions, but also offered remedies for other illnesses such as skin problems (4) or eye problems (2). Washing the infected parts of the body with clean water would, of course, have had some positive effects for such issues. The waters of other yaksutŏ are classified as the special water used only by royal palace residents; one faithfully provided cool water in the heat of summer, yet never froze in winter, while another was known as a "cure all" (Paek Namsin, 1955:342–346):

Why are yaksutŏ waters in general considered especially effective in treating stomach disorders or indigestion problems? This may be due to the chemical composition of the rocks from which "mineral waters" spring. However, yaksutŏ water could also be healthier than the domestic water supplies in urban areas due to their locations in mountain forests. The effort required to reach these sites itself, hiking along wooded footpaths, could also be health-inducing. Consumers of mineral water may have to walk (some jog) several miles from their suburban houses to yaksutŏ [see Figure 14.1]. As visits are usually undertaken in the morning, this exercise along hilly routes can enhance the appetite for food as well as aid digestion of food consumed before the trip. Thus, the habit of walking along mountain slopes to any mineral water springs must have been a health-enhancing activity and this alone could have contributed to yaksutŏ waters becoming known as particularly effective in treating stomach issues. Rather than being scientifically proven, the effectiveness of yaksutŏ waters on certain diseases in many cases seemed to be based on people's perceptions and storytelling.

Worshiping deities at yaksutŏ

Most traditional yaksutŏ are associated with some type of Korean folk belief systems in one way or another. Even today, one may readily see the remains of an offering ritual at a yaksutŏ on a foothill of Seoul or near other major cities. A portion of cooked rice and remains of dried pollock (fish) or dried squid laying on a piece of rock near a yaksutŏ may well be signs that someone performed an offering ritual recently. Some yaksutŏ rituals can be civic-oriented public displays. On October 7, 2018, the local government head of the Keyang-ku District of Inchon Metropolitan City led a solemn ceremony at the Yaksutŏ Todang Kosaje.[3] Garbed in traditional ceremonial robes, officials offered deities a large table full of food including a cooked pig's head and various kinds of fresh fruits. Such traditional offering ceremonies for the good and prosperity of villages and districts still occur at numerous yaksutŏ and in the capital city of Seoul.

Kyung-Min Park has noted that such traditional Korean ceremonies are called "kosa" which is a generic term for describing ritual offerings to a local deity including mountain spirits, village guardian deities or the deity in charge of the yasutŏ. These rituals are performed annually on a designated date, or on a special occasion such as the completion of repair work or renovation of any structures at mineral water springs (2000:76). Kosa at yaksutŏ in Seoul seem to be somewhat secularized in comparison to the traditional and famous yaksutŏ offering ceremonies away from the capital city. In their prayers, kosa ceremony participants especially ask local deities for good quality mineral water in abundance (Park, 2000:76).

Even if a yaksutŏ does not have an image of a deity or a sacred altar for worship and offerings, the mineral water at such places is assumed to have a healing power for body and mind. However, many well-known yaksutŏ *are* affiliated with mountain spirits or dragon deities and their images or tablets are displayed nearby. For instance, the famous Pang'adari yaksu in the National Park at Odaesan Mountain (The Mountain of Five Plains) has a shrine for a dragon god and a shrine for a mountain spirit where people perform religious rituals and offer prayers with special petitions (Yi Hakju et al., 2014:242). At the Namchŏn yaksu of Inche County in Kangwon Province, people pray and present petitions by a sacred painting of the mountain deity— the very image of which is believed to possess mystic power (ibid). In her study, Kim Ŭisuk commented that every traditional yaksutŏ bears traces of candles from prayer and worship and that these sites have been associated with people's traditional shamanistic folk beliefs (Kim Ŭisuk, 1995:345; Yi Hakju et al., 2014:242). Yaksutŏ remain sacred places to varying degrees and visitors behave accordingly. In some

FIGURE 14.2 This site's name, Sangsŏnam Yaksu, literally means "superior Supernatural deity rock medicinal water": 上仙岩藥水, 상선암약수. The sacred precincts of this holy well are marked with *kŭmkichul* (taboo ropes) that signify an area not to be disturbed or polluted. This site is in Kasanni Village of Tansŏng-Myŏn, in Tangyang County of the North Ch'ungchŏng Province. The sign reads: Spiritual (miracle) water well: 靈泉 령천; Keep it clean when you use 사용 깨끗이. Photo by Professor Won-suk Choi, used with permission.

cases, in order to draw mystic spiritual power from the resident deities, shamanistic offerings (called "kut" in Korean) are still made.

Many traditional yaksutŏ are associated with folk beliefs in nature spirits— perhaps because of the curative powers believed to emanate at such places (Yi Hakju, 2014:242). Folk religious rituals and prayers can relate to individual worries (such as a health issue or hopes for a child's performance on a university entrance examination) or to larger familial fortune or concerns, success in the harvest or in fishing, or even to invocations for a business's prosperity. Some yaksutŏ petitions may require elaborate ritual sequences performed by shamans or Buddhist monks. Korean shamanism engages the spirit world (populated by a pantheon of gods and spirits) and Korean Buddhism syncretized many aspects of indigenous tradition, including an emphasis on Sansin (the Mountain Spirit). While the form of the ritual offerings may vary from those derived from indigenous shamanism to those more overtly shaped by Korean Buddhism, they are made to nature spirits, and principal among these are either mountain spirits or dragon gods (see Kim Ŭisuk, 1995:345).

Chugok yaksutŏ at Chunch'ŏn in the Kangwon Province still holds an annual "yaksuche" or "offering ceremony to the deity of yaksutŏ." This ceremony is commonly known as Chugok yaksuche and is documented in detail by Kim Ŭisuk. The following is a summary of her description of the ceremony and its offering table as prepared by locals:

> The local people call the offering ceremony the "Sanche" ("the offering ceremony to the mountain-deity"). It is always held on the 1st day of the Third Moon and the 1st day of the Tenth Moon according to the lunar calendar.
>
> Women organize the ceremony and the other participants-spectators are also mostly women. Two food offering tables are prepared. A large offering table is for the Mountain Spirit (god) and a smaller one for the Dragon King (Yongsin) is placed on a lower slope. The Mountain Spirit table receives more food: the boiled head of a pig (*toejimŏri*), cooked vegetables (*namul*), fresh fruits and traditional Korean rice cakes in layers (*siruttŏk*) in two steamers (*siru*) with lit candles and burning incense. For the Dragon King, devotees offer less food: a rice cake without layers in one steamer, along with fresh fruits and cooked vegetables (*nambul*). On both tables, they position brass cups or bowls of fresh water from the yaksutŏ (1995:346–349).

People bow before the food-laden tables as a gesture of honoring and worshipping the deities. As in any other Korean sacred ritual, candle light, incense and clean fresh water are offered in the ceremony. In traditional shamanistic rituals in Korea, a pig's head (steamed or boiled) played an important role, probably because in Korean folk religion, a pig is considered as an incarnation of a deity or as a messenger to a god or spirit. Folk religious beliefs still play an important role in yaksuche. The size of the tables relates to the status of the offering recipients in the spirit world and to their earthly domains. While the greater Sansin presides over the entire mountain, the dragon god/king Yongsin seems to control only the particular yaksutŏ. At some well-known yaksutŏ, shamans gather to worship the deities which guard the sacred springs in order to strengthen their own powers. For example, Pangadari yaksutŏ and Sambong yaksutŏ are sacred mineral water springs that are popular with shamans. These sites each have a mountain spirit and a dragon king, and shamans perform special worship ceremonies there to draw mystic and psychic power from these deity-guardians of the sacred wells (Kim Ŭisuk, 1995:348).

From sacred springs to secular wells

Many yaksutŏ that were traditionally accepted as sacred mineral springs are now often treated like ordinary natural springs, especially in urbanized areas. City dwellers may go to yaksutŏ as pleasant destinations for walking or other exercise and enjoy drinking the natural spring waters without belief in their medicinal powers or supernatural protectors. Interviewing yaksutŏ-visitors around Seoul, Park noted that many contemporary visitors credited the healing effects of yaksutŏ mineral water to the pleasant exertions of walking through wooded areas to reach these sites (2000:50).

Rather than altars or offering tables, some secularized yaksutŏ nearby Seoul or within its urban fringe now have warning signs posted by the city health office that their waters are polluted and "not suitable for drinking." In fact, nine percent of yaksutŏ waters have been deemed unsuitable for human consumption, according to a Ministry of Environment survey. Yaksutŏ water in unguarded and open public spaces can easily be polluted by humans as well as by wild birds and animals. As these places lose their numens in popular belief, they literally lose their protection, as humans no longer act as they would in sacred space. Those on urban margins are particularly at risk. At a distance from cities and on wooded mountain slopes, devotees may still seek fortune, physical healing and interaction with the spirit world at traditional Korean sacred wells or yaksutŏ where indigenous supernaturals yet reign.

Notes

1 www.kossge.or.kr/enviro/gw2.htm.
2 Abridged and translated from Buyeo County home page: http://tour.buyeo.go.kr/_prog/history/?mode2=H04&site_dvs_cd=tour&menu_dvs_cd=0305
3 A photo-feature of the event was even presented in the local newspaper, see: "Yaksutŏ Todang Kosaje (Offering ceremony at Todang Mineral Water Spring)" by Mun Huikuk in the *Inchŏnilbo-Inchŏn Daily Newspaper* (October 12, 2018).

References

Buyeogun County Munhwa Kwankwang Homepage, Buyeogun부여군 > history/culture 역사/문화 > folktales and legends 설화와 전설 > Koran yaksu legend1고란약수전설. Accessed 10 October 2018. http://tour.buyeo.go.kr/_prog/history/?mode2=H04&site_dvs_cd=tour&menu_dvs_cd=0305.

Kim, Ŭisuk 김의숙. 1995. *Kangwondo Minsok Munwharon* 강원도 민속 문화론 (*A Study of Folk Culture of Kangwon Province*). Seoul: Chipmundang 집문당.

Mun, Huikuk. 2018. Yaksutŏ Todang Kosaje (Offering Ceremony at Todang Mineral Water Spring). *Inchŏnilbo-Inchŏn Daily Newspaper*, 12th October.

No, Sasin, Yang Sŏngji, Kang Himeng, Yi haeng, Yun Unbo and H Unpil, eds. 1969–1970. *Sinjŭng Tongguk Yŏji Sŭngnam* [新增 東國 興地 勝覽; Newly Revised Edition of the Augmented Survey of the Geography of Korea]. 7 vols. Minjok.

Paek, Namsin. 1955. *Sŏul Taekwan (A Grand Survey of Seoul).* Seoul: Chŏngchi Sinmunsa.

Park, Kyung-Min. 2000. Tosijiyŏk Yasu Tsyong-ui Sahoemunhwajok Uimi-dp Kwanhan Yŏnku (An Anthropological Study of the Socio-cultural Meaning of the 'Yak-su' in City) Department of Anthropology, Seoul National University MA Thesis, in Korean with English abstract.

Yaksutŏ hwankyŏng 약수터 환경, Accessed 10 August 2018. www.kossge.or.kr/enviro/gw2.htm.

Yi, Hakju, Ryu Siyŏng and Song Un'gang. 2014. Changso maketing-e Ttaŭn Munhwa kontench'ŭ konseptŭ wonhyŏng pakul siron (Finding the Originality of the Concept on Cultural Contents for Place Marketing – The Case of Kaein yaksutŏ), *Kuche ŏmun* 61:233–250.

Yi, Kwangyul. 2014. ŏkkŏp-ŭi Sewol Ttulko Semsot-ŭn Pomul Yaksu – ch'oyonkinommul 'yaksu'. *Wolgan munhwchae Sarang* (The Monthly, Loving Culture). Accessed 14 August 2018. https://m.cha.go.kr/cop/bbs/selectBoardArticle.do?nttId=17073&bbsId=BBSM-STR_1008....

15

SACRED HIERARCHY, FESTIVAL CYCLES AND WATER VENERATION AT CHALMA IN CENTRAL MEXICO

Ramiro Alfonso Gómez Arzapalo Dorantes

Southwest of Mexico City, Chalma is Mexico's second most important place of pilgrimage and the focus of an annual calendar of folk religious rituals that binds regional communities together. Many pilgrims still follow the arduous five- to six-day trail on foot through the hills around Chalma to a spring, tree and cave complex that was sacred in multiple pre-Colombian eras and which now serves as a ritual preface to visiting Our Lord of Chalma (Christ). Water veneration at Chalma is pre-Hispanic and pre-Aztec. The story of the site's conversion to Christianity has many versions (Sardo, 1979; Benuzzi, 1981; Ingham, 1989; Shadow and Shadow, 1990, 2000). In one, Augustinian friars first sought out the site in the late 1530s when they learned of a pilgrimage in which natives bathed in a spring before visiting an image of Oztotéotl (the Dark Lord) in a cave. They preached against idol worship and a crucifix with an image of a black Christ miraculously materialized in place of the idol. As the crucifix appeared about a decade after the Virgin Mary's 1531 apparition in Guadalupe (now a suburb of Mexico City), some devotees consider the Virgin of Guadalupe to be the "mother" of the Chalma image. In 1683, an Augustinian monastery was founded beside the cave and the current church structure of the pilgrimage complex dates to the 1830s. An ancient and contemporary site of healing and purification, the waters at Chalma have inspired an elaborate system of pilgrimage and the town's pre-eminence in an annual cycle of Lenten fairs.

Saints and the Lenten festive cycle

Diverse communities across the Mexican states of Morelos, México, Hidalgo and Guerrero are linked by a complex network of interrelations based on the patronage of saints and the hierarchical relationships of these saints with each other. These sacred town protectors "visit" one another and some pay homage to others. Mediated by the dynamics of popular religiosity, relations between towns and villages reflect those between their supernatural patrons. A complex of religious fairs honoring the saints also involves the movement of people between communities in ways that shape political, social, economic and religious realities (Báez-Jorge, 1998). Saints receive visits of other patrons in their own towns or villages and then must reciprocate with visits to each. Only the saint at the top of this Central Mexican socio-religious hierarchy, Señor de Chalma, hosts guests, but never visits elsewhere. Señor here translates as the Lord and is generally an image of Christ crucified. The following table indicates the communities involved in the organization of these fairs, their associated saint and their location.

What Bonfil Batalla called the "Cycle of Lent Fairs" in 1971 still flows through a constant and intricate relationship between the communities that is negotiated around feasts to their saints, but acknowledges the over-riding regional importance of the Señor de Chalma (Gómez Arzapalo Dorantes, 2009). Some communities honor the same "saint" or vision of Christ, but through local representations and stories. For example, the towns of Mazatepec and Ocuilan both honor Cristo del Calvario (Christ of the Calvary). His image in Mazatepec is painted on a flat rock where the "apparition" that inspired the painting dates to September 14, 1826, while in Ocuilan the focus for veneration is a statue that dates back to 1537. In Amayucan, Morelos and Tepalcingo (all in the State of Morelos), locals assert that their Christs are "twins." Amecameca (in the State of Mexico) has its Señor del Sacromonte (Lord of the Holy Mount), whose feast is part of the Cycle of Lent Fairs, corresponding to the First Friday of Lent, but the stewards (mayordomos) of Sacromonte go to Chalma a week before in preparation for their own town's celebrations. These supernatural figures and saints preside over the communities they inhabit and are required to move around in the form of statues/figures in order to visit, pay homage and sustain relations with other beings—also of a sacred order—which reside in other places. Since they are conceived as part of the community, saints participate in the rights and obligations of every inhabitant.[1] The saints have agency and can reshape social, political and economic relationships between

TABLE 15.1 The Lenten festive cycle and patron saints

Date of festivity	Location and State	Saint
Ash Wednesday	Amecameca, Mexico	Señor del Sacromonte
First Friday	Amecameca, Mexico	Señor del Sacromonte
Second Friday	Cuautla, Morelos	Señor del Pueblo
Third Friday	Tepalcingo, Morelos	Señor de Tepalcingo
Fourth Friday	Atlatlauhcan, Morelos	Señor de Tepalcingo
	Tlayacapan, Morelos	Virgen del Tránsito
	Amayucan, Morelos	Señor del Pueblo
	Miacatlán, Morelos	Cristo de la Vidriera
Fifth Friday	Mazatepec, Morelos	Cristo de Mazatepec
	Ocuilan, Mexico	Cristo del Calvario
Sixth Friday	Amecameca, Mexico	Señor del Sacromonte,
	Chalcatzingo, Morelos	La Dolorosa y el Santo Entierro

communities. For example, deciding to extend her stay in a town she was visiting, the Virgen del Tránsito mediated difficulties between the communities and brought them together. Through these supernatural visitations, people in diverse communities are united across the region and share the relationships their sacred protectors are conceived as having. These relationships are maintained through visitations during the Lenten Fairs.

The town of Amecameca initiates the cycle of fairs on the First Friday of Lent which is reckoned on a different calendar than church practice. In the Catholic liturgy, this day corresponds to Ash Friday. For the official Catholic Church, the week starts on Sunday "the Day of the Lord," so that all liturgical cycles also begin on this day. Because of this, although Ash Wednesday starts the Lent period, it is not considered as the first week of this liturgical period. The days previous to this first Sunday of Lent are called "ash days"; this is Ash Wednesday, Ash Thursday, Ash Friday and Ash Saturday. However, folk liturgical practice deviates by deeming the official Ash Friday as instead the First Friday of Lent and thereby adds a fair for the so-called "Sixth Friday of Lent" (non-existent in the official Catholic liturgy) and Holy Friday becomes the Seventh Friday of celebration. Chalma's regional ritual importance is recognized throughout the Lenten Fairs as town stewards travel there with the statue of their patron to visit Señor de Chalma in preparation for their own fairs. For example, during the Wednesday previous to Ash Wednesday, also known as Carnival Wednesday, the Amecameca stewards who are in charge of the First Friday fair, along with their families and helpers, go on a discreet pilgrimage to the Sanctuary of Chalma, asking *this* Christ for the success and safety of the fair. They carry a "pilgrim" image of the Señor del Sacromonte. The Señor del Sacromonte "visits" the Señor de Chalma for this purpose and "hears mass" in his sanctuary. In contrast, the townspeople of Ocuilan begin the cycle with a more exuberant pilgrimage to Chalma on the morning of Ash Wednesday. They take an image of the Christ of Calvary; they sing, pray, eat and drink during their journey and when they arrive to the sanctuary, they dance, visit the spring and go to mass, spending the whole day near the shrine and return to Ocuilan at sunset.

It is clear that popular religiosity, as a historically determined social process and in its complicated constitution, incorporates elements of official religion selected by the dwellers of a certain town or community, according to their own experience and concrete historical needs, which correspond to their particular location and economic, political and social organization (Carrasco, 1991; Chance and Tylor, 1985). A creative selection of supernatural beings related to natural forces and collective material needs can result in an operational logic that is completely illogical for the official church (Broda, 1991). As the most important pilgrimage site in the region, Chalma takes pre-eminence in the rituals of the festival cycle. The religious/ritual significance of the cave and spring in pre-Hispanic times means that Chalma's centrality in maintaining regional harmony might also have pre-Colombian aspects. Chalma is not visited merely in the Lenten season, but every day of the year. Before visiting the town's pilgrimage church, pilgrims stop for prayers and folk liturgies at much older sites of natural sacrality (Turner and Turner, 1978).

FIGURE 15.1 The Ahuehuete and Chalma's waters. Photograph by author.

Water ritual in the Chalma pilgrimage

On the road pilgrims take to the sanctuary of the Señor de Chalma, there is a place called the "Ahuehuete." This is a most important point in the pilgrimage where ritual purification takes place before the pilgrims arrive at the sanctuary and present themselves to the Señor de Chalma. The spot is named after a huge evergreen Montezuma cypress tree (said to be 1,000 years old in popular lore). This species of cypress, native to Mexico (*Taxodiummucronatum*), is long-lived and particularly found near water. The word Ahuehuete is of Nahuatl origin and one of its probable etymologies (from *Atl* for water and *Huehuetl*-for old) is the Old Man of the Water. Pilgrims circle the centuries-old tree thrice before ritually bathing in Chalma's waters. In thanksgiving for safe delivery of a child or in hopes of future offspring, people hang umbilical cords and baby booties on the tree (Claassen, 2011:500). From beneath the Ahuehuete flows a stream, nourished by local springs and also by the water flowing from the springs and pools around the high-mountain Cempoala Lake. This stop on the way to the sanctuary is symbolic of purification for the pilgrims. Here, the faithful wash in the spring water which is contained in pools. Stairs allow multitudes of people to wash at the same time. Folklore suggests that pilgrims who skip the visit to the tree and spring will turn into stones. Those who enter the water without having faith, or who do something disrespectful to the spring or tree, can also turn into fish or mermaids, or lose their souls. Visiting the spring has traditionally entailed dancing and perhaps did so in pre-Christian times. Indigenous rites were thus blended into site-specific Christian ritual practice. A popular saying invoked when someone faces a challenging task is that it cannot be done without "going to dance at Chalma."

The water is considered curative for a variety of health ailments. Women seeking fertility collect water closest to the tree with which to anoint themselves, and babies and young children are often immersed in the water by their families as a blessing. The holy spring water is considered effective to not only cleanse the body, but also the spirit. This cleansing prepares the pilgrims so that when they arrive in the presence of the Señor de Chalma, they are considered pure and worthy of favors requested from the Lord.

Water veneration and layered cosmovisions at Chalma

The cultural and symbolic value attributed to these waters developed in the context of an older, indigenous and local cosmovision. In indigenous beliefs, the ravine at Chalma is in itself a holy place and home to certain divinities such as Tláloc (the celestial waters) who was god of water, rain and lightning. His consort Chalchiuhtlicue (the earthly waters) was the goddess of running water and was also called Matlacueye, a name which means "She of the Blue Skirt" (de Orellana, 1972:71). Also associated with the surrounding mountains was Tepeyólotl (the heart of the hill or also, the master of the hill) and, in the specific case of the ravine where the sanctuary of Chalma is located dwelled Tezcatlipoca—the smoking obsidian mirror that reflects the face of those who come to him. In fact, the cave where the Señor de Chalma appeared on the ravine is the same where cultic practices were devoted to Oztotéotl, all the way back to pre-Aztec times, and which evolved into worship of Tezcatlipoca for the Aztecs in that same place. Appropriately associated with caves, Oztotéotl was the god of darkness and night. So the natural topography personified particular deities and the landscape features became depositories for the blessings of the holy entities, especially those that sustain life, animals and crops.

Sacred sources of water, then, cannot be understood if de-contextualized from this layered worldview. They are part of the sacred environment that frames the Christian sanctuary, giving it a broader symbolism. Chalma's springs are holy since they are found in a natural environment where the divinities who protect nature live, and it is necessary to create a pact with them for a successful agricultural cycle. The water of the spring where people purify themselves is also associated with the celestial water which will fertilize the fields during the rainy season. The regional and hierarchical cycle of saints feasts centered around Señor de Chalma demonstrates a religious experience fostered by place and one which stresses coexistence and reciprocity with those who inhabit the world (natural, human and divine) to achieve an equilibrium that benefits all.

Beyond the ritual bath and the purification of the spirit, the pilgrims save water in containers in order to take it back to their places of origin where, after being blessed in the sanctuary, it will be used for different ritual purposes. The most common of these are the blessing of the corn seeds before the sowing, and the blessing of the wells, springs and pools in their places of origin, since they believe that they will be more plentiful and will be strengthened when the holy water of Chalma is poured over them. It is also used for medicinal purposes, to be drunk by those who are sick and those who were unable to go on the pilgrimage. It is also especially valuable for the spiritual protection of children. To prevent them from being affected by the "evil airs" as well as by the "evil eye," parents may place a glass of this water under

FIGURE 15.2   After purification in the spring waters, pilgrims don their flowery crowns before visiting the sanctuary of the Señor de Chalma. Photograph by author.

their cribs or next to their beds with a "reindeer eye" (a little round and decorated piece of wood or glass which is generally red). The sprinkling of Chalma water in the house or in the barn provides special protection for the family and their animals, keeping away all evils which could have been "thrown" on them.

In this way, the natural context of the springs inspires the cultural conception of the water's purity and power. Emerging from under the sacred tree and by a sacred cave, this water appears where it has not yet been touched by humans and their work; so it issues from abodes of the various sacred entities that guard the holy landscape surrounding the sanctuary of Chalma. Pilgrims' purification in these waters restores a balanced and healthy interaction with the non-human neighbors of the world: natural and supernatural. This neighborly interaction guarantees the wholesome development of joint activities such as the cycle of corn, where human, natural and divine beings interact. It is believed that in pre-Christian times, pilgrims also bathed in the spring before entering Oztotéotl's cave. Chalma's current sacrality is a product of Colonial period reformulations of ancestral Mesoamerican indigenous cosmovision with Spanish Catholicism for an agricultural way of life in a particular environment. It is important to emphasize that after the act of purification in the spring waters at the Ahuehuete, pilgrims are crowned with flowers which they wear on the last part of their journey to the sanctuary of Señor de Chalma. Especially after long days of walking in their pilgrimage, devotees are renewed in strength by bathing in the waters at the Ahuehuete and, once again full of energy, can go on to the last part of their journey in order to meet the powerful Christ of Chalma.

Note

1 Beliefs and religious practice are united in a concrete social practice as Félix Báez points out:

> certainly, economics does not create religions, but it determines their shape and their ulterior transformations. In this framework, religious ideologies cannot be explained as products of conscience devoid of all relation with the material world; so to say, as archetypes.
>
> (Báez-Jorge, 2000:408)

In the towns under Señor de Chalma, the phenomenon of popular religiosity clearly manifests complex social dynamics and the interdependence which exists between material life and collective representations.

References

Báez-Jorge, Félix. 1998. *Entre los naguales y los santos*. Xalapa: Universidad Veracruzana.

Báez-Jorge, Félix. 2000. *Los oficios de las diosas*. Xalapa: Universidad Veracruzana.

Batalla, Bonfil. 1971. Introducción al Ciclo de Ferias de Cuaresma en la región de Cuautla Morelos, México. *Anales de Antropología* 8:167–202.

Benuzzi, Slivia. 1981. *A Pilgrimage to Chalma: The Analysis of Religious Change (Katunob, Occasional Papers in Mesoamerican Anthropology)*. Greeley: University of Northern Colorado Press.

Broda, Johanna. 1991. Cosmovisión y observación de la naturaleza: el ejemplo del culto de los cerros en Mesoamérica. In *Arqueoastronomía y Etnoastronomíaen Mesoamérica*, edited by Johanna Broda, Stanislaw Iwaniszewski and Lucrecia Maupomé, 461–500. Mexico: Instituto de Investigaciones Históricas.

Carrasco, Pedro. 1991. Sobre el origen histórico de la jerarquía político-ceremonial de las Comunidad es indígenas. In *Historia, antropología y política. Homenajea Ángel Palerm*, edited by Modesto Suárez, 306–326. Mexico: Alianza Editorial Mexicana.

Chance, John and William B. Taylor. 1985. Cofradías and Cargos: A Historical Perspective on the Mesoamerican Civil-Religious Hierarchy. *American Ethnologist* 12:1–26.

Claassen, Cheryl. 2011. Waning Pilgrimage Paths and Modern Roadscapes: Moving through Landscape in Northern Guerrero, Mexico. *World Archaeology* 43(3):493–504.

de Orellana, Margarita. 1972. The Worship of Water Gods in Mesoamerica. *Arqueología Subacuatica* 152:70–74.

Gómez Arzápalo Dorantes, Ramiro Alfonso. 2009. *Los santos, mudos predicadores de otra historia: la religiosidad popular en los pueblos de la región de Chalma*. No. Sirsi i9786077527084. Xalapa and Veracruz: Editora de Gobierno del Estado de Veracruz.

Ingham, John M. 1989. Chalma and Tepoztecatl; Further Reflections on Religious Syncretism in Central Mexico. *L'Uomo* 2:61–83.

Rodríguez Shadow, María and Robert Shadow. 2000. *El pueblo del Señor: las fiestas y peregrinaciones de Chalma*. México: Universidad Autónoma del estado de México.

Sardo, Joaquín. 1979. *Relación histórica y moral de la portentosa imagen de Nuestro Señor JesucristoCrucificadoaparecidoenuna de las cuevas de San Miguel de Chalma*. Mexico: Biblioteca Enciclopédica del Estado de México.

Shadow, Robert D. and María J. Shadow. 1990. Símbolos que amarran, símbolos que dividen: hegemonía e impugnación en una peregrinación campesina a Chalma. *Mesoamérica* 11(19):33–72.

Turner, Victor and Edith Turner. 1978. *Image and Pilgrimage in Christian Culture*. New York: Columbia University Press.

PART V

Medieval Europe

Archaeological evidence of votive depositions is demonstrating the long-lived sacrality of springs across Europe. Edicts of theological authorities from at least the fifth century onward indicate that periodic bans on their veneration were unsuccessful. Some water sources underwent *Interpretatio Christiana* and became the sites of early churches and/or were dedicated to the veneration of saints. A merger of saint cults with sacred natural places was mediated through folk liturgies and repeatedly emplaced across Eastern and Western Europe long after Christianization was secure. Just as in other faiths and other regions of the world, identifying or rededicating sacred places is a long and still-ongoing process. Kate Craig considers the creation and curation of a holy well associated with St. Theoderic (Thierry) outside of Reims and ecclesiastical attempts to recognize the site's power, yet make its importance secondary to that of the nearby monastery of Mont d'Or. Her study illustrates the complexities of negotiating sacrality. Andy Seaman then untangles a Welsh mystery as he discusses a well with an unknown location and a vague dedication to "Twelve Saints." Welsh medieval holy wells and springs served as places of curing, penance, divination, baptism and boundary marking, and medieval documents referencing the well in that latter role point to three potential venues for the site, while the same documents suggest the identity of the saints. In Iceland, which officially became Christian only in the year 1000, saints are thinner on the ground. Margaret Cormack considers the predominance of a thirteenth-century healing bishop and unofficial saint, Guðmundr Arason, in the majority of Iceland's holy well dedications. Springs and lakes blessed by Guðmundr became miraculous and although some ecclesiastics did not favor his holy well creations, Cormack finds the sites were subsequently supported through comparisons with the River Jordan's sacrality. Guðmundr's springs are still known across Lutheran Iceland today.

16

BETWEEN *FONS* AND FOUNDATION

Managing a French holy well in the *Miracula Sancti Theoderici*

Kate M. Craig

Based on his analysis of eighteenth-century geographical surveys, Jean Hubert (1967) estimated that over 6,000 holy wells existed in France. Furthermore, he noted that the vast majority of the considered toponyms did not associate these wells with any form of Christian veneration or saint's cult. He concluded that medieval Christianity had provided only an incomplete veneer over "pagan" practices which had continued, uninterrupted, in rural France until the modern day. Hubert's equation of non-Christian-identified holy wells with pre-Christian practices and Christian-identified holy wells as only superficially converted indicates older rifts in the interpretation of medieval religion. Medieval European holy wells, along with other physical sites of popular veneration, sit at an uncomfortable historiographical juncture (Schmitt, 1983; Christian, 1989). Their veneration was often assumed to represent a persistence of pagan or folk beliefs, in opposition to the elite and hierarchical culture of the organized church. As a result, it tended to be valorized as a type of resistance to the cultural domination of Christianity, or dismissed as an unchanging and "superstitious" practice disconnected from place and time.

While beliefs about the supernatural healing powers of certain water sources were indeed a longstanding feature of European culture, this level of generalization tends to conceal more than it reveals. More localized studies show the diversity of approaches to holy wells within medieval Christianity and especially, the nuances of their relationships to monasteries and the cult of the saints, in ways that undercut a simple model of pagan survival (Desmet, 1998). Investigating the approaches of the twin monasteries of Stavelot and Malmedy to their natural environment, Ellen Arnold (2013) identified multiple models for the spiritual links between holy wells and official cult sites in northern France. While some holy wells were in fact explicitly identified as pagan locations that were exorcised and converted by the saints themselves (as with the well associated with St. Remacle), other holy watery sites could be simply canals within the monastic enclosure that had performed miracles (St. Hubert), or the temporary resting place of traveling saint's relics (St. Quirin). Arnold's study demonstrates, first, that it is difficult to align medieval holy wells and their relationship to organized religion to a single pattern, and second, that certain medieval monasteries were both attracted by the potential of controlling a famous healing spring and cognizant of the difficulties of doing so.

This essay builds on these observations by examining a case study of the development and commemoration of a medieval holy well across the eleventh and twelfth centuries: that of St. Theoderic (Thierry, d. ca. 533) of the monastery of Mont d'Or near Reims. Though associated from the time of its appearance with the saint's power, this well was actively visited by those seeking healing and was thus an alternative sacred site to the monastery itself. The miracle stories authored by the hagiographer Adalgisus around the year 1000 show his desire to link the two spaces together and make the holy well secondary to the monastery, while at the same time acknowledging its power. Theoderic's spring (*fons*) followed the patterns identified by Arnold in some ways, and broke with them in others. The stories of the healing miracles at the fountain are very similar to the stories of miracles at other holy wells. However, the various iterations of the miracles of St. Theodoric created over the course of the eleventh and twelfth centuries, especially the revisions and continuations of Adalgisus, betray underlying tensions and collaborations between the spring and the monastery. Adalgisus in particular systematically "managed" the well through his text by linking its healing powers to the saint and, more importantly, the monastery. His work demonstrates a process of engagement less direct than the exorcism/conversion of pagan sacred springs, but nonetheless active in its efforts to tie the holy well to a more spatially controlled sacred site. Overall, the evolving representations of Theoderic's fountain help demonstrate not only the diversity of ways in which medieval monks understood and depicted the connections between their communities and the sacred landscape, but also the complexities of the relationships between holy wells and official religious sites.

The textual origins of the fountain

The story of Theoderic's healing spring has to be traced through a complicated series of hagiographical texts; multiple authors, mostly anonymous, took up the theme of the fountain and worked and reworked it over time. The discussion that follows adopts the authorship identifications and chronology proposed by Nicholas Huyghebaert (1979). Crucially, Huyghebaert has shown that what had previously been identified as a single twelfth-century account (BHL 8066[1]) was in fact a composite of three iterative texts: a first series of miracles, written by a monk named Adalgisus around the year 1000, a second series, written by an anonymous author at the end of the eleventh century and finally, a third series written around 1130 under the abbacy of the famous William of Mont d'Or. What may at first appear to be a defect (Huyghebaert himself counseled that these texts only be used "with circumspection") is here an advantage, since it offers evidence for at least three phases of the evolution of Theoderic's miracles and the saint's relationship to the well.

The first appearance of a spring associated with St. Theoderic has very little in common with the other stories of holy wells. It appears only in the second *vita* (life) of Theoderic (BHL 8060), and relates that when the future saint's baby clothes were

TABLE 16.1 The hagiographical textual tradition regarding St. Theoderic

BHL 8059	First Vita
BHL 8060	Second Vita
BHL 8061–8064	Miracles attached to the Second Vita [8 miracles]
BHL 8066	Miracles, Adalgisus (ca. 1000) [27 miracles]
	Miracles, anonymous (late 11th c.) [7 miracles]
	Miracles, anonymous (ca. 1120) [11 miracles]

washed in a fountain, rather than dirtying the water, they purified it ("Vita altera s. Theoderici," 1867). The hagiographer connects this infant miracle to the chastity of the saint, a fitting prologue to the next chapter which deals with Theoderic's parents' attempt to marry him off against his wishes to remain a virgin. Though this does not seem to be the same fountain that later would come to be associated with the saint, it may have suggested potential connections between the saint and water sources. The *vita* continues with Theoderic's life as a monastic founder figure, and we hear no more about fountains until we reach a series of miracles attached to the end of the text ("Miracula s. Theoderici," 1867).

It is in two of these additions that the story of Theoderic's well properly begins. BHL 8063 describes the recent appearance of a new fountain in the woods next to the monastery. A man wandering lost, confused and suffering from fever, saw an elderly person in clerical dress, holding a golden staff in his hand and bending over the spring. As the sick man drew closer, the figure straightened up, at which point he fainted from fear. When he woke up, he was healed; the vision was gone, but a "great splendor" showed that the old man had headed toward the monastery. The old man is not explicitly identified as St. Theoderic, though the implication is certainly there. Since that time, this short text claims, many people had been healed in that place. The following text (BHL 8064), likely composed separately, gives an extremely abbreviated list of six miracles performed (for "Magenildis," "Adelwindis," a blind man from Monzon, a blind woman from Monzon, "Fulbert," and "Ammalricus"). These miracles are given a single sentence of description each: five of them are performed at the fountain, and one is performed when the man in question enters the church of St. Theoderic.

These two attachments are of uncertain date and origin. Nicholas Huyghebaert notes that they deserve to be studied more closely, but in the absence of a critical edition, it is unclear when, or to whom, they should be attributed. However, the text composed by a monk of Mont d'Or named Adalgisus around the year 1000 references an earlier volume of miracles that he revised. Since the first eight chapters of Adalgisus' work report the same stories regarding the origin of the fountain and six miracles as BHL 8063/4, it seems likely that Adalgisus inherited this material from an earlier source (either BHL 8063/4, or a common ancestor). In other words, by the time Adalgisus was writing, it is likely that the stories of the discovery of the miraculous fountain, the vision of the old man in the woods and the performance of these six miracles already existed in some form.

Adalgisus and the fountain of the past

It is Adalgisus' work that represents and explores most fully the relationship between monastery and spring. The section of BHL 8066 that Huyghebaert attributes to Adalgisus comprises 27 chapters of which only seven do not mention the fountain in some context ("Alia miracula s. Theoderici" 1867; Paris BNF lat. 5612).[2] Indeed, Huyghebaert himself described this section of the work as having a special "hydrological" vocabulary that differentiates it from the two later compositions. While this emphasis may suggest that Adalgisus embraced the fountain wholeheartedly, in fact his work should be read as an attempt to explain and rationalize the well.

Already in Adalgisus' retelling of the stories of the appearance of the fountain and the first six miracles, there seems to be a conscious effort to provide an appropriate frame of interpretation. In the first place, the saint is more directly identified in the story of the spring's appearance: the feverish wanderer in the woods does not just see an old man in clerical clothing, but rather he sees the "holy confessor of God, Theoderic" (dead at that point for around 350 years). The old man's path also takes on a more definitive and directed shape in Adalgisus' version—not just a "great splendor," the saint's route to the monastery is indicated by "a line of light, like a ray of great brightness"[3] (one imagines a kind of glowing trail through the forest). However, despite these more absolute identifications, a sense of spatial separation between the two sites remains, as when Adalgisus explains that "some people were healed at the health-giving fountain, other people at the tomb of St. Theoderic."

Adalgisus' struggle to frame the well's existence is also demonstrated by two peculiar comparisons included in this section of his text that reveal a process of reflection over the nature of healing waters and their place in the Christian tradition. When describing the initial appearance of the fountain, Adalgisus claims that according to people who had seen both of them, the spring and the Jordan River had exactly the same color and taste and thus might be suspected to have similar power. Later, at the end of his eighth chapter, he raises an odd rhetorical question: to what should this most powerful health-giving well be compared? Strangely, he did not return to the earlier equivalence between the fountain and the Jordan. Instead, the text takes a quasi-chemical turn, as Adalgisus lays out what we might call a medieval spiritual theory of springs. He begins by acknowledging that the reputations of springs vary, and that each one of them has some kind of reputed properties (whether good or bad). He then claims that this means that each one was created by God for an immutable purpose, and each has its unique form of operation:

> Obviously, a great diversity of waters is spoken of, some of which are said to beget sterility, others fertility, some drunkenness, others sobriety, some uncountable illnesses, and others health. In fact the creator of all things formed each one of these, even lifeless bodies, so that each one of them was created for something, and works by a method that is fixed though secret, but something is inborn in all fountains of repute.
>
> *("Alia miracula s. Theoderici," 1867)*

While not alive, according to Adalgisus all noteworthy springs have hidden "characters" as ordained by God. He therefore concludes that Theoderic's fountain is best compared to the New Testament Pool of Siloam, because Christ used its waters to heal a blind man, as the waters of the fountain had supposedly healed several blind individuals. This implied that the power to heal was innate to the waters of the Pool, though activated by Christ, and that Theoderic's spring had analogous properties. Using Biblical episodes to interpret contemporary events was a time-honored tradition for medieval authors, but Adalgisus' explanation suggests a broader desire to integrate ideas about the powers of springs into a kind of Christianized hydrology.

Adalgisus and the fountain of the present

Whether we privilege Adalgisus' experimental comparison to the Jordan or his theoretical comparison to the Pool of Siloam, overall the first eight chapters of Adalgisus' work are completely centered on the fountain, as both a subject for analysis and the primary site of miracle-working. In these chapters (the material he inherited and revised), the monastery is only mentioned as the site of a miracle once when the man in question refused to go to the spring. There is, however, a marked change in the roles of both fountain and monastery in the continuation of Adalgisus' text. The ninth chapter (following the labeling in the Paris manuscript) begins with a striking claim: the spring *stopped* performing miracles, and disappeared "into the bowels of the earth." Since its purpose was to demonstrate the merits of the saint, Adalgisus concluded, its mission had been accomplished for the time being. How much time passed between the fountain's disappearance and reappearance? Adalgisus tells us that the generation alive at the time of these first miracles passed away, bringing his narrative and the reader up to "our times." However, the first miracle story suggests that the location of the holy well had not completely passed out of memory, as a woman took her feverish son "to the old place." His cure demonstrated that the fountain had been reactivated, so to speak, and thus the contemporary section of Adalgisus' narrative began.

A new narrative pattern emerges in these contemporary miracle stories. In the first six chapters (9–14), as in the earlier section, the person in need of healing goes to the fountain as the location of interest and is healed there. However, in each of these chapters, there is always a coda: the final lines indicate that before returning home, the person visited the monastery to thank the saint (whether with prayers or a gift). In other words, Adalgisus begins this part of the text—the part corresponding to his present day—by systematically pointing out that people healed at the spring finished their visit at the monastery. This motif of the fountain and monastery working in tandem is nowhere more evident than in Chapter 13. The description of the malady is slightly bizarre; according to the text, a man was walking through the woods when a kind of viscous liquid seems to have fallen on him, rendering him blind. In order to be healed, he starts at the fountain, then goes to the monastery (*ad templum*), then back to the spring, where he is healed, then back to the monastery to complete his vows (*vota vovit*). Healing, in this case, was achieved through alternating between the sacred spaces of the monastery and the holy well, and no longer exclusively through visiting the holy well.

As Adalgisus' text progresses further, the fountain begins to be subtly marginalized in favor of the monastery. In Chapter 15, the monastery is depicted not simply as the place where a person is expected to go after receiving healing, but is itself the location of the healing process. A blind man visits the fountain first, is *not* healed, but in coming to the monastery afterward receives his cure there. This marks a quiet overall shift in the text; the holy well is increasingly depicted as a secondary location, and finally (in Chapters 17, 19, 20, 22, 24 and 26), healing miracles occur exclusively at the monastery with no mention of the fountain. Though the spring remains part of Adalgisus' narrative up to the end, and continues to be cited as a location for receiving healing, in these contemporary miracles, it is always attached to the monastery in some way. This series taken as a whole, then, betrays some level of inquietude on Adalgisus' part regarding the fountain's central role (to the near-exclusion of the monastery) in the earlier material he reworked; thus, he seems to have made an effort to tame the fountain when retelling contemporary miracles by consistently and clearly presenting it as working in tandem with the monastery. Adalgisus' argument, so to speak, was that the spring needed the monastery, and not vice versa.

Continuations, disappearances and afterlives

The two later series of miracles suggest that over the course of the eleventh century, the relationship between fountain and monastery continued to evolve ("Alia miracula s. Theoderici" 1867; Paris BNF lat. 5612). In the first text, written in the late eleventh century, there are hints that the monastery had exerted more explicit control over the space of the holy well. When a sick woman was carried to the fountain, she needed to ask the "custodians" for permission to enter. The anonymous author of this series also indicates that "we" witnessed this miracle personally, giving the impression that monastic representatives were on site, in charge of determining access, and ready to formally celebrate any miracles performed. The spring also seems to have developed an international reputation, as an Englishwoman crossed the Channel to test its healing powers. Despite this perception of control and interest, only four of the seven miracles in this series mention the fountain. An even more surprising transition occurred between the second and third series: the spring disappeared completely from the hagiographical tradition. This third and final text (written ca. 1130) dealt solely with miracles performed by Theoderic's relics, often during movements of the saint's reliquary.

Today, there is a holy well dedicated to St. Theoderic near the village of Auménancourt-le-Petit, on the banks of the Suippe, about 12.5 km to the northeast of the old monastery. A small monument with the statue of the saint, erected shortly before 1869, marks its position. Various eighteenth-, nineteenth- and early twentieth-century scholars noted the presence of a "fontaine de Saint Thierry" at Auménancourt, though the current placement may not necessarily correspond to the medieval fountain's location (Du Broc de Ségange, 1887; Jadart and Demaison, 1911). Regardless, this most recent incarnation of Theoderic's fountain illuminates one of the themes of its history (and perhaps, the history of other holy wells): the contrast between the image of a holy well as timeless and unchanging, and the historical reality in which the reputations, interpretations and memories of holy wells might evolve over time. The story of Theoderic's spring across the eleventh century is a story of evolution and entanglement.

Although Adalgisus in particular sought to explain the nature of the fountain and actively link its power to the monastery, his work cannot be read as a simple example of antagonism or unilateral imposition of monastic control over competing, "popular'" sacred sites. Rather, spring and monastery existed alongside one another, providing one example of the complex processes by which a holy well might be created, forgotten, rediscovered, exploited, sidelined and commemorated. As a case study, the textual history of Theoderic's fountain suggests that understandings of holy wells, the sources of their power and their operation were fluid and actively discussed within medieval Europe. Though certainly some sacred springs were venerated before and outside official Christian practices, even fountains formally associated with saints had complex histories of activity that reflected the interest and engagement of both laypeople and ecclesiastics.

Notes

1 Hagiographical texts are identified by their catalog number within the *Bibliotheca Hagiographica Latina* (BHL), published by the Société des Bollandistes.
2 The edition of the texts appearing in the *Acta Sanctorum* is incomplete, and so I have also used the manuscript BnF lat. 5612.
3 All translations from the Latin are the author's.

References

Alia miracula s. Theoderici. 1867. In *Acta sanctorum quotquot toto orbe coluntur*, 2nd ed., July I:64–72. Paris: Victor Palmé.

Arnold, Ellen F. 2013. *Negotiating the Landscape: Environment and Monastic Identity in the Medieval Ardennes.* Philadelphia: University of Pennsylvania Press.

Christian, William A. 1989. *Local Religion in Sixteenth-Century Spain.* Princeton, NJ: Princeton University Press.

Desmet, Yves. 1998. Le culte des eaux dans le Nord de la Gaule pendant le haut Moyen Age. *Revue du Nord* 80(324): 7–27. doi:10.3406/rnord.1998.2860

Du Broc de Ségange, Louis. 1887. *Les saints patrons des corporations et protecteurs spécialement invoqués dans les maladies et dans les circonstances critiques de la vie*, edited by Louis-François Morel. Vol. 2. Paris: Bloud et Barral.

Hubert, Jean. 1967. Sources sacrées et sources saintes. *Comptes rendus des séances de l'Académie des Inscriptions et Belles-Lettres* 111(4): 567–573. doi:10.3406/crai.1967.12178

Huyghebaert, Nicholas. 1979. Les *Miracula Sancti Theoderici* et leurs auteurs. In *Saint-Thierry: une abbaye du VIe au XXe siècle: Actes du colloque international d'histoire monastique*, edited by Michel Bur. Saint-Thierry: Association des Amis de l'Abbaye de Saint-Thierry.

Jadart, H. and Louis Demaison. 1911. *Répertoire archéologique de l'arrondissement de Reims: Communes rurales des trois cantons de Reims.* Reims: F. Michaud. "lat. 5612." Paris: Département des Manuscrits. Bibliothèque nationale de France.

Miracula s. Theoderici. 1867. In *Acta sanctorum quotquot toto orbe coluntur*, 2nd ed., July I:63–64. Paris: Victor Palmé.

Schmitt, Jean Claude. 1983. *The Holy Greyhound : Guinefort, Healer of Children since the Thirteenth Century.* Cambridge: Cambridge University Press ; Editions de la maison des sciences de l'homme.

Vita altera s. Theoderici. 1867. In *Acta sanctorum quotquot toto orbe coluntur*, 2nd ed., July I:58–63. Paris: Victor Palmé.

17

FINNAUN Y DOUDEC SEINT

A holy spring in early medieval Brycheiniog, Wales

Andy Seaman

Wells and springs have been venerated in Wales since the prehistoric period. Over 1,000 holy wells have been identified through their names (which often include that of a saint), association with a church or chapel, and/or local tradition and folklore. Some, such as St. Winefride's Well (Denbighshire), are enclosed within elaborate structures and continue to attract large numbers of visitors, but many are marked by little more than a stone surround or appear as entirely "natural" springs. Despite their relative ubiquity, there have been relatively few academic studies of Welsh holy wells, the major exception being Francis Jones' seminal study first published in 1954 (with a second edition published in 1992). Jones drew together a list of holy wells from across Wales, and attempted to explore their veneration from prehistory through to the early twentieth century. Archaeological studies have been limited in number and scope, and whilst the Welsh Archaeological Trusts (organisations responsible for the curation of historic sites and monuments in Wales) have recently undertaken surveys of well structures (e.g. Ings, 2011), there have been comparatively few excavations or interpretive studies that have looked at the landscape contexts of holy wells.

During the medieval period (*c.* 400–1600 AD), wells and springs were associated with a range of functions including healing, divination, baptism, penitentials and boundary marking, but comparatively few examples are documented before the twelfth century (Edwards, 1994). *Finnaun y Dodec Seint* (modern Welsh *Ffynnon yr Deuddeg Sant* or Spring of the Twelve Saints) is therefore significant, since it is recorded in an early eleventh-century boundary clause attached to an earlier (*c.* eighth century) charter contained in an important collection of documents known as the *Book of Llandaff* (Evans and Rhys, [1893] 1979:146, 369–370). Charter 146 is one of a small group of charters that refer to grants of land within Brycheiniog, a region and at times kingdom in southeast Wales (see W. Davies, 1982:83, 91). The charter records the supposed donation of an estate at *Lann Cors* (Llan-gors, Powys) by King Awst of Brycheiniog and his sons Eiludd and Rhiwallon sometime in the early to mid-eighth century (W. Davies, 1979:98; Coe, 2004). The Spring of the Twelve Saints provides us with a rare opportunity to examine a documented early medieval holy spring, but the evidence is limited; the charter is the only reference to the spring in a primary source, and inquiries amongst local inhabitants of Llan-gors and neighbouring parishes suggest that knowledge of the spring within living memory is scanty. Neither the location of the spring nor the identity of the "Twelve Saints" is known. The sparsity of the evidence inevitably curtails interpretation, but clearly indicates the spring's significance as a sacred feature in the early medieval landscape. This essay considers three possible sites based on the boundary clause, suggests that the saints are the Twelve Apostles, examines potential associations between the spring and a church, and explores how a sacred spring served as a boundary marker of an important estate.

Source material: Charter 146 in the *Book of Llandaff*

The *Book of Llandaff* is an early twelfth-century collection of documents relating to the purported early history of the Norman episcopal see at Llandaff (Glamorgan). It includes 158 charters that claim to record grants of property made in favour of the see between the sixth and the eleventh centuries. The *Book* was compiled under the influence of Urban, the first bishop of Llandaff appointed under Norman rule, who was at the time of its compilation pursuing a series of disputes over diocesan boundaries and episcopal properties with the bishops of Hereford and St. David's (J. Davies, 2003:17–26). Although the charters were part of Urban's legal campaign and are demonstrably fraudulent (Brooke, 1986:16–49), Wendy Davies has exhumed a considerable number of original records under Urban's layers of later editing and interpolation (W. Davies, 1979). While no reliable evidence suggests that Llandaff was a major ecclesiastical centre prior to the eleventh century, she argues that many of the charters were derived from genuine records compiled at, and related to, other monastic houses in South Wales.

The Spring of the Twelve Saints

I will refer to the "Spring" rather than "Well" of the Twelve Saints, because whilst the Welsh word *ffynnon* can mean "spring, fountain, or well," its use in the *Book of Llandaff* was restricted to describing springs and occasionally the streams flowing from them (Coe, 2001:924). Nevertheless, there are sufficient examples to demonstrate that both springs and wells were considered sacred in medieval Wales. Springs feature in at least 28 of the 118 boundary clauses in the *Book of Llandaff*, and some of these appear, on the basis of their names, to have been considered sacred (Jones, 1954:2, 55). The *Finnaun i Cleuion* of charter 227b, for example, can be interpreted as the "Spring of the Sick," a name that must refer to the healing properties of its waters (Coe, 2001:281; cf. Jones, 1954:75). Many wells and springs are associated with saints' names, and some churches are dedicated to multiple numbered saints (for example, *Llantrisaint*, "Church of [the] Three Saints," in Anglesey), but this is the only example of a well or spring dedicated to "The Twelve Saints." A small number of references to churches dedicated to the Twelve Saints elsewhere in the *Book of Llandaff* suggest that their cult was popular in early medieval South Wales, but we can only speculate as to who they were.

Stories surrounding groups of saints occur frequently in hagiography and folklore, and Egerton Phillimore suggested that the well's dedication to twelve saints was associated with a variant of a story of seven saints produced by multiple birth (Phillimore, 1936:411). Noting that Llan-gors church was dedicated to St. Paulinus, Gilbert Doble suggested that the twelve saints represented the disciples of Paulinus mentioned in Wrmonoc's ninth-century *Vita Pauli Aureliani* (Doble, 1971:199, n100, 226). Charles Thomas linked the dedication to a list of male names appended to two medieval texts, known as the *De Situ Brecheniauc* and *Cognatio Brychan*, which purportedly relate to the early history of Brycheiniog (Thomas, 1994:151). However, the dedication most likely referred to the Twelve Apostles and this was undoubtedly the inspiration behind the trope of the saint and 12 followers. Tentative evidence may be found elsewhere in the *Book of Llandaff* where it is recorded that *Lann I Doudec Sent* (Church of the Twelve Saints) was consecrated by Bishop Herewald (d. 1104) in the *cimiterium* (cemetery or parish) of *Lann Custenhin* (Evans and Rhys, [1893] 1979:276; Coe, 2001:431). Jon Coe tentatively identified *Lann Custenhin* (the Church of Constantine) as Welsh Bicknor, a formerly Welsh parish now in Herefordshire (2001:300–301).[1]

We are on more stable, but still uncertain ground, when attempting to locate the Spring of the Twelve Saints. No spring or well of that name is recorded on the Ordnance Survey, Tithe or estate maps of the Llan-gors area, and whilst Francis Jones (1954:55) referred to the spring, he did not include it in his list of Welsh holy wells, presumably because he could not locate it and did not consider it to be still in existence. William Rees (1932) placed it within the neighbouring parish of Cathedine, while Doble favoured a location near Penllanafel closer to Llan-gors church (1971:152, n13), and Thomas (1994:161) placed it further south (labelled 3 in Figure 17.1).[2] They did not specify their evidence for these locations, so the search for the spring must start with the boundary clause itself. Fortunately, this is quite detailed and we are able to identify a number of features with some confidence. A translation reads as follows:

> From the mouth of the Spring of the Twelve Saints in Llangorse Lake upwards along the brook as far as the spring-head, to the end of Llywarch Hen's dyke. Along the dyke until it falls into the Llynfi. Along it downwards as far as the end of Brynn Eital. Leftwards across to the end of the hill, to the source of the Nant Tawel. Along the stream as far as the Llynfi. Along the Llynfi as far as the lake. Along the lake as far as the mouth of the Spring of the Twelve Saints where it began.

> *(Coe, 2001:975–976)*

The direction of the perambulation and the location of other named features suggest the spring must rise and flow into Llangorse Lake from the east, and its head must be located close to Llywarch Hen's dyke. The latter is an interesting feature in its own right that appears to refer to Llywarch Hen, the legendary king of Welsh poetic tradition (Sims-Williams, 1993:53; Seaman, 2019B). Llywarch Hen's dyke can be identified as the prominent boundary that is demarcated by a hollow-way (a sunken lane worn down by repeated use over many years) and field-bank that demarcates the upper limit of the post-medieval enclosed fields on the lower slopes of Mynydd Llan-gors (see Figures 17.1 and 17.2). This feature, which served as the

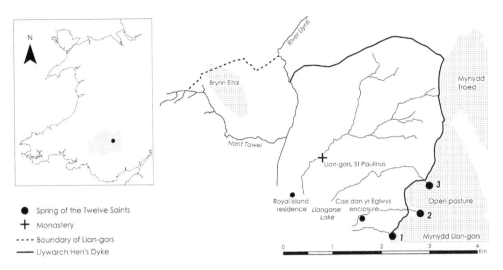

Spring of the Twelve Saints

✚ Monastery

---- Boundary of Llan-gors

——— Llywarch Hen's Dyke

FIGURE 17.1 Location map, showing Wales and the Kingdom of Brycheiniog (insert), and Llangorse Lake, the course of the early medieval boundary clause, and the likely locations of the Spring of the Twelve Saints.

FIGURE 17.2 Llywarch Hen's dyke (topped with trees) running from left to right, with Llangorse Lake in the background. A spring, labelled no. 2 in Figure 17.1, rises in the foreground and flows down towards the lake. Photograph by author.

later medieval parish boundary, represents what is known in Welsh as a *pen clawdd* (head-dyke): a land boundary that separates lowland infield from the unenclosed upland pastures. Post-medieval agricultural improvement has altered the courses of the streams flowing into Llangorse Lake from the east, but if the identification of Llywarch Hen's dyke is correct, then the likely candidates for the Spring of the Twelve Saints can be whittled down to several springs that rise close to it (labelled 1 to 3 in Figure 17.1). One of these is the spring identified by Thomas (labelled 3 in Figure 17.1), but the two springs further south have the greatest potential.

The first candidate appears as an "Old Well" on the nineteenth-century Ordnance Survey map very close to the point where the medieval parish boundary crossed Llywarch Hen's dyke (labelled 1 in Figure 17.1).[3] This well survived until the 1970s, but at some point during that decade, the area was cleared, ploughed and planted as a conifer plantation. A recent harvest of the planation reveals that no physical trace of a well structure survives. Nevertheless, the author has identified a spring that rises within metres of the grid reference where the "Old Well" must have been located, and the course of a stream flowing from the spring down to the lake is evident.

The second candidate is one of two springs that rises in close proximity, 730m to the north-east (labelled 2 in Figure 17.1).[4] There is some local tradition that places the spring here, and supporting evidence may be found when we consider whether there was a church or chapel dedicated to the Twelve Saints at Llan-gors.[5]

Was there a Church of the Twelve Saints at Llan-gors?

Many holy springs and wells had known associations with churches or chapels; indeed, they were sometimes incorporated into the buildings themselves, as at St. Trillo's Chapel (Caernarfonshire) where a spring rises below the altar (Jones, 1954:24–27). Physical remains of church structures dating to the early medieval period (400–1100) are very rare in Wales, but it is reasonable to assume that many churches were associated with springs. In this regard, it is worth considering a church named *Lann i Doudec Seith* (Church of the Twelve Saints) in an eleventh-century list of extra-diocesan properties in the *Book of Llandaff* (Evans and Rhys, [1893] 1979 255; n.b. this is not the same as the church called *Lann I Doudec Sent* referred to earlier). The church is listed within the same territory as Llan-gors and its position in the text implies that it was located close to Llan-gors and neighbouring Llanfihangel Tal-y-llyn (Coe, 2001:431, 444, 794). Thus, given the reference to the Spring of the Twelve Saints in the boundary clause, it is reasonable to assume that this church was located within the vicinity of Llan-gors. Indeed, it has sometimes been identified as a chapel within that parish (Richards, 1969:128). However, no church/chapel of that name exists now nor can one be identified in later medieval sources. Historians have, therefore, been left to speculate as to where the church was located; Rees (1932) identified *Lann I Doudec Sieth* with the church at Cathedine (now dedicated to St. Michael), whilst Thomas (1994:132) suggested that the Twelve Saints may have been the original dedication of an early church at Llangasty Tal-y-Llyn (now dedicated to St. Gastyn). This is little more than speculation, however. Local tradition places the church close to farms named Llan-beilin, Capel and Cwrt Y Prior.[6] These place-names are attested on the 1832 Ordnance Survey map, and could be suggestive of a church in the vicinity. However, the place-name element "Capel" was not in general use before the sixteenth century (Roberts, 1992:43), and Llan-beilin (the *Llan* element possibly meaning "church") is recorded as Llwyn Beiliau (*Llwyn* meaning "bush" or "grove") on the 1840 Tithe map.[7] Thus, both need not be early, and Cwrt Y Prior probably relates to the fact that the rights to the church of St. Paulinus in Llan-gors itself were granted to Brecon priory in the twelfth century (Cowley, 1977:175). Firm evidence for a medieval church or chapel in the vicinity of these farms is therefore lacking. Indeed, since the Church of the Twelve Saints is not recorded outside of the *Book of Llandaff*, and is noticeably absent from the charters granting the church of St. Paulinus to Brecon Priory, it is possible that its presence was interpolated by redactors who were familiar with the reference to the spring in the boundary clause.

However, the name of a field that appears in ninetieth-century records and collaborative archaeological evidence suggests that there may have been a church or chapel elsewhere on the eastern side of Llangorse Lake. The field-name, *Cae dan yr Eglwys* (field below the church), suggests that this field was located downslope of a church. It is, therefore, interesting to note that a NW-SE-aligned rectangular earthwork enclosure is visible on the north-east, upslope of *Cae dan yr Eglwys* (see Figure 17.1).[8] The enclosure is approximately 85m in length and 30m in width, and whilst not aligned east–west, could represent the remains of church and cemetery enclosure. As we can see in Figure 17.1, a stream flowing from the two springs identified earlier as the second strong candidate for the Spring of the Twelve Saints runs immediately adjacent to this field and enclosure before entering Llangorse Lake *c.* 230m to the south-west. Thus, whilst very tentative, it is possible that this is evidence of a Church of the Twelve Saints.

Holy springs, place-stories and boundaries

Springs are frequently associated with healing and baptism in the hagiography of Welsh saints (see examples in the *Lives* of Brynach, Winefride and David; Sharpe and Davies, 2007:117; Wade-Evans, [1944] 2013:7, 301). However, this was just one of their functions, which may have included roles in penitentials, divination and practical necessities such as the cleansing of vessels used in the Eucharist (Morris, 1989:87; Rattue, 1995; Bhreathnach, 2014:135). There also seems to have been an association between holy springs and the definition and protection of boundaries. The coincidence of holy springs with the boundaries of parishes and manors has long been noted (Jones, 1954:55; Rattue, 1995:95), and as we have seen, springs are named as features in at least 24% (28) of the boundary clauses in the *Book of Llandaff* (Coe, 2001:277–288). This phenomenon could reflect nothing more than the fact that springs were convenient features with which to define territories, but there is likely to be more to the relationship than pure practicality. Sometimes, the association of holy springs with boundaries may have reflected perceptions of watery places on the margins of settled land as liminal, possibly pagan places, the power of which required defusing by that of the Church (Rattue, 1995:75, 96; Semple, 1998). This need not apply in all cases however, and it is the active role that springs and their associated hagiotoponyms played in the definition of boundaries that will be considered here.

Llan-gors is known to have been a focus of high status activity in the early medieval period, and has reliably been identified as a royal, and latterly, ecclesiastical estate within the Kingdom of Brycheiniog (Seaman, 2019 A; Lane and Redknap, 2019). Thus, the estate's boundary demarcated an area over which particular rights and obligations were maintained, and knowledge of its course and the rights it conferred had to be actively maintained through its inscription on both the landscape and the cultural memory of local inhabitants. For this reason, whilst the text of early medieval charters was usually written in Latin, the boundary clauses were more often in the vernacular, so that when read aloud they could be understood by those living and working on the land (Kelly, 1990:56–57; Howe, 2008:37). At a local level, perambulations of the site and the performance of rituals at particular points along the route would have maintained knowledge of the boundary (Howe, 2008:39). The oral traditions associated with the boundary features and their place-names, especially hagiotoponyms such as the "Spring of the Twelve Saints," gave structure to processes of cultural memory. Anthropological studies, such as those of the Western Apache, have shown that "place-stories" had the power to perpetuate tradition and engender particular understandings of the world through the establishment of social norms and the legitimisation of claims to land (Tilley, 1994:32–33; Basso, 1996; Gardiner, 2012). For the most part, such onomastic tales do not survive from early medieval Wales. However, the Llan-gors boundary clause mentions "Llywarch Hen's dyke" that ran adjacent to the spring (see Figures 17.1 and 17.2) and this landscape feature was associated with a collection of early Welsh poems known as *Canu Llywarch Hen*. These poems focus on a legendary ruler named Llywarch Hen, and were originally composed sometime between the eighth and mid-tenth centuries, but survive in documents of the thirteenth century and later (see Koch, 2003).

Patrick Sims-Williams has argued that the Llywarch Hen poems were composed at Llan-gors. Their themes (such as inter-British feuding, battles against the Anglo-Saxons and the defence of borders) resonate with what we know of Llan-gors at that time as a royal estate in a border territory that was threatened by its neighbours (Sims-Williams, 1993). When the antecedents of the Llywarch Hen stories were performed during seasonal festivals and perambulation of the boundary of the estate, they would have become rooted in the concrete details of a feature that could be "visited, seen and touched," and therefore acquired mythic value and didactic relevance (Tilley, 1994:33; Seaman, 2019 A). The onomastic tales associated with the Spring of the Twelve Saints are lost to us, but we can note that place-stories which associate saints with the protection of ecclesiastical property are common in medieval hagiography (W. Davies, 1995). Thus, the spring and dyke were not just convenient features with which to construct a boundary clause; they were places that helped tell a story, and were a part of how an important royal and latterly ecclesiastical estate was defined, both physically and metaphorically.

The question of continuity

The sanctity of some sacred springs is likely to have stretched back to the Romano-British period or earlier (Woodward, 1992:51–53), and early medieval writers, such as Tírechán, refer to the Christianisation of "pagan" springs and wells (Charles-Edwards, 2000:47; Ray, 2014:79–81). Nevertheless, it is not possible to argue that devotional use of *all* medieval holy springs originated in the pre-Christian era, and many may have acquired their significance later (Morris, 1989:87). In the absence of firm evidence, we are unable to say precisely when the Spring of the Twelve Saints was recognised as sacred, but it must have been prior to the early eleventh century when the boundary clause was written. Potentially, it could have been before King Awst and his sons made their grant in the early to mid-eighth century. It is likely to have been after the Reformation, when devotion of holy wells was denounced as a superstition and indeed some were destroyed (Jones, 1954:58–63), that the Spring of the Twelve Saints slipped from local memory. Nevertheless, the Reformation did not entirely extinguish the significance of wells and springs for both Protestants and recusant Catholics for whom they continued to serve as religious foci. Indeed, their waters were sought throughout subsequent centuries, but now more often out of antiquarian interest or "for health reasons or as pleasant holidays as distinct from holy days and wakes" (ibid:64). Many of Wales' holy wells were lost during the nineteenth and twentieth centuries, through the combined effects of physical destruction and the erosion of the cultural memory that kept their traditions alive. Nevertheless, wells continue to be visited today, by both tourists and pilgrims of different faiths. Indeed, the tying of rags to trees and fences close to wells, a practice that was previously widespread throughout much of Britain and Ireland, but not Wales (ibid:10–11), has become increasingly common, suggesting that the long-held belief in the properties of *dŵr swyn* (holy water) remains active in twenty-first-century Wales.

Notes

1 The association with Constantine might derive from associations medieval Welsh knew from the wider world: the emperor Constantine I was buried in the Church of the Holy Apostles in Constantinople (Krautheimer, 1992:69–70). I am grateful to Graham Jones for drawing this to my attention.
2 Around SO157271.
3 SO 14923 26035.
4 At approximately SO 1547 26523.
5 Colin Preece, Llan-gors resident, personal communication, August 2017.
6 About SO153282; Colin Preece, Llan-gors resident, personal communication, August 2017.
7 IR 30/45/42.
8 At approximately SO 14320 26410.

References

Basso, Keith H. 1996. *Wisdom Sits in Places*. Albuquerque: University of New Mexico Press.
Bhreathnach, Edel. 2014. *Ireland in the Medieval World AD 400–1000: Landscape, Kingship and Religion*. Dublin: Four Courts Press.
Blair, John. 2005. *The Church in Anglo-Saxon Society*. Cambridge: Cambridge University Press.
Brooke, Christopher. 1986. *The Church and the Welsh Border in the Central Middle Ages*. Woodbridge, VA: Boydell.
Charles-Edwards, Thomas. 2013. *Wales and the Britons 350–1064*. Oxford: Oxford University Press.
Charles-Edwards, Thomas. 2000. *Early Christian Ireland*. Cambridge: Cambridge University Press.
Coe, Jon. 2004. Dating the Boundary Clauses in the Book of Llandaf. *Cambrian Medieval Celtic Studies* 48:1–43.
Coe, Jon. 2001. The Place-Names of the Book of Llandaf. PhD diss., University of Wales Aberystwyth.
Cowley, F. G. 1977. *The Monastic Order in South Wales 1066–1349* (2nd edition). Cardiff: University of Wales Press.

Davies, John. 2003. *The Book of Llandaff and the Norman Church*. Woodbridge: Boydell.

Davies, Wendy. 1995. Adding Insult to Injury: Power, Property and Immunities in Early Medieval Wales. In *Property and Power in the Early Middle Ages*, edited by Wendy Davies and Paul Fouracre, 137–164. Cambridge: Cambridge University Press.

Davies, Wendy. 1982. *Wales in the Early Middle Ages*. Leicester: Leicester University Press.

Davies, Wendy. 1979. *The Llandaff Charters*. Aberystwyth: The National Library of Wales.

Doble, G. H. 1971. *Lives of the Welsh Saints*. Cardiff: University of Wales Press.

Edwards, Nancy. 1994. Holy Wells in Wales and Early Christian Archaeology. http://people.bath.ac.uk/liskmj/living-spring/sourcearchive/ns1/ns1ne1.htm

Evans, J. Gwenoguryn and John Rhys. [1893] 1979. *The Text of the Book of Llan Dâv*. Reprint, Aberystwyth: National Library of Wales.

Gardiner, Mark. 2012. Oral Tradition, Landscape and the Social Life of Place-Names. In *Sense of Place in Anglo-Saxon England*, edited by Richard Jones and Sarah Semple, 16–30. Donington: Shaun Tyas.

Howe, Nicholas. 2008. *Writing the Map of Anglo-Saxon England: Essays in Cultural Geography*. New Haven, CT: Yale University Press.

Ings, Mike. 2011. *Medieval and Early Post-Medieval Holy Wells: A Threat-Related Assessment*. DAT Report No. 2012/7. Carmarthen: Dyfed Archaeological Trust.

Jones, Francis. 1954. *The Holy Wells of Wales*. Cardiff: University of Wales Press.

Kelly, Susan. 1990. Anglo-Saxon Lay Society and the Written Word. In *The Uses of Literacy in Early Medieval Europe*, edited by Rosamond McKitterick, 32–62. Cambridge: Cambridge University Press.

Koch, John T. 2003. *The Celtic Heroic Age: Literary Sources for Ancient Celtic Europe and Early Ireland and Wales*. Aberystwyth: Celtic Studies Publications.

Krautheimer, Richard. 1992. *Early Christian and Byzantine Architecture*. New Haven, CT: Yale University Press.

Lane, Alan and Mark Redknap, eds. 2019. *The Llangorse Crannog: An Early Medieval Island Residence of the Kings of Brycheiniog*. Oxford: Oxbow.

Morris, Richard. 1989. *Churches in the Landscape*. London: Dent.

Phillimore, Egerton. 1936. Notes on Place-Names. In *The Description of Pembrokeshire: Part IV: Denbighshire, Flyntsheere*, edited by Henry Owen, 408–412. London: Honourable Society of Cymmrodorion.

Ray, Celeste. 2014. *The Origins of Ireland's Holy Wells*. Oxford: Archaeopress (Oxbow).

Rattue, James. 1995. *The Living Stream: Holy Wells in Historical Context*. Woodbridge: Boydell.

Rees, William. 1932. *South Wales and the Border in the Fourteenth Century*. Southampton: Ordnance Survey.

Richards, Melville. 1969. *Welsh Administrative and Territorial Units: Medieval and Modern*. Cardiff: University of Wales Press,

Roberts, Tomas. 1992. Welsh Ecclesiastical Place-Names and Archaeology. In *The Early Church in Wales and West*, edited by Nancy Edwards and Alan Lane, 41–44. Oxford: Oxbow.

Seaman, Andy. 2019 A. Llywarch Hen's Dyke: Place and Narrative in Early Medieval Wales. *Offa's Dyke Journal* 1, 70–89.

Seaman, Andy. 2019 B. The Llan-gors Charter Material. In *The Llangorse Crannog: An Early Medieval Island Residence of the Kings of Brycheiniog*, edited by Alan Lane and Mark Redknap, 414–421. Oxford: Oxbow.

Semple, Sarah. 1998. A Fear of the Past: The Place of the Prehistoric Burial Mound in the Ideology of Middle and Later Anglo-Saxon England. *World Archaeology* 30(1):109–126. doi:10.1080/00438243.1998.9980400

Sharpe, Richard and John Reuben Davies. 2007. Rhygyfarch's *Life* of St David. In *St David of Wales: Cult, Church, and Nation*, edited by J. Wyn Evans and Jonathan M. Wooding, 107–155. Woodbridge: Boydell.

Sims-Williams, Patrick. 1993. The Provenance of the Llywarch Hen Poems: A Case for Llan-gors, Brycheiniog. *Cambrian Medieval Celtic Studies* 26:27–63.

Thomas, Charles. 1994. *And Shall These Mute Stones Speak? Post-Roman Inscriptions in Western Britain*. Cardiff: University of Wales Press.

Tilley, Christopher. 1994. *A Phenomenology of Landscape: Places, Paths and Monuments*. Oxford: Berg.

Wade-Evans, A. W. [1944] 2013. *Vitae Sanctorum Britanniae et Genealogiae: The Lives and Genealogies of the Welsh Saints*. Reprint, Cardiff: Welsh Academic Press.

Woodward, Ann. 1992. *Shrines and Sacrifice*. London: English Heritage/Batsford.

18

GVENDARBRUNNAR OF MEDIEVAL ICELAND

Margaret Jean Cormack

Iceland was first settled in the late ninth century by seafarers from Scandinavia and the British Isles. The holy wells in these areas today are generally associated with saints, but evidence of their "special" status may extend to the prehistoric period. On arriving in Iceland, the settlers entered a landscape void of pre-existing traditions, and although they soon ascribed the presence of supernatural beings to rocks and cliffs, bodies of water appear not to have attracted similar associations (Cormack, 2007). When Guðmundr Arason, holy man and future bishop, began blessing water sources, it cannot have been to exorcise evil beings, as was the case when he blessed cliffs, but rather to purify existing waters of more ordinary hazards. Twenty-one such blessings are mentioned in medieval writings about him, though these narratives also assure us that he blessed springs throughout the country. Today, geologist Árni Hjartarson has counted over 255 "special" water sources in Iceland. These are identified as such either through their traditional name or because of unusual properties such as healing, never freezing or never running dry.[1] About ten are hot springs; the remainder include springs, pools and rivers, and some are mere hollows in rocks that fill with rain water. The vast majority of these—some 230—are associated with Guðmundr Arason, a thirteenth-century bishop of Hólar with a reputation for sanctity. These sites are known as *Gvendarbrunnar* (Guðmundr's springs). Of the remainder, the names of 15 either evoke saints or priests (including one Lutheran priest) or incorporate the elements "cross" or "church" in their names. Six names contain the word "consecrated" and five make reference to the well's healing properties. Unlike traditional prohibitions against the domestic use of holy well water in other countries, some Icelandic sites served as sources of drinking water; indeed, the city of Reykjavík derives its water supply from the *Gvendarbrunnar* in Heiðmörk. There are no formal rituals associated with any of them, although people apply or drink the water from those with a reputation for healing.

Modern Scandinavian languages make a distinction between a "well," meaning a human-made source of water, or at least a source surrounded by a human-built structure, and a "spring," or a naturally occurring water source. These terms appear in modern Icelandic as *brunnur,* pl. *brunnar,* from Old Norse *brunnr,* for a human-made well, and, for natural water sources, *kelda,* pl. *keldur,* which is identical to the Old Norse form of the word. However, these terms were not always so distinctive. The *Kulturhistorisk leksikon for nordisk middelalder* (the Cultural Historical Lexicon of the Nordic Middle Ages/KLNM) notes that *brunnr* originally denoted a spring, watering place, brook, or other source of water, even a stream.[2] A *kelda* was a natural "water source which broke forth by its own power," a spring, small stream or swamp; this last meaning is the one that tends to dominate in modern Icelandic usage.[3] In the Middle Ages, the term could be applied to hot springs (*Biskupa sögur,* hereafter BS, II 5). In the following, "well" and "spring" are both used for natural water sources. "Holy well" is used to refer to any water source with which curative or other miraculous properties are associated, whether or not it has been modified by human hands. In modern Iceland, the vast majority of holy wells are associated with Guðmundr Arason.

Guðmundr Arason lived from 1161 to 1237, and was elected the bishop of Hólar in northern Iceland in 1203. Although never formally canonized, he was venerated as a saint in the diocese of Hólar. We know about his life from sagas (vernacular prose narratives) that were largely composed in the first half of the fourteenth century to promote his sanctity.[4] These depict Guðmundr's episcopacy as the height of Iceland's church-state conflict, in which excommunications and sentences of outlawry flew back and forth. It may seem surprising, in such a tumultuous period, that Guðmundr's practice of blessing water(s) attracted much notice. It was, however, such religious innovation for which Guðmundr was best known; his reputation for piety and miracles may well have been part of the reason for his election as bishop.

Water blessed by Guðmundr was of two types: holy water, which was created as part of the Sunday ritual of any priest, and that from springs he blessed. The first sort of holy water could be sprinkled over the congregation, fields or cattle, and was considered to have apotropaic properties. Although it was regularly produced by parish priests, Guðmundr appears to have developed a reputation for producing holy water that was exceptional in quality. We are told that at the translation of St. Þorlákr's relics to the cathedral of Skálholt in 1198, the presiding bishop, Páll Jónsson, asked Guðmundr to bless a whole kettle of holy water for curing people, on an occasion at which one might have expected that water sanctified by the relic of the new saint himself would have been used (GB 61; BS I 455). Implicit in many miracles attributed to Guðmundr, such as the quenching of a fire at Hólar (below), is the assumption that people had containers of water he had blessed ready to hand. In a vision, no less a person than the Virgin Mary confirms Guðmundr's ability to bless holy water exceptionally well (GB 48; BS I 438).

Like others, Guðmundr used water in which relics had been dipped (BS I 445), but since he himself was a holy man in the eyes of many of his contemporaries as well as later hagiographers, water that had been in contact with him could have healing properties. Water in which his hands had been rinsed after touching the Eucharist revived withered palms left over from Palm Sunday, and water in which he had washed his hands before administering confession brought about cures (GB 51, 55; BS I 441, 451). When a bishop wearing full pontifical vestments failed to put out a fire using regular holy water, and then relics, water that Guðmundr had blessed successfully extinguished the flames (BS I 445-46). There is nothing original in any of these stories; such accounts are hagiographic commonplaces.[5]

In addition to the weekly blessing of holy water, the church recognized blessings for a variety of purposes, including blessings specifically for newly dug wells, for wells that had been polluted by dead bodies or by impure substances, and more generally for wells or water that had been otherwise contaminated. However, blessings for springs or running water have not survived, and may not ever have existed (Franz, 1909:610–621).[6] It was precisely Guðmundr's blessing of such springs that was considered problematic by both laymen and clergy. His political opponents urinated in one of the springs he had blessed (which nonetheless continued to perform miracles) (GB 63; BS I 457). They were also skeptical of the relics he let people kiss (BS I 449). Bishop Árni of Skálholt is said to have blocked up a spring that Guðmundr had blessed at a major church—presumably with the knowledge of the parish priest at the time (GB 229; BS 612).[7]

In the sagas about Guðmundr, requests to bless springs come from farmers rather than priests, and appear to be associated with farms rather than with chapels or churches, where saints' wells were often to be found in mainland Scandinavia. This may, however, be due to the fact that medieval Iceland had no towns, and since churches or chapels were found on all major farms, the distinction between "church" and "farm" can be a misleading one. Árni Hjartarson's survey of contemporary *Gvendarbrunnar* shows that only about 20—less than a tenth of the total number—were associated with churches, and a comparable number provided the water supply for farms. The fact that Guðmundr is being asked to bless what are apparently water sources of farms does, however, put the *brunnar* of his sagas in a different category from holy wells in other countries, which are unlikely to be used for such purposes; indeed, there are stories of the wells taking objection to such usage (White, 1906–1915 III:340).[8]

The natural waters Guðmundr blesses are nonetheless miraculous.[9] A lake which he blesses immediately fills with fish, a story explicitly compared to an episode in the saga about St. Martin of Tours.[10] A similar tale is found in the *Dialogues* of Gregory the Great (book 1, 1959:7), and in a story of Iceland's saintly hermit *Ásólfr alskik*.[11] Lacking a bucket or pail, a woman carried blessed well-water home in her linen hat and lost none of the liquid on a walk that required her to pass five farmsteads.[12] In stories probably inspired by the *Dialogues* of Gregory the Great, a bucket full of Guðmundr's water falls down a mountainside without spilling a drop.[13] When men are playing backgammon at night and women refuse to bring them oil for lamps so they can finish their game, they are able to burn Guðmundr's water instead.[14] Although the water from *Gvendarbrunnar* was believed to have miraculous properties, people did not bring offerings to them, or visit them on specific days, as was done in the British Isles and Scandinavia.

We cannot know whether Guðmundr was the first Icelander to bless springs, although it is likely. *Hungrvaka*, a chronicle of Icelandic bishops of Skálholt before 1200, informs us that Bishop Bjarnharðr of Saxony blessed "churches and church bells, bridges and springs, fords and waters, cliffs and small bells, and these things seem to have manifested his true nobility and excellence" (*Biskupa sögur*, 2002:12). The implication is that he may have been a saint. While it is possible that early bishops did perform such blessings, it is equally likely that the statements that they did so are back-formations based on Guðmundr's activity. The alliterating pairs in the Icelandic passage about Bishop Bjarnharðr raise the suspicion that it is a rhetorical creation aimed at aggrandizing him rather than an accurate record of traditions about him. St. Þorlákr Þórhallsson is said to have blessed and sprinkled holy water as Guðmundr did, and we are told, in general terms, how much it was valued and used, first locally, later throughout the country. It is likely that Þorlákr used holy water in these traditional ways during his episcopate, and it may have been kept and used much as Guðmundr's was; however, it is never claimed that St. Þorlákr blessed springs, nor are there specific accounts of miracles that involve water he blessed. The passage which summarizes the effectiveness of his blessings is part of a generic list that might have been created to promote his sanctity; it forms part of an apology for people's unwillingness to attribute miracles to him during his lifetime.[15]

New holy wells could be regarded as suspicious by religious authorities, and fourteenth-century Icelanders were aware that Guðmundr's blessing of springs was problematic.[16] His sagas credit him with defending his practice to his ecclesiastical superior, the Archbishop of Nidaros. The date of the meeting and the historicity of the speech are open to question, but the contents illuminate fourteenth-century views on the subject. The speech takes up several themes, some of which can be found in other vernacular Icelandic religious writings, more or less word for word.[17] Guðmundr begins with a downright denial of his ability to sanctify things, on Biblical and theological grounds, quoting Paul in Titus 1:15 (via the saga of St. Ambrose) that all things are pure to the pure (GB 132, BS I 576, cf.; HMS vol. 1 34, 52).[18] He mentions, more or less in passing, the necessity of purifying wells into which dead bodies or other impurities have fallen; this was a known liturgical practice. He also argues that the end proves the validity of the means; whatever men may think, his actions are pleasing to God since people who truly believe and who are predestined to be cured by water from these springs, will be.

Most of the argument, however, concerns the fact that God had *already* sanctified *all* water, at its creation, at the wedding at Cana, and, most effectively, by His own baptism in the River Jordan. In medieval belief, these last two events were thought to have occurred on the same date, the feast of Epiphany, and sermons commemorate them on that day (Jan. 6). The idea that the River Jordan became holy as a result of Christ's baptism was well-known, appearing, among other places, in a skaldic verse (*Poetry from the Kings' Sagas* 2 part 2:506–507). It is mentioned in sermons for Epiphany, including two in the *Icelandic Homily Book*, a vernacular work from around 1200. In the first, we are told, seemingly as an afterthought to a translation of Gregory the Great's 10th gospel homily, that the day is the anniversary of the two events and that, when Christ was baptized in the River Jordan, He thereby "sanctified all waters so that they would be usable for baptism."[19] This is a standard interpretation, although it should be remembered that priests must still exorcise water as part of the baptismal ritual. The second sermon is also found in the *Norwegian Homily*

Book (1200–1225), which contains an excursus on the Virgin Mary not found in the Icelandic homily.[20] Both homilies state that

> the water was baptized by Christ rather than Christ baptized by the water, because when the Savior of the world stepped down into the water, he made all waters and springs holy as a symbol of his baptism, such that every man may be purified in the spring of Christ, wherever he is baptized in the name of the Lord.[21]

Only in Ælfric's sermon for Epiphany does a similar explicit mention of springs appear: "When he went into the water, the water and all springs (*wyllspringas*) were hallowed through Christ's body for our baptism."[22] The excursus in the Norwegian passage compares the activity of the Holy Ghost at Christ's conception to that at His baptism; "The same spirit that was with him in his mother's womb came over him in the likeness of a dove at his baptism. And that which then purified Mary now sanctified all waters."[23] The author of Guðmundr's speech states that the Holy Spirit in the form of a dove sanctified (literally "chrismed") the water.[24]

Thus, although the source texts clearly refer to the sanctifying of water specifically for the purpose of baptism, the idea that Christ's baptism in the Jordan sanctified all waters—including springs—was available for the author of Guðmundr's saga to use.[25] In fact, this assumption would seem to make Guðmundr's blessings unnecessary, and the author is careful to invoke other theological issues, such as faith and predestination, as well. However, just as baptismal and holy water need a priestly ritual to "activate" them, so wells and rivers needed Guðmundr's blessing before they could display miraculous properties—for those who believed in them.

In Guðmundr's sagas, the archbishop, impressed by Guðmundr's arguments, explicitly permits his "blessings and prayers, both over humans and animals and all [kinds of] water."[26] This permission came with the caveat that he does not know how his successors will react. With this passage, the saga's author approves a theological basis for Guðmundr's activity, while anticipating the skepticism of later Icelandic bishops such as Árni of Skálholt. In fact, the bishops of Hólar undoubtedly encouraged the idea that Guðmundr's water, of whatever origin, was "special" and provided proof of his sanctity, although they never managed to obtain his canonization from Rome. In present-day Lutheran Iceland, baptismal water, the only kind of water blessed by a priest, is thought by some to have healing properties. Guðmundr's reputation lives on in the numerous water sources in the countryside. Whether they all were actually blessed by him or associated with him by later generations, their common name is *Gvendarbrunnar*.

Notes

1 Personal communication, September 16, 2018.
2 KLNM II col. 324–330 and *Ordbog over det norrøne prosasprog*, hereafter ONP, http://onp.ku.dk/
3 KLNM X col. 53–59, entry *källa*, ONP entry *kelda*.
4 Stefán Karlsson, "Guðmundar sögur biskups."
5 For a discussion of miracles in Icelandic hagiography, see Whaley (1994/1992), "Miracles in the Sagas of Bishops: Icelandic Variations on an International Theme." For more on

Guðmundr's water-blessings, see Joel Anderson, "The Miraculous Water of Guðmundr Arason."

6 See also Leclercq and Cabrol (1907–1953), *Dictionnaire d'archéologie chrétienne et de liturgie.* Vol. 2 part 1 cols. 685–713.

7 Two successive bishops of Skálholt named Árni ruled from 1269 to 1320.

8 For example, a recurring theme in stories about Irish holy wells is that they dry up when someone uses their waters for domestic purposes such as washing clothes or potatoes.

9 The miracle accounts do not always specify what kind of water is being used, holy water or water from a spring Guðmundr had blessed; although the latter is occasionally referred to *brunnvatn*, for example in GB:237 and BS I 616, it is often necessary to rely on the context to determine what kind of water "Guðmundr's water" is.

10 GB:192-93, BS I:594; cf. *Heilagra Manna sögur* (hereafter HMS) I:572.

11 *Íslendingabók Landnámabók* (1968:62).

12 GB:71, 197-198; BS I:461, 596.

13 GB:71; BS I:461, cf. Gregory, *Dialogues* book 2:97.

14 GB:198-99, BS I:596, cf. Gregory *Dialogues* book 1:25.

15 Statements about Þorlákr's holy water are hedged round with caveats. If it was sprinkled over animals, "sickness or weather or animals *hardly* ever harmed them," "grandaði því náliga hvárki sóttir né veðr eða dýr," *Biskupa sögur* (2002:60–61), my italics. Joel Anderson ("The Miraculous Water of Guðmundr Arason":28) has suggested that the motif of not praising a living saint in *Þorláks saga* may have implicit reference to Guðmundr, who was already recognized as such.

16 In England, several bishops prohibited veneration of new springs; see the index of *Councils and Synods* under the heading "superstition."

17 Due to the limitations on length of this article, the following comments are necessarily abbreviated; a forthcoming study will provide a detailed comparison of the texts.

18 For the saga of St. Ambrose, see Wolf (2013:24–27). The relevant sections of the speech are in GB:131-35, BS I:575-78, cf HMS I 34.

19 "helgaþi aoll votn svo at til skírnar være hæf" *Homilíu-bók*:60). Andrea de Leeuw van Weenen (*The Icelandic Homily Book* 9) accepts Vrátný's identification of the homily as a translation of Gregory's 10th gospel homily.

20 *Homiliu-bók*:79–80; *Gammal norsk homiliebok*:57–59. Two of the texts are also found in a manuscript dated c. 1150. Linguistic forms suggest that the translations were made in the first half of the twelfth century (Erik Gunnes, *Gammel norsk homiliebok*, 1971:9).

21 *Gamal norsk homiliebok*, 58–59. var hældr vatnet scirt af Cristi an hann scirðisc í vatneno. Því at þa er grøðare hæims ste niðr í vatnet. þa hælgade hann oll votn ok brun í tacne sinnar scirnar. sva at hvær ma ræinsasc í Crist brvnne hvarge sem hann vil scirasc í nafne drotens. Cf. *Homiliu-bók*: 79–80.

22 "Ða ða hé into ðam wætere éode. ða wæs þæt wæter and ealle wyllspringas gehalgode þurh cristes lichaman to urum fulluhte" (*Ælfric's Catholic Homilies, Second Series*, 1979:22). See also Æfric's sermon for the octave of Pentecost, in which Christ is said to "gehalgian ... ealle wæterstréamas mid his ingange," (*Homilies of Ælfric. A Supplementary Collection.* I 416 and 467).

23 Ðvi at hinn same ande sa er með honum var í moðor qviði. sa kom yfir hann í dufu líki í skirn. Oc sa er þa læysti Mariam. nu hælgade hann oll votn." *Gamal norsk homiliebok*, 58.

24 GB:131, 133; BS I:575, 577. Chrism is a consecrated blend of oil and balsam used in anointing at baptism; it was agreed that Christ was chrismed at his baptism in the Jordan. The claim that the water itself was chrismed appears to be unique to the Icelandic text. The speech contains additional exegesis on the River Jordan which is not, however, relevant to Guðmundr's springs.

25 See also Stefán Karlsson, "Greftrun Auðar djúpúðgu."

26 "vígslur ok yfirsöngva, bæði mönnum ok fénaði ok öllum vötnum" GB:143; BS I 583.

References

Ælfric's Catholic Homilies. Second Series. Text. 1979. Edited by Malcolm Godden. London: Early English Text Society and Oxford University Press.

Anderson, Joel. 2008. The Miraculous Water of Guðmundr Arason and the Limits of Holiness in Medieval Iceland. MA thesis, University of Iceland.

Biskupa sögur II. 2002. Edited by Ásdís Egilsdóttir. Reykjavík: Hið íslenzka fornritafelag.

[BS] *Biskupa sögur.* 1858–1878. Edited by Guðbrandur Vigfússon, Jón Sigurðsson, Þorvaldur Bjarnarson, and Eiríkur Jónsson. Copenhagen: Hið íslenzka bókmenntafélag.

Cormack, Margaret. 2007. Holy Wells and National Identity in Iceland. In *Saints and their Cults in the Atlantic World*, edited by Margaret Cormack, 229–247. Columbia: University of South Carolina Press.

Councils and Synods with Other Documents Relating to the English Church. 1981. Vol. 1, Edited by Dorothy Whitelock, Martin Brett and Christopher N. L. Brooke. Oxford: Clarendon Press; Vol. 2, 1964. Edited by Frederick Maurice Powicke and Christopher Robert Cheney. Oxford: Clarendon Press.

Franz, Adolph. 1909. *Die Kirchlichen Benediktionen im Mittelalter.* 2 vols. Freiburg im Bresgau: Herdersche Verlagshandlung.

*Gammal norsk homiliebok Cod. AM 619 4to.*1931. Edited by Gustav Indrebø. Oslo: Kjeldeskriftfondet.

Gammelnorsk homiliebok. 1971. Translated by Astrid Salveson, Introduction and Commentary by Erik Gunnes. Oslo: Universitetsforlaget.

Gregory the Great, *Dialogues.* 1959. Translated by Odo Zimmerman. Washington, DC: Catholic University of America Press.

[GB] *Guðmundar sögur biskups* II. Guðmundar Saga B. 2018. Edited by Stefán Karlsson and Magnús Hauksson. Copenhagen: Museum Tusculanum Press.

[HMS] *Heilagra manna søgur: Fortællinger og legender om hellige mænd og kvinder efter gamle haandskrifter.* 1877. Edited by Carl R. Unger. 2 vols, [n.p.]. Oslo: B.M. Bentzen

Homilies of Ælfric. A Supplementary Collection. 1967. Edited by John C. Pope. London: Early English Text Society and Oxford University Press.

Homilíu-bók: Isländska homilier efter en handskrift från tolfte århundradet. 1872. Edited by Theodor Wisén. Lund: Gleerup.

The Icelandic Homily Book, Perg. 15 4o in the Royal Library, Stockholm. 1993. Edited by Andrea de Leeuw van Weenen. Reykjavík: Stofnun Árna Magnússonar á Íslandi.

Íslendingabók Landnámabók. 1968. Edited by Jakob Benediktsson. Reykjavík: Hið íslenzka fornritafélag.

Karlsson, Stefán. 1976. Greftrun Auðar djúpúðgu. In *Minjar og Menntir. Afmælisrit helgað Kristjáni Eldjárn 6. desember 1976.* Edited by Guðni Kolbeinsson, 481–488. Reykjavík: Menningarsjóður.

Karlsson, Stefán. 1993. Guðmundar sögur biskups. In *Medieval Scandinavia: An Encyclopedia*, edited by Phillip Pulsiano, Kirsten Wolf, Paul Acker and Donald K. Fry, 245–246. New York: Garland.

[KLNM] *Kulturhistorisk leksikon for nordisk middelalder fra vikingetid til reformationstid.* 1956–1978. Edited by Johannes Brøndsted. Copenhagen: Rosenkilde og Bagger.

Leclercq, Henri and Fernand Cabrol. 1907–1953. *Dictionnaire d'archéologie chrétienne et de liturgie.* Paris: Letouzey et Ané.

[ONP] Ordbog over det norrøne prosasprog. http://onp.ku.dk/

Poetry from the Kings' Sagas 2: From c. 1035 to c. 1300. 2009. Edited by Kari Ellen Gade. Turnhout: Brepols.

Whaley, Diana. 1994/1992. Miracles in the Sagas of Bishops: Icelandic Variations on an International Theme. *Collegium Medievale* 7:155–184.

White, James Grove. 1906–1915. *Historical and Topographical Notes etc. on Buttevant, Castletownroche, Doneraile, Mallow and their Vicinity.* Cork: Historical and Archaeological Society.

Wolf, Kirsten. 2013. *The Legends of the Saints in Old Norse-Icelandic Prose.* Toronto: University of Toronto Press.

PART VI

Contested and shared sites

The layered biographies of sacred watery sites can make their numens and associated folk devotions contested in popular visitation and by religious authorities. Different perspectives, both between and within faiths, may shape the experience and stewardship of a site. Particularly within international traditions, the degree of syncretism or even hybridity manifested in local sacred site practices can vary by the age, gender, ethnicity and class of devotees. For some individuals and communities, indigenous beliefs in water spirits may operate as an unsyncretized, parallel worldview beside their observances related to a dominant faith. Like other sacred sites, hallowed water sources are also venerated simultaneously by those with different and even conflicting ideologies. In Europe, the space of a holy well might be simultaneously occupied by Christians, Newagers and Neopagans. The sacrality of these life-giving sites is now also contested for devotees around the globe by secular day-trippers and tourists.

The mikvah is generally an indoor pool that Jewish women use for ritual purification, but Robert Phillips examines a current controversy about men's increasing use of outdoor springs for ritual bathing. He focuses on Mei Niftoach, a natural spring on the outskirts of Jerusalem, where formerly shared space has become gendered and also contested between observant and secular Israelis. Offering a microgeographical analysis of sacred springs in Finnish village landscapes, John Björkman identifies social dimensions of their spatiality and patterns in their historic vernacular rites. Those springs located on village or parish borders and furthest from village centers offered a place apart for the young. Not only were youths freed there from the supervision of adult relatives and the farm owners for whom they worked, but such locations also had more links to dangerous supernaturals (wizards rather than saints) and were venues for more borderline activities such as scrying. In a different type of space apart, generational identity also emerges as significant in Jean Marie Rouhier-Willoughby's analysis of cultural memories about three holy and miraculous springs in Western Siberia located on former prison camps. While the springs' contemporary sacrality stems from twentieth-century martyrdoms and post-socialist Orthodoxy, devotees relate contrasting sub-narratives about the gulag system, World War II and Soviet identity along generational lines.

Examining curative springs that have remained sacred sites across centuries of religious and political changes in North Macedonia, Snežana Filipova considers the multi-confessional folk beliefs and practices of contemporary pilgrims. She focuses on springs associated with Sts. Mary, George and the indigenous Naum that attract both Orthodox Christian and Macedonian Muslim devotees. Jens Kreinath considers the shared sacred topography of Hatay, in the southernmost province of Turkey, through four sacred water sanctuaries also associated with nearby sacred rocks and trees, and visited by members of Christian and Muslim communities who hold distinctive beliefs within their own respective faiths. Rather than "antagonistic tolerance," both the North Macedonian and Turkish cases note a ready amicability of interaction at shared shrines that have undergone sequential sacralization.

19

A HIGHER LEVEL OF IMMERSION

A contemporary freshwater mikvah pool in Israel

Robert Phillips

Water takes a central role in the Torah,[1] beginning in Genesis, which says that the world was brought to life by God who created "an expanse in the midst of the water" (Genesis 1:6 Stone Edition Chumash, 2000). This association of water with the sacred has been a continuous feature of Jewish belief and ritual over the past thirty-three centuries. For the most part, the narrative of the Torah takes place in what is known today as the southern Levant also referred to in religious terminology as "Canaan," the "Holy Land" and the "Land of Israel." This geographic region stretches from the Sinai Peninsula in the south to southern Lebanon in the north and extends eastward into Jordan, encompassing most of the present-day state of Israel. Based on a reading of some portions of the Torah, especially those dealing with the Israelite exodus from Egypt into the Sinai Desert, one might get the impression that all of the southern Levant is an arid desert. In fact, this is partially correct in that there is only one river, the Jordan, within the borders of the current state of Israel. If we include all of the southern Levant, then we also have the Litani River, contained within the borders of the modern state of Lebanon.

Israel is made up of four distinct physiographic regions (Metz, 1988). The Negev region in the south of Israel is considered a desert, and at 12,000 square kilometers, makes up over half of the country's land mass. To the east, the Central Hills, encompassing much of Judea and Samaria, are also considered arid. However, the two other regions—the coastal plain and the Jordan Rift Valley—tend toward a more Mediterranean climate, characterized by long hot dry summers and cool rainy winters. During the rainy season (late October to mid-March), streambeds (*wadis*) swell to overflowing but are dry the rest of the year. While contemporary Israel has state-of-the-art irrigation and water engineering systems in place, this has not always been the case.

In the recent past, wells and springs complemented natural rainfall and rivers and were an important component of the overall ecosystem in that they played a significant role in satisfying various water needs. Throughout the Torah, wells and springs figure prominently through several interwoven narratives. For instance, Miriam's Well (*Be'erah shel Miriam*) is credited with helping the millions of Israelites who left slavery in Egypt survive for 40 years in the parched desert of what is now known as the Sinai Peninsula. During their wanderings, the Israelites were accompanied by a rock from which a plentiful supply of water continuously flowed. According to commentators, it was named in the merit of Moses' older sister Miriam, who is considered both a prophetess and a righteous woman within the Jewish world. Part of the honor bestowed on Miriam comes from the fact that she is seen to embody properties of water, especially its ability to adapt to its surroundings. Figuratively, this refers to Miriam's ability to adapt her faith according to circumstances. Miriam is also connected to water via her role in leading the Israelite women in the singing of the celebratory "Song of the Sea" (Exodus 15:1–18), that followed the defeat of Pharaoh and his armies during the crossing of the Red Sea.

After Miriam's death in the desert, the well ceased to function, causing a water crisis of sorts. The people then approached Moses and his brother Aaron, asking them to speak with God as they were thirsting for water. God commanded Moses to speak to a rock and demand that it produce water. Still angry with the rebellious Israelites, Moses instead struck the rock. Water issued forth from the stone, satisfying the people. However, because Moses was filled with rage and the fact that he did not follow directions, God told him that neither he nor his brother will enter the Promised Land. Other instances feature wells as places where marriages are initiated. For instance, Eliezer is sent by Abraham to find a wife for his son, Isaac. He meets Isaac's future bride, Rebecca, at a well outside a distant village. She graciously offers him water from the central well for his thirsty camels (Genesis 24:10–27 Stone Edition Chumash, 2000). Eliezer determines that the extra kindness of watering the camels is the sign that she is the bride for Isaac. Later in the narrative, Jacob meets his future wife Rachel when he single-handedly moves a large stone from atop a well so that she can water her flock of sheep (Genesis 29:1–12 ibid.). Finally, Moses meets his wife Tzipporah at a well, after repelling some intimidating shepherds (Exodus 2:15–21 ibid.).

It should be noted that there is a difference between ordinary dug wells and step wells. Biblical-era dug wells were hand-excavated to a depth below the groundwater table. Once the hole was dug and the water rose to the surface, a heavy rock was often used as a cover. A clay pot attached to a rope was then used to retrieve the water. The Torah twice mentions the well of Bethlehem located by the gate of the city (1 Samuel 23:15 and 1 Chronicles 11:17 ibid.). This type of well stands in contrast to step wells which were dug at an incline with stone steps leading down to an exposed subterranean pool.

Mikva'ot

> Only a spring and a pit, a gathering of water, shall be clean.
> *(Leviticus 11:36 Stone Edition Chumash, 2000)*

In addition to wells acting as places where holy events unfold, naturally occurring springs have also been used as holy sites of ritual purification. Mikvahs have been found in many places associated with Judaism, including the first-century CE mikvah found at the ruins of Herod's fortress at Masada. Rituals, including hand washing (*netilat yadayim*) and washing of the dead (*taharah*), can incorporate spring water. Natural and artificial bodies of water are also used for purification through full bodily immersion. Pre-marital and post-menstrual women take part in immersion rituals (as do those individuals undergoing the last step of conversion to Judaism). In contemporary times, Jews of both sexes have come to use ritual baths known as mikva'ot (singular mikvah) to facilitate the completion of these rites.

On the most basic level, a mikvah (lit. a gathering or a collective) is a pool of clean water, such as a spring, in which a person who has become ritually impure immerses themselves in order to once again become ritually pure. Immersing oneself in the mikvah is not about physical cleanliness, but rather spiritual purity. Similarly, ritual hand washing, noted earlier, is to be performed on hands that are already clean. Among those who adhere to the Jewish laws of family purity (*taharat ha-mishpachah*), a woman is considered a *niddah* (lit. "to be separated") during and after her monthly menstrual period (see Metz, 1988; Kaplan, 1993). One week after her flow ceases, she visits the mikvah. Immersion occurs after sundown on the seventh day. The immersion is valid only if the waters of the mikvah completely enclose every part of her body, from the hair on her head to the tips of her toes (see Slonin, 2006). Natural mikva'ot include springs, lakes and oceans.

In contemporary times, large Jewish communities have constructed mikva'ot and incorporated them into synagogues and Jewish community centers. Others, with

FIGURE 19.1 The spring at Mei Niftoach. Faces intentionally blurred to protect identity. © Ori~Creative Commons CC0 License.

more resources, have them built into new homes. Regardless of where the mikvah is being built, a key to its construction is the satisfaction of an intricate set of requirements. A mikvah must be built into the ground or constructed as an integral part of a building. Thus, portable receptacles such as whirlpool baths and bathtubs can never function as mikva'ot. A mikvah must contain at least 200 gallons of rainwater that was collected in accordance with Jewish law (Ibid). It must also use water from two sources—rainwater and tap water. The sources of water are separated by a wall with the rainwater and tap water only connecting through a hole two inches in diameter. When the tap water comes into contact with the rainwater, it is made holy through that contact, known as *hashoko* (to kiss, contact, touch). While indoor mikva'ot are most common in contemporary Jewish communities, other individuals and communities around the world use naturally occurring mikvahs in the form of natural springs.

Mei Niftoach

Mei Niftoach[2] (literally "spring of the corridor"), also known by the Arabic name Lifta, was a small village located at the crossroads of two highways in the center of Jerusalem, just below the Giv'at Sha'ul interchange which connects Highways 1 and 50. The site was abandoned by Arab residents during the Civil War of 1947–1948 and is now in ruins, though there are many homes still partially intact and the architecture is unmistakably Arabic, with strong notes of Ottoman period construction. The currently undeveloped land bears traces of what was once farmland and terraces surrounded by almond, fig and olive trees as well as wild opuntia (cactus fruit). While Arabs were the most recent occupants of the site, Mei Niftoach has seen continuous settlement since ancient times and is noted in the Biblical Book of Joshua as the line of demarcation between the tribes of Benjamin and Judah (Joshua 15:8–9 and 18:15 Stone Edition Chumash, 2000). The spring at the center of Mei Niftoach is mentioned in both verses. Joshua 15 refers to it as the "spring of the waters," whereas Joshua 18 calls it the "well of the waters."

The current pool at Mei Niftoach is approximately 10 meters across. It is pie-shaped and originates with a sealed perennial spring in which there is a 60-meter-long tunnel that carries the water to the larger reservoir (Israel Antiquities Authority, 2008). In the past, the water flowed from the spring to two separate pools. From there, irrigation channels extended from the lower pool out into the fields. The spring itself is approximately 2 meters deep when full and is lined with rectangular blocks of Jerusalem stone (various types of pale limestone). There are no stairs in the pool, but people will sometimes pile stones in a corner to create a makeshift set of steps in order to facilitate access.

Mei Niftoach spring as mikvah

While the spring at Mei Niftoach is not in any way a "designated" or "official" mikvah, many men from Jerusalem and environs have adopted it as a place in which to immerse themselves. Jewish men have used mikva'ot, such as the one in Mei Niftoach, for thousands of years for various reasons all surrounding notions of purity and pollution. According to the Babylonian Talmud, at the beginning of the Second Temple Period (530 BCE–70 CE), Ezra the Scribe "ordained that a healthy man whose [seminal] emission is voluntary must immerse in forty se'ahs, and a healthy man whose [seminal] emission is involuntary must use nine kabs [before studying Torah] (Talmud)."[3] This practice never caught on with men in general because regardless of whether their seminal emissions were involuntary or voluntary, they still had to immerse before Torah study and when they did not have the opportunity to do so, they would have been unable to study.

In more recent times, men immerse at different times for various reasons, including before the beginning of the Sabbath on Friday afternoon, before his wedding in the case of a groom, and before Yom Kippur (the Day of Atonement). Others, whose circumstances allow, immerse daily. This practice permits them to emulate kohanim (Temple priests) who were commanded to immerse before beginning Temple services. The other reason for daily immersion is to "submerge" the ego and to subsequently allow one to pray unfettered. In fact, the Hebrew word for "immersion" is an anagram for the word "humility," indicating that immersion will lead to humility. In a contemporary twist, observant egalitarian men sometimes immerse in a mikvah in tandem with their wives' menstrual cycles (Heilman, 2015). Regardless of the reason, sources (USCJ, 2019) indicate that the highest level of purity is achieved by immersing in a naturally occurring spring, such as the one located in Mei Niftoach. For many men, the preference for immersing in an outdoor spring over an indoor mikvah has to do with connecting—with both nature and their forefathers who had used the spring in past times. It could even be argued that the use of springs is a reflection of the recent upsurge in observant Jewish men and women reconnecting to nature as a religious value (see Tirosh-Samuelson, 2001).

The use of the spring at Mei Niftoach as a mikvah has not come without controversy. Men's immersion in outdoor springs has been on the increase for the past decade and the practice has been featured in Israeli popular media including the television serial *Srugim* and the film *Eyes Wide Open* (2009). Beginning in 2015, newspapers have reported conflicts between men and women at Mei Niftoach and other outdoor springs including Nebi Samuel, just north of Jerusalem (Hasson, 2015, 2018a, 2018b). The main issue is that observant men desire to use these springs as ritual baths, whereas groups of young women are there to cool off with a swim. Because the men remove all of their clothing when immersing in the spring, women initially stayed away. But, with more and more men and women wanting to use these springs, conflict was inevitable. Some women have claimed to have endured violence or sexual harassment for simply showing up at the springs. At a spring in Ein Itamar, south of Jerusalem, unknown persons took it upon themselves to use concrete to block the channel that brings water to the pool from the spring, making it unusable. Although that situation was peacefully resolved, tensions continue.

Conclusions

Waters, religious historian Mircea Eliade explained in the 1950s, are "spring and origin, the reservoir of all the possibilities of existence; they precede every form and support every creation" (Eliade, 1987 [1957]:130). As described earlier, and supported by

Eliade's sentiments, waters—including wells and springs, through their ability to make pure the unclean—are sites of possibility. It could also be argued that in past times, wells and springs functioned as gathering places where things happened and events unfolded. In biblical times, the meeting of Rachel and Jacob and of Moses and his wife Tzipporah happened at a well, thus sealing the fate of the Jewish people. The current controversy about usage of outdoor springs also sheds light on contemporary gender relations in Israel as well as conflicts between religious (observant) and secular Israelis.

Beginning with the establishment of the State of Israel, numerous redevelopment plans have been put forward for Mei Niftoach. Some have focused on preserving the character of the village with a heritage center and nature preserve, while others have proposed luxury villas be built on the site. A multitude of issues, including development costs, the fragile state of many of the remaining stone buildings and environmental concerns, have prevented any of these plans from being implemented. In early 2017, the Israeli government announced that the site had been renamed the Mei Niftoach Nature Reserve (Lavie, 2017).

Notes

1 The Torah, which contains the five books of the Hebrew Bible, is known more commonly to non-Jews as the "Old Testament." The Torah is referred to elsewhere as the Chumash, the Pentateuch and the Five Books of Moses.
2 This name has also been transliterated from the Hebrew as Mei Naftoach and Mei Neftoach. Mei Niftoach is used in this work as it is the most common transliteration.
3 A se'ah is an ancient unit of measure that is roughly equivalent to 7.3 l. Similarly, a kab is equivalent to the volume taken up by 24 medium-sized eggs.

References

Artscroll. *Stone Edition Chumash*. 2000. Brooklyn: Mesorah Publications, Ltd.
Eliade, Mircea. 1987 [1957]. *The Sacred and the Profane: The Nature of Religion*. New York: Harcourt.
Hasson, Nir. 2015. Jerusalem's Religious Gender War about to Cause New Splash. *Haaretz*, September 29. Retrieved September 01, 2019. www.haaretz.com/.premium-jerusalems-religious-war-takes-to-the-water-1.5403118
Hasson, Nir. 2018a. Men and Women, Religious or Not, Battle for Rights at Israeli Springs. *Haaretz*, June 29. Retrieved September 01, 2019. www.haaretz.com/israel-news/.premium-men-and-women-religious-or-not-battle-for-rights-at-israeli-springs-1.6221515
Hasson, Nir. 2018b. Water Cut to Spring Near Jerusalem to Prevent Female Swimming. *Haaretz*, July 17. Retrieved September 01, 2019. www.haaretz.com/israel-news/.premium-water-cut-to-spring-near-jerusalem-to-prevent-female-swimming-1.6280253
Heilman, Uriel. 2015. Do You Know the Mikvah Men? *Times of Israel*, December 14. Retrieved September 01, 2019. www.timesofisrael.com/do-you-know-the-mikvah-men/
Israel Antiquities Authority. 2008. Mei Niftoach: A Preliminary Urban Survey. Retrieved September 01, 2019. www.iaaconservation.org.il/Projects_Item_eng.asp?site_id=3&subject_id=6&id=114
Kaplan, Aryeh. 1993. *Waters of Eden: The Mystery of the Mikvah*. New York: NCSY/Union of Orthodox Jewish Congregations of America.
Lavie, Dan. 2017. According to Natural Laws: Four New Reserves in Israel. *Israel Hayom*, April 7. Retrieved September 01, 2019. www.israelhayom.co.il/article/487969

Metz, Helen Chapin. 1988. *Israel: A Country Study.* Washington, DC: GPO for the Library of Congress.

Slonin, Rivkah. 2006. "Introduction." In *Total Immersion: A Mikvah Anthology,* edited by Rivkah Slonin, 21–38. Jerusalem: Urim Publishers.

Talmud b. Berakoth 22B.

Tirosh-Samuelson, Hava. 2001. Nature in the Sources of Judaism. *Daedalus* 130(4):99–124.

USCJ (United Synagogue of Conservative Judaism). 2019. *Mikvaot,* Chapter 1, *Mishnah 8.* http://learn.conservativeyeshiva.org/mikvaot-1-8-htm/

20

WATERS AT THE EDGE

Sacred springs and spatiality in Southwest Finnish village landscapes

John Björkman

The knowledge of sacred springs in Finland has mostly been forgotten. Archival sources, however, tell us that they were still in common use in the nineteenth century and local history associations have pointed me to many undocumented sites. Sacred springs in Finland have not been much studied. They are briefly mentioned in some archaeological surveys from the early twentieth century (see e.g. Tallgren, 1918), in some presentations of regional folklore and customs (Harva, 1935; Sarmela, 1994) as well as in later studies on vernacular faith (Toivo, 2016). Finnish sacred springs have had two main historical purposes: as sites of healing rituals and as gathering places for the young for midsummer revelries. These traditions have died out, but the sources suggest that they were still practised in the late nineteenth century and perhaps in the early twentieth. This essay queries the kind of space sacred springs occupied in the social and cultural landscapes at their recorded time of use.

To consider the spatiality of these sites, this study draws on descriptions of 68 sacred springs found in the folklore archives of the Finnish Literature Society, the *Finlands svenska folkdiktning* compendium of Finnish and Swedish folklore, literature on local history and lore, archived newspaper articles and, in some cases, oral lore. Material derives mostly from the mid-seventeenth century to the early twentieth. Thirty-two of these springs can be located on digitised village maps from the eighteenth to twentieth centuries. Of these, six have been lost and the author has exactly located eighteen in the field.

The meaning of these vernacular sacred sites relates to how communities worked and lived to a large extent off the land. Appreciating their location in relation to village geography identifies unexpected patterns. A geographical perspective on folklore or vernacular religion is in no way new. However, the focus has so far mostly been on a larger scale seeking regional differences. A closer, microgeographical perspective using cartographic material on the village level can bring new insights.

Southwest Finnish villages in the seventeenth through nineteenth centuries

Despite having endured numerous wars, calamities and shifts in both ruler-ship and religion, Southwest Finland is a region characterised by structural sta-bility. Catholicism (and with it, Swedish rule) was slowly introduced from the west in around the twelfth century, whereas the sixteenth-century conversion to Lutheranism was more sudden.[1] However, archaeological findings and place-name research have shown that the region was organised into proto-parishes and villages already in the Iron Age (which lasted until the mid-twelfth century in Finland). This territorial structuring remains to this day (see Tallgren, 1933; Orrman, 2003:72–77).

The best source material which we have to understand the cultural-spatial layout of Finnish villages approximately 200 years ago are maps drawn for "the great par-tition," a process of redistribution of land among the landowners in each village, initiated in 1757 (see e.g. Saarenheimo, 2003:349–365). Partition maps of Southwest Finnish villages from the late eighteenth and early nineteenth centuries show us dif-ferent ways in which space has been divided culturally. Most villages had a unitary central open area, a "heartland" with grain fields, pastures and meadows. The farm buildings were generally in a relatively dense group on one edge of this area. Pro-viding sustenance for the people, the heartlands comprised the most valuable land and were visible from the farms. Socially, this means that this space was most closely supervised by the farm owners.[2] Outside this "heartland" were the village outlands, which were mostly forests intertwined with outer meadows. These "secondary" lands could be characterised as a separate "space," and they were even sometimes drawn on separate maps from the heartlands. Outlands provided fuel and timber, and were where the cattle and sheep of the village grazed in the summer.

Sacred springs in Finland Proper

> On the meadow of Varttola, in Haltiahaka (was a healing spring). It healed eye diseases. Coins and needles were left there. If you stole them from the spring, you would be afflicted by disease. You had to leave without looking back.
>
> *(SKS KRA Paimio, translated from Finnish by the author)*

Sacred springs seem to be more common in Southwestern Finland than other parts of the country. The most common reason for visiting healing springs was particu-larly to heal eye and skin diseases. Those hoping for a cure left a needle or a coin "sacrifice" at the site. Devotees collected water at the spring that was thought to ease childbirth and also employed the water in baptism. Going to a healing spring is sometimes referred to in the sources as a "pilgrimage." As the aforementioned quote makes clear, the coins left in the spring were usually connected to a taboo: taking coins left by others brought affliction with the diseases they were sacrificed to heal. Other taboos prohibited a backward glance or stopping to urinate when leaving the spring.

The sacred springs are associated with different supernatural beings, animals, saints, legends, myths and divinities. These beings and stories serve to make the spring sacred or mythic, a *place* with a special meaning, and power. The most typical "patron" for sacred springs in Southwest Finland is St. Henry, a missionising saint alleged to have converted the pagan Finns into Christianity in the twelfth century. The motif of St. Henry preaching to the pagans at a spring and then using the spring water to baptise converts is popularly associated with multiple sites including the spring of St. Henry on the island of Lapila, the Bishop's spring in Rymättylä, the Ristinkylä spring in Taivassalo, the Kupittaa spring in Turku and possibly the Heikinlähde, also in Turku (see Tallgren and Montin-Tallgren, 1918:49).

Many other springs are named after saints as well, such as St. John, St. Bridget (of Sweden) or St. Gertrude. Some springs are named after animals, especially bears. One spring name contains the word "hiisi," which can mean "sacred site" or "giant" (see Koski, 1967, 1970). Some spring names contain the word "sampas" which can refer to the mythic Sampo (a supernatural bestower of fortune and prosperity, see e.g. Tarkka, 2012). The word can also mean "border marker." Some descriptions of sacred springs mention *haltija* (the Finnish term for local spirit) and implied that springs had spirits residing in them.

Locations of sacred springs

The majority are located more or less peripherally, either on the outskirts or borders of villages, or even further out, in parish backwoods. Historian Raisa Maria Toivo has noted that after pilgrimages to specific churches became prohibited in the Lutheran era, the customs became redirected to more peripheral locations (2016:51). Analysing the locations of sacred springs on partition maps, a very interesting feature becomes apparent: 15 springs lay on village or parish borders, or they lay on hills which mark such borders. It is also noteworthy that many, but not all springs that lie on borders, have a solitary erratic boulder in their proximity, but there are also springs with such boulders that are not connected to borders. In addition, there are known "border stones" which have springs next to them.

Although geographer Yi-Fu Tuan says that "Nature, other than the human body itself, doesn't seem to provide convenient yardsticks for the measurement of space" (1979:391), it seems that features which "stick out" in the terrain, such as springs and large solitary boulders, can be just that, and often these types of "yardsticks" gain a sacred character. A close comparison to the boulders viewed as special when found near sacred springs are the "blue stones" of central Russia; Linguist Arja Ahlqvist suggests that blue stones were markers of orientation in the landscape. They are also used as border markers for villages so that a village is said to reach "up to the blue stone," or conversely, the stone is said to lie between this and that village (2012:442–443).

However, in the written records about Finnish sacred springs, the boulders are rarely mentioned. One exception is formed by the "bishop's stone" and "bishop's spring" in Rymättylä (see Tallgren, 1918:75). Some descriptions also mention trees in connection with the springs, such as the spring and birch of Witigsuo in Lieto or the spring and oak of St. Henry on the island of Lapila. A possible explanation to why tradition around springs has prevailed, whereas tradition around sacred stones and trees has more frequently disappeared, is provided by historian of religion Therese Zachrisson. The church in medieval Sweden (which included present-day Finland) forbade the worship of trees, groves, cairns or stones, but springs or wells were not mentioned. Thus, the spring cult was able to endure much longer (2017:225). It is possible that the springs and their surroundings once served as sites of more complex rites.

In the seventeenth and eighteenth centuries, many of the old sacred healing springs were re-employed by the upper layers of society as mineral springs (see Zachrisson, 2017:215–219). A well-known example in Finland is the spring of Kupittaa on the outskirts of the city of Turku (which was the administrative capital of Finland at the time). In 1649, academy student Petrus Magnus Gyllenius wrote in his diaries that people gathered at the spring on Midsummer's Eve to light fires and play games (Gardberg and Toijer, 1962:108). Only four decades later, Elias Tillands stated that the water of said spring had a health-improving effect, and a sanatorium was established there. Later, in the eighteenth and nineteenth centuries, the sanatorium developed into a bath-house for the upper classes (Hyvönen, 2011:40–57).

Sacred springs and youth revelry

The custom of gathering at sacred springs to celebrate St. John's Eve is best known in the region around Turku and was assumed by Uno Harva to be a Swedish influence (1935:50). Many records of midsummer traditions even from other regions especially mention "scrying" in a spring or well at midnight (foretelling the future over a reflective surface). The most popular subject was discovering one's future love:

> In the region of Hinnerjoki people used to run three times backward around a spring on midsummer's night so one could see one's groom-to-be or hear extraordinary things.
>
> *(SKS KRA Uusikaupunki < Hinnerjoki. Salokannel, Tyyne KRK 9:115.*
> *1935, translated from Finnish by the author)*

Anthropologist Matti Sarmela has released a collection of "tradition maps," illustrating regional variations of folk tales, beliefs and festival customs (1994). According to Sarmela's material, 90% of participants at midsummer spring celebrations in the area of study were youth (map 25). The focus on scrying for one's future groom/fiancé also makes it clear that the rites were for the unmarried and allowed young people to imagine themselves taking over the role of farm master or mistress. Depositing coins or needles into the spring is also mentioned in the context of scrying.

Midsummer revelry, involving drinking and noise-making at sacred springs, was also known in Sweden. According to Zachrisson, "worldly" behaviour such as drinking, dancing and playing was not seen as contradictory to the sacrality of the place (2017:203–205). Cultural geographer Ronan Foley has brought up similar customs at holy wells in Ireland. Celebrations would first begin with pious activities such as rounding rituals and prayer, but would at midnight turn into revelry with music, drinking, nudity, sex and violence. Foley describes these customs as "unhealthy and unholy performances," conflicting with the sacred and therapeutic nature of the holy well (2013:56–57). However, is this a projection of modern conceptions of sacrality onto older vernacular ways of venerating a sacred site? As Veikko Anttonen has pointed out, our view of "the sacred" has changed over time and older forms of vernacular religion could have encompassed very different views on sacrality (1996:158). According to one of the sources Foley cites, being on sacred ground was seen to free the revellers from "normal" repercussions of such activities (2013:57). To consider such vernacular conceptions of the sacred, this essay presents two case examples of sacred springs in Finland Proper that were particularly known as sites of youth gatherings on St. John's Eve.

The spring of Muhkuri

In the early 1800s, the young Erik Julin, the 15-year-old son of a pharmacist who had recently moved to Turku, took part in midsummer rites at the spring of Muhkuri in the village of Pitkämäki, and described the event in his diaries:

> During the Catholic era the spring of Muhkuri at Pahaniemi was sacred; sacrificial feasts were held there. Still on midsummer's eve 1812 people spoke of making a pilgrimage to Muhkuri, to sacrifice for coming luck.
>
> Together with many others I visited said spring on the midsummer night in 1812 and sacrificed a copper coin into the spring like the others. I do not know if this sacrificial feast has brought any luck, but I wait and hope. The number of people gathered kept growing, and soon old ladies with coffee pots and liquor bottles showed up. This lead to disturbing behaviour, brawls and noisemaking, which caused the police to empty the site and prohibit further gatherings.
>
> *(Dahlström, 1918:16–17, translated from Swedish by the author)*

Julin's description is one of the more detailed of the midsummer revelries at a sacred spring.

It is worth noting that Julin was not a member of the agrarian population, but a member of the bourgeois. The village of Pitkämäki, although part of the city today, was definitely countryside in the early nineteenth century, belonging to the rural parish of Maaria. Yet, it seems that people went there not just from neighbouring villages but also from the city. In what Julin referred to as a "pilgrimage" at Muhkuri, bourgeois city-dwellers and villagers gathered to mingle. Not just village and farm borders, but even social borders were erased.

Muhkuri is a wooded hill at the southern edge of the village of Pitkämäki, formerly of Maaria parish (Julin erroneously states that the spring is in Pahaniemi, which is a neighbouring village). The hill lies on the village border, but on the side of Pitkämäki. The hilltop offers a good view of the surrounding landscape. The partition map of Pitkämäki (drawn in 1785, approximately 20 years before the young Erik Julin's midsummer visit) shows the four farms of the village laid out in a row from east to west at the northern edge of the village heartland. The open heartland consists of grain fields and meadows with the farms on the northern edge. On the south side of the opening is the hill of Muhkuri, and behind it the village border against the lands of Isoheikkilä manor. North of the farms is a broader wooded area.[3] The location of the Muhkuri hill could thus be considered peripheral in the village space, outside the open view of the heartlands, outside the lands directly controlled by the farm masters and bordering to another village. Thus, Muhkuri can be seen as a "yardstick" which defines the cultural landscape; it limits the open heartland and divides the landscape between the two villages of Pitkämäki and Isoheikkilä.

A sacred spring at such a liminal spot was a great attraction for people on a liminal holiday (the longest day of the year, after which the days grew shorter). In agricultural life, St. John's Eve also marked the end of the relatively leisurely period of early summer, when the young had more free time, and marked the beginning of the work-intensive high summer and harvest periods, when the youth would not have much freedom for merry-making. The harvest period was characterised by rites and celebrations performed at the farms, with the farm masters and mistresses taking the main roles. At midsummer, however, people came away from the farms and village centres, and even from the nearby city, to celebrate in manners which placed the youth at the centre. A gathering outside the farms (areas socially controlled by the farm owners) allowed the youth to interact on their own terms and engage, unobserved, in unruly behaviour as described by Julin.

FIGURE 20.1 The sacred spring at Kungsbacken in the Swedish-speaking parish of Kimito lies at a village border. A large solitary boulder can be seen in the background. Photograph by the author.

FIGURE 20.2   The Ämmälähde (Crone's Spring) on Inkisvuori Hill in the backwoods of the parish of Nousiainen, where young people gathered at midsummer. The hill, which formerly marked the parish border, offers a vantage point over the surroundings. Photograph by the author.

The spring of Ämmälähde

> Looking into a spring normally happened on Midsummer's Eve, but it had to be a natural spring, or one whose waters ran to the north. Looking into it, one would see one's future groom, and other life events of the coming year. One such spring was the Ämmälähde, at Mustakulma of Ojankulma. At this spring the old owner, the great witch who could fly in the air on his horse, the father of Inkisvuori, would punish his old lady by submerging her in the spring when she was in an unpleasant mood to him.
>
> *(SKS KRA. Nousiainen. Leivo, F. 2059. 1936)*

In the backwoods of the prehistoric parish of Nousiainen, on the hill of Inkisvuori lies the sacred spring of Ämmälähde (known as "The mother's spring" or "the crone's spring"). The Ämmälähde Spring is connected both with Midsummer's Night celebrations and also with stories of an infamous male figure, a "great witch" or warlock called the old man of Inkisvuori hill. The folklore archives contain stories of this "father" of Inkisvuori: using an axe, he tried to break into the church of Nousiainen at night, but was interrupted. Several stories involve his flying horse: he used it to win racing bets and escape from prison.

The name "Ämmä" (mother/crone) is repeated in many sacred springs in Southwest Finland and elsewhere. The Votes are a Finnish ethnic group and in Votian folk belief, "Vesi-ämmä" or "vesi-emä" is a common name for water spirits, roughly meaning "mother of the water" (see Västrik, 1999:17, 19). It could be assumed that a story of the old man of Inkisvuori punishing his wife in the spring is a later folk etymology applied to an older name, which might originally have referred to a water spirit.

The Ämmälähde Spring is among the most peripherally located springs in this sample. On a map drawn in 1770, the spring did not belong to a village, but was used as a border marker when defining the boundary between the parishes of Nousiainen and Masku. The Inkisvuori Hill is clearly drawn out on the map, which interestingly also marks a resting place for cattle on the hill.[4] Herding cattle in the woods was typically a task for the youth, who had to know the locations of good springs for watering. The location is very far from any farms, but must have been familiar to the youth involved in herding.

Being further away from the centres of habitation might have enhanced the spring's association with stories of an infamous wizard. In the eighteenth and nineteenth centuries, the nearest villages were approximately 4 km from Inkisvuori Hill. Charged with an atmosphere of danger, the spring perhaps was then particularly attractive to youth who had to wander several kilometres through relative wilderness to gather there on Midsummer's Night.

Concluding analysis

In the scope of what can be presented in this paper, cartographic material such as historic village maps can provide new insights into vernacular sacrality. A noteworthy finding is that many sacred springs are located on village or parish borders. Sacred springs can act as landmarks or yardsticks, dividing the landscape into cultural territories. The sacred seems to be related to spatial divisions, where the spatiality also has social dimensions: the central spaces of the farms are under the social control of the farm owners. The young and unmarried use places which are outside the space, and therefore social control, of the farms. From the point of view of the farm, they are spaces of secondary value, used by people of secondary status. But for the young and unmarried, that space is a space of freedom.

Scrying for one's future spouse in a spring not only expresses romantic desires, but also a longing for social upheaval, to occupy the primary space in the village as a master or mistress of a household. Being outside the actual farms also represents potential futures elsewhere, made possible by attendance of people from outside the village. This is also manifested spatially: the sites are usually located on hills offering a wide view over the surrounding landscape, which forms an "alternative" central space to that of the farms, as well as a "view" over potential futures outside one's own farm or village. In spatial terms, the sacred springs on the outskirts of villages offer a refuge from the authority present at the farms, and being on a border opens up the possibility to gather as a group not defined by the border. The "sacred" quality of these sites for the youth gathering there seems to have been in their role as places outside the confining borders of the everyday life, as venues for manifesting and performing their identity as a group in manners which were in stark contrast to later conceptions of "sacrality."

Notes

1 On how the Reformation affected vernacular rituals, see Toivo (2016).
2 On spatiality as a social practice of control and dominance, see Lefebvre (1991:289–292).
3 Maanmittauslaitoksen uudistusarkisto. Turku. Pitkämäki; Isojako käsittäen Pitkämäen, Metsäkylän, Suikkilan ja Teräsrautilan kylät 1785–1785 [A105:56/2-5]. http://digi.narc.fi/digi/slistaus.ka?ay=281092
4 Maanmittauslaitoksen uudistusarkisto. Nousiainen. Kartta ja asiakirjat riitamaasta Maskun ja Nousiaisten yhteismaan välillä 1770–1770 [A74:57/1-7]. http://digi.narc.fi/digi/slistaus.ka?ay=217628

References

Archival Sources: SKS KRA. The Finnish Literature Society, Folklore archives.
Maanmittauslaitoksen uudistusarkisto. Archives of the National Land Survey of Finland.

Secondary sources

Ahlqvist, Arja. 2012. Blue Stones in the Context of Traditions of Worshipping Stones. In *Mythic Discourses. Studies in Uralic Traditions*, edited by Anna-Leena Siikala, Frog and Eila Stepanova, 434–467. Helsinki: Finnish Literature Society.

Anttonen, Veikko. 1996. *Ihmisen ja maan rajat. 'Pyhä' kulttuurisena kategoriana*. Helsinki: Suomalaisen kirjallisuuden seura.

Dahlström, Svante. 1918. *Erik Julins anteckningar om Åbo stad*. Åbo: Åbo tryckeri och tidnings aktiebolag.

Foley, Ronan. 2013. Small Health Pilgrimages: Place and Practice at the Holy well. *Culture and Religion* 14(1):44–62. doi: 10.1080/14755610.2012.756410

Gardberg, Carl Jacob and Daniel Toijer. 1962. *Diarium Gyllenianum eller Petrus Magni Gyllenii dagbok 1622–1667*. Karlstad: Värmlands museum.

Harva, Uno. 1935. *Varsinais-Suomen henkistä kansankulttuuria*. Vol III.I of *Varsinais-Suomen historia*. Porvoo: Werner Söderström.

Hyvönen, Arja. 2011. Kupittaan vettä. *Vesi kaupungissa ja kulttuurissa*: 40–57. Turku: Turun museokeskus.

Koski, Mauno. 1967. *Itämerensuomalaisten kielten hiisi-sanue. Semanttinen tutkimus I*. Turku: Turun yliopisto.

Koski, Mauno. 1970. *Itämerensuomalaisten kielten hiisi-sanue. Semattinen tutkimus II*. Turku: Turun yliopisto.

Lefebvre, Henri. 1991. *The Production of Space*. Oxford: Blackwell.

Orrman, Eljas. 2003. Suomen keskiajan asutus. In *Suomen maatalouden historia I. Perinteisen maatalouden aika. Esihistoriasta 1870-luvulle*, edited by Viljo Rasila, Eino Jutikkala and Anneli Mäkelä-Alitalo. Helsinki: Finnish Literature Society.

Saarenheimo, Juhani. 2003. Isojako. In *Suomen maatalouden historia I. Perinteisen maatalouden aika. Esihistoriasta 1870-luvulle*, edited by Viljo Rasila, Eino Jutikkala and Anneli Mäkelä-Alitalo. Helsinki: Finnish Literature Society.

Sarmela, Matti. 1994. *Atlas of Finnish Ethnic Culture 2. Folklore*. Helsinki: Finnish Literature Society.

Tallgren, Aarne Michaël. 1918. *Suomen esihistorialliset ja ajaltaan epämääräiset kiinteät muinaisjäännökset*. Helsinki: Suomen muinaismuistoyhdistys.

Tallgren, Aarne Michaël. 1933. Hiisi ja moisio. Yritys muinaissuomalaisten asutus- ja yhteiskuntahistorian selvittämiseksi. *Virittäjä* 37:319.

Tallgren, Aarne Michaël and Jenny Maria Montin-Tallgren. 1918. *Maarian pitäjän paikannimistö I*. Turku: Uusi Aura.

Tarkka, Lotte. 2012. Sampo. Myth and Vernacular imagination. In *Mythic Discourses. Studies in Uralic Traditions*, edited by Anna-Leena Siikala Frog and Eila Stepanova, 143–170. Helsinki: Finnish Literature Society.

Toivo, Raisa Maria. 2016. *Faith and Magic in Early Modern Finland*. Hampshire: Palgrave Macmillan.

Tuan, Yi-Fu. 1979. Space and Place. Humanistic Perspective. In *Philosophy in Geography*, edited by Stephen Gale and Gunnar Olsson, 387–427. Boston, MA: D. Reidel Publishing Company.

Västrik, Ergo-Hart. 1999. The Waters and Water Spirits in Votian Folk Belief. *Electronic Journal of Folklore* 12. doi: 10.7592/FEJF1999.12.spirits

Zachrisson, Therese. 2017. Mellan fromhet och vidskepelse. Materialitet och religiositet i det efterreformatoriska Sverige. PhD diss., University of Gothenburg.

21

MEMORY AND MARTYRS

Holy springs in Western Siberia

Jeanmarie Rouhier-Willoughby

This chapter addresses the issue of memory of the Soviet-era gulag system through the lens of three holy springs in western Siberia in Omsk, Iskitim and Petukhov Log. All three are located on the territory of former prison camps, and their holiness is tied to this history. The local Orthodox dioceses have developed religious complexes on these sites, so that the faithful may bathe in the miraculous springs, collect water and attend services. Interviews with believers and participant observation in all three locations demonstrate that legends about the springs enable a reframing of the Soviet Russian past. The oldest generations focus nearly exclusively on the religious dead as the source of the sites' holiness, while younger generations in contrast emphasize victimization in their narratives. These differences are the result of narrators' own experiences of the former USSR.

The name Siberia invokes images of frozen tundra—a treeless, snow-covered moonscape similar to Antarctica. However, the West Siberia Plain, covering over a million miles of territory between the Ural Mountains and the Yenisey River, is a lush land of forests, rivers and marshes. While the northernmost portion is indeed above the Arctic Circle, the vast central plain is covered with forests of pine, larch and spruce merging southward into forest-steppe with its birch forests, grasslands and bogs. The holy spring of Lozhok, in the Novosibirsk Oblast' (an administrative unit roughly equivalent to a region or province) near the city of Iskitim, lies in the heart of the forest-steppe region. The beauty of the surrounding landscape belies its horrific past. Lozhok stands on the site of a former gulag camp[1] that was in operation from 1929 to 1956, a quarry where prisoners mined lime and rock for construction projects across the USSR (Applebaum, 2003:247; Zatolokin, 2007:17, 25).

While the Romanovs had long used Siberia as a place of exile and imprisonment for disruptive elements in society (whether criminals or political dissidents), the systematized incarceration of political prisoners and criminals known as the gulag was introduced by the Soviet leader Joseph Stalin beginning in 1929 (Applebaum, 2003:46–47) and continued until his death in 1953. The camps provided cost-effective labor during the shift from an agrarian to an industrial economy in the Soviet Union. The gulag system also helped Stalin consolidate his power and dispose of enemies who could be denounced as counter-revolutionaries under Article 58 of the Soviet constitution. All told, 28.7 million prisoners passed through the camps between 1929 and 1953 (Applebaum, 2003:582).[2]

Locals credit the sanctity of the Lozhok spring to the deaths of 40 priests and monks who were executed by gulag prison guards at the site. Still others say that 12 priests were buried alive there. A variant account tells how a group of priests interned in the camp asked the guards for water. The guards instead gave them salted fish to torment them, whereupon the priests prayed for water, and the spring bubbled up in answer to their prayers. These legends are common knowledge among the laity and the priests of the local congregation.

Events tied to gulag history thus have served as a source for the perceived holiness of this site, as they do also with two other holy springs in western Siberia, one in Omsk on the grounds of Achairskii Abbey and another in Petukhov Log, a tiny town in Gornaia Shoriia. Stories of the Petukhov Log spring, located on the site of the 17th Gorshor Camp (1938–1940), locals report that a group of 12 camp prisoners composed of priests and members of their congregation refused to work on Easter Sunday. The guards threatened them, but they were steadfast and were then beaten to death (or shot) and thrown into a common grave. The spring is believed to have emerged immediately afterward. People saw a flame in the sky soon after the massacre that led them to the spot that has been revered since that time. The Omsk spring, unlike the other two, is said to have arisen in the post-socialist period. The land was ceded from a local collective farm after the fall of the USSR to rebuild Achairskii Abbey, a religious complex destroyed by the Soviet authorities after serving as a prison camp (one common fate for remote religious sites during the Soviet period). The spring began to flow as the cornerstone of the new abbey was set, according to relatively recent local legend.

Visitors to the springs typically bring bottles with them to take water home, although they may also buy them on site. When bathing in the holy springs, people, especially women, are advised to wear a white shift, although this proscription is often ignored except on high holy days such as Christ's Baptism (January 19 in Russian Orthodoxy) or after formal religious processions to the site. When bathing, the devout immerse themselves completely thrice, crossing themselves before each immersion. Those who are concerned about the water temperature may simply wash their faces or immerse or bathe an ailing limb. Typically, people also buy candles to light in the nearby churches or, in the case of Lozhok, at the outdoor candle stand. The prayers said during the candle lighting are for the dead, often for one's own relatives or for the souls of the dead in general. People also pray to the saints, especially to Nicholas the Wonderworker or the Mother of God, for healing or other assistance. People are strongly discouraged from throwing coins into the springs (although some do), and caretakers remove them. The springs have been credited with healing miracles for a wide range of afflictions including paralysis, cancer, difficulty conceiving a child, skin ailments, addiction and even have assisted with finding a spouse. While the spirits of camp victims are never seen, some visitors have experienced visions of St. Nicholas, the Mother of God, or Christ.

In the years since the fall of the USSR, the Russian Orthodox Church has grappled with the issue of how to address the victims of the Soviet system. The 1936 Constitution of the Soviet Union allowed for freedom of religious worship and the separation of the church and state (Petrone, 2000:185–186). Despite this official stance, religious institutions of all faiths had been systematically oppressed from the Bolshevik Revolution to the fall of the USSR in 1991. Their lands and buildings were confiscated, destroyed or repurposed; religious figures were imprisoned and executed and official institutions produced anti-religious materials.[3] In 1996, the Church canonized Nicholas II and his family, naming them (and many others) to be Russian New Martyrs and Confessors in the Church role of saints. The Church has taken the position that anyone who died at the hands of the Soviet authorities, regardless of his/her personal beliefs, suffered to some degree for the Orthodox faith. While certainly not all have been canonized, this position supports the idea that those who died in the gulag, whether priests or not, were exemplars of these "new martyrs." In fact, in his history of the camp and the spring, Father Igor Zatolokin, the Lozhok priest who spearheaded the construction of a memorial park near the spring, makes specific reference to this issue:

> for many years believers prayed at the spring for the repose of the dead and those who suffered during the years of the persecution of Orthodox Christians, saying the prayer of the New Russian Martyrs. And on the basis of prayers to the New Martyrs, the waters of the spring, which existed even before the many horrible events that transpired here, became blessed, people who came here began to be healed of various illnesses. In the neighborhood of Lozhok the Holy Spring flows—like a non-corporeal memorial to all those innocents who suffered. This water is blessed by the torments of the people who suffered in this terrible punishment camp.
>
> *(2007:22)*

He expressed similar views in a personal interview:

> This fresh water spring has always been associated with people's suffering. You have those [stories about] forty martyrs, the shootings, and all. But it seems to me that it [the spring's holiness] is connected primarily with the camp, which was here during the times of repression, which were intense in our region.
>
> *(interview with the author, 8/7/2013)*

The priest's official views are having some effect on local belief, at least among the most devout. For example, Nadezhda,[4] who works at the icon kiosk on the site of the spring, stated that it was holy simply because there had been a camp on that site without reference to religious martyrs in particular.

Father Ivan Gensiruk of St. George's Cathedral in Tashtagol, near the Petukhov Log spring, has similarly expressed skepticism about the massacre of priests and their flock when he granted me an interview. He repeated that there was no historical basis for the events described in the stories. Rather, he focused, like Father Igor, on the camp and all its victims, in keeping with official doctrine about the Order of Russian New Martyrs and Confessors. Sister Veronika, a nun at the Achairskii Abbey, also rejects the local legend, arguing that the spring had been there for a long time before the abbey was built.

This conflict between official doctrine and local stories reveals the heart of the dilemma for the laity. Religious officials strive to control the narrative about the horrors of the atheist past, particularly after decades of absence from believers' lives. Many of the laity, however, revere the USSR and its leader during the time of the camps' operation. As Stalin is being rehabilitated in the context of Putin's Russia, the dichotomy between these two views has deepened. The people's saint, Matrona of Moscow, is one example of this shift. Matrona was born Matrona Dmitrievna Nikonova in 1885 in the village of Sebeno in the Tula region and died on May 3, 1952 in Moscow, where she was buried in Danilovsky Monastery. She was canonized in 1999. The most famous story about St. Matrona is not recorded in her official saint's life (Khudoshin, 2009), but is widespread among the laity. The legend tells how Stalin asked Matrona to take the Kazan icon of the Virgin Mary in an airplane around the borders of the Soviet Union during World War II. Matrona agreed and so saved the country from being overrun by German forces. According to the newspapers *Moscow Komsomol* and *Pravda,* this event led to the painting of an icon depicting Matrona blessing Stalin, which was "discovered" in St. Olga's Cathedral in St. Petersburg in 2008 (although the parish priest reported that it had long been known in the area) (Kormina, 2010:12; Rouhier-Willoughby and Filosofova, 2015:1543–1544). It seems that even Stalin himself, like much of Russia, is being re-Christianized in the post-Soviet world.

The beliefs expressed in the Siberian holy spring legends are the key to understanding how the memory of the gulag and indeed of the USSR has been reframed in western Siberia. The camps were erased (and the buildings destroyed after their closure), but the springs in Iskitim and in Petukhov Log served as tangible memorials to the religious dead and as a locus symbolizing the continuity of faith throughout the socialist era. While it is clear that untold numbers of people died in these camps, in the local imagination (at least among the oldest residents—those who came of age in the Stalin era), the sites are sacred specifically because of the religious victims. The experiences of younger generations (these consultants' children and grandchildren) are quite different and, as a result, their narratives about the spring differ significantly, as will be discussed later. These sites have provided a space for people to grapple with the local past, from the prison camp system to the country's positive achievements. Since it was local women who proclaimed the springs to be holy, the sites also validate the lay devotion. Aliona moved to the region in 1959 and soon thereafter witnessed how local women interacted with the spring. As she reported to me in an interview:

> I went out for lunch. A whole trail of *babushkas* comes walking along … A whole trail of little, old *babushkas*. Some with bottles. It amazed me that one is carrying a mug, and she's already exhausted, the mug is half full of water, half had poured out. I say, '*Babushkas*, where are you coming from?'[…] they say, 'From the holy spring.' And I say, 'How do you know that it's holy?' 'It's even written about in the Gospels that it's holy.'

Inna, another local resident, reported that women were essential to the work of establishing the Church of the Ever-full Chalice in Lozhok, near the holy spring. In her retirement, she took up the cause for the construction of the church and indeed of raising money to support both its construction and the development of the holy spring complex.

> And then, I, when I came here, I was always searching for a place to pray. I was soul sick … I wanted to thank God, as they say. And I would go to pray in Iskitim, when they were building the cathedral. […] I worked for the glory of God, I worked, so that Russia would not perish. I worked, so that Orthodoxy would not die, for my people, for the country … I would go on foot, 2 kilometers on foot. I would carry bags on my back, a box for donations. I would get there and sit at the table there, I would get to the spring and spread it all out, and father, as a matter of fact Father Igor, blessed me. You will, he says, go to the spring and sell things. I said, I will, Father. And I took that task upon myself and I went there to sell items. People started to come there sometimes, the people started to realize that they were selling icons and candles there. Folks started to come. And little by little we began earning money.

The money earned from the sale of religious items at the spring went toward church construction as well as to the beautification of the spring and buildings there. The women of this generation were the most involved in not only the preservation of the belief in the spring during the Soviet era, but in the resurgence of the Orthodox Church after its fall.

World War II emerged as a common motif in narratives about these springs among the oldest generation. One reason for this motif was that these people had arrived in the region and begun their interaction with the camps as a direct result of the disastrous effects of World War II. The Lozhok camp, for example, represented a chance to rebuild disrupted lives through gainful employment. Anastasia and Aliona both worked at the quarry after the war.[5] Anastasia was employed there while the camp was still in operation, while Aliona arrived after it had been closed. Aliona came to the region because she could not find a decent position in Novokuznetsk where she had studied and when she was taken on as a master at the lime kiln, the buildings were still in existence, and the people who had been imprisoned there ran the operation. Because these past experiences validate their struggle for identity as (Soviet) Russian citizens, they cannot simply condemn that history outright. By framing themselves first as victims and, ultimately, as victors in this struggle, their narratives provide a sense of agency for the oldest generation.

As a result, the post-socialist experience has threatened the identities they had crafted as Soviet Russian citizens. During the Soviet era, they could contend that they had not suffered in vain, pointing to the USSR's superpower status and to their own successful lives. In addition, as victims themselves, they were protected from being accused of complicity in the camp system. In the post-socialist period, these beliefs are more easily challenged. Past suffering for a beloved nation that no longer exists has led to doubt and personal crises. One key to reframing one's Soviet Russian identity and the perception of the nation itself, at least among those who profess faith in the holy springs, is the assertion of one's enduring belief in God. The oldest generation consistently emphasized that they were raised in devout families and maintained religious practices throughout their lives. Elizaveta, for example, reported that,

> from childhood, in my soul, I wondered why they had forbidden the church […]. But we didn't have a church in our village […]. So, we would ask Father from the nearby village of Viatskie Poliany to visit us for several years. And he came […]. And I remember how they baptized us. They baptized me first. I was, well, how old was I, maybe 10?

Her friend Liubov told a similar story:

> During the Soviet era they forbade baptism. I had two grandmothers, one on one side, one on the other, who arranged it on the quiet, because they were afraid, since our father was a party member, they baptized both me and my brother.

Nadezhda also said that her parents were both believers, and that she and her sisters even wore kerchiefs as a sign of devotion while in school, as she does to this day. Even Aliona, who initially doubted the testimony of the local *babushkas* that the spring was holy, reported that she had always, from childhood, said the "Our Father" each night, even though she was a Pioneer and a member of the Komsomol (the Pioneers and Komsomol were official groups to introduce children and teens to the values of the USSR. They were essential pathways for powerful positions in the Communist Party as adults). However, she explained that not until she was in her fifties had she "matured" and begun to attend church.

The religious victims at the heart of the local legends are a key to the oldest generation's reconceptualization of Soviet Russian history. Because narratives about the spring foreground only the religious dead, narrators can focus their attention on the most negative trait of the USSR from their point of view: that religious belief was restricted. In essence, these martyrs redeem the violent past of the Soviet prison camp system. In this view, the holy springs are a sign from God that they (and, by extension, the nation) have been forgiven for this sin of building the country at the hands of unjustly accused prisoners. This is a particularly apt metaphor for the Omsk spring, which emerged when Achairskii Abbey was being rebuilt, a palpable sign that the country was on the right course spiritually at last. At their heart, the beliefs about the holy springs enable the local populace to safely negotiate the complex strands of Soviet Russian history and their roles within it. These narratives allow them to disagree with the most significant shortcoming of Soviet society, the restriction on religion and also to re-Christianize Soviet Russia, to assert that faith had its role even in an atheist state.[6]

Evgenia Svitova, an Iskitim journalist and museum director, who has written several books dedicated to the spring and to those repressed during the Stalin era, stated that a dual motivation for locals is to uncover their past and the Soviet Russian past.

She said that all Siberians are exiles searching for their roots, which distinguishes them from European Russians. Interviewees express this position as well. Margarita said that her visit to both Lozhok and Achair springs

> made a strong impression. Because there was namely a strong feeling of history … the memory of that which happened here, the number of people who perished on this spot, and that it is necessary to remember[7] these people somehow.

Margarita also emphasized the horrors of the Lozhok camp, saying that

> from the outset it was the death camp of all death camps … those people who died there are martyrs. And martyrs are generally the same as the saints. Therefore, so much blood was spilled, so many innocent people … died there … that it became a holy spot, that now there is a holy spring there.

Two local Lozhok women born in the 1980s reported that they frequently visited the holy spring (as it was called throughout their childhood), but that they had only learned the spot's history as adults. One of them, Maria, stated that the spring was considered holy because of the number of innocent victims who died there, but she also made a specific point of noting that the shooting of priests was "a legend," using a term chosen to denote doubt about its veracity.

Younger generations must reconcile the horrific past with these springs' draw as local attractions known for their natural beauty. In that sense, they are less concerned with re-Christianizing the USSR or dealing with their identity crisis as Soviet Russian citizens, but with coping with the history of their nation. Achair is likewise a major tourist destination. Not only is the abbey particularly lovely, but the spring itself is warm (in contrast to the other two springs, which are quite cold). As a result, visitors to Omsk make the trip to bathe in the spring. They often have no awareness of the history of the site. The abbey has placed a large billboard near to the bathing area to discourage unseemly behavior by visitors to this holy spot, again with little success given the "pool parties" that persist at the bathing area there.

The view that the natural beauty of these springs itself redeems the violence of the camp recurs in interviews, regardless of the person's own religious beliefs or age. In essence, the lovely surroundings are a sign that the evils of the past have been forgiven, and that the current generation should not consider itself to be culpable for those past sins (or has the power to overcome them). They are a sign from God that Russia, particularly Siberia, so associated with the camps, has been forgiven for the horrors of the gulag system. Alla, a young journalist, mentioned this view of Siberia and the role of martyrdom in the sanctity of the site:

> Many died with no requiem mass, many without baptism, yes, and many in inexplicable circumstances of many kinds, like in the war, in the camps … So, everyone understands that they need our help … that we have to pray for them … in general, for the whole country, yes, for the Soviets.

To give a sense of the intricacies of this dilemma for western Siberians, regardless of their generation, consider the case of Anatoly, the grandson of one of two priests

FIGURE 21.1 Sacred spring at Achairskii Monastery.

FIGURE 21.2 Sacred spring in Lozhok.

from the Novosibirsk region that has been beatified as a New Russian Martyr and Confessor. At his home in Berdsk in May 2016, he told me the story of how his father took his aunt's last name after his grandfather had been arrested and executed by the Bolsheviks in October of 1937. Using this cover, he was allowed to distance himself from the label of "enemy of the people" attached to political prisoners and ultimately get an education. Later that evening, Anatoly related how he had worked as a laser specialist at a top-secret factory designing materials for the space program. Showing off his awards and complaining about how the fall of the USSR had destroyed his beloved work place (which now makes only electric razors), he concluded by saying, "I'm a Soviet person." The obvious dissonance between these events in his family history, while perhaps more extreme than in many families, illustrates the complex negotiations facing those grappling with the Stalinist and Soviet legacies in contemporary western Siberia. The springs serve as one locus for such negotiations and foster the creation of competing narratives about memory and Russian identity in the context of the socialist past and the post-socialist present.

Notes

1 The gulag was composed of Soviet-era forced labor camps that were most prominent from the 1930s to the 1950s under Joseph Stalin. Gulag is an acronym for Glavnoe Upravlenie Lagerei i Mest Zakliucheniia (Main Administration of Camps and Places of Detention). While the term refers to the governmental administrative body, the word now denotes the entire prison camp system including the camps themselves.
2 Statistics on the number of deaths in the gulag are yet to be compiled or released, but Applebaum (2003:583) estimates at least 2.7 million died and this figure does not reflect those who fell victim to Stalin's purges before they even reached a camp.
3 For a discussion of the Russian Orthodox Church during the Soviet era, see Davis (2003).
4 To preserve the anonymity of participants in the study, pseudonyms are employed.
5 Note that the camps employed locals as well as relied on forced labor. Many residents worked in the prison proper, e.g., as guards, but others were essentially day laborers, working in the quarry alongside the prisoners.
6 In fact, some people I interviewed did not mention the gulag at all, rather attributing the holiness of the springs to persecution of religious during the post-revolutionary period in the 1920s. This version of the legend is gaining traction and is consonant with the rehabilitation of Stalin as primarily the victor in World War II who rebuilt a devastated country, shifting attention to the "true" enemies, the Bolsheviks that instituted the atheist policy in the first place.
7 Margarita used the religious expression *pominat'* ("to commemorate" as during a mass for the dead or in vernacular commemorations of one's relatives on anniversaries of their deaths) rather than the usual verb for "to remember" (*pomnit'*). This choice is significant, since the sites are associated with Orthodoxy and indicate her familiarity with doctrine.

References

Applebaum, Anne. 2003. *Gulag.* New York: Anchor.
Davis, Nathaniel. 2003. *A Long Walk to Church.* New York: Routledge.
Khudoshin, Aleksandr. 2009. *Zhitie sviatoi blazhennoi staritsy Matrony Moskovskoi i ee chudotvoreniia XX–XXI vv.* Moscow: Idel Press.

Kormina, Zhanna. 2010. Politicheskie personazhi v sovremmennoi agiografii: kak Matrona Stalina blagoslovila. *Antropologicheskii Forum* 12:1–28.

Petrone, Karen. 2000. *Life Has Become More Joyous, Comrades.* Bloomington: University of Indiana Press.

Rouhier-Willoughby, Jeanmarie and Tatiana Filosofova. 2015. Back to the Future: Popular Belief in Russia Today. In *The Changing World Religion Map*, edited by Stanley Brunn, 1531–1554. New York: Springer.

Zatolokin, Igor. 2007. *Lozhok.* Iskitim: Novisibirsk Diocese.

Interviews

Aliona, Master of Lime Kiln, DOB 1936, Interviewed 8/12/2013 in Lozhok.

Alla, Journalist, DOB 1983, Native of Novosibirsk, Interviewed in Novosibirsk, 5/8/16.

Anatoly, Laser Engineer, DOB Unknown, Approximately 55–60 Years of Age, Interviewed 5/4/2016 in Berdsk.

Anastasia, Gulag Laborer and Railway Worker, DOB 1929, Interviewed 8/12/2013 in Lozhok.

Elizaveta, DOB and Profession Unknown, Approximately 60–65 Years of Age, Interviewed 8/7/2013 in Lozhok.

Evgeniia Svitova, Journalist and Museum Director, DOB 1979, Interviewed 5/6/2016 in Lozhok and 5/4/2018 in Iskitim.

Igor Zatolokin, Priest, DOB 1973, Interviewed 8/7/2013 in Lozhok.

Inna, Accountant, DOB 1938, Interviewed 7/3/2015 in Lozhok.

Ivan Gensiruk, Priest, DOB 1968, Interviewed 4/22/2016 in Tashtagol.

Liubov', DOB and Profession Unknown, Approximately 60–65 Years of Age, Interviewed 8/7/13 in Lozhok.

Margarita, Teacher, DOB 1973, Interviewed 6/16/2014 in Akademgorodok.

Maria, Teacher, DOB 1983, Interviewed 5/6/2016 in Lozhok.

Nadezhda, Former Cook, Now Works at the Icon Kiosk at the Lozhok Holy Spring, DOB 1958, Interviewed 8/7/2013 in Lozhok.

Veronika, Nun, DOB Unknown, Approximately 35–40 Years of Age, Interviewed 4/30/2016 in Naberezhnyi.

22

SACRED AND HEALING SPRINGS IN THE REPUBLIC OF NORTH MACEDONIA

Snežana Filipova

The name "Macedonia" is the oldest surviving name of a country in Europe. The ancient Macedonians enter the historical record in the mid-first millennium BC as ethnically, linguistically and culturally distinct from their neighbors. Multiple influences successively shaped the area. The Slavs were once thought to have arrived in the region in the sixth century AD, but new genetic research would seem to indicate their presence at least by the Bronze Age. Romans conquered the ancient Kingdom of Macedonia in the second century BC. During much of the medieval period, the territory of Macedonia was part of Byzantium. Serbian rulers took the region of Macedonia from Byzantium in the thirteenth century and the Ottomans arrived in the next. In the twentieth century, the Kingdom of Yugoslavia (1918–1941) and the Socialist Federal Republic of Yugoslavia (1963–1992) united Balkan Slavs. From this state, Macedonia peacefully succeeded in 1991. Today, Macedonia is home to just over two million people who are predominantly identified as ethnic Macedonians (southern Slavs). Ethnic Albanians are the largest minority group, but Macedonia is also populated by smaller numbers of Turks, Romani, Bosnians, Serbs and Bulgarians. While the majority of the population is Eastern Orthodox (belonging to the Macedonian Orthodox Church), some Macedonians and Romani people were converted to Islam several centuries ago. From the Middle Ages into the nineteenth century, over 1,100 churches were constructed in Macedonia. In this period, churches were often built on top of ancient temples, synagogues, *domus ecclesiae* and the earliest Christian sites, though many were built in the vicinity of powerful water sources.[1] In turn, many of these were replaced by, or refashioned into, mosques by the Ottomans beginning in the fifteenth century.[2]

Shared sacred sites

With centuries of cultural layering, many Orthodox sacred sites have become significant to Macedonians of different religious confessions. For example, one of the most prominent travel writers of Ottoman times, Evliya Çelebi, wrote in the seventeenth century about the mosque of Husamedin-Paša in the town of Štip (1967). Today, the shrine, called the Husamedin-Paša Mosque by the Muslims and the Church of St. Elijah by the Christians in Štip, is revered equally by both religious groups in the town, and each group claimed priority in its use. Other examples of religious shrines shared by Christians and Muslims include the Church of St. Nicholas/H'd'r Baba Tekke in Makedonski Brod, the Monastery of the Holy Virgin Prečista in Kichevo and the monastery of the tenth-century St. Naum near Ohrid.

In the first half of the nineteenth century, Sultan Mahmud allowed the building of new churches where they had previously not existed. Turkish law, however, required them to be only 1.5 m above ground so that builders had to dig their foundations below ground. In the mid-twentieth century, a small portion of churches that had been converted into mosques returned to their original faith: for example, the Church of St. Sophia in Ohrid and, in the year 2000, the old Church of St. Clement in Plaošnik. In the socialist period, selected large churches and mosques were used as monuments of culture or tourist sites, and some are still functioning as art galleries or as part of archaeological and national museums. Yet, today, several shrines and sacred springs remain sites of continuous multi-confessional visitation.

Many sacred shrines are near (or may actually encompass) sacred springs. One of the largest spring-associated shrines is that of the Holy Virgin Prečista in Kičevo, and the church of St. Naum near Ohrid is beside several healing springs. Shared sacred springs and their associated shrines have brought Christians and Muslims together in the Balkans for centuries. In this text, "shrine" denotes a site which is thought to be particularly holy, that houses a particular relic[3] or cult image which is the object of veneration, or a place where people seek spiritual guidance.[4] The only religious feast that unites several different ethnicities (Macedonians, Serbians, Albanians, Roma people, Vlahs [Aromani] and Turks) in the Republic of Macedonia is dedicated to St. George who is *Gjurgjovden* in Macedonian and *H'ederles or Ederlezi* in the Albanian and Roma languages. His day is celebrated on the 6th of May on which morning picnics and music are enjoyed in the early spring weather.[5] Maria Couroucli notes that those St. George shrines that attract mixed pilgrims in the Balkans and in Anatolia are usually situated next to springs and other liminal places (2012:45). One of the most famous holy springs associated with St. George's day is encompassed by the church of St. George at Krivi Dol in Skopje.[6]

Macedonian folk beliefs about healing waters

There are 1,100 sacred water sources in Macedonia. Macedonian folklore recalls older beliefs that water and its surrounds were places where various demonic creatures assembled, such as fairies, dragons and devils. Belief in fairies was very widespread and explains many toponyms. In Macedonian folk tradition, it was the fairy presence that was believed to give certain water sources their miraculous and healing powers (Vražinovski, 1998:102–104). As elsewhere in the world, many legends, stories, poetry and songs praise the magic and miraculous characteristics of the water and these evolved over time and in response to competing religious beliefs and authorities. In a syncretic formula of indigenous beliefs and Christianity, Our Lord was held to be born from a drop of water that fell down on a blade of grass (Vražinovski, 2006:19).

The Slavs, like other peoples, often used water springs as open-air sanctuaries or built wooden or stone temples in their vicinity. Holy wells have been regarded as places of healing into the twenty-first century and certain wells were associated with particular afflictions (Bowman, 2009). As happens elsewhere, petitioners tie strips of cloth on nearby trees and as the cloth decays, a cure is affected.

In the vicinity of Skopje, there are several popular holy water sources or healing mineral water springs. Some of these were frequented by indigenous tribes and re-employed by the Romans from the second century BC. These include the water sources and *thermae* (imperial bathing complexes) in Katlanovo and at Strumica in the village of Bansko where the Early Christian shrine of the 40 martyrs was later built (Taseva and Sekulov, 2017). Many of these pre-Christian sacred sites became the preferred location for churches: for example, sacred springs preceded St. George's Church in Krivi Dol, the Church of St. John the Baptist at Kapištec and the Church of St. Panteleimon in Nerezi. Archaeological excavations performed in 1975 in the village of Krupište, near Štip, discovered under the post-Byzantine Church of St. Nicholas (built in 1625) a three-naved Early Christian basilica with a narthex, dating from the late fifth to early sixth century. The basilica was constructed over a sacred spring and belonged to an Early Christian complex in which the cult of water was probably celebrated (Алексова, 1983:85–100). At the Church of the Holy Virgin in Volkovo, the water spring is inside the church—as is the healing water source in the nineteenth-century church of St. Panteleimon at village Pantelei near Kočani. That is also the case with the Church of St. Nikita at Kisela Voda, the Church of the Nativity of the Holy Virgin at Stopanski Dvor, St. George at Krivi Dol, all in Skopje, and the Church of the Holy Virgin at Katlanovo; yet, these are newly built churches probably replacing older ones beneath.

Outside the Macedonian capital of Skopje are springs and *thermae* at the Church of the Holy Virgin in Veljusa, at Vodoča near Strumica, at the village of Negorci near Gevgelia (where waters are thought to cure sterility and cardio-vascular problems), and at Debarski Banji (where spas supplied with formerly sacred water still treat rheumatism and skin ailments). In the Ohrid region, "St. Naum's springs" (the spring sources of the river Crn Drim) are known to heal eye problems (the most powerful of the springs is named Ostrovo). Their healing powers have been (and are) respected across faiths (in 1926, Djemail Zizo, a Muslim from Resen, gifted St. Naum's monastery with a bell in thanksgiving for his brother's deliverance from a near-fatal illness).

The first Friday after Easter is known as Bright Friday. The day commemorates the discovery of a life-giving spring (where golden fishes lived) by the future Byzantine Emperor Leo I (457–474) in Constantinople. The waters were immediately employed to cure a man's blindness (hence the "bright"). In Macedonia, the day is called *Balaklija* after the name of the spot in Constantinople (Istanbul) where the miraculous water source was situated. Macedonian churches hold festivals and large gatherings beside local spring waters. At the Monastery of St. Jovan Bigorski, there is a recently built shrine dedicated to Bright Friday where, after the liturgy, monks circumambulate the shrine (in *litii*) and pay their respects to the Mother of God.[7] In the Church of St. George in the nearby village of Rajčica, there is a fresco depicting this holiday in which a man is resurrected after being washed with the water from a spring dedicated to the Holy Virgin. Because the Virgin Mary washed Christ's wounds, people visit springs with healing water (which can be beside or within churches) and wash their eyes and face, or throw the water thrice behind their backs.

Holy springs often have associated sacred stones which are curative and are believed to enhance fertility. Such stones are dispersed throughout Macedonia. Among the most famous are those at Govedarov Kamen in Sveti Nikole and at Crn Kamen in Veles. At Goverdarov Kamen, a supernatural spring emerges from a stone and ritual visits involve both stone and water. A woman who seeks a baby is to wash her face in the spring water on St. George's day. She also wraps the stone with a belt of red and white wool that she and her husband have woven. Then, the man she has chosen to be godfather to the longed-for-child wraps the belt around her waist. Bright Friday is also a day when childless couples, or those with an ill child, visit a healing waterfall at Crn Kamen in Veles. Devotees pass a stone thrice under the water in prayers and keep the stone at home in hopes of an answer to their petition in the coming year.

Co-confessional sacred springs today

Despite centuries of contestation and compromise, many spring shrines, themselves likely sacred before they entered a historical record, are the focus of continuous multi-confessional visitation. For example, Orthodox believers and Muslims share a veneration for the holy spring at the Monastery of the Holy Virgin Prečista in Kichevo. Legends tell of a "self-migrating" (or "flying") icon that was left to bless the land for the planned monastery in the fourteenth century. The icon repeatedly removed itself to perch beside a spring until the monastery was built there. After Ottoman destructions, the vanished icon would reappear beside the spring on a particular bush which prompted the monastery's repeated reconstructions. The festival of the patron saint of Holy Virgin Prečista is attended by several thousand people. Orthodox practice is to celebrate the birth of Mary on the 28th of August and people gather at the site on the prior eve. Muslims, mainly from Romani families, as well as some Albanians, are present at the festivities. Women crawl through a stone-lined entrance to the spring and under the holy icon of the Virgin Mary. There is a widespread belief among ordinary devotees that the western part of the church was actually built for and belongs to the Muslims who were previously Orthodox and later forced to receive Islam. Thus, the same families, where some of the members stayed Orthodox and others became Muslims, could be together in the same church. Presently, the local Christians generally demonstrate understanding and acceptance of the presence of Muslims at the shrine (even though they are not relatives to any of the villagers).

Visitors to shared spring shrines may write their wishes on a paper and place this near an icon or icons, or say their prayers and leave a piece of cloth or an item of clothing at the place designated for such votives, or fix these on a nearby tree. Sometimes, they leave a gift (which they are either told or think is appropriate) next to an icon or iconostasis of the nearby church (sometimes, these votives might be money, towels or new and still-packaged articles of clothing such as socks or shirts). Whatever their faith, they might also make a small financial donation to the church for its physical maintenance.

The present-day church of the monastery of St. Naum near Ohrid was erected on the foundation of the Church of the Holy Archangels built by St. Naum in the early tenth century. A saint known for healing miracles, and a kind of psychiatrist, his monastery once had a hospital. Today, his shrine remains extraordinarily popular and attracts numerous visitors throughout the year, but especially on his feast day (July 3), due to Christians' deep faith in the miraculous and healing power of St. Naum. A large number of Muslim visitors to St. Naum's shrine, especially his tomb, relates to their equating Naum with the mystical Bektashi saint Sar' Salt'k.[8] In a representation of St. Naum, he sits in a two-wheeled chariot pulled by a deer and a lion, which are traditional symbols of the Bektashi Order (an Alevī-related branch of Islam) and some Muslims (wrongly) believe that this place is one of Sar' Salt'k's tombs (Ibrahimgil, 2001:375–390, 380). Sar' Salt'k is a holy dervish miracle-worker, an Islamic warrior (*gazi*), and an epic hero, whose cult appears in many places throughout the Balkans. Thus, some Muslims, who visit this monastery, bow before the tomb of St. Naum believing that it is the tomb of Sar' Salt'k.

Beginning on days before the July 3rd feast day, pilgrims camp out on the shore of Lake Ohrid near the St. Naum's springs and in other open areas on the monastery grounds. Until a hotel's construction about 25 years ago, pilgrims used to eat at the monastery and sleep near the saint's tomb (to which devotees would press their ear to hear Naum's hearbeat). During the days of the pilgrimage, participants also play folk music, visit with each other and enjoy an annual bazaar near the lake. Naum's feast day celebrations are attended by people from different religious and ethnic communities from various parts of Macedonia. A large number of the visitors are Muslim Roma.

The sharing of shrines by members of two religions was common in the Balkans during the Ottoman period and afterward. Holy places in Orthodox Christianity are also visited frequently by Macedonian Muslims since everyone, irrespective of confession, can pray there or ask a priest for a prayer. Macedonian Muslim belief in the miraculous power of icons and relics recognized by Orthodox theology is sometimes named Crypto-Christianity or bi-confessionalism to justify their practices of visiting churches and observing both Christian and Muslims festivities. While each group mostly perceives the tradition and religion of the other group as inferior and embraces their own site interpretations, there are "two codes of coexistence," and both groups consider neighborliness an important value and try to maintain peaceful coexistence by paying and receiving visits, exchanging festive foods and respecting each other's customs (Bielenin-Lenczowska, 2008). The sacred springs which are frequent features of shared shrines likely predate both faiths and may have been liminal meeting spaces for diverse peoples through the ages. These places of grace and healing continue to inspire today's Macedonians.

Notes

1 According to the published list of churches and mosques, there are now 767 Orthodox churches. Јелена Павловска, Наташа Никифоровиќ, Огнен Коцевски, 2011. Карта на верски објекти во Република Македонија. Скопје: Менора. On the latest data see Filipova (2018).
2 When visiting the city of Bitola in 1911, Jovan Hadži Vasiljević interviewed the citizens and thus found out that the Church of St. George had been turned into the Nil mosque

at the old Pekmez bazaar, while the Church of Resurrection had been turned into the Hazreti Ishak mosque at Bit Pazar, the Church of the Holy Doctors had been turned into Zandandžik mosque and the Church of the Holy Apostles had been turned into the Hajdar Kadi mosque at the Sheep Bazaar. Јован Хаџи-Васиљевић. 1911. Битољ, Кроз стару Србију и Македонију *1879* године. Београд.

3 See Filipova (2010 and 2012).

4 Some Islamic traditions entail shrine veneration. For Shia and Sufi Muslims, shrines are considered places to seek spiritual guidance. The most venerated shrines are dedicated to various Sufi saints and are widely scattered throughout the Islamic world. As Glenn Bowman emphasizes, popular assumptions about the fundamental exclusiveness of religious identities, practices and communities are thrown into question by the existence of shared shrines. In the Balkans and the Middle East, these have brought Muslims, Christians and Jews together around objects, tombs and sites believed to deliver spiritual protection and other benefits (Bowman, 2009:27–52).

5 Several decades ago, it was mostly the Roma people who celebrated this holiday at the same time as Orthodox Macedonians and Serbians. In 1988, the Bosnian director Emir Kusturica filmed the *Time of the Gypsies* (Serbian: Дом за вешање, *Dom za vešanje*, literally "Home for Hanging"), where this holiday was documented.

6 Some scholars (e.g. Jovan Trifunovsk) tentatively locate the lost Church of St. Georg/ Gorg either where the archbishop's residence now stands or where a new church erected after World War II is situated (Filipova, 2001).

7 The *litii* is part of Orthodox ritual and is a procession featuring an important icon which usually takes place outside the church and involves circumambulating the church multiple times.

8 The face of St. Naum in a painting entitled "St. Naum Reins in a Bear instead of an Ox" is thought by some Muslims to be that of the Bektashi saint, Sar' Salt'k. Just as many Christian churches were built over the tombs of martyrs and relics and reliquaries were placed under altar tables, some branches of Islam have also venerated the graves of holy persons, sometimes called wali.

References

Алексова, Блага. 1983. Крупиште, Штипско, археолошки истражувања 1975, АММ X–XI: 85–100.

Bielenin-Lenczowska, Karolina. 2008. Visiting of Christian Holy Places by Muslims as a Strategy of Coping with Difference, *Anthropological Notebooks* 15(3):27–41.

Bowman, Glenn. 2009. Identification and Identity Formations around Shared Shrines in West Bank Palestine and Western Macedonia. In *Lieux saints en partage: Explorations anthropologiques dans l'espace méditerranéen*, edited by Dionigi Albera and Maria Couroucli, 27–52. Arles: Actes Sud.

Çelebi, Evlija. 1967. *Putopis: Odlomci o jugoslovenskim zemljama*. Sarajevo: Svjetlost.

Couroucli, Maria. 2012. Chthonian Spirits and Shared Shrines: The Dynamics of Place among Christians and Muslims in Anatolia. In *Sharing the Sacra: the Politics and Pragmatics of Inter-Communal Relations around Holy Places*, edited by Glenn Bowman, 44–60. New York: Berghahn.

Filipova, Snežana. 2001. Култот на Свети Ѓорѓи и политичката ситуација во Македонија во средниот век [The Cult of St. George and the Political Situation in Macedonia in the Middle Ages]. *Makedonsko Nasledstvo (Macedonian Heritage)* 16:18–37.

Filipova, Snežana. 2010. Continuity in Choosing Cult Objects' Locations in the Ancient and Medieval Period in the Republic of Macedonia. In *Aeternitas Antiquitatis: Proceedings from the Symposium of the Association of Classical Philologists-Antika*, edited by Valerij Sofronievski, 67–83. Skopje: Association of Classical Philologists-Antika,

Filipova, Snežana. 2012. Early Christian Reliquaries and Encolpia and the Problem of the So-Called Crypt Reliquaries in the Republic of Macedonia. In *Rome, Constantinople and Newly Converted Europe: Archaeological and Historical Evidence*. Vol. II, edited by Maciej Salamon, 113–130. Krakow and Leipzig: Geisteswissenschaftliches Zentrum Geschichte und Kultur.

Filipova, Snežana. 2018. Cultural and Religious Geography in the Medieval and New Age Period in Today's Republic of Macedonia. In *International Scientific Conference Proceedings: Geobalcanica*, edited by Tomasz Komornicki et al., 317–323. Skopje: Geobalcanica. doi: 10.18509/GBP.2018.35

Ibrahimgil, Z. Mehmet. 2001. *Balkanlar'da Sarı Saltuk Türbeleri, Sempoziyum Bildiriler kitabı, Balkanlar'da kültürel ve Türk Mimarisi Uluslararası Sempozyumu Bildirileri*. Vol. 1, 375–390. Ankara: Atatürk Kültür Merkezi Başkanlığı.

Taseva, Slavica and Vane Sekulov. 2017. *The Great Bath of the Late Roman Thermal Spa in the Village of Bansko*. Skopje: Ministry of Culture of the Republic of Macedonia.

Vražinovski, Tanas. 1998. *Narodna mitologija na Makedoncite*. Skopje: Matica Makedonska.

Vražinovski, Tanas. 2006. *Makedonska narodna mitologija (1–5)*. Skopje: Matica Makedonska.

23

WATER SANCTUARIES OF HATAY, TURKEY

Jens Kreinath

The religious geography of Hatay, the southernmost province of Turkey, is shaped through a tapestry of sanctuaries of shared religious heritage. This chapter features four of the most prominent sites that illustrate the religious significance of water, namely: a waterfall in Harbiye attributed to the Greek myth of Apollo and Daphne; a rivulet ascribed to the water of life through the legend of St. George and al-Khidr, the Green One; a sacred well in the oldest Christian cave church in Antioch associated with St. Luke; and a water pool linked to a visit of the Virgin Mary. By reconstructing the legends and rituals in conjunction with the geography and environment of these sacred springs and water wells, this essay demonstrates how devotion to both deities and saints is integrally tied to the materiality and sacredness of abundant water resources providing the basis for interreligious relations in this region.

The veneration of sacred springs and water wells is shared among various religious communities across the Eastern Mediterranean and Northern Levant, commonly known as "the Fertile Crescent" (Hanauer, 1907; Mithen and Black, 2011). Like anywhere else, communities in this region depend on the available resources to make a living, and only an abundance of water can guarantee the necessary soil fertility around human settlements. Aside from providing such water resources, sacred springs and holy wells are elevated as fountains of incomparable refreshment for the thirsty or even employed in healing the sick. The locations of sacred springs and holy wells and the landscapes in which they are located are thought to be enchanted and charged with invisible forces that are considered the mysterious carriers of the water's healing power (Hawting, 1980; Ghabin, 2012). Often, the special quality of water as sacred springs or holy wells resembles notions of the fountain of life.

In various religious traditions that emerged in the Fertile Crescent, water is not only perceived as primordial matter out of which all living things emerge but also as a spiritual matter offering the renewal of life, purification of the soul, and the promise of eternal life. Considering that water "draws to itself all images of purity" (Bachelard, 1983 [1942]:14) and that it "symbolizes the whole of possibility" (Eliade, 1996 [1949]:188), it comes as no surprise that sacred springs and holy wells in Hatay represent fertility, ablution, and rejuvenation in the local religious traditions that emerged under various spheres of influence.

Water's often vague and elusive symbolism is significant for comparative research in the history of religion. The material manifestations and historical contexts of sacred waters along with associated rituals at sanctuaries near sacred springs or holy wells offer particular insights for understanding regions where multiple religious traditions coexist (Astarita, 2006). Focusing on Hatay, the southernmost province of the Republic of Turkey, this chapter presents four local sites visited by members of different Christian and Muslim communities.

Aside from the differences of religious traditions attributed to the examples of sacred springs and holy wells discussed later, these sites of veneration are all (1) recognized as some of the most important natural and cultural landmarks in the region, (2) associated with religious traditions that are at least 2,000 years old, despite their lack of documented history of veneration, (3) related to the veneration of saints or deities, and (4) visited in conjunction with the veneration of nearby rocks and trees. The four examples briefly discussed in this chapter address two sacred springs and two holy wells. The sacred springs include the waterfalls at Şelale (in Arabic: *Beit el-ma*) in present-day Harbiye (formerly named Daphne) and the water rivulet next to the Moses Tree (*Musa Ağacı* in Turkish) in Hıdırbey Köyü. The sacred wells entail the baptismal in the rock of the St. Peter Grotto (Turk.: *St. Pierre Kilisesi*) in Antakya and both the Virgin Mary Pond (Turk.: *Meryem Ana Havuzu*) and the Virgin Mary Valley (Turk.: *Meryem Ana Vadisi*) near Arsuz.

Şelale in Harbiye

The Şelale in Harbiye is a massive waterfall that originates with multiple springs directly pouring out of the mountain. Since the foundation of the city, this site has been associated with the myth of Apollo and Daphne; the temple there is dedicated to Apollo, and the surrounding village is named after Daphne.

FIGURE 23.1 Two of the many sacred springs bursting out of the mountain at the Şelale in Harbiye (formerly Daphne). Photographs by author.

Geographic locations and physical features

Şelale is located in the southernmost outskirts of Harbiye, a small town near Antakya. It is near the main road that connects Harbiye with Antakya in the north and Şenköy in the south. Bursting out of a mountain at multiple locations, the springs stretch across hundreds of meters covering the several promontories and collect in various basins and ponds before flowing into a valley and entering the Orontes River (Turk.: Asi Nehri). Near the water springs, numerous souvenir shops and bars or even fish restaurants have been established along the serpentine walkways running up and down the mountain slope. Along the path, small terraces or basins overflow with massive amounts of water which pour out at every corner over the smooth rocks underneath, filling the air with enchanting sounds of tinkling, bubbling water.

Myths and legends attributed to the site

Alexander the Great was likely the first to discover this site after exploring the region following his decisive victory against the Persians in the Battle at Issus (Downey, 1959:682). According to legendary accounts, it is this region where Alexander drank the sweetest water he had ever tasted. While he founded Alexandretta (present-day Iskenderun), it was his general, Seleucus I, who laid the foundation for the town of Daphne (present-day Harbiye) and also the cities of Seleucia (present-day Samandağ) and Antioch (present-day Antakya) (Norman, 2000:25). Always relying on oracles and divinations in founding these cities, Seleucus I believed that he had discovered the original location for the myth of Daphne and Apollo when he saw the aged evergreen laurel trees near the water springs named after Daphne (Latin: *Daphne laureola* or *Lauris nobilis*). The discovery of the sacred springs of Daphne and the foundation of the Apollo temple by Seleucus I is most elegantly described by the fourth-century Greek scholar Libanius:

> And this suburb, Daphne, much famed in song, Seleucus elevated to the dignity of a shrine, dedicating the place to the god, since he found that the myth was true. For Apollo, when he was enamored of Daphne but could not win her, pursued her; and as she was changed by her prayer into a tree … [Seleucus] once rode out to hunt, taking his dogs with him, and when he came to the tree which had once been a maiden, the horse stopped and smote the ground with his hoof, and the earth sent up a golden arrowhead. … I suppose that in [Apollo's] grief over the transformation of the maiden he shot all his arrows, and the tip of one, broken off, was hidden by the earth and was preserved for Seleucus, as a warning to adorn the spot and to consider it as what it actually was, a shrine of Apollo. There was indeed the miracle in which, they say, the spring on Helicon was produced when Pegasus struck the rock with his hoof; but this event here was the more miraculous because it is more natural for springs than for the tips of arrows to spring up from the earth. Seleucus however lifted the tip of the arrow and saw a serpent coming straight upon him, hissing with its head in the air. But as the serpent came on, it looked at him mildly, and vanished. When this serpent was added to the

omens that appeared from the earth, his conviction grew that the god walked abroad in this place. And at once a sacred closure was laid out and trees and a temple were provided, and the grove speedily flourished and was guarded by strong prayer. And Daphne was everything to Seleucus. For in addition to these signs from heaven which met his eyes, there also impelled him an oracle which he had received from Miletus, as support against his adversity, from which he had drawn courage. This oracle promised him coming good fortune, and commanded him, when he won the rule over Syria, to make Daphne sacred to the god.

(Downey, 1959:663–664)

Called the palaces of the nymphs, the springs were Daphne's chief glory. Ironically, the associated temple, dedicated to her offender, was located in the middle of a grove called "the Daphnaion" (Malalas, 1986:107).

Rituals of veneration performed at the site

The healing spring waters of the sanctuary of Apollo at Daphne were among the most widely venerated sites in antiquity where pilgrims prayed and offered sacrifices (Malalas, 1986:144; Norman, 2000:55–57; Cribiore, 2007:26). Even Julian the Apostate made a sacrifice there to Apollo and then laid down to sleep and receive visionary dreams (Malalas, 1986:178). The site became contested when Christians buried the relics of a martyred bishop of Antioch, Babylas, next to the Apollo temple, hoping to convert the site (Mayer and Allen, 2012:96–97). When Julian the Apostate stopped receiving oracles from Apollo there, he commanded the removal of Babylas' remains (Christensen-Ernst, 2012:46, 50–51). Later, the temple of Apollo was mostly destroyed in a fire on the night of October 22, 362, and Julian again blamed the Christians (Teitler, 2014:280). Although the Apollo temple survived most of the major earthquakes common in this region with some remains still visible to travelers during the eighteenth century, no traces of the temple can presently be found. The water springs are still identified with the myth of Apollo and Daphne. While the practices of divination or dream incubation are carried out at neighboring sacred sites by Arab Alawites who predominantly inhabit this region (Kreinath, 2014), they no longer take place at Şelale. Coins are frequently left in the numerous water basins for purposes of vows and wish-making, and, at times, one can find rags tied around twigs near the waterfalls for the same purpose.

Musa Ağacı in Hıdırbey Köyü

Located in Hıdırbey Köyü are a spring and a tree venerated across faiths. The Moses Tree (Turk.: *Musa Ağacı*) is a sycamore that is believed to be the oldest tree in the Hatay region and is estimated by some to be between 2,000 and 3,000 years old (Kalaycıoğlu, 2011:11; Zubari, 2016:107). The tree is located next to a rivulet in the slope of the Moses Mountain (Turk.: *Musa Dağı*). Different local legends explain the tree's origins as sprouting from either Moses' rod or Aaron's rod planted there in the ground. Alternately, the tree is said to have grown from the lance with which St. George killed the dragon who occupied the spring. The spring itself is thought to be that from which the water of life originated.

Geographic locations and physical features

The Musa Ağacı is located at the center of a village called Hıdırbey Köyü, near a small rivulet, known as the Hıdırbey stream (Turk.: *Hıdırbey Deresi*). In the northern district of Samandağ, Hıdırbey Köyü is one of seven former Armenian villages in the area now inhabited by Turkmen. It is located on a small plateau on the labyrinthine slopes of Moses Mountain (Turk.: *Musa Dağı*) that connect another former Armenian village, Yoğunoluk, with Vakıflı, which is presently the only remaining ethnic Armenian village in all of Turkey. Hıdırbey Köyü was referred to as Kheder Beg or Iddeyr by the native Armenian population, who lived there until 1939 when it was annexed to Turkey. The spring of the Hıdırbey stream originates some 50 meters above the *Musa Ağacı* and flows 2 km before reaching the Orontes River (Turk.: *Asi Nehri*), supplying drinking and irrigation water along its course. Where the Hıdırbey stream reaches Samandağ, it is called *Favvar*—Arabic for overflow—because its basin spills over on rainy days during the winter season.

Myths and legends attributed to the site

Because of its age and location where the Hıdırbey stream runs down the slopes of the Musa Dağı, this tree became an integral part of the local appropriation of the Qur'anic story "Where the Two Waters Meet" which is about Moses (Turk.: Musa) encountering al-Khiḍr (Turk.: Hızır), a mystical saint, who was in folk traditions also known as the Green One and often identified with the Green Man (Kreinath, 2019). In the Islamic tradition, al-Khiḍr is also associated with Alexander the Great (Dawkins, 1937). According to Arabic, Persian, and Early Ottoman versions of the Romance of Alexander the Great (Turk.: *Iskender-name*), Al-Khiḍr is depicted as a cousin of Alexander and, born under a fortunate star, was a fierce general during the Persian War who achieved immortality by finding the water of life (Arab.: *abu-hayat*) (Franke, 2011; Cheetham, 2012). In the local folklore of Hatay, Hızır is also known as St. George (Turk.: Mar Corcus), a man who killed the dragon occupying the spring of life close to Hıdırbey Köyü (Kızıldağlı, 1994:35). This legend of Hızır (aka Mar Corcus) frames the local legend of Hızır's encounter with Musa. In this story, the *Musa Ağacı* is the spear with which the dragon was killed; whereas other accounts hold that the tree grew where Musa forgot the stick of Aaron (Kızıldağlı, 1971:6013; Kreinath, 2015:134). Armenian legends describe the *Musa Ağacı* as "a notable, a verdant place, or a venerable spot associated with the Christian Saint George and/or the Muslim Khidr" (Shemmassian, 2016:81). According to Armenian traditions, sycamore trees are considered sacred since Anushavan—one of the female descendants of the founder of ancient Armenia—was given to a secret forest of sycamores that flourished close to Armenia's legendary capital city and resided there as a living sacrifice (Thomson, 1978:107–108; Kreinath, 2019:63). According to these traditions, the heathen priests of Armenia used to pray among the trees and make their predictions about the future by hearing the voice of the leaves (Villa and Matossian, 1982:127, 129–130; Kreinath, 2019:72).

Rituals of veneration performed at the site

Until recently, Christians and Muslims visited the *Musa Ağacı* to perform prayers and make wishes; at one point, visitors could even enter the tree, as it had split open in the middle. Visiting the sycamore or plane tree, people traditionally tied pieces of their clothing there or said prayers while touching the tree. It was also a tradition in Hıdırbey Köyü that elderly women visited the tree on Saturday nights to burn candles and pray. It was possible to see traces of the smoke left from burning candles in the tree with every niche or pinhole of the blackened wood filled with small crumbled scratches of paper or tissue. *Musa Ağacı* is now protected under a historic preservation initiative and continues to be a major attraction, mainly visited for wish-making, family celebrations, and life-cycle rituals (from name-giving and circumcision ceremonies to weddings and funerals). This site is considered sacred for many Muslims, Christians, and Jews in Hatay (Prager, 2013:42; Kreinath, 2015:134).

St. Pierre Kilisesi in Antakya

One particular holy well in Hatay is highly important for Eastern Orthodox and Catholic Christians living in Antakya. It is a baptismal located in the St. Peter Grotto in the very rock of the St. Pierre Kilisesi, the oldest church in the history of Christianity. After its restoration, the grotto was transformed into a museum with the permission of the ministry of tourism and remains accessible for special Christian services.

Geographic locations and physical features

Located east of the Orontes River in the foothills of the Stauris Mountain near the Parmenios River, this grotto is near both the Eastern or Aleppo Gate (later called the Gate of St. Paul) on the main road to Reyhanlı, and the famous Iron Gate that is built over the Parmenios River connecting the Stauris Mountain with the Silpius Mountain. Right above the St. Pierre Kilisesi is the massive rock-hewn bust traditionally called the Charonion, or the Tyche of Antioch, attributed to Antiochus IV, who ordered it to be carved for apotropaic purposes after the town had been devastated by a plague. The cave that is now St. Pierre Kilisesi extends over 42 feet (13 m) in length, 31 feet (9½ m) in width and 23 feet (7 m) in height. The oldest remains of the church date from the fourth or fifth century and include traces of black and white marble mosaics and some barely detectable frescos. The rock formations of the cave are left in their natural condition on the northeastern and southeastern corners of the church. On the southeastern corner, a basin on the ground retains water from flows along the nearby rocks.

FIGURE 23.2   Devotee receiving sacred water from the holy well at the Senpiyer Kilisesi in Antakya (formerly Antioch). Photograph by author.

Myths and legends attributed to the site

Although there is no reliable data available on the construction and early use of the St. Pierre Kilisesi, it is believed that this grotto was the place where St. Peter preached the Gospel of Jesus and laid the foundation for the Christian church in Antioch (Acts 11:26). According to local legends, St. Paul was baptized there and the relics of St. Ignatius, the first bishop of Antioch, have been venerated at his grave nearby (Mayer and Allen, 2012:81–87). The St. Pierre Kilisesi is also the place where St. John Chrysostom is believed to have given sermons and performed baptisms. He is also said to have lived as an ascetic in one of the cells near the grotto. It is probably for these reasons that this place is, according to some traditions, also known as the St. John Grotto (Förster, 1897:141; Jacquot, 1931, vol. 1:278). One account, given by Wilbrand of Oldenburg who visited during his pilgrimage to Jerusalem in November of 1211, identified the site as the St. John Grotto. He wrote that the cave church at the foot of the mountain was "built over the house of St. Luke the Evangelist" (Pringle, 2016:73).

Rituals of veneration performed at the site

On the inner right wall of the cave, a small spring oozes from the mountain rock and collects in a basin carved out of the rock. This water is sought by Christians and even Alawites who attribute to it a beneficent, if not miraculous, healing virtue.

They drink it and wash the wounds of the ailing (Jacquot, 1931, vol. 1:275). During the festival of St. Peter and Paul, one part of the religious service is celebrated either inside or in front of the grotto. One of the highlights of the service is drinking the well water and/or anointing one's face, neck, and arms with it. In the past, it was used for baptisms and taken home and given to those who were ill.

Meryem Ana Havuzu near Arsuz

A holy well dedicated to the Virgin Mary is located near Arsuz (formerly Rhosus), a coastal village just south of Iskenderun. The Virgin Mary Pool (Turk.: *Meryem Ana Havuzu*) with its large water basin can be found on a secluded plateau in the otherwise uninhabited upper slopes of the Musa Dağı. The Virgin Mary is believed to have visited the place and bathed in the pool during her travels between Antioch and Ephesus.

Geographic locations and physical features

The Meryem Ana Havuzu, also known by locals as Seydi, is in the neighborhood of Hacı Ahmetli in the Gözcüler village some 6 km southeast of Arsuz. It is known for its natural beauty and legends regarding the Virgin Mary. This site can only be reached on a forest path from Gözcüler. It is a place of vast mountains with rugged roads, deep valleys, and forests covered with pine trees. The river flowing through this valley is known by local Christians in Arsuz as the Virgin Mary River (Turk.: *Meryem Ana Deresi*). Nearby is also a site referred to as the resting place of the Virgin Mary (Turk.: *Meryem Ana Makamı*).

Myths and legends attributed to the site

The Meryem Ana Havuzu is associated with visits from the Virgin Mary on her way from either Jerusalem to Ephesus or vice versa. According to one legend, Meryem Ana came on her way from Jerusalem to Ephesus, first to Antioch, and after crossing the Musa Dağı on a forest path, descended the mountain into the coastal region of Arsuz. The Virgin Mary stopped at the site, where she realized that hot water flows from one side and cold water from the other. It is said that the Virgin Mary took a bath in the lake into which both streams flow. It was believed that the hot water symbolizes sin, while the cold water symbolizes holiness. In another legend attributed to the Meryem Ana Havuzu, the Virgin Mary was fasting on her way to Antioch. Upon her arrival, she began looking for something with which to break her fast. She saw a fish jump from the water and land on a stone at her side—the heat of the sun grilled the fish. According to another local legend, the Virgin Mary only ate half of the fish, and the remaining carcass jumped back into the water as a sign for the miraculous nature of this site.

Rituals of veneration performed at the site

Orthodox Christians from Arsuz perform a pilgrimage to the Meryem Ana Havuzu on the feast of the Assumption of the Virgin Mary beginning in the evening of August 14. Their procession begins at the St. Hanna Church (Turk.: *Maryo Hanna*

Kilisesi) in the center of the town. Since it is believed that the Virgin Mary broke her fast on August 14 (the day before her Assumption), local Christians break their fast during the festival of the Assumption of the Virgin Mary on that day. During this feast, offerings are given, candles burned, and prayers made. Among local Christians, the pilgrimage to the Meryem Ana Valley is also called the Feast of Seydi. Some Orthodox Christians visit the Meryem Ana Havuzu and stay there overnight for prayers and dream incubation. Ritual bathing during that night is also considered to heal and bless participants.

Conclusions

Although it is impossible to unpack all the nuances of the local legends and historical accounts, this brief essay explains the ritual significance of sacred waters representative of broader patterns in Hatay. Considering the geographic location and the material features of each landmark, the stories commonly attributed to the sites—and the rituals performed there—account for the religious significance of sacred springs and holy wells and their association with the patronage of deities or saints. Historical and ethnographic information, used in conjunction with textual sources of mythical narratives commonly associated with these sites, thus explicates the various layers of meaning that sacred water can acquire through sequential sacralization by multiple faiths.

References

Astarita, Tommaso. 2006. *Between Salt Water and Holy Water: A History of Southern Italy*. New York: W.W. Norton.

Bachelard, Gaston. 1983 [1942]. *Water and Dreams: An Essay on the Imagination of Matter*. Translated by Edith R. Farrell. Dallas: The Pegasus Foundation.

Cheetham, Tom. 2012. *Green Man, Earth Angel: The Prophetic Tradition and the Battle for the Soul of the World*. New York: State University of New York Press.

Christensen-Ernst, Jørgen. 2012. *Antioch on the Orontes: A History and a Guide*. Lanham, MD: Hamilton Books.

Cribiore, Raffaella. 2007. *The School of Libanius in Late Antique Antioch*. Princeton, NJ: Princeton University Press.

Dawkins, Richard M. 1937. Alexander and the Water of Life. *Medium Aevum* 6(3):173–192.

Downey, Glanville. 1959. Libanius' Oration in Praise of Antioch (Oration XI). *Proceedings of the American Philosophical Society* 103(5):652–686.

Eliade, Mircea. 1996 [1949]. *Patterns in Comparative Religion*. Translated by Rosemary Sheed. London: University of Nebraska Press.

Förster, Richard. 1897. Antiochia am Orontes. *Jahrbuch des deutschen Archäologischen Instituts* 12:103–149.

Franke, Patrick. 2011. Drinking from the Water of Life–Nizāmī, Khizr and the Symbolism of Poetical Inspiration in Later Persianate Literature. In *A Key to the Treasure of the Hakīm: Artistic and Humanistic Aspects of Nizāmī Ganjavī's Khamsa*, edited by Johann-Christoph Bürgel and Christine van Ruymbeke, 107–125. Leiden: Leiden University Press.

Ghabin, Ahmad. 2012. The Zamzam Well Ritual in Islam and Its Jerusalem Connection. In *Sacred Space in Israel and Palestine: Religion and Politics*, edited by Marshall J. Breger, Yitzhak Reiter and Leonard Hammer, 116–135. London and New York: Routledge.

Hanauer, James E. 1907. *Folklore of the Holy Land: Moslem, Christian and Jewish*. London: Duckworth and Co.

Hawting, Gerald R. 1980. The Disappearance and Rediscovery of Zamzam and the 'Well of Ka'ba'. *Bulletin of the School of Oriental and African Studies* 43:44–54.

Jacquot, Paul. 1931. *Antioche, centre de tourisme.* 3 vols. Beyrouth: Comité de tourisme d'Antioche.

Kalaycıoğlu, Mithat. 2011. *Hatay Halk Bilimi: Kültür ve Hoşgörü Kenti* [Folkloristics in Hatay: The City of Culture and Tolerance]. Hatay: Antakya Belediyesi.

Kızıldağlı, Edip. 1971. Hatay'da Hızır İlyas Efsaneleri [Myths of Hızır İlyas in Hatay]. *Türk Folklor Araştırmaları* 13:6012–6013.

Kızıldağlı, Edip. 1994. *Hatay Masalları* [Tales of Hatay]. Antakya: M. Tekin.

Kreinath, Jens. 2014. Virtual Encounters with Hızır and Other Muslim Saints: Dreaming and Healing at Local Pilgrimage Sites in Hatay, Turkey. *Anthropology of the Contemporary Middle East and Central Eurasia* 2(1):25–66.

———. 2015. The Seductiveness of Saints: Interreligious Pilgrimage Sites in Hatay and the Ritual Transformations of Agency. In *The Seductions of Pilgrimage: Sacred Journeys Afar and Astray in the Western Religious Tradition*, edited by Michael A. Di Giovine and David Picard, 121–143. Farnham: Ashgate.

———. 2019. Tombs and Trees as Indexes of Agency in Saint Veneration Rituals: Bruno Latour's Actor-Network Theory and the Hıdırellez Festival in Hatay, Turkey. *Journal of Ritual Studies* 33(1):52–73.

Malalas, John. 1986. *The Chronicle of John Malalas.* Translated by Elizabeth Jeffreys, Michael Jeffreys and Roger Scott. Melbourne: Australian Association for Byzantine Studies.

Mayer, Wendy, and Pauline Allen. 2012. *The Churches of Syrian Antioch (300–638 CE).* Leuven: Peeters.

Mithen, Steven, and Emily Black. 2011. Overview and Reflections: 20,000 Years of Water and Human Settlement in the Southern Levant. In *Water, Life and Civilisation: Climate, Environment, and Society in the Jordan Valley*, edited by Steven Mithen and Emily Black, 469–480. Cambridge: Cambridge University Press.

Norman, Albert F. 2000. *Antioch as a Centre of Hellenic Culture as Observed by Libanius.* Liverpool: Liverpool University Press.

Prager, Laila. 2013. Alawi Ziyara Tradition and Its Interreligious Dimensions: Sacred Places and their Contested Meanings among Christians, Alawi and Sunni Muslims in Contemporary Hatay (Turkey). *Muslim World* 103(1):41–61.

Pringle, Denys. 2016. *Pilgrimage to Jerusalem and the Holy Land, 1187–1291.* New York: Taylor and Francis.

Shemmassian, Vahram L. 2016. Armenian Musa Dagh in the Nineteenth and Early Twentieth Century. In *Armenian Communities of the Northeastern Mediterranean: Musa Dagh—Dört-Yol—Kessab*, edited by Richard G. Hovannisian, 79–121. Costa Mesa: Mazda Publishers.

Teitler, Hans C. 2014. Avenging Julian: Violence against Christians during the Years 361–363. In *Violence in Ancient Christianity*, edited by Albert Geljon and Riemer Roukema, 90–107. Leiden: Brill.

Thomson, Robert W. 1978. *Moses Korenats'i: History of the Armenians. Translation and Commentary on the Literary Sources.* Cambridge, MA: Harvard University Press.

Villa, Susie H. and Mary A. Matossian. 1982. *Armenian Village Life before 1914.* Detroit, MI: Wayne State University Press.

Zubari, İsmail. 2016. *Samandağ: Doğu Akdeniz'in Asi Coğrafyası* [Samandağ: The Rebellious Geography of Eastern Mediterranean]. Hatay: Samandağ Hizmet Vakfı.

PART VII

Sacred waterfalls

When punctuating sacred topographies formed by multiple linked sites, waterfalls are usually the places where pilgrims or devotees receive knowledge or spiritual protection and, being the most visibly dynamic manifestation of water sources, can be associated with spirits linked to nature's other elements. Flanked by two guardian *kami* stones and a sacred camphor tree, Japan's highest waterfall in the Wakayama Prefecture, Nachi Falls, is home to one of Japan's annual fire festivals (both water and fire being elemental purifying forces). The sacred water falls of PhiPhidi in South Africa's Limpopo Province are part of a linked sacred topography that also includes the supermundane Lake Fundudzi and the Thathe Vondo Sacred Forest. Advice-giving sprits dwell in different and named parts of the falls, its pool and its offering rock that received beer and millet gifts (before being quarried away to create a road for tourist access). Especially when associated with other natural features, Burmese waterfalls can be considered auspicious stops on special types of pilgrimages for vow-taking.

Elizabeth McAlister opens this section of the volume with a relatively new sacred waterfall created by an earthquake in 1842. In the Haitian mountains, the waters of Sodo receive transformative powers from the indwelling spirits of an Afro-Haitian cosmology. To "work" their healing energies, devotees must learn about the *chemin dlo*—the water path. Vodouist Catholics offer devotions to creolized African spirits and Catholic saints that can be seen as counterparts so that Sodo's largest spiritual gathering happens on the July 16th feast day of Our Lady of Mount Carmel. For the Lower Elwha Klallam people, a Coast Salish tribe on Washington State's Olympic Peninsula, the Elwha River watershed is a sacred landscape that encodes right interactions between humans, non-human animals, spirits and ancestors. Cailín Murray considers sacred waters of the Olympic Mountains where guardian spirits could be acquired. Because of Indigenous dispossession, ritual engagement of these sites is limited. The hot springs considered the site of creation in Klallam cosmology are now between two hydroelectric dams, and, at the region's most sacred waterfall and

pool, Marymere Falls, a viewing platform that protects the waters from tourist dese-
cration also hinders veneration. Ellen Schattschneider considers "Buddhist-inflected
Shinto" on Japan's Akakura Mountain where ascetics practice arduous rituals recognizing visible and invisible water sources across the sacred landscape and their
associated divinities and spirits. Seeking insights from the realm beyond the waters,
practitioners venerate a waterfall dedicated to the Buddhist fire deity Fudo Myôô.
Spirit mediums there may have the sensory experience of a fire's warmth from the
otherwise cold waters. Prayerful immersion under the falls is thought to alter both
devotees' minds and material beings to enable their path through the successive levels of awareness toward Enlightenment.

24

SACRED WATERS OF HAITIAN VODOU

The pilgrimage of Sodo

Elizabeth McAlister

Every July in Haiti, thousands of pilgrims flock to a mountainside waterfall for the Roman Catholic Feast of Notre Dame du Mont Carmel, known as the Miracle Virgin. Haiti's biggest pilgrimage site, the towering cascade is called "Sodo" (pronounced So-DOE). Sodo is the Creole spelling of "Saut d'Eau," which in French means waterfall. The great waterfall of Sodo was created during an earthquake on May 7th, 1842 (Laguerre, 1989:86). It lies high in the mountain range between the towns of Mirebalais and Saint Marc. Pilgrims come for summer vacation and many stay for weeks around the time of the Virgin's July 16th feast. During the month of the feast, the nearby town of Ville Bonheur swells with pilgrims and vacationers, who rent rooms and houses from the villagers.[1]

The dramatic cascade was understood by farmers in the region to be a natural dwelling place of various water spirits in the Afro-Haitian cosmology called Vodou. It is indeed a beautiful place. Clear, frothy mineral water falls hundreds of feet, bouncing off boulders and through twisting tree roots into pools below. As the cool spray splashes from the rocks, tiny rainbows glisten in the air. Pilgrims, hot from the seven-hour walk through the mountains, step under the falls and are sometimes possessed by the spirits. Their faltering steps and wide-eyed expressions become the visual currency of the ubiquitous foreign photographers who ring the falls, fighting for the best spots for their tripods in the undergrowth.[2]

In July 1849, sometime after the creation of the waterfall by the earthquake, rumors began to circulate that a farmer had sighted the Virgin Mary in a nearby palm tree. President Faustin Soulouque, Haiti's ruler from 1847 to 1859, appointed members of his legislative cabinet to study the apparitions at Sodo. After satisfying himself with their report, he ordered the (now baby-blue) chapel built in honor of Notre Dame du Mont Carmel, the *Vièj Mirak* (Miracle Virgin) (Laguerre, 1989:87).[3] Since the apparition, the pilgrimage at Sodo has been a site of multi-fold spiritual power.

Even before Our Lady revealed herself there, the waterfall was already inherently charged with powerful energy. Ancestral spirits (called *lwa*) of the water include the

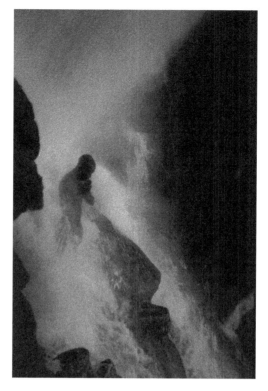

FIGURE 24.1 Pilgrim at the waterfall at Sodo. Photo by Phyllis Galembo, used by permission.

ancient serpent Danbala Wèdo and his rainbow wife Ayida Wèdo, as well as the lady with the fish tail, Lasirèn, a spirit called Simbi Dlo (Simbi of the water), and others, named and unnamed. These spirits appear through the *chemin dlo*, the water path (Courlander, 1960:70). Water is part of the life source, and the water path is also a vehicle for water-borne energies. Fresh water—springs, rivers, ponds and lakes—inherently carries the potential to serve as a conduit for spiritual force. Water is one of the four elements that Vodou initiates are taught to respect as natural spiritual forces. Water has properties of fluidity that lend themselves to ritual transformation. Of the four elements including earth, air and fire, water is the only one that can purify what is soiled. Ritual baptisms and baths make use of the spiritual properties of water, often with added herbs and other strengthening agents (Beaubrun, 2010:137).

Water is thought to have covered the earth in primordial times (as in the biblical story) and likewise is where the unborn baby floats, suspended in the womb. Fresh water is used in almost all rituals, drawn from wells or springs and stored in a *cruch* (clay pots with clay lids), which keeps it as cool as the earth from which it came. The most basic morning ritual of everyday life in the Haitian countryside is to light a candle and *jete twa gout dlo* (pour three drops of water) onto the earth from the *cruch*. With this simple act, the person engages the four elements and prepares for a day that will bring the heat and growth of fire and the transformation of water to move life forward.

With its life-giving and purifying energy, water forms a central space in Afro-Haitian cosmology. A body of water is said to divide the ordinary world of humans and the invisible world of the spirits and the ancestors. This world is often called *nan Ginen* (Ginen, or a mythical African realm), and elders in the Afro-Creole tradition talk about traveling *anba dlo* (under the waters) to undergo initiations and gain mystical knowledge. It is sometimes said that springs, caves and grottoes lead to the spaces deep in the earth, below the water, which are inhabited by alternative, human-like beings (Beaubrun, 2013:129). Springs, rivers and natural waterfalls are often "owned" by a spirit, whose energies can be "worked" by humans for healing treatments.

Simbi is a water spirit served in Haiti and some temples have a small cement basin built and filled with spring water for Simbi to dwell in the form of turtles or snails or snakes. Simbi most likely derives from the Kongo cultural heritage of Haiti, since *basimbi* spirits were and are a class of spiritual beings in Central African culture. Closely related to the recently deceased ancestors, the *basimbi* are a type of reconfigured ancestor spirit. They are thought to have passed through the under-the-water world of the deceased, living instead in lakes, streams and territories of the clans to which they are related (Jacobson-Widding, 1979:79). Note this Haitian prayer song for Simbi and Danbala:

Simbi Dlo, anye, Danbala Wedo, anye (x2)	Simbi of the Water, anye, Danbala Wèdo, anye (x2)
Simbi ou poko konnen mwen	Simbi you don't yet know me
Simbi ou poko konnen mwen la	Simbi you don't yet understand me
Simbi Dlo, anye a	Simbi of the Water, anye a

This text is cryptic in ways typical of prayer songs in Afro-Haitian religion, and does not impart a narrative or clear message. In this text, we learn only that Simbi lives in the water, Simbi is associated with Danbala Wèdo and with the mystery of knowing and unknowing. However, we can observe that the song is about—and is also an invocation of—the spirit "Simbi-of-the-water," and would be used in a religious ritual to call Simbi to possess a spirit medium (McAlister, 2012b).

A water spirit appears as a woman with a fish tail named Lasirèn (the Siren). Stories circulate of people who spot her on a rock or a riverbank, combing her long hair and looking into a mirror. She entices people to follow her under the water, where they might be lost forever. Or, they might reappear after a year and a day, having spent time learning secret knowledge in the land *anba dlo* (under the water). Said by some to be the wife of Agwe Towoyo, the ruler of the sea, and by others to be the wife of Labalèn, a whale, she is also considered one of the many versions of the spirit called Ezili, a female power who is thought by some to "walk with" St. Philomena. Ezili is often closely associated with water, and also with seduction, beauty, wealth and magic. Images of Lasirèn are particularly popular in paintings and textile arts, which are collected widely by museums and galleries throughout the world.

Ezili in her various forms is associated with the Virgin Mary; yet, Haitians of all classes who travel to Sodo in July with their families are likely to say that they are

FIGURE 24.2 Sequined Vodou flag for the water spirit Lasirèn by the artist Evelyn Alcide. Photograph by Grete Viddal, from her collection, used by permission.

there to celebrate Our Lady of Mount Carmel. Elders who serve the spirits in the system of Afro-Haitian spirituality explain that the Our Lady of Mount Carmel "walks with" her counterpart Ezili Dantò, the powerful Afro-Haitian goddess. Dantò's co-existence with the Vièj Mirak is an example of the great mystery of "le mélange," the syncretism of African and Catholic symbolisms. Like the Virgin of Guadalupe in today's Mexico City who appeared to an Amerindian man at the site of an Aztec goddess, Notre Dame du Mont Carmel at Sodo is a powerful national figure resonant with multiple layers of meaning. When pilgrims make the trip through the mountains to Sodo, they visit the church, the waterfall and the palm grove where the Blessed Virgin appeared—a three-fold spiritual site.

When pilgrims go to Sodo, and light a candle, sing to the Virgin and *fè demann* (make requests), they are addressing Notre Dame du Mont Carmel and Ezili Dantò *at the same time*. This overlapping, simultaneous practice of both Catholicism and Vodou, has puzzled outsiders—both Haitian intellectuals and foreigners—for generations. Within anthropology, "syncretism" was the term and theory developed by Melville Herskovits to understand the processes of change that arose with culture contact (Herskovits, 1941). However, scholarly formulations failed to examine the politics of syncretism, that is, the uneven power relations in which cultures met one another and changed. Syncretism came to describe an "impure" religious tradition, saturated with local, unorthodox strains. More recent terms to describe cultural mixings have included "creolization," "symbiosis" and "inter-culture" (Desmangles, 1992; Stewart and Shaw, 1994; McAlister, 2002).

The received way of thinking about Vodou and Catholicism is to imagine them as a pair of binary opposites. It is true that Catholics have affirmed their own status by stressing their apartness from Vodou. A Catholic who is not at all involved in serving the *lwa* identifies as a *fran katolik*, a "straight Catholic," and there are some in the upper classes who know nothing of Afro-Haitian religion. The upper classes were (and are) generally literate, French-speaking, politically enfranchised, light-skinned and emphatically Catholic. On the stage of cultural politics, Vodou was (and is) held up as the pagan, Satanic superstition of the poor, dark, non-literate and disenfranchised majority. Politically, then, Catholicism has always positioned itself in opposition to Vodou.[4]

In practice, it may be more helpful to imagine these two traditions occupying either end of a continuum, with Roman Catholicism on the one end and Vodou on the other. Any given actor in Haiti falls within the continuum, some as Catholics, some as Vodouists and the vast majority living their lives in the middle going through the rites of passage of the Catholic Church while simultaneously maintaining contact with traditional healers and the *lwa*, especially in times of crisis. Even this continuum model must be complicated with further qualifications. Both the Afro-Haitian religion and the Catholicism that evolved in Haiti were constructed in dialectical relation to the other in a process of *creolization*. In this sense, there is simply no "pure Catholicism" or "pure Vodou" in Haiti. To a degree that some advocates in each tradition might not like to admit, each has incorporated the other into its philosophies and practices. Each tradition is, therefore, constitutive and revealing of the other (McAlister, 1998).[5]

Catholics throughout Latin America make *promesas* (promises) to the saints, in which they ask for a favor, and in return make a sacrificial vow. Some promise to return to a church on its feast day each year, others make pilgrimages barefoot and still others donate family treasures to the saint's shrine. In Haiti, people will also *fè demann* (make a request) and tell the saint what they will give in return. Often, the requests to the saints are governed by the logic of Vodou. If a prayer is answered, they might bring an offering to a Vodou temple, for example.

For Catholics, the Virgin Mary and the saints are intercessors; they carry our prayers to God. If they grace us with our wish, we are blessed, but if they do not, we must accept things as they are as God's will. For Vodouist Catholics, things are slightly different. If one saint does not give what we want, we may berate it, argue with it and ultimately turn to a different saint with the same wish. Just as we can punish them by turning away, they can punish us if we do not live up to our promise.

The fact that people do the spiritual work of Afro-Haitian religion in church settings does not mean that they are not also fully participating Catholics. Light blue clothing, speaking prayers during fireworks, writing letters to the Virgin—all these things have a place in the ritual vocabulary of Catholicism, even if they are seen by the priests at the church as the quaint expressions of the "folk."

The spiritual works of Vodouist Catholics are achieved in a process of religious code-switching through language, color and leaving of offerings of spiritual significance. It is possible, then, to communicate with Ezili Dantò *and* Notre Dame du

Mont Carmel on the same public stage. Devotions to Our Lady can also be spiritual work for Ezili Dantò. Despite generations of experience of church repression of Vodou from France and Rome both during colonial and post-colonial periods, it is quite possible to serve Ezili Dantò and the Blessed Mother Miracle Virgin at the festival at Sodo coded in both Catholic and Afro-Creole themes. The celebrations are multifaceted and full of life.

Struggling entrepreneurs may arrive early to set up food stalls, market stands or gambling houses. Rich vacationers build or rent houses and arrive in private cars with the family to spend a few weeks enjoying the extended festivities. This small mountain village also turns into a crossroads of the emigrant diaspora. Haitians working abroad time their trips home from New York, Miami, Boston, Montreal, Martinique, Guadeloupe or the Bahamas to coincide with the festival of the Vièj Mirak.

Nights in Ville Bonheur before and after the feast are a series of ongoing parties with all social classes who come together in the village. The wealthy sit on their porches, enjoying whiskey, telling jokes and listening to Haitian *konpa* dance music on portable radios. Young sons may go out into the night in search of the many *bouzen*, prostitutes, who come into the town especially for the feast. The less well-to do stroll through the streets, tend their businesses or stop in at one of the many Vodou prayer rituals that enliven the village during the month of July. Street life is full and lively. By the light of the *tèt gridap* (kerosene lamps) or the burning torches set around the town, people recognize old friends, acquire new ones, make economic transactions and perform the spiritual work they need to do in order to affect change in their lives.

Traveling Vodou societies may bring their entire personnel, who set up their drums and call out the songs of the *lwa*, sometimes called *zanj* (angels) of Vodou. The popping of fireworks can be heard as various Vodou societies perform prayers and salutes. The noise and smell of the firecrackers "heats up" the prayers that carry messages to the Miracle Virgin. The sound of bursting gunpowder is also an aural semiotic sign for Ezili Dantò, the goddess who "walks behind" the Vièj Mirak. In prayer services for Dantò and the rest of the spirits in the Petwo rite to which she belongs, whips are cracked and gunpowder is lit to create the slaps and pops that Petwo spirits like.

Each year, some Vodou societies bring food to ritually distribute to the poor. Streets are also lined with kiosks that sell *griyo* (fried pork), rice and beans, *soup joumou* (pumpkin soup), soda, liquor and black, sugary Haitian coffee. Market stands sell inexpensive metal amulets tied with blue and white ribbon for pilgrims to pin on their clothes. One can purchase candles and blue and white braided cords to tie around trees—or waists—as part of a ritual devotional promise. There are head scarves printed with images of the Blessed Virgin, candles and images of other saints, as well as plants, roots and spices that can be made into herbal treatments and spiritual baths.

The most powerful baths are taken up at the Sodo waterfall. It is common to see pilgrims stripped down to their underwear, standing in the water pooling under the big cascade and being rubbed vigorously by a priest with herbs and the sacred water, starting with the head, and then the arms, back, torso and legs. With this prayerful bath using the waterfall's charged ancestral energies, the supplicant is once again entering into contact with the transforming power of the womb. The secrets of the fluid ancestral water and the grace of the Blessed Virgin together open up new possibilities, healing and a kind of grace. Water envelopes humans in the beginning in the womb, and the end in the watery ancestral realm of *nan Ginen*. At the waterfall, the power of the water can be found in the middle of life, just when it is needed to heal, renew and refresh.

Notes

1 This chapter revisits and expands a previously published essay (McAlister, 1998).
2 See, for example, Chapman (2017).
3 He was subsequently crowned Emperor of the Haitian Republic and the de facto head of the Roman Catholic Church.
4 Throughout Haitian history, the Catholic Church has launched waves of repression against Vodou practitioners in "anti-superstition campaigns" (Desmangles, 1992). In the twenty-first century, Evangelical Protestants have taken up violent campaigns against traditional religion (McAlister, 2012a).
5 Although the history is too lengthy to elaborate here, it is important to note that upon the Haitian Revolution in 1804, ties were officially cut with the Vatican, and a Catholicism in Haiti evolved with its own national flavor. In 1860, a Concordat was signed initiating the relationship with Rome anew. By that time, Afro-Haitian spirituality had established itself as the worldview of the vast majority (Desmangles, 1992).

References

Beaubrun, Mimerose P. 2013. *Nan Dòmi: An Initiate's Journey into Haitian Vodou.* San Francisco, CA: City Lights Books.

Chapman, Catherine. 2017. Voodoo Believers Bathe in a Haitian Waterfall. *Daily Mail.com.* www.dailymail.co.uk/news/article-4763926/Voodoo-believers-Haiti-bathe-healing-waterfall.html

Courlander, Harold. 1960. *The Drum and the Hoe.* Berkeley: University of California Press.

Desmangles, Leslie G. 1992. *The Faces of the Gods: Vodou and Roman Catholicism in Haiti.* Chapel Hill: University of North Carolina Press.

Herskovits, Melville. 1941. *The Myth of the Negro Past.* Boston, MA: Beacon Press, 1958.

Jacobson-Widding, Anita. 1979. *Red-Black-White as a Mode of Thought.* Stockholm: Almquist and Wicksell International.

Laguerre, Michel. 1989. *Voodoo and Politics in Haiti.* New York: St. Martin's Press.

McAlister, Elizabeth. 1998. The Madonna of 115th Street Revisited: Vodou and Haitian Catholicism in the Age of Transnationalism. In *Gatherings in Diaspora: Religious Communities and the New Immigration*, edited by R. Stephen Warner and Judith G. Wittner, 123–160. Philadelphia, PA: Temple University Press.

———. 2002. *Rara!: Vodou, Power, and Performance in Haiti and Its Diaspora.* Berkeley: University of California Press.

———. 2012a. From Slave Revolt to a Blood Pact with Satan: The Evangelical Rewriting of Haitian History. *Studies in Religion/Sciences Religieuses* 41(2):187–215. doi: 10.1177/0008429812441310

———. 2012b. Listening for Geographies: Music as Sonic Compass Pointing toward African and Christian Diasporic Horizons in the Caribbean. *Black Music Research Journal* 32(2):25–50. doi: 10.5406/blacmusiresej.32.2.0025

Stewart, Charles and Rosalind Shaw. 1994. *Syncretism/Anti-Syncretism: The Politics of Religious Synthesis.* New York: Routledge.

25

THE OLYMPIC MOUNTAINS AND THE SACRALITY OF WATER IN THE KLALLAM WORLD

Cailín E. Murray

The ancestors of Lower Elwha Klallam people, a Coast Salish tribe on Washington State's Olympic Peninsula, engaged with water as a sacred and powerful substance, particularly with regard to their major salmon stream, the Elwha River, as well as lakes, waterfalls and hot springs located in the Olympic Mountains. Historic Klallam cultural values, beliefs and practices shaped, and were shaped by, their relationships to water. Today, the sacrality of water exists within a larger relational framework that includes humans, animals, plants, spirits, ancestors, physical places and the past. The acquisition of knowledge and special skills through encounters with spirits known to dwell around sacred sources of water produces greater awareness of culturally specific concepts concerning respectful relationships between humans and non-humans and the transformative nature of power.

The sacred Elwha watershed

Along the indigenous Northwest Coast of North America, stretching from Alaska and British Columbia to the boundary between southern Oregon and northern California, watersheds, for millennia, have defined dwelling places for extended kin groups (Thornton, 2012:123). Dwelling in these locations establishes a deep sense of kinship between people and the landscape. Coast Salish[1] winter villages which comprised extended families residing together in cedar plank longhouses were often located at the mouths of rivers, along beaches fronting the salt water. Such was the case for the winter village of ʔéʔɬxʷaʔ, a Klallam place name mispronounced by newcomers as "Elwha" which is the name that now appears on maps.

As the largest watershed on the Olympic Peninsula, the Elwha includes 321 square miles of drainage and 70 miles of rivers and tributaries. The river courses 45 miles (72 km) from its headwaters in the Olympic Mountains to where it merges with brackish wetlands and an estuary, emptying into the Strait of Juan de Fuca and the central Salish Sea. The river was home to three villages, in all, and multiple use sites.

Hydroelectric development in the early twentieth century limited access to many places on the river. With the recent removal of two dams and the restoration of the Elwha to a wild state, Lower Elwha Klallam people, whose reservation it borders, are re-establishing their connections to sacred places that were previously flooded (Boyd, 2001; Crane, 2011).

From the Hoko River to Discovery Bay, historic Klallam villages were strung like beads along the Strait of Juan de Fuca. For villagers, the river provided access to resources and a sense of belonging to a specific place. The first Klallam people were bathed by the Creator in the waters of the Elwha (Wray, 2008:49). The salmon runs each season were the gifts of Salmon People, mythic figures that lived beneath the waters in villages of their own. The Animal People of Klallam stories behaved like humans and were motivated by emotions like love or greed. Coast Salish people emphasized similarities between humans and animals, not differences. Hence, the Animal People could also assume human form (Collins, 1952:353). For example, relationships with the salmon were governed by principles of kinship and reciprocity. The bones of the first salmon caught each spring were ritually returned to the river. By treating the first salmon respectfully, humans hoped the Salmon People would reciprocate with robust seasonal runs.

Thus, the watershed is a sacred landscape. The Elwha supported runs of all five species of Pacific salmon, which made it a highly valued fishery for centuries. It is also a storied place filled with sacred meanings. Klallam people view these aspects of the landscape as indivisible. Secular and sacred ways of "knowing" the landscape are not exclusive to one another. One story shared by Klallam people speaks directly to issues of respect for Salmon People as well as their role in providing sustenance. A boy was making fun of spawned out salmon in the Elwha River, who were nearing the end of their lives. The Salmon People heard this and turned the boy into a fish. Each season, his parents would recognize their son among the runs because he alone wore a strip of cedar bark.

As a liminal space, the river draws together humans, animals and spirits. Stories of mysterious occurrences, often at dusk or at night, are still shared. A Klallam fisherman was setting his net one night. He brought his two large dogs, who huddled against him, frightened and whimpering. As he prayed for fish, "something not human" began hurling large rocks at him from the opposite river bank. He continued to pray and it stopped. Other Klallam fishermen have reported being chased by the Wild Man, known as Sasquatch or čičəy'íqʷtən, on the wooded fishing trails next to the river. One summer, reservation children were seeing "Sasquatch" in the woods near the river. The children grew fearful, so elders in the community intervened by holding an event where they shared teachings about how humans remain safe from encounters with spirit power.

The Wild Man is a particularly powerful guardian spirit regarded by some Klallam as a "different breed" that is harmless and always provides help if asked (Wray, 1997:60). Others, especially Klallam with strong Christian faith, view "him" as malevolent. Traditional Klallam stories often associated čičəy'íqʷtən with water and mountains, which is a characteristic shared by similar figures around the world. In one story, an orphan boy found spirit power when he encountered a "large man" bathing in a mountain pool. The being was "a sort of giant whose noise could be heard, but who could not be seen. Yet this little boy saw him." The boy imitated the giant, by stepping into the pool and scrubbing himself with yew wood. After that, "the man disappeared and the boy fell unconscious," a state necessary for spirit power to be engaged (Gunther, 1923).

It is telling that the boy is instructed by this primordial figure in how to properly receive a vision and power. The longevity of the practice of bathing in cold water to prepare for encounters with spirits, or to ask for assistance, has been noted by various observers of the Klallam, into the present. Myron Eells, a nineteenth-century Protestant missionary and amateur ethnographer, wrote that in order to obtain spirit power, Klallam children bathed daily in the river or the saltwater, "sometimes ... for hours ... to gain the favor of their tamahnous" (Castile, 1985:405). "Tamanous" means spirit power and is a word from Chinook jargon, a regional trade language spoken by Native Americans, fur traders and settlers to the Pacific Northwest. Klallam people still use "tamanous" in this context.

Colonialism and indigenous cultural survival

With the arrival of Europeans to the region in the late eighteenth century, the Klallam and their neighbors suffered outbreaks of new contagious diseases. Waves of epidemics, integration into the global economy through the fur trade and later the arrival of American settlers led to significant demographic changes among the Klallam, including loss of their traditional village sites to newcomers and development. Many Klallam were forced to choose between relocation to Native American reservations in places that were not "their country," or the uncertainty of landlessness and squatting within their familiar territory (Boyd, 2001).

Klallam elders *chose* to share knowledge with anthropologists like Erna Gunther (1927) and John P. Harrington (1981/1942). They wanted to document their history and language as well as colonial disruption of Klallam lifeways (Boyd, 2006). They recalled when the potlatch[2] and traditional religions were discouraged by federal Indian agents and their sacred objects sent to museums or private collections. This was also a time when Klallam men were dragged from their beds and arrested for fishing, when Klallam children smuggled home the salmon they caught, and Klallam mothers cooked them with all of their windows closed for fear that the Washington State "fish cops" would smell the evidence and arrest them. It was not until the 1970s that the treaty-protected rights of western Washington tribes to fish were upheld in federal district court (*United States v. Washington*, 384 F. Supp. 312 (W.D. Wash. 1974), aff'd, 520 F.2d 676 (9th Cir. 1975)) or that the U.S. Congress assured the religious freedom of Native Americans by passing the American Indian Religious Freedom Act (1978).

Thus, the context in which knowledge of sacred sites was shared with early ethnographers was influenced by a history that was often at cross-purposes with the goals of cultural survival. Added to this were people's justifiable anger, the intergenerational grief many experienced and a fear of sharing too much with outsiders. This legacy requires contemporary researchers to demonstrate respect for the lingering impact of historical events and accept without judgment, the partiality with which knowledge is imparted.

Klallam sacred sites and sacred waters in the Olympic Mountains

Certain locations were especially known as places to engage with guardian spirits, receive visions and gain personal power. The Klallam encountered the beings that provided tamanous and specific skills, on the ocean and in lakes, ponds, hot springs and waterfalls. In traditional Coast Salish societies, people were born to different ranks and could improve their circumstances and their children's, through advantageous marriages. So, prestige and power were partially a function of kinship. High-ranking families also possessed intangible and tangible forms of power like good names or ceremonial objects. At the same time, individuals, in early adolescence, were expected to acquire power through their own efforts and unique experiences by visiting remote and dangerous places (Suttles, 1987:104). Sometimes, they would enhance the danger. For example, in a story told of a deep pool within Lake Crescent, a man weighted himself with a boulder to sink to the pool's depths in the hopes of finding his power (Wray, 1997:60).

Water is a powerful medium that is always changing: its color, its texture, its temperature, its velocity, its temperament. The Coast Salish, like people around the globe, possess stories of human encounters with monsters that personify bodies of water as powerful, willful and intelligent. Such water sources are also associated in the Northwest with mythic figures like the Animal People. Klallam stories associated with water often reminded people who spent a great deal of time fishing and hunting on rivers and in the ocean, to never forget water's impermanence or its capricious tendency to give and take. Similarly, the Animal People are fickle mythic beings that are both creators and destroyers (see Collins, 1952). These qualities demonstrate their power, their free will and the need for humans to treat them accordingly. Since individual salmon runs were influenced by many environmental factors, they could, in fact, be unreliable at times. This would be explained as the consequence of disrespect toward Salmon People. Sometimes, stories cautioned people about their desires because these carried a price. A man who had hunted many sea otters gave his wife a pelt that she wore to the beach. There, the pelt came to life and dragged her out to sea. Her husband built a magic canoe that took him to the whirlpool where Otter People had taken her down to their village. He jumped through this portal and was helped by other Animal People to retrieve her, but listeners are reminded that flaunting a pelt near the home of Otter People violated contracts of respect and reciprocity (Gunther, 1923).

Animal People belonged to a world that was a strangely unfinished place. For Klallam and other Coast Salish, a figure known as "Transformer" or "Changer" (*xáy'əs*) came to finish the world for the new humans, providing them with all they required to live. Changer stories explained landscape forms like distinct peaks in the Olympics, sand spits and familiar bodies of water. Some Coast Salish, like the Klallam, view Changer as having created them. Klallam people are intimately connected to the Elwha watershed, having been emplaced there by the Creator when they were made. Animal People also remained associated with specific places through place lore passed between generations which communicated ethics and responsibility.

In the twenty-first century, sacred sites remain central to Klallam ways of knowing the world and their unique place in it. At the same time, many indigenous sacred sites, especially those on public lands, are now threatened by development, pollution or over-use by the general public (McLeod and Maynor, 2001). This was the case with hydroelectric development on the Elwha River, that decimated fisheries, polluted water and flooded sites. What follows are accounts of three Klallam sacred water sites that face human-created challenges. Klallam access and use these sites differently from their ancestors, but these watery places retain their sacrality.

Thunderbird's home

At the headwaters of the Elwha River, in the Olympic Mountains, is a cave. "That is where Thunderbird lives," consultants were told as children in the 1960s and 1970s. Thunderbird, or čínəkʷaʔ, is a "lightening monster" who appears as an enormous bird. Elders shared that his size darkens the sky and his flapping wings cause the thunder. Lightening bursts forth from his mouth (Castile, 1985, 253). Thunderbird also helps chase salmon up the river to spawn. He is a harbinger of danger and also a bringer of life, since he signals when the fish are running. The design on the flag for the Lower Elwha Klallam Tribe reflects these meanings.

People sought spirit power by bathing at "Thunderbird's home"—near a spot where the first dam was later built. Klallam warriors sought Thunderbird spirit power by carving his head onto their war clubs (Castile, 1985:144). A sky filled with thunder and lightning was a sign the Klallam were going to war (Harrington, 1981 [1942]:0007; Wray, 1997:146–148). The spirit power which Myron Eells called "Tamahnous water" was also associated with Thunderbird's cave. Those who possessed this power could call a person who was far away and "he came." They could also "do evil" at a distance and cause harm to specific individuals. This power was gained by washing one's hands and arms in "black water" found in natural rock basins at the headwaters of the Elwha (Castile, 1985:375).

Marymere Falls

Bodies of water in the Olympic Mountains, like waterfalls and lakes, were favored by adolescents in search of their tamanous. Guardian spirit acquisition was essential for a young person's future and a critical step included seeking a vision. This required a child to demonstrate respect, courage and fortitude "by fasting and bathing in remote forest lakes or along lonely shores" (Suttles, 1987:204). In one Klallam story, a father wanted his son "to be a great man," so he deprived him of food and water. One day, the boy visited a waterfall. "Anyone that went there was supposed to die. The boy took a bath in the waterfall and nothing hurt him." When he awoke, he heard voices and followed them to a clear pond. When he looked into the water, he could see a village. He weighted himself with a large stone and jumped in. In the village, he met a man who gifted him with an old spirit power and bathed him in salt water. The boy, in time, became a skilled whale hunter (Gunther, 1923).

FIGURE 25.1 Marymere Falls viewpoint, Olympic National Park. ID 74249921 ©
Kyphua/Dreamstime.com.

One of the most famous sacred waterfall sites is Marymere Falls which resides
within the boundaries of the Olympic National Park. Hikes to the falls with extended family remain strong in the living memory of tribal citizens. It is a place
people go to reflect and pray. To reach Marymere Falls, hikers trek through a lowland old growth forest dominated by western red cedar. At the falls, people walk up
a narrow set of steps built by park personnel. At the top is a viewing platform, with
a sturdy railing to discourage hikers from climbing down to the pool and the falls.
A few people at one time can view the falls from the platform. Sometimes, a line
of hikers must wait for their turn. Klallam people hiking to Marymere Falls may
find their ability to fully engage with the site disrupted by federal park rules like
avoiding the actual water, and by feeling pressure to rush so that others may access
the platform. The presence of other stakeholders, who may not care for the smell
of tobacco offerings, for example, can also inhibit full use of the site. As a Klallam
sacred site, Marymere Falls illustrates the tensions that exist on public lands across
the U.S. between indigenous people practicing their religions, often in understated
ways that outsiders misinterpret, and federal laws that protect the rights of *all* visitors
to access these places.

The Olympic hot springs and the Klallam creation site

The Olympic wilderness areas are known for naturally occurring hot springs that are accessible only on foot. Hikers are cautioned that they use them at their own risk since they are not maintained and may contain harmful bacteria. For Klallam people, the hot springs are linked to personal quests for purification and spirit power and are also associated with supernatural monsters (Wray, 1997:149, 2008:49). In one account, the hot springs are the tears of two dragons that bitterly fought for territory. In another, "Boston Charlie," a turn-of-the-century Klallam "medicine man," made regular expeditions to the hot springs "for spiritual cleansing" (Valadez, 2000:40). On one trip, he became lost for several days. After he was found, he reported being kept alive by the actions of a *čičəy'íqʷtən* who provided him with berries and dew-soaked leaves (Wray, 1997:55).

The Klallam creation site is connected to the hot springs. Now located where two hydroelectric dams were constructed on the Elwha River, this site is called *spčúʔ*. Unlike the Abrahamic religions, North American indigenous people conceptualize their ancestral origins in direct association with map-able topography. Furthermore, the places themselves serve as mnemonic devices for recalling oral tribal histories. So, protecting these places becomes a serious matter of cultural survival.

Origins stories of tribes vary. Some arrived to earth through an opening in the sky; others emerged from the ground or even migrated. Some, like the Klallam, were created in specific places. The name of the Klallam creation sites, *spčúʔ*, references tightly woven baskets used for carrying water and cooking food (Wray, 2008:49), and, most particularly, a wide flat rock with two naturally occurring basket-shaped holes. It was in these rock depressions that the Creator bathed the first Klallam people, like a mother would prepare salmon in a watertight basket for her family. *Spčúʔ* is also the place the Klallam visited, since time immemorial, in order to learn their future roles in life.

Before approaching *spčúʔ*, knowledge seekers were expected to first purify themselves in the hot springs. They would then approach the creation site, reach into the holes and what they pulled out provided clues. A handful of shells suggested wealth, deerskin identified a hunter, while grasses indicated a weaver. This site was inaccessible to generations of Lower Elwha Klallam people because at the turn of the twentieth century, it was flooded by hydroelectric development (Boyd, 2001). With the recent removal of both dams and restoration of the Elwha River, *spčúʔ* is a place tribal citizens visit once more to ponder their past, present and future.

Conclusion

In the distant time of the Great Flood, the ancestors heeded the warnings of wise elders and prepared by stocking their canoes and then getting into them. When the waters rose, Klallam people used sturdy cedar bark rope to tie themselves to peaks in the Olympic Mountains and were saved. These peaks remain visible from the Elwha valley (Harrington, 1981:607, 609–610; Wray 1997:149). The story of the Great Flood is one of survival and resilience through reliance on tamanous. It is a story that was told often in the decades leading up to removal of the dams from the

Elwha River. Just as their ancestors required spirit power to face challenges, so do living Klallam people. For these reasons, continuing access to sacred sites like *spčú?*, the Olympic hot springs or Marymere Falls matters. For Klallam people, water binds humans, animals, plants, spirits, ancestors and places of significance to each other in a relational framework. Their relationship to salmon, and the Salmon People, endures as tribal citizens fish commercially and for subsistence. Treaty negotiations between their ancestors and the United States government in 1855 ensured their rights to take fish in their "usual and accustomed" places. With the removal of the dams and restoration of river habitat, the Elwha's salmon runs are returning in far greater numbers. Much of the Klallam story, past and present, has revolved around their interactions with place, in particular with sacred bodies of water, like those associated with the Elwha River and the Olympic Mountains. For the Klallam, as for all people, water both brings and takes life, and offers wisdom and fortitude in between.

Notes

1 Coast Salish refers to the related languages and dialects linking most of the indigenous peoples of the central Northwest Coast.
2 The potlatch is common to all indigenous cultures of the Northwest Coast. Its roots are in ceremony, belief and the validation of indigenous legal principles regarding the transfer of tangible and intangible forms of property and wealth.

References

Boyd, Colleen. 2001. Changer is Coming: History, Identity and the Land Among the Lower Elwha Klallam Tribe of the Olympic Peninsula. Ph.D. diss., University of Washington, Seattle.

Boyd, Colleen. 2006. 'That Government Man Tried to Poison All of the Klallam Indians': Metanarratives of History and Colonialism on the Central Northwest Coast. *Ethnohistory* 53(2):331–354.

Castile, George Pierre. 1985. *The Indians of Puget Sound: The Notebooks of Myron Eells*. Seattle: University of Washington Press.

Collins, June McCormick. 1952. The Mythological Basis for Attitudes toward Animals among Salish-Speaking Indians. *The Journal of American Folklore* 65(258):353–359.

Crane, Jeff. 2011. *Finding the River: An Environmental History of the Elwha*. Corvallis: Oregon State University Press.

Erna Gunther Papers, 1871–1981. Unpublished stories, 1923. Box 2/14, Accession 0614-001. University of Washington Libraries, Special Collections, Seattle.

Gunther, Erna. 1927. Klallam Ethnography. *University of Washington Publications in Anthropology* 1(5):171–314.

Harrington, John Peabody. 1981. [1942]. *The Papers of John Peabody Harrington in the Smithsonian Institution, 1907–1957*. Vol. 1. *Native American History, reel 16, frames 0002-1234. Language and Culture of the Alaska/Northwest Coast*. Milwood, NY: Krause International. Microfilm, thirty reels.

McLeod, Christopher and Malinda Maynor. 2001. *In the Light of Reverence*. DVD. Directed by Christopher McLeod. Bullfrog Films, Oley, PA.

Suttles, Wayne. 1987. *Coast Salish Essays*. Seattle: University of Washington Press.

Thornton, Thomas F. 2012. Watersheds and Marinescapes: Understanding and Maintaining Cultural Diversity among Southeast Alaska Natives. In *Water, Cultural Diversity and*

Global Environmental Change: Emerging Trends, Sustainable Futures, edited by Barbara Rose Johnston, 123–136. London: Springer.

Valadez, Jamie. 2000. Elwha Klallam. Lower Elwha Klallam Language and Cultural Program. Report Prepared for the Lower Elwha Klallam Tribe.

Wray, Jacilee. 1997. Olympic National Park Ethnographic Overview and Assessment. Report prepared for Olympic National Park.

Wray, Jacilee, ed. 2008. *From the Hands of a Weaver: Olympic Peninsula Basketry through Time*. Norman: University of Oklahoma Press.

26

BACK INTO THE LIGHT

Water and the indigenous uncanny in northeastern Japan

Ellen Schattschneider

This paper considers the symbolic politics of water at Akakura Mountain Shrine, a popular Buddhist-inflected Shinto institution in northeastern Japan long associated with female charismatic spirit mediumship. Women ascetics undertake transformative, ritualized climbs along a mountain stream and perform vision-granting austerities at a sacred waterfall dedicated to the fierce Buddhist deity Fudô Myôô. These ascents continue across the annual cycle, as the waterfall is obscured from sight by winter snows and then gradually made visible again during the warm months. Through their rituals, the shrine's congregation collectively reproduces itself and its relationship to mountain divinities through complex transpositions of the mountain's water, understood as gifts of "the dragon princess," an avatar of ancient indigenous capacity. The invisible and visible water flows may be understood in reference to Freud's discussion of the uncanny, forces that, in principle, should be hidden and yet which unexpectedly return to our vision, signaling fissures in structures of psychic and politico-historical repression.

Sacred water and the "uncanny"

What precisely do people consume when they drink sacred water from an ancient landscape? What do they immerse themselves within when they plunge into churning waters associated with divinities and ancestors? This essay explores uncanny traces of indigenous or autochthonous agency at Akakura Mountain Shrine in northeastern Japan's Aomori Prefecture. Water at this site can be read through Freud's approach to "the uncanny," which he interprets as an instance of the strangely familiar that evokes forces and desires which are subject to partial, though never complete, repression. As Freud famously writes of the *unheimlich* or the uncanny, "'*Unheimlich*' is the name for everything that ought to have remained … secret and hidden but has come to light" (from Shelling, quoted by Freud, 1925 [1919]:224). Mysterious flows of healing water encapsulate a set of profound and perhaps intractable cultural

FIGURE 26.1 Waterfall at Maple Slope, Shin-Kiyomizu Temple, from the series One
Hundred Views of Osaka (Naniwa hyakkei) from the Japanese Edo period, early 1860s (Bunkyû era) by Nansuitei Yoshiyuki. Used with permission from the Boston Museum of Fine Arts.

conundrums associated with native and newcomer, the immortal and the mortal, the intimate self and the alien other, life and death, and civilization and its
antecedents—central problems that are, in principle, hidden and yet which episodi-
cally are brought back, in Freud's terms, "into the light."

Water has rich symbolic affordances associated with the uncontainable surplus
of meaning, with the upwelling of forces, desires and presences beyond conventional knowledge, with the unanticipated bursting through that which was previously contained or repressed. Water, the very environment in which we come to
life within the womb, is the most familiar of forms, but also the most mysterious,
transcending all efforts to fully comprehend and organize it. Water is thus, we might
argue, inherently uncanny, simultaneously familiar and strange. Sacred healing water magnifies this inherent paradox exponentially, presenting its consumers with a
fundamental mystery in tangible form: how might we both belong to civilization
while longing for and depending upon that which is emphatically not subject to
civilization's reigning protocols? Sacred waters offer not so much answers, then, as
deep and abiding questions.

Sacred waters often embody precisely an enigmatic tension between the world of
the here and now and the other world that transcends our conventional experience.

Therapeutic water, coming from rather mysterious environs, enters into domestic spaces and human bodies in ways that are held to activate forces deeply beyond normal human experience. Within our physical bodies, subject to all manner of decay and disease, sacred waters are believed to simulate precisely that which is drawn to something beyond the bonds of regular humanity. That "beyondness," in both instances, bears significant traces of the indigenous or the autochthonous.

Watery symbolism pervades Freud's discussion of the *unheimlich*, usually glossed as "uncanny" in English. As Freud orders the relationship between the *heimlich* (familiar) and the *unheimlich*, he comes to the realization that the two terms migrate toward each other in usage. He observes that, "What interests us most in this long extract is to find among its different shades of meaning the word *heimlich* exhibits one which is identical with its opposite, *unheimlich*. What is *heimlich* thus comes to be *unheimlich*" (Freud, 1925 [1919]:224). Thus, the familiar moves toward the unfamiliar—what has been comfortable and visible becomes hidden and more fleetingly understood.

Freud comments on the image of water welling up out of earth as simultaneously unexpected but nonetheless always anticipated—it has "always been there." While the water wells up from another level of existence, this water is intimately associated with the human world: water is a highly evocative switch point between different levels of mind, strange and familiar, hidden and revealed, terrifying and life-giving. These thoughts preface consideration of Japanese sacred water.

Water and indigenous agency in Akakura Mountain Shrine

Akakura Mountain Shrine, founded by a woman known as Kudô Mura in the early 1920s, rests on the slopes of Akakura Mountain, the eastern face of volcanic Mount Iwaki, which towers over the Tsugaru plain of western Aomori Prefecture, the northernmost section of Honshu, Japan's principal island. This region is widely recognized as the final redoubt on Honshu of the Ezo, the indigenous ancestors of the Ainu, before their explosion northward or their assimilation into the Japanese national system.

For centuries, perhaps millennia, the rugged mountain-scape of Akakura, the site of Iwaki's most recent eruption in the late eighteenth century, has been associated with ascetic practice, often pursued by women, who gain capacity as spiritual healers and spirit mediums through challenging exercises on mountain sites. They gain charismatic power through meditation under a mountain waterfall and prayer-filled climbs through the rocky traces of previous volcanic eruptions. Akakura has particularly close associations with the enigmatic, ancient figure of "Onigamisama," the Demon Queen who is believed to have dominated the area before the coming of the Yamato civilization, the precursor of the imperial Japanese state system. Onigamisama is said to have been subdued or at least pacified, through the ministrations of the great Yamato general Sakanoue Tamuramoro, who may, some legends suggest, have entered into sexual congress with the Demon Queen. At times, Sakanoue possesses the bodies of female spirit mediums associated with the shrine, and they take on his violent, conquering masculine attributes. The avatar of the mountain at times manifests itself as a bearded old man, who some link to Sakanoue himself, although the avatar can also appear in dream visions as a dragon closely linked to the Demon Queen, or as two dragons in combat or play above the mountain, reenacting the sexual congress between the imperial conquering male and the indigenous goddess. High at the apex of the central mountain gorge is a great multicolored-stone valley, or gash, often interpreted by my informants as reminiscent of feminine genitalia; from this sacred maternal opening gush forth the sacred waters of the mountain's stream, which descends past the shrine to the plain below and into the Iwaki River, which feeds the region's extensive irrigation system.

Near the turn of the twenty-first century, Akakura Mountain Shrine had about 1,000 adherents; several hundred participated in its two largest annual observances, oriented in different ways toward a sacred stream that descends from the snow-capped mountain's highest reaches. Each May 1st, a mountain opening rite centers on the hanging of a sacred rice straw rope above the sacred waterfall of Fudô-taki, which initiates the six-month period of shugyô or ascetic discipline in the mountain's upper precincts. A great summer festival, in turn, culminates in the "cooking pot ritual" in which rice and salt—thrown into a social pot during the ritual process—are cooked in the mountain's sacred water (gathered from the waterfall's small river) accompanied by prayers chanted by spirit mediums; if all goes well, the boiling pot should emit an unearthly resonating hum, indicating that the mountain divinities have entered into the shrine's precincts, and into the ritual cooking pot, to bless its human members.

Off and on throughout the year, several ascetics reside within the shrine, rising at 4:00 AM to present sacred water and food offerings to the divinities, and then to undertake acts of spiritual austerity, such as cold water ablutions or daily pilgrimage climbs up and down the mountain. In the shrine's kitchen, a special tap is reserved for the water of the *kamisama* (divinities); only those who have undertaken shugyô (ascetic discipline) are allowed to touch this tap, although anyone may be served this sacred water.

For members of the congregation, these underlying psychic and historical dynamics and tensions are worked through each year in a succession of ritual undertakings on the mountain-scape. The annual ritual cycle at Akakura commences with the Dragon Princess Rite, in which 30 or 40 hardy parishioners participate. Each February, dedicated worshippers climb through snowdrifts (or travel by snowmobile) up to the shrine, and form a human chain to pass buckets filled with frigid water pulled from the sacred stream, and hand it off in a long hand-brigade from the river to the shrine, to be emptied into a special ritual *ofuro* (bathtub) in one of the outbuildings dedicated to the shrine's foundress, Kudô Mura. Chanting by priests and other female ritual specialists helps further to purify this water (as it is offered to the foundress, Kudô Mura) as it is poured into the sub-shrine's *ofuro*. During the year, this water, which is considered *kusuri* (medicine) by congregants, will be dispensed to the congregation; members are enjoined to take the water home and to judiciously apportion it to their family members, to protect them from illness and misfortune during the coming year.

The image of the Dragon Princess is a complex composite. It explicitly references the Devadatta (Chapter 12) of the *Lotus Sutra*, in which the daughter of the Dragon King presents her jewel to Shakyamuni Buddha. The passage is usually glossed as exemplifying the capacity of any soul, "even" female ones, to attain awareness and full Buddhahood. In most readings and iconographic depictions of the chapter's climax in Japan, the princess is transformed into a man and flies away to the domain of a Buddha himself, also depicted as male. However, there is an alternate tradition of reading the passage in Japan, celebrating the passage as a positive exemplar of women's spiritual agency and power. This reading is famously celebrated in the mid-twelfth-century *Heike nôkyô* Buddhist scrolls, which show the princess retaining her female form (Abe, 2016).

Although members of Akakura Mountain Shrine are not familiar with the *Heike nôkyô* or with sophisticated Buddhist commentaries on the Devadatta, they clearly share the long-term sensibility that dedicated spiritual action by female figures is profoundly efficacious. Many consult blind female *itako* shamanesses and seek healing from *kamimsama* women spirit mediums. They honor Akakura as a sacred landscape where women undertake spiritual austerities, sometimes for weeks or months at a time, and they return with gifts of healing and foresight. The Dragon Princess is a clear exemplar of women's special spiritual capacities, especially in the service of safeguarding their family, including their ancestors who need their aid as they traverse posthumous pathways toward Buddhahood.

At the same time, the Dragon Princess at Akakura has clear associations with the ancient figure of Onigamisama, the Demon Queen whose reign long proceeded the coming of Buddhism or the region's incorporation into the Yamato imperial state system. Her presence is sensed as the womblike *Ubaishi* (Old Woman Rock) high on the mountain overlooking the sacred stream that meanders through the central gorge. Here, female worshippers must crawl six times through a narrow tunnel under a great boulder, reenacting the soul's movement and rebirth through the six domains of existence.

Water rituals

The dragon at Akakura is evocative of radical, piercing transformations of the soul. As a young farm wife, the foundress Kudô Mura is believed to have first been summoned to the mountain's sacred three-peaked summit by a dragon, which bore her on its sinuous back at night in a dream vision. This nocturnal journey is celebrated in a votive painting that overlooks the main sanctuary of the *honden*, the shrine's principal hall of worship. In other shrine votive paintings, created by worshippers inspired by other sacred dream visions, the dragon at times divides itself into two equal beings, one female and the other male, dancing in the sky around the mountain's peaks. Indeed, one reading of the three peaks of the mountain summit is that the mountain is flanked by a male dragon to the right, a female dragon to the left and the unity of these opposites in the middle. The dragon and its component elements have strong associations for shrine members with libidinal energies and reproductive fecundity; each year, through the fusing and intertwining of differently gendered divine elements, the entire congregation is reborn through the womb-world of the mountain as a faithful united collectivity, bound together through the divine energies that descend to the human world through the mountain's sacred stream (Schattschneider, 2003).

For example, in preparation for the spring Mountain Opening rite, congregation members gather to twine together an enormous rice straw rope (*shimenawa*), created from the rice straw left behind from the previous harvest. These rice plants had been watered, it is explained, by the water which is a gift of the divinities that descends from the mountain's summit. On May 1st, the congregation reciprocates this gift by carrying the rope, which measures over two hundred feet, up the mountain path to the Fudô-taki (Waterfall of Fudô-sama) sacred gorge. Congregants stand in the deep snowpack above the location of Fudô-taki, a waterfall dedicated to the Buddhist deity Fudô-sama, known for his fearsome appearance and his flaming sword, which cuts away impurities and the rope he also carries to tie up demons. Here, during the warmer months, female ascetics chant sutras under the falling waters and may be gifted with sacred visions of the divinities. In early May, however, the sacred Waterfall of Fudô-sama remains invisible under the deep snowpack; its generative forces remained hidden and not yet "brought back to light."

Upon reaching the waterfall zone, men and women divide into separate groups. Women hold up the center part of the sacred *shimenawa* rope, while men attach guide ropes to either end, then scrambling up the gorge's banks to tie the guide ropes to properly positioned trees. They hoist the rope with rhythmic motions that are humorously compared to the male role in coition. Women, in turn, help launch the rope skyward, until it spans the gorge, high above the still-hidden Fudô-taki Waterfall.

Significantly, attached to the center of the *shimenawa* rope is the Hinomaru, the Japanese rising sun national flag and symbol of Amaterasu, progenitor of the imperial line. Ancient demons who are thought to dwell in the forest below the gorge are partisans of the Demon Queen. Unsuspecting novice ascetics may be tempted by the demons, who may call out an individual ascetic's name: and it is generally believed that those who turn around when called will be lost forever.

In that sense, the elevation of the national flag over the demon-haunted forest might be read as signifying the triumph of the expanding, imperial system over the indigenous past. Yet, the whole tableau, of the arcing rope, the flag, the waterfall and the forest, exemplify the needed balance between opposing forces—male and female, conquering alien and autochthonous native—that are held to be necessary for reproducing and sustaining life. Venturing each year into the upper reaches of the mountain, so closely shrouded about with ancient indigenous energies, is believed to be spiritually dangerous but absolutely vital, to overcome the dangers that beset every family in its journey through time. The living and their honored dead need the turbulent, unpredictable energies of long-vanished native worlds, epitomized by the transformative force of the Waterfall of Fudô, if they are to successfully traverse the pathways ahead.

The Rising Sun image, elevated far above the temporarily snow-covered waterfall, recalls the ancient mytheme of Amaterasu who, offended by her salacious brother, hid herself within a cave, plunging the world into darkness. Only once did sunlight and life return to the world, when she was seduced out of the cavern by a mirror in which she glimpsed her own captivating image. Similarly, with the coming of spring, all that which was hidden will once more come back to life, and the life-giving frozen waters of the mountain-scape will be transformed once more into liquid water, returning life to the rice fields in the plain below. Freud described the uncanny as waters that suddenly bubble up out of a dry, cracked river bed. Such an image resonates with the *Oyamabiraki* (Mountain Opening Rite). For Freud, the unconscious is always "with" us (familiar), but nonetheless largely out of conscious sight and knowledge (unfamiliar)—as are the still-frozen and snow-hidden waters of the Fudô-taki Gorge at the Mountain Opening Rite. Congregants make offerings and pray at the frozen, snow-covered Fudô-taki Waterfall while knowing that the river flows unseen below them and will soon reappear as spring progresses.

The transformative power of the mountain waters is made most tangible to the congregation three months later, at the Summer Festival, when all gather to witness the cooking pot rite (*kamado*). Rice and purifying salt are placed in a large pumice stone cooking pot, along with water drawn from the sacred mountain stream. After preparation by male Shinto priests, women spirit mediums gather to sing and chant over the heating pot. They are aided by the congregants who sing the shrine's hymn, *Saigi! Saigi!* (Opening! Opening!) If all goes well, the pot begins to emanate a strange, unearthly hum that seems to penetrate the bodies of all persons present. At this moment, the mountain divinities have fully descended from the mountain's upper reaches and have suffused the shrine itself, and the cooking pot, with their unruly, boiling energies. As soon as the hum is perceived, congregants queue up quickly and hurry forward to throw in a handful of rice and salt; later, they will all receive a small packet of this very same rice, now partially cooked, to place on their household altars as an offering.

Ritual specialists emphasize that the rite will only "work" if all those present are united in their hearts and minds in unified dedication, as the water begins to boil. The gods are attuned to their mortal subjects, and will not manifest themselves within the heating water without mortals' dedicated, collective efforts. The process appears to be closely analogous to conception within the womb, which likewise depends on the transformative blessing of divinities and ancestors to provide the vital spark of life. In a Durkheimian sense, the energizing of the heated, womblike waters is an instance of "collective effervescence," in which the social collectivity powerfully experiences the strength of its intangible unity in material, bodily exhilaration and exultation.

The cycle begins again with the February Dragon Princess Rite. The collective line of worshippers in a bucket brigade, passing the water-filled buckets from the stream to the shrine, becomes a kind of serpentine dragon. Their coordinated, dedicated labor, sustained by the previous year's gifts from the *kami*, is foundational to the year that will follow. The water is transported up to the *ofuro* (again, bath tub) in the shrine building which is dedicated to foundress Kudô Mura and presided over by her carved image. Into this tub are deposited, in essence, the combined energies of the dedicated, united worshippers, which will be re-consumed, in tiny amounts, by all their fellow faithful. The rite's participants usually bring along bottles or jugs to fill up with healing water to take home with them. Through the coming year, other persons, usually in the company of *kamisama* spirit mediums, will visit respectfully to take a small amount of water for healing purposes. They will be enjoined only to drink a capful at a time; the water is so powerful that only a little dose at any one time is safe.

These sacred waters are not simply signs of the indigenous. Rather, each dose of water is a complex hybrid form, a compromise formation, infused by a continuing dance between the indigenous and foreign, the subjected and the subjector, Dragon Princess and Dragon King. Over the course of the annual cycle, the congregation labors mightily to coax the unruly powers of the mountain divinities down into the mortal realm. They must unite in the Dragon Princess rite to bring the trickling water from the nearly ice-covered stream up into the *ofuro* container of the foundress, where the waters will serve to cleanse body and soul of impurities. Each May, they must climb up the mountain carrying the sacred rice straw rope, made of rice straw nurtured by river waters that flowed from the mountain, back up the slopes to the gods' domain, to re-establish a necessary boundary zone between immortal and mortal zones—a border which can then be properly traversed by pilgrims returning to the ancient, pre-civilizational domains of the gods. After the snows and ice have melted, those same pilgrims must perform ascetic discipline under the raging waters of the waterfall and follow winding paths along the stream to the highest peaks, where they may be gifted with sacred dreams of the impossibly ancient divinities. They will, each July, gather to concentrate the power of the mountain waters in a metal bowl, to re-experience the heated energies of the divinities whom they themselves have cultivated. They will labor in the plains below in irrigated rice fields (triumphs of the civilizational project) until in the darkest depth of winter they once again return up the snowy volcanic slopes to a territory that precedes the coming of civilization, to once more access the irreducible powers of the autochthonous, life-sustaining flows born from the land itself.

This compromise is not seamless, and is often marked by painful and disturbing eruptions of normally contained psychic phenomena. Water, which embodies all manner of contradictions, does not fully resolve those divides. One year, the boiling water pot (*kamado*) failed to emit its customary hum, and a long-simmering dispute between the senior and junior branches of the shrine ritual specialists temporarily burst back into the open, as each side argued over the true locus of ritual efficacy and charismatic authority. At times, these ostensibly healing waters seem to release, in an almost hydraulic fashion, pent up frustrations that course through interior landscapes of anguish and struggle.

The Waterfall of Fudô Myôô

The Waterfall of Fudô Myôô is about an hour's hike up from the main shrine buildings. Fudô Myôô (the Immutable One) is the principal deity of the Five Buddhist angry Lords of Light. He is venerated at Akakura in the Godaimyôô (Five Lords) Hall. Fudô serves as the tutelary deity to many of the shrine's *kamisama* spirit mediums. The sword of Fudô is one of the shrine's most important ritual objects, and is used by mediums in special healing hits within the Godaimyôô Hall.

In popular Buddhist cosmology, Fudô is illustrative of the highly disciplined cultivation of mind necessary to achieve detachment from worldly concerns, centered on the paradoxical reconciliation of two seemingly opposed emotional states, violent fury and infinite compassion. His flaming sword slashes away at all earthly bonds, while his rope binds up all dangers that might beset the viewer seeking to move toward a higher state of being.

Below or within the frothing waters of the falls, worshippers pray intensely, reciting Hannya Shingyô and the Fudô-son-ken-Kudoku-no-mon prayer to the fire divinity Fudô Myôô. As Carmen Blacker notes in *The Catalpa Bow*, the dedicated medium is believed to possess such great internal heat herself that she may experience "heat" or even "fire" from the waterfall which is intimately associated with Fudô Myôô's own flaming sword (2004:91–92). At the waterfall, ascetics may experience revelatory visions of Fudô or of the mountain's principal divinity Akakura Daigongen in his various incarnations, including that of dragon—a being intimately associated with water, rain and waterfalls.

Here, at Fudô-taki, the persona of the shrine's foundress Kudô Mura is ever-present. This is where she came to make offerings to the mountain *kamisama* (spirits), cleansing herself in the waterfall praying to her tutelary deity Fudô-sama. Here, she brought her followers to be healed and learn the disciplines of ascetic practice. Every pilgrim (*deshi*) who comes here to pray and make offerings on her own journey of healing recalls the Kudô Mura's founding practice, venerating her as a guardian "ancestral" spirit. As noted earlier, the yearly mountain-opening ritual, Oyamabiraki, held in early May takes place in the snow field that still buries the mountain stream and waterfall, resonating with Freud's evocation of subterranean waters bubbling up from unseen dimensions.

After the snows have melted and pilgrims come to Fudô-taki on a daily basis, they, on occasion, immerse themselves in the waterfall itself, allowing the pounding flow of the waterfall itself to hit their head and shoulders as they stand or sit in prayer to Fudô-sama. It is understood that the "heat" of the deities combined with the sincerity of the pilgrim's prayers will "warm" the person so that they will not suffer from the frigid mountain waters. Indeed, this spiritual power will "dry" their white pilgrim's clothing the moment they emerge from under the falls. Classical images of pilgrims praying under sacred waterfalls suggest that while under the waterfall, their own bodily form gives way, as it were, to a more divine shape, suggesting a Bodhisattva seated in prayer.

This imagery is mirrored in one of the shrine's outbuildings, in which a massive stone statue of Kudô Mura is placed above the sacred *ofuro*. As at the waterfall, the sacred water source is normally inaccessible to regular worshippers—the *ofuro* container is covered, except when it is opened by followers to retrieve healing waters in small amounts. The foundress' form "stands guard" in a sense, over these waters—now turned into curative *kusuri* (medicine) to be used, not like ordinary water in ample quantities, but in very minute, judicious amounts.

The shrine's ritual specialists emphasize that the pilgrim's mind and bodily being are altered as she prays under the waterfall. The cascading water itself smooths out individual human variations and produces a more abstract heart-mind, moving the pilgrim toward a generalizable Bodhisattva configuration, suitable for guiding lesser beings through successive levels of awareness toward Buddhahood. This smoothing away of individual distinctions anticipates the trajectory of the soul after death, as an individual's identity is gradually assimilated into the house's collective *hotokesama* (ancestral spirit), who then divinely serve, and protect, the living. At the same time, the waterfall functions as an externalized projection of the heart-mind of the dedicated worshipper; here, she allows to come to light those aspects of her own psychic topography which have long been relegated to unconscious realms.

Conclusion: uncanny waters

Water presents itself as the most benign and neutral of substances, but its very transparency and neutrality (often insensible to smell or taste) renders it at times a potent signifier of precisely that which cannot be seen, especially those tableaus of our individual or collective past which we normally cannot allow ourselves to behold. Water at Akakura coveys an enduring, compelling sense of the strange familiarity of pre-Yamato indigenous energies. These waters may thus not only offer a chance to heal physical ills, but to re-awake and dramatize, if only distantly, the sociopolitical contradictions that can ail humanity. The sensations of communitas experienced at the waterfall, during the Dragon Princess rite, and around the boiling water ceremony (*kamado*), are so compelling precisely because they are an antidote, in microcosm, to the long under-acknowledged history of indigenous multi-ethnic presence that still haunts the ostensibly mono-ethnic Japanese collective imaginary.

Water itself, under certain circumstances, may enable the return of the repressed, including indigenous agency that has been long forgotten or put away, as well as psychic images and pressures long kept under control. To seek the waters, at many different levels, may occasion journeys of homecoming, where all is somehow familiar, yet oddly new again. Consuming, and being actively consumed by, sacred falling waters, tangibly refashions the developing mind, as it traverses domains where so much that has been forcibly hidden returns, unexpectedly, to light.

References

Abe, Ryuichi. 2016. Revisiting the Dragon Princess: Her Role in Medieval Engi Stories and their Implications in Reading the *Lotus Sutra*. *Japanese Journal of Religious Studies* 42(1):27–70.

Blacker, Carmen. 2004. *The Catalpa Bow: A Study of Shamanistic Practices in Japan*. New York: Routledge.

Freud, Sigmund. 1925 [1919]. The Uncanny. In *The Standard Edition of the Complete Works of Sigmund Freud*. Volume XVII (1917–1919). Translated from the German under the General Editorship of James Strachey, in collaboration with Anna Freud. London: Hogarth Press.

Schattschneider, Ellen. 2003. *Immortal Wishes: Labor and Transcendence on a Japanese Sacred Mountain*. Durham, NC: Duke University Press.

PART VIII

Popular pieties

The folk liturgies discussed throughout this volume are often in contrast, or even at odds, with official practices ordained by religious authorities. Devotions at sacred waters may be individualistic, specific to a clan or family, or an accretion of practices within a community across generations. While popular pieties can be highly localized, they often draw on more widespread paradigms and are regularly renegotiated with the evolving relevance of external influences. Considering the veneration of springs in Estonia as an aberration from European traditions, Heiki Valk sees their endurance in popular belief and their shrine-free natural appearance as resistant to multiple conquests and accompanying conversions to Roman Catholicism, Lutheranism and Orthodoxy. Recipients of votives and inspiring their own visitation rituals, Estonian springs were never Christianized; they remained sacred to local people, but never became holy. Martin Haigh examines the holy and healing wells of Wychwood Forest in England that once were the focus of community Palm Sunday festivals and are now engaged for nature therapy and by Newage and other alternative religious groups. In Poland, holy wells are overwhelmingly linked to the Virgin Mary. Wojciech Bedyński compares two sites associated with her apparitions. While five hundred years of devotions at one have remained mostly local in significance, veneration at the second (which began on Mary's birthday and at her instruction in 1877) became significant for Polish national identity during the country's partition, and pilgrimage there became an act of patriotism as well as piety. Examining holy well devotions in Post-Reformation Sweden as a dynamic form of popular Christian piety, Terese Zachrisson examines the case of St. Ingemo's Well to demonstrate how Swedish folk liturgies employed both aspects of pre-Reformation tradition and Lutheran teachings. The inclusive syncretism of water spirits such as the *naga* and Phra Uppakrut within Thai Buddhism is next considered by Rachelle Scott. Thai conceptions of *nam mon* (sacred water) can be critiqued as un-Buddhist, yet are also linked to religious authorities such as the monarch and the Buddha himself (who is said to have created and consecrated sacred wells in Thailand).

27

WITH SACRED SPRINGS, WITHOUT HOLY WELLS

The case of Estonia

Heiki Valk

Known in different parts of the world, sacred springs are also numerous east of the Baltic Sea—on the eastern fringes of occidental Europe. In this geographical area where historical, social and cultural processes were somewhat different than in the core areas of the European civilization, these sites have preserved some of their archaic features and meanings more vividly than in the central regions of Christian culture. This essay gives a brief insight into the topic on the basis of source material from Estonia where the tradition of sacred and offering springs survived into the twentieth century and is known in the present time. Most of these sites were used for healing practices but some were also believed to have higher supernatural powers. Ecclesiastical attitudes toward sacred and healing springs have differed in Estonia, as has popular faith in these sites. While Estonia was formerly a part of Catholic medieval Livonia and is presently Lutheran, sacred springs never converted. They did not become holy wells, have no Christian associations and retain their natural appearance without the shrines and superstructures that can characterize holy wells. The Orthodox Church, has, however, involved some of these springs within the Christian context.

Historical and confessional background

As late as 1200 AD, the eastern Baltic region—the territory of present-day Estonia, Latvia and Lithuania—formed an area where the Iron Age way of life still continued and pre-Christian religions were still practiced. These lands were neighbored in the West by the Catholic kingdoms of Sweden and Denmark and in the east by Orthodox Old Rus principalities. The seaway to Rus markets was attractive for German tradesmen who reached the Baltic Sea in the mid-twelfth century. Their attempts to get control over the waterways to Rus—the Daugava River in Latvia and the Gulf of Finland (north of Estonia)—culminated with the Livonian crusades. The territory of Estonia was brought within the realm of Western

Christianity in 1208–1227, being conquered from the south by the German colonists and crusaders, and from the north by the kingdom of Denmark (in 1219/1220) (Henricus de Lettis/Brundage, 2003).

The conquest of the area of present-day Estonia and Latvia resulted in the making of medieval Livonia—a confederation of small Catholic states—four bishoprics and the Livonian branch of the Teutonic Order which also acquired northern Estonia in 1346. In parallel to the conquest, the political, cultural, judicial and religious structures characteristic of medieval Western Europe were introduced in the newly Christianized areas. The conquest brought along a strong ethno-cultural polarization of the society where political, social and ecclesiastical power belonged to social nobility of German origin. The native elite lost its former position and identity or melted among the German-speaking nobility (Valk, 2009). The states of medieval Livonia collapsed as a result of the Russian invasion in 1558–1561. During the big Livonian War (1558–1583), the land was divided between Moscovian Russia, *Rzecszpospolita* (the commonwealth of Poland and Lithuania), Sweden and Denmark.

Southern Estonia remained Polish until 1625 when the land, together with the northern Latvia was conquered by the Swedes. During the Great Northern War (1700–1721), the Baltic provinces of Sweden were conquered by Russia in 1700–1710. Since then and until 1918, the territory of present-day Estonia and Latvia belonged to Russia. The ethno-social polarization of the society into German nobility and native (i.e. Estonian and Latvian lower classes) lasted until the early twentieth century.

The geographical distance from the cultural centers of Western Europe also shaped the socio-cultural climate of Estonia. From the thirteenth until the early twentieth century, cultural impacts from the core areas of Europe were mediated by the mainly German social nobility via towns, manors and the church organization. The reception of these cultural influences by native peasants was greatly hindered by ethno-social barriers until the time of national awakening in the mid-nineteenth century.

The Baltic states became independent in 1918, but were occupied by the Soviet Union in 1940. The occupation, temporarily replaced by that of Nazi Germany in 1941–1944, lasted until the re-gaining of the independence in 1991. Soviet occupation had a multifaceted impact on rural culture and the countryside. Although traditional farm life was destroyed in 1949 by forced transition to collective and state farms, isolation from modernization processes characteristic of the Nordic countries, as well as passive opposition to innovations, contributed to the preservation of tradition-based knowledge. Memories of the past, including awareness of sacred natural sites still survived among locals whose childhoods had passed on private farms. However, extensive land improvement which changed traditional landscapes into large fields of state and collective farms, and had involved ca. 85% of agricultural lands by the end of Soviet time, greatly reduced the number of folkloric sites. Many sacred springs were destroyed by bulldozers or drainage systems, or captured into metal or concrete pipes.

Local awareness about sacred sites has rapidly declined during recent decades. The countryside faces depopulation as the older generation (those born before the 1950s) dies or moves to live with children and grandchildren in towns. This is accompanied by the retreat and disappearance of place lore and the disruption of oral tradition. The topic of sacred springs of Estonia must also be regarded against the background of denominational history (changing faiths and doctrines). The Catholic period saw the gradual Christianization of the landscape of medieval Livonia. In addition to parish churches, the land was covered by a network of rural chapels by the 1420s. Big stone and timber crosses stood at roadsides and on local non-churchyard village cemeteries—a tradition which, although originating from the compromises of the crusade period, lasted until the early eighteenth century (Valk, 2001). Although Lutheran Reformation took place in the towns in 1525, the countryside remained Catholic until the establishment of the Swedish rule brought a formal transition to Lutheranism, the state religion of Sweden.

Political antagonism between Lutheran Sweden and Catholic Poland fostered a systematic fight by the Lutheran Church against the remains of Catholicism. The de-Catholicization of the country meant profound changes in the religious landscape: written data speak about the destruction of chapels and crosses. Popular assemblies on saints' days and burials on non-churchyard cemeteries were prohibited. Nevertheless, rudiments of popular Catholicism survived until the end of the Swedish rule and fully disappeared only by the 1820s.

The location of Estonia between two large Christian traditions also impacted the survival of sacred topography. Although belonging to the realm of Western Christianity, the Baltic countries border on Orthodox areas to the East. The confessional border between the Eastern and Western Churches also runs within Estonia and illustrates differences in confessional attitudes toward holy springs. The south-easternmost corner of Estonia, the Setomaa district has belonged to the Orthodox world since the Christianization. This area has a mixed population: the Setos, closely related to southern Estonians, have shared the land with the Russians for centuries. In addition, the Russian Empire strived to convert the Estonians from Lutheranism to Orthodox Christianity in the nineteenth century: numerous Orthodox congregations and churches were then founded in rural areas of Estonia.

Sacred springs in Estonia: number, distribution, general features

Sacred and/or healing springs are numerous in Estonia and a large amount of related data exists in Estonian folklore and archaeological archives. The tradition is also still known in the countryside in awareness of places and toponyms. Taking water and depositing coins as offerings is still practiced sporadically.

Although Estonia's sacred springs have been briefly considered by folklorists since the early twentieth century, the only systematic study of the topic is the archaeological graduate thesis of Toomas Tamla from 1974 (University of Tartu). As the topic concerned religion, further studies in the field were not approved by Soviet science authorities, and a short article could be published only in 1985 (Tamla, 1985). The survey, based on archaeological and more-easily-accessible folklore data, numbers 416 sacred springs in Estonia. Building on Tamla's work and adding information from the Database of Estonia's archaeological and lore sites held at the University of Tartu,[1] their number can now be estimated to be closer to 580. The real number would nevertheless be higher since not all have been recorded in the archives.

The total number of springs is actually estimated to be between 5,000 and 15,000 in Estonia, with about 3%–10% of them having been considered healing or sacred. The density of sacred springs in the country (45.339 km^2) is, on the average, 1 per 90 km^2. This is, however, greatly less than on the island of Ireland (70.280 km^2) with over 3,000 sacred springs (Ray, 2014:4), but more than in Latvia or Lithuania, where the numbers of sacred springs are ca. 100 and 150, respectively (Vaitkevičius, 2004:37).

The appearance of sacred and healing springs in Estonia depends on local landscapes and geological conditions. Although mostly emerging from rather flat land, in southern Estonia, they sometimes flow from outcrops of Devonian sandstone. Estonian sacred springs have retained their natural appearance, as a rule (Figures 27.1 and 27.2). Sometimes, these sites have turned into wells by being bordered with limestone or timber, but such impoundments are caused by practical purposes and not from cultural factors (i.e. not from aspirations to "cultivate" or "civilize" the sites, but to facilitate access to the water and to keep it clean). In Estonian popular practices, the external features of springs have never been accentuated to stress their special or religious meanings.

Toponymic evidence on sacred springs is diverse in Estonia. The springs often have no specific name but are named after adjacent farms or villages. A common name, referring to the healing functions, is *silmaallikas* (North Estonia) or *silmäläte* (South Estonia) which translates to "eye spring." In northern and western Estonia, larger sacred sites of pre-Christian tradition relate to the word *(h)iis* which designates pre-Christian sacred areas (Jonuks, 2007) and the name of the spring may

FIGURE 27.1 Saula Siniallik (Blue Spring), North Estonia. Photograph by the author.

FIGURE 27.2   Silmäläte (Eye Spring) in Tuderna, South Estonia. Photograph by the author.

emerge from the same stem: *hiis > hiieallikas*. In such cases, the border between a real micro-toponym (i.e. Hiieallikas) and indication of its location in a *hiis* site (or belonging to such group) remains unclear; this difference cannot be distinguished in spoken language. The name may also reflect general healing or offering functions (e.g. *Arstiallikas* means "doctor spring"; *Ohvriallikas* means "offering spring"). Many sacred springs have, however, unique individual names. Sometimes, the springs are attributed with the word *püha* (sacred). It also must be noted that the word *püha* usually does not correlate with the name "eye spring"; rather, it can refer to different levels of sacredness.

Functions and practices

Most of the sacred springs of Estonia (69%) are known for healing purposes and over two-thirds of these concern healing for the eyes (Tamla, 1985:127). As building chimneys on peasants' houses began only in the 1840s–1850s in Estonia, the need for eye healing due to smoke exposure was urgent and widespread.[2] Most often, washing or healing eyes is the only tradition related to the "eye springs," but some were once credited with even healing blindness.

The water of some springs was believed to heal skin diseases—hives, pimples, abscesses, measles, dandruff, papilloma, etc. Waters of different springs helped to heal wounds, ears, stomach ache, rheumatism, and even a case of leprosy is mentioned. Sometimes, the healing power is explained by the running of spring water toward the north or the east—a belief of Scandinavian background. Healing practices included drinking, washing and taking water home for drinking. Sometimes, it was considered necessary to wash or drink 3, 6 or 9 times. However, uttering Christian prayers for healing is not noted in folkloric data in Lutheran Estonia.

Often, but not always, gifts were offered to a spring for healing (most commonly a coin of small value). The earliest documented coin finds from the springs in Estonia are from the sixteenth century (Valk, 2015:21). In Estonian tradition, "silver white" (*hõbevalge*) was also offered into spring waters—this is silver dust scratched with a knife from some silver item, most often a coin or a brooch. More rarely, healing practices involved magic: in that to be healed, one must visit the spring alone or not look back when leaving. A most important factor, although not often stressed in folkloric data, is the need to believe in the supernatural healing help that a spring could offer.

The items left at springs may have different functions. It is possible to distinguish "real gifts," (i.e. those left for supernatural help) from those which acted merely as a means of magic transfer of diseases (i.e. those which had contacted with the diseased part of the body). These sites can have a precaution against removing such gifts; to do so would sometimes invite the same illness that prompted the deposition of the gifts. One might explain a thief's acquisition of the same illness through contagion, but the rational explanations do not work when the person who has taken gifts from the spring gets healed after bringing them back. Such cases do not make it possible to explain spring water healings only with practical or medical circumstances, but engage belief in supernatural factors.

Some springs were used not only for healing (and in rare cases for healing animals also), but were believed to provide assistance in broader terms of welfare and fortune. Petitioners might seek good luck with their households and cattle, and protection against other misfortunes beside diseases. Different gifts would be left with these petitions at sacred springs as compared with those left for healing. For this level of assistance, food or household products were offered (e.g. grain, wool or bread) and these might sometimes be "the first" or "new" piece of bread from a harvest or the first milking of a cow after the calf is weaned. The database contains rare notes of animal sacrifices and "the firstling" also related to qualifications for meat offerings.

A special site is Pühaläte Spring near Otepää, southern Estonia (Valk, 2015)—the source of the sacred river Võhandu. As late as in the 1640s, the locals considered the river to be the dwelling-place of Thunder to whom oxen were still sacrificed. Prior to that time, children were sacrificed in the case of long-lasting bad weather as noted in a book by Lutheran pastor Johann Gutslaff (1644). The same source notes punishments such as disease or even death for misbehavior in relation to the spring.

Supernatural springs might also predict the future. In the seventeenth century, the outcome of a planned enterprise could be foretold by throwing a coin into Pilistvere Uduallik Spring. If the coin floated on the water for a while, it meant good luck, but if it sank to the bottom immediately, this predicted failure (Westrén-Doll,

1926:14).[3] Water from the same spring was whisked over young women to make them more marriageable. Other springs could also bestow beauty, love and appeal.

Among the 416 Estonian sacred springs identified by Tamla, 12 were considered to be able to change the weather. The Siniallik (Blue Spring) of Laiuse was believed to give rain, if cleaned in a proper way. It could only be cleaned by three widows with the same name who wore either festive or white clothing and who brought bread, a broom and a songbook with them. Once when the spring was over-cleaned, the rain turned into a flood. In case of strong rains, hindering the flow of spring water by some means was deemed efficacious.

Springs had times when they were most powerful, for example Midsummer Eve, full moon (particularly a full moon that fell on Thursday), or at sunset. Using spring water in the moon light (particularly by that of an old moon) was considered good for healing. Springs could have multiple auspicious times for visitation and sometimes multiple roles. Their abilities were not always singular; several of them were multifunctional. The waters of eleven springs identified by Tamla were believed to have turned into alcohol (beer or vodka) on a certain day of the year, but we have no information about the beliefs or religico-magical practices associated with these sites.

The origins of the tradition of making offerings to Estonian springs are unknown. Although weapons and edged tools were deposited into Estonian water bodies since the Early Iron Age and into the Viking Age (Oras et al., 2018), this tradition of Scandinavian origin probably relates not to springs close to settlement sites, but to waters in mires and bogs. The earliest finds from sacred springs of Estonia, located at settlement sites are some eighth- to ninth-century spearheads, and there are also some jewelry items from the eleventh to thirteenth centuries (Tamla, 1985:137–139). Although the importance and number of sacred natural sites are considered to have greatly increased in Estonia only after the end of the Roman Iron Age and the Migration period (when cemeteries had lost their central place in cult and ritual activities, see Jonuks, 2009:317–320), the transcultural character of beliefs and rites related to sacred and healing springs suggests a much deeper temporal dimension.

Connections with Christianity and denominational aspects

Of special consideration are the connections of sacred and healing springs with Christianity and its denominations. The Estonian material enables us to see the peculiarities of the area of medieval Livonia, as well as internal differences of confessional character.

Areas of the Western Church

While sacred springs turned into holy wells in most European countries and became dedicated to (often local) saints, there is almost no folkloric and toponymic evidence about the connections of sacred springs with Christianity in Lutheran Estonia. Although the name of St. Olaf is often attached to sacred springs in Scandinavia, and such sites can bear the name of St. Mary (*Marienquelle* or *-brunnen*) or St. John

(*Johannisquelle*) in Germany, respective connections are almost fully missing in Estonia. On the contrary, the connection of springs with sacred areas of pre-Christian meaning and context (*hiis*-sites) survives in the toponymic evidence.

The situation has its roots already in the Catholic period. Although rural chapels were most numerous in the presently Lutheran areas of Estonia (as shown by written data and place names), connections between them and sacred springs do not emerge in folkloric and toponymic evidence. At the same time, data referring to former chapels does frequently relate to medieval village (or hamlet) cemeteries (Valk, 2001:24–25). Considering the information that does exist for the period, the lack of data linking churches and chapels with springs does not seem to derive simply from forgetting the tradition.

The missing connection with Christianity is the more noteworthy in that the blessing of water is important in the Catholic tradition, and this was so also in medieval Livonia. In 1585, the pope's legate, Antonio Possevino, described the religious practices of the Estonians and especially stressed the importance of using blessed water in their households (Possevino, 1973 [1585]:29–30). Even if blessed water originated from springs, there are no signs of their Christian dedication in the toponymic record.

The lack of human-made structures with Christian meaning is characteristic of Estonian sacred springs. If a spring was lined (mostly with timber), this derives from practical needs, not from the wish to stress the sacredness of the site. There also exists neither written nor folkloric or toponymic evidence referring to images or statues of saints at sacred springs. This speaks to major differences in the attitudes of the Catholic Church in relation to sacred springs, on the one hand, in medieval Livonia and, on the other hand, in Scandinavia, Germany, central, western and southern Europe and on the British Isles. When using the dichotomy of "nature/wilderness" *versus* "culture/civilization," the sacred springs of Estonia definitely represent the uncultivated or "wild" part of the world. The reason sacred springs were not integrated within Christian practice was, evidently, the generally neutral or tolerant attitude of the Catholic Church toward sacred natural sites in medieval Livonia, partly reflected also in the written sources (Pluskowski et al., 2019).

As noted earlier, the Lutheran church fought actively against the rudiments of popular Catholicism. Although data from the seventeenth century repeatedly includes complaints about the use of village cemeteries, and about popular assemblies at chapel sites and ruins, springs are rarely mentioned among "superstitious" sites. Most likely, the reason is that ritual activities at springs were of personal, not of social character, and the practical functions of springs, i.e. using them as sources of clean water, duly overshadowed their ritual aspects, at least in the eyes of ecclesiastical authorities. The lack of connections with Catholicism likewise probably reduced the interest of Lutheran church authorities in controlling sacred springs. In broad strokes, the situation is similar in Lutheran areas of Latvia which have a similar religious history to Estonia's. Thus, the attitude of the church organization toward sacred and healing springs can be regarded as factually indifferent in the area of medieval Livonia both during the Catholic and Lutheran periods. Additionally, no popular initiative for the Christianization of the sites seems to have developed.

The Orthodox tradition

As noted earlier, the Orthodox tradition in rural areas of Estonia occurs in two different contexts: (1) Setomaa (inhabited by the Seto people and which has been Orthodox since Christianization) (Valk and Grouchina, 2017), and (2) Orthodox congregations founded in Lutheran areas in the nineteenth century. Among people who changed their confession in the nineteenth century, traditions related to springs do not differ from that of the Lutheran Estonians.

In both Orthodox contexts, however, some sacred springs, which may have been venerated in pre-Christian times, *have* been brought into Orthodox practices. A famed site is the holy well at Petchory (Petseri) monastery which is used for healing by thousands of visitors and pilgrims. The church of Maly (Mõla), as well as two churches of Izborsk (Irboska) stand on healing springs, and the spring near Värska church has been Christianized, as well. Also in Lutheran areas of Estonia, sacred or healing springs at some nineteenth-century Orthodox churches (e.g. Kavilda and Kastolatsi) have been brought within ecclesiastical contexts; their waters have been blessed on Epiphany (January 6th/19th) which is an important part of the Orthodox tradition. At the monastery of Kuremäe (Pühtitsa) in north-eastern Estonia, the holy spring has acquired a pilgrims' bathing house.

When located apart from congregational churches, the springs of the Seto areas in Setomaa have however remained distinct from Orthodox Christian tradition and have retained their natural appearance. Locally sacred springs generally do not bear the names of saints or church holidays, and are not related to Orthodox village chapels, although there are some exceptions. In this, the Seto tradition differs from that of northwestern Russia where sacred springs are closely bound with Orthodox Christianity. However, the Seto people have sometimes also followed certain Orthodox ritual practices (crossing themselves or reciting a prayer) before taking water from sacred or healing springs.

Discussion: attitudes and perceptions

Two levels of contact with the supernatural can be distinguished in popular practices at Estonian sacred springs. The first involves practical or magic rites without active and direct communication with the supernatural: performing visitation rituals in a right way, in a right place, and sometimes also at the right time can produce the desired result. This category involves most of the healing practices, but also magic transfer of diseases via something which has contacted the diseased place. The second, higher level of supernatural contact is communication with a definite partner—either the animated, living spring itself or some supernatural being.

When comparing Estonian folklore on sacred natural sites, a distinct difference between springs and other sacred natural sites can be noted. While sacrilege or misbehavior related to sacred stones, trees and groves often results in a supernatural punishment, similar reprisals for transgressions at springs are rare. This difference in recorded folklore perhaps means that Estonian springs were places of lesser sacredness with weaker supernatural powers than other sacred sites in nature.

Although popular perceptions of these sites are poorly documented in recorded folklore, four different views of sacred springs can be distinguished here:

1. as a special nature site/part of living nature (probably animatistically perceived),
2. as an animated living being,
3. as a locus and living-place of local supernatural beings (spirits, fairies, gods), and
4. as a portal, gateway or altar—a place to encounter and communicate with supernatural beings and/or sacredness.

In Estonian folklore, the first two perceptions clearly predominate. Distinguishing between them is perhaps a convention for the present-day researcher more than a reality for people of the traditional world view. Animatistic perceptions are reflected in stories in which a spring disappears after being mistreated. Group 3 (that of local spring fairies) is most rare, while folkloric data about less than ten sites in Lutheran Estonia related to group 4 is known. Five of these mention the pre-Christian celestial or thunder god Uku, while a Christian layer appears at two springs of [St.] Mary (Maarja). Springs that serve as communication sites with other popular Christian saints are unknown in Estonia. Thus, it was not important for the natives to provide sacred springs with a Christian layer of values because these sites continued to be powerful and helpful on the basis of formerly existing tradition. Assistance from Christian sources of power was sought with offerings and prayers at churches and chapels, but former, pre-Christian practices also persisted. The lack of a Christian superstratum for springs does not indicate a rejection of Christian values among the natives of medieval Livonia; the numerous rural chapels as well as popular assemblies at Christian sanctuaries on holidays indicate acceptance of the faith. However, from the user's perspective, tools for different things seem to have been in different pockets.

As sacred springs became so strongly associated with the cult of saints in most of Christian Europe, the lack of such connections in medieval Livonia must have historical reasons and cannot be explained by the ecclesiastical attitudes alone. The unique process of Christianization must have played an essential role. While in Scandinavia the native elite led faith change, the situation was greatly different in Livonia: the new religion arrived by force in crusades. Although the archaeological record demonstrates that Christian ideology had diffused among Estonians immediately before the crusades (Jonuks and Kurisoo, 2013), church organization was imported from outside through conquest. This perhaps explains one of the peculiarities of Livonia's medieval Christianity: the lack of local saints (Selart and Mänd, 2018).[4] The archaeological record testifies to two parallel worlds in medieval Livonia— those of the German elite, following European cultural pattern, and that of the native peasantry. Sacred natural sites, including sacred springs, represent the latter.

Conclusions

The folkloric and toponymic evidence shows clear differences in attitudes toward sacred and healing springs within Estonia, between the popular and ecclesiastical levels and in the Western (Catholic/Lutheran) and Eastern (Orthodox) traditions. Folkloric and toponymic data from Estonian territories (Catholic since the early thirteenth century and Lutheran since the seventeenth century) indicates that sacred springs remained outside the Christianized landscape and largely untouched by the cult of saints. In the Orthodox context, sacred natural sites acquired a certain Christian superstrate in both ecclesiastical practice and popular attitudes.

The sacredness of Estonian springs differs greatly from that of Western European sites and those in Eastern European Orthodox areas. Although related to magic rites, ritual practices and beliefs, sacred springs have never been closely bound with Christian tradition. In Estonia (except for some sites in Orthodox Setomaa), springs were considered sacred and healing as part of nature; their sacredness emerges from their natural qualities and/or pre-Christian veneration. The position of the native people on spring sacrality is also expressed through the state of sacred and healing springs: they exist mostly in their natural form, having not been converted into holy wells. The lack of holy wells in what was medieval Livonia is a considerable difference from Scandinavia, Germany and most of Western Europe and reflects the specific way in which the region was Christianized.

Notes

1 The composite database linked to Estonia's National Register of Monuments aims to involve all existing information from archaeological and folklore archives. From the parishes for which data have been processed by the present time, 295 sacred springs have been recorded, whereby the former survey presents 211 springs from the same area, so that the growth of about 40% can be suggested.
2 Nowadays, the need for washing eyes after being in smoke can be experienced after visiting chimneyless smoke-filled saunas which are still popular in southern Estonia and included in UNESCO's list of intangible heritage.
3 Evidently, the coins were thin and light Swedish Schillings minted in Riga in the 1630s–1660s.
4 The only exception is Meinhard († 1196), the first bishop of Livonia, canonized in 1993.

References

Henricus de Lettis. [2003]. *The Chronicle of Henry of Livonia.* Translated and edited by James A. Brundage. New York; Columbia University Press.

Jonuks, Tõnno. 2007. Holy Groves in Estonian Religion. *Estonian Journal of Archaeology*, 11:30–35.

Jonuks, Tõnno. 2009. *Eesti muinasusund* [Prehistoric Religion of Estonia]. Tartu: Dissertationes Archaeologiae Universitatis Tartuensis 2, Tartu University Press.

Jonuks, Tõnno and Tuuli Kurisoo. 2013. To Be on Not to Be … a Christian. Some New Perspectives on Understanding the Christianization of Estonia. *Folklore. Electronic Journal of Folklore* 55:69–98.

Oras, Ester, Aivar Kriiska, Andrus Kimber, Kristiina Paavel and Taisi Juus. 2018. Kohtla-Vanaküla Weapons and Tools Deposit: An Iron Age Sacrificial Site in North-East Estonia. *Estonian Journal of Archaeology* 1:5–31.

Pluskowski, Aleksander, Heiki Valk and Sewerin Szczepanski. 2019. Theocratic Rule, Native Agency and the Transformation of the Sacred Landscapes of the Eastern Baltic after the Crusades. *Landscapes* 20:1–21. doi: 10.1080/14662035.2018.1561009

Possevino, Antonio. 1973 [1585]. *Kiri Mantova hertsoginnale=Lettera alla Duchessa di Mantova.* Tõlked: Vello Salo; sissejuhatus ja kommentaar: Vello Helk. Roma: Maarjamaa.

Ray, Celeste. 2014. *The Origins of Irelands Holy Wells*. Oxford: Archaeopress.

Selart, Anti and Anu Mänd. 2018. Livonia – a region without local saints? In *Symbolic Identity and the Cultural Memory of Saints,* edited by Nils Holger Petersen, Anu Mänd, Sebastian Salvado and Tracey R. Sands. Newcastle upon Tyne: Cambridge Scholars Publishing, 91–122.

Tamla, Toomas. 1985. Kultuslikud allikad Eestis [Cultic springs in Estonia]. In *Rahvasuust kirjapanekuni. Uurimusi rahvaluule proosaloomingust ja kogumisloost,* edited by Ülo Tedre. Eesti NSV Teaduste Akadeemia Emakeele Seltsi Toimetised 17: 122–146, Tallinn: Eesti NSV Teaduste Akadeemia.

Vaitkevičius, Vykintas. 2004. *Studies into the Balts' Sacred Places*. BAR International Series; 1228. Oxford: John and Erica Hedges Ltd.

Valk, Heiki. 2001. *Rural Cemeteries of Southern Estonia 1225–1800 AD*, 2nd edition. CCC Papers, 3. Visby and Tartu: Gotland University College, Centre for Baltic Studies; University of Tartu.

Valk, Heiki. 2009. From the Iron Age to the Middle Ages. Local Nobility and Cultural Changes in Estonia in the 13th Century. In *The Reception of Medieval Europe in the Baltic Sea region. Papers of the XIIth Visby Symposium held at Gotland University, Visby*, edited by Jörn Staecker, 273–292. Acta Visbyensia, XII. Visby: Gotland University Press.

Valk, Heiki. 2015. Pühast Võhandust, Pühalättest ja ohvrijärvest Otepää lähistel [Sacred Waters: The River Võhandu, Spring Pühaläte and Sacrificial Lake near Otepää]. *Ajalooline Ajakiri* 1–2:3–37.

Valk, Heiki and Lioubov Grouchina. 2017. Les sources sacrées du Setomaa [The sacred springs of Setomaa]. In *Missions du Musée de l'Homme en Estonie. Boris Vildé et Léonide Zouroff au Setomaa (1937–1938)*, edited by Tatiana Benfoughal, Olga Fishman and Heiki Valk, 667–683. Paris: Muséum National d'Historie Naturelle Publications Scientifiques.

Westrén-Doll. August von. 1926. Abgötterey zu Ausgang der schwedischen und Beginn der Russischen Zeit. In *Sitzungsberichte der Gelehrten Estnischen Gesellschaft 1925*, 7–25. Tartu: Gelehrte Estnische Gesellschaft.

28

THE HOLY WELLS OF WYCHWOOD FOREST, ENGLAND

Martin Haigh

Healing wells have long played a role in the folklore of Wychwood Forest. Some, like Bridewell, with ancient, pre-Christian and pre-Roman roots, remain active in the present day, although today there are few votive offerings and their healing functions largely forgotten. Until the mid-twentieth century, community engagement focused on Palm Sunday festivals, when local villagers processed to Bridewell and other wells to make curative Spanish Water, a mixture of well-water, liquorice, sugar and/or peppermint. Today, this tradition persists at the wells of Cornbury Park estate, but until 1990, Palm Sunday was the only day that the public was allowed access to its "Secret Forest," a large Wychwood fragment. Eventually, this event became a campaign for greater public access and declined once this was conceded. Subsequently, the tradition has recovered some spiritual associations through engagement with varied interest and alternative religious groups.

Wychwood is a former Royal hunting forest, a place where the deer hunting has been reserved for the monarch since at least the eleventh century. The "forest," of course, was never wholly wooded, but rather a patchwork that included fields, meadows and heath. In the Norman period, Wychwood had physical boundaries that ranged from the River Glyme in the East, the River Windrush in the Southwest, the River Thames (or Isis) in the Southeast and the Sars Brook in the North. In the following century, the Plantagenet kings expanded the forest boundaries, but the modern Wychwood Project landscape restoration initiative uses the Norman boundaries (Flitter and Spicer, 2000). Today, the Wychwood area is contained by West Oxfordshire District where it ranges from a few kilometres west and north of Oxford City to the Gloucestershire border.

In the heart of Wychwood, downslope from the little church at Wilcote, a processional avenue of ancient, battered and often hollowed-out ash trees leads towards a small drystone-walled circular enclosure that houses one of Wychwood's holy wells. Bridewell, also called "Lady's Well," is a small part of a spring line that extends for 50–100 m along the valley. In October 2015, the well seemed neglected and forgotten. Accessed by a loose wire gate, its interior was crowded with nettles and overgrown by gnarled elder trees, but the clear waters of the well inside were still visible. If it were possible to classify holy wells as "dead" or "alive," meaning that they show signs of spiritual usage, then this was one that had died in recent years. Its walls were intact, the fragile gate was in place, if only to keep sheep out, but the well itself was untended.

For those who recognise them, holy wells are, of course, liminal spaces—places where the mundane and supernatural intersect—places that connect beliefs and cosmologies with the banalities of everyday life (Ray, 2014). Here, emerging from solid stone, life-giving or better still, curative mineralised waters emerge perennially, a blessing to the world as wonderful as the rain that falls from heaven. In times when rocks and trees were awarded special significance to some community or clan, it is hardly a wonder that such places became linked with the supernatural.

In this case, the clue is in the name, Bridewell, whose origins, here, relate less to the Irish Saint Brigid (British: St. Bride) than perhaps to the earlier Indo-European "Celtic" Goddess Brigantia "whose very name may be far older than the Celts" (Phillips, 1976:3). Brigantia/Brigid, the exalted celestial (cf. Sanskrit: बृहती, *bṛhati*, meaning mighty, lofty, brilliant, from the dhatu √*bṛh* meaning expanding, shining and speaking), shares her festival day, Imbolc, with the onset of spring and her associations are with the spring season, fertility, healing, as well as with the Brigantes tribe of northern England. She was a goddess of springs, streams, water, fire and smith-craft, but she was also the one who leant over every cradle. St. Brigid's miracles mainly relate to healing and the tasks of women. Similarly, Brigantia was a goddess of protection and wisdom; in the twentieth century, she became very popular with Neo-pagans (Condren, 2010). However, the most miraculous aspect of Brideswell and of the other, more or less, still "holy" wells in Wychwood's environs is that they have survived at all, despite all of the changes in society and culture since the Iron Age. How could a well, perhaps originally sacred to a pre-Christian goddess, have remained "holy" into the present day (Rattue, 1995)? In this case, the tale is long, enigmatic, and only its bare bones are known.

History

It has long been thought that local water cults originated with pre-Iron Age peoples—certain rivers and water deities in the "Celtic" lands seem to possess pre-Celtic names (MacCulloch, 1911). Very little is known about what happened before the arrival of the Iron Age Dobunni people in the Wychwood area. However, archaeological finds suggest that it was well peopled in their time (Hooke, 1985). In Wychwood, as across England, the toponyms of rivers and valleys often retain Celtic elements, as, for example, at Combe village. Combe, like the Welsh *Cwm* (and Proto-Celtic **kumbā*), means valley. Similarly, Wychwood's River Windrush combines Old English (OE) and older Celtic roots, which translate as white or pure (*gwyn*) and filled with sedge (**reisko-*) (Ekwall, 1928). In any case, the Dobunni held waters sacred and many places in the Dobunni's lands honour St. Bride.

Bridewell survived the coming of the Romans, who inhabited a villa complex at North Leigh (2.5 km east) until the fifth century and who built Akeman Street (1 km north), the Roman road that cuts Wychwood Forest in half. In the

Romano-British world, Brigantia became linked with the Roman goddesses Minerva and Victoria. Bridewell also survived the arrival of Christianity, established by AD 312 in Civitas Dobunnorum, Corinium (now Cirencester), 45 km southwest of Bridewell. However, as elsewhere, its later survival may be linked to the *Epistola ad Melitum* (AD 601) of Pope Gregory the Great, whose advice, to the mission of St. Augustine to convert the Anglo-Saxons (AD 596–653), was that pagan sacred sites should not be destroyed but converted to Christian purpose (Marcus, 1997).

Bridewell also survived conquest by the initially pagan Saxons and Angles, the Hwicce for whom Wychwood is named. The oldest known reference to Wychwood, *Hwicca wudu*, appears in a Charter dated AD 862 (Hooke, 1985). However, the Anglo-Saxon chronicles describe the capture of Eynsham, 9.5 km southeast of Bridewell, in AD 571, and the lands beyond in AD 577 after the battle of Dyrham, where the British kings of the three cities, Bath, Gloucester and Cirencester, were defeated (Garmonsway, 1953). This conquest may have involved less ethnic cleansing than elsewhere; the territory seems to have retained some British connections. Indeed, Coates (2013) argues that the very word *hwicce* has a British origin (meaning "most excellent ones" cf. "people of the sacred cauldron," Yeates, 2008), while archaeological evidence suggests that the Hwicce included a large British element alongside Anglo-Saxon settlers with Middle Anglian links (Wilson, 1972). By AD 628, when the area became dominated by King Penda's Angles of the Kingdom of Mercia, the territory appears to have been Christian (Hooke, 1985). Bede's history of Anglo-Saxon conversions does not mention the Hwicce, perhaps because Christianity persisted in the Hwicce lands, although Manco (1998) thinks that conversion came from British sources to the west.

Bridewell also survived disapproval and suppression of "pagan practices" by Christian authorities from the tenth century (Bord and Bord, 1985). However, several holy wells around Wychwood have Saxon heritage, including Holwell, Abbey Well, Eynsham and, possibly, Minster Lovell's Ladywell (see Table 28.1) and holy wells remained an important aspect of England's landscape into the late medieval period. Bridewell even survived the Reformation of King Henry VIII and the later rise of Protestantism, which disapproved of saint cults. However, healing wells retained their function in folk medicine. It required the emergence of the National Health Service, after 1948, to undermine this long-lived healing role. Today, even healing wells are neglected and "despite the heroic efforts of a group of local historians, this aspect of British heritage is in rapid decline" (Walsham, 1999). However, in Wychwood, a few endure.

Holy wells of Wychwood

In India's Uttarakhand, where Hinduism has shaped sacred topographies for millennia, almost every spring has an associated deity (often local); Iron Age Britain would likely have had a similar indigenous system. Certainly, this notion seems to sustain hobbyists who catalogue holy wells. In Wychwood's environs, almost every spring and well is claimed as a sometime-holy well. These claims derive from historical charters and other ancient texts, the often doubtful etymology of place names, simple association with other sacred sites, and more rarely from recorded usage.

However, even among those with recorded folklore, few of Wychwood's holy wells remain active sacred sites.

Certainly, some long-disused sites are well documented. For example, the holy well near Asthall Leigh, central Wychwood, is attested in both mediaeval charters (thirteenth century) and local place names. However, sometimes place-name etymology can be unhelpful. For example, Holwell village, near Burford, 20 km southwest of Bridewell, claims its village pond as a Saxon holy well. The OE word for a stream is *w(i)elle*, while *holh* means hollow, so Holwell could simply mean stream in a hollow; *hālig* would mean holy, but this would more likely yield the prefix *hal*. Fortunately, Alexander (1912) finds this site named Halliwelle in a document from AD 1086, so its credentials seem secure.

Sometimes, the well's name may be evidence, for example: Ladywell, but equally, some names imply the opposite of holiness (e.g. Fulwell, near Enstone, meaning foul well, or "Slut's Well," probably meaning muddy well as a slut originally was one of slovenly appearance). Similarly, Fair Rosamund's Well in Woodstock's Blenheim Palace Park, which appears a textbook holy well, owes much to the landscaping of Capability Brown (1763–1773). Around AD 1155, it was a bathing place for Rosamund Clifford, mistress of King Henry II; hardly, a spiritual association, probably the wishing well on Blenheim Palace's Water Terrace, where visitors throw pennies, is closer to a holy well in spirit.

FIGURE 28.1 Bridewell (the Lady's Well), near Wilcote. Photograph by author.

The location may indicate that a well was formerly a sacred site. Holy wells, long disfavoured by the established church in England, tend not to be found in church grounds that did not pre-date Protestantism, but at a discrete distance (Bord and Bord, 1985). Ladywell at Minster Lovell is enigmatic and undocumented. However, many "Lady wells" are sacred springs (ibid) and this one is just 250 m from the Saxon church of St. Kenelm, a Mercian king, whose martyrdom is associated with the miraculous appearance of many sacred springs, including that at his popular mediaeval pilgrimage site at Winchcombe, Gloucestershire, 50 km to the west (Cope, 2013).

Celebrations: Spanish Water

In neighbouring Gloucestershire, Bisley village supports an annual, Ascension Day, "Blessing of the Wells" involving flowers and celebration, a ritual introduced in 1863 by the Reverend Thomas Keble, brother of Keble College Oxford's founder. Well-dressings are also well known in Derbyshire and Malvern. On the Summer Solstice, June 2018, the trees of Avebury, Wiltshire were draped with cloth clooties (clouties, cloughties), a practice common in Cornwall, but not Wychwood.

However, until the late twentieth century, on Palm Sunday, local people would process to Bridewell and the wells in nearby Cornbury Park. Their purpose was to collect well-water, which they mixed with peppermint sweets and liquorice (also known as "Spanish") to make a curative elixir, some to be consumed on the day, some to be stored for use during the year. Sprigs of long willow leaves were worn in lieu of palms and the village girls received new straw hats for this event, which were adorned with spring flowers primroses and violets (Mason, 1929). The origin of this tradition is not known and it is not much practised outside Wychwood and Derbyshire (Roud, 2006). Charles Dickens called Spanish-liquorice-water (also known as "sugarelly") "that intoxicating fluid" (1861:52). However, this mixture of powdered liquorice root with water and sugar was pungent rather than alcoholic and had a medicinal reputation. Liquorice has antiviral, antibacterial, anti-inflammatory, antioxidant and antidepressant medicinal qualities. It was a traditional treatment against common ailments including asthma and bronchitis.

However, Bridewell's Palm Sunday Spanish Water custom vanished between 1956 and 1984 (Bord, 2008). Today, this tradition persists only at the three holy wells in Cornbury Park, just 5 km northwest of Bridewell. Originally part of the Royal Hunting Forest of Wychwood, Cornbury Park estate was gifted to the Earl of Danby by King Charles I in AD 1642. Via several other aristocratic lineages, the Park passed down to the present owner Lord Rotherwick. All this while, this private estate was closed to outsiders. Consequently, a large 870 ha fragment of ancient semi-natural broad-leaved woodland survived. Today, most of this area is designated for planning purposes as a Site of Special Scientific Interest (SSSI), while 262 ha is a National Nature Reserve. In respect to "ancient" tradition however, local villagers were allowed to walk the footpaths to its holy well on Palm Sunday. Here, as at Bridewell, young girls, especially, would mix well-water with liquorice and sweets to make "curative" Spanish Water (Varner, 2009).

Restricted access was key to the persistence of the Palm Sunday festival in Cornbury Park. Until 1990, Palm Sunday was the one day each year that the public could enter Wychwood's "Secret Forest." Chipperfield records the reminiscences of a local resident:

> Because the forest was accessible only once a year and because of local and national publicity, the mystique of this ancient woodland, by the late 1980s, was attracting hundreds of people for the Palm Sunday walks ... It was possible to meet people from Cornwall one minute, then a family from Durham a few yards later, and cars would line both sides of the narrow lanes near the entry (2010)

Latterly, the walk became associated with political lobbying to make public access more available and, in 1990 the land owner Lord Rotherwick opened a public footpath from Finstock in the west to Charlbury in the east. The forest no longer "secret" and political goals met, the event declined. Today, Cornbury Park's Palm Sunday event persists, albeit intermittently, through the activities of local community groups, ramblers walking groups and spiritual seekers. On Palm Sunday 2017, the Christian mystics of the Anglican Wychwood Forest Church visited both the Wort Well and chalybeate Iron (Spa) Well in Cornbury Park. The congregation is part of the "Forest Church" movement that emphasises both the benefits of spending time in Nature and past traditions in which sacred places and practices were out-of-doors. In 2014, the Palm Sunday walk was undertaken by the Green Friends of the Hindu spiritual leader Mata Amritanandamayi, better known as *Amma* (Mother), who see Nature as a form of God.

TABLE 28.1 Selected holy wells and sacred springs of Wychwood and environs

Location	Function and source literature and map reference*
Badgers Well, Appleton	This eye healing well is south of the Thames in a nicely maintained drystone housing with pool (Woods, 2006). Map: SP4360201485
Bridewell (aka Lady's Well), Wilcote	On Palm Sundays into the twentieth century, children from Wilcote and Finstock would process to this healing Lady's Well with bottles containing liquorice and sugar to fill them with well-water and make Spanish Water—a practice thought ancient in origin if not form (Colvin et al., 2006). About 800m downhill and south of Wilcote church, at the end of an avenue of ancient Ash trees, the well is also associated with local tales of a ghostly coach and black dog (Briggs, 1974; Baggs et al., 1990, Rattue, 1990). Map: SP374148
Cyder Well, in Cornbury Park	One of three unadorned healing springs in Cornbury Park estate. The waters are used to make the Spanish Liquor cure-all (see Wort Well) into the present decade (see also Rattue, 1990). Map: SP336171
Well of Fair Rosamond, Woodstock	Formerly called Everswell, because it flowed always, it was re-named for King Henry II's mistress and became a celebrated part of Capability Brown's eighteenth-century landscaping of Blenheim Palace's parklands (Bord and Bord, 1985). Map: SP436164

Location	Function and source literature and map reference
Holewelle (aka Abbey Well), Eynsham	Holewelle, just south of Abbey Farm barn, is associated with Eynsham's Abbey, a Saxon Minster founded in 1005 (Rattue, 1990). Now in private gardens, the holy well featured in the "Eynsham in Bloom" open gardens event in June 2018. Map: SP431091
Holywell Barn, Asthall Leigh	The well outside Holywell Barn is likely that identified in the early thirteenth-century parish. Located at the end of Holywell Street, 1.5 km west of Asthall Leigh. The parish is crossed by Akeman Street and local Roman activity included a bath-house at Worsham Mill (Colvin et al., 2006). Map: SP295124
Holwell near Westwell and Burford	The church pond is locally known as a Saxon holy well. The earliest place-name evidence is *Halliwelle* (AD 1086) for "holy well" (O.E. *se haliga wiella*: Alexander, 1912:129). The site is thought to be the deep pond at the village's southern end, next to which a probably twelfth-century baptismal chapel was built (Rattue, 1990). Map: SP 232091
Physic Well, Cumnor	A mile west of Cumnor Village, south of the former Thames ferry at Bablock Hythe, this small square stone-walled healing well was called "long disused" in 1806, but was being cleaned and maintained as recently as 2011 (see also Rattue, 2006). In 1667 this "Physic" Well, was "much frequented by scholars of Oxford in search of a pick-me-up" (Mais, 1956:1). Map: SP441043
Serpent's Well, Chipping Norton	"Near Chipping Norton, in Oxfordshire, AD 1349, was a serpent with two heads, faces like women, and great wings after the manner of a bat" (William Henderson quoted in Pennick, 1997). The well was mentioned in field listings from the AD 1770 Enclosure Acts (Bennett, 2008). Map SP3127—but the true location, if any, is unknown
Spa or Iron Well, Cornbury Park	Chalybeate healing well, marked by a stone wall and square margin in the nineteenth century. The water was/is used to make the Spanish Liquor cure-all on Palm Sunday; one of the three holy wells in Cornbury Park estate. Map: SP348174

★ SP names the twenty-five 100km square maps of the UK's national grid. See: https://www.ordnancesurvey.co.uk/resources/maps-and-geographic-resources/the-national-grid.html.

Other holy wells of Wychwood:

- Curbridge possibly had a now lost well known as Ashmore or Kettle Well (Rattue, 1990) or even the Colwell Spring (SP317084), mistakenly called Coral Spring on some Ordnance Survey maps and modern planning documents (Gelling, 1953:310–316). Curbridge has a street called Well Lane.
- Baywell, Charlbury (SP357188) (Rattue, 1993). Blindwell, Crawley (SP330146) meaning overgrown well, close to two bowl barrows from 2400 to 1500 BC.
- Boar Well (SP343090) Witney (Rattue, 1990).
- Bradwell–near Holwell (SP244 086) mentioned in AD 997 (Alexander, 1912:61).
- Cold Well–Ascott under Wychwood (SP299173), Rattue (1990); Gelling (1953:336). There is a Coldwell brook so the "well" may simply be a stream from the OE *w(i)ella*.
- Cooper's Well, Ducklington (SP354073) (Rattue, 1993).
- Crane's Well, Cornwell (SP270271), Rattue (1990); Gelling (1953:346).
- Ease Well, Ramsden (SP342152) (also Cold Well; Crop Well; Hor Well with unknown locations). These are said to be healing wells. Ramsden lies on Akeman Street and there was a Roman villa, maybe bath-house, at Easwell Copse and an earlier bowl barrow just to the west.
- Fordwells, Asthall (SP309129), named from the spring and pool in the south-west corner of Lowbarrow copse, called Sewkeford (i.e. "Seofeca's ford") in 1300, (Gelling, 1953:300; Rattue, 1990; Colvin, 2006).

- Gadding Well, Finstock (SP355160). A traditional starting point for the Palm Sunday procession to Bridewell; "gadding" indicates movement from place to place, but also possibly a Gospel Oak via *Gatesdeneheved* (Gelling, 1954:389).
- Holy Well, Hanborough (SP426132), associated with a Gospel Oak (Bennett, n.d.). Rattue (1990) also mentions a Wotmell Well. These locations are unknown, although a spring is marked on the Ordnance Survey map on the edge of Pinsley Wood (a Wychwood fragment just north of Hanborough Church).
- Lady Well, Great Rollright (SP328142) is near the Rollright Stones stone circle (Gelling, 1954; Rattue, 1990).
- Ladywell, Minster Lovell (SP337116), 400m east of St. Kenelm's Church and north of Doctors Ditch.
- Leo's Rest Well, Charlbury (SP375193) just 200m southwest of the scheduled monument earthwork that may have been a Romano-British temple.
- Madley Well, possibly Blindwell, Eynsham Park, North Leigh.
- Pear Tree Well, Cassington (SP443120) Gelling (1953:253) thought "Pear" may be the OE *pyr* meaning stream.
- Ruddy Well, Stonesfield (SP394183), from OE *Rothere* meaning cattle Gelling (1953:281); piped to a village tap from 1897 until 1979 (Baggs et al., 1983).
- Seven Springs, Swinbrook (SP285143) Deerhurst priory established a hermitage at Lockeslegh in Taynton Woods by the 1330s, possibly on the site of earthworks near Seven Springs (Rattue, 1990; Colvin et al., 2006).
- Slut's Well, Wooton (SP439203), possibly St. Luke's Well but more likely OE "*slyte*" meaning muddy (Rattue, 1990).
- Showel Spring, Crawley, OE *seofan wiella* meaning seven streams (SP3421331), (Gelling, 1953:346; Rattue, 1990).
- Spurnell's Spring (or Well), Charlbury (SP392201), near the Romano-British site in Ditchley Park, this drains to the west to a pond called Devil's Pool (Rattue, 1990).

In the larger Wychwood environs, several holy wells receive attention from New Age spiritual seekers, and one is newly been (re-)created. The holy well at Holycombe, Whichford (Hwicce's ford), was (re)discovered and promoted by a "local geomancer and an itinerant dowser" (www.holycombe.com/). Meaning is always a work in progress. It may owe debts to folk and written memory, but it remains something defined in the present day by those who invest something of themselves in its preservation. In Wychwood, as elsewhere, the number of active holy wells is small. Those still preserved by village-based folk traditions are also fading away as those village communities transform into dormitory suburbs for incomers working in Oxford and elsewhere. However, Bridewell remains connected to healing through the work of the neighbouring Bridewell Organic Garden and vineyard, which provides a mental health recovery service involving "therapeutic horticulture." Like the wells of Cornbury Park, it also retains a glimmer of life through the activities of New Agers and those keen to preserve local history (Walsham, 1999).

On an initial visit to Bridewell, the author found little evidence of current engagement with the site as sacred. Returning later, the nearby elder tree had been pruned and the nettles cleared from the well enclosure. Over the clear water, a small stone pendant nestled discretely in a niche of the encircling stone wall. The well is still being tended years later in 2019. Nearby trees are now adorned with four weather-beaten clooties. Clearly, Bridewell remains "alive" for someone.

References

Alexander, Henry. 1912. *The Place-Names of Oxfordshire: Their Origin and Development.* Oxford: Clarendon.

Baggs, A. P., William John Blair, Eleanor Chance, Christina Colvin, Janet Cooper, C. J. Day, Nesta Selwyn and A. Tomkinson. 1983. Parishes: Stonesfield. In *A History of the County of Oxford: Volume 11, Wootton Hundred (Northern Part)*, edited by Alan Crossley, 181–194. London: Victoria County History.

Baggs, A. P., William John Blair, Eleanor Chance, Christina Colvin, Janet Cooper, C. J. Day, Nesta Selwyn and S. C. Townley. 1990. Wilcote: Introduction. In *A History of the County of Oxford: Volume 12, Wootton Hundred (South) Including Woodstock*, edited by Alan Crossley and C. R. Elrington, 296–299, London: Victoria County History.

Bennett, Paul n.d. Trees. *The Northern Antiquarian.* Available at: https://megalithix.word press.com/sites/trees/ (accessed 21 Nov 2019).

Bennett, Paul (2008) Serpent's Well, Chipping Norton, Oxfordshire. *The Northern Antiquarian*, September 18, 2008. Available at: https://megalithix.wordpress.com/2008/09/12/serpents-well-chipping-norton/ (accessed 21 Nov. 2019).

Bord, Janet. 2008. *Holy Wells in Britain—A Guide.* Leicester: Heart of Albion.

Bord, Janet and Colin Bord. 1985. *Sacred Waters: Holy Wells and Water Lore in Britain and Ireland.* London: Paladin Grafton.

Briggs, Katherine M. 1974. *The Folklore of the Cotswolds.* Lanham, MD: Rowman and Littlefield.

Cary, John. 1793. *Cary's New and Correct English Atlas Being a New Set of County Maps from Actual Surveys.* London: John Cary.

Chipperfield, John. 2010. Walkers Flocked to Explore 'Secret Forest' at Wychwood. *Oxford Mail*, 28th June.

Coates, Richard. 2013. The Name of the Hwicce: A Discussion. *Anglo-Saxon England* 42:51–61.

Colvin, Christina, Carol Cragoe, Veronica Ortenberg, R.B. Peberdy, Nesta Selwyn and Elizabeth Williamson. 2006. Bampton Hundred. In *A History of the County of Oxford, Volume 15: Part Three)*, edited by Simon Townley, 36–37. London: Victoria County History.

Condren, Mary. 2010. Brigit, Matron of Poetry, Healing, Smithwork and Mercy: Female Divinity in a European Wisdom Tradition. *Journal of the European Society of Women in Theological Research* 18:5–30.

Cope, Phil. 2013. *Borderlands.* Cardiff: Seren.

Dickens, Charles. 1861. *Great Expectations.* Peterboro: Broadview.

Ekwall, Eilert. 1928. English River-names. Oxford, Clarendon Press.

Flitter, Belinda, and Alan Spicer. 2000. The Wychwood Project. In *Discovering Wychwood: An Illustrated History and Guide*, edited by Charles Keighley, 98–110. Charlbury: Wychwood.

Garmonsway, George N. 1953. The Anglo-Saxon Chronicle (trans). London, Dent.

Gelling, Margaret. 1953. *The Place-Names of Oxfordshire. English Place Names Society.* Cambridge: Cambridge University Press.

Hooke, Della. 1985. *The Anglo-Saxon Landscape: The Kingdom of the Hwicce.* Manchester: Manchester University Press.

MacCulloch, John Arnott. 1911. *The Religion of the Ancient Celts.* Edinburgh: T and T Clark.

Mais, Stuart Petre Brodie. 1956. Frank Cheeseman in Discussion with S.P.B. Mais. www.bodley.ox.ac.uk/external/cumnor/documents/cheesman-1956.htm.

Manco, Jean. 1998. Saxon Bath: The legacy of Rome and the Saxon Rebirth. *Bath History* 7:27–55.

Marcus, Robert A. 1997. *Gregory the Great and His World.* Cambridge: Cambridge University Press.

Mason, Violet. 1929. Scraps of English Folklore, XIX. *Oxfordshire Folklore* 40(4):374–384.

Pennick, Nigel. 1997. *Dragons of the West.* Chieveley: Capall Bann.

Phillips, Guy R. 1976. *Brigantia: A Mysteriography.* London: Routledge.

Rattue, James. 1990. An Inventory of Ancient and Holy Wells in Oxfordshire. *Oxoniensia* 55:172–176

Rattue, James. 1993. An Inventory of Oxfordshire Wells: additions. *Oxoniensia* 57:354.

Rattue, James. 1995. *The Living Stream: Holy Wells in Historical Context.* Woodbridge: Boydell.

Ray, Celeste. 2014. *The Origins of Ireland's Holy Wells.* Oxford: Archaeopress/Oxbow.

Roud, Steve. 2006. *The English Year.* Harmondsworth: Penguin.

Varner, Gary R. 2009. *Sacred Wells: A Study in the History, Meaning, and Mythology of Holy Wells and Waters.* New York: Algora.

Walsham, Alexandra. 1999. Reforming the Waters: Holy Wells and Healing Springs in Protestant England. *Studies in Church History-Subsidia* 12:227–255.

Wilson, Mary E. 1972. The Archaeological Evidence of the Hwiccian Area. Doctoral thesis, Durham University.

Yeates, Stephen J. 2008. *The Tribe of Witches: The Religion of the Dobunni and Hwicce.* Oxford: Oxbow.

29

HOLY WELLS AND TREES IN POLAND AS AN ELEMENT OF LOCAL AND NATIONAL IDENTITY

Wojciech Bedyński

Many studies have proven that the cult of water, in particular sacred wells, is a common phenomenon for most of the world's cultures and religions (Logan, 1980; Ray, 2014). The cult of trees, springs, wells and lakes has pre-Christian connotations, which through *interpretatio Christiana* entered the new faith in its local dimensions.[1] Polish holy wells and trees are presumably a good example, although it is always difficult, if not impossible, to trace this process. Holy trees and holy waters were important to heathen inhabitants of what are now the regions of Warmia and Mazury where old Prussian tribes worshiped their gods in sacred groves (Hochleitner, 2005:490). When studying holy wells (and trees) in Poland, even when associated with fairly recent Marian apparitions, we seem to touch something very old, a certainly pre-Christian and universal veneration.

Holy wells have played an important role in Polish popular religiosity. The cult of water (and often trees) is present in almost all Marian sanctuaries in Poland. The most famous Polish sanctuary of Our Lady is at the Luminous Mount in Częstochowa, where hundreds of thousands of pilgrims journey every year (Jackowski and Kaszowski, 1996). Legend says that when a band of robbers attacked the local monastery in 1430 and stole the icon of the Madonna, their horses refused to budge from the spot. They slashed the picture with their swords and threw it aside. In the place where the icon fell, water miraculously started to flow. From that time, the water had healing powers. Other sanctuaries dedicated to the Virgin Mary are also known for their holy water sources, as at Studzieniczna, Grabarka,[2] Licheń or Gietrzwałd.

The use of holy water was part of pilgrimage rituals. People approached the well with empty bottles to bring the water back to their homes as a gift for relatives, especially the old or infirm who are unable to participate in pilgrimage. They also pray with the rosary, which is later often left as a votive on a fence or trees by the well. Sometimes, individuals wash their faces with the holy water or may wash white handkerchiefs that they hang on surrounding trees.[3] As Mircea Eliade wrote in his famous *Sacred and Profane*, the sacred is manifested in very simple objects, like stones, wells or trees (1959b:11–12). These simple places of hierophanies are found almost everywhere in the world. The tree, the well and the stone often have close associations in Poland and elsewhere (Bedyński and Mazur-Hanaj, 2011).

Gietrzwałd and Święta Lipka are two sanctuaries associated with the cult of Virgin Mary. Both are situated in the North of Poland in the so-called "Recovered Lands" that were once part of Germany. Święta Lipka is much older and the place cult may have preceded the appearance of the Christian faith in the region. While historical sources note that there was formerly a holy well at the site, today there is no sign of it. Two lakes exist on either side of the sanctuary and are connected with a small stream. The name of the shrine, Święta Lipka, literally means "Sacred Lime Tree." In the region of Mazury, this shrine resisted Reformation processes and remained a pilgrimage center for people from the region and from more distant areas. The cult has never been officially recognized by the Roman Catholic Church.

The holy well at Gietrzwałd in Warmia is unusual in being a well blessed by an apparition. The nineteenth-century apparitions of the Virgin Mary there were well documented in the press of the time which detailed the holy well's origins. The apparitions occurred between June 27th and September 16th in 1877 (Brzozowski, 2009:143–144). The main participants are also well known: the children to whom the Virgin appeared were the 13-year-old Justyna Szafryńska and 12-year-old Barbara Samulowska. The "Bright Lady" revealed herself on a maple tree at the site. Gietrzwałd is the only apparition site in Poland that is officially recognized by the Church and is one of just 12 such places in the world (Spiss, 2007:61).

Historical context

> Will the Catholic Church in the Polish Kingdom be liberated?
> Yes, if the people truly pray, then the Church will not be persecuted, and the orphaned parishes will receive priests.
>
> *(fragment of the Gietrzwałd revelations, 1877)*

Polish Catholicism had been a crucial factor in defending national identity in confrontation with dominant political powers. For over a century, from 1795 to 1918 (with short intervals during Napoleonic wars and Polish national uprisings), Poland was absent from the maps of Europe. Several generations of Poles lived under partitions and experienced Germanization or Russification which included politically supported Lutheranism or Orthodox Christianity. Resistance was strengthened simply by adherence to Polish Catholicism.

When Polish lands were divided into three parts ruled by Russian, Austro-Hungarian and German (Prussian) Empires, the Catholic Church was virtually the only universal institution that unified Poles. When Polish was forbidden at school in Prussia (1874), the church was also the only public place where people could freely use their language. As the chancellor of the new German Empire, Otto von Bismarck introduced the policy of *Kulturkampf* (culture struggle), which was directed against the Catholic Church in general, but particularly against the Polish minority in the state (Tylor, 1969:124). Poles who did not have German citizenship were forced to leave the country (1885–1890). In 1873, some of the priests in Warmia and Mazury were forced to leave their parishes (Trzeciakowski, 1970:173).

Two regions lying in the former German province of Eastern Prussia, Warmia (home to the holy well at Gietrzwałd) and Mazury (the location of the sanctuary at Święta Lipka), had very different histories. Although Polish cultural elements were present there, Mazury has never belonged to Poland.[4] Warmia was under the Polish crown between 1466 and 1772, but fell to Prussian control with the first partitions. While Prussia became Lutheran, Warmia resisted the Reformation when it reached this part of Europe in 1525.[5] The local "holy land," Warmia was a "Catholic peninsula in Protestant Prussian duchy" (Ewertowski, 2010:111). As elsewhere in Europe, adherence to Catholicism or Protestantism was formative of local and national identity.

The year 1877 was very special for Polish Catholicism and national consciousness. After the failure of the January Uprising against Russian rule (1863–1864), repressions were severe: thousands of Poles were killed in fighting or executed and many more were sent in exile to Siberia. The Russians ultimately canceled the autonomy of the Polish Kingdom in 1867 and even the name was abolished. After 1868, parish books had to be written in Russian and Catholic monasteries were closed which broke diplomatic relations between the tsar and the pope. Pope Pius IX supported Polish Catholics and expelled the Russian ambassador from the Vatican. In 1877, Pius celebrated the 50th anniversary of his episcopal ordination and, encouraging a non-violent struggle for independence, received a group of Polish pilgrims from all three partitions (Bielawny, 2018:46–47). This first national pilgrimage of over 600 Poles to the Apostolic See marked the beginning of "Positivism" in partitioned Poland (a social movement that awakened national consciousness in provinces and encouraged folk masses as resistance to all Germanization or Russification attempts). Only three weeks after the audience in Rome, the Gietrzwałd apparitions began.

Gietrzwałd

It is difficult to overestimate the importance of the Gietrzwałd apparitions of the Virgin Mary for Catholic public opinion in the end of the nineteenth century. In the year of the one hundredth anniversary of Polish Independence, a 2018 book by Krzysztof Bielawny was even entitled *Niepodległość wyszła z Gietrzwałdu* (*Independence came from Gietrzwałd*). Unlike the apparitions at Święta Lipka, those at Gietrzwałd have a strong political context. The Virgin Mary's appearance on a maple tree in 1877 in Warmia came at the peak of *Kulturkampf* when some priests had been expelled from their parishes and even imprisoned.

What happened in the small Warmian village Dittrichswalde (Gietrzwałd) between late June and early September 1877? On June 27th, a 13-year-old girl, Justyna Szafryńska, was walking home with her mother to Nowy Młyn, a nearby village, after passing her last exam before first communion. They paused to pray at the ordained time for evening prayer (9PM), but when her mother resumed walking, she found that her daughter had not followed her. She called to her and Justyna replied "Wait, mother, I will just see what is so white on the tree." This scene was witnessed by a priest Augustyn Weichsel, who asked the girl to come closer to the maple tree.

She later said that she was the Bright Lady sitting on a throne and an angel coming from the heaven. The angel bowed before the Lady and the vision disappeared (Rosłan, 1994:4).

The next day, Justyna visited the tree with a few friends and again saw the Bright Lady with angels, as did 12-year-old Barbara Samulowska. The Lady told them that she was the Virgin Mary and that she would remain in that place for two months. The girls asked that she might give healing for the sick and Mary told them that she wanted a chapel built with the image of the Passion and a figure of the Immaculate Conception. She also ordered the people to pray the rosary. Her daily reappearances attracted more and more people to the site and on their last day, September 16th, 1877, over 15 thousand people were said to have participated in the chapel dedication (Rosłan, 1994:11).[6]

Unlike veneration of holy wells elsewhere, well veneration started in Gietrzwałd on a known date: the 8th of September, 1877. Fr. Franz Hipler's publication in the same year on the apparitions gives us a quite detailed description of the holy well's origins (2017:54). It was the idea of the parish priest to have the young visionaries ask the Virgin Mary to bless the water of the nearby well. According to Hipler's narration, the well had long been used by the inhabitants of the village for their cattle until being abandoned and buried around 1870.

On July 24th, the children asked Mary to bless jars of water placed under "the tree of revelations." They asked if the people could bring water and carry it during the rosary, drink it and whether that water would cure those who were sick. For all these questions, the Bright Lady answered "yes." Hearing that, the priest had the girls ask if the water of the well could be blessed. On the 12th of August, the Virgin Mary replied "later." The same answer came on the 7th of September. Finally on the next day, 8th September, Mary herself told girls to inform the priest that if he wanted the well to be blessed that day, he should come before the evening rosary to the well with other priests and the visionaries. They should be there at seven and pray the Loretan litany.[7] About 50 people gathered by the well and prayed together. Suddenly, the visionaries saw the Lady as before on the tree. After the Loretan litany finished, the priests sang "Salve Regina," then "O Sanctissima" and the "Magnificat" and the vision ended for the day. Those gathered around the well heard strange voices and witnessed unusual weather phenomena, including strong wind, and they were afraid (Rosłan, 1994:11). The visionaries assured the crowd that the Bright Lady blessed the well and then the people. From that day, miracles started to happen after people drank the well's waters (Hipler, 2017:54–55).

The majority of miracles noted just after apparitions were connected with the water from the holy well. The other healing artifacts were fragments of the maple tree (leaves or bark). A contemporary account documents 14 such cases, adding that many more were noticed (Hipler, 2017:75). In fact, many are claimed in recent years (Rosłan, 1994:21–31):

> A thirteen-year-old girl called Olga Stach from Lidzbark was blind in one eye. After using Gietrzwałd water and praying for five days, she regained her sight. A 53 year old worker had been hit by a large branch and in result suffered from involuntary nodding of the head. All medical actions were ineffective.

FIGURE 29.1 Gietrzwałd holy well with queue waiting for the access to the well. Photo by author.

On September 8th he went on pilgrimage to Gietrzwałd, participated in the service, took water from the well and a leaf from the maple tree. He drank the water and put the leaf on his neck. After that he found himself cured.
Anna Bracławska from the village Schattens near Olsztyn was slowly becoming blind. Her mother pilgrimaged to Gietrzwałd for her intention on the 4th of November. She returned with the holy water and a maple leaf and started a 9 day novena to Our Lady. After this time, her daughter could see again.

(Hipler, 2017:71–73)

Gietrzwałd is called the "Polish Lourdes" not only because the character of the apparitions of the Virgin Mary is similar, but also because the site's reputation and role for this part of Europe are comparable. There are many Marian sanctuaries in Poland. Some of them are famous for miracles, icons and holy wells, but most of them are very old and date back to the Middle Ages. The Gietrzwałd well blessing via apparitions is more contemporary and well documented.

Święta Lipka

In the region of Mazury, but in the same part of contemporary Poland, is another famous Marian sanctuary—Święta Lipka. Veneration of the Virgin Mary and pilgrimages there are traced back to the fourteenth or early fifteenth century. According to the local legend (Spiss, 2007:90), Mary appeared to a man sentenced to death on the eve of execution. Although she rebuked him that he had not loved her through his life as she had loved him, she promised to save him. She gave him a piece of wood and a knife and instructed him to make a figurine of her and then hang it on the first linden tree he would meet on his way between the towns of Kętrzyn and Reszel. He had never carved before and there was very little light, but he did what the Lady told him to do. In the morning when the executioner raised the axe to cut off his head, the figurine fell from the bosom of his coat. It was so beautiful that the executioner inquired about it and was amazed that it had been made by a human. The man was given freedom and the executioner gave him back the wooden sculpture. He did what the Virgin Mary told him to do and he found a big linden tree by a stream and climbed the tree to hang the figurine.

This, according to the legend, was a beginning of the sanctuary where there was a holy well.[8] The subsequently-constructed church now stands in a place where a small stream of water flows into a lake and had to be constructed over wet ground on stilts. Miracles were reported including recoveries from serious diseases and regained sight. Animals were even said to kneel and pray at the site (Paszenda, 2008:20). When the Reformation began in the area (1525), the holy tree was cut and the figurine thrown into Wirowe Lake. The chapel was destroyed and the tree was even replaced by a gallows to scare the remaining Catholics. In 1619, the Polish king's secretary Stefan Sadorski bought Święta Lipka and rebuilt the chapel and gave it to the Jesuits (Paszenda, 1998:139). Święta Lipka has since remained a place of pilgrimage, but of a more local character than Gietrzwałd.

The healing holy well was still visited in the late seventeenth century and beyond (Paszenda, 2008:148). Well waters were carried home by pilgrims in hopes of cures, particularly for diseases of the eyes. In 1732, the well was enclosed with a wooden wall and a roof. A small figure representing that which had originally hung on the

FIGURE 29.2 Święta Lipka, the bigger lake. Photo by author.

linden tree was placed over the well. The wooden shrine can be seen on a photo from 1938, but the well was no longer actively venerated. The well was then lost, but an excavation in 1968 revealed a wooden platform hammered deeply into the wet ground at the site (Paszenda, 2008:149). While Częstochowa is the most famous Marian sanctuary in Poland (and one of the biggest in the world), Święta Lipka has been called the "Częstochowa of the North."

Local and national identity

Cultural landscapes are generally layered, but particularly so in multicultural regions such as Warmia and Mazury. As Tim Ingold has described them, landscapes contain the deeds of multiple generations and they exist in the minds and imaginations of individuals and nations (Ingold, 1993:152). Single landscapes can have dual or competing narratives depending on ethnic and religious identity and in relation to faith or a lack thereof in miracles and apparitions, as in Warmia and Mazury (Selin, 2003:99).

The two sacred well sites considered here reveal an interesting tension. The older sacred place, of more local appeal, Święta Lipka, was less inscribed by Polish cultural and political struggles from the end of the nineteenth century. The pilgrimage there has a half a millennium-long tradition, during which borders varied and access was sometimes impossible (for example, after 1920). The narrative of the place remained religious rather than political. In contrast, the narratives about Gietrzwałd explicitly addressed Polish national identity and it was underlined that the Virgin Mary had spoken in the Polish language during her appearances (Hipler, 2017:29). Gietrzwałd attracted over a million pilgrims within the first four years after the apparitions, which is a staggering figure considering that the Polish population in all three partitions was no larger than ten million in the period (Bielawny, 2018:11–12). Pilgrims came from Warmia, from the Russian partition, from Lithuania, Silesia and Lubelszczyzna because the message resonated not only spiritually, but politically and socially. Therefore, it became a manifesto of Polish identity on a cross-partition scale.

This differing local/national character of the two sanctuaries is evident even now. While Święta Lipka has magnificent Baroque architecture, it is a pilgrimage landscape that remains more self-contained and symbolic of local events. Gietrzwałd is a landscape now shaped by an elaborate infrastructure for pilgrim groups (including eating places, book stores and pilgrim hostels). Each weekend is like a religious fair at which pilgrims may obtain holy water from the well, devotional articles, and also candies, cakes and other Warmian products. The site draws pilgrims from across Poland, and also from around the world, particularly among the Polish diaspora.

Conclusion

Popular piety, such as devotion to holy wells or trees, revelations of the Virgin Mary, the cults of local saints and services in the Polish language, was a strong focus for Polish national and cultural identity through times of the partitions. Pursuing a pilgrimage was not only an act of piety, but also of patriotism. In Poland, holy wells are strongly connected with the cult of the Virgin Mary.[9] They are present in most, if not all, of the Marian sanctuaries around the country, such as Licheń, Studzieniczna, the Orthodox Grabarka, and the biggest and most important—Luminous Mountain in Częstochowa. Many of them lay in the areas where Polish sovereignty and identity were threatened. Święta Lipka, for example, lies only 500 m from the historical border between Catholic and Polish Warmia and Protestant and German Mazury. While Gietrzwałd and Święta Lipka are very different in character and historical context, they both illustrate Polish popular piety and Marian devotion manifested in the cult of sacred wells and trees.

Notes

1 See, for example, Grafdon et al. (2010:485) and Zucchelli (2016).
2 A sacred place of the Orthodox Church in Poland.
3 According to Paweł Pytka, this custom is a borrowing from Eastern Christianity and symbolizes leaving your suffering and illness behind (2010:294).
4 Although Polish culture was very present there due to the proximity of borders and strong immigration dating back to late Middle Ages.
5 The last Grand Master of the Teutonic Knights, Albrecht von Brandenburg-Ansbach (Hohenzollern) secularized his country and became Lutheran himself. At the same time, he recognized the authority of the Polish king, making Prussia a Polish fief. Warmia, which was then already a domain of the bishop as an integral part of the Kingdom, resisted Reformation and remained predominantly Catholic. This situation continued also after the partitions of the Polish-Lithuanian Commonwealth.
6 Meanwhile, Elżbieta Bylitewska from Woryty, and Katarzyna Wieczorek from Nowy Młyn, also claimed visions, but their claims were later disproved (Rosłan, 1994:16; Hipler, 2017:20). The girls asked many questions of the Virgin, but she mainly answered those about faith issues and advised them that the Church would not be persecuted and that they should choose a monastic life (Rosłan, 1994:11). The revelations were thought to provide divine guidance on relations with the Protestant population and to encourage the dedication of masses for their conversion (ibid:10).
7 The sixteenth-century Litany of the Blessed Virgin Mary.
8 Some have argued that the site had pre-Christian sacrality (Paszenda, 2008:25).
9 Not all of them, of course, are dedicated to her, but more are compared to those in either Ireland or Brittany. The most well-known Polish holy wells are those connected with Marian sanctuaries.

References

Bedyński, Wojciech and Remigiusz Mazur-Hanaj. 2011. *The Tree, the Well and the Stone*. Warsaw: In Crudo.

Bielawny, Krzysztof. 2018. *Niepodległość wyszła z Gietrzwałdu*. Warsaw: SPES.

Brzozowski, Kazimierz. 2009. Sługa Boża siostra Barbara Samulowska–wizjonerka z Gietrzwałdu. *Salvatoris Mater* 11:143–150.

Eliade, Mircea. 1959. *The Sacred and the Profane: The Nature of Religion*. Translated by Willard R. Trask. New York: Brace and World.

Ewertowski, Stefan. 2010. Kulturowy i gospodarczy wymiar "świętych miejsc" region Warmii i Mazur. *Studia Warmińskie* 47:109–122.

Grafdon, Anthony, Salvatore Settis and Glenn W. Most. 2010. *The Classical Tradition*. Cambridge, MA: Harvard University Press.

Hipler, Franz. 2017. *Objawienia Matki Boskiej w Gietrzwałdzie dla ludu katolickiego podług urzędowych dokumentów spisane*. Dittrichswalde: Wichert (reprint of the original publication from 1877).

Hochleitner, Janusz. 2005. Ziemia pruska w przekazach hagiograficznych poświęconych św. Wojciechowi (do XV wieku). *Komunikaty Warmińsko-Mazurskie* 4:485–491.

Ingold, Tim. 1993. The Temporality of the Landscape. *World Archeology* 25, No. 2:152–174.

Jackowski, Antoni and Ludwik Kaszowski. 1996. Jasna Góra w systemie ośrodków pielgrzymkowych świata. *Peregrinus Cracoviensis* 3:171–191.

Logan, Patrick. 1980. *The Holy Wells of Ireland*. Gerrards Cross: Colin Smythe.

Paszenda, Jerzy. 1998. *Pielgrzymowanie do Świętej Lipki dawniej i dziś. Peregrinus Cracoviensis* 6:137–162.

Paszenda, Jerzy. 2008. *Święta Lipka. Monografia*. Kraków: Wydawn.

Pytka, Paweł. 2010. Święte źródła prawosławia w krajobrazie wschodniego pogranicza Polski. *Problemy Ekologii Krajobrazu* 26:285–296.

Ray, Celeste. 2014. *The Origins of Ireland's Holy Wells*. Oxford: Archaeopress.

Rosłan, Jan. 1994. *Sanktuarium Matki Bożej w Gietrzwałdzie*. Tarnów: Wydział Duszpasterstwa Ogólnego Kurii Diecezjalnej.

Selin, Helaine, ed. 2003. *Nature across cultures. Views of Nature and Environment in non-Western Cultures*. Berlin: Springer.

Spiss, Maria. 2007. *Objawienia maryjne w Polsce*. Cracow: Wydawnictwo M.

Traba, Robert. 2015. *Regionalna" czy "narodowa*. In *Czas przekraczania granic*, edited by Iwona Liżewska, Kazimierz Brakoniecki and Robert Traba, 15–20. Warsaw: Narodowe Centrum Kultury.

Trzeciakowski, Lech. 1970. *Kulturkampf w zaborze pruskim*. Poznań: Wydawnictwo Poznańskie.

Tylor, Alan J. P. 1969. *Bismarck: The Man and the Statesman*. New York: Alfred A. Knopf.

Zucchelli, Christine. 2016. *Sacred Trees of Ireland*. Cork: Wilton, Co.; Collins Press.

30

VISITING HOLY WELLS IN SEVENTEENTH-CENTURY SWEDEN

The case of St. Ingemo's Well in Dala

Terese Zachrisson

This essay sheds shed light on a largely neglected aspect of popular piety in post-Reformation Sweden by closely examining one of the most well-documented, seventeenth-century examples of Swedish holy wells. Despite various attempts by clerical and secular authorities to undermine the cult of holy wells, traditional practices survived throughout the early modern period. Holy wells in a Scandinavian context have often been interpreted as "pagan survivals"—as a tradition that people of the middle ages and early modern eras engaged in as a parallel to, rather than as part of, their every-day Christian beliefs (for a recent example, see Kaliff and Mattes, 2017:169–170, 188). In contrast, this article argues that the cult of holy wells in Sweden needs to be understood as a dynamic part of popular Christian piety, with intermingling elements from both official and unofficial Christian practices.

Hundreds—if not thousands—of sacred wells and springs are scattered throughout the vast landscape of Sweden. In most cases, vague references to their names and locations are all we have left and the beliefs and traditions associated with these natural sanctuaries are forever lost to us. But luckily, there are some exceptions in this silence. One of the most interesting cases of the popular cult of holy wells, and one on which we have an unusual amount of information, is the well of St. Ingemo in the parish of Dala in the province of Västergötland.

In Sweden, most of these wells and springs were known as *offerkällor* (offering springs)—a name that highlights the centrality of votive practices associated with visits to such places. This distinguishes the Swedish tradition in relation to the other Scandinavian kingdoms, in which terminologies are more aligned with the English concept of holy wells (*hellig kilde* in Norwegian and *helligkilde* in Danish). This difference in terminology has sometimes obscured the fact that these sites were indeed considered holy, and that other traditions apart from the offerings were of great importance. There are also a number of springs and wells associated with the Trinity, the saints and the holy cross, where we lack evidence of votive practices. Therefore, I will use the term *holy well* as an analytical category, even if it is only sporadically evident in contemporary sources.

Interestingly, Christian law codes from Medieval Sweden (of which the earliest dates to the 1220s) explicitly forbade all cultic practices at groves, stones, hills and mounds—but never wells and springs (Hellström, 1996:200–201). This is a contrast to corresponding laws from England and parts of continental Europe (Walsham, 2011:37). If wells and springs indeed were part of Scandinavian pre-Christian belief and practice, they do not seem to have been important enough to worry early Christian legislators—the cult was only banned after the Reformation. Whether or not holy wells were ever a major aspect of medieval Christianity in the North has also been the subject of some scholarly debate. Danish historians Susanne Andersen and Jens C. V. Johansen have both argued that medieval evidence for the cult of holy wells in Denmark is scarce and that the cult did not become widespread until the post-Reformation era (Andersen, 1985:34; Johansen, 1997:69). The same scarcity can be noted in the Swedish material as well, but there are exceptions. One prominent example is St. Helen's Well in Skövde, which is mentioned in an *officium* from 1281 as well as in two letters of indulgence issued in 1373 and 1425 (Pernler, 2007:59–60, 122). It also seems unlikely that Scandinavia would have differed that much from other parts of Western Christendom in related matters.

In the province of Västergötland, on the border between the two parishes of Dala and Ljunghem, there is a natural spring partly covered with a flat limestone rock. For centuries, the water of the spring was considered to have healing properties. In later folklore records collected in the early twentieth century, the well is generally referred to as the Chapel Well (*Sw. Kapellkällan*). But before that it seems to have been associated with a locally venerated female saint by the name of Ingemo, of which we have next to no knowledge today. It has even been suggested that the name does not even refer to a saint at all, but that it is a form of folk etymology of a local place name (Linde, 1955:32–33). Compensation for the lack of sources regarding the mysterious saint is found in the unusual number of early sources discussing the ritual practices that took place at the site in the seventeenth century. Thanks to an odd combination of favourable circumstances, more sources are preserved regarding this particular well than almost any other holy well in Sweden (perhaps with the exception of the Holy Cross Well (*Helga Kors källa*) in Svinnegarn and St. Olaf's well (*Sankt Olofs källa*) on Österlen).

The earliest mention of St. Ingemo's Well is a short paragraph in an ordinance by Superintendent Sylvester Phrygius of the Skara diocese, issued at some point in the 1610s. It states that anyone visiting either of the wells of St. Helen, St. Ingemo, St. Thomas or of the Holy Spirit, for the purpose of healing, was to confess their sin publicly and pay a fine of nine *mark* (Hall, 1932:16). St. Ingemo's Well is then mentioned on several occasions in sources from the latter part of the seventeenth century. In a 1667 antiquarian report[1] by vicar Erik Kristoffersson, we are told that a woman named Ingemo had lived in the parish long ago, and that she had been "worshipped for a goddess" by the populace. By the ruins of a chapel once dedicated to her, there was a spring, to which "many of the simple-minded" still made offerings of coins and pins in order to cure their ailments. Furthermore, in close proximity to the well, within the old churchyard walls, there was a grove of old birch trees that were held in "such sanctity, that no one dare[d] break from them as much as a twig." Among these birches and ruins, people were erecting crosses, onto which they placed items of clothing (Ståhle, 1969:216–217).

In a letter to the cathedral chapter dated May 23, 1681, some of the villagers themselves describe the traditions surrounding the old shrine (Regional State Archives in Gothenburg, Skara domkapitel EVI:17:1). Apparently, Bishop Andreas Omenius had demanded an explanation from some trustworthy parishioners about the "superstitions" that had taken place at St. Ingemo's Well. The letter opens with a short statement about St. Ingemo herself, and in contrast to the pagan-sounding term "goddess" used earlier by the vicar, the villagers themselves refer to her as a "holy woman"—thus placing her in a more legitimate Christian context. Then, the ritual practised at the well and the associated grove of birches is described in detail. First, the supplicants were to circumambulate the grove thrice. Then, they went to the well itself, where they drank, washed and made offerings of coins, bread and other items. When this was done, they went back to the grove, where they were to kneel by a tree stump and make their prayers. The ritual was then concluded with supplicants leaving clothing worn by the sick at the tree stump.

Further, the villagers state that the site was visited primarily on Midsummer and during Pentecost. They were also careful to emphasise that these superstitions were not as common as before, and that many visited the well "without any superstition." Only nine *öre* in copper coins had been retrieved from the well the previous Pentecost, whereas in earlier years, the offerings could amount to two *daler* (≈64 *öre*). The truthfulness of this claim is difficult to attest, since the villagers had an obvious interest in making the bishop believe that the cult was on the wane in order to evade eventual fines and interventions. In the statement issued by the vicar only 14 years prior to the letter, there were no attempts to conceal the on-going practices. The letter ends with the transcription of a prayer to be read when conducting the rituals, something that makes the case completely unique in the Swedish material. The prayer shares characteristics with the multitude of spells and charms recollected from early modern witch trials, but it is of importance to note that the villagers themselves specifically refer to the text as a "prayer."

Fördenskuldh är iag kommen hijt	For this reason I am come,
att sökia hielp med största flijt	To seek help most eagerly
Widh thenna Brund och thenna Lundh	at this well and this grove
Som mången gör i thenna stundh	as many do at this time
Dess heliga watn iagh dricke inn	Its holy water I drink
Så ock bestryker skadan min	And anoint my injury
Medh Knäfall för S. Ingemo kiäll	Kneeling at St. Ingemo's Well
gör iagh min bön i thenna qwäll	I say my prayers on this night
Och håppas på the heliges nådh	And I hope for the grace of the holy ones,
aff hwilken wist hielp kommer ifrå	from where help is sure to come.
Tree ressor Lunden går iagh omkringh	Three courses around the grove I walk
Mitt lilla offer wti den ringh	My little offering in that ring

Nedlägger iagh tacknämmeligh	I place there gratefully
Och beder the låta behaga sigh	And pray that they will be pleased
Min sorg att lindra dagh från dagh	My sorrow to be eased day by day
Min lust att komma i förra lagh	My mood and vigour to be restored

A very similar version of the prayer was recorded in a document from 1671. Though the original has been lost, a transcript was published by folklorists Erik Gustav Geijer and Arvid August Afzelius in 1814. In addition to the "idolatrous and superstitious prayer" that was being read at the site, this record informs us that on the Midsummer Night of 1671, people had brought their sick and injured horses to the site, for which they were making offerings. Some of them also bared themselves and washed their bodies and others brought water from the well with them in bottles. Along with Midsummer and Pentecost, the feast of St. Peter is also mentioned as an important day for visiting the well (Geijer and Afzelius, 1814, vol. 1:244–245).

In addition to these written descriptions, St. Ingemo's Well is also depicted in two topographic works from the turn of the eighteenth century, Erik Dahlbergh's *Suecia Antiqua et Hodierna* and Johan Peringskiöld's *Monumenta Sveo-Gothorum*. Both volumes

FIGURE 30.1   St. Ingemo's Well in Dala. Engraving from Erik Dahlbergh's *Suecia Antiqua et Hodierna*, c. 1705. Photograph by the National Library of Sweden. National Library of Sweden, KoB Dahlb. III:71.

were compiled in the late seventeenth century, and they show a great degree of consistency in their depictions. The images are also in accordance with the written descriptions discussed earlier. Both the engraving from the *Suecia* and the drawing in Peringskiöld's manuscript for the *Monumenta* show a house-like structure above the well, which is placed just outside the walls of the former churchyard. A grove of trees can be seen within the walls and among some ruins. The crosses mentioned in the written sources also figure. In Perinskiöld's drawing, there are two small crosses and a larger one, which seem to be covered with some kind of fabric. In Dahlbergh's engraving, more crosses are visible. In addition to those within the walls, there are also some arrow-shaped crosses close to the well-house, possibly a variation of St. Anthony's cross (Skånberg, 2003:149, 185).

We have no way of knowing if a St. Ingemo ever existed. Neither do we know if there was cult continuity from the medieval era into the early modern, though many of the features described in the sources echo aspects of medieval popular piety. There are also clear parallels to Catholic folk liturgies at holy wells of later eras, such as the circumambulation, kneeling and the attaching of cloths to nearby objects (Ray, 2012:141–143). Twentieth-century recordings of later folklore from the area offer two different accounts of St. Ingemo's death. According to one version, she is said to have been a martyr decapitated for the sake of her faith ("Ingemo källa" on Ortsnamnsregistret, the on-line Swedish Registry of Place Names). In another, she is to have been a pious woman who lost her life in the Black Death. According to the latter legend, her fingers suddenly pointed upwards during her funeral procession

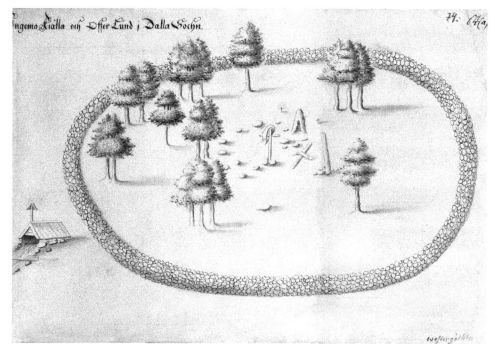

FIGURE 30.2 St. Ingemo's Well in Dala. Cropped drawing from Johan Peringskiöld's *Monumenta Sveo-Gothorum*, c. 1700. National Library of Sweden, MS Fh 9.

and the well sprung forth from the ground—a common theme in the origin myths of various wells and springs (Johansson, 1958:104).

There are few instances where we have such detailed evidence of traditional practices at a single holy well as in the case from Dala. But almost every aspect that is mentioned in the case reappears in the records of other holy wells from the same time period, suggesting that the only thing that is truly unusual about St. Ingemo's Well is its abundance of preserved sources. The practice of raising crosses at holy wells is often mentioned in seventeenth- and eighteenth-century sources. This highlights an important aspect of the cult of holy wells in a Scandinavian context that has rarely been properly emphasised by older research—that the cult was an aspect of *Christian* popular piety, and not a separate sphere of "magical" and/or semi-pagan belief. For instance, a vicar in a 1667 antiquarian report recalled that a large number of crosses at Holy Cross Well (*Helge korss kella*) in Mortorp had recently been destroyed in a wildfire (Ståhle, 1969:217), and when visiting the springs of the Virgin Mary in Torpa in 1719, an eye-witness reported that there were "some crosses, erected by those, that have benefited from the water" (Dal, 1719:29–30). The placing of votive offerings on these crosses is also evidenced from other sites, such as St. Nicholas' Well (*S. Nicolai kilde*) in Bohuslän (Nilssøn, 1885:164–165) and Holy Trinity Well (*Hellig Trefolldigheds killde*) and St. Helen's Well (*S. Ellenis kilde*) in Scania (Tuneld, 1934:60, 159–160).

As the term *Offerkälla* suggests, the most characteristic feature of Swedish holy well cults was the votive offering, and this aspect is mentioned in most documented cases throughout the early modern period. Monetary gifts were by far the most mentioned offerings and at some wells, coin findings indicate that this tradition was remarkably consistent throughout a vast period of time (Zachrisson, 2017:200–203). In 1901, when clearing one of *Barnabrunnarna* (Children's Wells) in Småland, almost six thousand coins were discovered. Only one coin from the middle ages was found (issued in the fourteenth century), which perhaps suggests that the well was cleared at some point during the Reformation. The remaining finds show a striking continuity in practice, being evenly distributed over the time period of 1573–1845 (Larsson, 1920:61–62; Golabiewski Lannby, 1992:8).

Trees connected to stories about various saints and those otherwise known as "holy" appear in some seventeenth-century antiquarian reports. For instance, Bishop Haquin Spegel wrote in 1683 that up until very recently, older inhabitants of the island of Gotland had "kept their superstitious habit" of praying underneath large trees (Spegel, 1901:53–54). In the diocese of Linköping, there were several stories of trees connected to the doings of St. Bridget (Ståhle, 1969:247–248, Pettersson, 1979:165). In addition, later sources from all over the Sweden often tell about healing trees (for example, "toothache pines") that were believed to absorb people's illnesses, and hollow trees which the sick would "pass through" in order to be healed (Skott, 2015:81–82). The pronounced connection between the grove of holy birches and the spring in the reports from Dala is, however, unusual.

The first known reference to St. Ingemo's Well was, as previously discussed, an edict from the diocese forbidding its use for healing purposes. Though holy wells could occasionally be embraced by local clergy (Zachrisson, 2017:226–227), the dominant attitude among the higher ranks of the Church was that holy wells were superstitious remnants of Catholicism and heathenry. This criticism is, however, remarkably late. During the sixteenth century, when Lutheran teachings gradually replaced those of the Medieval Church, little attention was paid to the popular cult of holy wells. In 1566, reformer and first Protestant archbishop in Sweden, Laurentius Petri, briefly mentioned Svinnegarn (the site of a famed holy well associated with the Holy Cross), when discussing "unnecessary peregrinations" and stated his disapproval of the way popish priests "with their incantations and unChristian consecrations" had been blessing wells and springs (1587:36, 69). Otherwise, Reformation-era writings were remarkably silent on the topic. But with the beginning of the seventeenth century, clerical hostility against holy wells grew.

Archbishop Laurentius Paulinus Gothus (in office 1637–1646) fought zealously against popular practices deemed "superstitious" and had an apparent distaste for the custom of visiting holy wells. The parish of Karlskyrka had a well dedicated to a local saint by the name of Karlung, and in his 1641 visit to the parish, Gothus reported encountering "much superstition" and a "foul well" (Lundström, 1898:69–70). Two years later, in 1643, he examined the conduct of the vicar of Svinnegarn parish, which housed the famed Holy Cross Well (Helga Kors källa). The vicar was being charged with neglect for failing to root out the "gross idolatry" committed at the well. The miraculous crucifix that once stood beside the well had already been removed by the mid-sixteenth century, but pilgrims had continued to flock to the site, which the Archbishop found deeply disappointing. The vicar, however, defended himself well, stating that these pilgrimages would continue regardless of what action he took—"even if her majesty would issue ten royal execution orders, it could not be abolished"—and that he had indeed done what little he could. The vicar got off with a stern warning to take such matters more seriously in the future, and to seek out the help of secular authorities in order to thwart the pilgrimage (Flentzberg, 1910:78–81).

Secular authorities too tried to abolish traditional practices in association with wells and springs. Two royal decrees were issued in 1665 and 1687, stating the punishments for those found guilty of making offerings to a holy well. Punishment was dependent on the circumstances and the severity of the crime, and could consist of fining, imprisonment, flogging and running the gauntlet (Schmedeman, 1706:453, 1142). Despite this legislation, active interventions against this form of popular piety were rare, and generally limited to wells attracting large crowds. One such intervention is mentioned in the diaries of vicar Gyllenius in 1649. When visiting Åbo, he recalls that the local magistrate had recently employed guards during Midsummer to "drive off the superstitious crowds" at St. John's Well in Kuppis (Gyllenius, 1882:138). Similarly, the governor of Blekinge deployed soldiers to prevent crowds from visiting the holy well of Edestad during Midsummer evenings in the early eighteenth century (Cronholm, 1976:265).

One of the reasons that traditional approaches to healing springs "survived" the Reformation for so long in the North might be the relatively late introduction of spa culture. By the later sixteenth century in Britain, mineral wells and spas were already arenas where traditional notions of healing waters could be merged and modified by medical science and Protestant ideas of providence (as thoroughly explored by Alexandra Walsham, 2008, 2011). When sources documenting St. Ingemo's Well were composed, this development had only just begun to take place in a Swedish context. Writing in 1683, royal physician Urban Hjärne concluded that "seven or eight years ago, there was a great silence on mineral wells in Sweden, they were as unknown to us as elephants and rhinoceroses" (Hjärne, 1683:1).

Hjärne published several works on the benefits of mineral wells. His arguments were characterised by the same kind of belief in divine providence that Walsham has noted in her British sources. God, in his benevolence, had scattered these healing sites throughout the landscape for the benefit of humankind. But present in the works of Hjärne was also an apparent need to proclaim his disapproval of the popular cult at holy wells. Not only were practices such as offerings an affront to God, they could also spoil the healing properties of the water (Hjärne, 1679:7). Similar criticism and warnings appear continuously in such works all-through the eighteenth century, indicating the difficulties in appropriating the popular cult of holy wells into "respectable" spa culture (see, for instance, Lindestolpe, 1718:4; Hülphers, 1770:4, 30). At the same time, the emergence of fashionable spa resorts served as an unintentional reaffirmation of popular conceptions of healing waters, and likely contributed to keeping traditional practices alive.

Traditional practices associated with holy wells might have also possibly survived in the Protestant North because of the mono-religious character of the region's development in the seventeenth century. On the British Isles and in Continental Europe, religious pluralism meant that visiting traditional sacred sites in the landscape (and what form these visits took) served as a denominational marker, with the development of distinct Protestant and Catholic practices at such sites (Walsham, 2005; Nye, 2002). In contrast, the Kingdom of Sweden lacked significant religious minorities, since Lutheranism was the only faith legally allowed. Though Calvinists were allowed to practise their faith to a limited degree within some towns, and foreign dignitaries were exempted from this law, ordinary citizens professing a different faith were to be exiled (Jarlert, 2005:250–251; Ljungberg, 2017:7, 230). Perhaps the general absence of the religious Other left boundaries more flexible for what could pass as Lutheran.

The case of St. Ingemo's Well is an excellent example to illustrate how Swedish popular piety utilised elements from pre-Reformation traditions as well as official Lutheran teachings and liturgy. The well of St. Ingemo was believed to have the power to heal the infirm bodies of humans and animals alike. The water was used for both drinking and washing, and the efficacy of the water was heightened by the use of powerful ritual tools: prayer, the raising of crosses, votive offerings, kneeling and circumambulation. Though these traditions were clearly taking place in a Christian context, the echoes of pre-Reformation piety placed them in the category of "superstition" in the eyes of the Lutheran church. From at least the early seventeenth century onwards, both secular and clerical authorities took a hostile stance against the popular cult of holy wells, labelling it superstitious and idolatrous. The cult was often described as "popish," and sometimes even pagan. But despite various attempts to undermine the practice, its survival was widespread throughout the early modern period. This likely points towards a general need for physical access points where petitioners could receive divine intervention, a need unaltered by the Lutheran Reformation.

Note

1 In accordance with the Gothicist movement of the Swedish empire, in 1666, the crown issued a decree for vicars to submit reports of "historical monuments" found in their parishes. Though the responses vary greatly in distribution, length and quality, these inventories are an invaluable source for early modern folklore and material culture.

References

Archival sources and online resources

Dahlbergh, Erik. 1667–1716. *Suecia Antiqua et Hodierna*. National Library of Sweden. https://suecia.kb.se/

Letter to Skara Cathedral Chapter, May 23, 1681. *Skara domkapitels arkiv (E VI:17:1)*. Gothenburg: Regional State Archives.

Ortsnamnsregistret, Ingemo källa, 1927. The Institute for Language and Folklore. Accessed June 14, 2018. www.sprakochfolkminnen.se/sprak/namn/ortnamn/ortnamnsregistret/sok- i-registret.html

Peringskiöld, Johan. c. 1700. Monumenta Sveo-Gothorum. Monumenta per Westrogothiam, Scaniam, Hallandiam, Blekingiam. Collection of Manuscripts (F.h.9). National Library of Sweden.

Printed sources and literature

Andersen, Susanne. 1985. Helligkilder og valfart. In *Festskrift til Thelma Jexlev: Fromhed of verldslighet i middelalder og renaissance*, edited by Ebba Waaben, 32–44. Odense: Odense Universitetsforlag,

Cronholm, Christopher. 1976. *Blekings beskrivning förf. Av Christopher Cronholm år c:a 1750– 1757*. Malmö: Blekingia.

Dal, Nils Hufwedsson. 1719. *Boerosia, Urbs per Regna Septemtrionis [...]*. Stockholm: Laurelius.

Flentzberg, Anton. 1910. Offerkällor och trefaldighetskällor. *Fataburen: Kulturhistorisk tidskrift* (5).

Geijer, Erik Gustav and Arvid August Afzelius. 1814. *Svenska folk-visor från forntiden*. Stockholm: Strinnholm och Häggström.

Golabiewski Lannby, Monica. 1992. *Ödetofta offerkällor: Barnabrunnarna och deras gåvor*. Växjö: Kulturspridaren.

Gyllenius, Petrus Magni. 1882. *Diarium Gyllenianum eller Petrus Magni Gyllenii dagbok 1622– 1667*. Helsinki: Reinhold Hausen.

Hall, Rudolf B. 1932. *Folkpedagogiska stiftsstatuter. 2. Påpud inom det nutida Sveriges gränser*. Lund: Fören. för svensk undervisningshistoria.

Hellström, Jan Arvid. 1996. *Vägar till Sveriges kristnande*. Stockholm: Atlantis.

Hjärne, Urban. 1679. *Een kort berättelse om the nys vpfundne surbrunnar tid Medewij vthi Östergöthland [...]*. Linköping: Kempe.

Hjärne, Urban. 1683. *Den lilla Wattuprofwaren [...]*. Stockholm: Henrich Keyser.

Hülphers, Abraham. 1770. *Kort berättelse, med förteckning uppå [...] mineral-brunnar [...]*. Västerås: L. Horrn.

Jarlert, Anders. 2005. Kyrka och tro. In *Signums svenska kulturhistoria: Stormaktstiden*, edited by Jakob Christensson, 249–299. Lund: Signum.

Johansen, Jens Chr. V. 1997. Holy Springs and Protestantism in Early Modern Denmark: A Medical Rationale for a Religious Practice. *Medical History* 41:59–69.

Johansson, Pehr. 1958. Folksägner och folktro i Västergötland. *Västergötlands fornminnesförenings tidskrift* 6(1):102–115.

Kaliff, Anders and Julia Mattes. 2017. *Tempel och kulthus i det forna Skandinavien*. Stockholm: Carlssons bokförlag.

Larsson, Ludvig. 1920. Barnabrunnarna i Ödetofta. *Hyltén-Cavalliusföreningn för hembygd-skunskap och hembygdsvård: Årsbok* 1:57–66.

Linde, Gunnar. 1955. Offerkällor och helgondyrkan i Västergötland. *Falbygden: Årsbok* 28: 8–42.

Lindestolpe, Johan. 1718. *Johan Linders Tanckar Om Suur-Brunnars Krafft och Werkan [...]*. Stockholm: L. Horrn.

Ljungberg, Johannes. 2017. *Toleranses gränser: Religionspolitiska dilemman i det tidiga 1700-talets Sverige och Europa*. Lund: Lund University.

Lundström, Herman. 1898. *Laurentius Paulinus Gothus: Hans lif och verksamhet (1565–1646). Vol. III. Paulinus såsom Ärkebiskop och prokansler (1637–1646)*. Uppsala: Almqvist and Wiksell.

Nilssøn, Jens. 1885. *Biskop Jens Nilssøns Visitatsbøger og Reiseoptegnelser 1574–1597*. Christiania: A. W. Brøggers Bogtrykkeri.

Nye, Jason K. 2002. Not Like Us: Catholic Identity as a Defence against Protestantism in Rottweil, 1560–1618. In *Religion and superstition in Reformation Europe*, edited by Helen Parish and William G. Naphy, 47–74. Manchester: Manchester University Press.

Pernler, Sven-Erik. 2007. *S:ta Elin av Skövde: Kulten, källorna, kvinnan*. Skara: Skara stiftsh-istoriska sällskap.

Petri, Laurentius. 1587. *Om Kyrkio Stadgar och Ceremonier [...]*. Wittenberg: A.A.A.

Pettersson, Sven. 1979. Birgitta-eken. *Vår hembygd* 3:164–165.

Ray, Celeste. 2012. Beholding the Speckled Salmon: Folk Liturgies and Narratives of Ireland's Holy Wells. In *Landscapes beyond the Land: Routes, Aesthetics, Narratives*, edited by Arnar Árnason, 139–159. New York: Berghahn Books.

Schmedeman, Johan. 1706. *Kongl. stadgar, förordningar, bref och resolutioner, ifrån åhr 1528. in til 1701 [...]*. Stockholm: Schmedeman.

Skånberg, Tuve. 2003. *Glömda gudstecken: Från fornkyrklig dopliturgi till allmogens bomärken*. Lund: Lunds universitet kyrkohistoriska arkiv.

Skott, Fredrik. 2015. Passing Through as Healing and Crime: An Example from Eighteenth-Century Sweden. *Arv: Nordic Yearbook of Folklore* 70:75–100.

Spegel, Haquin. 1901. *Rudera Gothlandica [...]*. Visby: Gotlands Allehanda.

Ståhle, Carl Ivar, ed. 1969. *Rannsakningar efter antikviteter*. Vol. 2. Stockholm: Almqvist and Wiksell.

Tuneld, John. 1934. *Prästrelationerna från Skåne och Blekinge av år 1624*. Lund: Gleerup.

Walsham, Alexandra. 2008. Holywell: Contesting Sacred Space in Post-Reformation Wales. In *Sacred Space in Early Modern Europe*, edited by Will Coster and Andrew Spicer, 211–236. Cambridge: Cambridge University Press.

Walsham, Alexandra. 2011. *The Reformation of the Landscape: Religion, Identity and Memory in Early Modern Britain and Ireland*. Oxford: Oxford University Press.

Zachrisson, Terese. 2017. *Mellan fromhet och vidskepelse: Materialitet och religiositet i det efterrefor-matoriska Sverige*. Gothenburg: University of Gothenburg.

31

THE BUDDHA'S THUMB, NĀGA LEGENDS AND BLESSINGS OF HEALTH

Sacred water and religious practice in Thailand

Rachelle M. Scott

Water has shaped the lives, economies and religions of people living in Thailand and other parts of South and Southeast Asia. One of the iconic representations of Thai culture is the "traditional" Thai house—a simple wooden structure built on long posts to protect families from unwanted visitors and seasonal floods. These houses mark how life in Thailand and other parts of Southeast Asia has been conditioned by the dangers and benefits of living near bodies of water. In fact, many Thai homes were built directly on the water for ease of transportation and fishing (Nithi and Mertens, 2006:34). Markets similarly occupied a space in boats or on the banks of rivers (*talad nam*), as did Buddhist temples (*wat*). Rivers were also sites of ritual and entertainment. Traditional Thai agriculture depended on the right amount of rain to ensure a plentiful harvest of rice, and rituals, such as boat racing, were a means for controlling the uncertainty of the rains (Kamala, 1997:27).

Given the impact of water over the lives of many Thais, it is not surprising that religious myths, rituals and festivals reflect the sacred power of water. While many surveys emphasize the fact that the vast majority of Thai Buddhists are practitioners of Theravāda Buddhism, the religiosity of Thai Buddhists in the past and in the present reflects the inherent hybridity of Thai religion in which practitioners selectively highlight or combine aspects of Theravāda Buddhism with elements of Brahmanism, Mahayāna Buddhism and numerous local traditions. The depth of this "inclusive syncretism" (Swearer, 1995) is apparent in Thai conceptions of sacred water. This chapter will examine a few examples of how Thai Buddhists envision sacred water, from legends of sacred wells, springs and water spirits to consecrated water and cleansing festivals and suggest that these legends and practices continue to occupy a prominent place within Thai religiosity despite radical cultural, economic and demographic changes in the twentieth and twenty-first centuries.

Sacred wells and springs in Thailand

The origin stories of sacred bodies of water in Thailand commonly relate how powerful beings contact and sacralize a particular place. Foremost among these beings is the Buddha, whose journeys to northern Thailand are recounted in local stories. In these vernacular texts (*tamnān*), the Buddha spreads dharma and converts the villagers through the power of his presence and the gift of relics (particularly his hair). Contact with parts of his body, even the most seemingly impure parts, makes mundane objects sacred. In the *Tamnān Ang Salung*, for instance, a towel used to cleanse the Buddha's feet turns to gold, and Indra and a *nāga* king construct a shrine over an area where the Buddha relieved himself (Swearer, 2012:152–154).

A similar local story describes how the Buddha created and consecrated a spring. In this story, the Buddha becomes thirsty while traveling, and when he discovers no water in the area, he touched the earth with his thumb and a spring miraculously appeared. The well, which contains this water, can be found at Mt. Kha Mo outside of Lamphun. Monks use the water from this well to consecrate a *ceitya* (a reliquary) during the Wat Haripuñjaya festival. According to tradition, it never goes dry, and women are forbidden from touching it (Swearer, 1976:57). However, this is not the only sacred water used during the festival. Monks also consecrate the *ceitya* (reliquary) with royal sacred water.

> On the morning of the full-moon sabbath, sacred water (*nam phra raja dāna*) blessed by the King of Thailand is sent from Bangkok to the provincial office. In the mid-afternoon it is placed in a palanquin and brought in a procession of government officials, boy scouts, and school children along with the water from Mt. Kha Mo, into the Wat compound now crowded once again with people. First the water sent by the King makes its way by pulley up the *ceitya* where it is used to lustrate the dome, followed by the water taken from the sacred spring. Then senior government officials and civil servants who had been in the procession anoint the *ceitya*. Afterwards the people who came to witness the event throw their own lustral water on the sacred mountain. After the *ceitya*-reliquary has been duly sanctified by lustral water from the King, the sacred well, and the government personnel, it is then draped with a new saffron cloth also sent by the King (Swearer, 1976:57–58).

This ritual demonstrates how sacred water in Thailand may be linked to religious authorities—whether the Buddha or the king.

The origin stories of other sacred wells in Thailand make similar claims of contact and consecration and emphasize the close association between religious and royal power. The sacred well (*bo nam saksit*) at Wat Pratu Khao in Nakhon Si Thammarat, for instance, was blessed by the temple's abbots whom many believed possessed miraculous powers. The water from this well was used in the past for important royal ceremonial rites, including royal weddings and coronations, but was also viewed as a powerful deterrent against dark magic and as medicine for the sick. While this Ayutthaya-era temple is in ruins, its healing properties remain potent. People continue to flock to the sacred site to either bathe or drink from the well. The well at Wat Lam Bo Tho in Songkhla province similarly links sacred water with the royal family. King Rama V (Mongkut, ruled 1851–1868) purportedly cured his sickness by drinking water from this well, and from that moment onward, legends emerged about the power of its healing waters, which led many to travel there. Recently featured on Thai PBS (2019), the water from Bo Namtip well, located in the Khao Plu cave in Chumphon province, was used to celebrate momentous events in the life of King Rama IX (72nd, 80th and 84th birthdays) and was used for the coronation of Rama X in May, 2019.

Spirits of the water

The Thai word for river is *mae nam* (mother water). Rivers bring life and fertility to communities. One source of life that emanates from these waters are spirits whose stories reflect their power and influence over our lives. Southeast Asian mythologies are replete with stories of water spirits—some of whom are of Indian origin while others are distinctly local. They all reinforce the strong connection between water and life, from the stories of *nāga* (water serpents) to water monks (Phra Uppakrut) and local spirits.

Tourist vendors in Thailand sell a wide variety of Buddhist items, from Buddhist amulets and statues to paintings and meditation manuals. Ubiquitous among the items for sale are statues of the Buddha, seated in a meditation pose, with a multi-headed serpent over his head. The serpent is a royal *nāga* named Mucalinda who sheltered the Buddha in the weeks following his awakening (*bodhi*). *Nāgas* feature predominantly in South and Southeast Asian stories, art and architecture. In both South and Southeast Asia, they are linked to fertility and water. In fact, many *nāga* stories involved *nagini* (serpent princesses) who mate with human males and produce children who possess the extraordinary power to produce rain. In the local *Nang Sa* legend, the Thai people descend from a water serpent (Tu, 2012).

Nāga stories in India and parts of Southeast Asia sometimes reflect a tension between the Buddha and *nāga* kings. In many of these legends, the Buddha encounters *nāga* kings who are irritated by his post-nirvanic glow and try to attack him, but he meets their attacks with lessons in the *dharma* (the truth). The *nāga* in these stories are frequently converted to the Buddha's teachings and become his protectors and guard his future relics. Thai temple architecture reflects the protective role of the *nāga* in Thai Buddhism. Nagas appear on finials, gables, arches, balustrades, along the tiers of temple rooves, and on carved stairs leading to shrines (Tu, 2012:163).

A local pond at Wat Hua Nongkaen in Burirum Province derives its sacrality from the *nāga* that dwells there. People travel from near and far to collect sacred water from the pond. Some will drink it; others will pour it over their bodies. As with other sacred ponds, they believe that the water has healing properties. Stories circulate within the community of miraculous healings and prophetic dreams. Those who are healed often bring *nāga* figurines and traditional Thai dresses to show their gratitude to the *nāga*. While the sacrality of this pond may appear to be solely a part of a local spirit tradition, it is promoted as a religious tourist destination (Thai PBS, 2015).

In northeast Thailand (and other parts of Southeast Asia), another water spirit occupies a place in popular religiosity. Phra Uppakrut receives offerings in the hope of "protection, good weather, and other boons" and is sometimes represented in shrines as a collection of stones taken from a river bed or pond and is also depicted as a monk, "seated cross-legged with his right hand in his bowl on his lap and gazing upwards over his shoulder at the sky" (Strong, 1992: 171–172).

The cult of Uppakrut differs from other water spirits in that he is a monk believed by many to be "devoted to meditation and strict in his adherence to discipline" (Strong, 1992:172). There are a number of mythic traditions involving Phra Uppakrut, but all associate him with water. Some myths describe him as the *nāga* who "foiled Māra's attempt to destroy the 84,000 *ceityas* built by King Asoka" (Swearer, 1995:45); others describe him as a water-dwelling novice born of the Buddha and a mermaid (Tambiah, 1970:169). "It is said that once the Buddha forced his semen (*beng nam asuchi* = forced out impure water) into the water and a mermaid swallowed it, became pregnant and gave birth to Uppakrut. He was subsequently ordained as a novice (or monk) and lives in the water, for he is a mermaid's son" (ibid). The invocation of Phra Uppakrut is an important part of the Bun Phra Wes festival in northeast Thailand. Villagers invite Phra Uppakrut to serve as the guardian of the festival prior to the annual recitation of the story of Prince Vessantara (Phra Wes) who was the Buddha in his penultimate life (ibid:163).

FIGURE 31.1   The guardian spirit Phra Uppakrut, sometimes thought to dwell in rivers and ponds. Wat (Temple) Phabong, Chiang Mai. Photograph by author.

FIGURE 31.2 *Nam mon* (consecrated water) at Wat Phra Singh, Chiang Mai, Northern Thailand. Photography by author.

Consecrated water

If you have the chance to speak to a Buddhist monk at a Thai temple, be forewarned that you just might get wet! It is common for Buddhist monks to sprinkle sacred water (*nam mon* or *nam saksit*) on practitioners after giving instructions in the Buddha's teachings. Monks similarly use this water to bless homes and businesses and to ward off disease and bad luck. In the past, villagers would take some of this water to sprinkle on their buffaloes to ensure the health of animals whose lives were vital to their household economies (Tambiah, 1970, 166). Similarly, women were given a particular kind of sacred water (*nam mon sadow kroh*) during childbirth to ease their pain and secure a good birth. This is especially necessary if there was an obstruction of the placenta, in which case a magic healer would "be summoned to prepare *nam mon* for the woman to drink" (Pranee, 2009:179). At weddings, guests pour "charged" holy water over the hands of the new couple from small (white plastic) conch shells to bless the new marriage (Olson, 1991:76).

This water is not inherently sacred; monks have consecrated the water with the power of the Buddha, his teachings (*dharma*) and his monastic community (*sangha*). A consecration ceremony may be as simple as monks lighting candles, chanting suttas (canonical texts) and dripping wax into the water (Olson, 1991:76). A more elaborate ceremony involves wrapping a cotton thread (*sai sin*) around a Buddha image, which is simultaneously wrapped around a bowl of water. Buddhist monks hold the thread as they chant from Pāli texts. Monks are thought to emanate beneficial and protective power as they chant the Pali. This power "travels through the cotton thread" and, "reinforced by the Buddha image," charges the water (Terwiel, 1975:212). The sprinkling or pouring of this water is not intended to aid a Buddhist on her path to nirvana, but rather "is performed for the happiness, prosperity, good health, and continuation of this existence" (Olson, 1991:76). Some Thai Buddhists link the origins of this practice to the *Ratana Sutta,* in which the Buddha purified a city plagued by famine, death and evil spirits with torrential rains. Following the rains, the Buddha instructed his attendant, Ananda, to further purify the city by sprinkling sacred water from the Buddha's alms bowl while chanting the *Ratana Sutta.*

In contemporary Thailand, the use of sacred water to bless a *ceitya*, Buddha images, or homes has been a subject of debate among modernist monks. The well-known modernist monk, Bhikkhu Buddhadasa, rejected the practice by saying: It is not important. It is magical (*saiyasāt*). It is something that came before Buddhism, is outside of Buddhism. This holy water (*nam saksit*) is for feeble-minded people (*khon panyā ōn*), but there are many people like this; there are many feeble-minded people in this world who feel they must pour holy water (Olson, 1991:79).

Bhikkhu Buddhadasa's critique of the practice reflects an anti-magical and anti-ritual strain within modernist Theravāda thought. Despite his critique and that of others, however, contact with sacred water remains a popular and wide-spread form of blessing within Thai Buddhism.

A recent story highlights the continued significance of sacred water in Thailand albeit from a very different source. On a Thai TV program (*Amarin News*), reporters investigated how many villagers in Phatthalung Province believed that the water emitted in sprays from the stink bean tree (*Parkia speciosa*) was miraculous and sacred. They tied colored cloth around the tree to mark its sacred status. Stories spread of miraculous healings after drinking the fluid from the tree or pouring it over one's body. Reporters told the villagers that the miraculous water was, in fact, urine from the cicadas dwelling in the trees, but this did nothing to deter their beliefs in its efficacy. Those who were interviewed for the program insisted that the sacred water led to miraculous healings, improved mobility and increased energy (*Amarin News*, 3/8/2019).

Water festivals

The most prominent festivals of the Thai calendar are celebrated with water. Water features predominantly in two of Thailand's most popular festivals, Loy Krathong and Songkran. Both festivals have origins outside of the Buddhist tradition, but they have become integral to the religious lives of Thai Buddhists. They highlight the agricultural cycle "from the rainy season and the planting of paddy rice through the cool harvest season to the hot and dry fallow season" (Swearer, 1995:35), and reflect numerous ideas about sacred water and its relations to life, purity and auspiciousness.

The floating lotus boats of Loy Krathong are iconic representations of Thai culture. On the full moon day of November, these boats (*krathong*) made from natural or human-made materials are set afloat in rivers, streams and ponds.

The purposes for these actions range from the expression of gratitude for wishes granted to the petitioning of forgiveness for immoral actions. The practice may partially derive from the Hindu festival of Diwali (Indian festival of lights) or the Chinese custom of floating lamps to guide the spirits of drowned persons. Buddhist-origin myths include a story of a *nāga* king who made offerings on the shore of the Nammada River to a Buddha footprint (an impression in a stone thought to signify the Buddha's former presence), and the story of Phra Uppakrut's thwarting of Mara's attempts to destroy Asoka's *ceityas*. Other explanations include offerings to departed relatives and Mae Khongkha (Mother Ganges, the goddess of the river) (Swearer, 1995:45).

The New Year's festival of Songkran has gained in popularity among tourists due to its water revelry. Today, trucks will drive through Thai streets with water cannons aimed at unwitting pedestrians. In fact, the Tourism Authority of Thailand (TAT) markets it as one of Thailand's most enjoyable festivals. The festival, however, is more than just a day full of water play. It is a celebration of the vernal equinox and the end of the hot dry season. Like many New Year's celebrations, it marks a period of new beginnings, from house cleaning to the purchase of new clothes. New Year festivals give center stage to water cleansing rites which include activities ranging from the ceremonial bathing of Buddha images, Buddha relics and Bodhi trees at monasteries, "to paying respects to elders with a water blessing, to unrestrained water fights with buckets and hoses" (Swearer, 1995:37). Many view the more somber ceremony of pouring water on the palms of elders or monks as a means by which to wash away offenses and procure blessings. All of the ceremonial bathings are viewed as merit-making opportunities. "The aspect of jocularity should not obscure the fact that pouring water over a senior person is essentially an act of great respect" (Terwiel, 1994:198). The festival's rain-making purpose is clearly represented in Chiang Mai, where Songkran celebrations conclude with the street procession of an image of Phra Singha Buddha which legend claims was crafted by a *nāga* king and possesses rain-making powers (Swearer, 1995:39).

Conclusion

Thailand's social and natural environment has dramatically changed over the past century. Mass deforestation has impacted and altered natural environments and communities and has led to unprecedented flooding, displacement and death. Cities have grown through urban migration, and modern temples have replaced riverfront wats. River routes have been replaced by paved roads, canals have been filled with concrete and waterways have become increasingly polluted. Within this context, Thai Buddhists have had to rethink traditional associations of water with sacrality, blessings and fertility. This chapter noted how some reformers have criticized the use of *nam mon* in Buddhist rituals, but stressed how sacred water, spirits and festivals continue to occupy a place within Thai religiosity.

The award-winning 2002 Thai film, *Mekong Full Party*, aptly captures the complexity of these issues. The film tells the story of Khan, a young orphan from Nong Khai, who returns home from a Bangkok university for the annual Naga Fireball Festival. As locals, tourists and vendors prepare for the festivities, we learn that

Khan has previously helped the abbot at a local temple to plant fireworks in the river to foster belief in the power of the nāgas. When Khan refuses to participate that year, the abbot "disappears" while planting the fireballs himself. The film leaves the audience wondering about the association of the abbot with the local nāga as the fireballs emerge from the river and light up the sky. The cultural tensions between consumerism (the heightened popularity of the festival), science (a scientist attends the festival to unearth the truth of the fireballs) and the power of tradition (the abbot's core teaching of "Do what you believe, believe in what you do") highlight modern cultural critiques at the same time as they reinforce the correlation between water and life in Thailand. The film has, in fact, fostered even more interest in *nāga* festivals and the myths that define them.

References

Kamala, Tiyavanich. 1997. *Forest Recollections: Wandering Monks in Twentieth-Century Thailand*. Honolulu: University of Hawaii Press.

Nithi, Sthapitanonda and Brian Mertens. 2006. *Architecture of Thailand: A Guide to Tradition and Contemporary Forms*. New York: Thames and Hudson.

Olson, Grant A. 1991. Cries over Spilled Holy Water: 'Complex' Responses to a Traditional Thai Religious Practice. *Journal of Southeast Asian Studies* 22(1):75–85.

Pranee, Liamputtong. 2009. Pregnancy, Childbirth and Traditional Beliefs and Practices in Chiang Mai, Northern Thailand. In *Childbirth across Cultures*, edited by Helene Selin and Pamela Kendall Stone, 175–184. New York: Springer.

Strong, John S. 1992. *The Legend and Cult of Upagupta: Sanskrit Buddhism in North India and Southeast Asia*. Princeton, NJ: Princeton University Press.

Swearer, Donald K..1976. *Wat Haripuñjaya: A Study of the Royal Temple of The Buddha's Relic, Lamphun, Thailand*. Missoula, MT: Scholars Press.

———. 1995. *The Buddhist World of Southeast Asia*. Albany: State University of New York Press.

———. 2012. Signs of the Buddha in the Northern Thai Chronicles. In *Embodying the Dharma: Buddhist Relic Veneration in Asia*, edited by David Germano and Kevin Trainor, 145–162. Albany: State University of New York Press.

Tambiah, Stanley J. 1970. *Buddhists and the Spirit Cults in North-East Thailand*. London: Cambridge University Press.

Terwiel, Barend Jan. 1975. *Monks and Magic: An Analysis of Religious Ceremonies in Central Thailand*. London: Curzon Press.

Thai PBS. 2015. Think Outside the Screen: Villagers Gather to Pay Respects to the Holy Pond in Buriram Province (คิดนอกจอ : ชาวบ้านแห่กราบไหว้บ่อน้ำศักดิ์สิทธิ์ จ.บุรีรัมย์" (17 ก.ย. 58). https://program.thaipbs.or.th/Kidnokjor/episodes/27493

———. 2019. Chumphon Province, Prepare to Draw Holy Water "Thip Pond" from Khao Phlu Cave, and Attend the Coronation Ceremony. (จ.ชุมพร เตรียมตักน้ำศักดิ์สิทธิ์ "บ่อน้ำ ทิพย์" ถ้ำเขาพลู ร่วมพิธีบรมราชาภิเษก).

Tu, Phan Anh. 2012. The Signification of Naga in Thai Architectural and Sculptural Ornaments. *DIALOGUE* 17(4):154–175.

PART IX

Hydrology, stewardship and biocultural heritage

This final section of the volume considers the environmental contexts of sacred springs and holy wells and their chemical and physical characteristics. Examining Lithuanian classifications of springs, Vykintas Vaitkevičius illuminates blendings of Baltic myth within the lore of Christianized springs and compares a selection by mineralization and hardness. He finds those with the highest iron content to be healing springs with the strongest associations to Baltic mythology, and those considered holy and having exclusively Christian associations to reflect a Catholic preference for colourless and odourless waters. Bruce Misstear and co-authors explore the distribution of Irish holy wells in terms of their physiographic settings, rock types and aquifer categories. They demonstrate that, because holy wells are located where aquifers are close to the ground surface, the majority are highly vulnerable to groundwater pollution. Jane Costlow considers the holy springs of Russia's Orel region as a focus for vernacular piety during Soviet suppression of religion and suggests that their renewed and open veneration is also witness to a resurgence of environmental stewardship. Working with Quechua-speaking farmers in the Peruvian Andes, Astrid Stensrud examines ritual practices that maintain relationships of reciprocity with sentient and demanding water beings. There, indigenous perceptions of mountain and water spirits exist side by side with Catholic devotions at sacred water sources; the two perceived waterworlds are competing and combined, but not syncretized. Glacial melt with climate change, and the concomitant variance of spring flow rates, have intensified the significance of collective ritual offerings to ensure environmental viability. Celeste Ray concludes the volume by considering Irish holy well ecosystems as sites of biocultural diversity (where culture and biology are interrelated and even co-evolved). Irreplaceable resources of archaeological, historical, spiritual and community significance, holy wells also serve as conservation patches for particular species of trees, plants and animals. Understanding the generationally-layered, local ecological knowledge about these sites and the cultural values that designate water sources as sacred is directly applicable in planning for socioecological resilience.

32

AT THE END OF THE FIELD, A POT OF NEMUNAI IS BOILING

A study of Lithuanian springs

Vykintas Vaitkevičius

The Baltic region was one of the last areas of Europe to be Christianised and Lithuania was the last pagan European nation, adopting Christianity only in 1387. Goddesses of Baltic mythology are thought by some to have Neolithic origins, and later gods have parallels with those of other Indo-European societies. During the early thirteenth-century emergence of the State of Lithuania, sacred watery sites (rivers, springs, lakes and bogs) were associated with fertility and military cults and the gods of the dead. Baltic myths are understood mostly through thirteenth-century Russian historical chronicles and fourteenth-century German missionary accounts. While Roman Catholicism arrived in parts of Lithuania in the late fourteenth century, today just over 85% of the Lithuanian population identifies as Catholic. Catholicism resisted the Protestant Reformation, the nineteenth-century Russian Empire and the Soviet suppression of religion. Particular watery sites, mainly springs, are thought miracle-producing and are important pilgrimage places. Water at such sites is called the tears of the Blessed Virgin Mary and regarded as efficacious for spiritual and physical healing.

In Lithuania, springs are defined as the concentrated and spontaneous emergence of underground water at the earth's surface (Juodkazis et al., 2003).[1] These landscape elements have their own tastes and smells. Their waters warm one up in winter and are cooling in summer. While they create and maintain life in nature, springs themselves are fragile. In the second half of the twentieth century, hundreds and thousands of Lithuanian springs were destroyed by land reclamation to increase hectares under cultivation and to improve soil productivity. The majority of surviving springs endure because of their location in large forests. However, these springs, flowing far away from areas dedicated to residential, recreational or economic purposes, are little known and rarely visited. In contrast, at spring sites on the outskirts of fields, the edges of woods, river banks and in areas accessible by hiking trails or motorways, people queue up to get spring water on weekends. Any attempt to appropriate a spring (the right to its water) is perceived negatively or even condemned. The understanding that a spring belongs to many (its near neighbours, the wider community and the people of the district) is considered to be an old and significant custom. Drinking water seeping from underground in an unusual way (not as a result of human excavation or drilling) must be equally used and shared by everyone. Spring waters are freely collected for domestic use and individuals who have moved away from their natal area may transport spring water from their home areas over long distances to have supplies where they now live. Few are interested in tests of the water's quality, as most people *a priori* believe that spring water is clean and healthy.

Comparison of 23 springs by mineral content and hardness indicated that those associated with Baltic mythology contain more iron than those associated exclusively with Christian veneration. The low iron concentration in springs with on-going Christian sanctity would seem to indicate Catholics' preference for transparent, colourless and odourless springs. Sites of Catholic devotion are generally called holy springs, while those springs connected to Baltic mythology are referred to as health-giving springs. The six exclusively Catholic springs in this study (those lacking additional connections to Baltic mythology) are generally visited individually, although families may go to these sites together once or twice annually, particularly on a saint's feast day. On first arriving at the holy site, devotees pray and then those who might be requesting healing may wash or anoint ailing portions of the body (the eyes, the mouth, the head or the legs). When a stream flows away from the pool of a spring, petitioners may walk barefoot in this water. Before departure, one may throw coins of low-denomination in the water, or leave candles or flowers (grown at one's own farmstead garden) beside the spring.[2]

Classifying springs in Lithuania

While springs can be classified by flow rate, abundance, temperature or chemical composition, currently in Lithuania, springs are divided into the "falling" ones, fed by underground, unpressurised water and the "rising" ones whose artesian waters emerge through natural pressure from intermorainal aquifers (for more detail, see Kadūnas et al., 2017:14–17). Lithuanian dialects provide their own classification of springs. A spring is *versmė* in the dialects of Eastern and Northeastern Lithuania, but *verdenė* in the North, *šaltenis* in the Northwest and *šaltinis* elsewhere in the country (Grinaveckienė et al., 1977:180–181, Map 104). *Šaltinis* and its derivative *šaltenė* originated from the adjective *šaltas* meaning "what is of a very low temperature," while *versmė* and *verdenė* derive from the verb *virti* meaning "to boil or bubble at high temperature."[3] Although *šaltinis* and *versmė* are opposites, these terms are interchangeable in everyday language, so that one might say *Maža versmelė, šaltas vandenelis* "A small *versmė*, cold water" or *Tę šaltiniai, tokis vanduo verda* "There are many *šaltinis*, and the water is boiling" ("Lietuvių," 1986: 487, 1997:802).

Mythological conceptions of springs relate to the meanings of the word *šaltinis* which can mean "gives the shivers" or people can shiver with *šaltinis* so that a blanket cannot warm them ("Lietuvių," 1986:487). The idea of *šaltinis* as a pot of water boiling on fire and yet staying permanently cold is part of many Lithuanian riddles. For example, "*At the end of the field, a cauldron is boiling. [What is that?]*

Versmė" (ALF file No. 1123, unit 56-22). Another goes, "*At the end of the field, a pot of many Nemunas is boiling.* [What is that?] *Versmė*" (ALF file No. 4094, unit 40). As the Nemunas is the largest river of Lithuania, this saying references the never-ending supply of infinite water at this source. In some other versions of the riddle, instead of the usual answer *šaltinis* or *versmė*, ants also appear, this would reference the constant movement of sand particles or tiny litter at the bottom of springs. For example, "*A pot of Nemunas is boiling at the edge of the forest.* [What is that?] *Ants*" (ALF file No. 1119, unit 42). More difficult to explain is why, instead of a spring or ants, the Sun or a fiery light is sometimes said to appear in the pot instead. "*A small cauldron is boiling at the end of the field.* [What is that?] *The Sun*" (ALF file No. 4018, unit 48-36) and yet the spring can be conflated with the sun, as in "*At the end of the field, the Sun is rising.* [What is that?] *Šaltinis* [A spring]" (ALF file No. 67, unit 24). The riddles mythically describe cold water flowing ceaselessly from a boiling pot in ways that are similar to descriptions of other natural phenomena such as: the Sun (which burns but never burns out, is also circular and radiates warmth in perceived ripples as the flow of cold water springs also ripples), the stone (that grows without roots), the rue plant (which is green in both winter and summer) and the fern (blooming without blossoms).

Lithuanian folklore identifies at least seven types of water, and formerly there were supposed to have been as many as nine! Water characterised by extraordinary features can be living, old, young, healthy, beautiful, fast and strong (firm). Thus, in fairy tales, different varieties of water are needed for different purposes. For example, an injured robber in a story asks a young woman to touch him with living healthy water for his wound to heal and then to touch him with young and beautiful water to make him young and handsome so that they can marry (Leskien and Brugman, 1882:162–163). It would follow that the waters of sacred springs can be living and old or young, and/or healthy, and/or beautiful/handsome, etc. These types of supernatural properties of springs that derived from Baltic religion seldom remained untouched by Christianity. Which miracles the water produced could change with Christianity to more curative remedies rather than the "vanity" of youth or beauty. Yet, many Christianised springs retain associations with older customs and with mythological phenomena and beings. This is evidenced by springs of the Aukštaitija Region (Figure 32.1).

The springs of Aukštaitija Region: a case study

In the Aukštaitija Region, which encompasses Eastern, Northeastern and Central Lithuania, 23 springs were investigated between 1999 and 2014; the findings are summarised below (Vaitkevičius, 2006; Kadūnas et al., 2017).[4] A general description of each is followed by water analysis in italics. Many of these sacred springs are considered curative and their waters are still deemed to be health-giving. The most common cures sought are for eye and skin problems. Many are recipients of votive offerings in the form of coins and some other objects. At least three (Budriškės, Palazduonis and Skudutiškis) are sites of apparitions of the Blessed Virgin Mary.

Almajas Spring (Ignalina district) is in a remote forest area, on the shores of a lake of the same name. In recent years, a shallow well shaft was excavated and a

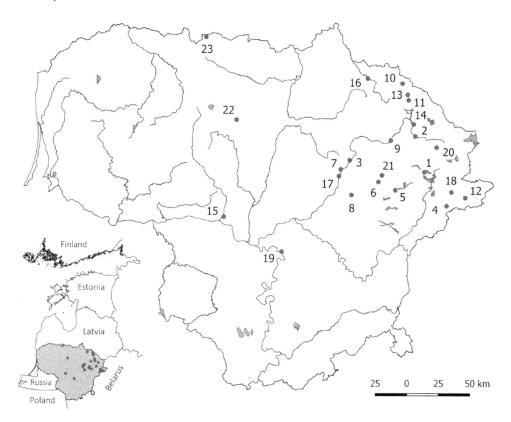

FIGURE 32.1 Springs noted in the chapter: (1) Almajas (Ignalina district); (2) Antalieptė (Zarasai district); (3) Ažuožeriai (Anykščiai district); (4) Bavainiškė (Švenčionys district); (5) Budriškės (Molėtų district); (6) Karališkės (Molėtų district); (7) Kavarskas (Anykščiai district); (8) Krapos (Ukmergė district); (9) Lygamiškis (Utena district); (10) Lukštai (Rokiškis district); (11) Mažeikiai (Rokiškis district); (12) Milašius (Ignalina district); (13) Obeliai (Rokiškis district); (14) Padustėlis (Zarasai district); (15) Palazduonis (Kaunas district); (16) Panemunis (Rokiškis district); (17) Riklikai (Anykščiai district); (18) Ropiškėlė (Ignalina district); (19) Rumšiškės (Kaišiadorys district); (20) Sabalunkos (Zarasai district); (21) Skudutiškis (Molėtai district); (22) Verduliai (Radviliškis district); (23) Žvelgaičiai (Joniškis district). Compiled and drawn by the author.

small wooden roof installed above it. Of the falling type, the spring is visited rarely and known only to the inhabitants of several of the nearest villages. They call the water healthy. *Water temperature is +7.4 °C, the yield is about 0.2 l/s (litres per second), the amount of dissolved minerals 527 mg/l (milligram per litre) and hardness 4.09 mg-eq/l (milliequivalents per litre); iron concentration in the water is low (0.2 mg/l), and no signs of contamination are recorded.*

Antalieptė Spring (Zarasai district) is on the forested left bank of the Šventoji River and is easily accessible from the township of the same name. The water of that rising spring was traditionally used to wash the face and rinse the eyes, and small coins were sacrificed there. People suffering from joint pains used to tie threads on the branches of trees around the spring, but local priests opposed that specific custom in the 1930s. *Water temperature is +7 °C, the amount of dissolved minerals 540 mg/l, the discharge varies from 0.04 to 1.2 l/s and hardness is 6.26 mg-eq/l; there is not much iron in water (0.4 mg/l), and no signs of contamination are recorded.*

Ažuožeriai Spring (Anykščiai district), also called the Queen's Quagmire (after an indigenous mythical figure), flows on the right bank of the Šventoji River, in a marshy area further away from homesteads (Figure 32.2). Many stories are told about the place. A century or so ago, ailments such as toothaches were treated there and prayers for success in dairying were also said at the spot. Offerings of food and money were thrown into the spring. A rising spring, the Queen's Quagmire was associated with one of the most outstanding pre-Christian sacred sites on the other side of the river, i.e. the Anykščiai Pinewood and the Puntukas Boulder (a glacial erratic and the second largest boulder in Lithuania). *Water temperature is +9.5 °C, the yield is 1.56 l/s, mineralisation 619 mg/l and hardness 6.87 mg-eq/l; the concentration of iron in the water exceeds the permissible rate by almost 20 times (3.95 mg/l), and nitrates were recorded.*

Bavainiškė Spring (Švenčionys district), also called *Lino verdenė*, streams from the shore of Sėtikis Lake, near a small village. It is maintained at the expense of the state and is visited by tourists. Previously, the rising spring is said to have been visited by numerous petitioners who rinsed their eyes and washed their skin to cure blemishes or sores. These devotees left coins in hopes of a cure. A woman who lived in the neighbourhood allegedly profited by selling the water. *The water temperature is +7.7 °C, the yield is 5.88 l/s, mineralisation 421 mg/l and hardness 4.93 mg-eq/l; iron concentration in the water is low (only 0.1 mg/l); however, the presence of sodium and chloride indicates pollution.*

Budriškės Spring (Molėtai district) is further away from the village, in a swampy forest area, at a rivulet called Šventoji [Holy]. "Unapproved," repeated apparitions of the Blessed Virgin Mary appeared on a hill nearby, and the water of this falling spring reportedly healed eyes. The place is infrequently visited now, but is still known in the district. *The water temperature is +6.4 °C, the yield is 0.5–1 l/s, minerali-sation 364 mg/l and hardness 4.45 mg-eq/l; no iron was found in the water; yet, light nitrate and nitrite contamination is present.*

Karališkės Spring (Molėtai district) is at the foot of a first millennium hillfort, next to a contemporary homestead. In the second half of the twentieth century, a wooden surround was installed. Early in the 1900s, ill individuals came at dawn to wash with the water of this falling spring. Before departing, they threw coins into the water. The water was allegedly considered to be healing because it was flowing in the direction of the Sun (e.g. to the East). *Water temperature is +9.6 °C, the yield fluctuates between 0.1 and 1 l/s, mineralisation is 558 mg/l, hardness 6.97 mg-eq/l and iron concentration 1.6 mg/l; nitrate ions are recorded.*

Kavarskas Spring (Anykščiai district), called after St. John the Baptist, flows abundantly in the town. Since at least the eighteenth century, a wooden cross has stood here and one reappeared after the restoration of independence in 1990. The site is well-tended and visited by local residents and guests of the town. The water of this falling spring was mainly used to rinse the eyes or other ailing body parts, while young girls washed with it to be beautiful. Today, people still gather there

FIGURE 32.2 (L) The Ažuožeriai spring, called the Queen's Quagmire (Anykščiai district); (R) The Lygamiškis spring, called Krokulė (Utena district). Photographs by author.

on St. John's Day, the day of the church feast in the nearby parish and on Pentecost (the seventh Sunday after Easter). *Water temperature is +8.2 °C, the yield is as much as 13–17 l/s, mineralisation 687 mg/l, hardness 8.72 mg-eq/l and iron concentration is insignificant—0.05 mg/l; however, economic activities in the town have produced an increased nitrate concentration (25 mg/l).*

Krapos Spring (Ukmergė district) is at a distance from the nearest settlement, but is close to a road, so that attendees at the church in Želva frequented the site on their way to or from services. Formerly, this rising spring was known as an eye cure and received coin offerings. *Water temperature is +10.3 °C, mineralisation is 592 mg/l, hardness 7.39 mg-eq/l and iron concentration is very high (2.4 mg/l). Small amounts of sodium and chloride indicate low-level contamination.*

Lygamiškis Spring (Utena district), called by an ancient name of Krokulė, flows on the Šventoji River's right bank opposite the Užpaliai township. A stone impoundment has existed there for at least a century or two (Figure 32.2). A small stone chapel stands nearby, and wooden shrines are mounted on wayside trees. The falling spring is especially frequented on the Day of the Holy Trinity, when people wash all parts of the body and wade in an east-flowing stream. Krokulė water is believed to protect both buildings and people from lightning and is brought home as a talisman. This water could be used for the dying in lieu of the consecrated water of last rites. Placards warn against throwing coins into the water as they are a source of contamination. *Water temperature is +6.8 °C, the yield is around 0.7 l/s, mineralisation 488 mg/l, hardness 6.06 mg-eq/l, iron concentration is very low (0.03 mg/l), and low sodium and chloride contamination is present.*

Lukštai Spring (Rokiškis district) runs in a secluded, forested place. No Christian symbols are present; however, a table and benches are employed at this site of regular prayer. On St. Peter's Day (June 29th), the site attracts numbers of Old Believers[5] from Lithuania and Latvia. This respected spring of falling water is used to wash faces and eyes and is taken home in bottles. *Water temperature is +7.7 °C, the* *yield is 1.6 l/s, mineralisation 488 mg/l, hardness 5.38 mg-ekv/l and iron concentration is insignificant (0.05 mg/l); however, some nitrates and ammonium are present.*

Mažeikiai Spring (Rokiškis district), called Šaltupėlis [Cold Rivulet], is far from several local farmsteads in the forests. After the reestablishment of Independence in 1990, a religious community embracing ancient Baltic religious perspectives, Romuva, has restored the site and secured its legal protection, but it is seldom visited. In cleaning the spring of falling water, they found many coins of the last few centuries. On their way to the Obeliai Church, devotees would formerly rinse their eyes, wash their knees and soak their feet there. *Water temperature is +10.1 °C, the yield is 0.5 l/s, mineralisation 461 mg/l, hardness 5.73 mg-eq/l and iron concentration is low (0.05 mg/l); some nitrate and ammonium ions are recorded.*

Milašius' Spring (Ignalina district), also known as the Cursed Spring, is near the Milašius' farmstead, seeping from under a stone. A 1926 description of the site (a spring of falling water) notes an unusual practice in the month of May when people would bring offerings to the spring at midnight. They left eggs and/or linen cloth. Those who did not bring gifts were said to later see frightening evil spirits in their dreams. *Water temperature is +11.3 °C, the yield 0.7 l/s, mineralisation 768 mg/l, hardness 7.82 mg-eq/l and iron concentration exceeds the norm by almost four times (0.8 mg/l); moreover, fairly high sodium concentration is recorded.*

Obeliai Spring (Rokiškis district), also called Raminta's Spring (after a Baltic supernatural figure), is in the Obeliai township, in a low place, on Lake Obeliai's shore. The spring of falling water is maintained and visited by local inhabitants who consider the water to be restorative. *Water temperature is +8.9 °C, the yield 0.55 l/s, the amount of dissolved minerals 598 mg/l, hardness 6.1 mg-eq/l, iron concentration has not been established and the indicators of contamination are insignificant.*

Padustėlis Spring (Zarasai district), also called the Čiegis' or Miraculous Spring, became a well in the front yard of a farmstead. Now roofed, it has a small water reservoir. Before storms, heavy rains or hail events (as well as other disasters), the Padustėlis Spring was said to change colour. The present owners of the farmstead found the spring "useful, but not miraculous"; however, they confirmed that the spring predicted the changes in weather and in their lives. *The temperature of the rising spring is +7.9 °C, the yield 1.25 l/s, mineralisation 609 mg/l, hardness 7.4 mg-eq/l and iron concentration exceeds the norm by almost 11 times (2.3 mg/l).*

Palazduonis Spring (Kaunas district) is in a secluded, forested place on the bank of the Lazduona Rivulet; however, a highway provides easy access. The site has long been frequented by those going to or from church feasts in Seredžius and Čekiškė. Next to the spring, a small stone chapel was re-built in the twentieth century. The site was scene to an "unapproved" apparition of the Blessed Virgin Mary. People rinse their eyes and wash their feet in the water. An offering box for site upkeep is mounted on a post. *The temperature of the falling spring is +9.3 °C, mineralisation is 347 mg/l, hardness 4.39 mg-eq/l and iron concentration has not been established; however, nitrites and ammonium are detected as a consequence of recent pollution.*

Panemunis Spring (Rokiškis district) is in a township, on the right bank of the Nemunėlis River. A cement impoundment contains the water, now covered with a small wooden roof. According to a story, a diseased elk that drank from the spring recovered, though was later shot dead by Count Krasitski. Its skull with antlers was hung on a wall of Panemunis Church with a statuette of the seated Virgin Mary between the antlers. The spring was visited on the Feast of the Holy Trinity (the first Sunday after Pentecost) and the Day of the Assumption of the Blessed Virgin Mary (August 15th). On the eve of those days, priests would consecrate the water which was used to wash wounds and the ailing parts of the body. Coin offerings are thrown into the spring. *Water temperature of the falling spring is +8.2 °C, the yield 0.02 l/s, mineralisation (902 mg/l); the water is very hard (10.49 mg-eq/l) and iron concentration insignificant (0.05 mg/l), while contamination is high—45 mg/l of nitrate ions.*

Riklikai Spring (Anykščiai district), called by an ancient name of Kregžlė, is not far from a village, on the bank of the Šventoji River. The spring is said to have been holy in pre-Christian times, and, as late as the early 1900s, girls and women used to wash with its water to be beautiful and healthy. Moreover, the water was "extremely delicious." *Water temperature of the falling spring is +11 °C, mineralisation (636 mg/l), the yield is about 4 l/s and hardness (8.35 mg-eq/l). Iron concentration has not been established, and the contamination is insignificant.*

Ropiškėlė Spring (Ignalina district) is in a remote area, in a deep, marshy ravine. Devotees stopped to wash with its water and offer coins when walking en route to the Ceikiniai Church. *Water temperature of the falling spring is +8.1 °C, the yield 0.1 l/s, mineralisation 584 mg/l, hardness 7.35 mg-eq/l, iron concentration insignificant (0.025 mg/l) and the level of contamination is low.*

Rumšiškės Spring (Kaišiadorys district), also called the Sunrise Spring, is in the historical village of Pieveliai (site of the Lithuanian Open-Air Ethnographic Museum). The place is well-tended, a cement impoundment has been placed inside and the water is readily consumed by the museum staff and visitors. As indicated by the name, the spring could have been considered healthy due to the direction of the water flow (eastwards). *Water temperature of the falling spring is +8.2 °C, the yield 0.01 l/s, mineralisation 455 mg/l, hardness 5.1 mg-eq/l, iron concentration has not been established and the recorded contamination is low.*

Sabalunkos Spring (Zarasai district), also called *Rudoji versmė* [The Brown Spring], is in the village of Sabalunkos and is easily accessible. A listed monument, the spring is occasionally visited by tourists. People believed that one who washed with the water of the Brown Spring before sunrise (if unseen by anybody) would become young again. *Water temperature of the rising spring is +7.2 °C, the yield 2.21 l/s, mineralisation 574 mg/l, hardness 6.91 mg-eq/l and iron concentration exceeds the norm by almost ten times; no contamination has been recorded.*

Skudutiškis Spring (Molėtai district) flows next to a village with a church. Its sanctuary is at the confluence of the Juodisa and another nameless rivulet. This spring is a widely known wonder-working place. The Blessed Virgin Mary is said to have appeared, possibly in the 1600s, standing on the stone beside the spring where a large chapel has been erected. The place attracts numerous devotees on the Feast of the Holy Trinity who rinse their eyes and wash the ailing parts of the body with the springs' water and that of the Juodesa rivulet next to it. It was customary to throw small coins into the spring. *The temperature and the yield of the falling spring water have not been established, mineralisation is 569 mg/l, hardness 6.34 mg-eq/l, iron concentration insignificant (0.27 mg/l) and the indicators of contamination are low (0.51 mg/l nitrate and 0.47 mg/l ammonium concentration).*

Verduliai Spring (Radviliškis district) is at the edge of the forest, easily accessible by car and visited by numerous domestic tourists. A cross of St. John is said to have once stood there, and offerings of food, linen and money used to be brought to the place. *The temperature of the falling spring is +10.1 °C, the yield about 0.5 l/s, mineralisation 516 mg/l, hardness 5.77 mg-eq/l, iron concentration 0.55 mg/l and contamination has been significantly increased (concentration of 39.36 mg/l chloride and 26.5 mg/l sodium).*

Žvelgaičiai Spring (Joniškis district r.) oozes in the marshy lowland, at a distance from settlements, yet close to the road. Well-tended at the expense of the state, the spring is within a regional park and is visited by numerous tourists. The local population once valued the water as health-giving. *The water temperature of the rising spring has not been established, the yield is 0.2 l/s, mineralisation 616 mg/l and hardness 7.41 mg-eq/l. No iron has been detected in the water, and the contamination has been found significantly increased (21 mg/l sodium and 67 mg/l chloride concentration).*

Findings and conclusions

Six of the 23 explored springs—those of Kavarskas, Lygamiškis, Lukštai, Palazduonis, Panemunis and Skudutiškis—still attract devotees, particularly on the occasion of church feasts, but also on any day of the year. Most of these sites have an overt Christian overlay with crosses or even chapels beside the waters. The remaining 17 springs are to be considered as historical sanctuaries due to the surviving memories about customs characteristic of either Baltic mythology or Christianity. Most of the visitors of the aforementioned sites are no longer local residents, but are returned natives, pilgrims or tourists.

In terms of physical qualities of the springs, all six of the exclusively Christian and 11 of the remaining springs are "falling," while six historical sanctuaries belong to the "rising" springs category. The water temperature of all the explored springs varies from +6.4 °C (Budriškiai Spring) to +11.3 °C (Milašius' Spring), while the average temperature of the springs is +8.85 °C. The flow rates vary from totally insignificant 0.01 l/s, at Rumšiškės, to spectacular at Kavarskas where a yield of 17 l/s once prompted plans to install a small hydro-power plant at the site. The explored springs are characterised by mineralisation, its degree amounting from 328 mg/l (Almajas Spring) to 902 mg/l (Panemunis Spring).[6] The iron concentration in the water of the explored springs varies from 0.025 mg/l (Ropiškėlė Spring) to 3.95 mg/l (Ažuožeriai Spring); attention should be paid to the fact that half of the explored springs have higher than the standard concentration of about 0.2 mg/l. The water hardness both in the historical and contemporary sanctuaries varies from 4.09 mg-eq/l (Almajas) to 10.49 mg-eq/l (Panemunis). However, in two-thirds of the cases, the water hardness varies between 6.06 and 8.72 mg-eq/l and just insignificantly exceeds the permissible hardness level for drinking water (6 mg-eq/l). Surviving Christian sites tend to be closer to settlements and are therefore more contaminated with nitrates, nitrites, ammonium and chloride.

The direction of the waters' flow could contribute to the significance of the sites. This was obvious in 18 cases and was measured. One can argue that the springs of the sanctuaries typically flow towards the east (8 cases), southeast (3), south (2) and southwest (2). Another three springs flow towards the north and northwest. There is no significant difference between the direction of the flow of the historical and the Christian springs, since, in the Christian sites, the water flows towards the east (at Kavarskas and Lygamiškis), the southwest (Lukštai) and the northwest (Panemunis). Due to the association of the east with sunrise, an east-flowing direction in the Baltic lands has long been considered significant and effective: people believed that the water flowing eastwards improved vision, cured diseases, returned one's strength and youth, and made the face and the skin beautiful (Vaitkevičius, 2004:45–46).

The water of most of the explored springs is thought to have medicinal properties. In 11 cases, after rinsing their eyes and washing the face and feet, after drinking water or filling their bottles with it, people used to make various offerings to the spring, and still do. These offerings usually take the form of small coins.[7] The relationship between the springs that visitors considered health-giving and those that visitors considered holy is not always easy to document. The chemical composition and physical characteristics of the so-called healthy and of the holy waters do not differ much. Certain differences do emerge when comparing the currently Christian and historically venerated sites. The indicators of mineralisation and hardness of their water are very similar; however, in the contemporary Christian sanctuaries, the water is relatively colder (varying between +6.8 and 9.3 °C) than the waters of historically venerated springs (which vary between +9.5 and 11.3 °C). Moreover, in as many as eight historical sanctuaries, the water contains significant quantities of iron (the indicator varying from 0.4 to 3.95 mg/l), while the highest iron concentration in the spring of a contemporary Christian site amounts to merely 0.27 mg/l (Skudutiškis).

To conclude, all of those categorised as health-providing springs were also ancient Baltic sacred places. The chemical and physical characteristics of their waters differ and could be used to treat different diseases, to promote human and animal health, and, of course, for magical purposes. However, as revealed by this research, Catholics selectively chose holy springs with waters that contained low iron concentrations and were therefore transparent, colourless and odourless.

Notes

1 This essay was translated by Laima Servaitė.
2 As churches were usually far away from these holy springs, the Soviets did not especially forbid their visitation.
3 In Latvian, *versme* means "heat, a flow of hot air."
4 In the periods of 1999 through 2005 and 2010 through 2011, the author collected data on the 23 springs (Vaitkevičius, 2006) and in the years 2012 through 2014, they were explored by a group of specialists of the Lithuanian Geological Survey (Kadūnas et al., 2017).
5 Russian Orthodox adherents to pre-seventeenth-century liturgical reforms who moved to Lithuania as refugees in the 1600s.
6 As a rule, the indicator varies between 558 and 636 mg/l and is slightly above that the high mineralisation rate (set at 550 mg/l).
7 In some cases, the water was used to cure diseases; however, no offerings were made (four springs), or, on the contrary, the facts of treatment were not known; nonetheless, the custom of sacrifice survived (two springs). In another four cases, the spring water was considered health-giving and was used by people; however, no data were recorded about associated rites.

References

[ALF] Archive of Lithuanian Folklore.

Grinaveckienė, Elena, Aldona Jonaitytė, Janina Lipskienė, Kazys Morkūnas, Marytė Razmukaitė, Birutė Vanagienė and Aloyzas Vidugiris. 1977. *Lietuvių kalbos atlasas. Leksika* [Atlas of Lithuanian Language]. Vilnius: Mokslas.

Juodkazis, Vytautas, Viktoras Kemėšis and Gailė Žalūdienė. 2003. *Enciklopedinis hidrogeologijos terminų žodynas* [Glossary of Hydrogeology]. Vilnius: Lietuvos geologijos tarnyba.

Kadūnas, Kęstutis, Petras Gedžiūnas, Zdislav Zanevskij, Rimantė Guobytė, Petras Pūtys and Danutė Balčiunaitė. 2017. *Lietuvos šaltinių katalogas. 220 versmių ir šaltinių* [Catalogue of Lithuanian Springs]. Vilnius: Lietuvos geologijos tarnyba.

Leskien, August and Karl Brugman. 1882. *Litauische Volkslieder und Märchen aus dem preussischen und dem russischen Litauen*. Strassburg: Verlag von Karl J. Trübner.

Lietuvių. 1986. *Lietuvių kalbos žodynas* [Academic Dictionary of Lithuanian]. Vol. 14 of *Lietuvių kalbos žodynas*, edited by Kazimieras Ulvydas. Kaunas, Vilnius: Lietuvių kalbos institutas.

Lietuvių. 1997. *Lietuvių kalbos žodynas* [Academic Dictionary of Lithuanian]. Vol. 18 of *Lietuvių kalbos žodynas*, edited by Vytautas Vitkauskas. Kaunas, Vilnius: Lietuvių kalbos Institutas.

Vaitkevičius, Vykintas. 2004. *Studies into the Balts' Sacred Places (BAR International Series 1228)*. Oxford: John and Erica Hedges.

Vaitkevičius, Vykintas. 2006. *Senosios Lietuvos šventvietės. Aukštaitija* [Ancient Sacred Places of Lithuania. Aukštaitija Region]. Vilnius: Diemedžio leidykla.

33

WHERE DOES THE WATER COME FROM?

A hydrogeological characterisation of Irish holy wells

Bruce Misstear, Laurence Gill, Cora McKenna
and Ronan Foley

This essay describes the hydrogeological settings of Irish holy wells, with the aim of addressing the question: are holy wells more common in certain geologies than others? This is the first attempt at classifying the distribution of Irish holy wells according to their geology and aquifer category (aquifer means a geological formation that can store and transmit groundwater in useful quantities). Some previous authors have considered the topographical settings of holy wells. For example, Logan (1980) describes the geographical settings of holy wells in terms of major landscape features such as the seashore, hills, mountains and bogs, whilst Brenneman and Brenneman (1995) report that that there are three main settings, or contexts, in which the wells are found: (a) in meadows or boggy areas "at the center of some bowl-like formation" (they refer to these as umbilicus or navel wells); (b) in rocky or mountainous areas; and (c) on or close to the seashore.

Water wells and springs

Before considering holy wells and their distribution in more detail, it is worth dwelling for a moment on water wells more generally, their history and the many different types of well. It is also relevant to discuss springs briefly, as many of the holy wells in Ireland are springs.

A water well can be broadly defined as "any hole in the ground that can be used to obtain a water supply" (Misstear et al., 2017). Wells have presumably been in existence since the time of the first humans. The earliest wells were probably shallow excavations along river valleys or around springs. However, when humans started to settle in villages and towns, defensive sites on high ground would have assumed greater importance, and so deeper wells would have become more common. No archaeological evidence of the earliest wells has survived. The oldest recorded well is in Cyprus and dates from between 7,000 and 9,500 BCE (Fagan, 2011). Another ancient well discovery in Europe is a 13 m deep hand-dug well in Germany dating from 5,090 BCE (Houben and Treskatis, 2007). In Mesopotamia, wells are known from the sixth millennium BCE (Miller, 1982), whilst Bromehead (1942) refers to a well in the Indus valley in Pakistan which dates from the third millennium BCE. Also in Asia, early well remains have been found in China, dating from around 3,700 BCE (Zhou et al., 2011).

Wells come in many different shapes and sizes. Traditionally, most wells were vertical shafts excavated by hand (referred to now as hand-dug wells, and often lined with brick, stone or concrete). The majority of hand-dug wells are only a few metres deep, although there are some examples of hand-dug wells extending to depths of several tens of metres. In the eastern desert of Ancient Egypt, a well was sunk to over 60 m in 1,300 BCE (Bromehead, 1942), and modern examples of deep hand-dug wells are found in countries such as Niger. Nowadays, water wells are mostly drilled by machine (and are commonly referred to as boreholes) and can reach depths of over 1,000 m, although the majority are less than 100 m deep (Misstear et al., 2017).

Springs are sites where groundwater issues from the land surface at a particular point; they may occur where the water table intercepts the ground surface in a topographic depression, or spring locations can be controlled by a particular geological feature such as the contact between two geological formations of contrasting permeability, or the presence of a fault or fracture zone. In Ireland, the largest springs are associated with fractures in karst limestones (where the rock fractures have been enlarged through chemical dissolution by groundwater), and many of these are regarded as holy wells. Prominent examples of holy wells at karst springs are St. Patrick's well in Clonmel, Tobernalt near Sligo and Ogulla well in County Roscommon (the flow of the latter spring, for example, ranges from 7 litres per second (L/s) in summer to 110 L/s in winter, with a mean flow of 39 L/s; Meehan et al., 2015). In contrast to springs, seepages occur where groundwater issues at the surface in a diffused manner, rather than at a particular point (Price, 1996).

Holy wells

In view of the essential nature of water for human livelihood and wellbeing, it is unsurprising that wells have become linked to religious beliefs in many societies. As Oestigaard (2013) notes, "water plays a fundamental role in many religious practices of the world's religions and is an important element in many of their underlying concepts." Let us now consider what constitutes a holy well. According to Logan (1980), "If it is necessary to define what is a holy well, it may be said that a holy well is any collection of water which for one reason or another is considered to be holy." However, such a definition is not specific to a well and could equally apply to a lake or rock pool. Ray (2014) notes that, in Ireland, "*toibreacha* (holy wells) and *toibreacha beannaithe* (blessed wells) are water sources, usually springs (but sometimes ponds or lakes), which are sites of religious devotion." She adds that, unlike shafts and holes purposely excavated by people for the collection of water, "holy 'wells' most commonly appear on their own and can also include seepage pools, or even the hollows of rocks or the cavities of trees … where dew and rain collect." Again, this definition is not fully satisfactory from a hydrogeological perspective, as many holy wells can include some degree of deepening, often around a pre-existing seepage or spring. Branigan (2012) describes a holy well as "a location where water issues from the earth and where the site is a focal point for supernatural divination, the curing of illness through ritual, the cursing of third parties, and/or the veneration of early Christian saints, Pagan deities, or elements of nature, specifically the water itself." This is a good definition, although the phrase "where water issues from the earth" applies more accurately to a spring or seepage rather than a well. In an article about the holy wells of County Limerick, Ó Danachair (1955) defines a holy well as "a well or spring at which prayers and ceremonies of a Christian religious nature have been performed in recent times." This is satisfactory in that both well and spring are included, but limits holy wells to sites of recent Christian devotion.

We define a holy well simply as a groundwater well or spring at which religious rituals have been, or are currently, performed. It is perhaps worth dwelling for a moment on the word "holy," and how its meaning differs from that of "sacred." According to Oestigaard (2013), the word holy implies possession of a divine quality, whereas sacred refers to objects that are respected or venerated. On that basis, holy wells might be more properly referred to as sacred wells. However, Oestigaard also notes that holy water can be regarded as having divine qualities. We might therefore reasonably term a well that contains "holy water" as a holy well. In any event, the phrase holy well is in common usage in Ireland and so is retained here. Again, many Irish holy wells are, in fact, springs, or could be termed "spring wells"—a site where a well has been created around a spring or seepage.

The geology and aquifers of Ireland

The geology of the Republic of Ireland comprises Precambrian and Palaeozoic bedrocks with a varied overburden. The Precambrian and Lower Palaeozoic rocks include igneous intrusives, volcanic rocks, metasediments, shales and sandstones, whilst the Upper Palaeozoic (Carboniferous) contains the country's main limestone formations (Holland and Sanders, 2009). The older rocks generally form a rim of higher ground around the coast, with mountains composed of granite and quartzite rising to about 1,000 m above sea level (ASL). The Carboniferous limestones mainly occupy lower ground in the Midlands and west, typically at elevations of 50–200 m ASL, although the famous limestone hills of the Burren in County Clare achieve elevations above 300 m ASL. Devonian sandstones are mainly found in the South and Southwest of the country, in Cork and Kerry. The overburden that covers most of the bedrock formations across the country consists of glacial deposits, river alluvium, lacustrine deposits and peat. The glacial deposits include tills and glacio-fluvial sands and gravels.

It is helpful to group geological formations into a small number of lithological groups when describing their main hydrogeological characteristics. The most productive aquifers in the country (i.e. the aquifers that give the highest well yields) occur within the Carboniferous limestones, Devonian sandstones (part of the non-sedimentary calcareous lithological grouping), Ordovician volcanic formations (notably those in County Waterford, part of the igneous lithological grouping), and in sands and gravels. The aquifers are classified by the Geological Survey of Ireland (2009) into three main groupings and nine sub-classes according to their extent and

TABLE 33.1 Aquifer classification in the Republic of Ireland (modified from GSI, 2009)

Category	Regionally important (R)	Locally important (L)	Poor (P) aquifers
Sub-category	• Karstified aquifers where conduit flow is dominant (Rkc) or where flow is more diffuse (RKd) • Fractured bedrock aquifers (Rf) • Extensive sand/gravel aquifers (Rg)	• Sand/gravel (Lg) • Generally moderately productive (Lm) • Moderately productive only in local zones (Ll) • Locally important karstified (Lk)	• Generally unproductive except for local zones (Pl) • Generally unproductive (Pu)

productivity (Table 33.1). About 70% of the country is underlain by aquifers that are described as "poorly productive"—a grouping that comprises classes Pu, Pl and Ll in the table (Moe et al., 2010).

The superficial deposits have a significant hydrogeological role even where they do not form aquifers themselves, in that they provide a protective cover to the underlying bedrock aquifers. The permeability and thickness of this cover material, therefore, determines the vulnerability of the underlying aquifers to pollution. The national groundwater protection scheme divides vulnerability into four categories, based mainly on the thickness and permeability of the subsoil cover: Extreme, High, Moderate and Low (Daly and Warren, 1998; DoELG et al., 1999; Misstear and Daly, 2000).

Hydrogeological characterisation of Irish holy wells using GIS

An analysis of the distribution of holy wells in the Republic of Ireland was carried out using ArcGIS with ArcMap 10.3.[1] A shape file was obtained containing National Monuments data on 2,996 wells, for which grid references were available for 2,676.[2] The analyses were performed using only those wells which had grid references. The distribution of holy wells was investigated by:

- elevation
- bedrock units
- main lithological groupings
- aquifer category
- groundwater vulnerability

The results of the GIS analysis are described in the following paragraphs. It is worth adding a couple of comments here:

- Not all holy wells are included in the analysis. For example, the 320 wells in the National Monuments database that do not have grid references were excluded.
- The distribution of a small number of the wells was not picked up in each analysis. Thus for example, of the 2,676 wells with grid references analysed for

vulnerability, a total of 68 wells were not included. The number of omissions in the different analyses varied from 48 to 107, representing only 1.8 to 4% of the total. In most cases, these appeared to be wells located on shorelines or map boundaries.

Results

The distribution of wells according to topographic elevation is shown in Figure 33.1, where 74% of wells are at elevations between sea level and 100 m ASL. Of the 19 wells identified as having elevations below sea level, all of these, as expected, are shoreline wells: six in Kerry, five in Donegal, three in Cork, two each in Waterford and Galway, and one in Wexford. In addition, many of the 958 wells in the 0–50 m elevation range are at or close to shorelines, either on the mainland or on islands. From a hydrogeological perspective, the location of wells close to the seashore, and often close to the high water level mark or in the intertidal zone, is not surprising, because groundwater, being less dense than sea water, commonly discharges to the sea in such areas and hence is easily accessible as a spring or via a shallow well. St. Colman's well at Salterstown, County Louth and the Abbey well in Ballyshannon, County Donegal are two such examples. When discussing well locations and the work of Brenneman and Brenneman (1995), Ó Giolláin (2005) mentions that "Other than those near the Medieval parish church, most wells are either on a height or by the seashore. Many are on the tops of hills or mountains." However, the current GIS analysis would suggest a more uniform topographical distribution, albeit that many medieval parish churches (probably the majority) lie in the elevation bands containing the largest numbers of wells—90% of wells lie between sea level and 150 m ASL.

Thirteen wells have elevations above 400 m: five in Cork, four in Donegal, two in Kerry and one each in Galway and Wicklow. Most of these are between 400 and 500 m ASL. Unsurprisingly, in view of their hill and mountain locations, all 13 of the highest wells lie in the Extreme (mainly X) vulnerability category, indicating that bedrock is at or close (within 3 m) of the ground surface. The high-elevation Cork and Kerry wells are all in Devonian Old Red Sandstone, whereas the Donegal and Galway wells are in Precambrian crystalline rocks (quartzites, gneisses and

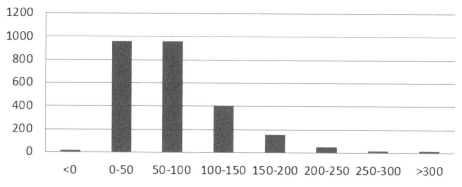

FIGURE 33.1 Number of Irish holy wells (*y*-axis) in different elevation bands (*x*-axis, m ASL) (n = 2,588).

TABLE 33.2 Number of wells in each main lithological group (n = 2,569)

Lithological group	Number of wells	Number of wells per 250 km²
Impure limestones	492	9.4
Pure limestones	686	10.4
Non-calcareous sedimentary	657	8.8
Igneous	215	11.2
Metamorphic	470	7.5
Sand and gravel	49	9.8

schists). The high-elevation Galway well (Gowlaunlee) is in Precambrian marbles, and the Wicklow well (Ballymoney) is in Lower Palaeozoic granite or other igneous intrusive. In terms of aquifer class, eleven of the elevated wells are classed as Poor (Pl or Pu) and two are in the Locally Important Ll category.

The distribution of holy wells according to the main lithological groupings is summarised in Table 33.2. It can be seen from the table that holy wells occur in all six main groupings. The right-hand column of the table shows the results "normalised" according to area, in this case number of wells per 250 km². This indicates higher densities in the pure limestone group (which might be expected as these form some of Ireland's most productive aquifers), but also in the igneous rocks (which often have poor aquifer characteristics).

The number of Irish holy wells in each aquifer category is shown in Table 33.3. Again, the results are normalised according to area. The majority of wells (1,782, or 68% of the total) are located in poorly productive aquifers (Ll, Pl and Pu categories) which underlie about 72% of the country. The highest densities occur in the regionally important (Rf and Rkc categories) and locally important (Lk) bedrock aquifers, and in the regionally important sands and gravels (Rg).

TABLE 33.3 Number of holy wells in each aquifer category
(n = 2,614)

Aquifer category	Number of wells	Number of wells per 250 km²
Rf	96	14.3
Rkc	368	11.4
Rkd	164	9.7
Rk	23	8.4
Lk	36	16.7
Lm	95	8.4
Ll	1,114	9.7
Pl	606	7.7
Pu	62	9.1
Rg	27	11.8
Lg	22	8.1

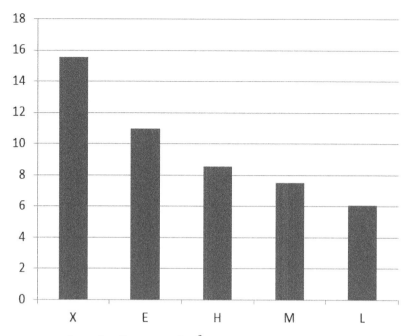

FIGURE 33.2 Number of wells per 250 km^2 in each groundwater vulnerability category (n = 2,608).

The distribution of holy wells according to groundwater vulnerability category (Figure 33.2) shows a clear pattern, with wells more frequent in the X and E Extreme and in the High vulnerability categories than in the Moderate and Low categories. This finding is not surprising, since field surveys by the lead author of more than 200 wells across the country have shown that the majority of these holy wells are springs or very shallow wells, and hence are more likely to be found where the subsoil cover is thin or absent, and the aquifer is close to ground surface (i.e. the X and E vulnerability categories especially).

Discussion and conclusions

The results of the GIS-based analysis show that Irish holy wells occur in all the main lithological groupings and in all the main aquifer classes in Ireland. Interestingly, they are nearly as numerous (in terms of wells per 250 km^2) in the poorly productive aquifers as they are in the regionally important aquifers. In contrast, a study by Mather (2016) reported that holy wells in England and Wales are more numerous in the less productive aquifers found in the West and Southwest (especially Cornwall and Wales) compared with the higher yielding aquifers in the East and Southeast. Mather attributes this pattern to water being more valued where it is scarcer (i.e. in the West and Southwest), and hence more likely to be venerated. However, additional non-geological explanations for this distribution might include the stronger legacy of Iron Age populations in the West and Southwest of Britain, and also possibly better survival rates of holy wells in these regions where there is less intensive agricultural development and less urbanisation than in the East and Southeast.

One clear trend in the distribution of holy wells in Ireland relates to groundwater vulnerability: the wells are more common in areas where the groundwater vulnerability is classed as Extreme or High, compared to Low vulnerability areas. This has important implications for water quality. Areas with Extreme or High vulnerability are at a greater risk of contamination from activities such as farming and on-site wastewater disposal, and shallow wells and springs are especially susceptible. On-going research involves field surveys of wells in all the major physiographical and hydrogeological settings across the country. This includes sampling of wells for water chemistry. Whilst the main purpose of the chemical sampling is to try and establish whether there are variations between the water chemistry of holy wells (with their associated reputations for particular cures) and the background water chemistry determined from non-holy wells, this work should also provide further insights into the susceptibility of these wells to pollution.

Notes

1 The geological information was sourced from the Geological Survey of Ireland (GSI). The various GIS layers were downloaded from www.gsi.ie/en-ie/data-and-maps/Pages/Groundwater.aspx4. The geology shape files were all in vector (polygon) format. The shape file with the elevation data, which was in the raster format and then converted to the vector format, was obtained from Maynooth University. An attributes table containing the topographical and geological information for the holy wells was built up during the GIS analysis.
2 Source: National Monuments Service, Department of Arts, Heritage, Regional, Rural and Gaeltacht Affairs.

References

Branigan, Gary. 2012. *Ancient and Holy Wells of Dublin*. Dublin: The History Press.
Brenneman, Walter L. and Mary G. Brenneman. 1995. *Crossing the Circle at the Holy Wells in Ireland*. Charlottesville: University Press of Virginia.
Bromehead, Cyril E. N. 1942. The Early History of Water-Supply. *The Geographical Journal* 99(3):142–151.
Daly, Donal and William P. Warren. 1998. Mapping Groundwater Vulnerability: The Irish Perspective. In *Groundwater Pollution, Aquifer Recharge and Vulnerability*, edited by Nicholas Robins, 179–190. London: Geological Society, Special Publication 130.
Department of the Environment and Local Government, Environmental Protection Agency and Geological Survey of Ireland. 1999. *A Scheme for the Protection of Groundwater*. Dublin: Geological Survey of Ireland.
Fagan, Brian. 2011. *Elixir: A Human History of Water*. London: Bloomsbury.
Geological Survey of Ireland. 2009. *Aquifer Classifications in the Republic of Ireland*. Dublin: Geological Survey of Ireland.
Holland, Charles H. and Ian S. Sanders. 2009. *The Geology of Ireland*, 2nd edition. Edinburgh: Dunedin Academic Press.
Houben, Georg and Christoph Treskatis. 2007. *Water Well Rehabilitation and Reconstruction*. New York: McGraw Hill.
Logan, Patrick. 1980. *The Holy Wells of Ireland*. Gerrards Cross: Colin Smythe Ltd.
Mather, John. 2016. Wonder Working Waters. *Geoscientist* 26(8):10–15.

Meehan, Robert, Monica Lee, Caoimhe Hickey and Natalya Hunter Williams. 2014. *Establishment of Groundwater Zones of Contribution: Mid Roscommon Group Water Scheme, Ogulla Spring*. Report prepared by the Geological Survey of Ireland in collaboration with the National Federation of Group Water Schemes with support from the National Rural Services Committee. Dublin: Geological Survey of Ireland.

Miller, Robert. 1982. Public Health Lessons from Prehistoric Times. *World Water* (October), 5:22–25.

Misstear, Bruce D. R., David Banks and Lewis Clark. 2017. *Water Wells and Boreholes*, 2nd edition. Chichester: John Wiley and Sons.

Misstear, Bruce D. R. and Donal Daly. 2000. Groundwater Protection in a Celtic Region: The Irish Example. In *Groundwater in the Celtic Regions: Studies in Hard Rock and Quaternary Hydrogeology*, edited by Nicholas S. Robins and Bruce D. R. Misstear, 53–65. London: Geological Society, Special Publication 182.

Moe, Henning, Matthew Craig and Donal Daly. 2010. *Poorly Productive Aquifers: Monitoring Installations and Conceptual Understanding*. Wexford: Environmental Protection Agency.

Ó Danachair, Caoimhín. 1955. The Holy Wells of Co. Limerick. *The Journal of the Royal Society of Antiquaries of Ireland* 85:193–217.

Ó Giolláin, Diarmuid. 2005. Revisiting the holy well. *Eire-Ireland* 40(1&2):11–41.

Oestigaard, Terje. 2013. *Water, Christianity and the Rise of Capitalism*. London: IB Taurus and Co.

Price, Michael. 1996. *Introducing Groundwater*, 2nd edition. London: Chapman and Hall.

Ray, Celeste. 2014. *The Origins of Ireland's Holy Wells*. Oxford: Archaeopress Archaeology.

Zhou, Yu, François Zwahlen and Yanxin Wang. 2011. The Ancient Chinese Notes on Hydrogeology. *Hydrogeology Journal* 19:1103–1114.

34

THE HOLY SPRINGS OF RUSSIA'S OREL REGION

Traditions of place and environmental care

Jane Costlow

The veneration of specific features of the natural landscape has long been a part of the religious and devotional practices of the eastern Slavic world. Historians, folklorists and popular writers convey stories and descriptions of sacred bodies of water, individual trees and forest groves, and large boulders (erratics) with "footprints" taken to be the impress of holy figures' passage through the landscape. Of these features, natural springs have been particularly beloved foci of local lore, veneration and practices of visitation. While it is well-nigh impossible to document the deep cultural history of these springs, scholarly traditions have assumed that many of the local cults are very long-lived, and may well have been associated with pre-Christian Slavic cultures (Panchenko, 2012a; Platonov, 2014). However, their endurance through the Soviet period and their renewed vitality in the present is well documented. This essay examines the holy springs of one particular part of European Russia—the Orel [pronounced *Or-yol*] region, to the south of Moscow. This part of central Russia is home to almost two hundred holy springs, sites that have received increasing attention and care in the decades since the fall of the Soviet Union. While the proliferation of natural springs in the region may be due to hydrology, the processes that have turned such features into valued sites of veneration, pilgrimage, tourism and storytelling are cultural. The springs of the Orel region and their role in the lives of both locals and visitors provide an intriguing window into the evolving meanings of water, place, healing and history in post-Soviet Russia.

Georgii Fedotov, the great historian and philosopher of Russian Orthodoxy, claimed in 1946 that "with [Russians] the tie between Christian and pre-Christian elements is perhaps stronger than in most of the nations of the West," a tie he attributed to the absence of a Reformation and Counter-Reformation in Russia, and a peasant life that remained "medieval" long into the nineteenth century (3). For Fedotov (1960), this link was nowhere more evident than in Russian attitudes toward the natural world: "In Mother Earth, who remains the core of Russian religion, converge the most secret and deep religious feelings of the folk" (12).

The notion that Russian peasants were, beneath a veneer of Christianity, essentially "pagan"—continuing traditional rites and rituals associated with the worship both of Moist Mother Earth (*mat' syra zemlia*) and of more local natural features—has in the past decades come under sustained critique (Levin, 1993; Milner-Gulland, 1997; Panchenko, 1998, 2012a). More recent scholars have tended to explore cultural and political tensions between the official church and popular or vernacular Orthodoxy. The modern era in Russia (beginning with the introduction of radical reforms under Peter the Great in the early eighteenth century) witnessed periods of hostility between state and church authorities and local religious practitioners, often revolving around cults of local saints and the veneration of springs, trees and footprint stones. Recent work on religious practices in the northwest of Russia documents ways in which the official church, in both the eighteenth and nineteenth centuries, attempted to discredit or ban popular veneration of local springs and the saints connected to them in an effort to "enlighten" society through submitting legends and vernacular accounts to more modern standards of proof (Platonov, 2014:61). Nonetheless, rituals of veneration associated with natural features "to some extent eluded the control of both parish priests and local authorities, and provided opportunities for 'informal' religious activities and social networks within village communities or groups of villages" (Panchenko, 2012b:322). Contemporary archival work provides copious evidence of the ineffectiveness of efforts to end practices which reformers and rationalists saw as superstitious (Platonov, 2014, 2016). The hostility of Soviet officials toward all manifestations of religious life was comprehensive and violent, and extended out beyond official houses of worship to natural sites. While these places' relative inaccessibility and hiddenness in the countryside often made them into refuges of both personal and collective faiths, they were also frequently targeted by anti-religious campaigns (Kormina, 2004; Panchenko, 2012a:49; Costlow, 2017, 2018).

The links between local memory, vernacular piety, the official church and evolving politics are all evident in the Orel region. Geologically, this is "a country of countless rivers" (Doklad, 2012:39), with its streams and small rivers entering European Russia's major watersheds: the Don, Dniepr and Volga Rivers all have their headwaters in this region. Located some 300 km south of Moscow, the Orel region (or *oblast'* in Russian, an administrative unit akin to states in the U.S.) is forested in the North, while in the South, the land opens out into expansive rolling fields scored with tree-lined gullies. As is the case with much of rural Russia, villages and towns are few and far between, with unevenly maintained roads winding through countryside that often bears few visible traces of the modern world. In the post-Soviet era, the region has struggled with the collapse of industries and collective farms that has led, in turn, to depopulation, particularly of rural areas. Politically, the region has been a locus of support for the post-Soviet Communist party, whose long-standing leader, Gennadii Zyuganov, is from Orel. Regional identity is connected both to memories of endurance during two years' occupation by German forces in World War II, and to a rich literary history. In the nineteenth century, Orel was home to writers like Ivan Turgenev, Nikolai Leskov and Ivan Bunin, and residents will tell you that the local Russian is the "purest" of all. In many ways, the region still lives up to Turgenev's characterization of it in one of his stories as a "backwater," but in 2017, it made headline news worldwide for being the site of the first monument to Ivan IV ("the terrible"), who is credited with founding the city in the sixteenth century.[1]

Orel's springs are distributed throughout the region, but the overwhelming majority are in rural areas, often accessible only on foot or by badly maintained roads. Soviet persecution of religious practices had two significant consequences for the springs (aside from attempts to actually pollute or destroy them). On the one hand, with the loss and/or destruction of religious *buildings*, such natural sites became all the more important, often serving as places of covert baptism and the celebration of religious holidays. On the other hand, more broadly shared knowledge about the springs, their locations and the legends/histories surrounding them was often lost or intentionally concealed. The recovery and publication of that knowledge has been facilitated in the Orel region by several different groups. In 2002, a local priest initiated a process of creating a map that would provide convenient information about known holy springs in the region (*Pravoslavnyi krest*). That map, in turn, became the basis for a website that provides abundant information about locations and directions, with compilations of whatever may be known about the history of the spring. (When such information is missing, the site invites the public to provide it.)

As of August 2018, the website *Orelrodnik.ru* (*rodnik* means "spring" in Russian) lists 178 holy springs in the Orel region. It is at present unclear just how many of these are officially consecrated by the church; a local priest's site that gave a much lower number—and insisted on the role of the church in shaping believers' interactions with holy springs—is no longer active. The springs and the sites surrounding them vary widely in the extent of information available, their accessibility and in the infrastructure at any given location. The site's authors highlight 20 "most famous" springs scattered in diverse locations throughout the region. These springs' stories feature various recurring themes, which situate local places in relationship to broader national and regional histories. Accounts of rediscovery and the process of restoration undertaken by local residents are part of what is cherished and highlighted. Descriptions often include accounts of miraculous origins and appearances of icons to believers, and may relate how a given spring has power to heal particular disabilities (failing eyesight, difficulties with conception, drinking problems). In other cases, the description is more generic: "You can take water from the spring, and dip in the *kupel'* (a ritual bathing pool) to wash away your sins and improve your health."

People come to springs for many different reasons, only some of which are explicitly religious. They may come to draw pleasant-tasting, clean water for drinking (a particularly valued—and free—alternative to municipal drinking water often delivered through rusting pipes); they may come for the peace and quiet of the place; or they may come to seek healing of particular physical or spiritual ills. For religious visitors, coming to the springs involves physical contact with the water, whether full immersion in the *kupel'* or simply dipping one's fingers and making the sign of the cross. The springs may also be the sites of organized communal events, particularly those connected to religious holidays like Epiphany (*Kreshchenie*, which is associated in Russian Orthodoxy with Christ's baptism).[2]

The infrastructure of the springs also varies widely, and sometimes includes little more than a pipe to move spring water into a small pool, or a few stones topped with an icon. Others are much more elaborate, and include enclosed bathing pools (*kupel'*) and small wells that allow visitors to collect water more easily. The Andreevskii spring site was first refurbished in the post-Soviet era by local authorities in the mid-2000s, and then in 2014, the structures were completely rebuilt and the site was officially reconsecrated. The *Orelrodnik* site contains links to photographs from before reconsecration, showing a simple wooden, roofed structure that is open on all sides and holds a small table with icons and field flowers. People of all ages mill about, dip their hands or wash their faces in the spring water. Photos from post-Consecration show much sturdier buildings that are no longer open-air, a reconstruction underwritten by a local agro-business concern. Other springs rely primarily on volunteer labor from locals, and are maintained either by nearby residents or, in one case, by children at a local school (Costlow, 2017:252).

Most sites include some kind of signage instructing visitors how to behave. The instructions at the Kuksha spring are typical—they are affixed both to a fence near

FIGURE 34.1   The Andreevskii spring in early winter. Photograph by Anton Khvostikov. Used by permission.

FIGURE 34.2 Small icon at the Gremiachii spring. Photograph by Anton Khvostikov. Used by permission.

the parking area and to the bathing house itself. The tone manages to be both firm and forbearing:

> In our efforts to preserve the holiness of this place, not only for you but for your children and grandchildren, we earnestly request that you be reverent in your behavior; please do not smoke, and especially do not drink alcoholic beverages at or near the spring. If at all possible women should wear headscarves.

The sexes are asked to enter the water separately (even if they are related), since there have been cases "when the water left the spring" after mixed-sex bathing. The authors of the instruction make a lengthy request that visitors do not throw coins into the pool, since such behavior "pollutes" the spring and is pleasing to demons rather than God. Instead, they implore visitors, Christ desires that each person should make what offering they can to the poor—rather than tossing coins into the pool, money should be sacrificed in acts of charity. Finally, the instructions invite each visitor to offer a prayer however small to St. Kuksha, "and to thank God that you have been able to visit this holy place."[3]

Stories are absolutely key to the springs, as they are to any sacred site (Kormina, 2004; Lane, 2012): the *Orelrodnik* site archives narratives of saints' lives, accounts of miraculous origins and histories of the faithfulness both of the springs themselves (withdrawing from the persecutors' wrath in the Soviet era) and of the locals who have worked in the post-Soviet era to restore them (see Costlow, 2017). As it does in so much Russian folk culture, the water in these instances has a kind of agency, refusing itself to those with evil intent.[4] Some of these narratives intersect with broader histories of Muscovy and the Russian lands, while others are not of national significance, but rather defend the dignity of a tiny village by attesting to the presence "even" here of saints, miracles and evidence of righteous perseverance. The Kuksha Spring in the northeast of the region, for example, is explicitly linked to the broader history of Christianity in the Slavic lands. The site is named for the monk (originally from the region) who returned to his birthplace from the famous Kiev Monastery of the Caves to baptize the region in the twelfth century; the spring is reputed to be the site of his martyrdom. The land that is home to the Kuksha Spring is now the site of a male monastery; the built structures at the site—set in deep woods—include a recently completed brick church and a modest log structure over the *kupel'*. The story of the Kamenets Spring similarly links the local site to national history. It is located at the site where a monastery was established in the sixteenth century and reputedly saved from "raiders from the [Mongol] Horde" by a thick fog that enshrouded it. According to legend, the Kamenets monastery miraculously vanished, and when the fog dissipated, the raiders saw neither the monastery itself nor those who had defended it; they seemed to have disappeared into the earth, with only the peeling of bells as a reminder of their vanished presence.

Such accounts of disappearance and protection are arguably part of a larger cultural trope that associates protection with righteousness and divine intervention manifest through bodies of water. The most famous such legend (which one scholar has called the single most powerful legend in Russia) is associated with the city of Kitezh, reputedly protected from Mongol raiders by being submerged beneath Lake Svetloyar, north of the Volga (Sheshunova, 2005; Costlow, 2013). All of these stories—like the practices and rituals of healing connected to the springs themselves—suggest water's miraculous powers, and the ability of bodies of water to shelter whole communities from malevolent strangers. Agency in these accounts is attributed both to the water itself and to the holy energies acting through it. Numerous descriptions of the Orel springs attribute agency to the springs themselves; signs at several of the sites urge visitors not to throw coins into the springs, and suggest that in the past, the springs have "dried up" in response to this profanation of their holy purity (Costlow, 2017:242). The legends surrounding Gromovoi Spring blend natural and divine intervention: the story is that the spring emerged as a result of a lightning strike; when locals considered filling it in, one of them had a "prophetic dream" in which a saint appeared to him and told him that the water in the spring had healing properties. The man took his ailing wife to drink and wash in the water—and she was healed. Springs in the Soviet era—referred to as "years of persecution"—repeatedly dried up or moved, exercising a kind of protective disappearance not unrelated to the legends of Kamenets or Kitezh.

Other springs highlighted on the *Orelrodnik* site have no major figure or national legends attached to them, but are nonetheless celebrated and beloved at the local level, with often quite poignant accounts of the springs' role in difficult lives. The Andreevskii Spring is considered "our own" (*svoim*) by residents of the local village, Maloarkhangel'sk, thanks to its relative accessibility and a good road. The *Orelrodnik* entry (written by a local journalist) notes that people go there on various occasions and for varying reasons: newlyweds go there as part of wedding celebrations, to dip in the *kupel'* on hot days and to gather water, which is considered healing. The writer is unsure just when these traditions began, but notes that after World War II, when there were no working churches in the region, people from 20 to 30 km would come to the spring for prayer services. The site's healing powers and holiness are connected to local stories of healing: in one, a sickly child who asked for Andreevskii water was healed; in another, a desperate mother during the war had a dream in which Nicholas the Wonderworker appeared to her and told her to go to the spring and take water to "sprinkle" her children; when she said she did not know the spring's location, he promised to show her the way. Soviet authorities attempted and failed to fill the spring in with brush and tree limbs. People claimed to be able to see the face of the Mother of God and Nicholas in the water.[5]

The springs listed on the *Orelrodnik* page are all accessible to the public, regardless of who actually owns the land on which they are situated. Some of the springs, as noted earlier, are affiliated with monasteries, while others are protected informally by local communities and caregivers. Several of the springs are explicitly protected under Russian environmental law as "monuments of nature," or as part of parkland. One of the most easily accessible springs is, in fact, located in a national park in the region's northeast; the "spring of the Kazan' Mother of God in the Orel Poles'e" includes a large area for parking, a small wooden chapel and large tented structure over the pool that emerges near the spring—along with a *kupel'* for ritual immersion. Whether such forms of protection will continue into the future is a question related to evolving land law, privatization of formerly state lands and the continuing development of post-Soviet agriculture. The commodification of what are still communally held sources of water also has the potential to threaten access. In the fall of 2016, the manager of the *Orelrodnik* site communicated his confidence that property law and restrictions on access are not currently, and would not become, problematic. Patronage and protection of the springs will no doubt continue to evolve.

The landscape of European Russia offers none of the spectacular features associated with visual traditions of the sublime, an absence that nineteenth-century artists struggled with as they sought to represent a distinctive Russian "motherland." The holy springs of the Orel region emerge from what Fyodor Dostoevsky called the "meager landscape" of central Russia, confirming a national mythology of spiritual riches hidden in the unremarkable (Ely, 2002). As post-Soviet Russians have begun to forge new forms of identity, the call of "Mother Russia" has been powerful. The revival of local springs can certainly be seen as part of a larger turn toward Orthodoxy and religious nationalism. Multiple other motives are at work as well, often allied to local history and a resurgence of interest in place-based memory and culture. Springs are socio-natural sites that receive environmental care as well as religious reverence.[6] In this light, holy springs offer an example of an emerging ethic of conservation and care grounded in specifically Russian traditions. Victor Shavyrin puts it this way:

> Looking at the question from a purely ecological perspective, and with the experience of past decades, it's time to admit it: protection of nature on the basis of rational thought alone is a dead end. We will be able to protect springs and thereby rivers only on the basis of a sacral relationship to them. That's why building chapels and outfitting springs is welcomed by everyone, regardless of their world view.
>
> *(2002:23)*

In this light, the care and veneration extended to these tiny springs suggest a resurgence not only of religious, but of civic life and of environmental stewardship.

Notes

1 www.rferl.org/a/russia-oryol-ivan-terrible/28086611.html and www.theguardian.com/world/2016/oct/14/russias-first-monument-to-ivan-the-terrible-inaugurated
2 The regional environmental authorities publish data on water quality in advance of these feast days, since they bring a high level of immersive contact.
3 Information sign on the *kupel'* at Istochnik sviatogo Kukshi, author's photograph, June 7, 2018.
4 Panchenko notes various traditional rituals that link miraculous icons and water, including the "ancient Russian custom that held that worn-out icons should not be thrown away but either lowered into water or buried in the cemetery" (1998:135).
5 http://orelrodnik.ru/rodnik/7/rodnik-7.html; www.orel-eparhia.ru/news/2014/08031; http://maloarhangelsk.ru/andreevsky-kolodez-2006/
6 I take the term socio-natural sites from Winiwarter (2017).

References

Costlow, Jane. 2013. *Heart-Pine Russia: Walking and Writing the Nineteenth Century Forest.* Ithaca, NY: Cornell University Press.
Costlow, Jane. 2017. *It Was Only a Tiny Spring*: Veneration, Value and Local Springs in Contemporary Russia. In *Water in Social Imagination from Technological Optimism to Contemporary Environmentalism*, edited by Jane Costlow, Yrjo Halla and Arja Rosenholm, 233–254. Leiden: Brill.
Costlow, Jane. 2018. Wayfinding, Map-Making and the Holy Springs of the Orel Region. In *Russia's Regional Identities: The Power of the Provinces*, edited by Edith W. Clowes, Gisela Erbsloh and Ani Kokobobo, 96–119. London: Routledge.
Doklad ob ekologicheskoi situatsii v Orlovskoi oblasti v 2011 godu. 2012. Orel.
Ely, Christopher. 2002. *This Meager Nature. Landscape and National Identity in Imperial Russia.* DeKalb: Northern Illinois University Press.
Fedotov, Georgii. 1960. *The Russian Religious Mind.* New York: Harper.
Kormina, Jeanne. 2004. Pilgrims, Priest and Local Religion in Contemporary Russia: Contested Religious Discourses. *Folklore* 28:25–40.
Lane, Belden. 2002. *Landscapes of the Sacred: Geography and Narrative in American Spirituality.* Baltimore, MD: The Johns Hopkins University Press.

Levin, Eve. 1993. *Dvoeverie* and Popular Religion. In *Seeking God: The Recovery of Religious Identity in Orthodox Russia, Ukraine, and Georgia*, edited by Stephen K. Batalden, 29–52. DeKalb: Northern Illinois University Press.

Milner-Gulland, Robin. 1997. *The Russians*. Oxford: Blackwell.

Panchenko, Alexander. 1998. *Issledovaniia v oblasti narodnogo pravoslaviia. Derevenskie sviatyni Severo-zapada Rossii*. St. Petersburg: Izd. Aleteiia.

Panchenko, Alexander. 2012a. How to Make a Shrine with Your Own Hands: Local Holy Places and Vernacular Religion in Russia. In *Vernacular Religion in Everyday Life*, edited by Marion Bowman and Ulo Valk, 42–62. London: Routledge.

Panchenko, Alexander. 2012b. 'Popular Orthodoxy' and Identity in Soviet and Post-Soviet Russia: Ideology, Consumption and Competition. In *Soviet and Post-Soviet Identities*, edited by Mark Bassin and Catriona Kelly, 321–340. Cambridge: Cambridge University Press.

Platonov, Evgenii. 2014. Kvoprosu o pochitanii rodnikov v XIX veke: Modeli povedeniia I praktika priniatiia resehnii. *Traditsionnaia kul'tura* 1:61–70.

Platonov, Evgenii. 2016. On the Veneration of Springs in the Nineteenth Century: Models of Behavior and Decisionmaking Practices. In *Meanings and Values of Water in Russian Culture*, edited by Jane Costlow and Arja Rosenholm, 51–64. London: Routledge.

Shavyrin, Viktor. 2002. Rodniki Orlovshchiny. *Mir i muzei* 1–2(7):122–125.

Sheshunova, Svetlana Vsevolodovna. 2005. Grad Kitezh v khudozhestvennoi literature i problema bifurkatsii russkoi kul'tury. *Izvestiia Russkoi Akademii nauk, otdelenie literatury i iazyka* 7–8: 12–23.

Winiwarter, Verena. 2017. The Many Roles of the Dynamic Danube in Early Modern Europe: Representations in Contemporary Sources. In *Water in Social Imagination from Technological Optimism to Contemporary Environmentalism*, edited by Jane Costlow, Yrjo Halla and Arja Rosenholm, 49–76. Leiden: Brill.

35

SENTIENT SPRINGS AND SOURCES OF LIFE

Water, climate change and world-making practices in the Andes

Astrid B. Stensrud

Water flows in a variety of ways in the Andes: it emerges from springs and glaciers, and flows in streams, rivers, canals and underground channels. Quechua-speaking peasant farmers in the Peruvian highlands depend on the water from glaciers, springs and rain for the irrigation of their fields and for domestic consumption. As the water flows through different uses, practices and relationships, it re-emerges in different ways: as vital force, a living being, the mother of life and/or an economic resource. People maintain relations of reciprocity with sentient beings in the surroundings to ensure fertility, productivity, wellbeing and water supply. Water is powerful as it has the force to sustain life, but can also destroy land and cause illness. Springs—called *manantial* in Spanish and *pukyo* in Quechua—are not only seen as sources of life, but they are also known to be dangerous and must be approached with great care. Therefore, they are often surrounded with ritual and are seen by many as "sacred." In the last few decades, however, farmers have experienced the effects of climate change: glaciers are melting and springs are drying. Collective ritual practices, such as making offerings to springs and paying tribute to mountains, have acquired new meanings. This chapter considers the contemporary collective work to maintain springs, streams, canals and ponds, and the ritual practices that ensure continued water supply in the southern Peruvian Andes, particularly in the regions of Cusco and Arequipa. The essay further discusses how water and springs emerge as living beings, and how their vitality and danger have been translated into holiness. With the effects of climate change, world-making practices related to water now acquire new significance and a sense of urgency. Inspired by Marisol de la Cadena (2015), Silvia Rivera Cusicanqui (2012) and Marilyn Strathern (2004 [1991]), this essay argues that in contemporary world-making practices, different and competing water-worlds are combined, but not mixed, and further suggests that these practices are as important as ever in the wake of climate change.[1]

The anthropology of water in the Andes

Several anthropologists working in the Andes have described how water is a vital force that circulates through the cosmos. Waters (in plural) circulate under, around and through the earth (Earls and Silverblatt, 1978), and surface to nourish crops. From their 1970s work in Colca Valley in the region of Arequipa, Ricardo Valderrama and Carmen Escalante noted that water is "a vital force, principle of life, a living being which, like ourselves, participates in the universe" (1988:206). Jeanette Sherbondy states that water is the essence of life itself and thus the most important element of the Andean cosmos; it is the dynamic principle that explains movement, circulation and the forces for change. The ocean—called *mamacocha* (motherlake) in Quechua—is associated with the origins of the world, and most origin stories in the Andes tell how people were created in water and emerged from lakes (1982, 1998). Catherine Allen's research in Cusco indicates that both God and the Sun are seen as sources of water, which is a manifestation of an animated essence or power—called *sami* in Quechua—that circulates through the world (2002:34–36). Peter Gose (1994) discusses the connections between water, death and agriculture. Dead bodies go to the underworld within the mountains where they are dried out to provide the living with water. The expelled water contains a pure vital force that plants can absorb and convert into life (1994:130–131).[2] However, to ensure that the dead give back water to the living, the latter have to engage in ritual drinking and libations. Hence, ritual work is needed to maintain the cycle of life. Since water is given to the humans by the mountains or the ancestors, humans have to reciprocate by offering gifts, called *pagos* (Allen, 2002 [1988]; Gose, 1994; Gelles, 2000).

In Colca Valley, offering *pagos* (also called *iranta*) to the earth, mountains and water springs is an intrinsic part of agricultural and irrigation practices. These *pagos* usually consist of a fetus from a llama or alpaca,[3] sugar, fat, food, alcohol, coca leaves, flowers and other items, and they are offered in return for water, crops, fertility and wellbeing. Water is in Colca known as a female life source that connects humans, plants, animals and spirits. Farmers in Colca note that the common name of water is *Yakumama*, which means water-mother, and that they also use a more specific name they consider most respectful "*Mama Choqesisa*," especially in ritual contexts in the higher parts of Colca. Pastoralists refer to Choqesisa as the source of water and the origin of alpacas, and there is a story of a young woman called Choqesisa who was the owner of alpacas and who entered a spring after the death of her baby, followed by her alpacas (Vásquez Soto and Estrella Canaza, 2010).[4] Water-beings such as lakes and springs (*qochas* and *pukyos*), and the earth-mother (*pachamama*), mountain-lords (*apus*) and other place-beings in the Andean landscape that may be referenced as earth-beings (*tirakuna*)[5] are not inherently benevolent or malevolent, but they are very demanding and can be quite capricious (Allen, 2002 [1988]).

In the pre-colonial Andes, there was no conception or reification of an evil spirit; the fetishization of evil in the form of the devil developed after the Spanish Conquest (Taussig, 1980). The earth-beings had to assimilate to the Christian religion or descend underground to the world within/below called *ukhu pacha* in order to become invisible, and some of these beings were identified with the devil (Cereceda,

2006). Similarly, places and objects used for rituals were identified as "sacred," earth-beings were called "gods" and practices related to them were translated to words with religious connotations, such as "sacrifice," "libation" and "spiritual." For example, *iranta* has been translated as "food for the gods" (Valderrama and Escalante, 1988:109). Marisol de la Cadena (2015) has argued that the interpretation of mountain-lords and other earth-beings as "spirits" allows native perceptions of mountains to be relegated to the sphere of "indigenous religion." However, Andeans do not necessarily see offerings as exclusively a religious practice, but as part of good agricultural stewardship. Hence, de la Cadena suggests that instead of an either–or analyses, these practices can be seen as both religious and not (de la Cadena, 2015:205). Whether making *pagos* to mountains and springs is understood as a form of religion or world-making, the practice is seen as more important than ever. When the environment, the weather and the water supply change, the need for making *pagos* becomes ever more pressing in order to secure the continued provision of water from the mountains.

Glaciers as sources of life and power

Peru contains 70% of the world's tropical mountain glaciers, which are the most visible indicators of climate change due to their sensitivity to increased temperatures and the visibility of their shrinkage (Orlove et al., 2008; Vuille et al., 2008:80). These glaciers are disappearing at an alarming pace, with serious consequences for the environment, for the water supply of rural and urban populations, for the livelihoods of farmers and pastoralists, and also for cultural practices (Bates et al., 2008; Bolin, 2009). Related cultural traditions include the pilgrimage to *el Señor de Qoyllur Rit'i* (the Lord of the Snow Star) in the region of Cusco. Every year, between Pentecost and Corpus Christi, tens of thousands of pilgrims walk to a place called Sinakara which is situated below a mountain peak and the glacier named *Qolqepunku* (Silvergate). They go to visit the Lord of Qoyllur Rit'i, who is called "the little father of the poor" (*el taytacha de los pobres*) since he is known to aid the needy. The origin story of the pilgrimage and the *Señor* begins with the appearance of a fair-skinned boy in white clothing to a poor, young alpaca herder. After they had played and shared bread, the alpaca herd multiplied. Later, when a delegation of priests and other authorities went to investigate the matter, the boy appeared in a sparkling white light beside a large rock and turned into a tree with the bleeding body of Christ hanging from it. The herder boy died on the spot and was buried beneath the same rock (Sallnow, 1987:207–214). The apparition, which today is known as the Lord of Qoyllur Rit'i, is painted on the rock which is now inside the altar of a church built around it in the 1960s. The boy can be interpreted as both Jesus Christ and Apu Ausangate, who is the most powerful *apu* in the area (Sallnow, 1987:211).

Most people agree that in this place, the Catholic Lord Christ exists side by side with the mountain-lords (the indigenous apus). Michael Sallnow (1987) observed that the association between the two powers does not mean that they are identical; indeed, they are sometimes seen to be competing for attention (1987:212). Some pilgrims do not bother to enter the church at all; they prefer to go up to the snow on Apu Qolquepunku. At the same time, the most conservative Catholic priests do not approve of what they see as pagan rituals. Although the combination of Catholic and non-Christian practices can be defined as a problem by the Church, it is not problematic for most pilgrims. Many pilgrims— perhaps the majority—go first to the church and afterward to the mountain. In this way, two different worlds are combined, but not mixed.[6]

FIGURE 35.1 Dancers descending from the glacier Qolqepunku during the pilgrimage festival of Qoyllur Rit'I. Photograph by author.

Ritual dancing is an important part of the pilgrimage, and the dancers dressed as *Ukukus* (bears)[7] go up to the snow on the final night, and, at dawn, bring down the crosses (which pilgrims had placed there earlier). Almost every year, people die during the pilgrimage. Some of those who perish are individuals dressed as *Ukukus*, perhaps exhausted from dancing and the long hike, and losing their footing in the dark, they stumble into glacier crevasses at night. Several pilgrims told me that it was a good sign that "the Lord" satisfied his appetite by eating an *Ukuku*. As one *Ukuku* dancer put it, "if the mountain eats a *Pablucha* [another name for *Ukuku*], it will be a good year." This perhaps alludes to the circulation of *sami*—the vital force—in the cosmos (cf. Allen, 2002 [1988]; Gose, 1994). The *Ukukus* leave a few drops of their own blood in the snow as a "sacrifice" to the mountain, and in return, they used to chop off large chunks of glacial ice, which they brought home to their villages to use as potent medicine (Bolin, 2009:233). However, due to glacial melt, this practice was forbidden in 2000, and the prohibition has been strictly enforced since 2003 (ibid:234). Since that year, the *ukukus* are only allowed to bring meltwater in bottles. The meltwater flowing from the glacier and natural springs in Qolqepunku has healing power.[8]

Climate change has altered and reduced ritual practices in the pilgrimage of Qoyllur Rit'i. In other places, however, ritual offerings have increased because of

climate change and dwindling water supplies. The ice cap on Hualca Hualca mountain (an extinct volcano) that rises majestically at 6,025 m in Colca Valley is the main
water source of various surrounding communities, among them Pinchollo village in
the district of Cabanaconde, province of Caylloma. Today, the farmers are worried
because the permanent snow is disappearing. While slow glacial melt seeped into
the underground water table and re-emerged in springs, the loss of glaciers is already
evidenced in lower spring flows. As one farmer noted, "If the glacier disappears,
there is no life anymore; there is no village anymore. The mountain supports us.
Who will contain the thaw?"

Earlier, the meltwater used to seep gradually into the ground, recharging the groundwater, flowing through the underground deposits and then re-emerging as springs.
However, when the glacier melts at a fast pace, the water tends to flow over the surface,
causing erosion. Farmers also report that the rain patterns have become irregular in the
past years: the rain often starts later and when it finally comes, the torrential rain falls
hard and goes straight to the river and gets lost in the ocean. The Colca River runs deep
and its water is not used for irrigation.

Many years ago, the farmers in Pinchollo started to receive allocations of irrigation water from the state-sponsored Majes Canal, which goes parallel to the
Colca River, bringing water from a highland dam and down to agribusiness in the
desert. Then, they stopped the practice of going up to the mountain top to make
collective offerings. However, more recently, they revived the tradition because
of the threat of climate change, this time with the support of an NGO, which
also funds projects of climate change adaptation. In October 2011, after a church
mass, the villagers walked up to the foot of the Hualca Hualca glacier where the
meltwater starts its descent toward the village. The peasant community's leader
expressed the mutuality and affection in the relationship between the humans and
the mountain Apu:

> We make an offering, a ritual, so that he [Hualca Hualca] will receive with a
> lot of good will and affection, and so that we will not lack water in the next
> year. The water is fundamental for us, for our plants, for the humans. We live
> from the water, and that is why we make this offering, with a lot of affection
> and devotion. And I know that tomorrow, the water will increase by 3 or 4
> litres per second. We have this hope and every year we do this.

The leader of the local water user commission—as a representative of the farmers—
was in charge of presenting Hualca Hualca with the *iranta*: a package of alpaca fetus,
llama fat, maize, coca leaves, sweets, fruit, flowers, wine and *chicha* (maize brew).
The representative asked him not to forget the people, to give them more water and
to protect the village. At that moment, a significant quantity of ice fell from a rock
overhang, which indicated that Hualca Hualca was thrilled and, offering immediate
reciprocity, he seemed to be saying: "look, here is the water!" People shared drinks
among themselves and with the Apu, and they played music and danced in honor of
Hualca Hualca. Later that day, the villagers stopped by a spring in a cave called "the
window" to make another offering. Drawing on oral traditions and knowledge of
well-publicized recent archaeological investigations, the villagers talked about the

FIGURE 35.2   One of the *pagos* that was offered to Apu Hualca Hualca. Photography by
author.

human offerings made in ancient times: in times of crisis, a young girl would be
chosen to go into "the window," where Apu Hualca Hualca summoned her into his
domain (see also Stensrud, 2016).[9]

Springs: nonhuman beings and world-making practices

In the past decades, farmers in Colca and in Cusco—as in the rest of the Andes—
have experienced changing weather patterns, irregular rain, unstable seasons, extreme temperatures and dwindling water supplies. These environmental changes
are increasingly explained by climate change. Mountain springs well up from the
groundwater, which is fed by rainwater and glacial meltwater, and during the last
few years, several springs have dried up completely. Springs are not only threatened
by climate change, however, but also by mines and urbanization. For example,
many springs in Cusco city have disappeared due to the city's expansion into the
surrounding hills. In one of the new neighborhoods, a spring in a family's backyard
was frequented by all of their neighbors to collect water for domestic use. After
lightening struck the spring, however, all the family's animals got sick from drinking
the water. The woman dwelling beside the spring made the spring dry by burying
garlic and other herbs and ingredients known for their "strong" and powerful properties. Water springs (*pukyu* in Quechua) are considered powerful and potentially

dangerous. Some say that "evil winds sleep in the springs" and that the springs may cause an illness called *pukyo* (the symptoms of which are rashes and blisters). Also in Colca Valley, there are some springs and lakes that are known to be particularly powerful and that should be approached with caution. When, for example, officials from the public water administration conduct inspections and measure the water flow rates in springs, they are encouraged by local farmers and engineers—who know the stories of particular springs—to select three coca leaves to make a *k'intu* (a bouquet of coca leaves for ritual exchange; see Allen, 2002 [1988]), breathe *samay* into the leaves and offer it to the spring by putting it under a stone.[10]

To give offerings to springs is an important part of the work of the water users' commissions, which are local associations that organize the distribution of irrigation water among farmers. These commissions also have to maintain respectful relations with the mountains and lakes, as well as with ponds, reservoirs and canals. The mountain-lords are the owners of water, and the springs and lakes are also living water-beings that have to be respected and cared for in order to continue receiving water. Twice a year the commissions offer food and alcohol to the most important water sources. Members hike up the mountains to make *irantas* to the high springs, located above 4,000 m of altitude. By each spring, the *paqu* (a ritual expert) prepares the ingredients for an *iranta*, and all participate by rolling balls of llama fat and making *k'intus* of coca leaves into which they blow their *sami* while addressing various beings: the place, the spring, the ancestors (*machulas*) and Lord Santiago who controls lightening. The *paqu* burns the *iranta* after summoning the water (*llamar al agua*). Individuals may vary the details, for example, seawater brought from the Pacific Ocean may be poured into a spring as seawater "will call for more water." After burning the *iranta*, the *paqu* places tiny ceramic goblets with *chicha*, sweet wine and holy water in a box in the earth beside the spring. One *paqu* explained "It is for the spring, to drink. This will be preserved here and it is for the whole year. It is . . . how should I put it . . .—it is [her] *pago*. Like we sometimes toast [drink], they are also thirsty." Through these ritual actions, springs and other water-beings are enacted as living nonhuman beings that can feel thirst and respond to human action (see also Stensrud, 2016).

Ponds and canals: partially connected worlds

Hydraulic infrastructure, such as ponds and canals, cannot be seen as separate from the entangled world of water-beings and earth-beings. Each year in August, the water users' commissions in Colca Valley organize collective work to clean all the irrigation canals and ponds. Some men and women walk up to the mountains and descend by foot while they clean the canals with shovels, while others clean the ponds by removing all the dirt that has gathered during the year. Before starting the work, it is important to make offerings to the mountains so that no accidents or deaths will happen. Proper offerings also have to be made to the ponds and canals that are going to be cleaned and repaired. The leader of one of the commissions explained:

> We make our *iranta* by the springs, and we pay (*pagamos*) and sprinkle with wine, and afterwards I make all the people pray [...] We also go to the

irrigation ponds to clean them on another day, and then we also make our *iranta* there. [...] We respect them so that they will supply us all year; so that there will be enough water in the ponds to sustain all our agricultural fields.

After the work is finished, all participants celebrate with food, drink and dance. When the water, which has been withheld during the work, is released, it is received with reverence and joy. People celebrate the water by drinking it and pouring *chicha* into it, and they also play festive music and dance around the canals and in the pond, while it slowly starts to fill with water.

Before starting to build a new infrastructure, it is even more important to make sure that the affected earth-beings are respectfully asked for permission to build in or near their abodes. In Canocota, a village in Colca Valley where 60% of the cultivated land is rain-water-dependent, the municipality was planning to build a dam by a lake called Casaccocha in order to use its water for irrigation, since the farmers can no longer rely on the regularity of rainfall with climate change. Located at the foot of a mountain, Casaccocha Lake is known to "have powers" so that the Apu first had to be begged for permission and an offering paid. In a village meeting, the mayor argued that the town should dedicate a church mass in the name of the Apu, and then offer the *iranta*: "only then can we go on with the project, and if God wills, nothing will happen."

In everyday life in the Andes (in public and private, in work and family life, in water user associations and municipalities), combining different and diverging world-making practices, like Christianity, earth-beings or secular modernity, is neither problematic nor paradoxical. For example, the engineer working for the Water Users' Board in Colca Valley often relates to water and water-bodies as living, sentient and responsive beings. However, he also relates to water as fluid matter that can be quantified and technically managed. He lives simultaneously, if always partially, in both worlds since they overlap and cannot be clearly separated. This dual reality is perhaps best described by the Aymara concept of "*ch'ixi*," which Silvia Rivera Cusicanqui (2012) uses to describe how indigenous and mestizo worlds can be combined without being mixed. *Ch'ixi* has many connotations and reflects the Aymara idea of something that is and is not at the same time. Hence, the notion of *ch'ixi* can illuminate the "motley" [*abigarrada*] quality of Andean society, expressing the parallel coexistence of multiple cultural differences that do not extinguish, but instead both antagonize and complement each other (Rivera, 2012:105).

Conclusion

Farming in the Andes has always depended upon irrigation, especially in the semi-arid areas like Colca Valley (Guillet and Mitchell, 1994), and relations of reciprocity to the living nonhuman beings in the landscape are an integrated part of practices of farming and irrigation. The effects of climate change, like changing rain seasons and drying springs, increase the need to ensure the water supply through different means. Offering gifts to mountains and springs is one very concrete way of maintaining respectful relationships between humans and earth-beings. It is also a way of creating a sense of control in a world of increasing uncertainty. In contemporary ritual practices, water sources are regarded as a variety of sentient and responsive beings in ways that disrupt the boundaries of nature and culture. Humans and water- and earth-beings participate in world-making practices from which partially connected worlds emerge. Water is an essential part of these worlds, both for the irrigation of cultivated fields and for the circulation of the vital force or *sami*.

Notes

1 The ethnographic descriptions and analysis in this chapter have been generated from extensive fieldwork in southern Peruvian Andes: particularly in Cusco (both in the city and in various districts of the Cusco region), and in Colca Valley of the Arequipa region. Fieldwork in Cusco was conducted in 2001–2002 (12 months), 2006–2007 (12 months) and 2008 (2 months) and in Colca Valley in 2011 (8 months) and 2013–2014 (5 months).
2 In some places, water is thought of as the blood of mother earth, while in other places, rivers are associated with semen, and rain with tears (Sherbondy, 1998).
3 South-American camelids (alpacas and llamas) often miscarry, and the aborted fetuses are collected and used in offerings.
4 According to the story, Choqesisa controlled her alpacas with the sound of her drum. While her husband was away on a travel, she gave birth. When the mother-in-law came to visit, she sent Choqesisa out to look after the alpacas, discovered that the grandson was a frog and killed him. Consumed by grief, Choqesisa entered a spring, followed by her husband and the alpacas (Vásquez Soto and Estrella Canaza, 2010).
5 *Tirakuna* is the Quechua plural of the Spanish *tierra* (earth) and is translated by Allen (2002:32) as "Earth Beings," "Earth Ones" or "Places." *Tirakuna* are said to be essentially the same as the earth-mother or the mountain-lords, and "seem to be localizations of the vitality animating the material Earth as a whole" (Allen 2002:33).
6 For more information on Qoyllur Rit'i, see Sallnow (1987) and Salas Carreño (2006).
7 The spectacled bear, or Andean bear (*ukuku* in Quechua), inhabits the rainforest on the eastern foothills of the Andes. As the only surviving bear species native to South America, it is today threatened due to habitat loss. Many oral stories in the Andes involve the wild and uncontrollable offspring of a peasant woman and a bear. In Qoyllur Rit'i, the *ukuku* is an ambivalent and tricksterlike, yet powerful, figure, who preserves order but also makes jokes and pranks (Sallnow, 1987:218–219).
8 The sanctuary of the Lord of Huanca, near Cusco city, also has a spring that is said to have medicinal and healing properties.
9 There are oral stories of human sacrifices in the area. In 1995, the "mummy Juanita" was found on the neighboring mountaintop Ampato. She was sacrificed as a young girl and is today displayed in a museum in Arequipa.
10 I observed this during fieldwork in 2011 in the district of Coporaque.

References

Allen, Catherine J. 2002 [1988]. *The Hold Life Has. Coca and Cultural Identity in an Andean Community*, 2nd edition. Washington, DC: Smithsonian Institution Press.

Bates, Bryson, Zbigniew W. Kundzewicz, Shaohong Wu and Jean Palutikof, eds. 2008. *Climate Change and Water*. Geneva: IPCC Secretariat.

Bolin, Inge. 2009. The Glaciers of the Andes are Melting: Indigenous and Anthropological Knowledge Merge in Restoring Water Resources. In *Anthropology and Climate Change: From Encounters to Actions*, edited by Susan A. Crate and Mark Nuttall, 228–239. Walnut Creek, CA: Left Coast Press.

Cereceda, Verónica. 2006. Mito e imagines andinas del infierno. In *Mitologías Amerindias*, edited By Alejandro Ortiz Rescaniere. Madrid: Editorial Trotta.

de la Cadena, Marisol. 2015. *Earth-Beings. Ecologies of Practice across Andean Worlds*. Durham, NC: Duke University Press.

Earls, John and Irene Silverblatt. 1978. La realidad física y social en la cosmología andina. *Actes du XLII Congrès International des Américanistes*. Vol. 4, 299–325, Paris.

Gelles, Paul. 2000. *Water and Power in Highland Peru. The Cultural Politics of Irrigation and Development*. New Brunswick, NJ and London: Rutgers University Press.

Gose, Peter. 1994. *Deathly Waters and Hungry Mountains: Agrarian Ritual and Class Formation in an Andean Town*. Toronto: University of Toronto Press.

Guillet, David and William P. Mitchell, eds. 1994. *Irrigation at High Altitudes: The Social Organization of Water Control Systems in the Andes*. Vol. 12. Washington, DC: American Anthropological Association, the Society for Latin American Anthropology Publication Series.

Orlove, Ben, Ellen Wiegandt, and Brian H. Luckman, eds. 2008. *Darkening Peaks: Glacier Retreat, Science, and Society*. Berkeley: University of California Press.

Rivera Cusicanqui, Silvia. 2012. Ch'ixinakax utxiwa: A Reflection on the Practices and Discourses of Decolonization. *The South Atlantic Quarterly* 111(1): 95–109.

Salas Carreño, Guillermo. 2006. Diferenciación social y discursos públicos sobre la peregrinación de Quyllurit'i. In *Mirando la esfera pública desde la cultura en el Perú*, edited by Gisela Cánepa and María Eugenia Ulfe, 243–288. Lima: CONCYTEC.

Sallnow, Michael J. 1987. *Pilgrims of the Andes: Regional Cults in Cusco*. Washington, DC: Smithsonian Institution Press.

Sherbondy, Jeanette. 1982. El regadío, los lagos y los mitos de origen. *Allpanchis* 17(20):3–32.

Sherbondy, Jeanette. 1998. Andean Irrigation in History. In *Searching for Equity. Conceptions of Justice and Equity in Peasant Irrigation*, edited by Rutgerd Boelens and Gloria Dávila, 210–214. Assen: Van Gorcum.

Stensrud, Astrid B. 2016. Climate Change, Water Practices and Relational Worlds in the Andes. *Ethnos: Journal of Anthropology* 81(1):75–98.

Strathern, Marilyn. 2004 [1991]. *Partial connections*. Walnut Creek, CA: AltaMira Press.

Taussig, Michael. 1980. *The devil and commodity fetishism in South America*. Chapel Hill, N.C.: University of North Carolina Press.

Valderrama, Ricardo and Carmen Escalante. 1988. *Del Tata Mallku a la Mama Pacha: Riego, sociedad y ritos en los andes peruanos*. Lima: DESCO.

Vásquez Soto, Milagros and Omar Estrella Canaza. 2010. *Fragmentos de la Historia del Distrito de Callalli*. Arequipa: Universidad Nacional San Agustín de Arequipa.

Vuille, Mathias, Bernard Francou, Patrick Wagnon, Irmgard Juen, Georg Kaser, Bryan G. Mark, and Raymond S. Bradley. 2008. Climate Change and Tropical Andean Glaciers: Past, Present, and Future. *Earth Science Reviews* 89:79–96.

36

FLORA, FAUNA AND CURATIVE WATERS

Ireland's holy wells as sites of biocultural diversity

Celeste Ray

In Ireland, as elsewhere, the holy well (*an tobar beannaithe*) is a water source, most often a spring, that is a site of religious devotion. These sacred sites might be deepened by human devotees, enhanced with stone impoundments and steps to aid water retention and access, and may be ornamented with superstructures, but they remain distinct from those human-excavated holes or shafts dug purposely for the collection of water for non-ritual use. Holy "wells" naturally occur and can even include seepage-fed pools. Generally dedicated to saint patrons, Irish holy wells often possess miraculous healing qualities like sacred water sources around the world. Charismatic, wells are also fickle and may "move" away from their miracle-working precincts if offended. The ritual engagements required to obtain cures and to placate wells and their patrons are folk liturgical practices unique to each well's topography—the arrangements of the natural and built features of a well's landscape setting (Ray, 2011, 2015). In contrast to liturgies (officially prescribed forms of public religious worship), folk liturgical practices are those accepted as efficacious through generations of repetition rather than by sanction of religious authorities. Circumambulating a well site while repeating particular prayers and movements in a set order is traditionally known as "paying the rounds" in Ireland. ("Paying" references the spiritual labor by which the sincerity of one's wellside requests is conveyed and a hopeful investment to secure a desired outcome.) Rounds may incorporate prayer, prostrations and circumambulations around other thaumaturgical features of a well's landscape called "stations" as a preface to approaching the well itself—the locality's ultimate source of grace. Stations can include unusually shaped boulders (sitting on which is thought to cure backaches), medieval church ruins or prehistoric burial mounds (beside which prayers are considered particularly efficacious) and sacred trees where devotees may leave votive offerings for wells' patron saints. The rounding process may also be called "the pattern" and the course followed between stations is called in Irish "*an turas*," which means "the journey" or "pilgrimage." Undertaken at any time, these localized pilgrimages are also the traditional feature of annual "patterns" or Patron days, when communities gather wellside on or near the associated saint's feast day.

Based on nineteenth-century Ordnance Surveys, William Wood-Martin suggested that the island of Ireland had at least 3,000 holy wells (1895:143). The Northern Ireland Sites and Monuments Record notes 187 (of which, just under two dozen remain active) and the National Monuments Service of the Republic has recordings of the location (or former location) of 2,996. Their continued existence is being gradually ground-truthed (verified) by field workers, but for most sites, historical information on the saint dedications, rounds or lore must be found in sources such as the published letters of the Ordnance Survey workers, the "Name Books" these surveyors prepared of toponyms, seventeenth to nineteenth-century antiquarian publications on folk traditions, the published archaeological inventories for 15 of the Republic's 26 counties and the 1930s Schools Folklore Collection (referenced below). While most counties in the Republic retain at least two dozen wells (excepting Monaghan), large counties like Cork, Galway and Clare have hundreds. Wood-Martin's figure has diminished in recent decades through residential, commercial and road construction and new farming practices. Holy wells might now flow within well-tended gardens, rest serenely as nearly forgotten pools in wooded areas, sit precariously beside busy roads, exist as unadorned depressions in the ground known to only a few families, or remain frequented pilgrimage sites in the middle of pastures.

Although over 70 holy wells may still be visited in County Dublin (where 30% of the Irish population lives), holy wells have stronger ties to familial and community identities beyond the capital city and its hinterlands.[1] Families may visit wells together on the anniversaries of a loved-one's death or on the occasion of a child's first communion. Family reunions can be held in conjunction with the local pattern day and neighbors may come expressly to see dispersed natives they know will be in attendance. Students may visit wells in groups for prayer before their "Leaving Certificate" examinations (which determine university placement) or before a football match (and bring holy well water to drink at the game). In today's "Post-Catholic" Ireland, many who have abandoned "the church" will attend pattern days when they will not attend mass, and will "do the rounds" at their local well in memory of the deceased loved ones who taught them how. At close to 200 holy wells across Ireland, communities still gather at their local well on the pattern day— now commemorated in a variety of ways. Few sites still host the "fun fair" patterns of past generations with vendors of religious and emphatically non-religious goods, games and unsaintly revelry; today's gatherings range from a few neighbors sharing in prayers, to group engagement in the rounds, a wellside mass, and/or children's sports competitions and shared meals.[2]

While some wells yield archaeological evidence of prehistoric origins, many have gained sacrality since the medieval era, as a paradigm for holy and curative wells was emplaced in new landscapes with population growth and with stimuli of other social-political factors (Ray, 2014, 2019). Whether isolated green spaces within towns, or encompassed by woodlands, holy wells and their immediate landscape contexts are ecosystems in themselves; otherwise, rare flora and fauna flourish in these often sheltered sites. They are nodes of both cultural heritage and biological diversity. Considering the relationship between curative wells and their associated flora and fauna, this chapter presents holy wells as sites of biocultural diversity (where culture and biology are interrelated and even co-evolved) (Maffi, 2001).[3]

FIGURE 36.1 (L): A prayer before St. Patrick's well at Three Trees on Co. Donegal's Inishowen Peninsula; (R): Sunlight reflects on the clear waters of St. David's well at Woodhouse (Tinakilly), Co. Waterford beside a large oak.

Blessed wells and "the cure"

In many parts of the globe, different watery sites offer different cures; Pliny the Elder even classified springs in his *Natural History* according to their perceived remedies for eyes, ears, head, bones, stomach, infertility and miscarriage, gout and insanity. Not all holy wells "have a cure;" those that do are known as "blessed wells." Obtaining the cure relates to site-specific folk liturgies and may involve drinking the waters, bathing the affected area in a stream that flows away from the source (to avoid cross-contamination) or more simply anointing the ailing with well water. To yield the cure, most wells require the afflicted to offer the rounds on multiple consecutive visits (most commonly three, but sometimes up to nine) and on particular days (sometimes consecutive Sundays or those around the patron saint's feast day). Before departing, visitors may leave a votive offering (rosary beads, a candle, a pebble or shell, or a religious image) in token exchange for aid granted or expected. Alternately, a petitioner's illness or concern may be symbolically deposited in personal effects or a "rag" (a strip of cloth or a ribbon) to also-symbolically cast off at the site.

Formerly, Irish wells specialized in diseases such as tuberculosis, scurvy, excessive bleeding and pertussis. A well dedicated to St. Lassair at Cill Lasrach near Kanturk, County Cork was even said to have the cure for anthrax! For rheumatism, Co. Leitrim residents could visit the turf-fire-heated sweathouse beside St. Hugh's holy well at Ballinagleragh. Near Clones in Co. Monaghan, sweathouse treatments also followed bathing in a "gallibois" well (from the Irish *galar buidhe* for jaundice), after which a swatch of one's garment had to be left on a wellside alder.[4] Some holy wells are rich in specific chemicals with beneficial properties such as potassium or magnesium and waters connected with skin complaints, for example, often contain sulfur. Chalybeate springs, containing iron salts, yield "strength-building" water. Those efficacious in improving mental health can have naturally occurring lithium, as do two in County Kerry's "Valley of the Mad."[5] Tested in 2012 by chemist Henry Lyons, the southern well yielded lithium at 12 parts per billion (three times what nearby Killarney tap water contains) and the northern well registered 55 parts per billion. While hardly comparable to prescriptive medicine, continued use possibly helped bipolar sufferers.[6] Transgenerational experience of local environments and communication of traditional ecological knowledge would have identified such blessed wells. The most common "cure" of Irish holy wells into the mid-twentieth century was for "sore eyes" and such sites are still known as *tobair na sul* (eye wells). Sore eyes are commonly dry eyes and have been treated with collyrium (mostly sodium chloride) since ancient times; major pharmaceutical companies such as Bausch and Lomb offer collyrium today as an eye wash. Sore eyes could be irritated by smoke from perpetually burning hearth fires in poorly ventilated homes so that getting fresh air and rinsing the eyes likely provided some relief, but waters with naturally occurring sodium chloride would also have been identified as an aid across the generations when a walking way of life enabled more ready acquisition of local ecological knowledge than in the automobile era.

Wells credited with easing the most common complaints (eye problems, aches of the body, stomach or head, warts and other skin complaints) compose the majority of surviving blessed wells today. Into the third-quarter of the twentieth century, most counties had wells famed for curing the most frequent ailments so that parents might march a child with a sore throat or even a sports injury to "the local" for a cure and, if that and medical advice failed, on to the next county's specialist source. On "bank holidays" in the second decade of the twenty-first century, when dentists and other medical offices are closed for a long weekend, wells credited with easing toothache and backaches have increased visitation. Cures for ailments of our times (for example, allergies, anxiety and even cancer) may now be attributed to blessed wells that once offered hope for consumption or measles.

Sacred trees and curative flora

Into the mid-twentieth century, most wells had larger numbers of stations and lengthier rounds. What remains in most places is an abbreviated liturgy for condensed well landscapes (nibbled away through land sales, re-use and agricultural expansion). Trees are some of the most enduring (if periodically replaced) features of well rounds; taboos against cutting them or even removing their dead branches mean they have been the most protected stations and their close proximity to the well generally means they are one of the last associated landscape features to be forgotten.

While tree cults have existed around the world wherever trees can grow, the first documented references to Irish trees sacred on their own account are to the *bili* (plural)/*bile* (singular) of the Late Iron Age and early Christian tuaths (tribal settlements with petty kings), and those of later parishes. Placenames across Ireland including the elements billy, billa, bellew, bell and bellia derive from a *bile* (Farrelly and O'Brien, 2002:273). Beyond the medieval era, trees considered sacred rather than storied were those associated with a religious foundation or a holy well.[7] Venerable wellside trees are now most commonly whitethorn, but also holly, ash or hazel, sometimes yews, and occasionally even imports such as Sitka spruce as at St. Brigid's well in Tully, Co. Kildare. Holy wells not only have trees, but can exist in them, usually at the site of a broken branch or indention where dew and rain water collect. Offended wells may migrate to the forks or trunks of trees and become known as "*tobar igcrann*" (the well of the tree) (Zucchelli, 2009:55) or, as A.T. Lucas noted *Tobar an bhile* (the well of the bile) as in Co. Waterford's Kilrush parish (1963:41) or Toberbilly, Co. Antrim. Wellside trees also gave their names to places: the tree by St. Pappin's now-neglected well gave its name to the area of Poppintree in North Co. Dublin.[8]

The seasonally self-renewing hawthorn, alder, ash, birch, willow or wych elm provides both symbolic and tangible affirmation that miracles, or at least change, can happen. Likewise, interviewees consider wellside evergreens as representing perseverance and the continual availability of divine help and guidance. The tree is the station where one surrenders disbelief, fear and anger in preparation for receiving grace. As the Indian sacred groves by Hindu temples (*kaavu*) are considered "the depository of sin and malevolence" (Uchiyamada, 1998:193), the wellside tree is a station of riddance in contrast to the giving waters of the well where devotees linger. An act of contrition may be said at the tree and votives, or symbols of affliction, may be tied to its branches before devotees bless themselves with well water.

The tree is seen to perform the sacrificial act of bearing devotees' concerns and further enabling the well to offer grace and healing. The decline or death of a wellside tree is sometimes read as a worrying sign about the health and power of the well and the burden of anxieties left there.

Holy well "cures" are traditionally related to a site's associated flora. Willow tree bark was the original source of aspirin and wells surrounded by willow trees are known as headache wells. Whooping cough was treated at wells with plentiful stitchwort; the presence of speedwell germander indicated "eye wells," and wells where comfrey proliferates are still considered ameliorative for arthritis and joint pain even though well devotees might not now be aware of comfrey's folk medicinal use. Between 1937 and 1938, Irish school children collected folklore nationwide and the resulting "Schools Folklore Collection" is a mine of folk healing traditions; in addition to noting the uses of specific wellside plants, children reported that leaves of any vegetation growing *in* a well could cure ailments.[9] Rushes are associated with the making of St. Brigid's crosses on her day (February 1st), but, growing around bodies of water and holy wells, they are perceived as physical water purifiers and those visiting a well which may have swollen due to heavy rains will not hesitate to take holy water from between the rushes. As in Iceland and other European countries, the dew or rain drops that collected on the leaves of Lady's Mantle (*Alchemilla*), often found near wells, were considered a good cure for headaches and, in Ireland, for other types of ailments such as diarrhea. Bone-setters used to place comfrey or "knitbone" in the bandages with which they treated broken bones (Munnelly, 2005:167). The herb contains allantoin which accelerates the body's natural cell replacement and seems to help skin conditions and bone mending. Although a ninth-century Triad listed the three signs of an abandoned place as being elder, corncrake and nettles (Kelly, 1976:117), wellside nettles can be used to make diuretic tea and anti-allergy tonics, and wellside elderflower infusions are considered helpful for bronchitis and catarrh (coupled with rounds at the site).

Popular perceptions of a plant's usefulness may relate to its appearance and season of growth. In typical folk medicine traditions of "like for like," ragwort and other yellow flowering plants such as buttercups, lesser celandine, vetchling and primrose were associated with treating jaundice (Logan, 1981:46), and liverwort, which grows on the edge of wells, was once boiled with milk to treat that condition in Ulster (Ballard, 2009:30). Yellow flowering plants, especially primrose, were formerly employed on May Eve against generalized evil connected with seasonal changes. For example, children collected marsh marigold before dusk on May Eve for protection against fairies and would scatter it around holy wells. Common names for the plant in Irish mean "the shrub of Bealtaine" (May 1st) (Mac Coitir, 2006:54). Also on May Eve, vervain was once mixed with holy well water to sprinkle on the boundaries of a farm for protection against disease and pests (Ibid:125). Certain plants are metonymic for a saint's feast day because of their seasonal appearance. One of the regional protectors of Munster (Ireland's Southwest) is St. Gobnait and though winter weather might still be expected for her day (February 11th), wellside snowdrops (*Galanthus nivalis*) are said to bloom without fail by the dawn.

Fauna and piscifauna

As natural water sources with supernatural patrons and powers, holy wells are liminal places. Even within towns, they can be perceived as an aperture between two realms of existence and attract seldom seen fauna which visitors associate with the power of the place. Particular wells are known as the haunts of tawny owls or endangered red squirrels.[10] People describe unusual interactions with animals at well sites (looking up after a prayer to find a bird or multiple birds observing them at a surprisingly close range, for example, or encountering ordinarily shy and elusive animals in a well's tranquil vicinity). Otherworldly owls appear in many Irish, Welsh and Scottish tales as good and bad omens and as wells are often in isolated locations, owls may live nearby. Some interviewees describe them as wells' nighttime guardians, but in Counties Laois, Tipperary and Limerick, consultants avoided well visitation at dusk or during the night "because of the owls" (which they considered inauspicious presences).

Folklore can credit well inhabitants with oracular abilities, supernatural longevity and control over the weather. Although legends associate a few wells with cows, birds, horses and deer, the more common genius loci is the prophetic fish. Seeing a fish in well waters after performing the rounds indicates that requests will be granted. Some perceive the direction and speed of piscine movements as also divinatory. Trout are most common (often appearing in twos and granted immortality by the well's associated saint), but salmon and eels are also said to show themselves to those whose petitions are favored. (These last are generally *Anguilla anguilla* which are long-lived snake-like catadromous fish with an average length of 60–80 cm.) Most consider these appearances to be supernatural visions, but fish have been introduced to wells to keep them clean and *Anguilla anguilla* do colonize varied fresh inland waters. Despite taboos against harming well residents, stories are still shared in the twenty-first century about disrespectful people or silly children (positioned at least two generations in the past) who caught and tried to grill the fish. The fish always escaped back to their wells, but bore marks of the offense ever after. Tales of sacred fish with such gridiron, tong or other sear marks are numerous in the Schools Folklore Collection. For Co. Mayo alone, they were recorded at Ballina, Carrowgarve, Cloonfad More, Derrymore, Killacorraun, Prison East, Skerdah Lower, Teevenacroaghy and Westport.[11] Analogous accounts of the near demise of holy-spring-dwelling fish are also found in Scotland, Wales, Cornwall, Brittany, Denmark and Germany, and in other historic eras. Le Roy Ladurie provides a remarkably similar narrative recorded by fourteenth-century Inquisitors ferreting out heretical Cathar beliefs in southern France. A villager of Bédeillac described a conversation in which he joined: "…we were talking about a certain spring …. Someone said that in the olden days someone had fried some fish near the fountain, but the fish jumped out of the pan into the fountain and you can still see them there, fried just on one side!" (1978:260). In Irish tales, the human culprits sometimes die. Even when the fish are caught accidentally while bringing water home for domestic use (to boil potatoes or "wet the tea"— explicitly forbidden uses of holy well water), and then returned to the well on discovery, harming the aquatic genii has repercussions. The ubiquity of these accounts, of course, reinforces respect for holy well water and its proper use. Stories of piscifauna are good indicators of a site's ongoing sacrality (locals may mention the miraculous fish when they no longer recall the saint patron or a well's cure).

Wells also teem with other aquatic life. Algae grows freely and might not even be brushed aside by those dipping in a cup to drink the waters or washing their faces and eyes. In fact, some faithful may rub a bit of the algae or moss from around the well (perceived to have concentrated powers) into the corners of their eyes, or on a bodily sore or injury, as at St. Bartholomew's well in Coolard, Co. Kerry, or St. Mochulla's well at Fortane, Co. Clare. Gordon D'Arcy notes that "if the green curtain" of algae is

FIGURE 36.2 Ireland's oldest Marian shrine is Our Lady's Island, Co. Wexford. Appearing to gaze at the rosary-wrapped figures of Joseph and Mary with the young Jesus, the lone amphibian to their lower right is said to frequent the island's holy well during pilgrimage season (from the eve before Mary's Assumption Day, August 15th, through her birthday, September 8th). Pilgrims traditionally began their rounds at a mainland holy well before circumambulating the 32-acre island nine times while praying the rosary. Situated in a "lake," actually a back-barrier lagoon on the edge of the Atlantic Ocean, the site is an important breeding ground for terns, black-headed gulls, the black-tailed godwit and whooper swans.

pushed aside, "an aquatic drama of invertebrates" can appear at holy well sites featuring "strange insects with stranger names" such as the water measurers and pond skaters which dance on the water's surface tension, along with water-boatmen, diving beetles and water scorpions (1988:138). Small shrimp-like crustaceans (*Gammaridea*) may also be found in some larger pools where they feed on vegetation and favor waters hosting starwort (*Callitriche stagnalis*) and watercress (*Nasturtium officinale*).[12] The ecosystems of well sites are appreciated by regular visitors who sometimes read meaning in the presence, absence or movement of these seasonal residents, which all attract frogs.

Just as "amphibian" derives from the Greek *amphibios* meaning to live a double-life, frogs' wellside presence has multiple interpretations. In European traditions, frogs have secret talents and transformative powers.[13] Although Biblical references to frogs are utterly negative (they were the second plague to visit the Egyptians in Exodus, and appear as spirits of devils in Revelations), and although frogs and toads were popular in representations of pestilence in general, frogs were generally considered benign in Europe by the middle ages, while the toad embodied evil and symbolized death (Robbins, 1996:25). Toads at a well are always profaning, but at some Irish wells, frog sightings affirm the granting of wellside petitions rather than signifying fish. Cian Marnell notes that this is the case at Tobar Mac Coille at Killeen, Co. Galway (1999:184) and Anna Rackard comments that the appearance of a frog, particularly if young, is considered a good omen at St. Caoidhe's well in Foohagh, Co. Clare (2001:30). School children reported in the 1930s that a cure could not be obtained from Co. Cork's Castletownbere well without being also granted a glimpse of the occupant frog and that in the same county, near Rusheen, a frog would emerge in water taken from St. Croabh Dearg's well to prevent its use for domestic purposes; the frog was considered "the spirit of the well" and otherwise appeared at nightfall (Dudley, 1937; Neville, 1937).[14] Some semiaquatic well residents can play a role in the curing practices of traditional healers—Protestants and Catholics with the gift for curing particular ailments (for example, bleeding, burns, ringworm, mumps, headaches, toothache and skin complaints). Licking the underside of a newt (a hungry one is most efficacious) not only relieves burns in Ulster, but also asthma if the chest of the afflicted is licked immediately after the newt (Ballard, 2009:28; see also Nolan, 1988:51). For Catholic healers, recruiting these assistants from holy well waters yields added potency.

With their permeable skin, frogs live in clean waters and while their limited presence is thought to indicate the purity of holy well water, more than two can be thought to be unlucky, if not cursed. Frog eggs, which must incubate submerged in water, evoke concern. A small clump of frogspawn is often acceptable (in part depending on the size of the well), but even visitors who highly regard well algae will refuse to touch water with clusters of the gelatinous masses. With sadness or disgust, some consultants have noted that the sight of large quantities of spawn caused them to cease consulting a well they once frequented; the spawn, followed by tadpoles, followed by a "colony" of frogs indicated a loss of sanctity to them. Eighty years ago, Helen Roe noted that a cursed well near Graiguenahown, Co. Laois was sometimes so completely filled with grown frogs that no water could be drawn from it, but that "after a time, the frogs disappear as mysteriously as they come" (1939:32). Recurring and seasonal frog colonization can send wells quickly into decline. Interviewees in Counties Leitrim, Limerick, Mayo and Kerry noted that large numbers of frogs perhaps indicated a misuse of the well—not an offense great enough for the well to move, but enough for the well to withhold blessings for a few years (of course, harming or moving frogs would only invite more trouble). Other consultants blamed the seemingly increasing frog relocations to wells on the eradication of their former habitats by rampant development with Ireland's transformative "Celtic Tiger" economic boom (1995–2007).[15]

Applications for studies of sacred watery sites

Due to increased groundwater withdrawals and disturbance of the aquifer system through rapid residential, commercial and road construction, many holy well sites have been outright destroyed or have lost their micro-ecosystems with contamination or diminished flow since the mid-1990s (Ray, 2019). Development happened so quickly that, for example, in 2006, over 27% of all housing in Ireland had been newly constructed in the decade since the previous census.[16] Between 2003 and 2019, the Irish have constructed over 800 km of "motorway" (the highest speed roads with two or more lanes in each direction) and have built or widened thousands of kilometers of lesser category roads.[17] Newly disposal capital from the economic revolution and even the government's former Training and Employment Authority (*An Foras Áiseanna Saothair* or *FÁS*) was directed at "doing up" holy wells in the interest of their preservation and providing employment, but often entailed concrete pavements and linings, along with fencing and ground clearance for seating which, of course, eradicated habitats. Such renovations can deflate rather than elevate the local cultural capital of their sponsors. They may have intended to honor their communities or deceased family members who were devoted to the site, but such enhancements are critiqued for their perceived disconnection from these places' enchantments.

Experiencing the impacts of Ireland's headlong transitions, holy wells are untapped indicators of local environmental health. These most protected water sources are like the proverbial canary in the coal mine; when they are contaminated by development or by fertilizer run-off, the local water table is also likely impacted. Noting flora and fauna levels at holy well sites and consulting older residents about perceived changes in holy well ecosystems can provide a measure against which to appreciate broader changes in both environmental health and local ecological knowledge.

After years of debate, domestic water charges were introduced in Ireland in 2015 for those homes connected to public water supply or to public waste water services, but then refunded in 2017 due to public outcry. Ireland's water culture and water abstraction rates (the third-highest in the EU) are based on a paradigm of bounty. However, famously water-logged Ireland has had multiple water crises in the twenty-first century (see Leonard, 2013). The European Court of Justice issued a warning to the Irish government over 2002 microbiological (*E. coli*) contamination in public and private water supplies. Record dry spells have led to water shortages in urban areas, and rapid development and new housing construction have outpaced infrastructure improvements. Galway City (supplied by the River Corrib) experienced an outbreak of cryptosporidiosis that required residents to boil their water for five months in 2007 (see Chyzheuskaya et al., 2017). Water stress in portions of Co. Roscommon put a "boil water notice" in place for six years from 2009 to 2015. Due to problematic water treatment, Dublin water supplies were restricted in 2013. Quality of drinking water in Ireland can no longer be taken for granted. Despite traditional taboos on doing so, during recent water crises, residents in impacted areas have taken their domestic water from holy wells. For example, before inland fracking (gas capture through hydraulic fracturing of gas-bearing rock) was banned in Ireland in 2017, the practice had County Leitrim residents making regular trips to St. Patrick's well under a massive ash tree at Miskaun Glebe to bring home what they considered the safest water for drinking and cooking in the vicinity.

In the last decade, anthropologists have considered water's role in shaping human societies and the significance of water inequities (Strang, 2004; Wagner, 2013; Hastrup and Hastrup, 2015). Their work points to the need for greater understanding of the religious significance of water and what motivates people to steward water sources in ways that enable both wildlife habitats and socioecological resilience. Documenting everyday water practices, "different forms of valuing water" (Orlove and Caton, 2010) and popular perceptions of the sacrality of water is essential for environmental studies today and for strategizing socioecological resilience in the face of predicted water crises. With urban water stress and rural contamination, better understandings of Ireland's water culture can further conservation in popular discourse and practice. Considered such a national shibboleth that they were chosen as the subject of the Irish Free State's first national folklore survey in 1934, holy wells offer ready examples (and documentation with time depth) for appreciating how people value and steward water. Holy wells are irreplaceable resources of archaeological, historical, spiritual and community significance and also serve as conservation patches. The folk liturgies that developed and evolved in relation to the unique topography of each site and the generationally layered knowledge and lore about holy wells and their associated cures, flora and fauna, exemplify the ways in which cultural tradition can enhance biological diversity.

Notes

1 See Gary Branigan's survey (2012).
2 Food and goods vendors still appear for the pattern days, for example, of St. Brigid at Faughart, Co. Louth (Feb. 1st), at Tobernalt, Co. Sligo (last weekend of July), for St. Moling in St. Mullins, Co. Carlow (last Sunday before July 25th) and St. Declan's at Ardmore, Co. Waterford (July 24th). At the last two, carnival rides, live music and candy floss are also available. Shared meals follow St. Declan's pattern day at Toor, Co. Waterford (around the saint's feast day July 24th) and the children's sports competitions at St. Peacaun's Co Tipperary (August 7th), for example.
3 Ethnographic fieldwork for this essay was made possible by a Jack Shand Research Grant from the Society for the Scientific Study of Religion, and two National Geographic Explorer Grants for research between 2010 and 2018.
4 Duffy (2007:35) also mentions this well.
5 Ireland has other mental illness wells; Donegal has "Madman's well" at Port a' Doruis and Gort na Leici's "Flagstone of the Sorrows."
6 "Gleann na ngealt." 2012. Dingle, Co. Kerry: Sibéal Teo. Broadcast on TG4 October 28.

7 The Tree Council of Ireland has created a remarkable database of Heritage Trees including categories for those of "religious significance" and "rag trees": https://treecouncil.ie/
treeregisterofireland/aacategory.htm
8 St. Pappin's well still exists on the edge of a property boundary wall.
9 For example, records from Trinity, Co. Wexford, NFC, No. 218:152.
10 Red squirrels are now endangered because of deforestation and the introduction of the
larger North American gray squirrel which can carry the squirrel pox virus.
11 The Schools' Collection: Ballina, Vol. 0146:38; Carrowgarve, Vol. 014:589; Cloonfad
More, Vol. 0249:149–150; Derrymore, vol. 0138D:18_039; Killacorraun, Vol. 0152:348;
Prison East, Vol. 0095C:07_021; Skerdah Lower, Vol. 0086:98; Teevenacroaghy,
Vol. 0138:311; Westport, Vol. 0137:148.
12 Thanks to Dominic Berridge (Wexford Wildfowl Reserve, National Parks and Wildlife
Services) for pointing out the *Gammaridea*.
13 In the German *Märchen* of the Frog Prince, the shape-shifting frog marries a woman
seeking water at his residence (a well or pond or pool).
14 St. Croabh Dearg is St. Red Claw or Red Branch and has her own fascinating folklore.
15 By 2005, the *Economist* ranked Ireland as having the highest quality of life in the world
and even after the international downturn, Ireland had the 11th highest GDP per capita
globally by 2016.
16 Government of Ireland. 2007. *Census 2006, Volume 6—Housing*. Dublin: Stationery
Office. See also Kitchin (2015:64–65).
17 See road project reports at: www.irishmotorwayinfo.com/inex/roads/misc/index.html

References

Ballard, Linda-May. 2009. An Approach to Traditional Cures in Ulster. *Ulster Medical Jour-
nal* 78(1):26–33.
Branigan, Gary. 2012. *Ancient and Holy Wells of Dublin*. Dublin: The History Press.
Chyzheuskaya, Aksana, Martin Cormican, Raghavendra Srivinas, Diarmuid O'Donovan,
Martina Prendergast, Cathal O'Donoghue and Dearbháile Morris. 2017. Economic
Assessment of Waterborn Outbreak of Cryptosporidiosis. *Emerging Infectious Diseases*
23(10):1650–1656.
D'Arcy, Gordon. 1988. Archaeology and the Environment: Conflict or Co-operation. *Ar-
chaeology Ireland* 2(4): 137–139.
Dudley, Dolores. 1937. *Holy Wells. Schools Folklore Collection. Vol. 278:61, Roll 13762*. Dublin:
National Folklore Collection, University College Dublin.
Duffy, Patrick. 2007. *Exploring the History and Heritage of Irish Landscapes*. Dublin: Four
Courts.
Farrelly, Jean and Caimin O'Brien. 2002. *Archaeological Inventory of County Tipperary. Vol. 1
North Tipperary*. Dublin: The Stationery Office.
Hastrup, Kirsten and Frida Hastrup, eds. 2015. *Waterworlds: Anthropology in Fluid Environ-
ments*. New York: Berghahn.
Kelly, Fergus. 1974. The Old Irish Tree-List. *Celtica* 11:107–124.
Kitchin, Rob. 2015. Housing. In *The Atlas of the Island of Ireland: Mapping Social and Economic
Patterns*, edited by Justin Gleeson, 63–76. Maynooth: All-Island Research Observatory.
Le Roy Ladurie, Emmanuel. 1978. *Montaillou: The Promised Land of Error*. New York:
George Braziller.
Leonard, Liam. 2013. The Water Crisis in Ireland: The Sociopolitical Context of Risk in
Contemporary Society. In *The Social Life of Water*, edited by John Wagner, 199–219. New
York: Berghahn.

Logan, Patrick. 1981. *Irish Folk Medicine*. Belfast: Appletree Press.

Lucas, A. Tony. 1963. The Sacred Trees of Ireland. *Journal of the Cork Historical and Archaeological Society* 68:16–54.

Mac Coitir, Niall. 2006. *Irish Wild Plants: Myths, Legends and Folklore*. Cork: The Collins Press.

Maffi, Luisa, ed. 2001. *On Biocultural Diversity: Linking Language, Knowledge, and the Environment*. Washington, DC: Smithsonian Institution Press.

Marnell, Cian. 1999. Healing Wells of Kiltartan. *Journal of the Galway Archaeological and Historical Society* 51:182–188.

Munnelly, Tom. 2005. Plant Lore from West Clare. *Béaloideas* 73:164–169.

Neville, Joan. 1937. *Holy Wells. Schools Folklore Collection. Vol. 0343:85–86, Roll 12395*. Dublin: National Folklore Collection, University College Dublin.

Nolan, Peter. 1988. Folk Medicine in Rural Ireland. *Folk Life* 27: 44–56.

Orlove, Ben and Steven C. Caton. 2010. Water Sustainability: Anthropological Approaches and Prospects. *Annual Review of Anthropology* 39:401–415.

Pliny the Elder. 1938. *Natural History*. Translated by Harris Rackham, William H.S. Jones, and David E. Eichholz (Vol. 10, Book 31). Cambridge, MA: Harvard University Press.

Rackard, Anna. 2001. *Fish Stone Water: Holy Wells of Ireland*. Cork: Arium.

Ray, Celeste. 2011. The Sacred and the Body Politic at Ireland's Holy Wells. *International Social Science Journal* (UNESCO/Blackwell) 205/206: 271–285.

———. 2014. *The Origins of Ireland's Holy Wells*. Oxford: Archaeopress/Oxbow.

———. 2015. Paying the Rounds at Ireland's Holy Wells. *Anthropos* 110:415–432.

———. 2019. Sacred Wells across the *Longue Durée*. In *Historical Ecologies, Heterarchies and Transtemporal Landscapes*, edited by Celeste Ray and Manuel Fernández-Götz, 265–286. London: Routledge.

Robbins, Mary. 1996. The Truculent Toad in the Middle Ages. In *Animals in the Middle Ages*, edited by Nona C. Flores, 25–47. New York: Garland Publishing.

Roe, Helen. 1939. Customs and Beliefs from Laoighis. *Béaloideas* 9(1):21–35.

Strang, Veronica. 2004. *The Meaning of Water*. Oxford: Berg.

Uchiyamada, Yasushi. 1998. 'The Grove is our Temple': Contested Representations of Kaavu in Kerala, South India. In *The Social Life of Trees: Anthropological Perspectives on Tree Symbolism*, edited by Laura Rival, 177–196. New York: Berg.

Wagner, John Richard, ed. 2013. *The Social Life of Water*. New York: Berghahn Books.

Wood-Martin, William Gregory. 1895. *Pagan Ireland; An Archaeological Sketch: A Handbook of Irish Pre-Christian Antiquities*. London: Longmans, Green and Co.

Zucchelli, Christine. 2009. *Trees of Inspiration: Sacred Trees and Bushes of Ireland*. Cork: Collins Press.

INDEX

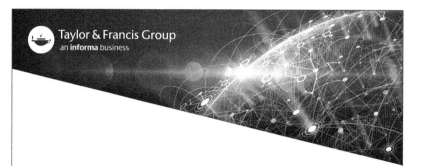